Who Was Who in the
GREEK WORLD

Contributors

John Chadwick, D.Litt., F.B.A.
Reader in Classics, Downing College, Cambridge
Minoan–Mycenaean essay

Audrey Griffin, M.A., D.Phil., A.I.L.
Research Assistant for the *Lexicon of Greek Personal Names*
Archaic Period (History)

E. L. Bowie, M.A.(Oxon.)
University Lecturer and E. P. Warren Praelector in Classics, Corpus Christi College, Oxford
Archaic Period (Literature)

Thomas Wiedemann, M.A.(Oxon.)
Lecturer in Classics, University of Bristol
Fifth Century BC (History), Fifth and Fourth Centuries (Prose)

Andrew Brown, M.A., Ph.D.
Head of Classics Department, Christ's Hospital Girls' School, Hertford
Fifth and Fourth Centuries BC (Poetry)

Christopher Tuplin, M.A.(Oxon.), D.Phil.
Lecturer in Ancient History and Classical Archaeology, University of Liverpool
404–323 BC (History)

E. E. Rice, M.A.(Cantab.), D.Phil.
Junior Research Fellow, Wolfson College, Oxford
Hellenistic Period (History)

Perilla K. M. Kinchin, M.A.(Oxon.)
Lecturer in Classics, Trinity College, Oxford
Hellenistic Period (Literature)

Richard Hawkins, M.A.(Oxon.), B.Phil.
University Lecturer and Tutor in Philosophy, Keble College, Oxford
Philosophy

R. R. R. Smith, B.A., M.Phil.
Fellow by Examination in Ancient History, Magdalen College, Oxford
Fine Arts

with additional entries by

Nicholas Horsfall, M.A., D.Phil.
Lecturer in Classics, University College London

David Mealand, M.A.(Oxon.), M.Litt.
Lecturer in New Testament Studies, University of Edinburgh

Who Was Who in the
GREEK
WORLD

776 BC–30 BC

Edited by
Diana Bowder

Phaidon · Oxford

Phaidon Press Limited, Littlegate House, St Ebbe's Street, Oxford

First published 1982

© Phaidon Press Limited

British Library Cataloguing in Publication Data
  Who Was Who in the Greek World
    1. Ancient Greece—Biography
    I. Bowder, Diana
    938'.0092'2   DF16

    ISBN 0-7148-2207-8

Set in Monophoto Apollo, and printed in Great Britain by BAS Printers Limited, Over Wallop, Hampshire

FRONTISPIECE: Knights on horseback, fragment of the Parthenon frieze (south), c. 447–432 BC. London, British Museum.

Contents

Chronological Table

776 BC	First Olympic Games (traditional date)
c. 750 BC	Foundation of Cumae (Cyme) in Italy
735 BC	Foundation of Naxos in Sicily
734 BC	Foundation of Syracuse
c. 730–710 BC	First Messenian War
c. 700 BC	Homer and Hesiod active
c. 680 BC	Gyges becomes king of Lydia
c. 675 BC	Reforms of Lycurgus at Sparta (?). Terpander active
c. 675–655 BC	Reign of Pheidon at Argos (?)
669 BC	Battle of Hysiae
657 BC	Cypselus becomes tyrant at Corinth
c. 650 BC	Second Messenian War. Orthagoras becomes tyrant at Sicyon, Theagenes at Megara. Archilochus and Tyrtaeus active
c. 638 BC	Voyage of Colaeus
c. 630 BC	Cylon's attempted *coup* at Athens. Foundation of Cyrene and Naucratis
627 BC	Periander succeeds Cypselus
c. 625 BC	Mimnermus active
c. 620 BC	Reforms of Dracon at Athens
c. 600 BC	Pittacus tyrant at Mytilene. Alcman, Alcaeus, Sappho, Thales active
594 BC	Reforms of Solon at Athens
c. 590 BC	First Sacred War
c. 585 BC	Death of Periander and collapse of tyranny at Corinth
c. 575 BC	Marriage of Megacles and Agariste
569–525 BC	Reign of Amasis in Egypt
561 BC	First tyranny of Peisistratus at Athens
c. 559–556 BC	Elder Miltiades goes to Thrace
c. 557 BC	Second tyranny of Peisistratus
556–553 BC	Ephorate of Chilon: Sparta adopts 'Orestes Policy'
c. 550 BC	Stesichorus, Hipponax, Theognis active
548 BC	Burning of temple at Delphi
546 (?) BC	Fall of Sardis. Battle of Pallene: third tyranny of Peisistratus
527 BC	Hippias succeeds Peisistratus
c. 525 BC	Pythagoras, Ibycus, Anacreon active
c. 523 BC	Death of Polycrates of Samos
521 BC	Darius I becomes king of Persia
514 BC	Assassination of Hipparchus
513 BC	Scythian expedition of Darius
510 BC	Expulsion of Hippias from Athens
508 BC	Reforms of Cleisthenes at Athens
506 BC	Failure of Cleomenes' expedition against Athens
c. 500 BC	Heracl(e)itus active
499–494 BC	Revolt of Ionian Greeks against Persia
494 BC	Defeat of Ionian fleet at Lade; destruction of Miletus
492 BC	Persians conquer Thrace, demand submission of Greece
490 BC	Persian punitive expedition against Eretria and Athens; battle of Marathon
487 BC	Constitutional reforms at Athens; archons selected by lot; introduction of ostracism
483 BC	Discovery of silver-deposits at Laureum allows Themistocles to propose creation of Athenian navy

480 BC	Xerxes' expedition against Greece; battles of Artemisium, Thermopylae, Salamis. Gelon defeats Carthaginian invasion of Sicily at Himera
479 BC	Battles of Plataea and Mycale
478 BC	Spartans recall Pausanias (1), leaving leadership of Greek Aegean states to Athens
477 BC	Founding of Delian League
c. 475 BC	Parmenides and Polygnotus active
474 BC	Hieron I of Syracuse defeats Etruscan fleet at Cumae (Cyme)
470 BC	Themistocles ostracized
c. 468 BC	Death of Simonides
c. 467 BC	Cimon's victory at the Eurymedon. End of Deinomenid rule at Syracuse
464 BC	Earthquake at Sparta: Third Messenian War (464–455)
462–458 BC	Democratic reforms of Ephialtes and Pericles at Athens
461 BC	Cimon ostracized
457 BC	Battles of Tanagra and Oenophyta: Athens controls Boeotia
456 BC	Athens takes control of Aegina; expedition to Egypt. Death of Aeschylus
454 BC	Collapse of Egyptian expedition; League treasury transferred from Delos to Athens
c. 450 BC	Death of Bacchylides
449 BC	Cimon defeats Persians at Salamis (Cyprus)
448 BC	Peace between Athens and Persia ('Peace of Callias')
447/6 BC	Athens loses Boeotia and Megara; revolt of Euboea
c. 446 BC	Death of Pindar
445 BC	Thirty Years' Peace between Athens and Sparta
444 BC	Athenians found 'Panhellenic' colony at Thurii
440–439 BC	Samos and Byzantium revolt
432 BC	Deaths of Empedocles and Pheidias
431–421 BC	Archidamian War. Thucydides begins history
429 BC	Plague at Athens; death of Pericles
428 BC	Death of Anaxagoras
427 BC	Gorgias comes to Athens
425 BC	Capture of 120 Spartans at Sphacteria (Pylos) by Cleon
c. 425 BC	Death of Herodotus
422 BC	Brasidas' victory and death at Amphipolis
421 BC	Peace of Nicias
418 BC	War between Sparta and Argos: battle of Mantinea
416 BC	Athens conquers Melos
415–413 BC	Sicilian expedition
413–404 BC	Decelean War
411 BC	Oligarchic regimes of 400 and 5,000 at Athens
410 BC	Alcibiades' victory over Spartans (and Syracusans) at Cyzicus
409 BC	Carthaginian invasion of Sicily; Hannibal conquers Selinus and Himera
408 BC	Defeat of Athenians at Notium
406 BC	Athenian victory at Arginusae. Deaths of Sophocles and Euripides
405 BC	Hannibal takes Acragas; Dionysius I forces peace on Carthaginians. Total destruction of Athenian fleet at Aegospotami
404 BC	Surrender of Athens; installation of regime of Thirty Tyrants
403 BC	Fall of Thirty Tyrants at Athens
401 BC	Battle of Cunaxa: defeat and death of Cyrus the Younger
c. 400 BC	Democritus and Zeuxis active
399 BC	Death of Socrates
396–392 BC	War between Dionysius I of Syracuse and Carthage
395–387/6 BC	Corinthian War
c. 388 BC	Plato's first visit to Syracuse. Aristophanes ceases activity
387/6 BC	King's Peace (alias Peace of Antalcidas)
383–(?)375 BC	War between Dionysius I and Carthage
382 BC	Spartan seizure of Cadmea at Thebes
379/8 BC	Liberation of Thebes
378 BC	Foundation of Second Athenian Confederacy. Raid of Sphodrias
375/4 BC	Common Peace
371 BC	(Common) Peace of Sparta. (July/August) Battle of Leuctra
371/70 BC	(Common) Peace of Athens
370/69 BC	First Theban invasion of Peloponnese (including Laconia); foundation of Messene
368 (?) BC	Foundation of Megalopolis
c. 366 BC	Plato's second visit to Syracuse
366/5 BC	(Common (?)) Peace

364 BC	Battle of Cynoscephalae; death of Pelopidas
362 BC	Battle of Mantinea; death of Epaminondas
360/59 BC	Philip II succeeds Perdiccas III of Macedonia
357–355 BC	Social War
357 BC	Philip II captures Amphipolis and Pydna; outbreak of war between Athens and Macedonia
355–346 BC	Third Sacred War
c. 350 BC	Praxiteles active
347 BC	Death of Plato. Aristotle moves from Athens to Assos
346 BC	Peace of Philocrates
344–343 BC	Timoleon liberates Syracuse from Dionysius II
342 BC	Aristotle becomes Alexander the Great's tutor
341 (?) BC	Timoleon defeats Carthaginians at river Crimisus
340 (late) BC	Athens declares war on Philip II
338 BC	(August) Battle of Chaeronea. Death of Isocrates
338/7 BC	Foundation of League of Corinth
336 BC	Philip II murdered; accession of Alexander III (the Great)
335 BC	Destruction of Thebes
334 BC	Battle of river Granicus
333 BC	(November) Battle of Issus
331 BC	Alexander visits oracle of Ammon at Siwah. (October) Battle of Gaugamela (alias Arbela)
330 BC	Burning of Persepolis. Murder of Darius III. Deaths of Philotas and Parmenion
328 BC	Murder of (Black) Cleitus
327 BC	Alexander's marriage to Roxane. The 'Pages' Conspiracy'
326 BC	Battle of river Hydaspes (Jhelum). Alexander's army mutinies at river Hyphasis (Beas)
c. 325 BC	Apelles and Lysippus active
324 BC	Exiles' Decree. Macedonian mutiny at Opis. Death of Hephaestion
323 BC	(June) Death of Alexander the Great. Death of Diogenes of Sinope
323–322 BC	Lamian War
322 BC	Battle of Crannon; abolition of Athenian democracy; death of Demosthenes. Death of Aristotle
320 BC	Death of Perdiccas. Conference at Triparadeisus: Antipater becomes regent
319 BC	Death of Antipater
317 BC	Olympias murders Philip III Arrhidaeus
316 BC	Cassander disposes of Olympias and imprisons Roxane and Alexander IV
310 (?) BC	Alexander IV murdered
305–304 BC	Demetrius Poliorcetes besieges Rhodes
301 BC	Battle of Ipsus: death of Antigonus
297 BC	Death of Cassander
294 BC	Demetrius Poliorcetes declared king of Macedon
c. 290 BC	Death of Menander
283 BC	Death of Demetrius Poliorcetes in captivity
283–246 BC	Reign of Ptolemy II; Callimachus, Theocritus, Apollonius Rhodius, Ctesibius, Erasistratus active
281 BC	Battle of Corupedium: death of Lysimachus
280 BC	Antiochus I succeeds Seleucus I
279 BC	Gallic invasion of Macedonia and Greece. Death of Ptolemy Ceraunus
277 BC	Antigonus Gonatas established as king in Macedonia
c. 274–271 BC	First Syrian War between Ptolemy II and Antiochus I
272 BC	Death of Pyrrhus of Epirus
270 BC	Death of Epicurus
266–262 BC	Chremonidean War
263 BC	Eumenes I succeeds Philetaerus as ruler of Pergamum. Death of Zeno of Citium
261 BC	Antiochus II succeeds Antiochus I
260–(?)253 BC	Second Syrian War between Ptolemy II and Antiochus II
251 BC	Aratus frees Sicyon
c. 253/c. 249 BC	Revolt of Alexander of Corinth
246 BC	Ptolemy III succeeds Ptolemy II; Eratosthenes active. Seleucus II succeeds Antiochus II
246–241 BC	Third Syrian (Laodicean) War between Ptolemy III and Seleucus II
244 BC	Agis IV becomes king at Sparta
241 BC	Death of Agis IV. Attalus I succeeds Eumenes I. War of the Brothers between Seleucus II and Antiochus Hierax
239 BC	Demetrius II succeeds Antigonus Gonatas
235 BC	Cleomenes III becomes king of Sparta
229 BC	Antigonus III Doson succeeds Demetrius II
226–225 BC	Death of Antiochus Hierax. Seleucus III succeeds Seleucus II
223 BC	Antiochus III succeeds Seleucus III

222 BC	Battle of Sellasia: defeat of Cleomenes III
221 BC	Philip V succeeds Antigonus III Doson. Ptolemy IV succeeds Ptolemy III
220–217 BC	Social War between Philip V's allies and Aetolia
219–217 BC	Fourth Syrian War between Ptolemy IV and Antiochus III
217 BC	Peace of Naupactus. Battle of Raphia
213 BC	Death of Aratus of Sicyon
211–205 BC	First Macedonian War
205 BC	Peace of Phoenice
204 BC	Ptolemy V succeeds Ptolemy IV
202–195 BC	Fifth Syrian War between Antiochus III and Ptolemy V
200–197 BC	Second Macedonian War
197 BC	Battle of Cynoscephalae. Eumenes II succeeds Attalus I
192–188 BC	Syrian War between Rome and Antiochus III
189 BC	Battle of Magnesia
188 BC	Peace of Apamea
187 BC	Seleucus IV succeeds Antiochus III
182 BC	Death of Philopoemen
180 BC	Ptolemy VI succeeds Ptolemy V
179 BC	Perseus succeeds Philip V
175 BC	Antiochus IV succeeds Seleucus IV
173–164 BC	Maccabean Revolt in Judaea
171–168 BC	Third Macedonian War
170–168 BC	Ptolemy VIII declared king of Egypt. Sixth Syrian War between Ptolemies VI and VIII, and Antiochus IV
168 BC	Battle of Pydna
165/4 BC	Seleucus IV succeeds Antiochus IV
160 BC	Demetrius I established as Seleucid king
159 BC	Attalus II succeeds Eumenes II
150 BC	Demetrius I killed by Alexander Balas
149–148 BC	Rise of Andriscus in Macedonia; Macedonia becomes Roman province
146 BC	Achaean War; sack of Corinth
145 BC	Alexander Balas killed by Demetrius II. Death of Ptolemy VI
142 BC	Diodotus Tryphon usurps Seleucid throne
139 BC	The Seleucid Demetrius II captured by Parthians. Attalus III succeeds Attalus II
138 BC	Antiochus VII deposes Diodotus Tryphon
133 BC	Pergamum bequeathed to Rome on death of Attalus III
132–130 BC	Revolt of Aristonicus
125 BC	Demetrius II killed by Alexander Zabinas
123 BC	Antiochus VIII deposes Alexander Zabinas
116 BC	Death of Ptolemy VIII; civil war begins between Ptolemy IX and X
114/13 BC	Civil war begins between Antiochus VIII and IX
c. 100 BC	Meleager active
96 BC	Cyrene bequeathed to Rome by Ptolemy Apion. Death of Antiochus VIII
95 BC	Antiochus IX dies; civil war begins among Seleucid descendants
88 BC	Death of Ptolemy X
88–84 BC	First Mithridatic War; Sulla in Greece
83 BC	Tigranes I becomes Seleucid king
81 BC	Death of Ptolemy IX. Second Mithridatic War
80 BC	Accession of Ptolemy XII
74–63 BC	Third Mithridatic War
74 BC	Nicomedes IV bequeaths Bithynia to Rome
64 BC	Pompey makes Syria a Roman province
51 BC	Ptolemy XII succeeded by Ptolemy XIII and Cleopatra VII
51–47 BC	Alexandrian War
47 BC	Death of Ptolemy XIII
44 BC	Death of Julius Caesar. Death of Ptolemy XIV
31 BC	Battle of Actium
30 BC	Death of Mark Antony and Cleopatra; Egypt becomes Roman province

Attic krater, c. 460 BC (?), depicting the murder of Aegisthus by Orestes, a scene described by *Aeschylus in his *Choephori* (*Libation Bearers*), 458 BC. Courtesy, Museum of Fine Arts, Boston (William Francis Warden Fund).

Introduction

Like the previous volume *Who Was Who in the Roman World*, *Who Was Who in the Greek World* aims to provide a scholarly and readable account of the lives, achievements, and works of all the more notable personages who appear in the history of the period covered. The entries are illustrated, wherever possible, by portrait busts and coins, works of artists, maps of campaigns, monuments constructed, and other pictorial documentation, to give the reader a vivid, informed, up-to-date, and rounded view of the subject of each short biography. Important non-Greeks with whom the Greeks came into contact are included, in addition to the Greeks themselves, who come not only from Greece itself but from the lands of early colonization in Asia Minor and the north Aegean, the Black Sea, Sicily, southern Italy, North Africa, and elsewhere, and, later, from the countries of the Hellenistic 'diaspora' over much of the Middle East.

The book begins at 776 BC, the traditional date of the first Olympiad – the first Olympic Games ever celebrated – and the dawn of Greek 'protohistory' as it has been called, for until at least the sixth century BC hard facts and known persons are difficult to come by. The period of legend that comprises several centuries before 776 is almost – but not quite – excluded, for here the borderline between legend based on fact and pure myth is an impossibly fine one, and this area is properly the preserve of the poet and the dictionary of mythology rather than of the historian (Greek or modern) and biographer. An exception has been made in the case of a few representative figures from the Greek Bronze Age, for the magnificent achievements of archaeology in digging up Minoan and Mycenaean palaces prove the existence of powerful kings and princes, and the literary tradition has handed down names such as Minos and Agamemnon, Nestor and Odysseus, which may or may not be the names of real Bronze Age leaders who lived in the palaces. The present state of our knowledge of the palaces and the tablets with Linear B writing, and their

possible relation to some of the most famous *Homeric (and other) heroes, is explained in a special section of the Introduction, written by Dr John Chadwick (who was associated with Michael Ventris in his brilliant decipherment of Linear B). At the other end of 'Greek history', the closing date for the book, 30 BC, is that of the fall of the last major Hellenistic kingdom – Ptolemaic Egypt under *Cleopatra (VII) – to Rome in the person of Octavian, soon to become Augustus, the first Roman emperor. In the period of Rome's advance into the eastern Mediterranean, there is inevitably some overlap with the Roman volume, which has been dealt with as follows. Only the major architects of that advance during the second century BC – men such as *Flamininus, *Scipio Africanus, and Aemilius *Paullus – and others such as *Mummius, destroyer of Corinth, and *Scipio Aemilianus, great patron of Greek culture, are included here; and they are looked at from the point of view of Hellenistic history, with broader consideration of their careers omitted. By the first century BC the Hellenistic world was rapidly becoming Roman, and it is in the Roman volume alone that the reader will find such figures as Sulla, Lucullus, Pompey, Caesar, Antony, and Octavian; while *Mithridates (VI), for example, is in both books, but the entry here concentrates on his dealings with Greece and Asia Minor. Some of the Greek intellectuals and poets whose influence was mainly felt by the Romans are included here, whether they were in the Roman volume or not, as representatives of those who helped to carry Greek culture to Rome. From 30 BC virtually the whole of the Greek world was incorporated in the Roman, and it is *Who Was Who in the Roman World* that must be consulted. However, advantage has been taken of the fact that it was not until AD 72 that the last minor Hellenistic kingdom, Commagene, became part of Roman Syria, to include a few figures from beyond the lower time limit of 30 BC, much as, beyond the upper limit, a small selection of representative Bronze Age and early Dark Age heroes is included in Dr Chadwick's excursus in the

Introduction, and perhaps *Daedalus in the main text. The main ones are *Heron of Alexandria, whose very uncertain date may be as late as AD 100, but whose work forms a pendant to Hellenistic science; and the *Evangelists and St *Paul, in deference to the ancient view that Christianity was the fulfilment of Greek philosophy.

The form of each entry is as follows: the heading normally consists of the name, a brief identification or description, and one or more dates. The date or dates of a person's birth and/or death almost invariably follow the name, in brackets. Dates of an office held, on the other hand, follow the mention of that office on the right-hand side of the heading, and this is also the case with less precise dates, e.g. 'Philosopher, 2nd century BC'. A date of death following, exceptionally, the office indicates that the person died in office (generally killed in battle or executed). Inclusive dates, e.g. '493–490 BC', are indicated by a hyphen, meaning that the person held office (or lived) from one date to the other. The stroke convention shows that the office was held (or the person was born or died) somewhere between the dates given, e.g. 'Archon 493/490 BC'. As the (variable) Greek year did not coincide with the Roman (and modern) year, many dates are in this form. In the body of the entry (and elsewhere), cross-references are indicated by an asterisk at the beginning of the name (that under which the person is classified, if more than one). A double asterisk against a name distinguishes a 'representative' Bronze Age hero on whom there is a brief entry in the Minoan-Mycenaean section of the Introduction. Cross-references to entries in *Who Was Who in the Roman World* are given in the bibliography at the foot of the entry concerned. At least one bibliographical reference, whether to an ancient source or to a book for further reading, appears at the foot of every entry. In the case of writers whose works are preserved, the existence of an edition in the Loeb Classical Library series, with text and English translation, is assumed (there is a complete list of 'Loebs' at the back of every volume), and is only mentioned specifically in the bibliography if several writers share a single volume (e.g. *Minor Attic Orators, Papyri*).

The book also contains additional information of various kinds. A chronological table, comprising major events and their dates and the regnal dates of Hellenistic kings, accompanies this introduction and the outline history of the period covered which forms part of it. At the end of the book, an index of (historical) persons mentioned in other entries, but not important enough to be given their own entry, supplements the main text. This is followed by a glossary, in which technical terms used in the entries, such as offices held and specialized literary and philosophical terms, are explained. The general

bibliography includes all the abbreviations used in the main text, and a few extra works, not mentioned elsewhere, for further reading. In addition to the maps illustrating some individual entries, there are a number of general maps at the end of the book: virtually all geographical names appearing in the text are to be found on the appropriate one of these. Finally, several stemmata (family trees) show the family connections of Spartan and Hellenistic kings.

The entries are arranged in alphabetical order; Romans with more than one name are classified by that under which they appear in *Who Was Who in the Roman World*. Kings and queens appear before other individuals of the same name. The numbering of homonymous persons has only been resorted to where there is no other means of distinguishing them (e.g. *Thucydides, *Thucydides son of Melesias; *Zeno of Citium, *Zeno of Elea, *Zenon); where they are numbered, they appear in chronological order or, if contemporary, in order of fame or importance.

In any book on ancient Greece, the most pressing preliminary problem is that of the transliteration of Greek names and words. This has been dealt with according to the golden mean of *Aristotle – i.e. moderation. There are basically two systems of transliterating Greek names into the Roman alphabet. One is Latinization, i.e. spelling them as the Romans themselves spelt them, notably with 'c' for kappa, 'ch' for chi, 'ae' for alpha iota, 'oe' for omicron iota, 'u' for omicron upsilon, 'y' for upsilon, '-us' for the '-os' ending, and '-der' for the '-dros' ending – e.g. Aeschylus, Cleon, Lysander, Oenopides, Pericles, Thucydides. The other is direct transliteration – e.g. Aiskhulos, Kleon, Lusandros, Oinopides, Perikles, Thoukudides. Broadly, the Latinized form (with the exception of epsilon iota, in which the 'e' is retained, as are final 'n's where custom is not too strong – as it is with Plato, Phaedo, and the two famous Zenos) has been used for all personal names, to avoid the confusion resulting from the direct transliteration of familiar names (e.g. Kroisos ('as rich as *Croesus*'), Drakon ('Draconian measures'), Hektor, Platon, Alexandros the Great). In only two cases has this been departed from: the sculptor Endoios and the vase-painter Exekias will be more familiar to readers in their transliterated forms and the Latinized versions would be uncomfortable (Execias) or almost unrecognizable (Endoeus). The most important consequence is that names beginning with kappa and chi should be sought under C, not K. Where the direct transliteration is different from the Latinized form (or there are etas and omegas), it is given in brackets immediately after the Latinized form in the first sentence of the entry. The chosen system of transliteration is that of the *Concise Oxford Dictionary*, with 'k' and 'kh' for kappa and chi, 'u' for upsilon, and a long vowel sign 'ē' for eta and 'ō' for omega. The names are almost all given in the Attic form used by most Greek writers – here again it is the most familiar form that is selected; a few names of Dorians (Spartans and others) have their Doric alternative given as well (alpha replacing eta and sometimes other vowels). As for geographical names, the vast majority of these appear in their familiar Latinized – or even Anglicized (e.g. Athens, Corinth) – form: thus Epirus, not Epeiros; river Maeander, not Maiandros; Mycenae, not Mukenai. The most obvious exceptions are some Aegean islands (and a few other place-names ending in '-os'), well known by their modern Greek names (Lesbos, Samos, Knossos, etc.), and a few hybrids (Ceos, Cos, Cnidos) established by usage. Titles of works in Greek are generally current in Latin translation or Latinized or semi-Latinized form, and these – again the more familiar forms – have been used. Other Greek words and technical terms are also treated flexibly, the most common form being chosen.

I should like to thank my contributors for their enthusiasm and helpfulness, and willingness to respond promptly to last-minute requests for information, which have made working on this book – and reverting to my earlier love of the Greeks – a great pleasure. As before, I have also been given much support and practical assistance by my husband and by Phaidon.   D.B.

The Homeric Heroes

JOHN CHADWICK

The records kept by the ancient Greeks did not go back further than the eighth century BC, the date at which alphabetic writing was introduced. But a dim recollection of earlier events was preserved in the oral tradition of epic poetry, and Homer and other poets told of a period when the southern mainland of Greece had been rich and powerful.

Archaeology over the last hundred years has established a framework for the early history of Greece. Civilization began in the third millennium BC, and the Bronze Age is divided into three major periods: Early Helladic, very roughly 2500–2000 BC, Middle Helladic 2000–1600 BC, Late Helladic or Mycenaean 1600–1100 BC. For linguistic reasons it seems probable that the ancestors of the Greeks arrived at the break between the Early and Middle Helladic periods. The Late Helladic culture seems to be a development from the preceding period under the influence of Minoan Crete. The Minoans were not Greek-speaking, but the Greeks of the mainland eventually displaced them as the leading power in

the southern Aegean, and took over Crete itself in the fifteenth century. The Heroic Age of the poets is therefore probably to be identified with the Late Helladic period, especially the fourteenth to thirteenth centuries when the civilization based upon Mycenae was at its height. A series of destructions around 1200 BC led to its collapse and disappearance.

We do not know if any of the Greek heroes are historical characters. For the fourteenth and thirteenth centuries BC we have administrative documents from Pylos and Knossos (as well as a few discovered at Thebes, Mycenae, and Tiryns), written in Linear B, a syllabic script; they contain accounts, but there are no monumental inscriptions recording the names of occupants of tombs or episodes of political importance such as the exploits of kings. These tablets were preserved by the accidental baking of their clay in the fires which destroyed the palaces, and they are testimony only of a limited sphere during a limited period. Since alphabetic writing was introduced into Greece only in the eighth century BC, the preceding centuries are a dark age, illuminated by what archaeology can deduce and by stories the Greeks themselves told of their past. The legends and oral traditions must have become confused, contaminated by myth and folk-tale. Archaeology can confirm the main sequences and localizations, but can tell nothing of the personalities.

We may wonder whether heroic characters were invented later to give colour to the traditional stories and provide illustrious pedigrees for noble families. The classical Greeks had no such misgivings. To them episodes such as the Trojan War were historical fact. Monumental Bronze Age remains, such as the walls of Tiryns and Mycenae, were visible to the classical Greeks, proof to them of the reality of the heroes their legends described. The propagandist purpose of the restoration of the bones of Theseus from Scyros (476 BC) by *Cimon shows that Bronze Age history was real to the fifth-century Greeks.

Such beliefs have persisted. Archaeologists have been romantics, their searches directed by the text of *Homer, and they have named their discoveries after legendary figures. Evans called the palace at Knossos in Crete 'the Palace of Minos', Blegen that at Ano Englianos in Messenia 'the Palace of Nestor', but in fact the discovery of the buildings does not vouch for the authenticity of the names. Schliemann claimed to have verified the *Iliad* by unearthing a fortified city in the Troad, which he called Troy and the rich treasure found there 'Priam's treasure'. In fact the site at Hisarlik has provided no inscriptional evidence to fix its pre-classical name, and the treasure, from Troy II, is at least 1,000 years older than Troy VIIA, the city destroyed in the thirteenth century BC. Crowded dwellings and numerous large storage jars let into floors suggest a siege. Archaeology tends to confirm the main outline of the story, but of Priam and his sons there is no trace.

At Mycenae, another site where Schliemann excavated, the beehive tombs and two groups of shaft graves with their rich treasure must have been burial-places of wealthy rulers, but we do not know whether any of them were called Agamemnon or Atreus or any other of the names from Mycenaean legend. At Ano Englianos the Linear B tablets give us the name Pylos for the site, but the Homeric geography of the kingdom does not match what we know from the tablets.

The Catalogue of the Ships in *Iliad* ii describes a Greece unlike that which existed at any historical period. But the passage shows signs of having been designed for a different purpose – note, for instance, the preponderance of Boeotians, who figure little in the rest of the poem – and it is hard to accept it as an accurate record, though it is of course true that most classical cities had a Mycenaean predecessor. The absence of Thebes has been explained as being due to its eclipse before the end of the Mycenaean period, but the archaeological evidence for this is disputed; it was certainly active in the early thirteenth century. But sherds of Mycenaean pottery from Ithaca cannot guarantee the existence of Odysseus, nor a palace at Thebes confirm the legend of Oedipus.

Although the Linear B tablets do not reveal the names of the kings at Pylos or Knossos, since the title alone suffices to describe them, they do contain the names of hundreds of men and women, both nobles and humble folk. The script sometimes makes their interpretation uncertain, but there are enough clear examples for us to be able to recognize familiar Greek types of name, so we can be sure that the population was predominantly Greek.

If Nestor and Agamemnon are missing, at least 50 other heroic names can be identified as corresponding to the spelling habits of the script. Noteworthy are *a-ki-re-u* Akhilleus, *te-se-u* Theseus, *e-ko-to-ri-jo* (patronymic derivative of Hektor), *pi-ri-ja-me-ja* (feminine derivative of Priamos), *a-re-ka-sa-da-ra* (feminine of Alexandros).

The explanation of this undoubted fact is uncertain. It is possible, for instance, that the legendary characters were already sufficiently famous for relatively humble people to have been named after them. But this would involve supposing that the stories of the Trojan War were already current by the mid-thirteenth century BC, if not earlier, and this would destroy the identification of Troy VIIA as the 'Homeric' Troy. Perhaps the leading figures of the epics are historical characters, but transposed to a later period, as happened in

other oral traditions. Perhaps the epic tradition drew upon a genuine stock of Mycenaean names, but invented fictitious characters to bear them. Certainly the documents confirm that the Homeric names are appropriate for Mycenaean characters, but they cannot do anything to prove that Homer's history is correct.

Achilles (Akhilleus) Son of the sea-nymph Thetis and Peleus, king of Phthia in Thessaly; chief of the Greek heroes in the *Iliad*. He refuses to fight because of a quarrel with **Agamemnon, until at length the death of his friend Patroclus rouses him to kill **Hector.
BIBL. *Iliad, passim.*

Aeneas (Aineias) Son of Anchises and Aphrodite, Trojan leader in the *Iliad* and hero of Virgil's *Aeneid*. After the fall of Troy he fled with his father and his son Ascanius, and after many wanderings founded Lavinium, head of the Latin League.
BIBL. *Iliad* v. 467–8, etc.; Virgil, *Aeneid, passim.*

Agamemnon (Agamemnōn) Son of Atreus and brother of **Menelaus, he was king of Mycenae and overlord of the Greeks at Troy. He allowed the sacrifice of his daughter Iphigeneia to appease Artemis, and on his return from Troy was murdered by his wife Clytemnestra and her lover Aegisthus. The legend of an important king of Mycenae answers well to the pre-eminent position of the surviving remains of a major fortress from the Mycenaean period.
BIBL. *Iliad, passim*; *Odyssey* i. 35 ff., etc.; Aeschylus, *Agamemnon*; Euripides, *Iphigeneia in Aulis*; McDonald, *Progress into the Past*; F. H. Stubbings, *Prehistoric Greece* (1972).

Ajax (Aias) Son of Telamon, king of Salamis, a bulwark of the Greek army at Troy. *Sophocles' play *Ajax* tells how Athena, in revenge for the destruction of her statue at Troy, drove him to madness and suicide when he did not receive the arms of the dead **Achilles.
BIBL. *Iliad* iii. 225–9, etc.; *Odyssey* xi. 543 ff.; Sophocles, *Ajax.*

Codrus (Kodros) King of Athens, whose house succeeded that of **Theseus (q.v.); his father Melantheus, a descendant of Neleus, had been expelled from his Pylian kingdom by the Dorians (see below). Since an oracle decreed that the Dorians could only take Athens while he lived, he deliberately courted death in battle.
BIBL. Herodotus ix. 97; Pausanias I. xix. 5, etc.

Hector (Hektōr) Eldest son of **Priam (q.v.) and Hecuba, husband of Andromache and father of Astyanax; he led the bravest Trojans in battle. He was killed by **Achilles (q.v.) in revenge for the death of Patroclus. His body was eventually ransomed by Priam.
BIBL. *Iliad, passim.*

Heracleidae (Hērakleidai) Since Heracles' son Hyllus was a Dorian by adoption, the Dorian conquest of the Peloponnese was regarded as a return of the sons of Heracles (Heracleidae) to reclaim their legitimate inheritance, the kingship of Mycenae and Tiryns, of which Heracles had been cheated through Hera's jealousy. The royal houses of the three Dorian states in the Peloponnese (Argos, Sparta, and Messenia) all claimed Heraclid descent.

BIBL. Herodotus ix. 26; Apollodorus ii. 167 ff., etc.; Pausanias I. xli. 2, III. i. 5–6, v. iii. 5–6, VIII. v. 1.

Menelaus (Menelaos) King of Sparta, the younger brother of **Agamemnon (q.v.), husband of the beautiful Helen whose abduction by Paris caused the Trojan war. After the sack he was reunited with her and returned to Sparta after many wanderings and adventures. There were undoubtedly Mycenaean settlements in the vicinity of Sparta, but no major palace has yet been discovered. On one site there is evidence that Helen and Menelaus were worshipped as heroes in the archaic period.

BIBL. *Iliad*, passim, esp. iii. 21 ff.; Euripides, *Helen*.

Minos (Minōs) Son of Zeus and Europa, king of Crete and ruler of a great empire by his fleet. Athens was forced to pay a yearly tribute of youths and maidens to the Minotaur, half-man, half-bull, kept in the Labyrinth belonging to Minos, until at length this was foiled by **Theseus (q.v.). The huge palace of Knossos with its complex plan has been thought to be the origin of the myth of the Labyrinth. It was at least a major administrative centre down to its destruction in the fourteenth century BC. Minos was killed in Sicily by the craftsman *Daedalus, and in the *Odyssey* he appears as a ruler of the dead.

BIBL. *Odyssey* xi. 568, xix. 178; Plutarch, *Life of Theseus* 15; Herodotus vii. 170; A. Cottrell, *The Minoan World* (1979); McDonald, *Progress into the Past*.

Nestor (Nestōr) Son of Neleus, garrulous and aged ruler of Pylos, who gives counsel to the Greeks at Troy. A large Mycenaean palace has been excavated in the south-west Peloponnese and can be shown to have controlled the Messenian kingdom, but there is no evidence for the name of its ruler at the time of its destruction at the end of the thirteenth century BC.

BIBL. *Iliad*, passim, esp. i. 247 ff., xi. 655 ff.; J. Chadwick, *The Mycenaean World* (1976); McDonald, *Progress into the Past*.

Odysseus (Odusseus) Son of Laertes, father of Telemachus, king of Ithaca, the resourceful central figure of the *Odyssey*, which recounts his ten years of wanderings after the fall of Troy. On his return he is reunited with his faithful wife Penelope, after slaying her suitors. Traces of Mycenaean occupation have been found on Ithaca, but there is no confirmation that it was an important administrative centre.

BIBL. *Odyssey*, passim; *Iliad* x. 242 ff., xi. 312 ff., xix. 154 ff., etc.

Oedipus (Oidipous) Son of Laïus king of Thebes, exposed as a baby after an oracle declared that he was destined to kill his father. He lived, however, only to kill Laïus unknowingly. At Thebes he guessed the riddle of the Sphinx, was made king, and married the queen Jocasta, not realizing she was his mother. They had four children. On discovery of the truth Oedipus blinded himself and

Jocasta hanged herself. The site of Thebes is still occupied by the modern town, but what excavation has been possible clearly proves that it had an important palace in the Mycenaean period.

BIBL. *Iliad* xxiii. 679–80; Sophocles, *Oedipus Tyrannus*, *Oedipus Coloneus*.

Priam (Priamos) Son of Laomedon, king of Troy at the time of the Trojan war, when already an old man; father of 50 sons by his wife Hecuba and others. In the sack he was killed by Neoptolemus at Zeus' altar in his own palace. The existence of a Bronze Age fortress in a position overlooking the Dardanelles corresponding to Homer's description of Troy was established by Schliemann. Modern opinion inclines to identify the settlement of Troy VIIA, which was destroyed, probably by enemy action, in the middle of the thirteenth century BC, with the Homeric Troy.

BIBL. *Iliad* iii. 616 ff., xxiv. 495–7, 159 ff.; Virgil, *Aeneid* ii. 506 ff.; C. W. Blegen, *Troy and the Trojans* (1963); McDonald, *Progress into the Past*.

Theseus (Thēseus) National hero of Athens. In his youth, on the road from Troezen, his mother Aethra's city, to Athens he slew various bandits and beasts, and later in Crete the Minotaur with Ariadne's help. He succeeded his father Aegeus as King of Athens, and united Attica into a single state. He fought beside his friend Peirithous against the Centaurs, and accompanied him to the Underworld. One version says that he was imprisoned there permanently, another that he was rescued by Heracles and was eventually murdered on Scyros. There is clear evidence for Mycenaean occupation on and around the Acropolis, but subsequent rebuilding and destruction, especially that by the Persians in 480 BC, has destroyed what traces might have been left by a palace.

BIBL. *Odyssey* xi. 631; Plutarch, *Life of Theseus*, *Life of Cimon* 36.

The Dorian Invasions

The collapse of the Mycenaean civilization used to be attributed to the arrival from the north of a new wave of Greek invaders. But it now appears that this was not the major cause of the collapse. None the less, a persistent tradition, recorded by *Thucydides as well as *Herodotus and supported by references in *Pindar and other early poets, related that following the Trojan War attacks were launched on the Mycenaean strongholds by Dorians under the leadership of the Heracleidae or 'descendants of Heracles'. These invaders came from northern Greece and occupied most of the Peloponnese. Implausible accounts of their wanderings are given by Herodotus (i. 56), but all indications agree that they came from the general area of the Pindus mountains. There is archaeological evidence of extensive fortifications constructed in the thirteenth century at Mycenae, Tiryns, and Gla in Boeotia. Remains of a Mycenaean wall crossing the Isthmus of Corinth suggest that attempts were made to prevent an incursion from the north into the Peloponnese.

Since the classical inhabitants of all the Peloponnese except Arcadia called themselves Dorians, it has been accepted that their ancestors conquered this area, and that the Doric dialects extend from north-western Greece (Epirus, Acarnania, Phocis, and Locris) to the Isthmus and Megara, embracing all the Peloponnese except Arcadia, and the islands of Melos, Thera, Crete, and the southern Dodecanese. There is, however, singularly little archaeological confirmation of this extension. Mycenaean sites were destroyed equally in Boeotia and Attica, and there is no clear indication of invasion from the mainland to account for the presence of Dorians in the islands.

It is certain that migrations did take place inside Greece during the Dark Ages, but their scale and origins are totally obscure. In particular, it now seems unlikely that the Doric dialects were imported from any other area, since most scholars now accept that the Greek language was created inside Greece. A massive invasion of Greek-speakers from north-western Greece is improbable in view of the inhospitable nature of the country and the lack of known inhabited sites; but it is not impossible that some leading families of the Peloponnese could trace their ancestry back to that area. It has recently been suggested that the Doric dialects were already established in southern Greece in Mycenaean times, and the apparent change of dialect after the collapse of the palace-based economy is simply due to the expulsion of an aristocratic class whose dialect was different from that of their subjects. On this view, the formation of the classical dialect divisions dates largely from the Dark Ages, and the Doric dialect cannot be attributed to any groups of northerners who reached the Peloponnese at this time.

The Mycenaean collapse was followed by a Dark Age of which little is known. Material culture was reduced to a low level: there are no stone buildings, and luxury goods seem to be almost unknown. Foreign trade is non-existent, or on a small scale. Only in the production of fine pottery can we see a continuous tradition; and here the decoration popular with the Minoans and Mycenaeans gives way to a new style characterized by formal patterns, known as Geometric. The introduction of iron ultimately led to the production of superior weapons and a change in fighting techniques. The chariot had long since ceased to be the basis of military power, and the heavily-armed infantry now dominated the battlefield. This correlates with the change from monarchical to oligarchical government.   J.C.

Outline History 776–30 BC

By 776 BC, the first Olympiad and traditional beginning of early Greek history, the Greek world – comprising mainland Greece, the Aegean islands, and the coast of Asia Minor – had settled down after the invasions and upheavals that brought the Bronze Age to a close and ushered in the Iron Age. It was also becoming literate with the gradual adoption of the modified Phoenician alphabet. This enabled the first systematic records to be kept, sacred records such as lists of priests or of Olympic victors, and secular ones such as lists of kings and annual magistrates in the emerging *poleis*. The *polis*, or city-state, the basic unit of political organization in this country of small plains and valleys sharply divided from each other by mountains and sea, was formed by the grouping of villages and small towns in each geographically delimited area. Sometimes a dominant 'city', as we would recognize it, such as Athens or Corinth, was the centre of the political unit, but this was by no means always the case, especially in northern Greece. This type of political organization, within which a wide variety of constitutions was possible, was to prove an ideal framework for the innovative turbulence of the Greek mind, but also a potent source of conflict and disunity, which was to prove the undoing of Greece as an independent country and put it beneath the power first of its near relation Macedon, and then of Rome, who gave it the name 'Graecia' which has passed into western European languages instead of the Greeks' own name, Hellas.

The early records of archaic Greece were later used as sources by the first historians, especially *Herodotus, known as the 'Father of History', and mark the dividing line between history proper – at first recorded only tenuously – and prehistory, part of which in the case of the Greeks is illuminated by a literary tradition in which, as Dr Chadwick points out, it is generally impossible to disentangle truth from fiction. Gradually, as the succeeding Dark Age came to an end, trading relations with the more highly developed countries of the eastern Mediterranean were re-established, and the introduction of the alphabet was one of the fruits of this renewed contact. The painted pottery, hitherto Geometric – decorated with close-set bands of patterns with only an occasional little scene of stylized figures (like the huge Dipylon Vase in Athens) – began to show eastern influences, depicting animals such as panthers on a rosette-scattered background in an 'orientalizing' style. Much of this ware was Corinthian, Corinth with her access to two seas being well placed to become a major seafaring power.

The populations of the city-states were expanding

rapidly, and a solution was found, in the period *c.* 750–*c.* 550 BC, in the sending-out of overseas colonies, to the Black Sea and the northern Aegean, to Sicily and southern Italy, to northern Africa (Cyrenaica), the south of France (notably Marseilles), and even Spain. In an age when most city-states were ruled by aristocracies, the expeditions to found colonies were made up of landless men and their families and led by a member of the ruling class who had for some reason fallen foul of it (e.g. *Archias; compare *Dorieus). The expedition would take brands from the city's sacred hearth, and the new settlement retained sentimental ties with its 'metropolis' or mother-city, but not usually political ones. The main colonizing cities were maritime ones with a confined territory and a seafaring tradition, such as Corinth, Megara, and Chalcis in Euboea. Another maritime power, Aegina, was the first to issue its own coinage, *c.* 650 BC, borrowing the idea from the Lydians of Asia Minor.

Cultural life, too, was flourishing. In the field of literature, the epic of *Homer and *Hesiod was followed by a more personal 'lyric' poetry, no longer chanted in kingly halls but sung among boon companions after dinner: the drinking-songs, love-songs, fables, and attacks on political enemies composed by *Sappho and *Alcaeus, *Archilochus, and others. Architecture and art were developing, too, with stone temples replacing wooden ones, with sculptured stone and terracotta decoration and statues in the round (the latter at first showing Egyptian influence). The archaic period (roughly 776–500 BC), which largely coincides with the period of colonial expansion, was an age of adventure and individualism, in which Greek navigators in their small boats braved the dangers to explore the whole Mediterranean and even beyond, and Greek mercenary soldiers were to be found as far afield as Babylon and Egypt. The talented man of noble family had plenty of scope for his ambitions, and exceptional individuals might become wise lawgivers to whom their cities turned for the solution of their problems: this was the age of the *Seven Sages, such as *Solon of Athens and *Pittacus of Mytilene in Lesbos. Or, generally later in the period, they might take advantage of popular discontent to become despots – 'tyrants'.

Neither Athens nor Sparta, the two most celebrated city-states of ancient Greece, played a very large part in the colonizing movement. Sparta, in the earlier part of the period, was engaged in extending her control over the southern Peloponnese, notably by the conquest of Messenia in the late eighth century BC (see *Aristodemus of Messenia, *Theopompus of Sparta), and in developing her unique constitution: two kings, five annually elected 'ephors', a council of elders (the Gerousia), and an assembly of free citizens (Spartiates) who lived the life of soldiers among a large population of serfs (helots) and non-citizens. Throughout her history Sparta showed a strong conservatism and reluctance for military adventure, lest she lose too much manpower and the helots revolt. As for Athens, the size and fertility of the plains of Attica long saved her from the pressures which drove neighbouring Megara and Corinth to send colonies overseas, but once the land was all in use and increasingly subdivided, the owners of small plots began to get into debt, and many were forced to sell their families into slavery and become bond-slaves themselves. It was this crisis which Solon dealt with in 594 BC by freeing the bond-slaves and reforming the constitution, establishing a council drawn from those of moderate property in addition to the old aristocratic council, the Areopagus.

The classic constitutional pattern followed by the majority of the Greek city-states was: monarchy, aristocracy, tyranny, then democracy or oligarchy. In the sixth century BC very many cities were governed by a tyrant, an ambitious noble who had set himself up as unconstitutional ruler, relying on the support of the *demos*, the people, who still had no voice in the government. Some even succeeded in founding a dynasty, for example the Cypselids of Corinth (see *Cypselus, *Periander). Solon had hoped, by his just solution of the problems afflicting Athens, to remove the causes of the discontent that normally lay at the root of tyranny; but, in 546 BC, *Peisistratus succeeded where *Cylon had failed, and became tyrant of Athens, handing on power on his death to his son *Hippias. Many tyrants ruled well, built up the power and prestige of their cities (e.g. *Polycrates of Samos, in addition to those already mentioned), and were noted for the brilliance of their courts; but the inevitable corruption attendant on the wielding of absolute power led to the word *tyrannos*, which originally meant simply 'king', acquiring the connotations of the English 'tyrant'. However, when the archaic-period tyrannies ended, through death or deposition, the *demos* to which the tyrant had looked for support against rival nobles was more politically aware and ready to assert its rights: there could be no going back to rule by the 'best', the *aristoi*, i.e. the nobles, but equally there was in most cases no reason to give political franchise to every humblest citizen in the State. Political power still lay in the hands of those best able to defend the city and fight its wars, the class of men able to afford their own armour and maintain themselves on campaign, fighting as 'hoplites', heavy-armed soldiers. This was the normal basis of an oligarchy, 'rule by the few', which remained a common type of constitution. In Athens the existence and stability of true democracy, in which every full citizen had the right to vote conclusively on matters in the Assembly, to be empanelled as a juror, and to be elected to any of the State offices, was linked especially with the rise of her powerful navy, which was promoted by *Themistocles at the time of the Persian Wars (490–479 BC), in a brilliant identification of the true path for Athens' self-interest. For the large numbers of oarsmen were drawn from the common people, who thus acquired a strategic importance greater than that of the richer hoplites, who fought on land or as marines. (Indeed the destruction of her fleet at the end of the Peloponnesian War, in 404 BC, was to lead to an immediate attempt to establish an oligarchy – but democracy proved too deep-rooted.) The conditions necessary for Athens' emergence as a naval power were created under the Peisistratid tyrants in the sixth century, with her rise to economic pre-eminence, eloquently witnessed by the clean sweep of the market made by her beautiful black-figure pottery (see *Exekias). And it was in the last decade of the sixth century, after the removal of the Peisistratids with Spartan assistance (see *Cleomenes I), that *Cleisthenes, to prevent the threatened return to the chaos of aristocratic faction, broke the political dominance of the nobles by setting aside the clan basis of political organization, and established a democratic constitution, comprising a Council of Five Hundred chosen by lot, an assembly of all citizens, and ten annually elected 'generals' (*strategoi*), who formed the main executive. Meanwhile Sparta, her own territory already secured, had in the course of the sixth century been building up a system of defensive alliances known to us as the Peloponnesian League, to which even Athens belonged for a time (and of major Peloponnesian states only Argos, bitter foe of Sparta, remained aloof). For Sparta was unquestionably the most powerful Greek state militarily – at least on land.

Across the Aegean, the expanding power of Persia was beginning to impinge on the Greeks. Already the Greek cities of the coastal areas of Asia Minor (Ionia) had fallen under Persian control, and by 513 BC, when *Darius I first crossed the Bosporus, the strait between Asia and Europe, he also controlled the northern Aegean. His fleet comprised the large Phoenician navy and those of the Ionian cities and islands, and the free Greeks of the mainland were powerless to stop its advance across the Aegean. Indeed, in 499 BC a Persian force tried to capture Naxos, largest and richest of the Cyclades in the central Aegean. Its failure to do so was a cause of the Ionian Revolt (499–494), for the cities of the Ionian seaboard were growing restive under the tyrants through whom Persia maintained her control, and hoped, through winning support from mainland Greece, to throw off the Persian yoke;

prematurely. For though under its leader *Aristagoras of Miletus some initial successes were gained, disunity among the Ionians and the scantiness of help from the mainland combined to sink the enterprise, and Persian control was re-established. In 492 Thrace and Macedonia were added to the Persian domains. Then, in 490, Darius sent an expedition under *Datis and *Artaphernes to Greece itself, to punish Athens and Eretria for sending a few ships to the Ionian rebels. Eretria (in Euboea) was destroyed, but the Athenians under *Miltiades, with reinforcements only from neighbouring Plataea – the Spartan forces, fetched by the runner *Pheidippides, did not arrive in time – decisively defeated the invaders when they landed at Marathon, and marched quickly back to Athens to foil an attempt by the Persian fleet to take the city in their absence. The Persian threat was removed for ten years, but in 480 BC King *Xerxes himself mounted a huge expedition by land and sea, invading Greece from the north. This time there was ample warning, as Xerxes had a canal dug across the stormy promontory of Mount Athos and a bridge of boats made across the Bosporus, and the Greeks, led by Sparta, decided to hold the pass of Thermopylae in northern Greece, keeping their fleet – including a very substantial Athenian contingent – at Cape Artemisium (Euboea) near by. The subsequent events – the fierce and prolonged fighting, the Persian discomfiture, the turning of the pass by a force led by a traitor, and the final stand of King *Leonidas with 300 Spartans – are among the most famous in all history. After an inconclusive naval engagement off Artemisium, the Greek fleet retreated to Salamis and Athens was abandoned. But the sea-battle in the narrows at Salamis, in which the comparatively few Greek ships threw the Persian fleet into confusion and crippled it, gave the Greeks control of the sea. Xerxes retreated to Persia, leaving *Mardonius to continue the campaign on land. In 479 the Greek forces, led by the Spartan *Pausanias (1), marched out to Plataea, where they defeated the Persian land army and killed Mardonius. On the same day the Greek fleet destroyed the remnants of the Persian fleet off Cape Mycale (Asia Minor) and proceeded to clear the Aegean and free the Ionian and north Aegean cities. With similar success the Greeks in Sicily defeated a Carthaginian invasion (see *Gelon, *Hamilcar).

The recall of Pausanias to Sparta left the Athenians with the leadership of the allied forces, and they organized the newly liberated cities of the Aegean into the Delian League, whose transformation into a reluctant Athenian empire dominated the events of the 'Pentekontaetea', the 'fifty years' between the Persian Wars and the Peloponnesian War (which began in 431 BC). As long as the Athenian 'alliance' was operating, even intermittently, against Persia – the highlight was the victory under *Cimon at the river Eurymedon in c. 467, and in the 450s the allies were even involved in a rebellion in Egypt (see *Inarus) – there was a moral justification for Athens' dominating position within the League, and for the allies' payment of tribute towards the war effort; but in 449/8 she negotiated some sort of peace with Persia (the 'Peace of *Callias' son of Hipponicus (1)). Thereafter, in the great age of *Pericles' ascendancy at Athens, the enemy was coming more and more to be seen as Sparta, to whom, as the 'yoke-mate of Athens', help had been sent in 462 when she was threatened with destruction after an earthquake and a helot revolt, but who now stood in the way of Athens' imperialist ambitions. In 445, at the end of Athens' ten-year domination of Boeotia, a Thirty Years' Peace was signed with Sparta, and Periclean Athens reached the peak of her power and prosperity and of an artistic and intellectual life expressed, above all, in the Parthenon and the Propylaea of the Acropolis (see *Pheidias, *Ictinus) and in the tragedies of *Sophocles and *Euripides.

But Athens' uncompromising attitude to Sparta and her allies led to the outbreak of the Peloponnesian War in 431, most of it chronicled by *Thucydides, the greatest historian of antiquity. The first half of the war – the Archidamian War (431–421) – was won by Athens, whom the Peloponnesians were unable to dislodge from her position or even seriously damage, despite the outbreak of the plague in 430. The main theatres of war, apart from Attica itself, annually ravaged by the Spartans, were north-west Greece, Pylos, and Thrace. After the death of Pericles in 429, the main war-leaders at Athens were *Cleon and *Demosthenes, son of Alcisthenes (not to be confused with the fourth-century orator), and at Sparta King *Archidamus II, after whom the war is named, and *Brasidas. In the years of uneasy peace that followed the 'Peace of *Nicias' (421), the cautious Nicias and the brilliant but unstable *Alcibiades vied for Athens' favour, and the latter's intrigues with Argos led to a Spartan victory in 418. Even before the outbreak of the war Athens' attitude to her subject 'allies' had become increasingly arrogant, and in 416 she cruelly destroyed the independent island of Melos, thereby losing all claim to moral authority as enlightened leader of Greece. 'Those whom the gods wish to destroy they first make mad', and the launching of the great Sicilian expedition by Athens in 415, in an attempt to extend her sphere of influence westwards, is a superb example of the Greek concept of atē or divinely sent infatuation. With no clear-cut purpose and incompetently led, by Nicias (who had opposed the idea) and Alcibiades (who soon deserted to Sparta on the threat of arrest), the expeditionary force and large reinforcements brought by Demosthenes were wiped out by the Syracusans in 413.

Sparta, meanwhile, had renewed the war, fortifying Decelea as a base in Attica (hence the name 'Decelean War' for the second part of the Peloponnesian War) and depriving Athens of the revenues from the silver mines at near-by Laureum. She also began to intrigue with Persia (see *Tissaphernes), getting money to build her own fleet to oppose Athens at sea. It says much for the extraordinary energy of the Athenians that despite the loss of their forces in Sicily and internal troubles in 411, when an attempt was made to replace the democracy by a moderate oligarchy (see *Peisander, *Phrynichus (2), *Theramenes), they set about building a new fleet, and won several naval victories (some under the recalled Alcibiades) over the Peloponnesians (after the last of which, at Arginusae in 406, they rejected an offer of peace (see *Cleophon), and mass hysteria led them to execute their victorious generals for failing to rescue survivors from disabled ships – see Theramenes). But the partnership between the Persian satrap *Cyrus the Younger, who held the purse-strings for the Spartan fleet and was glad to pay off Persia's old scores against Athens, and *Lysander, the Spartan admiral, was destined to bring Athens to her knees, and in 405 incompetence and treachery resulted in the destruction of Athens' last fleet at the battle of Aegospotami. Her supply-lines from the Black Sea region (see *Spartocids) cut, she was starved out, and surrendered to Sparta on honourably generous terms in 404.

Both the great city-states of fifth-century Greece had, however, exhausted themselves by their long war against each other, and the first half of the fourth century was to see the rise to prominence of some of the lesser, though still powerful, cities, notably Thebes in Boeotia. From 404 to 395 and again from 387/6 to 379, it is true, Sparta was the dominant state of the Greek world. But the bad feeling generated by Lysander's replacement of democracies at Athens (see *Critias, leader of the 'Thirty Tyrants') and in the cities of the Aegean world by narrow oligarchic juntas long outlived the reversal of that policy in 403/2, and Spartan efforts to secure the liberation of the Ionian Greeks from Persia from 399 onwards won her no credit from old enemies (Athens, Argos) and dissident erstwhile friends (Thebes, Corinth). Instead, tempted by promises of Persian help, these states went to war with Sparta in 395 (the 'Corinthian War'), and were only brought to heel by the new Spartan–Persian rapprochement in 387/6, which resulted in the King's Peace. At the cost of surrendering the Ionian Greeks to *Artaxerxes II, Sparta was able to enforce the principle of city autonomy elsewhere, thereby breaking up the Boeotian League (Thebes' power-base), dissolving the democratic united state of Corinth–Argos, and isolating Athens. In the subsequent years Sparta strengthened her position by interference in certain Peloponnesian cities (Mantinea, Phlius), by the occupation of the Theban acropolis in support of a pro-Spartan faction, and by military defeat of the Olynthian confederacy in northern Greece. But, with the liberation of Thebes by counter-insurgents (winter 379/8) and the rapid growth of the Second Athenian Confederacy (founded in 378), Sparta was toppled from her pre-eminent position. Unable to defeat the Boeotians on land or the Athenians by sea, she twice renewed the King's Peace (this time from a position of weakness) in 375/4 and 372/1. Immediately after the second renewal King *Cleombrotus invaded Boeotia to enforce autonomy, but was catastrophically defeated at Leuctra (371), when the Theban citizen-army, spearheaded by the Sacred Band (see *Gorgidas), delivered a devastating attack on his right wing. The formation of the Arcadian League (370) and the Theban liberation of Messenia (Spartan subject territory since the eighth century) completed Sparta's discomfiture. However, the Thebans proved incapable of imposing themselves upon the complexities of Peloponnesian politics (*Pelopidas was slightly more successful in Thessaly) and could achieve little against Athens (which had joined the Spartan camp in 370/69), and the period of largely illusory 'Theban hegemony' ended with *Epaminondas' death at Mantinea in 362, although Boeotia remained a military force to be reckoned with. Meanwhile Athens gradually abandoned the principles of the Second Athenian Confederacy in favour of imperialist ambitions which she lacked the resources to fulfil, and any credibility her confederacy had was shattered by the Social War (357–355), by the end of which she was also financially exhausted.

The opening decades of the fourth century had seen a dramatic rise in the use of mercenary soldiers, not only by foreign powers such as Persia and Carthage, but also by the Greeks themselves. Nor was it only ruthless despots like *Dionysius I of Syracuse – who by the aid of large numbers of highly paid mercenaries carved out an empire for himself in Sicily and southern Italy and kept at bay the Carthaginians who by now controlled the west of the island – who made use of them, but free city-states including Athens. Part of their advantage lay in their being more mobile than the slow-moving hoplites, but the decline in citizen-armies was one symptom of the general decline in the city-state as an institution. Once welded together by corporate religious feeling and worship, both within the city and on the Panhellenic plane, it had formed the setting for political innovations which, with the

astonishing flowering of intellectual and artistic life that followed in their train, made ancient Greece one of the great civilizations of the world. Now the system of city-states, with its potent tendency towards internal and external disunity allowed full play, was collapsing in confusion; and this was despite the general level of prosperity, which was much more widespread than in the fifth century. The political future lay with the once backward nation-state of Macedon to the north, now emerging to prominence and then pre-eminence under its able and energetic King *Philip II.

In 360/359 Philip was elected king by the Macedonians, a people partly of Greek descent, and he soon put to good use, against the numerous enemies who were devouring his country piecemeal, the knowledge of military matters and diplomacy which he had gained while a hostage at Thebes in 367–364. By 354 he ruled over an enlarged Macedonia and had won the enduring loyalty of the finest citizen-army in the Greek world, staffed by the king's Companions. Intervention in the Sacred War (355–346), which was declared by Thebes and others after Phocis seized Delphi and used the temple treasures to pay large numbers of mercenaries (see *Onomarchus), gave him some control over Thessaly. In 349–348 he reduced the promontory region of Chalcidice, despite ineffectual opposition by Athens, where the great orator *Demosthenes was by now urging resistance to Philip. His policy of mercy and generosity to defeated foes, shown especially in the treatment of Phocis at the end of the Sacred War, increased greatly the influence he won by military means. Although an ally of Macedonia (under the Peace of *Philocrates), Athens remained a focus of resistance, but when war was renewed in 340 because of Philip's threats to Athenian interest in the Black Sea approaches, her attempts to unite the Greeks against him, which were attended by partial success, ended in the catastrophic defeat at Chaeronea in Boeotia in 338, when the entire Theban Sacred Band was annihilated and huge numbers of Athenians captured by the full Macedonian army under Philip and his son *Alexander (the Great). Athens had no alternative but to submit to Philip's generous terms, and he henceforth controlled the whole of Greece, which was organized in the 'League of Corinth' (from which a weakened Sparta alone stood apart). Order was also restored at this time to Sicily and south Italy, which had gradually disintegrated into chaos after the accession of *Dionysius II of Syracuse; and this was the work of a Corinthian of outstanding ability and integrity, *Timoleon, during the years following 344.

The next step for Philip was to lead the newly united Greeks against their traditional enemy Persia, in a crusade (such as advocated by *Isocrates) to free their fellow Greeks of Ionia: the days of 'medizing', when Persia could play off the different Greek factions against each other, were over. But in 336, after his vanguard had already reached Asia Minor, Philip fell victim to an assassin's knife, leaving the twenty-year old Alexander the Great on the throne. He first reduced to order the tribes of the lower Danube, and then, in 335, turned back to Greece, where Demosthenes, with Persian gold, had been fomenting a revolt at Thebes. After a bloody battle the city of Thebes was destroyed and razed to the ground, and with it perished the possibility of genuine co-operation between Greeks and Macedonians. Alexander, however, was now free for the great Persian expedition, and crossed to Asia Minor in 334. He faced a Persia which, though theoretically strong and certainly immensely wealthy, had suffered internal dissensions (e.g. the Satraps' Revolt (late 360s: see Glossary)) and had on occasion shown considerable practical inefficiency (e.g. in permitting *Evagoras' revolt to last a decade, or allowing Egypt to remain independent for some 60 years down to 343/2). By the end of 331, after three masterly battles, he had definitively conquered *Darius III and subjugated much of Persia; he had also stormed the 'impregnable' city of Tyre, received Egypt into surrender, and founded Alexandria. In 330–327 he extended his control over the north-eastern satrapies of the Persian empire. Then, having organized the government of the Persian empire as successor of Darius, he set out eastwards on a further campaign of conquest and exploration to India (327–324), from which mutiny by his long-suffering soldiers eventually made him turn back. He died of a fever at Babylon in 323, on the eve of yet another great expedition. The 13 years of his reign had changed the course of history in the entire eastern Mediterranean and further east, for several centuries to come.

Alexander left behind him vast armies of seasoned troops and a number of experienced and ambitious generals, who proceeded to manœuvre and fight each other for control during the Age of the Successors or Diadochi (323–301), before the settled pattern of the Hellenistic monarchies emerged. The first few years were marked by the attempt of the regent *Perdiccas to retain control of Alexander's empire, though *Ptolemy (I) had established Egypt as an independent kingdom from 321. An effort by Athens and other Greek states to break away (see *Hyper(e)ides) was foiled by *Antipater in the Lamian War of 323–321, which led to the Macedonian occupation of Athens, the imposition of an oligarchy, and the death of Demosthenes. After Perdiccas' death in 320, the scene was dominated by *Antigonus, self-proclaimed king in Asia Minor and Syria from 306. But his successes and apparent territorial ambitions

led the other generals – *Cassander, *Lysimachus, Ptolemy, and *Seleucus (I) – to form a shifting pattern of alliances against him and his son *Demetrius Poliorcetes (who held Greece from 307 to 301 and again from 294), and he was finally defeated and killed at Ipsus in 301. With Antigonus died the last chance of Alexander's empire being held together; but his son Demetrius temporarily became king of Macedon (294–288), before an ill-judged attempt to recover his father's Asian possessions led to his defeat by Seleucus, and his grandson *Antigonus Gonatas succeeded in establishing himself and his dynasty (see stemma, p. 237) on the Macedonian throne from 277. The antecedents of this last event, from 294, included the occupation of Macedon by Lysimachus and *Pyrrhus of Epirus – a character well known to Roman history; the disintegration of Lysimachus' kingdom in Thrace and Asia Minor, bulwark against the northern barbarians, after his defeat and death at Corupedium in 281 by Seleucus, in consequence of a dynastic quarrel (see *Agathocles, son of Lysimachus, *Arsinoe II, *Ptolemy Ceraunus); and the invasion of Greece and Asia Minor by hordes of marauding Gauls (see *Brennus): those in Greece were defeated by Gonatas and others, while those in Asia, troublesome for many years, finally settled down and became 'Galatians'. Magna Graecia, during this period, saw the tyranny of *Agathocles of Syracuse (317–289) and his expedition to Africa against Carthage, and the adventures of Pyrrhus in Italy and Sicily in consequence of his alliance with Tarentum (280–275), and his 'pyrrhic victory' over the Romans.

By this time the Hellenistic world had taken shape (see map, p. 232). The Ptolemies of Egypt also held Cyrenaica, Coele-Syria (a bone of contention with the Seleucids), and Cyprus, and had a number of client states in the Aegean and Asia Minor. Seleucus and his successors (see stemma, p. 236) ruled Syria, part of Asia Minor, Babylonia, and for a time much of Persia, while *Eumenes I of Pergamum (263–241), like the dynasts of Bithynia (see *Nicomedes I) and Cappadocia (*Ariarathes III), soon succeeded in winning independence for his kingdom from Seleucid control. The Antigonids of Macedonia exerted some control and influence over Greece (the domination of Corinth played a key role), though it varied with events. In Asia, Greek ruling-classes were grafted on to native populations of differing races and levels of civilization, and, though inevitably diluted, a certain degree of homogeneity of Greek culture emerged. As this new world settled down, intellectual and artistic life began to flourish. Building on the system established by the Pharaohs, the Ptolemies set up a bureaucracy (see *Zenon) designed to exploit the peasants and place vast resources, and thus great patronage, in their own hands. The foundation of the scholarly institutions, the Library and Museum (see Glossary), at their newly created capital enabled the Ptolemies to make Alexandria the greatest cultural centre of the Hellenistic world, especially under *Ptolemy II Philadelphus – so much so that 'Alexandrian' became the label for a particular kind of poetry, erudite and polished. Large numbers of poets, scholars, doctors, scientists, and others settled at Alexandria or visited it for a time: *Callimachus, *Apollonius Rhodius, *Theocritus, *Eratosthenes, *Aristarchus of Samothrace, *Herophilus, *Erasistratus, and *Ctesibius are some of the names that spring to mind. Antioch and Pergamum, as well as Athens – still the chief home of philosophy that *Plato and *Aristotle had made it in the fourth century (see *Theophrastus, *Carneades, *Diogenes of Sinope, *Epicurus, *Zeno of Citium, etc.) – were other centres of this upsurge of cultural activity. Trade also flourished and, together with embassies, festivals, athletic events, and the like, helped to link the various parts of the Hellenistic world.

No fewer than six Syrian Wars were fought between the Ptolemies and the Seleucids, five of them within a century (see Chronological Table). The fact that Coele-Syria was, anomalously, in the possession of the former was a main factor, and others came into play as well, notably in the Third Syrian, or Laodicean, War (246–241) between *Ptolemy III and *Seleucus II, fought after the murder of one rival queen (*Berenice Syra from Egypt) and her child by the other (*Laodice), after the death of *Antiochus II. Civil war then broke out between Seleucus II and his younger brother *Antiochus Hierax, to whom he had entrusted the government of Asia Minor during the Laodicean War, and, while Seleucus was thus preoccupied in the west of his domains, part of his Iranian possessions began to break away, with the independence of Bactria under *Diodotus I, and the rise of *Arsaces of Parthia. The extreme eastern parts had been ceded to the Indian king *Sandracottus even before 300 BC, and the Seleucid empire, too widely spread and too little coherent, would continue to exhibit a tendency to disintegrate, especially in the east, under its largely western and Mediterranean-orientated kings. The Ptolemies, whose hostility to the Seleucids played more than a little part in this, were also ready to fish in troubled waters in Greece, to prevent any resurgence of Antigonid ambitions overseas, for example in the War of *Chremonides (266/5–261), a revolt of Athens and a Peloponnesian coalition (see *Areus I) against Antigonus Gonatas, which ended in the Macedonian occupation of Athens. A decade later, *Alexander of Corinth rebelled against Gonatas and declared Corinth and Euboea independent. *Aratus of Sicyon now makes his first

appearance, liberating his city from a tyrant in 251, and joining it to the Achaean League, of which he became the leader, making the League the major power in the Peloponnese. For some time he pursued anti-Macedonian policies, especially in the liberation of Corinth from Antigonus Gonatas, who had repossessed it after the death of Alexander (245). But the revolutionary ideas and aggressive policies of *Cleomenes III of Sparta (235–222) – with the support of *Ptolemy III – drove Aratus into the arms of Gonatas' second successor *Antigonus Doson, who defeated Cleomenes at Sellasia in 222.

The Seleucid *Antiochus III (the Great) acceded in 223, and the 17-year old *Philip V of Macedon in 221. Both were in due course to be worsted by the Romans, who, at this point, had done no more than establish a protectorate in Illyria after operations against pirates. Antiochus initiated the Fourth Syrian War, but was seriously defeated by *Ptolemy IV at Raphia in 217. Ptolemy's victory, however, was gained at the price of enrolling native troops, and internal troubles followed under this weak king and his over-mighty ministers, *Agathocles and *Sosibius. Antiochus proceeded to restore the situation in Asia Minor after the revolt of *Achaeus, and then, to repair Seleucid prestige, set off on an anabasis of reconquest in the east, which took him to India. Philip, meanwhile, began by fighting a 'Social War' on the side of Aratus of Sicyon and the Achaean League against Aetolia and her allies (220–217), but then was influenced against Rome by a dethroned Illyrian, *Demetrius of Pharos, and, after varying fortunes, emerged successful from the Romans' First Macedonian War (211–205), ended by the Peace of Phoenice. In the same year 205 Antiochus returned from the East, and he and Philip turned against the Egypt of *Ptolemy V, in the Fifth Syrian War (202–195), which at last gave Coele–Syria to the Seleucids (c. 202). Philip soon found that he had a Second Macedonian War against Rome on his hands (200–197), and this ended in his decisive defeat by *Flamininus at Cynoscephalae (197), from which time on he was a reluctant ally of a Rome which, in 196, made a declaration of freedom for the Greeks. Antiochus, who fatally underestimated Rome's strength, suffered a first defeat in Greece in 191, as an ally of the Aetolians, then lost the control of the sea to the Romans and their allies Rhodes and Pergamum, and finally suffered a crushing defeat at Magnesia ad Sipylum in 189 (see *Scipio Africanus). By the Peace of Apamea, which ended Rome's First Syrian War (192–188), Antiochus gave up all Asia Minor to the Taurus Mountains (to the benefit of Rhodes and the Pergamum of *Eumenes II), and was saddled with a huge indemnity, which led indirectly to his death (187). Rome, from beyond the frontiers of the Hellenistic world, was now its major power, and the

Hellenistic monarchies were irreversibly weakened, through internal causes and warfare among themselves as well as through their defeat by Rome.

The next generation brought *Ptolemy VI to power in Egypt in 180, *Perseus in Macedon in 179, and *Antiochus IV in 175. Dynastic quarrels between Ptolemy VI and the notorious *Ptolemy VIII Physcon (died 116) preoccupied the Egyptians for over half a century, together with the Sixth Syrian War against Antiochus IV (170–168), and intrigues with legitimate and illegitimate occupants of the Seleucid throne in the years following 150 (see *Alexander Balas, *Demetrius II). Antiochus' aggressive policy of hellenization caused a serious Jewish revolt under the Maccabees (see *Judas Maccabaeus) in (now Seleucid) Palestine in 173–164, and Judaea later became independent. As for Perseus, his ambitious policies, building up again the power of Macedon, played into Rome's hands and led to the Third Macedonian War (171–168), in which he was defeated and captured by L. Aemilius *Paullus at the battle of Pydna (168). The historian *Polybius was among the hostages sent to Rome after this. Macedonia was divided into republics, but did not become a Roman province until after the elimination of the pretender *Andriscus by *Metellus Macedonicus in 148. Two years later, the rash policies of two leaders of the Achaean League led to the sack of Corinth by *Mummius and the *de facto* annexation of Greece as a Roman province attached to Macedonia (146).

There now remained only two of the three main Hellenistic kingdoms, Seleucid Syria and Ptolemaic Egypt, and the balance which had made possible the third-century floruit of Hellenistic civilization was gone for ever. Rome did not yet possess any territory in Asia, but, already in 168, Antiochus IV had obeyed Roman directions to give up conquered Egypt. Nor was the first Roman territory long in coming: in 133 *Attalus III of Pergamum died, leaving his kingdom to Rome in his will, and, despite the revolt of *Aristonicus (132–130), Pergamum became the Roman province of Asia. In Seleucid Syria, *Demetrius II was put to flight by one pretender, *Diodotus Tryphon, was a captive in Parthia for ten years (139–129), and lost his throne and life to another pretender (125). While he was a prisoner, his brother *Antiochus VII campaigned against Parthia, but initial success ended in disaster and death (129), and the permanent loss of Iran. *Antiochus VIII spent much of his reign (126–96) fighting his half-brother *Antiochus IX (113–95), and the Seleucid kingdom came to an end in a welter of civil wars between the five sons of the former and one son of the latter (see Later *Seleucids): from 83 (to 69) *Tigranes I of Armenia occupied the throne at the request of the Syrians,

weary of anarchy, and in 64 BC Pompey made Syria a Roman province. This was part of the general settlement of the East after the Mithridatic Wars (88–63) fought by Rome and *Mithridates VI of Pontus (120–63), who had occupied large areas of Greece and Asia Minor. Bithynia was bequeathed to Rome in 75/4, and Pompey amalgamated it with the new province of Pontus, Mithridates' kingdom.

The Hellenistic world had now shrunk to the remaining Ptolemaic possessions: Cyrene had already been bequeathed to Rome by *Ptolemy Apion in 96. As with the Seleucids, so with the Ptolemies: after the death of Ptolemy VIII in 116, dynastic troubles continued to afflict them. The brothers *Ptolemy IX and X (116–81, 116–88 repectively) were at each other's throats, and, of the Later *Ptolemies, only Auletes (Ptolemy XII– 80–51 BC) and his famous daughter *Cleopatra VII (51–30 BC) managed some continuity of rule. Cleopatra's alliance with Antony brought the civil war between him and Octavian to Egypt, and the consequences of backing the losing side were her own death and the incorporation of Egypt as a province in the Roman Empire. The shrunk Hellenistic world thus virtually disappeared (though the very last Hellenistic kingdom, Commagene (see *Antiochus IV of Commagene), was not absorbed into Roman Syria till AD 72), but 'captive Greece led her conqueror captive' and made her civilization truly Graeco-Roman; moreover, when Rome went down before the barbarians in the fifth century AD, the Greek world survived for many centuries more as the Byzantine Empire.   D.B.

Biographical Dictionary

Achaeus General of Antiochus III, floruit *c.* 246–213 BC.

A Seleucid prince, the son of Andromachus, Achaeus (Akhaios) supported *Seleucus II against *Antiochus Hierax in their fraternal war, and, although he married the latter's daughter Laodice, he and his father helped to defeat Hierax in 226 BC. In 223 Achaeus accompanied Seleucus III on his expedition to regain some of the Seleucid territory lost to *Attalus of Pergamum. When Seleucus was killed, Achaeus was proclaimed king by the army, but he refused the throne in favour of the legitimate king *Antiochus III. The new king appointed him governor of Seleucid Asia across the Taurus Mountains, and he easily reconquered much Pergamene territory. When the king was distracted by various internal revolts, Achaeus, who had grown powerful in Asia Minor, revolted in 220 and declared himself king in Phrygia. His army refused to march against Antiochus, but Achaeus maintained himself in a separate 'kingdom', and helped Byzantium against Rhodes in 219.

Coin portrait of Achaeus, general of the Seleucid king *Antiochus III (enlarged).

Antiochus turned his attention to Achaeus in 216, and Attalus joined him against their mutual enemy. He was driven to his capital Sardis in 215, but took refuge on the acropolis. His mercenaries betrayed him to Antiochus, who, after mutilating and beheading him, crucified his body and sewed his head into an ass's skin. Asia Minor was completely recovered by 213.

BIBL. Will, *Hist. pol.* ii; Bevan, *House of Seleucus*; H. H. Schmitt, *Untersuchungen zur Geschichte Antiochus des Grossen und seiner Zeit* (1964).

Achaeus of Eretria Tragedian, born 484/481 BC.

Little is known of the work of Achaeus (Akhaios) of Eretria in Euboea, although critics placed him in a canon of five great tragedians (with *Aeschylus, *Sophocles, *Euripides, and *Ion of Chios), and some considered him second only to Aeschylus as a writer of satyr plays.

BIBL. D. F. Sutton, *The Greek Satyr Play* (1980).

Acusilaus Mythographer, *c.* 500 BC.

Acusilaus (Akousilaos) of Argos is said by *Hecataeus to have been the earliest prose writer to try to systematize the myths of the epic heroes within a genealogical framework. His three books were entitled *Genealogies* or *Histories*, and covered the period from the creation of the world and the gods down to the Trojan War. His date is uncertain; Josephus puts him 'shortly before the Persian expedition against Greece'.

BIBL. *FGrH* i, no. 2; Diels and Kranz, *Vorsokratiker*, no. 9 (73); *Roman World* *Josephus.

Adea (alias Eurydice) Macedonian princess, died 317 BC.

Adea, *Philip II's great-niece, married *Philip Arrhidaeus in 322 BC, but an alliance with *Cassander was thwarted by *Olympias, who defeated her army at Euia and forced her to commit suicide.

BIBL. Berve, *Alexanderreich*, no. 23; Macurdy, *Hellenistic Queens* 49 ff.

Adeimantus Athenian commander, late 5th century BC.

A supporter of *Alcibiades, Adeimantus (Adeimantos) was involved in the accusations of profaning the Eleusinian Mysteries. Elected *strategos* on Alcibiades' return to Athens, he took part in an expedition to Andros (407 BC), and in the battles of Arginusae (406) and Aegospotami (405). Before the latter battle, he opposed Philocles' motion that those captured should have their right hands cut off, and he was therefore spared when other Athenian captives were executed. Inevitably, he was accused of treachery.

BIBL. Xenophon, *Hellenica* I. iv. 21; vii. 1; II. i. 30–2.

Aeneas Tacticus Military writer, 4th century BC.

Aeneas (Aineias) 'the Tactician' was the first soldier to write up his ideas on military practice in the form of a series of handbooks, of which one, dealing with besieging cities, survives. Interestingly, it suggests that suppressing potential opposition inside a city is as important a

component of defence as repulsing the invader outside.
There is no reason to identify the writer with Aeneas of
Stymphalus, leader of the Arcadian League in 367 BC.

BIBL. Loeb, ed. W. A. Oldfather (1923); ed. L. W. Hunter
and S. A. Handford (1927).

Aeschines (c. 390–314 BC) Athenian orator.

Aeschines (Aiskhinēs) is paired with his bitter personal
and political enemy *Demosthenes. In the face of *Philip
II's expansionism, Aeschines supported *Eubulus in
advocating a common peace which would give all Greek
states security and obviate the need for anyone to turn to
the Macedonians. In 346 (or possibly 348), Eubulus' and
Aeschines' diplomatic initiative failed, and Aeschines and
Demosthenes were sent to arrange a separate treaty
between Athens and Philip. Demosthenes was responsible
for persuading Athens to accept this peace (Decree of
*Philocrates); but, before it was ratified by Philip, the
Macedonian army had moved against central Greece.
Demosthenes' proposal for resistance was rejected;
Aeschines counselled resignation to the military facts.

Demosthenes' supporter Timarchus proceeded to
prosecute Aeschines for having taken bribes from Philip;
he replied with the Against Timarchus, successfully
accusing Timarchus of notorious immorality. In 343
Demosthenes again attacked Aeschines in On the Embassy;
Aeschines replied, and was acquitted. In 339, as one of the
Athenian representatives on the Amphictyonic Council,
he made such a vigorous attack against the Amphissans
that open war resulted, and Philip was given an excuse to
intervene to restore order (the 'Fourth Sacred War').

In 336 Ctesiphon proposed that Demosthenes should be
publicly crowned for his services to Athens; Aeschines
accused him of having made an unconstitutional proposal,
but did not proceed with the prosecution until 330. His
speech, the Against Ctesiphon, was answered by
Demosthenes' On the Crown; the jury overwhelmingly
accepted Demosthenes' case, and Aeschines left Athens for
Rhodes, where he taught rhetoric until his death at the
age of 75.

BIBL. Davies, Athenian Families, no. 14625 II; T. T. B.
Ryder, introduction to T. Saunder's trans. of Demosthenes
and Aeschines (Penguin Classics, 1974); Kennedy, Art of
Persuasion, 236–45.

Attic krater showing the murder of **Agamemnon by Aegisthus.
Date uncertain: perhaps late enough to show the influence of
Aeschylus' Oresteia. Boston, Museum of Fine Arts.

Aeschylus (525/4–456/5 BC) Tragedian.

Born at Eleusis, Aeschylus (Aiskhulos) had begun his
career as a dramatist by the 490s BC. He fought in the
battle of Marathon (490), in which his brother Cynegeirus
died a heroic death, and very probably in that of Salamis
(480). According to a persistent but confused tradition, he
was at some time put on trial for revealing the secret rites
of the Eleusinian Mysteries in a play, but was acquitted.
He became the most popular tragedian of his day, winning
13 victories (the first in 484) in the competitions at
Athens, and also visiting Sicily to produce plays for
*Hieron I of Syracuse. It was on a later visit to Sicily that
he died, at Gela; the only distinction recorded in the
grave-epigram which he is said to have written for himself
was his courage at Marathon. The Athenians paid him the
exceptional honour of allowing posthumous revivals of his
plays. He is himself a character in *Aristophanes' Frogs,
where his style is skilfully and affectionately parodied.

For at least part of his career he took the leading role in

Herm bearing the name 'Aeschines', from a villa near Tivoli.
Copy of a late 4th-century BC original. Vatican Museum.

his own plays, as was normal at this period. He is said to have been responsible for reducing the choral part in tragedy, and for introducing the second actor (without whom tragedy could only have been in a very limited sense 'dramatic'); later, according to some authorities, he introduced the third, who is required in his *Oresteia* (but see *Sophocles). Many, perhaps most, of his plays belonged to connected tetralogies.

He is said to have written 90 plays; we know the titles of over 70; seven survive under his name, of which six are certainly authentic. *Persians* (472) is the only surviving tragedy on a historical subject, and depicts the (supposed) despair of the Persian court (see *Atossa) after the Greek victory at Salamis. *Seven against Thebes* (467) is the third play of a tetralogy about the family of **Oedipus, and concerns Oedipus' son Eteocles, who dies killing his brother Polyneices and defending Thebes. *Suppliant Women* (once thought to be the earliest play, but now dated between 466 and 459) is almost certainly the first play of a tetralogy about the daughters of Danaus; in the surviving play the Danaids, fleeing from Egypt to avoid marriage with their cousins, reach Argos and are befriended by its king Pelasgus.

Agamemnon, *Choephori* (*Libation-Bearers*), and *Eumenides* together form the *Oresteia* (458), the only connected trilogy that survives. In the first play **Agamemnon returns to Argos from his victory at Troy and is murdered by his wife Clytemnestra; in the second their son Orestes avenges his father by killing his mother and her lover Aegisthus; in the third, Orestes, pursued by the avenging Furies of Clytemnestra, is tried and acquitted before the Council of the Areopagus at Athens, and the Furies are placated by Athena. Parts of *Eumenides* must represent Aeschylus' reaction to *Ephialtes' democratic reform of the Areopagus, but it is uncertain whether he was reacting against the reform or in favour of it, or simply appealing to both sides for unity and patriotism.

The seventh play, *Prometheus Bound*, was until recently accepted as authentic by most scholars, but is now thought to be probably post-Aeschylean. It seems to have belonged to a connected tetralogy about Prometheus; but there are many problems.

Among the fragments that also survive are some interesting scraps of Aeschylus' satyr plays, a genre of which later critics considered him the greatest exponent.

Each of the authentic plays, while fairly simple in plot, invests a single event with great moral and religious significance, exhaustively exploring its multiple causes and implications. The presence of the chorus is exploited throughout, the action being consciously projected out to it and to the world; in two plays (*Suppliant Women* and *Eumenides*) it is itself given a central role in the action, though this must have been unusual. Characterization tends to be subordinate to the deeds which the *dramatis personae* perform, rather than being developed for its own sake; but this does not prevent Aeschylus' Clytemnestra from being one of the most impressive characters in Greek tragedy. All the plays are remarkable for the power and complexity (and often obscurity) of their verbal imagery; this is especially true of the *Oresteia*, where the moral and emotional significance of the action is conveyed largely through patterns of imagery sustained for whole plays and even for the whole trilogy. Telling use is also made of visual effects (e.g. the 'carpet' in *Agamemnon*, the robe in

Choephori), though the impression given by some ancient critics, that Aeschylus was addicted to grandiose spectacle, is not to be trusted.

Divine and human causation work together in Aeschylus (see, e.g., *Persians* 742, *Agamemnon* 1505–8). Events are intelligible in purely human terms (except in *Eumenides*, where the gods themselves take the stage), but the influence of divine forces can be detected throughout. Above all, the supremacy of Zeus is constantly emphasized; but prayers are often addressed to him more in desperation than in hope. He and the other gods ensure that crime is punished and are in that sense 'just', but they are much less concerned to see innocence rewarded; indeed in some plays it seems that the punishment of crime must always involve further crime, creating an unbreakable cycle (*Seven* 742–65, *Agamemnon* 757–71). Scholars have given particular attention to passages (*Seven* 653–719, *Agamemnon* 205–27, *Choephori* 269–305) in which a character feels compelled by the gods to commit an act of bloodshed that will bring pollution, but also shows a positive desire for that act. In *Eumenides*, however, while he does not negate the grim vision of the earlier plays, Aeschylus expresses an emotional faith that the cycle can be broken, linking this to his faith in the future of Athens.

BIBL. Lesky, *Greek Literature*; M. Gagarin, *Aeschylean Drama* (1976); O. Taplin, *The Stagecraft of Aeschylus* (1977).

Aesop Author of fables, traditionally *c.* 600 BC.

As early as the fifth century BC, a semi-legendary figure called Aesop (Aisōpos) was thought to have invented the genre of the fable, a short story in prose or verse, always ending with a moral, and generally using animals to symbolize different human character-types or status groups. An early collection of fables ascribed to him was made by *Demetrius of Phalerum.

In the course of time a whole series of folk-tale elements were woven around the figure of Aesop to produce a romantic biography: he was a Phrygian or Thracian slave bought by the Samian I(a)dmon and manumitted, met *Solon at *Croesus' court, visited the king of Babylon, and was murdered by the Delphians (a late Egyptian version of the romance makes Apollo his persecutor).

BIBL. Herodotus ii. 134 f.; Aristophanes, *Wasps* 1446; B. E. Perry, introduction to Loeb ed. of Babrius and Phaedrus (1965).

Aesop and the Fox: scene on the inside of an Attic red figure cup of *c.* 470–450 BC. Vatican Museum.

Agariste Wife of Megacles, married *c.* 575 BC.

As the daughter of *Cleisthenes of Sicyon, Agariste (Agaristē) was a desirable bride, and her father organized an epic-style competitive wooing for her, which, however, was reduced to near-farce by the drunken antics of Hippocleides (see *Philaids). Agariste married the Athenian *Megacles, and later brought about the breakup of their daughter's marriage to *Peisistratus, by passing on to Megacles the girl's complaint that Peisistratus was maltreating her.

BIBL. Herodotus i. 61, vi. 126–31; Davies, *Athenian Families*, no. 9688.

Agatharchides Historian and geographer, 2nd century BC.

An outstanding figure of the intellectual life of Alexandria, Agatharchides (Agatharkhidēs) of Cnidos served as private secretary to two ministers of *Ptolemy VI, one of them *Heracleides Lembus. He was thus a man of public affairs, and the broad scope of his writings classifies him as a 'world historian' in contrast to many parochial, antiquarian writers of his time. Although Agatharchides was a prolific writer, the relatively few existing fragments of his work do not adequately reproduce the scope, content, or worth of his works. The *Events in Asia* quote *Phylarchus and were used by *Diodorus Siculus, and the *Events in Europe* were quoted by Athenaeus. One quotation by Josephus reveals a contemptuous attitude to the Jewish religion.

Agatharchides' geographical work in five books, *On the Red Sea*, was written in his old age, and was left unfinished both because of his age and because *Ptolemy VIII's persecutions of scholars (145 BC) forced him to flee from Alexandria (perhaps to Athens) and forgo the research material available there. Its uneven excerption by the Byzantine scholar Photius shows that it contained a description of the geography, anthropology, zoology, and ethnography of southern Egypt, the eastern desert, and beyond. He included a *periplous* of the Red Sea and the Arabian Gulf. This highly personal work contained much that was irrelevant to his subject but of interest to him. Although he castigated the 'Asianic' prose style, he may himself be considered a 'rhetorical' writer in loose contact with the Peripatetics. Agatharchides was indebted to *Eratosthenes, and was used by *Pos(e)idonius, *Artemidorus of Ephesus, *Strabo, and Diodorus. His works and literary style received the highest praise from Photius.

BIBL. *FGrH* 86; E. H. Bunbury, *A History of Ancient Geography* (1879) ii; Fraser, *Ptolemaic Alexandria*; *Roman World* *Athenaeus, *Josephus.

Agatharchus Painter, active *c.* 440–410 BC.

Son of Eudemus of Samos, Agatharchus (Agatharkhos) seems to have worked at Athens, where he decorated the walls of *Alcibiades' house – the first recorded instance of such luxury. He was apparently arrogant about the speed and facility of his technique. He painted a stage-set for a play by *Aeschylus (not necessarily during the poet's life), and wrote a treatise on it. The importance of this scene-painting and its 'commentarium' was to do with some advance, unclear to us, in optical perspective, for it inspired *Anaxagoras and *Democritus to work out rules of perspective. The advance is unlikely to have been to

full pictorial perspective with one vanishing point, which was achieved, if at all by ancient painters, not until later in the Hellenistic period, when scene-painting (*skenographia*) came to mean perspective painting.

BIBL. Vitruvius vii, *praef.* 11; Robertson, *History of Greek Art* 411 ff.

Agathocles Tyrant and king of Syracuse, 317–289 BC.

Son of one of *Timoleon's new Syracusans, Agathocles (Agathoklēs) served at Croton against the Bruttians in 325 BC. Remaining in Italy he was driven from Croton and Tarentum under suspicion of revolutionary activities, and then helped Rhegium against oligarchic Syracuse (322). When the Syracusan oligarchy fell, he returned home, helped defend the city against the exiled oligarchs and the Carthaginians, and was again expelled for alleged plotting. Further internal revolution restored the oligarchs, whereupon Agathocles raised an army, but was able to return peacefully after Carthaginian mediation. Elected 'General and Guardian of the Peace', he staged a bloody coup against the rich, emerged as *strategos autokrator* (317), instituted social reforms in Syracuse, and began the subjugation of eastern Sicily. When the Carthaginians intervened and blockaded him in Syracuse, he escaped, invaded Africa, and nearly captured Carthage. The African venture ended in disarray in 307, with Agathocles abandoning his army, but a negotiated peace with Carthage and brutally firm treatment of the Sicilians (e.g. massacres in 307/6 in Segesta and Syracuse) kept him in power, and he adopted the title 'King'. In the later, poorly documented, part of his career his interests turned to Italy and the Adriatic (he took Corcyra *c.* 299) and he made marriage alliances with *Pyrrhus and *Ptolemy I. He died in 289 (some said he was poisoned), having made the empty gesture of 'restoring self-government to the Syracusans'.

BIBL. Berve, *Tyrannis* 441 ff.

Agathocles, son of Lysimachus (died *c.* 282/1 BC).

Eldest son of *Lysimachus by Nicaea, Agathocles (Agathoklēs) married Lysandra, the daughter of *Ptolemy I and Eurydice, who, as the widow of *Cassander's son *Alexander V, had taken refuge in Thrace from *Demetrius Poliorcetes after he had murdered her husband. Agathocles fought bravely for his father against Demetrius, who threatened Thrace from Asia, but was murdered by Lysimachus in unknown circumstances, possibly with the contrivance of his step-mother, *Arsinoe (later II) and *Ptolemy Ceraunus. Lysandra and their children fled to *Seleucus I, but their fate – perhaps determined by Ceraunus, whose path to the throne they hindered – is unknown.

BIBL. Tarn, *Antigonos Gonatas*; Will, *Hist. pol.* i.

Agathocles and **Sosibius** Ministers of Ptolemy IV, floruerunt *c.* 240–*c.* 203 BC.

Agathocles (Agathoklēs) and Sosibius (Sōsibios) were ministers under *Ptolemy IV who to a large extent ran the government because of the king's neglect of public affairs. Sosibius had served under *Ptolemy III from *c.* 240 BC (and Agathocles probably did so too), but the accession of the young king gave them real power. They assassinated all who might have exerted alien influence on him: his uncle, brother, mother (*Berenice II), and *Cleomenes III of Sparta (an exile in Alexandria). Both of them controlled negotiations with *Antiochus III in the Fourth Syrian War and enrolled 20,000 natives in the army, which proved fatal to Egypt's internal peace.

The ministers were probably responsible for dismissing Queen *Arsinoe III from court, and, when Agathocles' sister became the royal mistress, they had another means of controlling the king. His premature death in 204 threatened their power: so that Arsinoe did not gain the regency over *Ptolemy V (with disastrous consequences to themselves), they concealed the king's death until her assassination could be arranged. Sosibius died c. 203, whereupon Agathocles and his clique seized power; but one unsuppressed opponent fomented the riots in which Agathocles, his mother, sister, and family were dragged into the stadium and torn limb from limb by the mob, which *Polybius describes in a colourful passage.

BIBL. Polybius xv. 25–34, with Walbank, *HCP*; Will, *Hist. pol.*

Agathon (c. 447–c. 401 BC) Tragedian.

Agathon (Agathōn) of Athens produced tragedies there for some years before departing about 407 BC, like *Euripides, for the court of *Archelaus of Macedon, where he died. *Aristotle mentions a tragedy of his (*Antheus*) in which plot and characters were entirely invented (not mythical), and another which contained enough material for an epic; he also says that Agathon was the first to write choral odes that were mere interludes irrelevant to the play's action. He thus took to their logical conclusion tendencies visible in the later work of Euripides. A few fragments survive.

Agathon is a character in *Aristophanes' *Thesmophoriazusae*, where he is mocked for effeminacy, and in *Plato's *Symposium*, which purports to describe a party held at his house to celebrate his first victory as a tragedian in 416.

BIBL. Lesky, *Greek Literature*; P. Lévêque, *Agathon* (1955).

Agesilaus Eurypontid king of Sparta, c. 400–360 BC.

Agesilaus (Agēsilaos) became king unexpectedly, *Agis II's son Leotychidas having been declared illegitimate. Here and in his undertaking of the Persian War in 396 BC *Lysander's influence was important, but Agesilaus soon became his own man. Successful campaigns in Asia Minor were cut short by the Corinthian War (395–387/6), though without a reliable fleet his position was in any case precarious. Returning to Greece, he won an unproductive victory over the confederate states at Coronea (August 394), and then fought in Corinthia, Argos, and north-west Greece. In 387/6 he gladly enforced *Artaxerxes II's rescript (the 'King's Peace'). He defended both *Phoebidas and *Sphodrias and twice invaded Boeotia after 379/8, but prolonged convalescence then kept him out of public life until 371, when his unbending hostility to Thebes was a proximate cause of the Spartan defeat at Leuctra. In the 360s hopes of financial profit for Sparta led him to associate with *Ariobarzanes and to join *Tachos as a *condottiere*. He died at Cyrene in the winter of 361/60 or 360/59. *Xenophon's encomium (*Agesilaus*), which praises Agesilaus for all the virtues (especially ones of self-denial), fails to convey any real impression of the man, and his stress on the king's hostility to Persia must be set against his willing acquiescence in the King's Peace.

BIBL. Xenophon, *Agesilaus*; Plutarch, *Agesilaus*; G. Cawkwell, *CQ*, n.s. xxvi (1976).

Agesipolis Agiad king of Sparta, 395/4–380 BC.

During the Corinthian War (395–387/6 BC) Agesipolis (Agēsipolis) invaded the Argolid with considerable success, and after the King's Peace effected the dioecism of Mantinea (c. 385) and took part in the Olynthian War, during which he died of a fever (summer 380). Contrasts were drawn between *Agesilaus' aggressive policies and Agesipolis' gentler attitude towards allies, but the record does not altogether bear this out.

BIBL. Poralla, *Prosopographie*, no. 14; D. G. Rice, *Historia* xxiii (1974); G. Cawkwell, *CQ*, n.s. xxvi (1976).

Agias (or Hegias): see Cyclic Poets

Agis II Eurypontid king of Sparta, 427/6–c. 400 BC.

Agis was the son and successor of *Archidamus II. In 426 and 425 BC he commanded the Peloponnesian expeditions which devastated Attica. During the Peace of *Nicias, he led the army which re-established Spartan control over the Peloponnese at Mantinea (418). With the start of the Decelean War (413), he made Decelea the base for a permanent Spartan occupying force in Attica; in 405 he organized the final blockade of Athens together with *Pausanias (2). In 402/400 he forced Elis back into the Spartan alliance.

BIBL. Thucydides v. 57 ff., vii. 19, 27, viii; Xenophon, *Hellenica* ii. 2, iii. 2; A. W. Gomme, *Essays in Greek History* (1937) 132 f.

Agis III Eurypontid king of Sparta, 338–330 BC.

After receiving Persian money and collecting a mercenary army (from survivors of Issus (see *Alexander the Great) and fresh levies in Crete in 332 BC), Agis III, son of *Archidamus III, rebelled against the Macedonian hegemony. He was not widely supported and, while he was engaged in besieging the recalcitrant Megalopolitans, *Antipater entered the Peloponnese and defeated the rebels, Agis being among those killed (late 331 or early 330).

BIBL. E. Badian, *Hermes* xcv (1967); G. Cawkwell, *CQ*, n.s. xix (1969); E. N. Borza *C. Phil.* lxvi (1971); A. B. Bosworth, *Phoenix* xxxix (1975); E. I. McQueen, *Historia* xxvii (1978).

Agis IV Eurypontid king of Sparta, 244–241 BC.

Agis acceded to the Eurypontid throne of Sparta at a time of financial crisis, and proposed the cancellation of debts and the redistribution of land. Such controversial measures failed to pass in the conservative Gerousia. Agis' retaliatory political strategy involved deposing his co-king Leonidas II and the opposing ephors. His uncle Arcesilaus persuaded him to cancel debts but not to redistribute land, a compromise which alienated those for and those against change. In 242 BC Agis aided *Aratus of Sicyon in a joint defence of the Peloponnese against the Aetolians. His absence weakened his support at home, and he returned to find that his uncle had turned against him and assumed extraordinary powers. He was summarily tried and executed by the opposition in 241.

BIBL. Jones, *Sparta*; Forrest, *History of Sparta*.

Part of the base of the statue of Nemesis at Rhamnus by
Agoracritus, *c.* 430 BC. Roman period copy (heavily restored).
From left to right: Tyndareus, one of the Dioscuri, Helen, Leda.
Stockholm, National Museum.

Nemesis of Rhamnus, by Agoracritus, *c.* 430 BC. Roman period
copy. Copenhagen, Ny Carlsberg Glyptotek.

Agoracritus Sculptor, active *c.* 440–400 BC.

Widely reported as the pupil and lover of *Pheidias,
Agoracritus (Agorakritos) of Paros probably worked
mostly in mainland Greece, based perhaps in Athens. He
is listed by Pliny as a marble-sculptor, but two bronze
statues by him are recorded. His most famous work was
the cult-statue of Nemesis at Rhamnus (before 431 BC),
which a popular or local tradition attributed to Pheidias,
who allowed him to sign it as a love-gift. The signature
was on a small plaque on the apple branch held in the
goddess's left hand, and no doubt recorded the true
authorship of the statue. Fragments of the statue have
been excavated, from which Roman copies of the whole
figure have recently been identified. Fragments of the
relief figures of the base were also found, from which a
Roman copy of part of its composition has been
recognized: the girl Helen being presented to her real
mother Nemesis by her foster mother Leda, as in one
version of the story. Agoracritus' style, apparently hard to
tell apart from that of Pheidias, seems related to the more
advanced figures of the Parthenon pediments, and points
to the rich drapery styles of the late fifth century.

BIBL. G. I. Despinis, *Symvoli stin meletin tou ergou tou
Agorakritou* (1971); Robertson, *History of Greek Art*
351–5; *Roman World* *Pliny the Elder.

Agoratus Athenian political agent, late fifth century BC.

Agoratus (Agoratos) claimed, perhaps falsely, to have
gained Athenian citizenship for his part in the
assassination of *Phrynichus (2). *Lysias, *Oration* xiii
belongs to a trial concerning his anti-democratic activities
in the revolution of 404 BC.

BIBL. Kirchner, *PA*, no. 17.

Agyrrius Athenian politician, floruit 403–389 BC.

Agyrrius' (Agurrhios) only recorded public offices are
council-secretaryship (403/2 BC) and generalship (390/89).
He was particularly associated with public finance
(reduction of comic poets' pay; restoration of *theorika*;
introduction and increase of pay for attending the
Assembly) and business (he was chief of a tax-consortium

in 402/1, and agent of *Pasion in the 390s). After accusations of embezzlement he spent many years in prison as a state-debtor.

BIBL. Kirchner, *PA*, no. 179; Davies, *Athenian Families* 278 f.

Alcaeus Lyric poet, *c.* 590 BC.

An aristocrat from Mytilene in Lesbos, Alcaeus (Alkaios) played an active role in the power-struggles which rent its oligarchy. Ancient reconstructions, undoubtedly based, precariously, on poems, indicated a family alliance with *Pittacus which overthrew the tyrant Melanchrus *c.* 612–609 BC; a plot against the next tyrant Myrsilus, the failure of which exiled Alcaeus, his brother Antimenidas, and Pittacus to nearby Pyrrha; then Pittacus' desertion of Alcaeus for Myrsilus, on whose death, prematurely celebrated by Alcaeus (fr. 332), Pittacus was himself appointed to crush Alcaeus and his fellow exiles (*c.* 590?). They probably had to leave Lesbos: a papyrus commentary (*Suppl.* 282) associates 'the battle at the bridge' with 'the second exile', survived by Alcaeus for a 'third return' linked with a war of *Alyattes and Astyages (no earlier than 584 BC).

Conflict dominated his songs: attacks on his opponents' ancestry and behaviour (frs. 72, 348); distress at his rural exile (fr. 130); a confident inventory of gleaming armour (fr. 357); recollections or fantasies of storms imperilling guerrilla operations at sea (frs. 6, 326, interpreted as allegories of the ship of State by some ancients and moderns). But they also exploit themes conventional in symposia (where they were sung): hymns to gods (fr. 34); good cheer while storms rage outside (fr. 338); drinking, garlands, and pretty boys (frs. 38, 48, 430). One addressing Antimenidas welcomes him on return from fighting for Babylon's king, Nebuchadrezzar (fr. 350); another, addressed to Melanippus, posed as a despatch reporting Alcaeus' abandonment of his shield on the battlefield like *Archilochus (fr. 428). Alcaeus also draws on mythology, but not for its own sake: the tale of Helen is told (fr. 42) to stress how she destroyed a city, and **Ajax's rape of Cassandra is vividly narrated to warn Pittacus of the workings of divine justice (*Suppl.* 262). As antiquity observed, his poetry's strengths were moral fervour and invective vigour.

BIBL. Text: Lobel and Page, *PLF*; Page, *Suppl.*; *Greek Lyric Poets* (Loeb). Comm.: D. L. Page, *Sappho and Alcaeus* (1955); Campbell, *Lyric Poetry*; Kirkwood, *Greek Monody*.

Alcaeus of Messene Epigrammatist, *c.* 200 BC.

An active patriot, Alcaeus (Alkaios) treats politics alongside more conventional subjects in his extant epigrams. Adulation of Macedon's *Philip V (unless Epigram 1 is sarcastically hyperbolic) turns to virulent vituperation – 'poisoner' (2, 3), 'coward of Cynoscephalae' (4) – while *Flamininus, Greece's liberator, is compared and contrasted with *Xerxes (5).

BIBL. Gow and Page, *Hellenistic Epigrams*; F. W. Walbank, *CQ* xxxvi (1942), xxxvii (1943).

Alcamenes Sculptor, active *c.* 440–400 BC.

Alcamenes (Alkamenēs) was probably an Athenian, but may have come from the Athenian-controlled island of Lemnos in the Aegean. Nine of his dozen or so recorded

Fragment of a papyrus text of the poems of Alcaeus, from Oxyrhynchus, in Egypt. 2nd century AD. Oxford, Bodleian Library.

Left: Hermes, by Alcamenes. Roman period copy. Istanbul Archaeological Museum. *Right*: marble group of Procne and Itys from the Acropolis, dedicated and probably made by Alcamenes, *c.* 420 BC. Athens, Acropolis Museum.

works were made at or near Athens, and he was known as both a pupil and a rival of *Pheidias. One of his commissions was for *Thrasybulus in 404/3 BC; so he must have been a younger contemporary of the great master. Pausanias attributed the west pediment of the temple of Zeus at Olympia, built in the 460s, to Alcamenes, but this is almost certainly a mistake – perhaps for an unknown elder Alcamenes.

All his recorded works were of gods and in marble, except for a chryselephantine cult-statue of Dionysus and a bronze athlete. His most famous statue was the Aphrodite in the gardens outside the walls of Athens; we do not know what it looked like. There was a marble group of Procne and Itys on the Acropolis dedicated by Alcamenes which has been recovered, and it is reasonable to suppose that he also made it. Many copies and adaptations of the Roman period of his Hermes at the Gate and probably of his triple-bodied Hecate from Athens exist. Both show an unusual and early interest in conscious archaism – unless they too should be attributed to the conjectured elder Alcamenes. Plausible guesses have been made to identify Roman copies of his Ares and Aphrodite in Athens and of his conjectured cult-statues of Hephaestus and Athena for the Hephaesteum at Athens. He has also been tentatively associated, on grounds of technique and style, with the sculptures of the Erechtheum on the Acropolis. But we know nothing for certain of his artistic personality.

BIBL. L. Capuis, *Alkamenes* (1968); Harrison, *AJA* xxxi (1977); Robertson, *History of Greek Art* 284–7; *Roman World* *Pausanias.

Alcibiades Athenian political leader, died 404 BC.

To the ancients, Alcibiades (Alkibiadēs) was the stock type of the sophisticated aristocrat, endowed with all possible advantages, brilliant and 'outstanding both in his vices and in his virtues' (Nepos). His father *Cleinias' family had supported *Cleisthenes; his mother was an *Alcmaeonid. His father died at Coronea (446 BC); Alcibiades was brought up by his uncle and guardian *Pericles, and came under the influence of various sophists including *Socrates. The extent of his wealth can best be illustrated by the fact that he entered seven chariots at the Olympics of 416, coming first, second, and fourth.

Although a hereditary *proxenos* of Sparta at Athens, Alcibiades first appeared as *strategos* in 420, trying to arrange an alliance between Athens and several Peloponnesian states opposed to Sparta (Elis, Mantinea, and Argos). The defeat of this alliance by King *Agis II at the battle of Mantinea (418) discredited Alcibiades, who was not re-elected. In the following year *Hyperbolus tried to eliminate him by re-introducing the obsolete procedure of ostracism, but, by some adroit political manœuvring, Alcibiades had Hyperbolus ostracized instead. He was re-elected *strategos*, and led an expedition to conquer Melos, which had supported Sparta during the Archidamian War (431–421). In 416 he strongly supported an appeal for Athens to send an expedition to support the Sicilian city of Segesta against its rival Selinus. Alcibiades was appointed to command the expedition, together with his opponent *Nicias and *Lamachus. Soon after his arrival in Sicily, he was recalled on suspicion of implication in the *Hermocopid affair. At Thurii he

escaped from the Athenian ship which was bringing him back; his property in Attica was confiscated, and he now put himself at the disposal of Sparta, advising the Spartans to send *Gylippus to Syracuse and occupy Decelea.

With the collapse of Athenian authority in the wake of the Sicilian disaster (413), Alcibiades accompanied a Lacedaemonian fleet to Ionia; he first tried to arrange an agreement between Sparta and the Ionian satrap *Tissaphernes, but then advised Tissaphernes that it was in Persia's interest not to allow either Greek state to achieve an outright victory. Alcibiades saw that only a change in government would allow him to return to Athens. He was in contact with the oligarchs who organized the coup of 411, suggesting that he would be able to mediate between an oligarchic Athens and Tissaphernes. But Tissaphernes stood by the Spartan alliance, and Alcibiades turned to the democrats at Samos instead: through the agency of *Thrasybulus he was elected *strategos*, and in that capacity destroyed the Spartan fleet under Mindarus at Cyzicus (410). In 408 he returned to Athens, ostentatiously escorting the annual religious procession to Eleusis overland for the first time since the Spartans had occupied Attica. (One of the charges on which he had been exiled had been profaning the Eleusinian Mysteries.)

In spring 407 the arrival of *Lysander and *Cyrus the Younger meant that the initiative in the Aegean war passed back to Sparta and Persia. An Athenian flotilla was defeated at Notium; although Alcibiades was not present, he was held responsible and not re-elected. Rather than face trial again, he retired to his estates in Thrace and took no more part in the war. After the installation of the regime of the Thirty (see *Critias) at Athens in 404, Lysander and the oligarchs felt that they would only be secure if Alcibiades, as a potential focus of democratic opposition, were eliminated; he fled to *Pharnabazus (in Phrygia), who killed him.

BIBL. J. Hatzfeld, *Alcibiade* (2nd ed., 1951); Davies, *Athenian Families*, no. 600; Westlake, *Individuals in Thucydides*, ch. 12; *Roman World* *Nepos.

Alcidamas Rhetorician, 5th or 4th century BC.

Alcidamas (Alkidamas), from Elaea in Aeolis, was a teacher of rhetoric, mainly at Athens. He was a pupil of *Gorgias, and developed his theories about rhetoric in opposition to those of *Isocrates; his one surviving speech (*On Those Who Write Written Speeches, or On the Sophists*) stresses the need for spontaneity and for a speaker to react on the spot to immediate changes in the mood of his audience. He wrote a systematic textbook on oratory entitled the *Mouseion*; it contained much anecdotal material which made it extremely useful for later students of oratory, and considerable papyrus fragments survive.

BIBL. W. Steidle, *Hermes* lxxx (1952); Guthrie, *Greek Philosophy* iii, 311 ff.

Alcidas Spartan leader, floruit 427/6 BC.

In spring 427 the Spartans sent Alcidas (Alkidas) to support the revolt of the Mytilenean aristocrats against Athens. *Thucydides describes his hesitation, and how he arrived too late to help; instead he sailed along the Ionian coast executing the people he was supposed to 'liberate' from Athens. He supported the aristocrats at Corcyra the following summer, but lost a naval engagement against the

Athenian and Corcyrean fleets. When the Spartans founded Heraclea in Trachis (426), he was sent out as one of the oecists.

BIBL. D. Lateiner, *GRBS* xvi (1975); Westlake, *Individuals in Thucydides*, ch. 9.

Alcmaeon: see **Alcmaeonids**

Alcmaeon of Croton Natural philosopher, *c.* 500 BC.

A younger contemporary of *Pythagoras, and no doubt influenced by him, Alcmaeon (Alkmaiōn) wrote a book on nature. He was best known for his medical theory that health consists in the proper balance of opposing powers in the body (hot and cold, wet and dry, etc.). He was perhaps the first Greek philosopher to argue that thought, or intellect, is what distinguishes men from animals, and to distinguish carefully between thought and sensation. He also gave detailed accounts of how sense-organs work. A wider interest in the nature of man may be indicated by his virtually unintelligible remark, 'Men perish for this reason, that they cannot join the beginning to the end.'

BIBL. Guthrie, *Greek Philosophy* i. 5.

Alcmaeonids Athenian family.

The Alcmaeonids (Alkmaiōnidai) were one of the leading Athenian aristocratic families. An early member of the family, Megacles (Megaklēs), was responsible for suppressing *Cylon's attempted *coup* (*c.* 630 BC), incurring a curse which was often brought up against the Alcmaeonids by political opponents. At the beginning of the sixth century the head of the family was Alcmaeon (Alkmaiōn), who commanded the Athenian forces in the First Sacred War (*c.* 590) and was enriched by the king of Lydia. His son *Megacles became a leading rival of *Peisistratus, and consequently the family spent some time in exile under the tyranny. During this time they rebuilt the temple at Delphi, which had been burnt down in 548, on a more lavish scale than they had originally undertaken to do, thereby winning the support of the oracle. Megacles' son *Cleisthenes reformed the Athenian constitution, but after *c.* 500 the family went into decline, partly because of alleged pro-Persian tendencies – another *Megacles (son of Hippocrates) was ostracized in 487/6. Its only other distinguished member was *Pericles, whose mother was an Alcmaeonid.

BIBL. Herodotus i. 64, v. 62, vi. 115, 121–31; Davies, *Athenian Families*, no. 9688.

Alcman Lyric poet, *c.* 610 BC.

Alcman (Alkman) was probably Laconian (the view of *Crates of Mallos, that he was from Sardis, doubtless treated fragment 16 as sung *propria persona*). He was best known for songs composed for performance by Spartan choirs on ritual occasions. Meagre quotations may preserve scraps of hymns to Apollo (frs. 45–50), Aphrodite (fr. 55), Athena (fr. 43), and the Dioscuri (fr. 2): but his skill is best displayed in a 100-line papyrus fragment (1) of a *partheneion* originally of (probably) ten 14-line stanzas in dactylic/trochaic metre. The vestiges of the first half narrate a myth involving sons of Hippocoon, and draw morals about mortal limitations and divine punishment; in the second the choir of maidens sings of the beauty of its leaders, Agido and Hagesichora, and stresses its dependence on them and on Aotis, whose identity

Fragment of a papyrus text of Alcman's *Partheneia* from Oxyrhynchus, Egypt. Late 1st century BC or early 1st century AD. Oxford, Bodleian Library.

(Artemis Orthia is often suggested) is as obscure as the nature of the performance. Alcman's briefly-drawn pictures of beauty and finery, and his rich imagery of light and race-horses, convey the opulence and self-confidence of aristocratic festivals, while erotic innuendos (compare fr. 3, also from a *partheneion*) show the poet's skill and licence in composing songs for (?) *rites de passage* of nubile girls. Other songs were for (less formal?) performance by youths in Spartan messes. In which category the ancients found the more explicit mentions of love (see fr. 58) that made him 'inventor of love-poetry' is obscure.

His works circulated in six books, and his grave was shown in Sparta near those of the Hippocoontids and Heracles.

BIBL. Text: Page, *PMG*. Commentary: D. L. Page, *Alcman: the Partheneion* (1951); Campbell, *Lyric Poetry*; Bowra, *Lyric Poetry*.

Aleuadae Thessalian dynasty.

In the classical period, Thessaly was ruled by a small number of extremely wealthy families: notably the Aleuadae (Aleuadai), based on Larissa, the family of Antiochus of Pharsalus, and the Scopadae of Crannon. After the death of most members of the Scopadae when their banqueting-hall collapsed (probably at Pharsalus, *c.* 510/500 BC), the Aleuadae became predominant; their leader Thorax (Thōrax), who was recognized as *tagos* or king of Thessaly, supported Persia in 480. In the period after 404, Thessalian politics was centred on their opposition to the family of *Lycophron of Pherae and his successor *Jason. The Aleuadae leaders Aristippus (Aristippos) and Medius (Mēdios) appealed for help first to *Alexander II of Macedon, then to the Theban *Pelopidas, and finally to *Philip II (356). Philip annexed

Thessaly and divided it into tetrarchies (342); several Aleuadae received appointments as tetrarchs.

BIBL. Hammond and Griffith, *Macedonia* ii, index.

Alexander I, 'Philhellene' King of Macedon, c. 494–452 BC.

As a vassal of Persia, Alexander (Alexandros), son of Amyntas, supported the invasion of Greece and extended Macedonian power into Thrace (whose mines financed the first Macedonian coins). Later generations remembered him for organizing the Macedonian army. Representing himself as a Greek, he invited poets like *Pindar and *Bacchylides to his court, and competed at Greek festivals. Although he pretended that he had secretly given support to the Athenians during the Persian invasion, his attempts to interfere in Greek politics were resisted by Athens; *Cimon's conquest of Thasos and the foundation of Ennea Hodoi (c. 465 BC) prevented further Macedonian expansion into Thrace.

BIBL. Hammond and Griffith, *Macedonia* ii. 98–114; P. A. Brunt, *JHS* xcvi (1976).

Alexander II King of Macedon, 370–368 BC.

Alexander's (Alexandros) short reign was marked by an unproductive intervention in Thessaly (thwarted by *Pelopidas) and (some have believed) a reorganization of the Macedonian army (the creation of so-called 'foot-companions'). His murder, during a war-dance, was credited to *Ptolemy Alorites.

BIBL. Hammond and Griffith, *Macedonia*, ii. 180 ff., 705 f.

Alexander III (the Great) (356–323 BC) King of Macedon 336–323 BC, and Persia 330–323.

After an education at the hands of various tutors, notably (from 342 BC) *Aristotle, which left him with tolerably well-developed literary and scientific interests, Alexander (Alexandros) had his first taste of power in 340 as viceroy of his father, *Philip II, in Macedonia, when he suppressed a Thracian revolt and founded Alexandropolis. In 339 he fought in Scythia, and in 338 played a leading role in the battle of Chaeronea, visiting Athens afterwards as part of an escort for the ashes of the Athenian dead. In 337 a furious and nearly fatal quarrel with Philip (apropos of Princess *Cleopatra-Eurydice) led to Alexander's flight to Illyria. He soon returned, but there was further trouble about the proposed marriage of *Philip Arrhidaeus to a daughter of Pixodarus of Caria, after which four of Alexander's close friends were exiled. That he connived at Philip's murder (336) is, however, not a necessary inference. His accession was readily accepted in Macedonia (though there were certain precautionary 'liquidations'), but he had to underline his claims to the *hegemonia* (leadership) of the Corinthian League by a swift descent on central Greece, and false reports of his death in 335 provoked a Theban revolt, which was suppressed with exemplary ruthlessness.

The remainder of his reign falls into four periods. 1. The first period, 334–330, covers the conquest of Persia up to the death of *Darius III. The latter's defeat was chiefly encompassed by three great victories, at the river Granicus (334), Issus (late 333), and Gaugamela (*alias* Arbela: late 331), but between and after these Alexander marched through Anatolia, Phoenicia, Palestine, Egypt, Mesopotamia, Persis, Media, and Hyrcania, receiving or enforcing submission as he went – a strategy imposed in the Levant and Egypt by Alexander's decision to neutralize the Persian navy not by reliance on the allied Greek fleet (which was disbanded in 334) but by direct control of its bases. It was the time taken by, above all, the siege of Tyre (332) that permitted Darius, whose first inclination after Issus was to attempt a negotiated division of empire, to regroup for a final encounter. Other notable events during this period were the cutting of the Gordian knot (333), the visit to Ammon's oracle at Siwah (331), the foundation of Alexandria (official date 6 April 331), the acquisition of some 180,000 talents from the Persian imperial capitals (331), the burning of Persepolis (330),

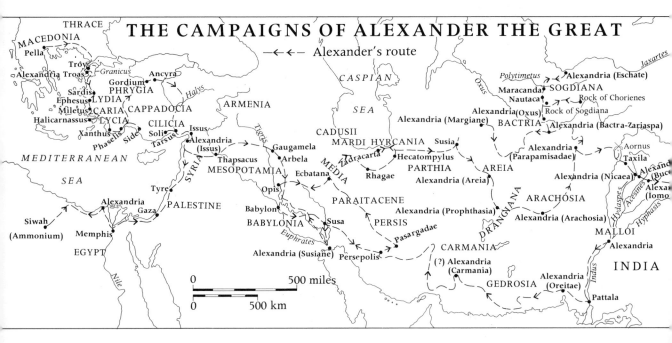

THE CAMPAIGNS OF ALEXANDER THE GREAT

—←—←— Alexander's route

Alexander the Great at Issus: Roman (c. 100 BC) mosaic from the House of the Fauns, Pompeii, copying a painting of the later 4th century BC. Naples, Museo Nazionale.

Left: coin portrait of Alexander the Great as Ammon; minted at Magnesia by Lysimachus. *Right*: late Hellenistic alabaster head of Alexander the Great. Brooklyn Museum Collection.

and the hectic pursuit of Darius from Ecbatana to somewhere east of Tehran (c. July 330). Alexander had claimed the Achaemenid throne in 332, and his troops hailed him 'King of Asia' after Gaugamela. But Darius' murder by *Bessus underlined Alexander's position as the new Great King (and precluded the embarrassment of a captive Darius). The Greek allied contingents were now disbanded. The 'crusade' was over, and further fighting would be against recalcitrant 'subjects' and would-be usurpers.

2. In 330–327 Alexander faced the resistance of Bessus (captured 329) and the nationalist opposition led initially by *Spitamenes (329–328/7) and only terminated by the capture of the Rocks of Sogdiana (where *Roxane was taken) and Chorienes. This was the period of the first orientalization of court protocol, the marriage to Roxane, the foundation of eight Alexandrias, and the occurrence of certain ugly incidents at court (the deaths of *Philotas and *Parmenion (330), the execution of *Alexander the Lyncestian (330), the murder of (Black) *Cleitus (328), and the 'Pages' Conspiracy' (327)).

3. In 327 Alexander entered India, capturing the almost impregnable Aornus (Pir-Sar) on the way. Resistance from *Porus was eliminated at the river Hydaspes (Jhelum; 326) – perhaps Alexander's most remarkable victory, involving the crossing of a major river in face of an army which included numerous elephants – but the inexorable eastward advance was finally halted at the river Hyphasis (Beas), where the army refused to endorse a march to the Ganges. Instead of returning to Afghanistan, Alexander set off down the Indus to subdue the peoples of south-west India, which was achieved only with considerable carnage. (Alexander himself was nearly killed by the Malloi.) Preparations for a co-ordinated advance of army and fleet along the coast of Baluchistan and Iran were upset when *Nearchus was delayed by monsoons, and Alexander had to cross the Gedrosian desert unsupported. That even one quarter of the army survived represents a

remarkable achievement. Alexander's emergence from Gedrosia was marked by celebrations in Carmania which some sources describe as a Dionysiac revel, and by a purge of satraps and other officials whose deportment during the king's absence in India was deemed unsatisfactory. (One notable delinquent, *Harpalus, escaped.)

4. Alexander's final 18 months were marked by (a) new army dispositions involving increased use of Iranian troops and the disbandment of Macedonian veterans (whose initial reaction was mutiny (at Opis in 324)); (b) the Exiles' Decree, which infringed Greek autonomy and caused immense local problems by ordering the repatriation of almost all Greek exiles; (c) the request for divine honours (if this is historical); (d) the death of *Hephaestion; and (e) preparations for an Arabian campaign. The last was ready to start when Alexander fell ill. His death (10 June 323) was inevitably ascribed to assassins (e.g. *Antipater, acting through his son Iolaus), but natural causes (pernicious malaria?) remain a more probable explanation. Alexander's supposed last words, that he left his kingdom 'to the best man; for I foresee that grand funeral games will be provided by my Friends', are at least *ben trovato* – and his corpse itself became one of the interim prizes (won by *Ptolemy I).

More copiously documented than *Philip II, Alexander is not much less elusive. Some aspects, naturally, are less controversial than others. Of his resourcefulness and sureness of touch as tactician and leader of men the record of conquest speaks for itself, though only with Engels' recent book (see below) has appropriate attention been drawn to his mastery of logistical problems. Militarily speaking he simply outclassed all opposition, whether in formal battle or in hit-and-run or siege warfare. There is naturally room for argument about the intricacies of battle narratives or about the precise details of army reorganization and the like, but what is at stake is more the credit of ancient sources than that of Alexander.

Administrative complexities were not a major preoccupation, and Alexander contented himself here with general retention of the Persian satrapal organization (with all the associated local administrative structures), the establishment of garrisons, and the foundation of cities (chiefly in the East). Matters such as the status of the Asiatic Greeks can provoke disagreement, but administration generally only acquires special interest where matters of policy obtrude (e.g. the appointment of *Iranian* satraps or the tolerance shown to a *Cleomenes of Naucratis). It is questions of politics (especially the ramifications of 'orientalization') and personality (was Alexander a cynical, or a paranoid, tyrant? Did he regard himself as divine?) that really divide historians. Old pictures of Alexander as proponent of universal brotherhood or (worse) Aryan world domination certainly overstate and/or misinterpret such phenomena as the adoption of Persian court ceremonial, attempts to impose *proskynesis*, the marriage to Roxane and the mass marriage of Alexander and 91 Companions to Iranian ladies (Susa, 324), the incorporation of oriental contingents into the army, the training of Iranians as 'Macedonian' troops, or the use of Iranian satraps (only three of whom survived until 323 anyway). There is much here that is merely pragmatic. This is less true of the intimations of divinity. That the denomination 'son of Ammon (Zeus)' was used of Alexander must be accepted (whatever the exact events at Siwah that engendered or encouraged it), and that a request for divine honours was issued to the Greeks in 324 remains a distinct possibility. Neither phenomenon can be regarded as a reasonable practical response to political or administrative problems, and both suggest a personality dangerously out of touch with reality (note the reaction to Hephaestion's death). On the other hand the murder of Cleitus arguably shows Alexander in no worse a light than Philip (who nearly killed his son at a drinking-party in 337); and the rights and wrongs of the executions of Philotas, Alexander the Lyncestian, the Pages, *Callisthenes (?), and certain Iranian satraps are not always easy to judge. In any event we ought not to be shocked to discover that Alexander was not a soft-hearted ruler. Of his long-term plans (if any) little can be said. A document was circulated posthumously claiming that he envisaged the conquest of Carthage, the building of roads and harbours from Egypt to Gibraltar, the erection of six 1,500-talent temples in Greece and Macedonia, and the transplantation of populations between Asia and Europe, but it was certainly partly or wholly inauthentic. What really lay beyond the conquest of Arabia is unknown, and was perhaps unknown to Alexander.

BIBL. H. Berve, *Das Alexanderreich* (1926); W. W. Tarn, *Alexander the Great* (1948); J. R. Hamilton, *Alexander the Great* (1973); R. Lane Fox, *Alexander the Great* (1973); F. Schachermeyr, *Alexander der Grosse. Das Problem seiner Persönlichkeit und seines Wirkens* (1973); *Alexandre le Grand. Image et Réalité* (Fondation Hardt, Entretiens xxii (1975)); D. Engels, *Alexander the Great and the Logistics of the Macedonian Army* (1978).

Alexander IV King of Macedon, 323–c. 311 BC.

The posthumous son of *Alexander and *Roxane, Alexander (Alexandros) became nominal king (jointly with *Philip III Arrhidaeus) immediately on birth. Brought to Macedonia in 320 BC by *Antipater, he and his mother fled to Epirus after the regent's death (319), and Alexander eventually became sole king, after Philip had been disposed of by *Olympias (317). Captured by *Cassander in 316 he did not long survive the Peace of 311, which, by securing Cassander's position only so long as Alexander was a minor, rendered his continued existence superfluous. His death marked the end of the Argead dynasty.

BIBL. Will, *Hist. pol.*; R. M. Errington, *JHS* xc (1970).

Alexander V King of Macedon, c. 295–294 BC.

Alexander (Alexandros), youngest of the three sons of *Cassander and Thessalonice (a daughter of *Philip II), contended for the Macedonian throne with his brother Antipater (Antipatros) after the death of their consumptive elder brother Philip IV. He was the first husband of Lysandra, a daughter of *Ptolemy I. While Antipater murdered his mother for siding against him, Alexander unwisely summoned the aid of *Pyrrhus of Epirus and of *Demetrius Poliorcetes, who both welcomed an invitation to intervene in Cassander's old territory. Alexander was installed on the throne by the former but murdered in uncertain circumstances by the latter. Antipater, who had married a daughter of *Lysimachus, fled to his father-in-law, as did his brother's widow Lysandra, when Demetrius seized the Macedonian throne.

BIBL. Tarn, *Antigonos Gonatas* 13.

Alexander II of Molossia King, 272–c. 240 BC.

The son of *Pyrrhus of Epirus and Lanassa (daughter of *Agathocles of Syracuse), Alexander (Alexandros) may have played some part in his father's plans in Sicily, but there is no evidence that he accompanied Pyrrhus there in 278 BC. Although Pyrrhus died fighting *Antigonus Gonatas, the latter allowed Alexander to take the Epirote throne in 272. Epirus was allied to Athens against Macedon in the War of *Chremonides (266/5–261), and Alexander invaded Macedon when Gonatas was occupied with the siege of Athens. He was defeated by the future *Demetrius II, who drove him from Epirus to take refuge in Acarnania. Aetolia and Acarnania restored him to his throne (c. 259(?)), perhaps as a counterweight to Macedon, but he later divided Acarnania with the Aetolians. When he died, leaving a widow with two young sons, the Aetolians invaded his half of Acarnania; in desperation the queen mother married her daughter Phthia-Chryseis to Demetrius for protection.

BIBL. Hammond, *Epirus*; G. N. Cross, *Epirus* (1932); P. R. Franke, *Alt-Epirus und das Königtum der Molosser* (1955).

Alexander Aetolus Poet, c. 280 BC.

From Pleuron in Aetolia, Alexander (Alexandros) was contemporary with *Aratus at the court of *Antigonus Gonatas, but was also retained by *Ptolemy II at Alexandria (chronology unclear), where under *Zenodotus he tackled the preliminary editing of the new Library's tragedies and satyr plays. Though he was counted in the tragic *Pleiad, only one play-title survives. Other fragments show him to be a versatile poet in favourite Hellenistic forms, from learned epyllion and narrative elegy to epigram and the kind of indelicate verse associated with *Sotades.

BIBL. Webster, *Hellenistic Poetry*.

Coin portrait of Alexander Balas, claimant to the Seleucid throne.

Alexander Balas Seleucid pretender, 150–145 BC.

The supposed younger son of *Antiochus IV, Alexander (Alexandros) was installed in Cilicia as claimant to the Seleucid throne by *Attalus II of Pergamum, who resented the support given to a Cappadocian pretender by the legitimate Seleucid king *Demetrius I. Demetrius' unpopularity at home and abroad paved the way for Balas' recognition by Rome, Pergamum, *Ariarathes V of Cappadocia, *Ptolemy VI, and the Jewish leaders. Their military alliance led to Demetrius's death in 150 BC, after which Balas' position was secure. Having little aptitude for anything beyond the perquisites of kingship, Balas placed himself under the political protection of Ptolemy, whose daughter *Cleopatra Thea he married. In 147 the usurper was threatened by Demetrius' son, *Demetrius II, but, when Balas tried to kill Ptolemy for pursuing Egyptian interests in Coele-Syria, the latter switched his support to Demetrius. Balas was defeated and killed in a battle against them in 145.
BIBL. Bevan, *House of Seleucus* ii; Will, *Hist. pol.* ii.

Alexander of Corinth (c. 290–c. 245 BC) *Strategus* and king.

Inheriting the *strategia* in Corinth and Euboea after the death of his father, the younger *Craterus, Alexander (Alexandros) revolted from *Antigonus Gonatas of Macedon sometime during the period c. 253–c. 249, and proclaimed himself king. After consolidating his position regarding Athens, Argos, *Aratus of Sicyon, and the Achaean League, Alexander became a severe obstacle to Macedonian strategy on the mainland, but died c. 245 leaving his widow Nicaea as ruler in Corinth. Antigonus promised her the hand of his heir *Demetrius II, and, thereby, a future as queen of Macedon, but, although she acquiesced, Corinth and its citadel were taken from her – apparently by deceit or stealth – and no marriage occurred.
BIBL. Will, *Hist. pol.* i.

Alexander of Epirus King, 342–331/30 BC.

Alexander (Alexandros), *Olympias' younger brother, grew up in Macedonia and then replaced King Arrybas in 342 BC to secure *Philip II's control of Epirus. It was during celebrations of his marriage to Princess *Cleopatra that Philip was murdered. In 334 he went to help Tarentum against local Italian enemies, but relations became strained and, after defeat at Pandosia (331/30), he was murdered by a Lucanian exile. In distant Parthia his illustrious namesake (*Alexander the Great) ordered general mourning for the occasion.
BIBL. Berve, *Alexanderreich* no. 38; Hammond and Griffith, *Macedonia* ii.

Alexander the Lyncestian Macedonian general, died 330 BC.

The son-in-law of *Antipater, Alexander (Alexandros), son of Aeropus, survived alleged implication in *Philip II's murder (his brothers were executed), and initially prospered under *Alexander the Great, attaining command of the Thessalian cavalry. He was eventually arrested in 334/3 BC or autumn 333 (date and circumstances are disputed) and executed in autumn 330.
BIBL. Berve, *Alexanderreich*, no. 37; Bosworth, *Arrian* 162 f.

Alexander of Pherae Tyrant, 369–358 BC.

Alexander (Alexandros), *Jason's nephew, became tyrant and *tagos* of Thessaly after murdering Polyphron. For five years he sought effective power in Thessaly despite repeated Theban opposition, but defeat at Cynoscephalae (364 BC) heralded the abandonment of such ambitions and submission to Theban suzerainty. He was eventually murdered by his wife Thebe and her brothers, an event which inspired *Moschion's *Men of Pherae* and played a part in *Aristotle's *Eudemus*. Alexander's reputation for tyrannical brutality may be somewhat exaggerated.
BIBL. Berve, *Tyrannis* 290 f.

Alexander Polyhistor Historian, floruit 80–c. 50(?) BC.

A Milesian Greek called 'Polyhistor' ('Very Learned') because of the vast scope of his knowledge, Alexander (Alexandros) was a captive at Rome in the time of Sulla, was freed, and became the pedagogue in a Roman family. In the tradition of *Crates of Mallos, Alexander wrote on poetry, grammar, and philosophy, but also on *Pythagoreanism, and he composed histories of Rome, Delphi, Chaldaea, and the Jews. Although a gentile, Alexander recorded much secular, apologetic Jewish literature and Greek Jewish poetry of the Hellenistic Age, which is partly preserved in Eusebius. He is pre-eminent among those who hellenized Jewish historical tradition and thus made it comprehensible to the Graeco-Roman world. According to the *Suda*, he died in a fire in Laurentum.
BIBL. *FGrH* 273; PW i. 1449 (Alexandros (88)); J. Freudenthal, *Alexander Polyhistor* (1875); A. Momigliano, *Alien Wisdom* (1975) 121 ff.; *Roman World* *Eusebius of Caesarea, *Sulla.

Alexis Comic poet, active before 350–after 280 BC.

The very long career of Alexis of Thurii in south Italy, during which he is said to have written 245 plays, spanned the transition from Middle to New Comedy. He may have played an important part in that transition (he was allegedly the teacher, or even uncle, of *Menander), though he treated mythical themes as well as ones from contemporary life.
BIBL. Lesky, *Greek Literature*; Edmonds, *Attic Comedy* ii; Webster, *Later Comedy*.

Alyattes King of Lydia, c. 610–560 BC.

Alyattes (Aluattēs) continued his predecessors' policy of conquering Ionia, and took Smyrna after a siege. He then attacked Miletus, and after a long war was persuaded by a trick to give up hope of winning and make peace. Like *Gyges, he sent offerings to Delphi. His tomb was considered a remarkable structure.

BIBL. Herodotus i. 18–22, 25; Strabo xiii. 627.

Amadocus Thracian (Odrysian) kings, 5th–4th centuries BC.

Amadocus (Amadokos) was the name of two Odrysian dynasts. The first was a friend of *Alcibiades and later an Athenian ally (390/89 BC). The second, his son, caused the breakup of the Thracian kingdom created by *Cotys (358) and, in search of local advantage, was successively allied with Athens and with *Philip II.

BIBL. *PW* i. 1713.

Amasis (1) Egyptian Pharaoh, 569–*c*. 525 BC.

Amasis encouraged the Greeks to settle in Egypt at Naucratis, and made alliances with several Greek states, including *Polycrates' Samos (it was he who advised Polycrates to throw away his ring in order to end his excessive good luck). He died shortly before the Persian invasion, and his reign was remembered as a time of peace and prosperity.

BIBL. Herodotus ii. 162–82; iii. 1–4, 10, 39–43.

Amasis (2) Potter, active *c*. 560–530 BC.

Amasis was one of the leading potters working at Athens in the archaic period, and, judging by his name, was probably from Egypt. We have nine vases signed by him as potter, all decorated by the same painter, called the 'Amasis painter', to whom over a hundred vases painted in the black-figure technique have been attributed. It is possible that, as with his great contemporary *Exekias,

Lekythos (oil bottle) by the Amasis painter, showing an evening procession: a groom transports his newly-wed bride to his house. Mid-6th century BC. New York, Metropolitan Museum.

potter and painter were the same man. He decorated a large variety of vase shapes, specializing in amphorae. He painted a considerable range of subjects, showing a strong interest in genre scenes, which were new to vase-painting.

BIBL. Beazley, *ABV* 150 ff.; *Paralipomena* 62 ff.; S. Karouzou, *The Amasis Painter* (1956); Boardman, *Black Figure* 54–6.

Amynander King of Athamania, floruit *c*. 210–*c*. 189 BC.

Ruler of a country which occupied the mountainous region between Macedonia and Aetolia, Amynander (Amunandros) had a vested interest in the fortunes of his neighbours, and inevitably became involved in the struggles between Greece and Rome. On the eve of the First Macedonian War (209 BC) Amynander, representing Aetolian interests, met *Philip V with other states to try to prevent war, but in 207 he was bought as Philip's ally, and allowed him free access through Athamania to Aetolia. He attended the negotiations leading to the Peace of Phoenice in 205.

In the Second Macedonian War, Rome had elicited his support against Philip by 200 BC, and he used *Flamininus' men to besiege Thessalian strongholds. Flamininus sent Amynander to Rome in 198 to argue for the renewal of the consul's command. He fought at Cynoscephalae, and the peace agreement allowed him to keep what he had conquered. In 192–1 his third switch of allegiance allied him with *Antiochus III and the Aetolians against Rome and Philip; the latter drove him from his kingdom in 191. After Antiochus' defeat at Magnesia in 189, the Aetolians helped to obtain the restoration of his kingdom from Rome. He was pardoned and restored, despite his treachery, and probably died a few years later.

BIBL. Hammond, *Epirus*; Walbank, *Philip V*.

Amyntas III King of Macedonia, 393/2–370/69 BC.

Amyntas (Amuntas) acceded by means of murder after the disturbed period following *Archelaus' death, and, despite problems with Olynthus and the Illyrians, retained his throne for over 20 years and died a natural death, an achievement (in Macedonia) quite as notable as his fathering of *Philip II.

BIBL. Hammond and Griffith, *Macedonia* ii. 172–80.

Anacharsis Scythian prince, 6th century BC (?).

Anacharsis (Anakharsis) was said to have travelled in Greece and become an enthusiast for its culture, but to have been put to death for trying to introduce Greek religious rites into Scythia. Later writers made him a guest of *Solon and one of the *Seven Sages.

BIBL. Herodotus iv. 76–7; Diogenes Laertius i. 101 ff.

Anacreon Lyric poet, *c*. 520 BC.

From Teos (Ionia), whose colony at Thracian Abdera he may have joined *c*. 540 BC, Anacreon (Anakreōn) was in Samos by *c*. 538, invited, according to Himerius, by *Polycrates' father. An anecdote in *Herodotus presents him banqueting with Polycrates at his overthrow *c*. 522 BC: thence a warship despatched by *Hipparchus brought him to Athens. Here his patrons included Critias, grandfather of the oligarch *Critias, and probably *Pericles' father *Xanthippus; his role as entertainer at symposia was depicted on red figure vases; and his songs

Herm inscribed 'Anacreon the lyric poet', found in Trastevere, Rome. Roman copy of a Greek original of *c.* 440 BC. Rome, Palazzo dei Conservatori.

could still be requested by characters in *Aristophanes' Banqueters* (427 BC).

These songs were mostly short (some of six and eight lines seem complete) and their short metrical units, often in four-line stanzas, fitted his refined treatment of the old themes of wine, women (more often boys), and song – themes drawn from the symposia where they were sung. Sincerity is elusive, though perhaps discernible in fragment 395, on old age: instead Anacreon impresses by choice and placing of words, bowls over by telling imagery (e.g. striking personifications of Love (frs. 398 and 413)), and surprises by punch lines exposing new, humorous perspectives (fr. 358). Although elegiac and iambic poems survive (including full-blooded abuse (fr. 388)), it was his songs for the lyre, collected in five books, which with their praise of Smerdies' locks, Cleobulus' eyes, and Bathyllus' sex-appeal (fr. 402) established his poetic image and were imitated in theme and metre by later *Anacreontics*. Surviving statues, perhaps copies of one attested on the Acropolis at Athens, predictably portray him drunk, and legend has him die choking on a grape-pip.

BIBL. Herodotus iii. 121; Page, *PMG*; Campbell, *Lyric Poetry*; Bowra, *Lyric Poetry*; Kirkwood, *Greek Monody*; *Roman World* *Himerius.

Ananius Iambic poet, *c.* 500 BC (?).

To Ananias or Ananius (Ananios) are ascribed three trimeters invoking Apollo (Dionysus in *Aristophanes, Frogs*, seems to think they are by *Hipponax); three choliambic fragments (two also ascribed to Hipponax), and nine trochaic tetrameters on the seasons for fish and meats, alluded to by *Epicharmus.

BIBL. Aristophanes, *Frogs* 661 ff.; West, *IEG*.

Anaxagoras (*c.* 500–428 BC) Philosopher.

Born at Clazomenae, Anaxagoras spent much of his life

in Athens. As a friend of *Pericles, he was charged with impiety by opponents who wished to undermine Pericles' dominant position, and was condemned to death in his absence. He died in exile in Lampsacus, where he may have founded a philosophical school. He had a reputation for unworldliness.

Bronze coin portrait of a philosopher of Clazomenae, probably Anaxagoras, shown standing with his left foot on a rock and holding a globe.

His one work, of which quite large parts survive, was an attempt to explain the universe, from its origins to such details as meteorology and the nature of life and thought. His system is obscure and hard to interpret consistently. The following account overlooks many difficulties.

In the beginning 'all things were together', i.e. everything formed a homogeneous mass in which no distinct qualities could be discerned. A rotation in this mixture caused wetness, dryness, cold, and other qualities to be separated, and from these were compounded the things that make up the present world. Anaxagoras agreed with *Parmenides that nothing comes into existence or is destroyed. He resolved the problem of *apparent* generation and destruction by saying that every kind of substance contains portions of every other kind. Thus he could explain how, say, smoke, fire, and ash come into existence out of wood, by claiming that the wood already contained them. All that happened was a rearrangement of the constituent parts.

The only exception to this principle of universal mixture was mind (*nous*), which is mixed with nothing, but present everywhere. Mind planned the course of the universe and started the original rotation. This is perhaps the first Greek example of an explanation of the world in terms of ends or purposes, a kind of explanation central to the systems of *Plato and *Aristotle.

BIBL. Guthrie, *Greek Philosophy* ii; Kirk and Raven, *Presocratic Philosophers*.

Anaxandridas Agiad king of Sparta, *c.* 560–525 BC.

As king of Sparta, Anaxandridas helped to carry out the 'Orestes policy' of *Chilon, but there is some evidence that he himself opposed it. When Anaxandridas' wife had failed to produce an heir after several years of marriage, the ephors urged him to divorce her and marry another who would not fail in this important duty. Anaxandridas refused to do this, but agreed to bigamy as a compromise. The new wife, a relative of Chilon, soon gave birth to *Cleomenes, but the first wife then became pregnant too, and gave birth to *Dorieus. The choice of this name appears to indicate Anaxandridas' dislike of the 'Orestes policy', which tended to play down the Dorian origins of the Spartan kings. Anaxandridas then returned entirely to his first wife, and had other children by her, while his second wife remained neglected for the rest of her life.

BIBL. Herodotus i. 67–8, v. 39–41; Forrest, *History of Sparta* 82 f.

Anaxandrides Comic poet, active *c.* 380–after 349 BC.

Anaxandrides (Anaxandridēs) of Rhodes (?) won his first victory in 376 BC, and is said to have written 65 plays. Several fragments survive.

BIBL. Lesky, *Greek Literature*; Edmonds, *Attic Comedy* ii; Webster, *Later Comedy*.

Anaxarchus Philosopher, floruit 340–337 BC.

Little can be guessed of the philosophy of Anaxarchus (Anaxarkhos) of Abdera. He admired *Democritus and taught *Pyrrhon the sceptic, with whom he accompanied *Alexander the Great on his campaigns. Late reports say that he offended Nicocreon, a Cypriot tyrant, who, after Alexander's death, had him pounded to death in a mortar with iron pestles.

BIBL. Diogenes Laertius ix. 58–60.

Anaxilas (-aos) Tyrant of Rhegium, 494–476 BC.

Anaxilas (or Anaxilaos) belonged to a family of Messenian origin; he seized power in Rhegium (south Italy) by overthrowing an aristocratic regime of one thousand in 494 BC. An attempt to control Zancle on the Sicilian side of the Straits in 493, by settling Samian refugees from Ionia there, failed when these preferred to rely on the support of *Hippocrates of Gela. In 490 Anaxilas occupied Zancle himself, expelled the Samians, and resettled the city with Messenians; hence the name Messana. He had married Cydippe, daughter of Terillus, tyrant of Himera, who was expelled by *Theron of Acragas in 483; in the following years, Anaxilas welcomed Carthaginian intervention in Sicily as a counterweight to the Deinomenids (see *Gelon, *Hieron I). This policy failed when Hieron defeated *Hamilcar at Himera in 480. Although Hieron married Anaxilas' daughter, friction continued until Anaxilas' death. His sons ruled Rhegium until 461 (see *Micythus).

BIBL. Dunbabin, *Western Greeks*, chs. 13–14; E. S. G. Robinson, *JHS* lxvi (1946).

Anaximander Natural Philosopher, mid-6th century BC.

Possibly a pupil of his fellow Milesian *Thales, Anaximander (Anaximandros) was the first to write a book on natural philosophy. Its subject-matter ranged from the origins of the universe to meteorology, geography, and a theory of the evolution of man. A few obscure words of the book survive. He held that the origin or source of things was the 'unlimited' (*apeiron*), by which he probably meant a mass of stuff without determinate qualities and unlimited in extent and duration. Our world and innumerable others were produced from the 'unlimited', and are surrounded and governed by it. He evidently had a notion of justice operating on a cosmic scale, by which he probably wished to explain how encroachments by one element on another are always compensated for (e.g. rain by evaporation, coastal erosion by silting). He was the first, later sources say, who 'dared to draw a map of the world'.

BIBL. Guthrie, *Greek Philosophy* i. 72–115; C. Kahn, *Anaximander and the Origins of Greek Cosmology* (1960).

Anaximenes of Miletus Philosopher, mid-6th century BC.

A younger contemporary of *Anaximander, Anaximenes (Anaximenēs) wrote a book on natural philosophy of which a few doubtful words survive. His account of the origins and workings of the universe seems to have been more elaborate than Anaximander's. For him, air was the origin of things. Other things came into being from air by condensation (e.g. clouds, water) or rarefaction (e.g. fire). Like Anaximander's 'unlimited', Anaximenes' air was not only what things were made from, but had a 'divine' role. He is reported to have said, 'Just as our soul, being air, controls us, so breath and air enclose the whole world.'

BIBL. Guthrie, *Greek Philosophy* i.

Andocides (*c.* 440–390 BC) '*Attic orator'.

Andocides (Andokidēs) came from a wealthy family; his ancestors can be traced back to the mid-sixth century BC. After the episode of the mutilation of the Hermae in 415, he was arrested on suspicion of involvement in both this and the parodying of the Eleusinian Mysteries (see *Hermocopids, *Alcibiades). Andocides admitted involvement, implicating many wealthy young friends. Although he was released, a subsequent Decree of Isotimides imposed *atimia* (loss of civic rights) upon him and he left Athens, making a living as a merchant. Attempts to return to Athens in 411 and in 410 resulted in imprisonment by the oligarchy of the Four Hundred, and failed. He returned under the general amnesty which followed the fall of the Thirty Tyrants (see *Critias) in 403. In 391 he was a member of an Athenian delegation sent to Sparta to negotiate an end to the Corinthian War; the terms were rejected by the Athenians, and Andocides was prosecuted and went into exile again.

Andocides was not a professional speech-writer: he both composed and delivered his orations. Consequently the argument is often very loosely constructed, but the narrative is vivid, with bitter personal attacks on his opponents. Three genuine speeches survive: *On his Return* (411/10), pleading to return to Athens; *On the Mysteries* (399), denying that the Decree of Isotimides still applied to him (the sixth speech of the *Lysian corpus, *Against Andocides*, gives the case for the prosecution); and *On the Peace* (391), urging acceptance of his agreement with Sparta.

BIBL. *Minor Attic Orators* i (Loeb); Davies, *Athenian Families* no. 828; J. L. Marr, *CQ* xxi (1971); G. A. Kennedy, *AJP* lxxix (1958).

Andriscus Macedonian pretender, *c.* 153–148 BC.

An adventurer from Adramyttium in the Troad, Andriscus (Andriskos) claimed to be Philip, son of *Perseus and legitimate heir to the throne of Macedon. Sent to Rome probably in 153 BC by the Seleucid king *Demetrius I (to curry favour with Rome in his own struggle against *Alexander Balas), Andriscus was not considered a serious threat by the Senate, and escaped to Asia Minor. He was recognized by a Thracian chieftain, fought his way to mastery in Macedonia, and was threatening Thessaly by 149. Rome awoke to the danger, and finally sent *Metellus Macedonicus in 148 with a large army and the fleet of *Attalus II of Pergamum. Andriscus was defeated, and, after regrouping his forces in Thrace, was captured, exhibited in Metellus' triumph, and executed.

BIBL. Will, *Hist. pol.* ii, 326 ff.

Androcleidas Theban politician, early 4th century BC.

A leading political figure in 395 BC (he reputedly received money from *Timocrates of Rhodes), Androcleidas (Androkleidas) was associated with the anti-Spartan moves which provoked *Phoebidas' seizure of the Cadmea, the stronghold of Thebes (382). He escaped to Athens, but was assassinated there by *Leontiades' agents.

BIBL. Buckler, *Theban Hegemony* 38 f.

Andronicus of Rhodes Peripatetic philosopher, mid-1st century BC.

Andronicus (Andronikos) acquired copies of *Aristotle's works from a library in Rome, and published them in the order in which they are still usually presented. None of his own works on Aristotle's life and philosophy survives, but he revived interest in the Peripatetic school in its founder, and did much to preserve Aristotle's philosophy for posterity.

BIBL. I. Düring, *Aristotle in the Ancient Biographical Tradition* (1957).

Androtion Athenian historian and political leader, mid-4th century BC.

Androtion (Androtiōn) was a pupil of *Isocrates; like Isocrates, he believed that Athens should be opposing Persia rather than Macedonia. During the Social War (357–355 BC) he was sent on an embassy to King *Mausolus of Caria, and served as *strategos*. In 355/4 he served on a committee to prepare for war against Persia; he was subsequently accused of putting forward an unconstitutional proposal by *Eubulus (the speech was written by *Demosthenes (*Or.* xxii)), but acquitted. He was exiled sometime after 344, possibly for insulting a Persian embassy to Athens, and lived at Megara.

Androtion's *Atthis*, a history of Attica in eight books down to 343 BC, makes **Theseus rather than *Solon the founder of Athenian democracy; scholars now believe that he had no political motive for his innovation, but was simply trying to be original. Although lost, his work is important as a major source of *Philochorus and of the Aristotelean *Constitution of Athens*.

BIBL. *FGrH* iiiB, no. 324; Jacoby, *Atthis*; Davies, *Athenian Families*, no. 913; P. Harding, *Phoenix* xxviii (1974).

Antalcidas Spartan diplomat and general, floruit 393/2–c. 361 BC.

In 393/2 BC Antalcidas (Antalkidas) attempted to end the war with Persia by ceding the Asiatic Greeks. This proved unsuccessful, but in 388/7 he persuaded *Artaxerxes II to issue a rescript declaring that (i) Asia Minor (plus Cyprus and Cnidos) was his, (ii) all other Greek cities were to be autonomous, and (iii) he would assist the military imposition of these conditions. Sparta's enemies, confronted by a Spartan–Persian alliance (its effectiveness exemplified by Antalcidas' operations in the Dardanelles in 387), were compelled to accede to this 'King's Peace'. Antalcidas' subsequent career is ill-documented. He was in Persia in 371, was ephor in

370/69, and committed suicide after a further, unsuccessful, visit to Artaxerxes (c. 361?). He is represented as a political enemy of *Agesilaus, though the latter happily condoned the King's Peace.

BIBL. Hamilton, *Sparta's Bitter Victories*; J. Buckler, *GRBS* xviii (1977); D. Whitehead, *LCM* iv (1979); Hofstetter, *Griechen*, no. 18.

Marble statue of a girl (a 'kore') from the Acropolis, by Antenor. Late 6th century BC. Athens, Acropolis Museum.

Antenor Sculptor, active c. 530–500 BC.

Antenor (Antēnor) made the famous bronze group, now lost, of the Athenian tyrant-slayers, *Harmodius and Aristogeiton, who killed *Hipparchus in 514 BC. The group was stolen by *Xerxes in 480, to be returned about 150 years later by *Alexander the Great. In the meantime it had been replaced in 477/6 by another group by Critius and Nesiotes, of which we have Roman copies. The appearance of Antenor's group is unknown. An over-lifesize female figure from the Acropolis almost certainly belongs to a base signed by him; it is a last great gasp of the archaic kore statuary type. He also perhaps designed or worked on the marble pediment of the temple of Apollo at Delphi (c. 520–510), paid for by the *Alcmaeonid opponents of the Athenian tyrants.

BIBL. Deyhle, *AM* lxxxiv (1969); Boardman, *Sculpture (Archaic)* 83–4; Robertson, *History of Greek Art* 103–4, 185–7.

Anticleides Historian, 3rd century BC.

An Athenian historiographer about whom little is known, Anticleides (Antikleidēs) may have been active in

the first half of the third century BC. His history of
*Alexander the Great, quoted by Diogenes Laertius, is
unknown in content, style, or worth. An account of Delos
is similarly shadowy. He was perhaps best known in
antiquity for his work *Nostoi*, accounts of various Greeks
returning homeward from their expeditions. This random
collection of stories of both mythical and historical
homeward journeys, in chronological order, is perhaps
reminiscent of Alexandrian *aetia* (see *Callimachus) with
their artificial, tenuous connections of subject. Anticleides
seems to have been fond of ingenious rationalization and
clever fabrication. The dictionary of ancient words and
phrases (the *Exegeticus*) which is often attributed to him
may be the work of another.

BIBL. *FGrH* 140; PW i. 2425 (Antikleides 2); Pearson,
Lost Histories 251 ff.; *Roman World* *Diogenes Laertius.

Antigonus (I) Macedonian dynast, *c*. 381–301 BC.

Antigonus (Antigonos) Monophthalmus ('One-eyed')
was appointed satrap of Phrygia by *Alexander the Great
in 333 BC, during his march through Asia Minor. After
Alexander's death, Lycia and Pamphylia were included in
his domain. In 321, threatened by the increasing authority
of the regent *Perdiccas, Antigonus, together with the
other Macedonian generals *Ptolemy (I) and *Lysimachus,
joined *Antipater and *Craterus; at the conference of
Triparadeisus following Perdiccas' death, he was
rewarded by being appointed Macedonian *strategus*
(supreme commander) in Asia.

In the following years the Macedonians were divided
between the usurping generals and *Polyperchon,
Antipater's successor as *strategus* in Europe. Between 319
and 316 Antigonus campaigned in Asia Minor against
*Eumenes of Cardia, who had remained loyal to the court.
His success was such that, by 315, *Cassander, Ptolemy,
and Lysimachus formed an alliance against him; an
invasion of Egypt by Antigonus' son *Demetrius
Poliorcetes was defeated at the battle of Gaza in 312, but
in the following year a general peace agreement left
Antigonus as the recognized ruler of the whole of Asia
Minor and Syria (leaving provinces east of the Euphrates
to *Seleucus (I)).

Following the murder of the boy king *Alexander IV
and his mother *Roxane by Cassander in 309, Antigonus
sought to strengthen his position by sending his son
Demetrius to conquer Greece (the 'Four Years' War',
307–304); Demetrius captured Athens in 307 and held it
against Cassander, but failed to capture Rhodes in 305/4.
Following a naval victory over Ptolemy at Salamis in
Cyprus in 306, Antigonus was the first of the Macedonian
commanders to proclaim himself king. In 301 he was again
attacked by a coalition of the other four surviving
dynasts, and defeated and killed at the battle of Ipsus. His
Asian empire was split up among the victors, but
Demetrius was able to maintain himself in Greece for a
time, and Antigonus' grandson *Antigonus Gonatas
ultimately became king of Macedon.

BIBL. Will, *Hist. pol.* i; P. Briant, *Antigone le Borgne*
(1973); C. Wehrli, *Antigone et Demetrios* (1969).

Antigonus II Gonatas (*c*. 320–239 BC) King of Macedon,
277–239 BC.

The son of *Demetrius Poliorcetes and *Phila, and
grandson of *Antigonus (I), Antigonus Gonatas (Antigonos

Coin portrait of Antigonus II Gonatas in the guise of the Greek
god Pan (enlarged).

Gonatas – the meaning of the nickname is unknown),
served as his father's trusted general in Greece, and upon
the latter's death in 283 BC took the title of king. He
entered the fray for the throne of Macedon after the death
of *Lysimachus in 281, and finally established himself
there *c*. 277, having won a great victory over the Gauls at
Lysimacheia. At about the same time he allied himself
with the Seleucids, marrying his own niece Phila II, the
daughter of *Seleucus I. He finally consolidated his power
in the Peloponnese against the combined forces of
*Pyrrhus of Epirus and *Cleonymus of Sparta, fighting
battles at Sparta and at Argos, where Pyrrhus was killed
in 272. Athens rose against him in the War of
*Chremonides (266/5–261), but the lack of decisive support
for Athens by *Ptolemy II and the inability of *Areus I of
Sparta to join forces with her enabled Antigonus to
besiege the city, which capitulated in 262 and was
occupied by a Macedonian garrison. His possible
involvement on the side of *Antiochus II in the Second
Syrian War, and on that of *Seleucus II in the Third
Syrian War, has been suggested because of his two naval
victories (at Cos and Andros) over the Seleucid rivals, the
Ptolemies, but the battles cannot be dated. By a
treacherous ploy in *c*. 245 Antigonus was able to regain
possession of Corinth from the widow of his governor
*Alexander of Corinth (q.v.), who had revolted in
253–249, but the city was 'liberated' a few years later by
*Aratus of Sicyon. As a result of this, Antigonus
supported, tacitly rather than actively, the forays of the
Aetolians into the Peloponnese, since they threatened the
growing power of the anti-Macedonian Achaean League
and encouraged the rise of local tyrants who looked to
Macedon for protection.

Known as 'the Old Man', Antigonus died in 239, having
outlived all his royal contemporaries. Although his control
over Greece was insecure, and Pyrrhus had been able to
threaten him in Macedon, Antigonus re-established
Macedon as a nation and made it a kingdom to be ruled
by his descendants. He was himself a pupil of
*Menedemus and *Zeno of Citium, and the court of
Antigonus at Pella was a centre for writers and scholars,
including (among others) Menedemus, *Aratus of Soli,
*Alexander Aetolus, and *Hieronymus of Cardia.

BIBL. W. W. Tarn, *Antigonos Gonatas* (1913); W.
Fellmann, *Antigonos Gonatas, König der Makedoner, und die
griechischen Staaten* (1930); Will, *Hist. pol.* i.

Antigonus III Doson Regent and king of Macedon, 229–221 BC.

The son of *Demetrius the Fair, Antigonus (Antigonos – the origin and meaning of the nickname Doson are unknown) became regent for the future king *Philip V after the death of *Demetrius II of Macedon, and married the widowed Queen Phthia-Chryseis. He proved a blessing to a threatened Macedonia, and his loyalty to the child remained unshaken even when he himself was given the throne c. 227/6 BC. Assuming control, Antigonus defeated the warlike Dardani who had killed Demetrius II. Macedonia was threatened by the loss of all her Greek possessions except Euboea, but Antigonus turned the tide. He defeated the Aetolians and Thessalians in 228, and made an expedition to Caria in 227. The circumstances, cause, and purpose of the Carian adventure remain obscure, but some Macedonian influence was re-established in the Aegean and eastern Greece. Antigonus' chance to recoup his influence in Greece came from *Cleomenes III of Sparta, whose aggressions in the Peloponnese frightened *Aratus (of Sicyon) of the Achaean League into sending *Cercidas and Nicophanes secretly to Doson in 227/6 to elicit his support against Sparta and Aetolia. Doson agreed, and in 225–4 he was formally offered Acrocorinth in return for his military support. In that year, he occupied Corinth with a Macedonian garrison, and chased Cleomenes from Argos into Arcadia.

In 224 Doson founded the Hellenic League, an alliance of existing Greek federations under Macedonian hegemony. The federations were to be internally autonomous but interdependent in respect of foreign policy. This was potentially the greatest act of his reign (in view of the fact that Greece was shortly to face Rome), but his premature death prevented its fruition. In 223 Doson recovered Arcadia, and in 222 confronted Cleomenes at Sellasia, where the Spartan was decisively beaten. He returned to Macedon to deal with another Illyrian invasion, but a burst blood-vessel in his lungs worsened his already weak health. He died some months later in 221, after providing for the education of Philip and sending him to Aratus to learn about Greek affairs.

BIBL. Walbank, *Aratos of Sicyon*, and *Philip V*; Will, *Hist. pol.* i.

Antigonus of Carystus Sculptor and writer, late 3rd century BC.

If Wilamowitz was correct in assigning diverse notices to the same individual, Antigonus (Antigonos) of Carystus in Euboea had several strings to his bow, being (i) a sculptor working on *Attalus I's Gallic monument at Pergamum, (ii) a writer on works of art, (iii) a superior biographer of contemporary philosophers used by Diogenes Laertius, (iv) a less superior paradoxographer, reshuffling 'strange but true' stories from *Callimachus and others, and lastly (v) a lexicographer.

BIBL. Wilamowitz, *Antigonos von Karystos* (1881); Hansen, *Attalids*; *Roman World* *Diogenes Laertius.

Antimachus Poet and scholar, 5th–4th century BC.

Little is known of the life of Antimachus (Antimakhos) of Colophon, and only brief fragments of his work survive. His most important poems were an epic, the *Thebais*, perhaps in 24 books, concerning the 'Seven

against Thebes', and the *Lyde*, a long poem in elegiac couplets narrating the unhappy loves of heroes. He was also the earliest known editor of *Homer, and he made use of his Homeric scholarship in his own poetry. He is said to have been admired by *Plato, but, although his work foreshadows that of the scholar-poets of Alexandria, it was found tedious by *Callimachus and became a by-word for long-windedness.

BIBL. Lesky, *Greek Literature*; *Greek Elegy and Iambus* (Loeb) i; Pfeiffer, *Classical Scholarship* i. 93 f.

Antiochus I Soter Seleucid king, 281–261 BC.

Antiochus (Antiokhos) I was the son of *Seleucus I and his Bactrian wife Apama. He fought with his father against *Antigonus I at Ipsus in 301, and later governed Seleucus' Upper Satrapies. Seleucus gave him in marriage his own wife *Stratonice, and Antiochus succeeded as king when his father was killed in 281 by *Ptolemy Ceraunus. Although he enjoyed a long alliance with *Antigonus Gonatas (to whom he married his half-sister Phila II, the daughter of Seleucus and Stratonice), his reign was troubled by wars on many other fronts. The so-called Carian War against *Ptolemy II was concluded in 279. The unwise alliance of the Northern League with the Gauls (Galatians) forced him to face the rampages of the latter;

Coin portrait of Antiochus I Soter, Seleucid king (enlarged).

he defeated them in the famous 'Elephant Victory' in 275/4(?), for which he won the title 'Soter' (Saviour). He fought, and lost, the First Syrian War against Ptolemy II (274–271) (not taking advantage of a simultaneous attack on Egypt by his son-in-law *Magas of Cyrene), and in 261 he was deprived of large areas of northern Asia Minor by the revolt of *Eumenes I of Pergamum, which may have been supported by Ptolemy. By the end of his reign, Antiochus had founded numerous cities throughout his realm.

BIBL. Bevan, *House of Seleucus*; Will, *Hist. pol.*

Antiochus II Theos Seleucid king, 261–246 BC.

Antiochus (Antiokhos; 'Theos' ('god') is a deification title) was the younger son of *Antiochus I, but succeeded to the throne in place of his elder brother Seleucus, who had perhaps been executed for treason when co-regent. Antiochus' personality was reputed to be unpleasant. The Second Syrian War against *Ptolemy II occupied him after

260 BC; its details are obscure, but a peace concluded between 255 and 253 brought him large areas of Ptolemaic Asia Minor and a wife of the Ptolemaic house. His first queen, *Laodice, was sent to Ephesus, while *Berenice Syra, the daughter of Ptolemy and *Arsinoë I, lived at the court in Antioch from 253/2 and in due course bore a son. Antiochus appears to have maintained his Macedonian alliance as well, since at about this time his sister Stratonice II married *Demetrius II, the son of *Antigonus Gonatas.

Coin portrait of Antiochus II Theos, Seleucid king (enlarged).

After losing some territory to *Eumenes of Pergamum and seeing Bithynia become anti-Seleucid, Antiochus died at Ephesus in 246 in mysterious circumstances. Some said that as death approached he had pronounced Laodice's disinherited son, *Seleucus II, as heir, fearing the alternative of a Ptolemaic regency. Others considered this story as propaganda to cover his poisoning by Laodice and her son in revenge for their loss of the succession. The succession was violently contested by the rival queens (qq.v.).

BIBL. Bevan, *House of Seleucus* i; Will, *Hist. pol.* i.

Antiochus III 'the Great' Seleucid king, 223–187 BC.

The younger son of *Seleucus II, Antiochus (Antiokhos) succeeded to the throne after the death of his elder brother Seleucus III, and immediately faced several crises. The satrap of Media, Molon, revolted in 222 BC and was defeated in 221. Antiochus' overly powerful minister, Hermias (who unwisely incited him against Egypt in 221), had to be killed c. 220. Antiochus decided to pursue the invasion of Egypt (the Fourth Syrian War), and, although he nearly reached Alexandria in 219, he was utterly routed at Raphia in 217. Only after this could the king finally deal with *Achaeus, his cousin and general in Asia Minor, who had revolted and declared himself king in 220. Achaeus was killed in 213 with the help of *Attalus I of Pergamum.

When his power was consolidated, Antiochus made his famous anabasis in the East. He acquired Armenia (212), marched through Media (ravaging native temples to help his finances, 211–210), and regained Parthia (209). His two-year siege of *Euthydemus of Bactria became a stalemate and was ended in a compromise, whereby the Bactrian was recognized as an independent monarch (208–

206). He reached the borders of India (Paropamisadae and Arachosia) in 206/5: the ruined Mauryan empire could not oppose him, and he received elephants, victuals, and money. He returned to Antioch in 205/4 via Arabia. Antiochus apparently saw himself in the role of *Alexander the Great and *Seleucus I, and after his expedition he took the title 'Megas' ('the Great').

After the accession of *Ptolemy V in 204, Antiochus and *Philip V colluded to divide Egypt between them, but Antiochus invaded alone and conquered Coele-Syria c. 202. This attracted Rome's attention, but he ignored a Roman embassy in 200. In 196 he crossed with an army to Thrace and insulted a second Roman embassy. Peace with Ptolemy was concluded in 195, and Antiochus' daughter Cleopatra I was sent to him in marriage. When the Carthaginian general Hannibal, Rome's *bête noire*, came to the Seleucid court in 195, friendship with Rome was no longer possible. Antiochus proposed an alliance in 193, but *Flamininus presented him with terms difficult to accept. When Aetolia began agitating against Rome, she invited Antiochus into Greece in 192, but setting out from a base in Euboea he was defeated by the Romans at Thermopylae in 191 and departed for Asia. The war became a struggle for mastery of the sea off Asia Minor, where the Roman fleet was joined by those of Rhodes and Pergamum. The Seleucid fleet held its own under their admiral *Polyxenidas, but was defeated off Myonessus in

Marble portrait head identified as Antiochus III 'the Great', Seleucid king. Paris, Musée du Louvre.

190. When the Romans answered his offer of peace with the demand that he pay a substantial indemnity and retire beyond the Taurus Mountains, he decided to risk all in battle, since the terms could hardly be harsher. He was decisively defeated by *Scipio Africanus and *Scipio Asiagenus on the plain of Magnesia ad Sipylum in 189. After the Peace of Apamea, the Seleucid empire was no longer a Mediterranean power. Antiochus retreated to his eastern possessions, and in 187, in the course of robbing a temple in the Elymaean Hills to aid his payment of the indemnity, he was murdered by outraged natives.

BIBL. H. H. Schmitt, *Untersuchungen zur Geschichte Antiochus des Grossen und seiner Zeit* (1964); Bevan, *House of Seleucus*; Will, *Hist. pol.*; M. Holleaux, *Rome, la Grèce, et les Monarchies hellénistiques* (1921); *Roman World* *Antiochus III, *Hannibal, etc.

Antiochus IV Epiphanes Seleucid king, 175–165/4 BC.

The younger son of *Antiochus III, Antiochus (Antiokhos) 'God Made Manifest' was a hostage at Rome after the battle of Magnesia (189 BC), while his brother, Seleucus IV, spent his reign restoring the fortunes of the empire. A few contacts with other powers (notably the marriage of Seleucus' daughter to *Perseus) made a suspicious Rome demand the king's son *Demetrius (later I) as hostage instead of Antiochus. Seleucus was murdered in 175 when Antiochus was *en route* for home, and he was escorted to the throne by *Eumenes II of Pergamum, who was eager to have an allied neighbour to support him against Perseus. Antiochus consolidated his power by dubious means, and publicly obeyed Rome while privately repairing his foreign alliances. When the Sixth Syrian War erupted, Antiochus invaded Egypt three times (170–168), captured his nephew *Ptolemy VI, playing him off against his brother *Ptolemy VIII, and advanced to Alexandria. Antiochus was ordered out of Egypt by Rome, and he obeyed. Presenting his campaigns as great victories, he staged a festival in 166 which outshone the victory celebrations of L. Aemilius *Paullus after Pydna.

In reaction to Antiochus' policy of hellenization, a severe Jewish revolt broke out in 167 under *Judas Maccabaeus, but the king left for his eastern territories. He was seized by a fatal illness at Tabae in Persis in the winter of 165/4.

Antiochus' mental state has been debated: his clever

Silver tetradrachm with portrait of Antiochus IV Epiphanes, Seleucid king (enlarged).

political calculations argue for sanity, but his eccentric personal exhibitionism (such as dancing naked at a dinner party) verged on madness. His universally bad reputation cannot be easily discounted, even granting the prejudice of Roman and Jewish sources.

BIBL. *Roman World*; Mørkholm, *Antiochus IV of Syria* (1966); Bevan, *House of Seleucus* ii. 126 ff.

Antiochus VII Sidetes Seleucid king, floruit 138–129 BC.

Antiochus (Antiokhos), the second son of *Demetrius I, who was called 'Sidetes' because he had lived at Side, saw his chance for power while his brother *Demetrius II was a Parthian captive after 139 BC. He married his brother's abandoned wife *Cleopatra Thea, and easily defeated a partly successful claimant to the throne, *Diodotus Tryphon, in 138. By fomenting internal strife in the newly-independent Hasmonaean State in Judaea, Antiochus made a pretext to intervene there. He re-established Seleucid political, but not religious, control by 131. Now in a stronger position, Antiochus attacked the eastern satrapies to extend his power and, perhaps, to subdue his brother, who was still in Parthia. His series of brilliant military successes in 131/30 forced the Parthian king to negotiate, but he rejected the Seleucid's harsh terms in favour of releasing Demetrius (to oppose Antiochus) and allying himself with fierce Scythian tribes.

Coin portrait of Antiochus VII Sidetes (enlarged).

Antiochus spent a terrible winter in the East, and was decisively defeated and killed in his first battle against them in 129. His death marked the end of Seleucid claims in the East.

BIBL. Bellinger, 'The End of the Seleucids'; N. C. Debevoise, *A Political History of Parthia* (1938); Justin XXXVIII. ix. 10, x; XLII. i; Will, *Hist. pol.* ii.

Antiochus VIII Grypus Seleucid king, 125–96 BC.

Antiochus (Antiokhos), 'Hook-Nose', the son of *Demetrius II and *Cleopatra Thea, claimed the throne from Alexander II Zabinas, his father's usurper and murderer. Since *Ptolemy VIII (Zabinas' original supporter) had switched his allegiance back to Demetrius' family and had married Antiochus to his daughter by *Cleopatra III, Cleopatra Tryphaena, Antiochus was able to dispose of Zabinas by 123 BC, establish himself in Antioch, and murder his mother, who had tried to

Coin portait of Antiochus VIII Grypus, Seleucid king (enlarged).

dominate him. Antiochus faced a serious revolt from his half-brother *Antiochus IX in 114/13. Their struggle lasted for years and was aggravated by their queens; in 112 Grypus captured Antiochus' wife and killed her at the wish of Tryphaena, her sister. Tryphaena was killed in revenge by Antiochus. By 108 Antiochus was secure in most parts of his kingdom, and some years later married Cleopatra Selene, another daughter of Ptolemy VIII and Cleopatra III, perhaps in alliance with the mother against *Ptolemy IX. Antiochus spent much time feasting and writing poetry, and was assassinated by a minister in 96, leaving five sons.

BIBL. Will, *Hist. pol.* ii; Bellinger, 'The End of the Seleucids'.

Antiochus IX Cyzicenus Seleucid king, 113–95 BC.

Called 'Cyzicenus' because he had lived at Cyzicus, Antiochus (Antiokhos) was the son of *Antiochus VII Sidetes and *Cleopatra Thea; he married Cleopatra IV, the repudiated wife of *Ptolemy IX who was a daughter of *Ptolemy VIII (Euergetes II) and *Cleopatra III. In 114/13 BC he revolted against his half-brother *Antiochus VIII Grypus (q.v.), whose wife he put to death in 111 since she had ordered the death of his own wife. Although, by 108, his captured territories were limited to coastal regions, Antiochus made a second attempt at undivided power after his brother's assassination in 96. He married Grypus' second wife, Cleopatra Selene, but was helpless in face of the rivalries of Grypus' five sons for the throne. He was killed by one of them, *Seleucus VI (see Later *Seleucids), in 95.

BIBL. Will, *Hist. pol.* ii; Bellinger, 'The End of the Seleucids'.

Coin portrait of Antiochus IX Cyzicenus, Seleucid king (enlarged).

Antiochus X, XI, XII, XIII: see Later *Seleucids

Antiochus I of Commagene King, floruit 69–31 BC.

Through his mother Laodice, Antiochus (Antiokhos) was a grandson of the Seleucid king *Antiochus VIII Grypus, and was probably the third ruler to be designated 'king' in the small kingdom of Commagene, whose history is little known. 'Philoromaios' ('Friend of Rome') was one of Antiochus' many official titles, and he allied himself to Rome after she had defeated *Tigranes I of Armenia in 69 BC. Pompey extended the boundaries of Commagene in 64, and in return received troops from Antiochus in the Roman Civil War. Antiochus lost the friendship of Rome when he later supported the Parthians: he was besieged in his capital Samosata in 38 by the Romans Ventidius and, later, Mark Antony. He had either died or been dethroned by 31, when his brother became king. Antiochus is probably best remembered for the funerary monuments which he built for his father and himself. His father was honoured with a royal mausoleum at Arsameia (a city in Commagene), while his own monumental tomb was constructed at Nimrud Dagh on Mount Taurus. The latter is remarkable for its inscriptions, reliefs, and statues, which reflect a syncretism of Greek and Persian religion.

BIBL. R. Ghirshman, *Iran* (1962) 57 ff.; H. Dörrie, *Der Königskult des Antiochos von Kommagene* (1964); *OGIS* 383 ff.; *Roman World* Mark *Antony, *Pompey, *Ventidius.

Antiochus of Ascalon Philosopher, early 1st century BC.

Antiochus (Antiokhos) won a high reputation as a philosopher, partly, no doubt, because Cicero attended his lectures and wrote of him with respect. Taught by *Philon of Larissa, he rejected his scepticism and propounded a more dogmatic version of *Plato's philosophy. This led to something of a split in the Academy. He also adopted some Stoic doctrines on knowledge and ethics, but criticized the school for attaching no value to pleasures of the body.

BIBL. Dillon, *The Middle Platonists*; *Roman World* *Cicero.

Antiochus Hierax (*c.* 263–226 BC) Rival for Seleucid throne.

The second son of *Antiochus II and *Laodice, Antiochus (Antiokhos) the 'hawk' acted as joint ruler with his brother *Seleucus II, and as general of Asia Minor at the end of the Third Syrian War against *Ptolemy III (*c.* 242–241 BC). When peace was concluded in 241, Antiochus refused to renounce his powers, and the civil 'War of the Brothers' began. Antiochus had the support of two brothers-in-law, *Mithridates II of Pontus and *Ariarathes III of Cappadocia (who both stood to gain if the Seleucid empire was divided), and of the Gauls (Galatians). Fortunes wavered, and the empire was partitioned before 236.

Antiochus was undone by the Gauls, who turned on him. Re-buying their loyalty, he directed their energies against Pergamum, whose independence blocked his own territorial ambitions. *Attalus I decisively defeated them (*c.* 238–230?). Hierax renounced his Gauls, but in the next few years was defeated several times by Attalus, who captured extensive Seleucid lands. Defeated also by Seleucus' generals in Mesopotamia, Hierax fled to

Coin portrait of Antiochus Hierax, rival for the Seleucid throne (enlarged).

Ariarathes, to *Ptolemy III, and finally to Thrace, where he was murdered in 226.
BIBL. Will, *Hist. pol.* i.

Antipater Macedonian general and regent, died 319 BC.

A trusted lieutenant of *Philip II, Antipater (Antipatros) was *Alexander the Great's viceroy in Macedonia in 335 BC and from 334 onwards, and as such suppressed the revolt of *Agis III. Alexander supported him in quarrels with *Olympias, but in 324/3 planned to replace him with *Craterus (perhaps because Antipater was increasingly unsympathetic to Alexander's departures from old Macedonian *mores*). Alexander's death intervened (some held Antipater responsible), and Antipater remained in Macedonia and was able to defeat the Greek revolt of 323–322 (see *Hyper(e)ides), suppressing Athenian democracy along the way. In 321 he joined *Perdiccas' enemies and, emerging from Triparadeisus (320) as imperial regent, returned to Macedonia with the kings (*Philip III Arrhidaeus and *Alexander IV), but died in 319. Antipater could boast connections with literary figures (*Isocrates, *Aristotle) and himself wrote a (lost) work on King *Perdiccas III's Illyrian campaigns.
BIBL. Berve, *Alexanderreich*, no. 94; Lane Fox, *Alexander*; Will, *Hist. pol.* i.

Antipater, son of Cassander: see Alexander V

Antipater 'Etesias' King of Macedon, July–August 279 BC.

Grandson of *Antipater the Regent and nephew of *Cassander, Antipater (Antipatros) sat on the unsteady throne of Macedon in the confusion of 279 BC, when, after *Ptolemy Ceraunus' death, the army offered the throne to various candidates. He was nicknamed 'Etesias' (King of the Dog-Days) because his rule of only 45 days coincided with the period of the sultry Etesian Winds (mid-June to August). He was later killed or expelled by *Antigonus Gonatas and his army of Gauls.
BIBL. Tarn, *Antigonos Gonatas*.

Antipater of Idumaea Governor, floruit c. 70–43 BC.

The Arab governor of Idumaea in southern Judaea, Antipater (Antipatros) was involved in the fraternal struggle between the two sons of Alexander Jannaeus, the late High Priest and king of the Jews, in 67 BC. He supported Hyrcanus II and bought him the military

support of the Nabataean Aretas III. He represented Hyrcanus' cause before Pompey, who, depriving Judaea of many liberties and of its royal family, installed Hyrcanus as ethnarch in 63. The latter lived in the shadow of his adviser Antipater. In the restoration of *Ptolemy XII Auletes in 55, Antipater helped Gabinius (the Roman governor of Syria) by winning him passage through the Jewish garrisons in the Delta, but in 48 he persuaded the same troops (with the help of Hyrcanus, who was also High Priest) to admit the forces of Julius Caesar, who would depose Auletes' son *Ptolemy XIII. Antipater and Hyrcanus led Jewish troops on Caesar's side in the Alexandrian War in 47, and by way of thanks Caesar appointed him governor of Judaea. Antipater was murdered in 43, and was succeeded by his son Herod the Great.
BIBL. Will, *Hist. pol.* ii; F. M. Abel, *Histoire de la Palestine* (1952) i; *Roman World* Gaius Julius *Caesar, *Gabinius, *Herod the Great, *Pompey.

Antipater of Sidon Epigrammatist, c. 145 BC.

*Meleager asserts that Antipater (Antipatros) was born in Tyre (also, mischievously, that he died drunk); other traditions call him Sidonian. Two emotional pieces, probably contemporary, treat Rome's destruction of Corinth (146 BC), and he lived to be remembered as an exuberant improviser by Q. Lutatius Catulus. Antipater writes in the tradition of *Leonidas of Tarentum, whom he loves to paraphrase. Pleasantly expansive, with a speciality in riddle epitaphs, he inaugurates a productive Phoenician revival of epigram continued by Meleager.
BIBL. Gow and Page, *Hellenistic Epigrams*; *Roman World* Q. Lutatius *Catulus (1).

Antiphanes Comic poet, active from c. 385 BC.

An unusually prolific poet of Middle Comedy, Antiphanes (Antiphanēs) is variously said to have written from 260 to 365 plays. 134 titles are known, and we have many fragments; a famous one (fr. 191) complains at the ease of a tragedian's lot compared with a comic poet's.
BIBL. Lesky, *Greek Literature*; Edmonds, *Attic Comedy* ii; Webster, *Later Comedy*.

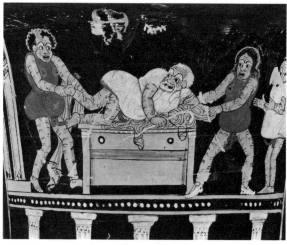

'Robbing of a miser' on a vase from Paestum, Italy, of c. 350/40 BC, suggesting how the comedies of Antiphanes, *Alexis, and *Anaxandrides appeared. Berlin, Staatliche Museen.

Antiphon (c. 480–411 BC) Earliest of the '*Attic Orators'.

Antiphon (Antiphōn) appears not to have participated in politics before the oligarchic *coup* which installed the regime of the Four Hundred in 411 BC. Antiphon, who was largely responsible for the *coup*, favoured an immediate peace with Sparta. He was opposed by *Theramenes. After *Phrynichus (2) had failed to negotiate peace-terms and had been assassinated, most of the oligarchs fled to the Spartans at Decelea, and Theramenes restored the democracy in a modified form ('the Five Thousand'). Antiphon was arrested, tried, and executed; *Thucydides says that his defence speech was outstanding.

Antiphon was the earliest professional Athenian speech-writer, composing speeches for others to deliver. This allowed him to pay as much attention to style as to content, carefully organizing his sentences ('periodic' style) and arranging his material with proems and epilogues. Three speeches survive: *The Murder of Herodes*, written on behalf of a Mytilenean accused of having killed an Athenian; and two on poisoning charges, *On the Choreutes* and *Against a Stepmother*. Lost speeches included two on behalf of subject states of the Athenian empire; but this does not indicate that Antiphon was opposed in principle to Athenian imperialism. There are also the *Tetralogies*, three sets of rhetorical exercises on fictitious murder cases, each containing two prosecution and two defence speeches. These are not necessarily by Antiphon (nor by the sophist Antiphon, one of several homonymous contemporaries).

BIBL. *Minor Attic Orators* (Loeb) i; Kennedy, *Art of Persuasion* 129 ff.; K. J. Dover, *CQ* xliv (1950).

Antisthenes (c. 450–360 BC) Philosopher.

A pupil of *Gorgias, and later a devoted follower of *Socrates, Antisthenes (Antisthenēs) became known as the

Inscribed herm of the philosopher Antisthenes, found at Tivoli. Probably a copy of the original made by *Phyromachus. Vatican Museum.

first of the 'Cynic' philosophers, although his connection with *Diogenes of Sinope and later Cynics is doubtful. Little is known of his philosophy, but much has been guessed, notably by scholars who have seen him as the anonymous target of some of *Plato's arguments. Practical philosophy interested him more than theory. For him, virtue was the end for men to aim at. It was teachable, and once acquired could not be lost. Pleasure was valueless, perhaps even bad: food, drink, warmth, and sex were needs to be satisfied, but with as little enjoyment as possible (if *Xenophon is to be relied on). *Aristotle thought him and his followers uneducated and silly.

BIBL. Guthrie, *Greek Philosophy*, iii.

Anyte Poetess, early 3rd century BC.

The perfectly assured talent of Anyte (Anutē), unexpected in an Arcadienne from Tegea, is preserved in 20-odd epigrams, her more substantial lyrics being lost. Quatrains are her preferred form: elegantly sensitive and artfully simple, they generally maintain an inscriptional appearance, dedicatory or sepulchral. Her epitaphs for animals established a popular 'sub-genre' of epigram. A few descriptive pieces – on Pan, and shady springs – contribute elusively to the pastoral developed by *Theocritus.

BIBL. Gow and Page, *Hellenistic Epigrams*; G. Luck, *MusHelv* xi (1954).

Anytus Athenian politician, c. 400 BC.

Anytus (Anutos) is best known as one of the accusers of *Socrates in 399 BC; the story that he was killed by an angry mob in revenge for Socrates' death is a fable. He first appears as commander of a maritime force which failed to hold Pylos in 409. In 403 he played a prominent role in the overthrow of the Thirty Tyrants (see *Critias), and served as *strategos* for the following seven years. He appears as a character in *Plato's *Meno* (where he is not overtly hostile to Socrates).

BIBL. Davies, *Athenian Families*, no. 1324.

Apelles Painter, active c. 340–300 BC.

Born in Colophon or Cos, Apelles (Apellēs) moved to Ephesus, where he studied under a local painter, Ephorus, otherwise unknown. Later he studied under Pamphilus, a master of the Sicyonian school. He was the most famous and highly praised of all Greek painters. He worked for *Philip II of Macedon and for *Alexander the Great, with whom he was on intimate terms and whose court painter he seems to have been. His main contemporary rival was the painstaking Protogenes of Caunus.

His paintings, now all lost, were mostly done in the eastern Aegean: Cos, Rhodes, Samos, Ephesus, and Smyrna. None is recorded in mainland Greece. Later in life he travelled to Alexandria, where he painted the famous 'Calumny' for *Ptolemy I and a portrait of an actor. More than half of his 30 or so recorded works are portraits, in which he is said to have excelled. We know of four of Alexander and six of members of Alexander's circle. A copy or a reflection of his famous 'Alexander with a Thunderbolt' at Ephesus may be preserved in a small wall-painting from Pompeii. His portrait of *Antigonus (I) the One-eyed (Monopthalmus) was, for obvious reasons, in profile. He also made a self-portrait – the first in painting that is recorded. His most famous picture was the

The Calumny of Apelles, by Botticelli, after a description of a painting by Apelles. Oil on panel, late 15th century. Florence, Uffizi.

'Aphrodite Anadyomene' at Cos, which showed the goddess wringing out her hair having just come out of the sea, though art critics preferred an equestrian portrait of Antigonus and an Artemis.

For Hellenistic art history Apelles stood at the apogee of the development of Greek painting; he was its culmination, its Titian. All the most important advances in naturalistic depiction, in chiaroscuro and perspective seem to have been made before him, and his particular contribution is hard to pin-point. His paintings' special quality was said (chiefly by himself) to be an inimitable grace or charm (*venustas, charis*). He was interested in techniques and made many innovations; he discovered a secret dark varnish or glaze, again inimitable, which toned down too florid colours and 'excited the colour white by the reflection of light' (referring to strong highlights on representations of wet or shiny surfaces, like eyes or glass?). He wrote treatises on his work, and as a person and artist seems to have been urbane, charitable, and hard-working.

BIBL. Pliny, *Natural History* xxxv. 79 ff.; Mustilli, *Enc. Art. Ant.* i, 456–60; Robertson, *History of Greek Art* 492 ff.

Apollodorus Painter, active *c.* 420–390 BC.

Apollodorus (Apollodōros) of Athens was known as the 'shadow-painter' (*skiagraphos*) and credited with the discovery of modelling with light and shade. He was said to have 'opened the doors of the art of painting through

which entered *Zeuxis' (q.v.) in 397 BC. Though he was clearly very important, we have no precise idea of his achievement, all his works being lost; only a few are recorded, among them a praying priest and an Ajax struck by lightning. He may have been the first to concentrate on easel rather than wall-painting.

BIBL. Robertson, *History of Greek Art* 411 ff.

Apollodorus of Artemita Historian, floruit *c.* 100–70 BC.

Apollodorus (Apollodōros) wrote a history of Parthia in at least four books. His work is lost, but originally included an account of Greek Bactria and the Greek conquest of India as an adjunct to his survey of Parthian history. Since his native city Artemita was east of the Tigris, Apollodorus may have travelled in the East, and he may have had connections with the court of Mithradates II of Parthia.

Trogus and *Strabo appear to have used the work of Apollodorus as an important source for the East; Strabo did not think Apollodorus very reliable, and stated that he often contradicted what was already known.

BIBL. *FGrH* 779; Tarn, *Greeks in Bactria . . .*; Narain, *Indo-Greeks*; Fr. Altheim, *Weltgeschichte Asiens im griechischen Zeitalter* (1947) i. 2 ff.; *Roman World* *Trogus.

Apollodorus of Athens Scholar, *c.* 140 BC.

Apollodorus (Apollodōros) began and ended life in Stoic circles at Athens. After prime years in Alexandria under *Aristarchus (of Samothrace) he decamped to its rival, Pergamum, probably fleeing *Ptolemy VIII. His authoritative *Chronica*, dedicated (in hope or gratitude?) to *Attalus II in 144/3, popularized without devaluing the fundamental chronographic researches of the third-century giant *Eratosthenes, versifying them deftly in iambic trimeters, but also improving accuracy and covering a longer period. A later supplement, probably genuine, reached at least 120/19 BC. Apollodorus' fine treatise on *Homer's Catalogue of Ships (see Introduction), used by *Strabo, carried on Eratosthenes' geographical labours, and work on *Epicharmus and *Sophron his study of comedy. *On the Gods* in 24 books is a considerable loss: fragments reveal Apollodorus' preoccupation with etymology, a Stoic streak well tempered by his Aristarchean training. The mythological handbook hung on his famous name is a first- or second-century AD compilation.

BIBL. *FGrH* 244; Pfeiffer, *Classical Scholarship* i, 252 ff.

Apollodorus of Carystus Comic poet, first comedy *c.* 285 BC.

Called 'Athenian' in the *Suda* – which allots him 47 plays and five victories – Apollodorus (Apollodōros) possibly gained Athenian citizenship as a successful practitioner of New Comedy in the generation after *Menander. His development of the master's gently observed middle-class intrigues attracted Terence to adapt him twice (*Hecyra*, *Phormio*).

BIBL. Webster, *Later Comedy* 205 ff.; *Roman World* *Terence.

Apollodorus of Pergamum (*c.* 104–*c.* 22 BC) Rhetorician.

A famed exponent of rigid adherence to strict rhetorical rules, Apollodorus (Apollodōros) taught the young Octavian. His handbook was translated into Latin by Valgius Rufus, a friend of Horace.

BIBL. Kennedy, *Rhetoric* 338 ff.; *Roman World* *Augustus (Octavian), *Horace.   N.H.

Apollodorus, son of Pasion *Athenian orator, mid-4th century BC.

Apollodorus (Apollodōros), son of the banker *Pasion, a man of persistent and somewhat hysterical litigiousness, is the author of six or seven of the (private) speeches in the *Demosthenic corpus, some connected with his father's business. In the public sphere he prosecuted at least five Athenian *strategoi*, and, in 349 BC, proposed the diversion of revenue surpluses to military use, which led to his own condemnation under a *graphe paranomon*. (See also *Neaera.)

BIBL. Kirchner, *PA* no. 1411; Schaefer, *Demosthenes*, Beilagen 130 ff.

Apollonis of Cyzicus Queen of Pergamum, *c.* 223–after 184/3 BC.

Apollonis (Apollōnis), the daughter of one Athenaeus, was married to *Attalus I of Pergamum in his late middle age. Their apparently happy family life was blessed with four sons, *Eumenes II, *Attalus II, Philetaerus, and Athenaeus, all of whom loved and honoured their parents (according to the language of numerous inscriptions and dedications) and co-existed without rivalry. In Cyzicus, Apollonis' sons Eumenes and Attalus erected in her

honour a temple whose relief sculpture illustrated various mythological scenes of filial piety and devotion; descriptions of these sculptures form the 19 epigrams of book iii of the *Greek Anthology*. After her death, Apollonis was associated in the divine ruler-cult with her husband.

BIBL. Hansen, *Attalids*.

Apollonius, finance minister: see *Zenon

Apollonius Molon Rhetorician, 1st century BC.

A native of Alabanda in Caria, Apollonius (Apollōnios) taught on Rhodes and visited Rome twice in the 80s BC as the Rhodians' ambassador. Caesar and Cicero – who pays him eloquent tribute – were his most distinguished pupils.

BIBL. Cicero, *Brutus* 304 ff.; Kennedy, *Rhetoric* 104 ff.; *Roman World* Gaius Julius *Caesar, *Cicero.   N.H.

Apollonius of Perge Mathematician, second half of 2nd century BC.

A younger contemporary of *Archimedes, Apollonius (Apollōnios) studied in Alexandria. He became known as the 'great geometer', largely through his work *Conics*, in which he investigated the properties of conic sections. Most of the work survives, some in Arabic translation. He also worked on contemporary theories (the epicyclic and the eccentric) about the apparent irregularities in the movement of planets.

BIBL. Heath, *Greek Mathematics*.

Apollonius Rhodius Poet and scholar, born *c.* 295 BC.

According to ancient tradition, Apollonius (Apollōnios), a 'pupil' of *Callimachus, was driven from Alexandria to retirement on Rhodes by the hostile reception of his epic, *Argonautica*; later he returned with the revised poem to acclaim and acceptance in the Museum. This is patently a largely fictional construction, complete with happy ending, round scanty facts (e.g. two known editions of the *Argonautica*); and the famous story of the quarrel with Callimachus, who is supposed to have attacked him in his *Ibis*, should not be uncritically accepted. A papyrus establishes that Apollonius, who was apparently a native Alexandrian, followed *Zenodotus as *Ptolemy II's chief librarian (a post which Callimachus never held). It is possible that he was edged out, not simply succeeded, by *Eratosthenes – which may have prompted withdrawal to Rhodes in a huff (though 'Rhodian' might be expected to derive from family origin rather than later residence).

Apollonius' scholarly activities are well attested: he wrote on *Homer, *Hesiod, and *Archilochus; his lost minor poems, foundation legends of various cities, were packed with antiquarian erudition. The same interests are plain in the *Argonautica*. The fairy-tale story of the Golden Fleece is laid out in four books: i–ii preparation and journey of the Argonauts to Colchis, iii the winning of the fleece, iv the voyage home. Sorting out the richly contradictory traditions of this ancient legend was itself a major scholarly undertaking; and Apollonius' fastidiously evolved Homeric language often interprets through usage difficult words which were the subject of learned dispute: this is poetry used like a learned journal. At the same time the old world of mythology is revitalized by imagination: the gods can be treated with subtle humour or effectively suspended disbelief, and there are fine similes and vivid descriptions, especially of light-effects. Apollonius' new epic – complex, sophisticated, morally casual – is extremely ambitious and not surprisingly somewhat uneven, especially for today's reader, who is as powerfully repelled by its geographical, ethnographical, and aetiological learning as he is attracted by the psychologically penetrating portrait of Medea in love (book iii), the model for Virgil's Dido. Medea herself is a split personality, tremulous maid and ruthless witch. Jason – glamorous, enervated, entirely dependent on Medea's magic for his success – is a hero created in deliberate opposition to the traditional type, represented aboard Argo by Heracles and Idas. The *Argonautica* is a thoroughly up-to-date, 'Callimachean' work, alluding frequently to the master's poetry. Nevertheless Apollonius is self-consciously asking to be placed in the tradition of Homer, who is constantly evoked in episode, detail, and language: here we might perceive a true disagreement with Callimachus, Apollonius asserting that epic *could* be creatively renewed, Callimachus that new poetry must not rival Homer (see *Callimachus, *Theocritus).

BIBL. Lesky, *Greek Literature*; C. R. Beye, *GRBS* x (1969); M. R. Lefkowitz, *ZPE* xl (1980); *Roman World* *Virgil.

Apries Egyptian pharaoh, 589–570 BC.

Apries (Apriēs, the Egyptian Hophra), the great-grandson of *Psammetichus, continued his dynasty's policy of friendship to the Greeks, making much use of Ionian and Carian mercenaries. After a generally prosperous reign, he sent an expedition against Cyrene which failed disastrously, and was overthrown by a rebellion led by *Amasis.

BIBL. Herodotus ii. 161–9, iv. 159.

Aratus Poet, born *c*. 315 BC.

Having left Cilicia for study in Athens, Aratus (Aratos)

Portrait herm identified by some as Aratus from its similarity to coin portraits of the poet. Rome, Villa Albani.

of Soli encountered *Antigonus Gonatas, probably through *Zeno of Citium, and was invited to court at Pella, where he celebrated the king's Celtic victory (277 BC) and marriage (276). After a spell with *Antiochus I in Syria he apparently returned to Macedonia. Aratus' alleged work on *Homer's text (see *Timon of Phlius) and varied poetic output – hymns, epicedia, short poems – were soon eclipsed by the brilliant success of his one extant poem, *Phaenomena*, a rendering into 1,154 hexameters of the prose treatise of *Eudoxus of Cnidos on the constellations, plus a work on weather signs. The matter is rebarbative and the treatment unrelieved to modern taste, but this learned didactic in the *Hesiodic tradition, fastidiously expressed, was hailed by *Callimachus as his kind of poetry, and remained lastingly popular. It magnetized commentators: 27 are named, including *Hipparchus of Nicaea, whose criticism of Aratus' astronomy survives. Latin translators included Cicero and Germanicus. Stoic fervour permeates the poem, especially the opening invocation to Zeus, and the digression on man's degeneration from the Golden Age (98 ff.) is welcome and attractive; but this is generally austere stuff with little poetic colouring (contrast Virgil's technique with similar material in *Georgics* i).

BIBL. *Phaenomena*, ed. J. Martin (1956); *SH* 83–120 (fragments); D. A. Kidd, *AUMLA* xv (1961); *Roman World* *Cicero, *Germanicus, *Virgil.

Aratus of Sicyon (271–213 BC) Head of the Achaean League.

When his father Cleinias was deposed in 264 BC from the tyranny of Sicyon, the child Aratus (Aratos) was raised in exile at Argos. He freed Sicyon from a later tyrant in a bloodless *coup* in 251 with the aid of *Demophanes and *Ecdelus. Initial rapport with *Antigonus Gonatas of Macedon gave way to an alliance with the Achaean League (which Sicyon joined), and friendship with *Alexander of Corinth made Macedonian friendship impossible. Aratus instead allied himself with *Ptolemy II, whose funds eased Sicyonian financial difficulties.

In a romantic adventure, Aratus liberated Corinth from Gonatas in 243 (see *Persaeus), and united her and other Peloponnesian cities to the League. When Gonatas allied himself with Aetolia against Achaea, Aratus summoned the help of his ideological enemy *Agis IV of Sparta, but peace was concluded in 241/40. Achaea and Aetolia later formed an alliance against Epirus and *Demetrius II of Macedon, *c*. 238. Aratus intervened in Attica and Argos, and was finally defeated before *c*. 233. He now faced a rival to his authority within the League: *Lydiadas of Megalopolis frequently opposed him for the office of *strategus* and in policy decisions.

Although Aratus had been staunchly anti-Macedonian, the threat of the aggressions of *Cleomenes III of Sparta in the Peloponnese forced him to make overtures to *Antigonus Doson in 227 through secret negotiations by *Cercidas of Megalopolis. Doson was formally invited to intervene in 225–224 for the price of Corinth, the city which Aratus had freed from Macedon. The influence of Aratus, who foresaw the potential of a new relationship between Greece and Macedon, can perhaps be seen behind Doson's foundation of the Hellenic League in 224. When Doson died, the future *Philip V was entrusted to

Aratus to learn about the Achaean mind and Greek ideals.

Aratus, Philip, and the Hellenic League fought the so-called 'Social War' against Aetolia and her allies in 220. Aratus outwitted the intrigues of Philip's ministers who wanted to subdue Achaea, and succeeded in keeping Achaea independent. With the Peace of Naupactus in 217, Aratus no longer had to play the role 'of a courtier' to Philip (Walbank): but he saw his own influence with the king eroded by that of *Demetrius of Pharos, in whose schemes against Rome Aratus refused to participate. When Philip intervened in Messene in 215 on Demetrius' advice, he was persuaded to withdraw by Aratus' appeals to his conscience. Philip's pillage of Messene in 214 gave great offence to Aratus, who realized his utter betrayal when he learned that Philip had seduced his daughter-in-law, Polycrateia. He died in 213, claiming that Philip had poisoned him.

Ineptitude as a military commander was one failure of Aratus. Although some claim that he was politically incorruptible and others that his character was severely flawed (in the betrayal of his own ideals, the use of immoral means, etc.), Aratus was on the whole a wise statesman who acted always for the good of the Achaean League with which he came to be identified.

Aratus wrote his memoirs in over 30 books of events until c. 220. Even granting a bias against Macedon, Sparta, and all enemies of the Achaean League, his trustworthiness as a source is debatable. He was admired by *Polybius, who agreed with his political views, but some have seen the memoirs as an attempt to excuse and glorify Aratus. The work remains only in quotations: it was the main source for Plutarch's *Life* of Aratus, and the main source of Polybius' account of the events before 220.

BIBL. FGrH 231; Tarn, *Antigonos Gonatas*; Polybius ii. 37–71, iv–v, with Walbank, *HCP*; Walbank, *Aratos of Sicyon* (1933); *Roman World* *Plutarch.

Arcesilaus of Cyrene: see Battiads

Arcesilaus of Pitane (c. 316–241 BC) Philosopher.

Arcesilaus (Arkesilaos) studied mathematics and philosophy, and was introduced to the Academy by his friend *Crantor, with whom he afterwards lived. Under his headship the school became a centre of scepticism. His method was to argue for and against a proposition, and thus arrive at contradictory conclusions, making it appropriate to suspend judgement on the issue. He published no works, perhaps because to do so would have committed him to dogmatic views. His pupils were said to fear his sharp wit.

BIBL. Diogenes Laertius iv. 28–45; Long, *Hellenistic Philosophy*.

Archelaus King of Macedon, 413–399 BC.

Archelaus (Arkhelaos) was a bastard son of *Perdiccas II by a slave-woman belonging to Perdiccas' brother Alcetas; by 436 BC he had apparently been declared legitimate, since his name appears in an alliance with Athens. On Perdiccas' death he killed Alcetas, together with his son Alexander, as well as his own brother, the legitimate king; *Plato (*Gorgias*) calls him 'The greatest criminal in Macedon'. *Thucydides says that he put Macedonia in a stronger position for war than all the eight kings who preceded him, building roads and forts and a

new capital at Pella, to which he invited intellectuals from all over Greece (including *Euripides); *Socrates refused. He reconquered Pydna and occupied parts of Thessaly. He was killed by his boy-friend Craterus while hunting in 399; his young son Orestes was quickly murdered by his guardian Aeropus, who seized the throne.

BIBL. Hammond and Griffith, *Macedonia* ii. 137 ff.: *SEG* xii. 16. 52 (alliance).

Archelaus of Athens Philosopher, 5th century BC.

An unoriginal philosopher, Archelaus (Arkhelaos) was a follower of *Anaxagoras and a teacher of *Socrates. His natural philosophy hardly differs from Anaxagoras', except that he believed that mind (*nous*) was mixed with other things, and was perhaps identified with air.

BIBL. Guthrie, *Greek Philosophy* ii.

Archias Founder of Syracuse, c. 735 BC.

Archias (Arkhias), alleged descendant of the **Heracleidae, and member of the Bacchiad dynasty, left Corinth (perhaps for discreditable personal reasons) as leader of the expedition which colonized Syracuse, while his brother Chersicrates occupied Corcyra. Thus Corinth acquired an important site in Sicily, and a strategic point on the route to it.

BIBL. Strabo vi. 269–70, viii. 380; Thucydides vi. 3; Plutarch, *Moralia* 772e–773b.

Archias, Aulus Licinius (c. 118–after 62 BC) Poet.

Aulus Licinius Archias was a native of Antioch. Epics on the victories of Marius and Lucullus are lost, and the ascription of epigrams to him remains confused. Cicero failed to secure a panegyric from him, but defended him most eloquently against the charge of false assumption of Roman citizenship.

BIBL. Gow and Page, *Garland of Philip* 3588 ff.; Cicero, *Pro Archia*; *Roman World* *Cicero, *Lucullus, *Marius. N.H.

Archidamus II Eurypontid king of Sparta, 476–427 BC.

Archidamus (Arkhidamos) succeeded his grandfather *Leotychidas when the latter was forced into exile. During the earthquake of 464 BC he saved Sparta by leading the army to face a potential helot attack. He played a major role in the subsequent repression of the helots at Ithome. During the diplomatic activity preceding the Peloponnesian War (the first ten years of which are named after him), Archidamus urged restraint; he was a *xenos* (guest-friend) of *Pericles. In 431, 430, and 428 he led the invasions of Attica, and in 429 directed operations against Plataea. His children were *Agis II, *Agesilaus, and *Cynisca.

BIBL. Westlake, *Individuals in Thucydides*, ch. 8.

Archidamus III Eurypontid king of Sparta, c. 360–338 BC.

Archidamus (Arkhidamos) was already active in *Agesilaus' lifetime (he rescued the survivors of Leuctra (371 BC), campaigned in Arcadia in 368 and 364, and fought in the streets of Sparta during *Epaminondas' invasion in 362). As king he is noted for his support of Phocis in the Sacred War (355–346) – for which some held him indirectly responsible – and for expeditions to Crete (to defend Lyctus against *Phalaecus) and Italy (to defend Tarentum from local barbarians). He died in Italy at the

Portrait herm of the Eurypontid king Archidamus III in cuirass and baldric, from Herculaneum. Naples, Museo Nazionale.

Ionic capital of *c.* 550 BC from Paros bearing an inscription of the 4th century: 'Archilochus of Paros, the son of Telesicles, rests here'. Paros.

battle of Mandurion. *Isocrates' *Archidamus* is a speech supposedly delivered by Archidamus in 366/5, and his *Epistle ix* accompanied a Panhellenist tract sent to him in 356/5.

BIBL. Poralla, *Prosopographie*, no. 158.

Archilochus Poet, *c.* 650 BC.

Archilochus (Arkhilokhos) of Paros, regarded, like *Callinus and *Mimnermus, as the 'inventor' of elegiacs, certainly antedates other surviving poets of trimeters, tetrameters, and epodes. The ancients ranked him next to *Homer and exploited the poems for biography: these presented him as the bastard son of Telesicles, the aristocratic leader of a colony to Thasos, whither Archilochus was driven by poverty, and mentioned both conflicts with Thracians and rival Naxian settlers and his passion for Neobule – her father Lycambes, reneging on an agreed marriage, provoked such invective from Archilochus that (legend elaborated) he and his daughters hung themselves.

Archilochus' frequent focus on affairs purporting to be his own, his jocular justification for abandoning his shield (fr. 5, from the few extant elegiacs), his dismissal of a conventionally handsome general (fr. 114), and coarse material in trimeters (frs. 42–6) have encouraged undue contrast with *Homer's world. Genre explains the difference: these are *our* (and antiquity's) earliest examples of songs for symposia that must long have existed, songs where one addressed companions (fr. 105 and five others addressed Glaucus, whose memorial archaeologists have found on Thasos), offered comments on life (fr. 128 'Take

it as it comes') or consolation (fr. 13), and narrated military or amatory exploits. These last occasion our earliest first-person declarations of passion (frs. 191, 193). Although invective was prominent in the epodes (against Lycambes, frs. 172–81), an exciting discovery of 36 lines narrating Archilochus' seduction of Neobule's younger sister in a flowery meadow shows that the epodes also admitted tenderer tones (fr. 196A). This poem's address to a companion undermines notions that Lycambes' family were mere characters in a drama, and its treatment of the incident augments our earlier knowledge both of Archilochus' skill in presenting conversation and character (carried furthest in frs. 19 and 122, where only late in the poem is the speaker discovered not to be Archilochus) and of how phraseology (especially dactylic) can be shared with or vary that of epic (although epic influence cannot be proved to be direct or Homeric).

BIBL. Text: West, *IEG* and *Delectus*. Commentary: Campbell, *Lyric Poetry*; West, *Studies* 1 ff., 118 ff.; Kirkwood, *Greek Monody*.

Archimedes (287–212 BC) Mathematician.

One of the greatest of Greek mathematicians, Archimedes (Arkhimēdēs) was also famous for mechanical inventions, although he is said to have despised mechanics. He was killed by a Roman soldier in 212 BC, when his native city Syracuse fell to Marcus Claudius Marcellus after a siege, during which machines devised by Archimedes had caused the Roman attackers many casualties. His well-known remark 'Eureka' (*Heurēka*) was allegedly made when, reflecting on his own displacement of water in a bath, he realized how he could calculate the proportions of silver and gold in a crown made for his friend *Hieron II, and absent-mindedly ran home naked. Among his other inventions was 'Archimedes' screw', a device for raising water that is still in use today, in some form, in many parts of the world. He claimed, 'Give me a place to stand and I will move the world', probably as a comment on the efficacy of pulleys. His surviving writings show great originality in his mathematical methods, some of them disapproved by purists.

BIBL. T. L. Heath, *The Works of Archimedes* (1897, reprinted 1957); Plutarch, *Marcellus*; *Roman World* M. Claudius *Marcellus.

Archinus Athenian politician, late 5th century BC.

Archinus (Arkhinos) was partly responsible for reducing comic poets' state pay (before 405 BC), and was later among the counter-revolutionaries who seized Phyle in winter 404–3 and overthrew the Thirty Tyrants (see *Critias). But in 403 he hindered radical alterations in the citizen body by forestalling the mass exodus of 'city men' to Eleusis and defeating *Thrasybulus' grant of citizenship to all non-citizens who had fought for the democracy. He also introduced special legal procedures to enforce the post-restoration amnesty, and was responsible for the official use of the 'Ionic' alphabet after 403/2.

BIBL. Kirchner, *PA* no. 2526; Hignett, *Athenian Constitution* 295 ff.

Archytas Mathematician, early 4th century BC.

A *Pythagorean philosopher, Archytas (Arkhutas of Tarentum) was also a successful general. His most famous mathematical achievement was that of doubling the cube, i.e. determining the length of the side of a cube that is double a given cube in volume. Among his mechanical inventions was a children's rattle, so that they could make a loud noise without breaking things.

BIBL. Heath, *Greek Mathematics*.

Arctinus: see **Cyclic Poets**

Areus I Agiad king of Sparta, 309/8–265/4 BC.

When Macedonia was distracted from interference in Greece by the Gallic invasion in 279 BC (see *Brennus), King Areus led an unsuccessful Peloponnesian attack on Aetolia in an attempt to reassert Spartan supremacy. He was recalled from fighting in Crete in 273 to repel an attack on Sparta by his uncle *Cleonymus, supported by *Pyrrhus of Epirus, against whom Areus was temporarily backed by *Antigonus Gonatas of Macedon. His enhanced prestige enabled him to form another Peloponnesian alliance, and in 266 he joined with Athens and *Ptolemy II against Gonatas in the 'War of *Chremonides'. His attempt to force the Isthmus in order to relieve Athens was given no support by the Ptolemaic fleet, and he was defeated and killed by *Craterus the Younger at Corinth in 264. Areus was the first Spartan king to act like a Hellenistic monarch; he glorified himself and his personal achievements on coins and inscriptions.

BIBL. Jones, *Sparta*; Forrest, *History of Sparta*.

Ariarathes III King of Cappadocia, c. 255–220 BC.

Ariarathes (Ariarathēs) was co-dynast with his father Ariaramnes until he pronounced himself independent of Seleucid authority and declared himself king, perhaps as early as c. 255 BC. His marriage to Stratonice, the sister of *Seleucus II, probably occurred in the context of the Third Syrian War, when the Seleucid badly needed neighbouring allies in his internecine struggle; in any case a friendly Cappadocia was a vital link between Syria and western Asia Minor. Ariarathes, however, supported *Antiochus Hierax against Seleucus II in the 'War of the Brothers'.

BIBL. PW ii. 816.

Ariarathes IV King of Cappadocia, 220–163 BC.

Cappadocia was officially independent of the Seleucids, but Ariarathes (Ariarathēs) was allied to them through his

Coin portrait of Ariarathes IV, king of Cappadocia (enlarged).

marriage in 193 BC to Antiochis, a daughter of *Antiochus III (q.v.). He thus sent forces in 189 to help the Gauls against Pergamum and Rome, and fought with Antiochus at Magnesia (189). Perhaps to escape the harsh indemnity imposed by the Peace of Apamea and to ally himself with Pergamum, the new Asian power, Ariarathes betrothed his daughter Stratonice to *Eumenes II. His fine was halved, and Cappadocia became an ally of Pergamum and Rome. He and Eumenes collaborated in the war against *Pharnaces of Pontus (q.v.) and obtained his surrender. Ariarathes may have helped Eumenes in his final subjugation of the Gauls in the early 160s, and died in 164/3.

BIBL. PW ii. 817.

Ariarathes V King of Cappadocia, 163–130 BC.

As a youth Ariarathes (Ariarathēs) studied philosophy in Athens with *Carneades, as a fellow pupil of the future *Attalus II of Pergamum. He succeeded to the throne despite the claims of a supposed elder brother, Orophernes, but when (on Rome's advice) he refused to marry the sister of the Seleucid king *Demetrius I, the latter incited Orophernes to seize the throne in 160 BC. The pretender retained his power despite the help of Attalus II, now Ariarathes' brother-in-law; Attalus retaliated by unseating Demetrius with the pretender *Alexander Balas, and welcomed Ariarathes in Pergamum, and together they attacked Cappadocia and drove the unpopular Orophernes to Syria. Ariarathes later sacked Priene when the temple of Athena refused to give him the usurper's treasure, and sent troops to Attalus in 155 during his war with *Prusias II of Bithynia. He supplied men and ships to Rome in 131 for use against *Aristonicus (q.v.). Ariarathes was killed in this war in 130, but his descendants were rewarded with much of Lycaonia.

BIBL. PW ii. 818.

Ariobarzanes Persian satrap, died c. 362 BC.

Satrap of Dascyleium after *Pharnabazus, Ariobarzanes (Ariobarzanēs) was a prominent rebel in the 360s BC, receiving help from King *Agesilaus and from *Timotheus (2) (to whom he gave Sestos and Crithote, getting Athenian citizenship in return). His betrayal by his son Mithradates, which led to his execution, was regarded by *Xenophon as exemplifying the moral degradation of contemporary Persia.

BIBL. PW ii. 832.

Reverse of a coin of Methymna (enlarged) showing Arion riding on a dolphin. 2nd or 1st century BC. London, British Museum.

Arion Lyric poet, *c.* 600 BC.

Arion (Ariōn) of Methymna in Lesbos figures in a tale of *Herodotus – which relates how a dolphin saved him when thrown overboard by avaricious sailors – as an outstanding singer to the lyre and the first composer of dithyrambs (at *Periander's Corinth). The *Suda* ascribes to him the invention of satyr choruses and tragedy (a magnification of his dithyrambic activity?) and two books of *prooemia*. Nothing survives (Page, *PMG* fr. 939 was composed *c.* 400 BC).

BIBL. Herodotus i. 23; Bowra, *Greek Margins*, 164 f.

Ariphron Lyric poet, 5th–4th century BC.

Ariphron (Ariphrōn) of Sicyon was famous for his *Paean to Health* (*Hygieia*), which is quoted by several later writers and in inscriptions.

BIBL. *Lyra Graeca* (Loeb) iii.

Aristagoras Ruler of Miletus, died 497 BC.

Aristagoras was left to administer Miletus while his cousin and father-in-law *Histiaeus was in Persia at the court of *Darius I. When Histiaeus suspected that he would not be allowed to return, he advised Aristagoras to rebel. This resulted in the Ionian Revolt (499–492 BC); Aristagoras travelled to Greece, and persuaded Athens and Eretria to support the rebels. Defeated by the Persians, he abandoned Miletus to found a colony at Histiaeus' fief of Myrcinus in Thrace, where he was killed in a battle against the Edoni.

BIBL. Burn, *Persia and the Greeks*; P. B. Manville, *CQ* xxvii (1977).

Aristarchus of Samos Astronomer, first half of 3rd century BC.

The main achievement of Aristarchus (Aristarkhos) was to put forward the heliocentric theory, that the sun and stars are fixed, and the earth moves round the sun. The theory was rejected by *Hipparchus and Ptolemy. His calculations, in a surviving work, of the size and distance of the sun and moon were much inferior to those of Hipparchus.

BIBL. T. L. Heath, *Aristarchus of Samos* (1913); *Roman World* *Ptolemy.

Aristarchus of Samothrace (*c.* 216–*c.* 144 BC) Scholar.

Aristarchus (Aristarkhos) was librarian at Alexandria after Apollonius Eidographus until he fled to Cyprus from the persecutions of (his ex-pupil?) *Ptolemy VIII in 145 BC; he died shortly afterwards. The personification of fine scholarship for later times, he was a worthy successor to *Aristophanes of Byzantium and the master of notable pupils (*Apollodorus of Athens, *Dionysius Thrax, and others). Aristarchus' systematic and wide-ranging commentaries (*hypomnemata*) represented a major scholarly advance on the monographs and lexica whose form had limited his predecessors' enquiries. A papyrus fragment reveals that he dealt not only with the classical poets but also with prose (*Herodotus). His fame rested chiefly, however, on his *Homeric studies: here he certainly produced a text, as well as a commentary (in two editions), of which excerpts survive. Scrupulous, circumspect, and penetrating, he refined critical methods, emphasizing the importance of the author's usage in interpretation. Here and in grammar he developed an analogist position opposed to *Crates of Mallos (q.v.).

BIBL. Pfeiffer, *Classical Scholarship* i.

Aristeas of Proconnesus Hexameter poet, 680/540 BC.

Aristeas is presented by *Herodotus as the writer of an *Arimaspea* (*Suda* says in three books) reporting a journey to the Scythian Issedones and their tales of their neighbours, the one-eyed Arimaspi, of *their* neighbours, gold-guarding griffins, and of *their* neighbours, the Hyperboreans. The journey took place during the six years after he had been taken for dead in a fullery and his body had disappeared (though he had also been encountered at this time on the Cyzicus road). Herodotus' tale that after his return to Proconnesus he again disappeared, to reappear 240 years later in Metapontum enjoining the cult of himself and Apollo, ought to give a date earlier than 680 BC, but some (e.g. Jacoby) prefer *Apollodorus of Athens' date (in *Suda*) *c.* 547. Apolline and *Pythagorean features of the biography encourage scepticism, but the existence both of a cult at Metapontum and of the *Arimaspea*, known to *Hecataeus and quoted still by Longinus (first century AD?), seems secure. *Suda* also attributes a prose Theogony.

BIBL. Herodotus iv. 14–16; (Jacoby), *FGrH* 35; J. D. P. Bolton, *Aristeas of Proconnesus* (1962); *Roman World* *Longinus.

Arist(e)ides Athenian leader, archon 489/8 BC.

In ancient tradition, Arist(e)ides (Aristeidēs) became the symbol of the just (and therefore impoverished) politician. Hence he was the subject of a series of unhistorical anecdotes: according to one, he wrote his own name on a potsherd for an illiterate voter at an ostracism who told him that, although he did not know who Aristeides was, he wanted him ostracized because he was fed up with hearing him called 'the Just'; according to another, he was so poor that there was no money for his funeral, nor for dowries for his daughters (see *Xanthippe). Ancient tradition also saw his open and straightforward character as the opposite of that of the wily *Themistocles; hence if Themistocles was a 'radical' leader, Aristeides had to be placed in the list of 'conservatives'.

Aristeides in fact belonged to the wealthiest of Solon's property-classes (since he was elected archon before the reforms of 487 BC); he was related to the ancient clan of the Kerykes of Eleusis, and *Callias (son of Hipponicus (1)) was a cousin. At Marathon (490) he agreed, as one of the ten *strategoi*, to let *Miltiades have supreme command on the day allotted to himself, thus contributing to the Athenian victory over the Persians. In 482 he was ostracized. He returned to participate in the battle of Salamis (480), where he occupied the strategic island of Psyttaleia. He was a *strategos* at Plataea (479), then commanded the Athenian ships serving in the Aegean under *Pausanias (1). When Sparta withdrew from the war against Persia, Aristeides was largely responsible for the formal organization of the Delian League, and in particular for the assessment of the tribute to be levied from those islands that did not wish to provide ships. Thereafter reliable information about him ceases; he may have died in 467.

BIBL. Davies, *Athenian Families*, no. 1695; Meiggs, *Athenian Empire* 42 f., 58 ff.

Ostracon cast against the Athenian leader Aristeides in 482 BC. Athens, Agora Museum.

Arist(e)ides of Miletus Erotic writer, late second century BC (?)

That he wrote the *Milesiaca* (*Milesian Tales*), is all that is known of Arist(e)ides (Aristeidēs), who may not even have come from Miletus. This work, apparently a collection of salacious stories embroidering a strong sub-literary tradition, had a considerable vogue: the name became generic for the ribaldly erotic and/or macabre material which influenced the picaresque novel – compare Petronius and Apuleius. Sisenna's Latin translation enlivened a tedious campaign: the Parthians made capital from capturing a copy in Roman baggage at Carrhae.

BIBL. S. Trenkner, *The Greek Novella* (1958); Perry, *Ancient Romances*; *Roman World* *Apuleius, *Petronius, *Sisenna.

Aristeus (-eas) Corinthian leader, died 430 BC.

Adeimantus, the father of Aristeus (or Aristeas), was the Corinthian commander at the battle of Salamis (480 BC); a hostile Athenian tradition recorded by *Herodotus made him an opponent of *Themistocles who tried to avoid the battle. Aristeus himself commanded the Corinthian volunteers who went to support Potidaea when it revolted from Athens in 432. He escaped from the besieged city, but in 430 the Peloponnesian League sent him on an embassy to Persia; he was captured in Thrace by *Sitalces' son Sadocus, handed over to the Athenians, and executed.

BIBL. Westlake, *Essays*, ch. 4.

Aristides: see **Arist(e)ides**

Aristion Sculptor, active *c.* 550–520 BC.

From Paros and perhaps trained there, Aristion (Aristiōn) later moved to Athens. For a long time he was known to us only from a few signed bases, one of which was for a grave statue of an unmarried girl, Phrasycleia. But in 1972 this statue, still in excellent condition, was found buried at Merenda (Myrrhinus) in Attica and is perhaps the finest surviving archaic kore.

BIBL. Mastrokostas, *Athens Annals of Archaeology* V (1972); Robertson, *History of Greek Art* 100–1; Boardman, *Sculpture (Archaic)* 75–6.

The statue of Phrasycleia by Aristion of Paros as discovered with another statue at Merenda in Attica; *c.* 530 BC. Athens, National Museum.

Aristippus, Thessalian: see **Aleuadae**

Aristippus of Cyrene (elder and younger) Philosophers.
  Two philosophers of this name, one a grandson of the
other, were connected with a school of philosophy at
Cyrene in North Africa, founded in the fourth century BC.
There is some confusion between them. The elder
Aristippus (Aristippos) went to Athens as a follower of
*Socrates. He is said later to have led a life of luxury. The
younger Aristippus probably contributed more to the
philosophy of the school, whose main tenet was that a
man's aim in life should be the pursuit of his own
immediate pleasure, especially pleasures of the body. This
was a more extreme doctrine than the hedonism of
*Epicureans, for whom freedom from trouble was the
chief end in life. Apart from ethics, other branches of
philosophy were despised, but the Cyrenaics also held
that our knowledge is limited to what we perceive at any
given moment, an extreme form of scepticism. Among
members of the school who diverged from the central
doctrines were Hegesias of Cyrene, who held life to be no
more valuable than death and denied the possibility of
altruism (his teaching was banned by *Ptolemy (I) Soter as
too conducive to suicide), and Anniceris, who admitted
the possibility of benevolence and selfless action.
  BIBL. Diogenes Laertius ii. 65–104.

Aristobulus of Cassandreia Alexander historian,
c. 300 BC.
  Aristobulus (Aristoboulos) served under *Alexander
the Great as a technical adviser (he restored *Cyrus' tomb
at Pasargadae), and wrote a history of his reign more than
a quarter-century after his death. A sober work of few
literary pretensions and tending to banish extravagances
due to flattery or hatred of Alexander, it became one of
Arrian's chief sources.
  BIBL. Pearson, *Lost Histories* 150–87; P. Brunt, *CQ*, n.s.
xxiv (1974); *Roman World* *Arrian.

Aristocrates Athenian politician, mid-4th century BC.
  In *c.* 353/2 BC Aristocrates (Aristokrates) proposed
special sanctions against anyone who might kill
*Charidemus. *Demosthenes, *Oration* xxiii was written for
a consequent *graphe paranomon.*
  BIBL. Kirchner, *PA* no. 1897.

Aristodemus of Cumae Tyrant, *c.* 504–492 BC.
  Aristodemus (Aristodēmos) fought against the
Etruscans, and became tyrant of Cumae (Cyme) on the
strength of his success. However, he was friendly to the
exiled Tarquinius Superbus, who took refuge at his court
and died there. Despite his military achievements and the
bloodthirstiness of his rule, he was nicknamed the
'Effeminate'.
  BIBL. Dionysius of Halicarnassus, *Roman Antiquities* v.
36, vi. 21, vii. 2–12; Livy ii. 21; A. Alföldi, *Early Rome
and the Latins* (1963) 47–72; *Roman World* *Tarquinius
Superbus.

Aristodemus of Messenia King, *c.* 710 BC.
  During the First Messenian War, an oracle promised the
Messenians success if they sacrificed a virgin of the royal
house, and Aristodemus (Aristodēmos, or Aristodamos)
offered his daughter. The Messenians later chose him as

king, and at first he was successful, but eventually the
war went against the Messenians, and in despair
Aristodemus killed himself on his daughter's grave.
  BIBL. Pausanias iv. 9–13.

Aristomenes Messenian war leader, *c.* 650 BC.
  Aristomenes (Aristomenēs), a member of the Messenian
royal house, became leader of the revolt against Spartan
rule which led to the Second Messenian War. He was
highly successful at first, but was eventually defeated,
largely because of the treachery of his Arcadian allies.
Most of his surviving followers retired to Sicily, where
they founded Messana (Messina), but Aristomenes himself
died in Rhodes while seeking fresh allies in the eastern
Aegean. Several distinguished families in Arcadia and
Rhodes claimed descent from him, and he was worshipped
in Messenia as a hero.
  BIBL. Pausanias iv. 14–24; Forrest, *History of Sparta* 70.

Ariston Eurypontid king of Sparta, *c.* 550–515 BC.
  Like his colleague *Anaxandridas, Ariston (Aristōn) had
a colourful married life. He appropriated his best friend's
wife, and declared that *Demaratus, born soon after their
marriage, could not possibly be his child. He later
changed his mind and accepted Demaratus as his heir, but
this initial repudiation was used by *Cleomenes in his
campaign to depose Demaratus.
  BIBL. Herodotus vi. 61–6.

Ariston of Ceos Head of the Peripatetic school, *c.* 225 BC.
  Little is known of the philosophy of Ariston (Aristōn), a
pupil of *Lycon. The little that is known about the lives
of *Aristotle and other early Peripatetic philosophers may
be partly due to his work. According to Cicero, he was
polished and elegant, but lacked the weight that we look
for in a great philosopher.
  BIBL. F. von Wehrli, *Die Schule des Aristoteles* (1967–9)
vi; *Roman World* *Cicero.

Ariston of Chios Stoic philosopher, mid-3rd century BC.
  A pupil of *Zeno of Citium, Ariston (Aristōn) became a
popular and persuasive lecturer (sometimes called 'the
siren'). He thought ethics the only worthwhile branch of
philosophy, and held that everything except virtue and
vice is morally indifferent. He founded a small school of
philosophy.
  BIBL. Diogenes Laertius vii. 160–4.

Aristonicus Pergamene pretender, died 128 BC.
  A possible member of the Attalid royal family (an
illegitimate son of *Eumenes II?), Aristonicus
(Aristonikos) led a large-scale revolt after the death of
*Attalus III and the passing of the Pergamene kingdom to
Rome by his bequest. Anti-Roman sentiment may have
motivated him; perhaps he was one of those claiming that
the will was false. The situation of general social unrest
throughout Asia Minor (the result of the numbers of
unsettled slaves, mercenaries, and metics) was certainly
exploited by Aristonicus, whether in pursuit of genuine
social improvement, or, more selfishly, of the throne of
Pergamum.
  Although Aristonicus had supporters in Pergamum, the
city tried to pacify its population, and his main strength
came from various Greek cities which he induced to revolt

by persuasion or force, and from peasants and slaves. To these he promised economic and social freedom in his ideal State of Heliopolis (City of the Sun). As the revolt spread and Greek cities as well as local dynasts were threatened, Roman envoys returning from Pergamum persuaded the Senate of the danger. Publius Licinius Crassus Dives Mucianus sailed with a large army, eagerly supplemented by Asians who feared Aristonicus (*Nicomedes II of Bithynia, *Ariarathes V of Cappadocia, and Mithridates V of Pontus, among others). Although Crassus was defeated and killed, the next consul attacked and defeated Aristonicus decisively in 130, and starved him into surrender. Pergamum came under Roman control, and Aristonicus was sent to Italy. He was probably strangled in prison in 128, although he might have been led in triumph in 126.

BIBL. Hansen, *Attalids*; Will, *Hist. pol.* ii.

Aristophanes Comic poet, active 427–after 388 BC.

Aristophanes (Aristophanēs) of Athens was the most celebrated poet of Old Comedy (the type produced in the fifth century BC), and his are the only Greek comedies preserved in medieval manuscripts. He must have been born about the middle of the fifth century. Little is known of his life; he seems to have lived on Aegina, or owned property there, at the time of his *Acharnians* (425), and to have been unsuccessfully prosecuted by *Cleon on a charge of traducing the magistrates in his *Babylonians* (426) and on a charge of falsely claiming citizen rights. He is mentioned in an inscription as holding public office.

He wrote about 40 plays, of which some were performed at the Great Dionysia and others at a lesser festival, the Lenaea. The first was the *Banqueters* of 427. Because of his youth he gave his first three plays (*Banqueters, Babylonians, Acharnians*) to another man to produce instead of doing so himself, and for some reason he did the same with some of his later plays; his last two were produced by his son, perhaps after his death. Despite his posthumous reputation, he does not seem to have won first prize particularly often.

Eleven plays survive. Except for *Peace, Lysistrata*, and *Plutus* they are called after the guise in which the chorus first appears. In *Acharnians* (*Men of Acharnae*, a village in Attica; 425) an Athenian makes a private treaty with Sparta (six years after the start of the Peloponnesian War) and enjoys the benefits of peace; characters include *Euripides and *Lamachus. *Knights* (424) is a savage attack on Cleon, who is beaten at his own game by an even viler demagogue. *Clouds* was produced in 423, but what we have is a version partly revised by the author about 418; the play ridicules *Socrates as (remarkably enough) a typical sophist. *Wasps* (422) attacks the alleged passion of the Athenians for serving on juries. *Peace* (421) celebrates the imminent Peace of *Nicias by showing the goddess Peace being brought down to earth. In *Birds* (414) two Athenians found an ideal city, Cloudcuckooland, among the birds. In *Lysistrata* (411) the women of Greece, led by Lysistrata, hold a 'sex strike', and thus compel the men to end the war. In *Thesmophoriazusae* (*Women Celebrating the Thesmophoria*, a women's festival; 411) the women of Athens plot against Euripides on account of his misogyny; characters also include *Agathon. In *Frogs* (405) the god Dionysus descends to the Underworld to fetch back the dead Euripides, but decides, after a contest

between the two tragedians, to fetch back *Aeschylus instead. In *Ecclesiazusae* (*Women Holding an Assembly*; c. 392) the women take control at Athens and institute a 'communist' society (showing some much-discussed resemblances to the ideal 'Republic' of *Plato). In *Plutus* (*Wealth*; 388) the god Wealth is cured of his blindness and so enabled to distribute his blessings according to merit.

Grave-relief of a comic poet, possibly Aristophanes, of c. 380 BC. Stockport, Lyme Park.

It is hardly possible for us to distinguish the characteristics of Aristophanes' work from those of Old Comedy generally. In any case, the most striking feature of the plays is their wild and uninhibited exuberance. The plots are outrageous 'wish-fulfilment' fantasies, which make no concessions to plausibility and not many to internal consistency; by the end they have often degenerated into a succession of slapstick routines. Scene-changes are common and often sketchily indicated, and such 'dramatic illusion' as exists is frequently broken by references to the theatre and the audience. There are no discernible restraints on the explicitness of the sexual and excremental jokes or on the scurrility and unfairness of the attacks on individual Athenians. Subjects for cheerful humour include torture, rape, blindness, and starvation, as well as the ubiquitous casual violence; and yet there are also passages of innocent and whimsical charm (notably in *Birds*). Verbal humour ranges from the feeblest of puns to ingenious parody of tragedy. Honesty, decency, and courage barely exist, the finest quality even of the 'comic hero' being generally a certain shrewd peasant cunning; if we identify with him, it is because he contrives to enact with impunity our more disreputable fantasies.

In Aristophanes' earlier work there are formal conventions governing, in particular, the structure of the *agon* (verbal contest between two characters) and the *parabasis* (the section of the play in which the story is temporarily forgotten and the chorus addresses the audience directly). In the course of his career, however, these conventions are progressively modified and abandoned; *Ecclesiazusae* and *Plutus* have no *parabasis* at all. Indeed these two plays exhibit in many respects the transition from Old to Middle Comedy.

Aristophanes writes for an audience deeply traditional in its attitudes (though capable of laughing at extremes of old-fashioned conservatism). While nothing good is said of any living politician or intellectual, it is the new-fangled ones – the demagogues and the sophists – who attract most vilification (Socrates and Euripides, who also upset traditional assumptions, are treated indiscriminately as sophists).

It is disputed whether the plays express any serious political views. Certainly their *main* purpose is to entertain, but it is possible to discern a consistent political outlook – not oligarchic, but resentful of attempts by the poor or low-born to acquire real power. If we wish to take seriously Aristophanes' attractive devotion to peace, we must be prepared to take this political snobbishness seriously also.

It is unlikely, however, that he had much real influence (Cleon was elected general shortly after a first prize had been awarded to *Knights*). Plato in his *Apology* does hold him partly responsible for popular prejudice against Socrates, but he treats him more indulgently in his *Symposium*; the fact that Aristophanes is there seen at ease in the company of Socrates and Agathon is evidence that his mockery was taken in good part.

BIBL. Lesky, *Greek Literature*; R. G. Ussher, *Aristophanes* (GRNSC xiii, 1979); K. J. Dover, *Aristophanic Comedy* (1972); G. E. M. de Sainte-Croix, *The Origins of the Peloponnesian War* (1972), 232 ff.

Aristophanes of Byzantium Scholar, born *c.* 260 BC.

Successor to *Eratosthenes as librarian at Alexandria (*c.* 200 BC?), Aristophanes (Aristophanēs) was a figure of central importance in its scholarship, consolidating and advancing on all sides the study of Greek poetry that was to be taken over by his great pupil *Aristarchus of Samothrace. He corrected and supplemented *Callimachus' *Pinakes*, and replaced the work of *Zenodotus, *Alexander Aetolus, and *Lycophron with fundamental recensions of *Homer, tragedy, and comedy. By developing analysis of metre he quite outclassed previous editing of lyric poetry, recognizing 'cola' and setting out the text accordingly. Particularly magisterial was his edition of *Pindar. Papyrus discoveries are steadily supplementing our knowledge of his editing: he extended the use of marginal signs to express opinions on the received text, systematized previously sporadic punctuation, and (of momentous consequence) introduced

accentuation. Traces of his methodical scholarship survive in introductions (*hypotheses*) to certain plays. A wealth of learning on dialect and usage was amassed in his great *Lexeis* (*Glossary*). He apparently played a part in the establishment of 'canons' of classical authors, as well as starting some scholarly hares, e.g. ending the *Odyssey* at xxiii.296, and introducing the principle of analogy (see *Crates of Mallos).

BIBL. Pfeiffer, *Classical Scholarship* i.

Aristophon Athenian politician, died early 330s BC.

Aristophon's (Aristophōn) services during the democratic restoration (404/3 BC) earned him *ateleia*, and he may have been ambassador to Sparta in 372/1, but the bulk of his recorded career comes between 363/2 (intervention, as *strategos*, in Ceos) and his death (aged nearly 100) in the 330s. He was chiefly active in the Assembly and law-courts (he allegedly survived 75 *graphai paranomon*); notable items are the attack on *Iphicrates and *Timotheus (2) after Embata (356), support of *Leptines' law (he himself proposed a law aimed at replenishing the public treasury), and isolated opposition to acceptance of the Peace of *Philocrates (346). He was considered a political enemy of *Eubulus (although they agreed about Thebes), but attempts to describe their fundamental political differences are dangerous.

BIBL. Kirchner, *PA*, no. 2108; Davies, *Athenian Families* 64 f.; Sealey, *Essays* 164 ff.; S. I. Oost, *CPhil.* lxxii (1977); C. J. Tuplin, *LCM* ii (1977).

Aristoteles Athenian politician, floruit 370s BC.

Aristoteles (Aristotelēs) proposed an important decree advertising the principles of the Second Athenian Confederacy, and visited Thebes as an ambassador in the same connection (early 377 BC). His 'elegant' forensic speeches failed to survive.

BIBL. Tod, *Inscriptions*, no. 123; Accame, *Lega Ateniese* 48–69.

Aristotle (384–322 BC) Philosopher.

Aristotle (Aristotelēs) was born at Stagira in Chalcidice, the son of a physician. At seventeen he went to Athens, and studied at *Plato's Academy until Plato's death in 347 BC. He then spent some time at Assos on the Asia Minor coast, on Lesbos, and at Pella in Macedonia, where for three years he was tutor to *Alexander – subsequently 'the Great'. In 355 he returned to Athens and established a school in the Lyceum, a public grove. A covered walkway (*peripatos*) where he taught gave its name to his school, the Peripatos. After Alexander's death in 323, Aristotle was charged with 'impiety' and withdrew to Euboea, where he died in 322.

His philosophy cannot be summarized briefly. Its scope is enormous, including logic, scientific method, natural sciences, psychology, philosophy of mind, metaphysics, theology, ethics, politics, literary criticism, and rhetoric, and each of these is discussed in elaborate detail. Moreover, his investigations are sometimes exploratory and inconclusive. Characteristically, he lists opinions that have been held on a subject (e.g. the soul, time, weakness of will) and points to their inconsistency. He then seeks answers that preserve what is best in the opinions, and also explain why the erroneous ones came to be held. This involves drawing subtle distinctions in meaning, and formulating tentative solutions which are scrutinized, and sometimes modified or rejected. Sometimes firm and systematic conclusions are reached, but often questions are left open, or the complexity and ingenuity of the arguments leave unclear just what Aristotle himself thought. A further problem is that, quite often, inconsistent passages are found in the same work, even adjacent to each other. Apparently, different thoughts, perhaps from different periods of his career, have been put together clumsily. (The works that survive may have been Aristotle's own lecture-notes, textbooks, even notes taken by pupils, or they may have been cobbled together by editors from all these sources. Some of them, though, are quite polished.) The following account gives only a rough and incomplete account of some of his views on the questions that most absorbed him.

Portrait of Aristotle. Vienna, Kunsthistorisches Museum.

Logic was not a science, in Aristotle's view, but a tool (*organon*) to be used in all sciences. He was the first to develop a systematic theory of logic. This was based on the syllogism, a form of argument in which all scientific explanation should ultimately be presented. He has been criticized both by ancient Stoics and by modern logicians for the narrowness of his logic (there are many valid forms of argument other than syllogisms), but, within its limits, his pioneering work remains impressive. A more serious complaint is that science must be pursued (and indeed was pursued by Aristotle) with empirical research, and

with forms of speculative or dialectical reasoning which do not seem to involve syllogisms. But it seems clear that Aristotle meant the syllogism to be the form in which a *completed* science was to be ideally presented. The struggles that precede its completion may take many different forms.

His 'natural philosophy' embraces subjects that would now be thought to belong to many different disciplines. The *Physics* is concerned with, among other subjects, the different kinds of 'causes' (i.e. the different sorts of explanation we can give of things); with philosophical problems about change; and with the analysis of such concepts as time, place, and the infinite. *De Anima* and other 'psychological' works investigate problems of the relation between body and mind, and of perception and its relation to thought. The biological works contain evidence of extensive research (Aristotle organized the acquisition of data on an impressive scale), and of attempts to determine the correct methods of classifying and defining species.

Metaphysics was, for Aristotle, the most general of all sciences: the study of *being*, i.e. of what there *is*, and what it means for things to *be* or *exist*. (He called this science 'First Philosophy'; 'Metaphysics' meant simply 'After Physics' in the systematic order of sciences.) He divided things into 'Categories' – substance, quality, quantity, position, time, action, and a few others. Since no single account of 'being' can apply to things in more than one category, he concentrates on the first category, substance. Substance is *first* because the other categories depend on it for their existence (every quality is a quality of a substance, every action the action of a substance, and so on), and the 'being' of things in other categories can be explained in terms of that of substance. Aristotle's exceedingly difficult investigation of substance concludes that concrete individual things are substances, especially those that are members of natural species (individual men, trees, etc.). (This contrasts with Plato's belief that 'Forms' were the primary entities.) However, he goes on to argue (in *Metaphysics* xii) that there is another substance which, unlike men and trees, is eternal and unchanging. This is the 'Unmoved Mover', by which the perpetual movements of the universe are explained. It is portrayed as a self-contemplating intelligence, and is Aristotle's God.

Ethics is practical philosophy, and its purpose is to determine what sort of life a man should live. For Aristotle, the good life for man is one of performing *well*, or in accordance with virtues, those activities that are characteristic of men. He discusses man's virtues in great detail, those of character, such as courage, liberality, and temperance (each of which he says lies at a 'mean' point between two 'extreme' vices), and those of the intellect. The latter involve him in an investigation of practical reasoning, and the connected problem of whether it is possible to act against one's better judgement – perhaps the hardest and most impressive sections of his ethical works. Politics form part of ethics, since man achieves a good life only in a society, indeed (Aristotle assumes) only in a Greek-style city-state (*polis*). His conception of the State as *natural*, with natural roles for women and slaves, makes the *Politics* one of his less endearing books to modern readers.

Later ancient and medieval commentators eventually gave Aristotle's philosophy the status of a complete and authoritative system. No doubt Aristotle was aiming for that, but he did not achieve it, and it is often when his intellectual efforts are least conclusive that they are most impressive.

BIBL. R. McKeon (ed.) *The Basic Works of Aristotle;* W. D. Ross *Aristotle* (6th ed., 1955); I. Düring, *Aristoteles* (1966).

Aristoxenus Philosopher, born 375/60 BC.

Born at Tarentum in southern Italy, Aristoxenus (Aristoxenos) became a pupil of *Aristotle in Athens, and wrote, it was said, 453 works on many subjects. His fame rests on his influential work on musical theory. Parts of his *Elements of Harmonics* (three books on the theory of scales) and part of a work on rhythm survive. Although influenced by *Pythagorean theory, he rejected the view that consonant intervals were to be determined only mathematically, believing that the ear was a proper test. He may have held that the soul is an 'attunement' of the body, a belief perhaps devised by *Philolaus.

BIBL. R. da Rios, *Aristoxeni Elementa Harmonica* (1954).

Arsaces I King and founder of the Parthian dynasty, *c.* 239(?)–before 209 BC.

After the Seleucid satrap of Parthyene declared independence *c.* 245 during the fraternal war between *Seleucus II and *Antiochus Hierax, he was invaded and defeated by the barbarian Arsaces (Arsakēs), possibly in 239–238 when his neighbour *Diodotus I of Bactria made more trouble in the area by also declaring independence. Arsaces gathered a great army from fear of Seleucid revenge and of the threat of Diodotus, but an alliance was concluded with the Bactrian's successor Diodotus II, for mutual security. The anticipated expedition against him by Seleucus may have taken place *c.* 230(?)–*c.* 227(?), and Arsaces was victorious – the day from which the Parthians reckoned their freedom. Arsaces was thus firmly established in a part of the former Seleucid territory, but died before the arrival of *Antiochus III in 209.

From this beginning the royal dynasty of Parthia grew into a world power. The 37 or so successors of Arsaces took his name as an official royal title.

BIBL. Will, *Hist. pol.* i; N. C. Debevoise, *A Political History of Parthia* (1938); J. Wolski, *Historia* viii (1959), 222 ff., xi (1962), 138 ff., and *Berytus* xi (1956/7), 35 ff.

Arsinoë I Queen of Egypt, *c.* 289/8(?)–*c.* 281(?) BC.

Arsinoë (Arsinoē), the daughter of *Lysimachus of Thrace and Nicaea, became *Ptolemy II's first queen in a dynastic marriage which probably either cemented the treaty between their fathers in 289 BC or acknowledged Ptolemy's association with his father on the throne in 285. After bearing three children (including the heir *Ptolemy III and *Berenice Syra), she was repudiated sometime after Lysimachus' death in 281, probably before 279 (although perhaps later at the instigation of *Arsinoë II), on charges of treason. She faded to total obscurity in Upper Egypt.

BIBL. Macurdy, *Hellenistic Queens*; Scholia on Theocritus xvii. 128; W. W. Tarn, *JHS* lv (1933), 60.

Arsinoë II Philadelphus Queen of Egypt, before *c.* 273–270 BC.

The daughter of *Ptolemy I and *Berenice I, Arsinoë (Arsinoē) was married to *Lysimachus of Thrace, and may

have conspired in the death of his son *Agathocles, which left her own three sons as the heirs. Widowed by Lysimachus' defeat at Corupedium in 281 BC, Arsinoë fled the breakup of his kingdom, hoping to establish her sons on the Macedonian throne. To this end, she married her half-brother *Ptolemy Ceraunus who claimed that throne, but he killed her two younger sons. When he died in 279, Arsinoë supported the claims to the Macedonian throne of her remaining son Ptolemaeus, which were dashed in 276 when *Antigonus Gonatas gained supremacy. Arsinoë returned to Egypt and married her full brother *Ptolemy II before 273, probably shortly after *c.* 276.

Portrait head of Arsinoë II Philadelphus, queen of Egypt. Alexandria, Graeco-Roman Museum.

A mature woman of experience and intelligence, Arsinoë had great power as sister, queen, and co-regent. After the First Syrian War (*c.* 274–271), won largely through her diplomatic skill, she was granted extraordinary honours and was deified as Arsinoë 'Philadelphus' (She Who Loves Her Brother). She formed around her a notable coterie of statesmen and men of letters, including the admiral Callicrates and the poet *Callimachus. She was worshipped as a goddess after her death, and her ideas on foreign policy influenced Ptolemy at least publicly until the War of *Chremonides.

BIBL. Will, *Hist. pol.* i; *CAH* vii. 704–5; Tarn, *Antigonos Gonatas.*

Arsinoë III Philopator Queen of Egypt, 221–204 BC.

The daughter of *Ptolemy III and *Berenice III, Arsinoë (Arsinoē) the 'Father-loving' was married to her full brother *Ptolemy IV. She is mentioned in the autobiography of *Eratosthenes as a cultivated woman

Marble portrait head of Arsinoë III Philopator, queen of Egypt. Boston, Museum of Fine Arts.

who found her husband's extravagances and debauchery disgusting. Probably because of her potential good influence on the king, she was sent away from court at an uncertain date by his manipulative ministers *Agathocles and *Sosibius. She endured replacement by the former's sister Agathoclea, through whom Agathocles' influence over the king could be strengthened. Ptolemy died unexpectedly in 204 BC; some days later the ministers had Arsinoë murdered, since she was the natural regent for her son *Ptolemy V, and would certainly have engineered their downfall.

BIBL. Will, *Hist. pol.* ii; *FGrH* 241 T 16 (Eratosthenes).

Artabazus

Several prominent Persians are found bearing this name in the 5th century BC. They all appear to have belonged to a family which provided the hereditary rulers of the Phrygian satrapy.

An Artabazus (Artabazos), son of Pharnaces, commanded the Parthian and Chorasmian units in *Xerxes' expedition of 480, and led the Persian army back to Asia after *Mardonius' death at Plataea. He may have been identical with the Artabazus who, together with Megabyzus, put down the rebellion of *Inarus in Egypt, fought *Cimon in Cyprus, and negotiated the Peace of *Callias (son of Hipponicus (1)) in 449.

BIBL. Olmstead, *Persian Empire*, chs. 18–19.

Artabazus, son of Pharnabazus Persian satrap, 4th century BC.

A grandson of *Artaxerxes II and son of *Pharnabazus, Artabazus (Artabazos) fought against *Datames and then briefly rebelled himself. A second revolt under *Artaxerxes III failed, despite Athenian and Theban help,

and he fled to Macedonia (c. 352 BC). *Mentor secured his return (c. 342), and on *Darius III's death he became *Alexander the Great's satrap of Bactria, but retired in 328.

BIBL. PW ii. 1299–1300; Hammond and Griffith, *Macedonia* ii.

Artaphernes (or Artaphrenes)

Artaphernes (Artaphernēs, or Artaphrenēs: Persian Vi(n)dafarnah) was the name of several prominent Persians of the late sixth and fifth centuries BC:

Artaphernes (1) was the half-brother of *Darius I. After the Scythian expedition of 513 he was appointed governor of Sardis, which he successfully defended against the Ionian Greeks in 498 during their revolt against Persia.

Artaphernes (2), son of Artaphernes (1), was the Persian commander at the battle of Marathon in 490 (see *Miltiades).

Artaphernes (3) was a Persian ambassador to Sparta in 425. He was captured by the Athenians and taken back to Ephesus.

BIBL. Olmstead, *Persian Empire*, ch. 11; J. A. S. Evans, *CPhil.* lxxi (1976) (Artaphernes (1)). Herodotus vi. 94–119 (Artaphernes (2)). Thucydides iv. 50 (Artaphernes (3)).

Artaxerxes I Macrocheir King of Persia, 464–424 BC.

The second son of *Xerxes, Artaxerxes (Artaxerxēs) 'Long-arm' came to the throne after he had killed his elder brother and his father's assassin Artabanus. An Egyptian revolt led by *Inarus was suppressed by the generals *Artabazus and Megabyzus in 454 BC. Repeated Athenian interference in Cyprus led to a Persian defeat at Salamis in 449; subsequently the 'Peace of *Callias' (son of Hipponicus (1)) brought an end to hostilities with Athens. Despite Spartan appeals for support during the early years of the Peloponnesian War (see *Artaphrenes (3)), Artaxerxes avoided involvement in Greek affairs.

BIBL. Olmstead, *Persian Empire*, chs. 21–2.

Artaxerxes II Mnemon King of Persia, 405–359 BC.

Despite his mother's favour for *Cyrus the Younger, Artaxerxes (Artaxerxēs) the 'Mindful' succeeded *Darius II and in 401 BC crushed Cyrus' rebellion at Cunaxa. He is perhaps best known for the 'King's Peace' of 386 (*alias* the Peace of *Antalcidas). His long reign is otherwise marked by repeated failure to reconquer Egypt, a weak settlement with the rebel *Evagoras of Cyprus, an unsuccessful war with the Cadusii, an era of satrapal revolt starting in the late 370s, and a plot on his life by his son Darius.

BIBL. Plutarch, *Artaxerxes*; Olmstead, *Persian Empire* 371–429 (with caution).

Artaxerxes III Ochus King of Persia, 359/8–338/7 BC.

Artaxerxes Ochus (Artaxerxēs Ōkhos) is mainly notable for the reconquest of Egypt after over 60 years of independence (343 BC). Earlier, his order to disband satrapal mercenary forces was generally obeyed, and his angry complaints about *Chares frightened the Athenians into climbing down (355). He was evidently a personality of unusual forcefulness and ability, but this did not save him from being poisoned by *Bagoas.

BIBL. Olmstead, *Persian Empire*; Hammond and Griffith, *Macedonia* ii.

Artemidorus of Ephesus Geographer, floruit *c.* 150–100 BC?

A scholar who based his work on personal research and secondary literary sources, Artemidorus (Artemidōros) was interested in both the physical geography and the anthropology of the lands he studied. He was himself a well-travelled man: sent on an embassy to Rome from Ephesus, he later visited Spain, the coasts of the Mediterranean, parts of the Atlantic coast, Egypt, Arabia, the Red Sea, and Ethiopia. He gave careful attention to the measurement of coastlines, distances, navigation, and the main routes of travel through countries. He used his secondary geographical sources variously, from consulting and copying *Agatharchides of Cnidos to correcting *Eratosthenes. His research culminated in a work in eleven books on the whole inhabited world: Europe (books i–vi), Libya (vii), Asia and Egypt (viii–xi). His work was much admired by the ancients, and he was *Strabo's main source for Spain and Portugal. His book was excerpted by a Christian writer and condensed into one book.

BIBL. E. H. Bunbury, *A History of Ancient Geography* (1883); H. Berger, *Geschichte der wissenschaftlichen Erdkunde der Griechen* (2nd ed., 1903); PW ii. 1329.

Artemisia I Carian queen, *c.* 480 BC.

Queen Artemisia was ruling Halicarnassus, Cos, Nisyrus, and Calyndria on behalf of her son at the time of *Xerxes' invasion of Greece. *Herodotus, a close relative, tells with pride of her heroic deeds at Salamis.

BIBL. Herodotus vii. 99; viii. 68 f., 87 f.

Asclepiades of Prusa Physician, early 1st century BC.

Asclepiades (Asklēpiadēs) left his native Bithynia to study for a rhetorical career in Athens, before settling down as an influential doctor at Rome. An independent-minded *Erasistratean, he brought to medicine an adherence to *Democritean atomism (maintaining that the atoms of the body should be kept in proper healthy motion) and a rejection of *Hippocratic humours, forging an eclectic and practical theory to which he added pleasant therapies (including abundant wine) and a good bedside manner. A thoroughly civilized man, he died at a ripe age popular and highly successful.

BIBL. PW ii. 1632–3; J. Scarborough, *Roman Medicine* (1969).

Asclepiades of Samos Epigrammatist, *c.* 300 BC.

Asclepiades (Asklēpiadēs), is revered by *Theocritus in his seventh idyll under his alias, or possibly his real name, 'Sicelidas'. Senior Hellenistic epigrammatist (he must also have used the metre called after him 'Asclepiads') and general literary arbiter, he gave his seal of approval to *Erinna (epigram 28) and *Antimachus (32). Asclepiades freed the epigram from its traditional inscriptional form, though that too is brilliantly used – e.g. for a poignant epitaph (31), or a *double entendre* dedication (6) – and made it the vehicle for lively vignettes presented as personal experience, drawing early symposium poetry into the compactness of his urbanely polished couplets. The epigrams are mostly erotic, encapsulating brief encounters with girls compliant and fickle; Asclepiades, an easy sensualist, accepts love's bitter-sweetness. He stands at the beginning of long chains of imitation and variation (by *Poseidippus (q.v.), *Callimachus, and others), and of the process of crystallizing into sharp, many-faceted convention the love-imagery of earlier poets: fire, torture, and the boy Eros – precocious, captivating, irrational, cruel. His *komos* epigrams (among those which show the clear influence of mime and comedy) also establish the lover-locked-out-on-the-doorstep as part of the package handed over to the Roman love poets.

BIBL. Gow and Page, *Hellenistic Epigrams.*

Asclepiodotus Military theorist, 1st century BC.

A few nuggets of historical value, possibly deriving from *Polybius, are preserved in the rigidly boring pages of Asclepiodotus' (Asklēpiodotos) treatise on obsolete military tactics, extant with diagrams. 'Asclepiodotus the philosopher' writes from duty to a certified branch of knowledge, not from interest or experience, probably regurgitating a work of his master *Pos(e)idonius.

BIBL. Loeb edition with Aeneas Tacticus (1923).

Asius Hexameter and elegiac poet, *c.* 500 BC (?)

From Samos, where fragment 13 depicts, perhaps satirically, the pomp of a religious procession, Asius (Asios) is also represented by twelve genealogical fragments and four elegiac lines on a beggar at the wedding of Meles (*Homer's father?). Dates from 600 to 400 are offered.

BIBL. Kinkel, *EGF* 202–6; Huxley, *Epic Poetry* 89 ff.; Bowra, *Greek Margins* 122 ff.

Aśoka King of the Mauryas, 269–232 BC.

Aśoka (or Ashoka), the Indian ruler and missionary of Buddhism, was the grandson of *Sandracottus

The palaestra at Ai Khanum, Afghanistan; one of many sites which reflect the extent of Greek influence in Asia (see Aśoka).

(Chandragupta) (q.v.) and served as viceroy in Taxila before himself acceding. He maintained contacts with several Hellenistic kings. Pliny records that *Ptolemy II sent an envoy to him, and in Aśoka's thirteenth Rock Edict, dated to *c.* 256 BC, ambassadors are mentioned to Ptolemy, *Antiochus II, *Antigonus Gonatas, *Magas of Cyrene, and *Alexander (of Corinth or Molossia). Another edict from Kandahar, preserved in a bilingual and a Greek version, extols the Buddhist doctrines of piety, obedience, and vegetarianism. After Aśoka's death the Mauryan empire declined, and finally split apart.

BIBL. J. W. Sedlar, *India and the Greek World* (1980); R. Thapar, *Aśoka and the Decline of the Mauryas* (1961), and *A History of India* (1968) i; *SEG* xx. 326; *Roman World* *Pliny the Elder.

Aspasia Wife of Pericles from *c.* 450/445 BC.

Aspasia was a Milesian who married the widowed *Pericles *c.* 450/445 BC. She had philosophical interests, and was highly regarded in the circle of *Socrates. As the wife of Athens' leading citizen, she was subject to unfounded abuse by the comic dramatists: *Eupolis in the *Demes* called her a *hetaira*, *Hermippus accused her of impiety. She was made responsible for Athenian intervention on behalf of Miletus against Samos in 441/40, and for the Megarian Decree discriminating against Megarian trade (432). Later biographical tradition held that in the 430s, when there was increasing resentment of Pericles' impregnable political position, she was prosecuted for impiety (like the philosopher *Anaxagoras).

Head of a woman, inscribed 'Aspasia', from a site near Civitavecchia. Roman period copy of a 5th-century BC Greek original. Vatican Museum.

Since she came from Miletus, her son, also called Pericles, was not born an Athenian citizen. After the deaths of Pericles' sons by his first wife in the plague (430), he was given a special grant of citizenship; he served as *strategos* at Arginusae (406), and was executed with the other *strategoi* after the battle (see *Theramenes).

BIBL. Plutarch, *Pericles* 24, 32; Davies, *Athenian Families*, no. 11811 IV.

Astydamas (1) and (2) Tragedians, 4th century BC.

The two Athenian tragedians called Astydamas (Astudamas) were father and son. The father produced his first play in 398 BC. The son probably won his first victory in 372, and was still active in 340.

BIBL. T. B .L. Webster, *Hermes* lxxxii (1954), 302 ff.; Xanthakis-Karamanos, *Fourth-Century Tragedy*.

Astyochus Spartan admiral, 412/11 BC.

After the destruction of the Athenian expedition to Sicily in 413 BC, various Athenian subject states in the Aegean revolted; the Spartans sent out a fleet under Astyochus (Astuokhos) in their support. He first operated successfully off Chios and Lesbos, then set up a base at Miletus. With the help of *Alcibiades he won the support of the Persian *Tissaphernes. But the Spartans were dissatisfied with his generalship, and his own forces mutinied.

BIBL. Westlake, *Individuals in Thucydides*, ch. 15.

Atossa Queen of Persia, late 6th to early 5th century BC.

Atossa was *Cyrus' daughter and, according to *Herodotus, wife of her brother *Cambyses (524 BC); after his death, she married first the pretender supported by the clerical faction (the 'False Smerdis'), and then the successful candidate, *Darius (I). Atossa was powerful enough to ensure the succession of her son *Xerxes in 486. She is a major character in *Aeschylus' *Persians* (performed in 472).

BIBL. Olmstead, *Persian Empire*, chs. 8, 16.

Attalus I Soter King of Pergamum, 241–197 BC.

The adopted son of *Eumenes I, Attalus (Attalos)

Marble portrait head of Attalus I Soter, from Pergamum. Berlin, Staatliche Antikensammlung.

The reconstructed Stoa built in the Athenian Agora by Attalus II Philadelphus, king of Pergamum.

inherited the dynasty, and soon received the titles 'King' and 'Soter' (Saviour) for his brilliant successes against the Gauls (Galatians) before 230 BC. In the Seleucid civil war between *Seleucus II and *Antiochus Hierax, Attalus defeated Antiochus and his Gallic mercenaries in 228 and won control of much Seleucid territory, maintaining it (possibly with Ptolemaic help) against the later attempts of *Seleucus III to recover it. *Achaeus, in revolt against *Antiochus III, deprived Pergamum of this territory and more, but by 213 Attalus had joined in suppressing this revolt. Attalus was by now married to *Apollonis of Cyzicus, by whom he had four sons.

As an ally of the Aetolian League and Rome against *Philip V of Macedon, Attalus' forces saw action during the First Macedonian War in 208. He returned to defend his kingdom against harassment by *Prusias I of Bithynia. In 201 Attalus and Rhodes defeated Philip in a sea-battle off Chios. After entering Athens triumphantly in 200, Attalus fought in the Cyclades, Chalcidice, and Euboea in the Second Macedonian War, and gained for Pergamum Andros and Aegina. A second campaign in 198 saw the completed conquest of Euboea and an attempt, with *Flamininus, to reason with *Nabis of Sparta. Attalus was struck with paralysis in Thebes in 197; he was taken back to Pergamum, where he died some months later.

BIBL. *Roman World*; Hansen, *Attalids*.

Attalus II Philadelphus King of Pergamum, 159–138 BC.

Attalus (Attalos) justifiably bore the title 'Philadelphus' (Loving his Brother) for his loyal service to *Eumenes II before succeeding him. He commanded Pergamene forces for Rome against the Gauls in 189–188 BC, and won massive booty. In 178 Attalus studied philosophy with *Carneades in Athens, along with the future *Ariarathes V of Cappadocia. When Eumenes' death was mistakenly

announced, Attalus assumed control and courted (if he did not actually marry) the 'widow' Stratonice – actions precipitate and near treason, but comprehensible and forgiven by Eumenes. Attalus fought with L. Aemilius *Paullus at Pydna in 168 and earned favour at Rome. He became joint ruler with his ailing brother in 161, since his nephew was a minor.

Succeeding in 159 at the age of 61, he legally married Stratonice. By 157 he had helped restore Ariarathes V to his rightful throne when that had been usurped, and in 156 he was forced into war by *Prusias II of Bithynia. He was in danger of defeat when Rome obtained peace in 154. Attalus placed *Alexander Balas on the Seleucid throne in 150 when *Demetrius I had caused Ariarathes' throne to be threatened again, and he finally rid himself of the plague of Prusias by replacing him with his son *Nicomedes II. He aided Rome against the Macedonian pretender *Andriscus, and sent a force under *Philopoemen to *Mummius at Corinth in 146. The art collection at Pergamum was substantially increased from Corinth's spoils. His last campaign was in 145 against Diegylis, a Thracian chieftain. He died in 138, still a friend to Rome.

BIBL. *Roman World*; Hansen, *Attalids*.

Attalus III Philometor King of Pergamum, 138–133 BC.

The reign and personality of the last Pergamene king Attalus (Attalos) the 'Mother-loving', the son of *Eumenes II and successor of *Attalus II, remain an enigma. Varying interpretations of the conflicting ancient sources present him as a popular benefactor who was well-disposed towards his people, or as a cruel, suspicious torturer of friends and officials. His zoological, botanical, and pharmacological preoccupations are well attested, whether their practical applications were for good or evil;

other interests included games, metalworking, and sculpture.

Attalus is best known for his will bequeathing Pergamum to Rome. His motives for this are not certain, but may have included recognition of the inevitability of Rome's control over Pergamum, the search for a means of defence against social unrest over the succession, or, least likely, rancour against his subjects or a putative successor. In any event, his action ended the dynasty of the rulers who have been called 'the jackals of Rome' (Tarn).

BIBL. Hansen, *Attalids*; *OGIS* 338.

Attalus Macedonian general, died 336 BC.

Attalus' (Attalos) prayer that *Philip II and *Cleopatra-Eurydice would have legitimate issue occasioned a violent quarrel between Philip and *Alexander in 337 BC. In 336 he and his father-in-law *Parmenion began the invasion of Asia Minor, but after Philip's murder he was liquidated for allegedly treasonable correspondence with the Athenians.

BIBL. Berve, *Alexanderreich*, no. 182; Hammond and Griffith, *Macedonia* ii. 676 ff.

'Attic Orators'

A list, probably originating with Alexandrian scholars or school-teachers, was made of the ten most widely read Athenian orators of the late fifth and fourth centuries BC. They are: *Antiphon, *Andocides, *Lysias, *Isocrates, *Isaeus, *Lycurgus, *Aeschines, *Demosthenes, *Hyper(e)ides, and *D(e)inarchus. The canon first appears in a work of *Caecilius of Calacte.

BIBL. Plutarch, *Lives of the Ten Orators* (Loeb vol. x,

1927); Kennedy, *Art of Persuasion*; R. C. Jebb, *The Attic Orators* (1893).

Autolycus of Pitane Astronomer, late 4th century BC.

Autolycus (Autolukos) applied the geometry of spheres to questions of astronomy. His works *On the Moving Spheres* and *On Risings and Settings* are the earliest complete treatises on Greek mathematics that have survived. In the latter, he distinguishes the true risings and settings of stars (as calculated mathematically) from their visible risings and settings.

BIBL. Heath, *Greek Mathematics* i. 348–53.

Bacchylides Lyric poet, active *c*. 485–*c*. 450 BC.

Like his uncle(?) *Simonides, Bacchylides (Bakkhulidēs) came from Ceos, though he is said to have lived in exile in the Peloponnese. He wrote much the same kinds of lyric poetry as his contemporary *Pindar: dithyrambs, paeans, hymns, processional songs, maidens' songs, dance-songs, victory-songs, love-songs, and encomia. He is also credited with some epigrams.

Little was known of his work until 1896, when a papyrus was found containing remains of 20 poems, several of them virtually complete. 14 are victory-odes, similar in form and function to those of Pindar but very different in style, sacrificing Pindaric grandeur and concentrated power in favour of fluency and lucid elegance. The most interesting, perhaps, are poems iii and v, both written for *Hieron I of Syracuse, the former telling the story of *Croesus and the latter describing a meeting between Heracles and Meleager in the Underworld.

The Sanctuary at Olympia, site of the Olympic Games; some of the victors were celebrated by the poets Bacchylides and *Pindar.

The remaining six poems were written for various purposes on mythical subjects; ancient editors apparently classed them as dithyrambs, but Bacchylides himself may not have done so. The most interesting of these are perhaps poems xvii and xviii, both concerned with **Theseus, the latter having the form of a dramatic dialogue.

There is some evidence that Hieron preferred Bacchylides to Pindar. The critic Longinus, however, made the opposite judgement, and most modern critics agree with him.

BIBL. Lesky, *Greek Literature*; *Lyra Graeca* (Loeb) iii; J. Stern (essay in English) in *Pindaros und Bakchylides*, ed. W. M. Calder and J. Stern (1970); *Roman World* *Longinus.

Bagoas Persian kingmaker, died *c.* 336 BC.

Bagoas (Bagōas) was a eunuch who poisoned *Artaxerxes III (whose trusted agent he had been) and replaced him first with Arses (Artaxerxes IV), whom he proceeded to murder, and then with *Darius III, who escaped a similar fate by killing him. His life-style and ambitious opportunism made him an *exemplum* of moral turpitude.

BIBL. PW ii. 2771–2.

Bardylis Illyrian king from *c.* 400 BC.

Bardylis (Bardulis) created a considerable Dardanian state in southern Yugoslavia, extending to the borders of classical Macedonia. He troubled *Amyntas III, and his defeat of *Perdiccas III (360/59 BC) precipitated a crisis from which Macedonia was saved as much by Bardylis' failure to press the advantage as by his subsequent defeat by *Philip II near Monastir.

BIBL. N. Hammond, *BSA* lxi (1966); Hammond and Griffith, *Macedonia* ii.

Barsine Mistress of Alexander the Great, died 309 BC.

Barsine (Barsinē), daughter of *Artabazus (son of Pharnabazus) and widow of *Mentor and *Memnon, was captured at Damascus (333 BC), became *Alexander's mistress, and bore him a son Heracles (327). On Alexander's marriage to *Roxane, she retired to Pergamum. 18 years later (309) *Polyperchon murdered Heracles and his mother after abandoning a plan to make the former king of Macedonia.

BIBL. Berve, *Alexanderreich*, no. 206; P. A. Brunt, *RFIC* ciii (1975).

Battiads Kings of Cyrene.

The descendants of *Battus (q.v.) and kings of Cyrene, the Battiads (Battiadai) bore the names Battus (Battos) and Arcesilaus (Arkesilaos, or Arkesilas) in alternate generations. Under Battus II (*c.* 583 BC) the expansion of Cyrene caused a war with the native Libyans and their Egyptian allies. His sons quarrelled over the succession, and some of them founded a new city at Barce, and incited the Libyans to attack Cyrene. Battus III called in Demonax of Mantinea to devise a new constitution for Cyrene, which limited the privileges of the king (*c.* 550). Battus' son Arcesilaus III refused to accept this and was forced into exile (*c.* 530), but returned and conquered Cyrene. He treated his opponents with extreme cruelty, and was eventually assassinated. His mother Pheretime appealed to

King Arcesilaus II superintending the weighing of produce. Painting on a Laconian cup from Vulci, in Etruria. Paris, Bibliothèque Nationale.

the Persian governor of Egypt, and, since Arcesilaus had paid tribute to *Cambyses, the Persians invaded Libya, capturing Barce but not Cyrene itself. The last Battiad king, Arcesilaus IV, won a victory at the Pythian Games (462), which was celebrated by *Pindar. He was overthrown by a democratic revolution in 440.

BIBL. Herodotus iv. 159–67, 200–5; Pindar *Pythian Odes* iv–v; Boardman, *Greeks Overseas* 155–6; F. Chamoux, *Cyrène sous la Monarchie des Battiades* (1953).

Battus Founder of Cyrene, *c.* 630 BC.

A native of Thera, Battus (Battos) was chosen by the Delphic oracle to lead a colonizing expedition to Libya. After various adventures they settled first on an offshore island and then on the mainland, calling their city Cyrene. Battus became its first king, and reigned for 40 years (see *Battiads). The account of the foundation given by *Herodotus is interesting for the light it throws on Delphi's role in the setting up of colonies: it was only under considerable pressure from the oracle that the Therans were persuaded to undertake colonization at all.

BIBL. Herodotus iv. 150–8; Boardman, *Greeks Overseas* 153–5.

Berenice I (*c.* 340–before *c.* 275 BC) Queen of Egypt.

The widow of a Macedonian, Berenice (Berenikē) accompanied to Egypt her relative Eurydice, the first queen of *Ptolemy I. Often wrongly considered Ptolemy's half-sister, Berenice gradually supplanted Eurydice in the

Coin portrait of Berenice I, Ptolemaic queen (enlarged).

king's affections and as his queen. Their children
*Ptolemy II and *Arsinoë II inherited the throne, and
Berenice's previous children were *Magas of Cyrene and a
wife of *Pyrrhus of Epirus. After her death Berenice was
deified and worshipped with her husband as the 'Theoi
Soteres', 'Saviour Gods'.

BIBL. Macurdy, *Hellenistic Queens*; Theocritus xvii.

Berenice II Euergetis Queen of Egypt, 246–221 BC.

The daughter of *Magas of Cyrene and Apama, Berenice
(Berenikē) was betrothed to the future *Ptolemy III in
honour of their fathers' reconciliation. When Magas died,
the marriage was to have united Egypt and Cyrene, but
Apama stopped the unification by breaking the
engagement and inviting the Macedonian *Demetrius the
Fair to be Cyrene's king and Berenice's husband. The
princess's strong character rebelled when a love affair
began between her mother and Demetrius: she had him
slain, although she spared her mother's life. Her betrothal
to Ptolemy was confirmed, and the marriage took place on
the death of *Ptolemy II in 246 BC. (Her title means
'Benefactor'.)

Coin portrait of Berenice II Euergetis, Ptolemaic queen (enlarged).

When Ptolemy left for Syria to support his sister
*Berenice Syra, his wife dedicated a lock of hair for his
return. The poet *Callimachus, in the *Lock of Berenice*,
recorded how the apotheosized lock was found among the
constellations by the astronomer *Conon of Samos.
Berenice's children included *Ptolemy IV and *Arsinoë
III. She became joint ruler with her son after her
husband's death (222/1), but was murdered, probably by
the ministers *Agathocles and *Sosibius.

BIBL. Callimachus, fr. 110 (Pfeiffer); Macurdy,
Hellenistic Queens; Will, *Hist. pol.* i.

Berenice Syra Seleucid queen, *c.* 253–*c.* 246 BC.

A daughter of *Ptolemy II and *Arsinoe I, Berenice
(Berenikē) 'Syra' ('the Syrian') was married to the Seleucid
king *Antiochus II *c.* 253 BC. The union, aided by a
magnificent dowry, signalled a *rapprochement* between the
bride's father and husband after the Second Syrian War
(begun in 260); but it entailed the renunciation of
Antiochus' first wife, *Laodice, while Berenice was
established at Antioch, where she bore a son. When
Antiochus died in 246, the sons of both queens were
proclaimed king; each was backed by strong supporters,

and the half-Ptolemaic prince had the additional aid of his
uncle *Ptolemy III, who came with a large army on his
behalf. Berenice and her son were murdered at Laodice's
instigation before help arrived, and the war of vengeance
which followed between Egypt and Syria was known as
the Third Syrian, or Laodicean, War (246–241).

BIBL. *CAH* vii. 715 ff.; Bevan, *House of Seleucus* i.
178 ff.; *Select Papyri* (Loeb) i. 93.

Bessus Persian satrap of Bactria, 4th century BC.

Bessus (Bēssos) organized the murder of *Darius III
(330 BC) and proclaimed himself king (as Artaxerxes V),
but his attempt to mount effective resistance to
*Alexander the Great foundered, and he was betrayed
and captured in 329. Alexander's desire to appear as
Darius' avenger and legitimate successor was served by
Bessus' subjection to public indignity, torture, and
execution.

BIBL. Berve, *Alexanderreich*, no. 212; Bosworth, *Arrian*.

Bias Ionian statesman, 6th century BC.

Bias of Priene was one of the *Seven Sages. Like other
members of the group, he distinguished himself in public
affairs, especially in negotiations between the Ionians and
Lydia. After the Persian conquest, he advised the Ionians
to emigrate *en masse* and found a new, free city in
Sardinia.

BIBL. Herodotus i. 27, 170; Diogenes Laertius i. 82 ff.;
Plutarch, *Moralia* 296a (*Greek Questions* 20).

'Portrait' herm of Bias, inscribed with his most famous saying:
'Most men are bad'. From a villa near Tivoli. Vatican Museum.

Bion Pastoral poet, *c.* 100 BC (?).

Little is securely known of Bion (Bíōn) from Phlossa near Smyrna, third – after *Theocritus and *Moschus – in the *Suda*'s list of pastoral poets. The *Lament for Bion* by an unknown disciple (*not* Moschus, as manuscripts assert) claims that he was poisoned, casting him – in extension of Theocritus' first idyll – as a dead herdsman in a Sicilian landscape, which presumably represents his spiritual home in pastoral-land rather than biographical fact. Clear echoes in this *Lament* guarantee the ascription to Bion of the anonymously preserved *Lament for Adonis*, a luxuriantly emotional and imaginative poem bewailing the death of Aphrodite's lover amid sympathetic nature. 17 little pieces (some apparently complete) anthologized by Stobaeus from the *Bucolica* are sweet in style and mostly prettily erotic or sententious in content. The Vienna bucolic fragment has been reasonably assigned to Bion.

BIBL. Gow, *Bucolici Graeci* and *Bucolic Poets*; Gallavotti, *RFIC* xix (1941).

Bion of Borysthenes Wandering philosopher, born *c.* 325 BC (?)

In Diogenes Laertius, Bion (Bíōn), from Olbia, otherwise known as Borysthenes, on the Black Sea, sketches a colourful autobiography: freedman father, prostitute mother, sold as slave to a rhetorician, inheritor of his master's fortune. He is describing himself to *Antigonus Gonatas, who is reputed to have helped him when he was old and ill in Chalcis (Euboea). A hostile biographical tradition portrays Bion as vulgar and abrasive. After eclectic study in Athens, where he was chiefly influenced by the Cynic *Crates of Thebes, he took to the road as a tub-thumping popular philosopher. The diatribe style he developed, influential, for example, on Horace's moral satire, was lively and hectoring, using every device to carry his ethical preaching – sarcasm, parody, imaginary objectors, comparisons from everyday experience. . . . Nothing substantial remains of Bion's writings, but his unoriginal follower Teles, anthologized by Stobaeus,

preserves the general effect, with frequent quotations.

BIBL. Diogenes Laertius iv. 26; J. F. Kindstrand, *Bion of Borysthenes* (1976); *Roman World* *Diogenes Laertius, *Horace.

Brasidas Spartan commander, died 422 BC.

Brasidas' father Tellis was a leading Spartan who participated in the negotiations leading to the Peace of *Nicias in 421 BC; he himself was eponymous ephor in 431/30. In 431 he saved Methone from an Athenian attack by sea, and in 425 he again distinguished himself at Pylos.

After the capture (by *Cleon) of the Spartan soldiers who had been cut off there, many Spartans were prepared to accept a peace with Athens. Brasidas advocated an offensive policy instead, collected an army of Peloponnesian mercenaries and helots, and marched north with the aim of weakening Athenian control over Chalcidice and Thrace, and ultimately over the vital corn-route from the Black Sea (see *Spartocids). On the way he prevented an Athenian force under *Demosthenes (son of Alcisthenes) from capturing Megara; in return for the support of *Perdiccas II, he took part in the Macedonian civil war between the king and his rival Arrabaeus. In the autumn and winter of 424/3 he detached Acanthus, Stagirus, Torone, and Amphipolis from Athens. In 423/2, despite an official truce between Athens and Sparta, he supported the revolts of Scione and Mende. He again campaigned in Macedonia against Arrabaeus, but quarrelled with Perdiccas, who then dropped his support for Brasidas and allied himself to Athens. In 422 Cleon arrived to restore Athenian hegemony in the north; after some initial successes, he was surprised by Brasidas outside Amphipolis, and both leaders were killed. Brasidas was buried at Amphipolis, whose citizens honoured him as their 'founding hero'.

BIBL. D. Kagan, *The Archidamian War* (1974); Westlake, *Individuals in Thucydides*, ch. 10.

Brennus Gallic chieftain, first half of 3rd century BC.

Brennus (Brennos) – this may be a title rather than a

The remains of the Temple of Apollo at Delphi, attacked by Brennus and his Gauls in 279 BC.

proper name – led one of the three bands of Gauls which invaded Greece in 279 BC, when, after they had killed the Macedonian king *Ptolemy Ceraunus, Macedonia was in a state of turmoil and vulnerable to attack. Brennus came through Paeonia and along the Axius river, being only temporarily halted by the Macedonian general Sosthenes as he made his way south into Thessaly. A collected Greek army faced him at Thermopylae. Brennus wisely created a diversion to draw off the fierce Aetolians to defend their homeland, for the harassment of which the Gauls paid dearly; but the pass was turned and the Gauls proceeded to Delphi. The battle at the walls of the sanctuary was blanketed by a blizzard so thick that the Gauls were unable to see either defenders or missiles. When Brennus was wounded, the Gauls retreated north and were harried along the way by the Thessalians. The Greek victory was naturally attributed to divine intervention, and became a legend second in national appeal only to the Persian Wars. Brennus killed himself in despair during the retreat.

BIBL. G. Nachtergael, *Les Galates en Grèce et les Sôtéria de Delphes* (1977).

Skyphos (drinking mug), by the Brygus painter, showing dancing revellers, *c.* 480 BC. Paris, Musée du Louvre.

Brygus   Potter, active *c.* 490–470 BC.

Brygus (Brugos) has left us over a dozen vases signed by him as potter; they are all cups and are mostly decorated by the same painter, the 'Brygus painter', the master of late archaic cup-painting. Well over 200 vases, mostly cups, have been attributed to the painter, who was a draughtsman of considerable power and facility in a wide range of genre and myth subjects, although he was perhaps at his best doing symposium scenes.

BIBL. Beazley, *ARV* 368 ff., and *Paralipomena* 365 ff.; A. Cambitoglou, *The Brygos Painter* (1968); Boardman, *Red Figure* 135–6.

Caecilius of Calacte   Historian and rhetorician, 1st century BC.

Caecilius, of Calacte in Sicily, was perhaps a Jew. He was an Atticist who wrote on the style of the *Attic Orators, a lexicographer, a historian, and a critic of rhetoric. He was a friend of Dionysius of Halicarnassus. He was severely criticized by Longinus for failing to give

an adequate account of 'the sublime' in a treatise on the subject.

BIBL. Kennedy, *Rhetoric* 364 ff.; Longinus i. 1, with Russell's commentary (1964); *Roman World* *Dionysius of Halicarnassus, *Longinus.   N.H.

Statue of a woman or goddess (perhaps Aphrodite or Europa). Marble copy of the Roman period of an original of *c.* 470/460 BC (see *Calamis). Baiae.

Calamis   Sculptor, active *c.* 470–430 BC.

Calamis (Kalamis) was perhaps an Athenian, and, with Pythagoras of Rhegium, was one of the most important bronze sculptors of the early classical period; unfortunately we have no evidence to associate safely any surviving sculptures with his name. About a dozen works by him are recorded, mostly gods, among which are a Zeus Ammon dedicated in Thebes by *Pindar, a colossal Apollo at Apollonia on the Black Sea, apparently 45 feet tall, a chryselephantine Asclepius in Sicyon, and a Sosandra on the Acropolis at Athens which was his best-known work and probably identical with his Aphrodite dedicated there by *Callias (son of Hipponicus (I)); it is often associated with a fine early classical draped statue known in several Roman copies.

BIBL. P. Orlandini, *Calamide* (1950); Dörig, *JDAI* lxxx (1965); Richter, *Sculpture and Sculptors* 158–60.

Callias, son of Calliades   Athenian politician, died 432 BC.

In 434/3 BC, to prepare Athens for the lengthy and costly war envisaged by *Pericles, Callias (Kallias)

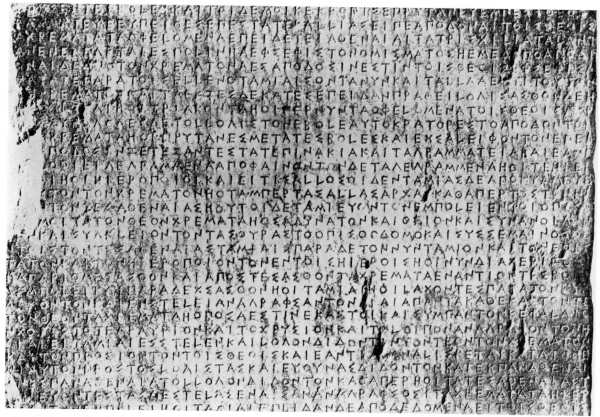

Inscription recording the financial decree moved by Callias, son of Calliades. Athens.

proposed transferring 3,000 talents to the temple of Athena on the Acropolis as a reserve fund (the 'Callias Decree'; the details are controversial). In the following year he proposed a military alliance with Rhegium and Leontini. In 432 he was killed while commanding Athenian forces at Potidaea. *Plato (in the *First Alcibiades*) suggests that he was a student of the philosopher *Zeno of Elea.

BIBL. Meiggs and Lewis, *Inscriptions* 58, 63, 64; C. W. Fornara, *GRBS* xi (1970); H. B. Mattingly, *GRBS* xvi (1975).

Callias, son of Hipponicus (1) Athenian political leader, 5th century BC.

The wealth and prestige of Callias' (Kallias) family is indicated by the fact that he is said to have won three Olympic chariot victories. (See also *Calamis.) His wife was Elpinice, daughter of *Miltiades and sister of *Cimon; the fact that he later apparently divorced her, and that his son Hipponicus married a former wife of *Pericles, has suggested that at some time in the 460s BC Callias transferred his support from the Cimonids to the supporters of *Ephialtes. If so, Ephialtes will have sent him to Susa on an embassy c. 461 to try to negotiate peace with the Persians. But it was not until after the victory at Salamis in Cyprus that hostilities ceased. From the fourth century on, Athenian orators and historians claimed that Callias had negotiated a formal peace agreement with *Artaxerxes' representatives in Cyprus in 449/8. Although the precise terms cited seem to be a fourth-century invention, Persia clearly did recognize Athenian

hegemony over the Delian League, while the Athenians gave up their claim for 'reparations' for the destruction of Athens in 480. This 'Peace of Callias' meant that work on the reconstruction of public buildings like the Parthenon could begin soon after.

Callias' son Hipponicus served as *strategos*, and died at Delium in 424; his grandson *Callias was *strategos* in 391.

BIBL. Davies, *Athenian Families*, no. 7826; D. Stockton, *Historia* viii (1959); H. B. Mattingly, *Historia* xiv (1965); Meiggs, *Athenian Empire* 487 ff.

Callias, son of Hipponicus (2) Athenian politician and *bon viveur*, died after 367/6 BC.

Callias (Kallias) played a part in fourth-century Athenian political and military life (*strategos* 391/90 BC, ambassador to Sparta 387/6, 375/4, 372/1, Spartan *proxenos*), but is more notable for his role in the Mysteries trial of 399 (see *Andocides, *Or.* i) and for a ruinously extravagant life-style which was already notorious in the 420s and whose least reprehensible aspect was association with sophists (on whom, according to *Plato, he outspent everyone). *Socrates moved in his circle, and *Plato's *Protagoras* and *Xenophon's *Symposium* are set in his houses at Athens and Piraeus.

BIBL. Kirchner, *Prosopographia Attica*, no. 7826; Davies, *Athenian Families* 263 f.

Callias of Sphettus Ptolemaic commander, floruit c. 295–c. 265 BC.

Callias (Kallias), of the Attic deme Sphettus, was known only in name as the brother of *Phaedrus (q.v.) until details of his political career emerged recently in an inscription from Athens. Exiled from Athens in the 290s BC, Callias returned in the service of the Ptolemies in 288/7, and, using Ptolemaic mercenaries from Andros, aided Phaedrus in gathering the harvest of summer 287 before the expected siege by *Demetrius Poliorcetes after the Athenian revolt in that year. In the diplomatic negotiations which raised this siege, Callias represented the Athenian democrats before *Ptolemy I's personal envoy, who arranged the treaty with Poliorcetes. Remaining in Ptolemaic service, Callias continued to work for the good of Athens by providing food and money, being appointed in return chief Athenian delegate to the first celebration of the Ptolemaieia festival in Alexandria. When the decree recorded in the inscription was passed in 270/69 to vote him full civic honours, Callias was in command of the Ptolemaic garrison in Halicarnassus, and was still interceding with Egypt for Athens.

BIBL. T. L. Shear, Jr., *Hesperia*, Suppl. xvii; Osborne, *ZPE* xxxv (1979), 181 ff.; Habicht, *Untersuchungen*.

Callias of Syracuse Historian, floruit *c*. 325–*c*. 285 BC.

Callias (Kallias) wrote the first known history of the reign of *Agathocles of Syracuse (besides that of the tyrant's brother Antandrus, of which nothing is known). The work, originally in 22 books, covered the history of Sicily during the years 317–289 BC, but so few fragments remain that no opinion of it independent of its ancient criticism is possible. Callias probably lived at Agathocles' court, and is the only ancient source favourable to the tyrant. *Diodorus Siculus, perhaps following *Timaeus, who hated Agathocles, attributes this distortion of truth to generous royal gifts given to Callias. The few remaining fragments of the history come from various excursuses with which the work abounded. One of these includes a catalogue of traditions on the founding of Rome. *Callimachus used Callias as a source for various stories pertaining to the West, and he is quoted in Dionysius of Halicarnassus, book i (on Rome).

BIBL. *FGrH* 564; PW x. 1628 (Kallias (22)); J. Perret, *Les Origines de la Légende troyenne de Rome* (1942), with review by Momigliano, *JRS* xxxv (1945); *Roman World* *Dionysius of Halicarnassus.

Callicrates of Leontium Achaean statesman, floruit 182–149/8 BC.

After the death of *Philopoemen in 182 BC, Callicrates (Kallikratēs) came to be identified with the 'anti-Philopoemenist' party in the Achaean League. Whereas Philopoemen had always espoused the right of the League to control its internal affairs (notably the chronic problem of faction in Sparta), a view now supported by Lycortas (the father of *Polybius), Callicrates argued that Achaea as Rome's client state should not oppose Roman wishes about Sparta. When the Spartan question arose again, violent dissension in the League led to an embassy to Rome in 180–179, where Callicrates argued for more positive Roman action in Achaea; the Senate's reaction was favourable, and they lavished praise upon him.

Callicrates was elected *strategus* of the League in 179/8, and, in accordance with Rome's policy, restored the disaffected parties in Sparta and Messene, which immediately solved the long-standing problem. When the party of Lycortas were sent as hostages to Rome in 167

after Pydna (see *Perseus), the policies of Callicrates reigned supreme until his death (149/8), although he did not himself hold another federal office in the League. His death removed the restraint on a new, more radical independence party (see *Critolaus and *Diaeus), whose defiance of Rome led to the Achaean War and the sack of Corinth (146).

Polybius presents Callicrates with extreme calumny, since he was diametrically opposed to the politics of Lycortas. If we look behind this partisan view, Callicrates was a realist who, by accepting the inevitability of Roman domination, made its effect more palatable and replaced internal discord with security and peace.

BIBL. R. M. Errington, *Philopoemen* (1969); *Roman World*; Walbank, *HCP*.

Callicratidas Spartan admiral, 406/5 BC.

Callicratidas (Kallikratidas) was a political opponent of *Lysander. Despite friction with him and with *Cyrus the Younger, Callicratidas was able to conquer Delphinium, Teos, and Methymna. He blockaded *Conon's fleet in the harbour of Mytilene, and then attacked an Athenian relief fleet at Arginusae; he was defeated and was drowned in the battle.

BIBL. Xenophon, *Hellenica* I. vi. 1–33; Diodorus Siculus xiii. 70–9, 97–9.

Callimachus Poet and scholar, *c*. 270 BC.

Callimachus (Kallimakhos) of Cyrene, a cardinal figure of literary history, apparently traced descent from his city's founder *Battus, calling himself, and often called, 'Battiades'. Tradition asserts, doubtless romantically, that he began as a humble schoolmaster in the suburbs of Alexandria: soon noticed by *Ptolemy II he was ensconced at court by the 270s BC, turning out elegant poems for the king's marriage to *Arsinoe II and later for her apotheosis. He lived on under *Ptolemy III and his Cyrenean queen *Berenice II (q.v.): the fanciful *Lock of Berenice* (fr. 110) is securely datable to 246/5.

While Callimachus, mysteriously, never became head of the Library, he was early employed there on cataloguing its contents, a task fraught with problems of categorization, disputed authorship, etc.: his mighty *Pinakes* (*Catalogue of all Greek Literature*, including biographical information, in 120 books) became an essential tool of scholarship, revised by *Aristophanes of Byzantium. Callimachus' innumerable learned prose works – *Rivers of the World, Foundings of Islands and Cities and their Changes of Name, Curiosities from All Over the World*, etc. – displayed a truly encyclopaedic delight in knowledge. That he was also a remarkable poet, the representative *par excellence* of the combination of scholarship and creativity characteristic of Hellenistic poetry, is best seen in the works preserved through the manuscript tradition: about 60 epigrams – dedications, epitaphs, and love-poems of beautiful economy and wit – and the six *Hymns* (*Hymn* v in elegiacs, the rest in hexameters). The *Hymns* are literary exploitations of a once functional form, public poetry converted for an élite audience on whose learned collusion it depends. Recondite erudition on cult and a delightful *faux-naïf* treatment of mythology are found side by side, and Callimachus' most appealing qualities – humour, imagination, an observant interest in human behaviour –

Fragmentary remains of the famous prologue to Callimachus' *Aetia (Origins)*, preserved in a 2nd-century AD papyrus. London, Egypt Exploration Society.

emerge clearly: the story of Erysichthon in *Hymn* vi, for instance, becomes a study in bourgeois values. Sophisticated but affectionate mischievousness modernizes the tradition.

In the epilogue of *Hymn* ii Apollo rejects the big, muddy river for the pure spring, an influential literary image. Callimachus later expressed more fully his commitment to the short, highly-wrought poetry inherited from *Philitas, in the prologue written for a collected edition of the *Aetia* (*Origins*), fragmentarily preserved on papyrus (fr. 1). Here he dismisses the 'single continuous poem' – not implying *Homer, whom he revered above

any other, but those who regurgitate him in the epic tradition – arguing that poetry must be measured by quality not quantity. Further images explore these ideas – the narrow, untrodden path versus the common highway, etc. The key words of the creed are *leptotes* ('slenderness', 'refinement') and *techne* ('art'). The question of form was paramount: here, with *Theocritus' support, Callimachus probably quarrelled with *Apollonius Rhodius (q.v.).

The elegiac *Aetia*, Callimachus' major poem, surviving in numerous fragments, put this preaching into practice: though long (four books containing about 7,000(?) lines) it was not continuous, stringing together in conscious variety aetiological accounts ranging from obscure ritual practices to the origin of the mousetrap. *Hesiod was evoked at the beginning and end (frs. 2, 112). Callimachus' famous hexameter epyllion *Hecale* demonstrated the correct (i.e. unexpected) treatment of heroic material: the story of **Theseus and the Marathonian Bull was narrated to focus with realistic detail on a pious old woman's hospitality, with an *aetion* thrown in. Callimachus' extraordinary metrical and linguistic virtuosity was on display in his 13 *Iambs*, in mixed iambic metres and on very varied subjects, reviving and broadening the tradition of *Hipponax. Miscellaneous lyric poetry further extended this versatility. Particularly interesting among other fragments is the *Victory Ode for Sosibius*, an elegiac recreation of the fifth-century epinician.

Callimachus' polemics (note 'a big book is a big evil' (fr. 465)) failed to put a stop to traditional epic; but, while such productions are largely lost, he survives in very numerous papyri and quotations. He also greatly influenced the best poets of Rome (Catullus, Propertius, and Ovid in particular).

BIBL. R. Pfeiffer, *Callimachus* (1949, 1953); *SH* 238–308; Gow and Page, *Hellenistic Epigrams*; W. Clausen, *GRBS* v (1964); *Roman World* *Catullus, *Ovid, *Propertius.

Callimachus of Aphidna Athenian general, died 490 BC.

Callimachus (Kallimakhos) was polemarch in 490/89 BC, the year of the Persian expedition sent by *Darius I to punish Athens and Eretria for supporting the Ionian Revolt. He was responsible for the plan to fight at Marathon. He died in the battle, and was commemorated in a painting in the Stoa Poikile.

BIBL. E. B. Harrison, *GRBS* xii (1971).

Callinus Elegiac poet, c. 650 BC.

Our only substantial piece (fr. 1, in 21 lines) of Callinus (Kallinos) of Ephesus exhorts his audience to display courage in battle (compare *Tyrtaeus). References to the Cimmerians' sack of Sardis (fr. 5a) and a prayer to Zeus to pity his city (fr. 2) may cohere, and place him c. 650: hence (like *Archilochus and *Mimnermus) he was labelled 'inventor' of elegiacs. He allegedly (fr. 6) ascribed the *Thebais* to *Homer.

BIBL. Text: West, *IEG*. Commentary: Campbell, *Lyric Poetry*; W. J. Verdenius, *Mnemosyne* xxv (1972).

Callippus Astronomer, late 4th century BC.

An astronomer from Cyzicus, Callippus (Kallippos) worked with *Aristotle in Athens. He improved on *Meton's attempts to correlate the cycles of the sun and the moon by introducing a cycle of 27,759 days (one day shorter than four of Meton's cycles). His calculation of the lunar month was only 22 seconds too long. He also elaborated and improved *Eudoxus' (of Cnidos) explanations of heavenly movements by introducing additional spheres.

BIBL. Heath, *Aristarchus of Samos*; D. R. Dicks, *Early Greek Astronomy to Aristotle* (1970).

Callisthenes Historian, died 327 BC.

Callisthenes (Kallisthenēs) of Olynthus was a relation (probably a grand-nephew) of *Aristotle. *Alexander the Great invited him to accompany him on his expedition against the Persian empire (beginning in 334 BC) as his official historian. Callisthenes saw himself in the role of *Homer to Alexander's **Achilles, and his account of Alexander was highly panegyrical; nevertheless he opposed Alexander's adoption of Persian customs such as *proskynesis*, and was executed.

Callisthenes' (lost) works included a monograph on the Sacred War (355–346), and a highly inaccurate history of Greece in ten books (386–355), as well as the *Achievements of Alexander*, going down to the battle of Gaugamela and including many ethnographic, antiquarian, and geographical digressions.

A number of medieval manuscripts ascribe to Callisthenes authorship of a romantic and almost completely fictitious biography of Alexander, hence called Pseudo-Callisthenes, or, more frequently, the Alexander Romance. Pseudo-Callisthenes appears to have been collated in c. AD 200 by an Alexandrian Greek who made use of the native Egyptian legend that Alexander's real father was the wizard Nectanebos; of Greek (especially Cynic) philosophical tracts about the Indian gymnosophists; possibly of a Hellenistic account in the form of a collection of spurious letters; and even of some genuine history. Pseudo-Callisthenes was translated into Latin as well as into almost every language between the Atlantic and India, and was one of the main sources of the medieval European romance of Alexander.

BIBL. *FGrH* iiB, no. 124; Pearson, *Lost Histories*. Pseudo-Callisthenes: ed. A. W. Kroll (1926/58); D. J. A. Ross, *Alexander Historiatus* (1963); R. Merkelbach, *Die Quellen des griechischen Alexanderromans* (2nd ed., 1977).

Callistratus Athenian politician, floruit 392/1–366 BC.

Callistratus (Kallistratos) attacked the envoys who favoured peace with Sparta in 392/1 BC, and was closely associated with the anti-Spartan Second Athenian Confederacy. Growing Theban power led him to a pro-Spartan stance and advocacy of the Common Peace of 372/1 and of Athenian assistance to Sparta in 370/69. The Theban seizure of Oropus (366) undermined his position, though his *apologia* (greatly admired by *Demosthenes) secured acquittal in court. A further impeachment (361), however, led to exile, which Callistratus spent in Macedonia, Thasos, and Byzantium. The Delphic oracle advised him to return to Athens, but he was executed after seeking sanctuary at the Altar of the Twelve Gods in the Agora.

BIBL. Kirchner, *PA* no. 8517; Davies, *Athenian Families* 277 f.; Sealey, *Essays* 133–63 (with caution).

Cambyses King of Persia, 530–522 BC.

Cambyses (Kambusēs, Persian Kambujiya), the son of *Cyrus, conquered Egypt, but later showed increasing signs of insanity, which the Egyptians regarded as a punishment for various outrages against their religion. He had his popular brother Smerdis killed as a possible rival, but an impostor claiming to be Smerdis started a rebellion (see *Atossa), and Cambyses died while hurrying back to Persia to meet this threat.

BIBL. Herodotus ii. l, iii. 1–39, 61–6.

Carcinus Tragedian, c. 370 BC.

This Carcinus (Karkinos) was the grandson of the Carcinus (also a tragedian) ridiculed by *Aristophanes. It is said that the grandson wrote 160 plays, won 11 victories, and worked at the court of *Dionysius II of Syracuse. *Aristotle refers several times to his work.

BIBL. T. B. L. Webster, *Hermes* lxxxii (1954) 300 f.; Xanthakis-Karamanos, *Fourth-Century Tragedy*.

Carneades (c. 213–129 BC) Philosopher.

The philosophy of Carneades (Karneadēs) of Cyrene strikingly resembles that of some modern British empiricists. As head of the Academy in Athens, he developed the moderate scepticism introduced by *Arcesilaus of Pitane. He believed that we can only know about the real world from appearances. We can never be sure whether an appearance is true, but can judge some more probable than others. His moral philosophy is similarly sceptical. On a visit to Rome in 156/5 BC he argued in one lecture that justice was a natural virtue, and in the next that it merely resulted from a compact. He was renowned for his ability in argument, and the evidence seems to justify the reputation. Although he published nothing, his friend *Cl(e)itomachus wrote about his philosophy, and much of it is preserved by Cicero. He produced an impressive rebuttal of a Stoic argument purporting to show that all events are causally determined.

BIBL. Long, *Hellenistic Philosophy*; *Roman World* *Cicero.

Cassander (c. 355–297 BC) Macedonian king.

Cassander (Kassandros) was the eldest son of *Alexander the Great's general *Antipater. In Babylon in 324 he defended his father against the accusations of Alexander's mother *Olympias. There was a tradition that the ensuing enmity led Cassander to murder Alexander by poisoning him.

At the conference of Triparadeisus in 321 Cassander was appointed commander of the Macedonian cavalry, but fear of *Antigonus, supreme commander (*strategus*) of the Macedonians in Asia, led him to return to Europe; here he was responsible for the execution of the Athenian orator *Demades. When *Polyperchon was appointed Antipater's successor as supreme commander in Europe in 319, Cassander felt his position threatened and formed an alliance with Antigonus and the other generals. He won control of several central Greek states, including Athens, which he placed under the rule of *Demetrius of Phalerum (317). He then had himself appointed *strategus* in Europe, in place of Polyperchon, by *Adea (Eurydice), queen of King *Philip Arrhidaeus. Polyperchon retaliated by calling upon Olympias for help: she occupied Macedon with an Epirote army and had Adea, Philip, and Cassander's brother Nicanor executed. But in 316 Cassander forced Olympias to surrender, had her condemned to death by the Macedonian army, and won control of the surviving king, *Alexander IV, and his mother *Roxane, who were imprisoned at Amphipolis. He then married Thessalonice, daughter of *Philip II, founding the city of that name in her honour.

In 315, in response to the hostility of Antigonus, Cassander allied himself with *Ptolemy (I) and *Lysimachus. While he managed to extend Macedonian control over Epirus, he lost Greece; the peace agreement of 311 declared Greece free, and recognized Cassander as ruler of Macedon, but only for so long as Alexander was still a minor. This induced him to have Alexander and Roxane put to death (309); and he followed the lead of Antigonus by proclaiming himself king from 305.

During the 'Four Years' War' (307–304) Cassander failed to dislodge *Demetrius Poliorcetes from Athens and other Greek cities; but after the defeat and death of Antigonus at Ipsus (301) his position as ruler of Macedonia was no longer threatened. He recognized the independence of Athens (299), and campaigned unsuccessfully against *Agathocles of Syracuse at Corcyra c. 299, dying soon after at the Macedonian capital of Pella.

BIBL. Will, *Hist. pol.* i.

Cebes Pythagorean philosopher, c. 400 BC.

A pupil of *Philolaus, Cebes (Kebēs) of Thebes was said by *Plato to have been one of those who took part in a discussion on immortality just before *Socrates drank the hemlock. An ethical work, *The Tablet*, is attributed to him, almost certainly wrongly.

BIBL. Plato, *Phaedo*.

Cephalus Athenian politician, floruit 390s–370s BC.

A notable orator (he supported *Andocides in 399 BC), Cephalus (Kephalos) was politically prominent in the 390s (when he took a strong anti-Spartan line), the 380s (in 384 he was involved in making an important alliance with Chios), and the 370s (in 378 he proposed military assistance to Thebes after the anti-Spartan counter-revolution there). In contrast to *Aristophon he boasted that he was never attacked by *graphe paranomon*. Like other Athenian politicians he had 'industrial' interests, in his case pot-making.

BIBL. Kirchner, *PA* no. 8277; Sealey, *Essays* 133–63.

Cercidas (c. 290–c. 220 BC) Poet and philosopher.

Cercidas (Kerkidas) was both a literary and a political figure in Megalopolis. Although few fragments of his work remain, he appears to have been a poet of considerable skill and unorthodox style. One meliamb is a vituperative poem about the gulf between rich and poor, which, since it advises helping the poor and healing the sick as a way of preventing social revolution, has been called 'the one expression of philanthropy in [Greek] literature' (Tarn). Such general dissatisfaction with the existing order may have come from Cercidas' Cynic leanings, but the poem transcends other moralizing literature when considered against the background of the contemporary reign of *Cleomenes III of Sparta (q.v.), who sought such social changes.

Even if Cercidas personally admired Cleomenes, political considerations outweighed ideological ones when the Spartan's aggression was recognized in the Peloponnese. *Aratus of Sicyon approached his family friends Cercidas and Nicophanes to ask the Megalopolitan Assembly and the Achaean League for permission to request help against Sparta and Aetolia from *Antigonus Doson. Visiting Macedonia in 227–226, they elicited a promise to that effect from Doson in the event of Sparta and Aetolia uniting. When events culminated at Sellasia in 222, Macedonian allies against Cleomenes included a Megalopolitan force under Cercidas. He may have fought the tyranny of *Lydiadas, and perhaps spent some time in Crete.

BIBL. Loeb edition with Herodas; A.D. Knox, *The First Greek Anthologist* (1922); J. U. Powell and E. A. Barber, *New Chapters in the History of Greek Literature* (1921), ch. 1; Walbank, *Aratos of Sicyon*.

Cersobleptes Thracian dynast, floruit 360–342 BC.

Despite *Charidemus' efforts, Cersobleptes (Kersobleptēs) was compelled by the combined hostility of Athens and two pretenders (Berisades and *Amadocus) to permit the division of *Cotys' kingdom, of which he retained the eastern part minus the Thracian Chersonese, which went to Athens (358/7). In due course the Macedonian threat drove him to friendship with Athens, but he was excluded from the Peace of *Philocrates (346) and eventually expelled by *Philip II (342/1).

BIBL. Demosthenes xxiii; Hammond and Griffith, *Macedonia*.

Chabrias Athenian general, floruit 390–356 BC.

Chabrias (Khabrias) was continually employed as a general between 390 and 356 BC, either by Athens (390–387/6, 379–369, 362, 359) or by foreign powers (Egypt in the 380s and c. 360), most notably, perhaps, during the first decade of the Second Athenian Confederacy, when his victory off Naxos (376) won him considerable civic honours (including *ateleia* and a monument in the Agora) and, along with other operations in 377 and 375, contributed significantly to the Confederacy's growth. His considerable wealth, much of it representing the profits of a successful military career, is said to have supported an extravagant off-duty life-style. Chabrias died fighting against rebel allies at the battle of Chios (356).

BIBL. Kirchner, *PA*, no. 15086; Davies, *Athenian Families* 560 f.; Parke, *Mercenary Soldiers*.

Chaeremon Tragedian, 4th century BC.

*Aristotle says that the tragedies of Chaeremon (Khairēmōn) were better suited to reading than to performance, and that his *Centaur* was a mixture of 'all the metres'. Fragments exhibit a very florid style.

BIBL. T. B. L. Webster, *Hermes* lxxxii (1954), 302; Xanthakis-Karamanos, *Fourth-Century Tragedy*.

Chandragupta: see **Sandracottus**

Chares Athenian general, floruit mid-4th century BC.

Chares (Kharēs) gained early notoriety for atrocities at Corcyra (361 BC). After the Athenians were worsted by rebel allies at Embata (356), he joined *Artabazus (son of *Pharnabazus) and defeated a Persian army (he called this a 'second Marathon'), but was recalled when *Artaxerxes III's threats terminated the Social War (355). He operated frequently against *Philip II in Thrace and the Hellespont

(353–340), and fought as *strategos* at Chaeronea (338). In 335 he fled to Sigeum and, despite an amicable meeting with *Alexander the Great in 334, joined the anti-Macedonians at Mytilene in 332. He last appears among the unemployed mercenaries at Taenarum in the 320s.

BIBL. Kirchner, *PA*, no. 15292; Davies, *Athenian Families* 568 f.; Parke, *Mercenary Soldiers*; Hofstetter, *Griechen*, no. 73.

Chares of Lindos Sculptor, *c.* 300 BC.

A pupil of *Lysippus, Chares (Kharēs) is best known as the sculptor of the Colossus of Rhodes, one of the seven wonders of the ancient world. The statue, which represented the island's patron deity, Helios (the Sun-god), was paid for from the booty left by *Demetrius Poliorcetes after the raising of his famous siege of Rhodes in 304 BC, and was no doubt a thanks-offering. It was made of bronze and stood over 100 feet high. The figure took 12 years to make, and was cast *in situ* in sections from the feet up. The legs and feet were fitted with clamped stone blocks inside to keep the statue stable. We do not have much idea what the Colossus looked like, but it did not stand astride the harbour as medieval legend supposed. It stood for little over half a century (*c.* 280–220) before it fell, breaking off at the knees during an earthquake.

BIBL. Robertson, *History of Greek Art* 476–7.

Chares of Mytilene Alexander historian, 4th century BC.

Chamberlain to *Alexander the Great, Chares (Kharēs) wrote reminiscences about the court (including such incidents as the *proskynesis* debate and the Susa marriages) and about oriental customs, natural history, and folklore. No special bias is discernible.

BIBL. Pearson, *Lost Histories* 50–60.

Charidemus Mercenary general, mid-4th century BC.

Charidemus (Kharidēmos) of Oreus in Euboea worked as a mercenary in western Thrace (368–362 BC, fighting both for and against Athens), western Asia Minor (in the employ of *Memnon and *Mentor and then independently, in which capacity he captured Troy), and finally in eastern Thrace (where he served *Cotys and *Cersobleptes). In 357 he negotiated a pact between Athens and Cersobleptes, became an Athenian citizen, and appears as an Athenian *strategos* in 351, 349/8 (when his life-style offended the Olynthians), and 338. In 335 he fled from *Alexander the Great to the service of *Darius III, who later executed him for insolence.

BIBL. Kirchner, *PA*, no. 15380; Davies, *Athenian Families* 570 f.; Parke, *Mercenary Soldiers*; Hofstetter, *Griechen*, no. 74.

Chariton Novelist, 50 BC/AD 100 (?).

Chariton (Kharitōn) claims to be secretary to the rhetorician Athenagoras, though the authenticity of this and even of his name has been suspected. His eight-book *Chaereas and Callirhoe* is the earliest of the few surviving Greek novels, an exciting adventure romance, simply constructed with features that later became standard: the lovers are separated (in Chariton after their marriage) but remain ever true to each other (Callirhoe repels even the king of Persia), and survive frightful ordeals – false deaths, pirates, distant travels, shipwreck, etc. – to be

reunited in a happy ending. Chariton chooses a classical setting, casting Callirhoe as daughter of the historical fifth-century BC Syracusan *Hermocrates. His simple style, recalling *Xenophon, is not concerned to Atticize, which some see as evidence that Chariton antedates AD 50. Papyri show that he was being read by the second century AD, but sure dating is elusive.

BIBL. Perry, *Ancient Romances*; B. P. Reardon, *YCS* xxv (1982).

Charon of Lampsacus Historian, 5th century BC (?).

The *Suda* gives a long list of historical works ascribed to Charon (Kharōn), of which only a local history of Lampsacus and an account of the Persian Wars are likely to be genuine. He is said to have been born in the reign of *Darius I, and cannot have written before that of *Artaxerxes I (beginning 465/4 BC); he is generally held to have been a contemporary of *Herodotus, although some believe that he was a contemporary and continuator of *Hellanicus. Charon may have been the source of the *Themistocles-story, since Themistocles was given Lampsacus as his fief by Artaxerxes.

BIBL. Pearson, *Ionian Historians*, ch. 4; H. D. Westlake, *CQ* xxvii (1977).

Charondas Lawgiver, 6th century BC.

Charondas (Kharōndas) of Catana in Sicily made laws for several Western Greek cities. However, he is not known to have created constitutions. *Aristotle says that his laws were very detailed and that he was the first to legislate against perjury. *Diodorus Siculus gives a long account of him, which is mostly legendary.

BIBL. Aristotle, *Politics* 1274a–b; Diodorus xii. 11–19.

Charops of Epirus Pro-Roman leader, died *c.* 159 BC.

The descendant of the elder Charops, an Illyrian chieftain who in 198 BC had helped *Flamininus to turn the Aous pass against *Philip V of Macedon and who had secured Epirote support for Rome, Charops (Kharops) the younger continued his family's affiliation to Rome, perhaps strengthened by his own education at Rome. The Roman victory over *Perseus at Pydna (168) gave prominence to pro-Roman Greek leaders, and many used Roman influence for their own political ends. As one of these, Charops might have been responsible for L. Aemilius *Paullus' order to ravage Epirus in 167, having persuaded a certain element in the Senate to sanction this in order to rid himself of an opposing faction at home. Charops was afterwards powerful in Epirus until his death, although he lost Roman support. *Polybius excoriates him as the most evil of contemporary Greek politicians.

BIBL. Polybius xxx. 12, with Walbank, *HCP*; *Roman World*; Hammond, *Epirus* 626 ff.; Scullard, *JRS* xxxv (1945), 55 ff.

Chilon Spartan statesman, ephor *c.* 555 BC.

Little is known about Chilon (Khilōn) apart from the fact that he was ephor, but he was considered important enough to be numbered among the *Seven Sages. He may have been responsible for the increase in the power of the ephorate which can be seen after his time; for the afterwards traditional Spartan policy of hostility to tyrants; and for the introduction of the 'Orestes policy',

'Portrait' of Chilon from a late 2nd-century mosaic from Cologne. Cologne, Römisch-Germanisches Museum.

whereby Sparta acquired the alleged bones of Orestes from Arcadia. This act was part of a wider policy of claiming Spartan connections for Bronze-Age heroes (seen, for instance, in *Stesichorus' *Oresteia*), and of using these rather than the 'return of the **Heracleidae' as the mythological justification for Sparta's leading position in the Peloponnese. Chilon apparently tried to give himself royal connections by making a female relative the second wife of King *Anaxandridas, and there is some evidence that her son *Cleomenes was sympathetic to his policies; Anaxandridas himself was apparently less so, although he helped to carry out these policies, and probably also resented having the second marriage forced upon him.

BIBL. Herodotus vii. 235; Diogenes Laertius i. 68 ff.; Forrest, *History of Sparta* 76 ff.

Chionides Comic poet, from *c.* 487 BC.

*Aristotle regarded Chionides (Khiōnidēs) and Magnes as the earliest poets of Attic comedy. Chionides was probably victor in the first recorded contest, *c.* 487 BC.

BIBL. Pickard-Cambridge, *Dithyramb . . .*; Edmonds, *Attic Comedy* i.

Choerilus of Samos Epic poet, died *c.* 400 BC (?).

Choerilus (Khoirilos) wrote in a more archaic style than his rival *Antimachus. He was the author of a *Persica*, concerning the Persian Wars. He was cultivated by *Lysander, and died at the court of *Archelaus of Macedon.

Choerilus is also the name of a later epic poet (Choerilus of Iasus) and of one of the earliest known tragedians.

BIBL. Lesky, *Greek Literature*; G. Huxley, *GRBS* x (1969).

Chremonides Athenian statesman, floruit 270–240 BC.

One of the sons of Eteocles of the deme of Aethalidae in Attica, Chremonides (Khremōnidēs) was a pupil of *Zeno of Citium, and an important nationalist politician in the

decades after Athens' revolt from *Demetrius Poliorcetes in 287 BC. He is probably best remembered in connection with the 'Chremonidean War', named after him as the proposer of the motion in the Athenian Assembly which allied the city to an anti-Macedonian coalition from the Peloponnese (led by *Areus I of Sparta), and which led to war with *Antigonus Gonatas in 266/5. Although Athens was supported by *Ptolemy II (more in words than in decisive military action), she surrendered in the spring of 261 and endured another Macedonian occupation

Chremonides and his brother Glaucon fled to Egypt, where the former served as admiral until *c.* 240. The Egyptian fleet under his command was defeated by *Antiochus II's ally, the Rhodian admiral Agathostratus, *c.* 258 in the battle for Ephesus during the Second Syrian War.

BIBL. Ferguson, *Hellenistic Athens*; Habicht, *Untersuchungen*.

'Portrait' statue of the philosopher Chrysippus, incorporating a plaster cast of the head in the British Museum. Paris, Musée du Louvre.

Chrysippus (*c.* 280–206 BC) Stoic philosopher.

The philosophy of Chrysippus (Khrusippos), third head of the Stoa, became orthodox Stoicism. His contributions to the school's thought are hard to disentangle from those of his predecessors *Zeno of Citium and *Cleanthes, but were probably considerable. In logic, he developed an impressive system based on propositions (unlike *Aristotle's syllogistic logic, which was based on subjects and predicates), and was thus able to accommodate forms of argument involving complex propositions such as conditionals. Although once a pupil of *Arcesilaus of Pitane, Chrysippus came to oppose his sceptical philosophy.

BIBL. Long, *Hellenistic Philosophy*; Rist, *Stoic Philosophy*.

Cimon Founder of the Athenian empire, died *c.* 450 BC.

Cimon (Kimōn) was related to one of the most powerful landowning families in Attica, the *Philaids; from his father *Miltiades he inherited an aggressively anti-Persian policy, and from his mother Hegesipyle connections with Thrace and the Chersonese. The historical tradition represents him as a pro-Spartan 'conservative' leader of the hoplite class, in contrast to the 'radical' spokesmen of the *nautikos okhlos* ('naval mob') *Themistocles, *Ephialtes, and *Pericles. These categories seemed illuminating in the nineteenth century, but they are not helpful. In fact it was Cimon who commanded the naval expeditions on which the Athenian empire was based.

Ostracon cast against Cimon in 461 BC, found in the Agora at Athens. Athens, Agora Museum.

After the expulsion of the Persians from Greece in 479 BC, Cimon commanded Greek expeditions to Cyprus and Byzantium, where he expelled *Pausanias (1), who was suspected of wanting peace with Persia. He also expelled the Persian general Boges from Eion, preventing *Alexander I of Macedon from developing his authority over Thrace. The colonization of Scyros and the transfer of the bones of **Theseus to Athens in 476 was a major propaganda operation; this, together with a systematic attempt to represent his father's victory at Marathon as much more glorious than Salamis, enabled him to eliminate *Themistocles. Cimon probably commanded the expedition against Naxos, the first unsuccessful defector from the Delian League, in *c.* 470/468. There followed the decisive victory over Persian land and sea forces at the river Eurymedon (between 469 and 466), the expulsion of the last Persian garrisons from the Chersonese, and the two-year siege of Thasos.

In 462 Cimon persuaded the Athenians to let him lead them on an expedition in support of the Spartans, whose *proxenos* he was at Athens. Following the earthquake of 464, the Spartans were engaged in a war against their Messenian helots which was to last for nine years; they did not relish the presence of Athenians in the Peloponnese, and soon sent Cimon's army home. His prestige collapsed: on his return to Athens he found himself unable to rescind constitutional reforms proposed by his opponent *Ephialtes, and in 461 the conflict was resolved through Cimon's ostracism. He was recalled after perhaps only five years in exile (after the disaster in Egypt in 454? – see *Inarus); he negotiated a five-year peace with Sparta *c.* 450, and then commanded a last expedition against the Persians in Cyprus, where he died

while besieging Citium. He was the father of *Lacedaemonius.

BIBL. Davies, *Athenian Families*, no. 8429; Meiggs, *Athenian Empire*, chs. 3–8.

Cimon: see also **Philaids**

Cinadon Spartan revolutionary, died 399 BC.

Cinadon (Kinadōn), a member of the class of 'Inferiors', organized an abortive conspiracy against the Spartiates (whom, he declared, most non-Spartiates would gladly eat raw) shortly after *Agesilaus' accession (*c.* 400 BC). Its precise aims (beyond the shedding of blood) are unclear.

BIBL. E. David, *Athenaeum* lvii (1979).

Cinaethon: see **Cyclic Poets**

Cinesias Dithyrambic poet, 5th–4th centuries BC.

Nothing survives of the poetry of Cinesias (Kinēsias), but it must have resembled that of *Timotheus (1). He is frequently mocked by *Aristophanes for his thinness, for the airy emptiness of his poetry, and for having defiled a shrine of Hecate (he appears in person in *Birds*, but the Cinesias in *Lysistrata* is a fictional character). He is treated with equal scorn by *Pherecrates (for musical innovation), *Plato (for lack of moral purpose in his work), and *Lysias (for blasphemous conduct).

BIBL. *Lyra Graeca* (Loeb) iii; Pickard-Cambridge, *Dithyramb*, . . .

Cleanthes (*c.* 331–232 BC) Stoic philosopher.

A boxer from Assos in the Troad, Cleanthes (Kleanthēs)

Large bronze statuette of a philosopher of the time of Cleanthes, possibly representing Cleanthes himself. From Brindisi. London, British Museum.

studied in Athens under *Zeno of Citium, while labouring at night for his living, and eventually succeeded him as head of the Stoa. What little is known of his philosophy suggests a strong interest in religion. His *Hymn to Zeus* touches (though only barely) on problems of free will. Nothing, he says, happens apart from Zeus, except what bad men do. He was reputedly industrious, patient, and slow-witted. It seems likely that his pupil *Chrysippus was a philosopher of much greater originality.

BIBL. Long, *Hellenistic Philosophy*; Rist, *Stoic Philosophy*.

Clearchus   Athenian politician, *c.* 450 BC.

Fragments of fifth-century inscriptions from various parts of the Athenian empire suggest that a law dating to the period 450/446 BC referred to a previous proposal by the otherwise unknown Clearchus (Klearkhos), which insisted that all the states of the Delian League use Athenian coins, weights, and measures; the minting of silver coins was forbidden. This enactment should be seen as a symbol of Athens' political hegemony, rather than as an instance of 'economic imperialism'.

BIBL. Meiggs and Lewis, *Inscriptions* 45; Meiggs, *Athenian Empire* 167–214.

Clearchus of Heraclea Pontica   Tyrant 364/3–353/2 BC.

A one-time pupil of *Isocrates and *Plato, Clearchus (Klearkhos) was exiled from Heraclea, but returned with a mercenary army and deceived his fellow-citizens into making him *strategos autokrator*, from which basis he became tyrant. As such he liberated the Mariandynoi (serfs), built the first public library, affected to be the son of Zeus, and appeared in public dressed as a god. After 12 years he was murdered, but his dynasty lasted until 288/7.

BIBL. Berve, *Tyrannis* 315 ff.

Clearchus, son of Ramphias   Spartan soldier, died 401 BC.

In the Decelean War (413–404 BC) Clearchus (Klearkhos) fought first in Attica, then at Byzantium. In 408 he defended Byzantium against the Athenians, but lost it because of the support of some Byzantines for Athens. At Arginusae (406) he was appointed by *Callicratidas to take his place. In 403 the Spartan government appointed him harmost over Byzantium as an opponent of *Lysander; but he refused to take orders from Sparta, was sentenced to death, and fled to Cyprus. He fought for *Cyrus the Younger in Thrace, and then became commander of Cyrus' Peloponnesian mercenaries during the march against *Artaxerxes II. His failure to carry out orders at the battle of Cunaxa led to Cyrus' defeat and death; soon after, Clearchus was captured and executed by *Tissaphernes.

BIBL. Xenophon, *Hellenica* i. 1; *Anabasis* i. 2; Diodorus Siculus xiv. 19–26.

Cleinias

Cleinias (Kleinias) was the name of several rich Athenians of the clan of the Eumolpidae in the fifth century BC.

One Cleinias, son of Alcibiades, commanded his own ship with distinction at Artemisium in 480 (*Herodotus vii. 17); some scholars identify him with the Cleinias, son of Alcibiades, who married Deinomache, granddaughter of *Cleisthenes. Father of the famous *Alcibiades, he died at

the battle of Coronea in 446. Another Cleinias proposed a decree of controversial date, perhaps 447, tightening up the payment of tribute by Athens' allies (Meiggs and Lewis, *Inscriptions* 46). *Xenophon (*Symposium* iv. 12 ff.) and *Plato (*Euthydemus*, *Axiochus*) mention a Cleinias, son of Axiochus, as one of *Socrates' associates.

BIBL. Davies, *Athenian Families*, no. 600.

Cleisthenes   (*c.* 565–500 BC) Athenian statesman.

Cleisthenes (Kleisthenēs) succeeded his father *Megacles as head of the *Alcmaeonid family. At first he was friendly to the Peisistratids, holding the archonship under *Hippias in 525/4, but later he went into exile. On his return to Athens after the expulsion of Hippias, he tried to get the better of his rival *Isagoras by proposing a programme of political reform. The Spartans then expelled the Alcmaeonids at Isagoras' request, but popular support for Cleisthenes was too strong, and he was able to return and carry out his reforms.

Fragment of the Athenian archon-list for the 520s BC, including the names of *Hippias, Cleisthenes, and *Miltiades. Athens, Agora Museum.

The chief of these was the reorganization of the tribal system. Cleisthenes replaced the four traditional Ionian tribes with ten named after local Attic heroes, each tribe made up of three *trittyes* (thirds), and the *trittyes* of demes. The deme, corresponding geographically to a village or a district of the city, became the local administrative unit, and it was membership of the deme which guaranteed citizenship. The *trittyes* were divided into three geographical groups – city, inland, and coastal – and each tribe contained one *trittys* from each group. It is generally supposed that the object of this geographical organization was to benefit Cleisthenes and harm his opponents by concentrating or dispersing their supporters. His other known act, the creation of a 500-member Council (50 from each tribe), appears to be simply a logical consequence of the tribal reform. It is disputed whether or not he introduced the system of ostracism; the story that he not only introduced it but became its first victim is, regrettably, probably untrue.

BIBL. Herodotus v. 66, 69–73; Aristotelean *Constitution of Athens* 20–1; Forrest, *Greek Democracy*, ch. 8.

Cleisthenes of Sicyon   Tyrant, *c.* 595–565 BC.

Cleisthenes (Kleisthenēs) made himself tyrant of Sicyon

The François Vase: a krater (mixing-bowl for wine) signed by *Ergotimus as potter and Cleitias as painter, c. 570/560 BC. *Right*: a detail showing the Calydonian boar-hunt and Diomedes in his chariot. Florence, Archaeological Museum.

by eliminating his two brothers, and perhaps because of this was rudely received when he tried to consult the Delphic oracle. He therefore joined the Amphictyons in the First Sacred War, the aim of which was to free Delphi from the control of the neighbouring city of Cirrha (Kirrha, Krisa). Cleisthenes' navy played an important part in the Amphictyons' victory (c. 590 BC) by blockading Cirrha, and he was rewarded with a share of the booty. He also fought a war with Argos which appears to have been largely on the propaganda level, involving an attempt to suppress the worship of the Argive hero Adrastus at Sicyon, and the renaming of the Sicyonian tribes to make them different from those at Argos.

BIBL. Herodotus v. 67–8, vi. 126–31; Griffin, *Sikyon* 40–59.

Cleitarchus of Alexandria (c. 350–c. 300 BC) Historian.

Cleitarchus (Kleitarkhos) wrote a lost history of *Alexander the Great in at least 12 books. It is often claimed, though there is no proof, that he was a native of Alexandria, and that he wrote in the first quarter of the third century BC. If one accepts that his history was written before that of *Ptolemy I (i.e. before c. 290), and that he need not have accompanied Alexander's expedition (perhaps because of his youth), he could have lived c. 350–c. 300 and written c. 315–300. Alexandria might then have been his adopted, not native, city. In any event, Cleitarchus' work suggests that he was somehow connected to that city, since his popularizing, rhetorical account of Alexander lies behind the later tradition of romantic Alexander-history which began there. Cleitarchus was popular in the Roman Empire, and was used by *Diodorus Siculus (book xvii) among others, although he was often criticized for inaccuracy.

BIBL. *FGrH* 137; W. W. Tarn, *Alexander the Great* (1948) ii; P. Goukowsky, *Essai sur les Origines du Mythe d'Alexandre 336–270 BC* (1978); Fraser, *Ptolemaic Alexandria* ii. 717, notes 3–4.

Cleitias Vase painter, active c. 575–550 BC.

Cleitias (Kleitias) was a master of developed Athenian black figure vase-painting. He worked regularly with the potter Ergotimus: they sign together four times and once each separately. About 16 vases have been attributed to Cleitias, of which the masterpiece is the François vase in Florence, which introduced a new interest in extended mythological narrative – 270 human and animal figures are depicted, over 100 of them accompanied by their names.

BIBL. Beazley, *ABV* 76–80, and *Paralipomena* 29–30; Boardman, *Black Figure* 33–4.

Cl(e)itomachus (c. 186–109 BC) Philosopher.

A Carthaginian originally called Hasdrubal, Cl(e)itomachus (Kleitomakhos) went to Athens at the age of 40 and studied under the sceptical philosopher *Carneades, whom he succeeded briefly as head of the Academy in 129 BC. His many works are lost. They were said to be long-winded. It is probably due to him that much indirect evidence of Carneades' philosophy survives.

BIBL. Diogenes Laertius iv. 67.

Cleitus ('Black Cleitus') Macedonian general, died 328/7 BC.

The brother of *Alexander the Great's wet-nurse, Cleitus (Kleitos) became commander of the royal cavalry squadron and later joint commander of the Companion Cavalry. He is chiefly famous for saving Alexander's life at the battle of the Granicus (334 BC) and losing his own at Alexander's hands during a drunken quarrel at Maracanda (autumn 328). The dispute concerned Alexander's supposed depreciation of the Macedonians and his orientalizing tendencies. As Cleitus' taunts infuriated Alexander, those present hustled him out of the room; but he returned by another entrance, whereupon the king ran him through with his spear. This grisly incident, about which Alexander was massively contrite when it was too late, became a natural topic of moralizing comment.

BIBL. Berve, *Alexanderreich*, no. 427; Lane Fox, *Alexander* 309 ff.

Cleitus ('White Cleitus') Macedonian general, died 318 BC.

An officer in *Alexander the Great's army, Cleitus (Kleitos) later decisively defeated the Athenian fleet at Amorgos (322 BC), ending the Lamian War. He received the satrapy of Lydia (321), but was expelled by *Antigonus and joined *Polyperchon's camp; he helped to engineer the fall of *Phocion. His attempt to thwart Antigonus' crossing of the Bosporus ended in total failure, and he was killed while trying to escape to Macedonia.

BIBL. Berve, *Alexanderreich*, no. 428.

Cleobulina Elegiac poetess, *c*. 600 BC (?).

To Cleobulina (Kleoboulinē), are attributed two riddles in elegiacs (fr. 2 already known *c*. 400 BC, fr. 1 known to *Aristotle) and a riddling hexameter, though the ascription of the latter is as dubious as Diogenes Laertius' attribution of 3,000 riddling hexameters to her father, *Cleobulus of Lindos.

BIBL. West, *IEG*; *Roman World* *Diogenes Laertius.

'Portrait' of Cleobulus, one of the *Seven Sages, from a late 2nd-century AD mosaic from Cologne. Cologne, Römisch-Germanisches Museum.

Cleobulus Tyrant of Lindos *c*. 600 BC.

Little is known of the life of Cleobulus (Kleoboulos), who was later known chiefly for his wise sayings (he was one of the *Seven Sages). He was said to have rebuilt the temple of Athena at Lindos, and the temple chronicle records a dedication by him after a campaign in Lycia.

BIBL. Diogenes Laertius i. 89 ff.; Lindian Chronicle C 23.

Cleombrotus Agiad king of Sparta 380–371 BC.

Cleombrotus (Kleombrotos) showed himself half-hearted about the Theban war of the 370s BC (and, if responsible

for the *Sphodrias raid, may have thought Athens the more proper enemy), though he evidently protected Phocis from Theban attack *c*. 375. In 371 he invaded Boeotia to enforce city autonomy, was disastrously defeated at Leuctra, and became the first Spartan king since *Leonidas to die in battle.

BIBL. Poralla, *Prosopographie*, no. 434.

Cleomenes I Agiad king of Sparta *c*. 525–488 BC.

As with other outstanding Spartan chieftains, Cleomenes' (Kleomenēs) successes provoked the resentment of his own community, resulting in his exile and death and in a historical tradition that was extremely hostile. The ancient sources (chiefly *Herodotus) are so sparse as to make any assessment of his career or policies highly hypothetical.

Cleomenes belonged to the Agiad family; his father was King *Anaxandridas, and his mother was Anaxandridas' second wife. It has been plausibly suggested that this made him a protégé of the ephor *Chilon, whose programme of military expansion in opposition to Argos he would then have inherited. In 519/18 he was asked by the Plataeans to support them against Thebes; he recommended an alliance with Peisistratid Athens instead. Some scholars put this event ten years later, in the aftermath of Cleomenes' intervention at Athens to expel the tyrant *Hippias. In any case he intervened in Athenian affairs again in 508, unsuccessfully supporting *Isagoras against *Cleisthenes; *c*. 506, in an attempt to restore Isagoras; and *c*. 504, to restore the Peisistratids. The opposition of the Peloponnesian allies and of the other king *Demaratus resulted in failure on each occasion.

Cleomenes' reported behaviour with respect to Athens

Spartan warrior of the time of Cleomenes I. Courtesy, Wadsworth Atheneum, Hartford, Conn.

makes it impossible to interpret his policy as being motivated by opposition to tyranny. Similarly, there is no trace of consistent hostility to Persia: Ionian ambassadors seeking support for their revolt in 498 met with no success. Although Cleomenes crushingly defeated Argos (later a pro-Persian state) at the battle of Sepeia (perhaps in 494), he purposely refrained from annihilating this old enemy of Sparta, giving religious reasons as his excuse. In 492/1 he led a Spartan force against Aegina; the pretext was that Aegina supported Persia, but there may have been other reasons. This expedition too was sabotaged because of Demaratus' hostility; Cleomenes tried to have him deposed with the help of a forged oracle, but this provoked such anger that he had to flee Sparta. One theory suggests that his attempt to organize opposition to Sparta among other Peloponnesian states may be connected with the failure of the Spartan army to arrive in time for the battle of Marathon. Cleomenes returned to Sparta, where – according to Spartans – he committed suicide by the macabre process of chopping himself up.

BIBL. Herodotus v. 39–91, vi. 51–85; G. L. Huxley, *Early Sparta* (1962), chs. 6–7; Forrest, *History of Sparta*, ch. 8.

Cleomenes III Agiad king of Sparta, 235–222 BC.

Son of the Leonidas (II) who had been deposed by *Agis IV, and married to (and perhaps inspired by) the latter's widow, Cleomenes (Kleomenēs) began a second programme of reform like that begun by Agis. After strengthening Sparta's position over *Aratus of Sicyon and the Achaean League, he staged a coup in 227 BC in which he rearranged the system of Spartan government, cancelled debts, redistributed land, and enrolled new citizens. More military successes in the Peloponnese could have made Sparta the head of the Achaean League, but, although Cleomenes demanded to be made commander-in-chief, Aratus refused to concede this. His growing strength and popularity because of the reforms threatened the balance of power; Aratus asked *Antigonus Doson of Macedon to aid the League against Sparta. Antigonus and Cleomenes, after gaining support in various Peloponnesian cities, met at Sellasia in 222. Cleomenes was defeated and fled to his ally Egypt, whence he hoped for restoration, but Ptolemaic help was refused by *Sosibius. He was killed in 219 while trying to escape from prison in the palace purges which attended the accession of *Ptolemy IV.

BIBL. Forrest, *History of Sparta*; Jones, *Sparta*; Will, *Hist. pol.* ii.

Cleomenes of Naucratis Satrap of Egypt, died 322 BC.

In 331 BC Cleomenes (Kleomenēs) was given control of Arabia-by-Heroönpolis, appointed collector of taxes for Egypt, and made responsible for the building of Alexandria, and from this basis he became effective satrap of Egypt, in which role he was eventually formally confirmed by *Alexander (the Great). His (personally profitable) financial activities caused considerable hardship in Egypt and elsewhere at a time of high corn-prices, but complaints to Alexander produced no result. After Alexander's death Cleomenes was made assistant to *Ptolemy I, who soon liquidated him (322).

BIBL. *OCD*, Cleomenes (3); J. Vogt, *Chiron* i (1971); J. Seibert, *Chiron* ii (1972).

Cleon Athenian leader, died 422 BC.

The hostility of the ancient sources (*Thucydides iii–iv and *Aristophanes, *Knights* both depict him as violent and over-confident, in contrast to *Pericles) has made Cleon (Kleōn) the typical demagogue, a man with no inherited landed property who supposedly represents commercial, imperialist interests against the traditional type of leadership exemplified by Pericles; this in turn endeared him to nineteenth-century Radical historians like George Grote.

There are hints that Cleon may have opposed Pericles' policy of restraint in the 430s BC. In 427 he was the author of the proposal that the whole population of Mytilene should be executed (see *Diodotus). After the occupation of Pylos in 425, he rejected moves for a compromise peace, and won a crucial victory by capturing the 292 Spartans blockaded on Sphacteria. He was also responsible for raising the annual tribute assessment from 460 to 1,460 talents. After Thucydides had lost Amphipolis to *Brasidas, Cleon led an Athenian army in Thrace, but died in battle together with Brasidas; their deaths removed the main opponents of a peace agreement ending the *Archidamian War – the Peace of *Nicias (421).

BIBL. Davies, *Athenian Families*, no. 8674; A. Andrewes, *Phoenix* xvi (1962); H. D. Westlake, *CQ* xxiv (1974); Westlake, *Individuals in Thucydides*, ch. 5.

Cleonymus Spartan pretender, floruit 305–270 BC.

The son of *Cleomenes II, Cleonymus (Kleōnumos) never renounced his claims to the Agiad kingship, which went instead to his nephew *Areus I in 309/8 BC. In 303 he accepted a commission from the Greek city of Tarentum in Italy, and fought there as leader of a mercenary force. He quarrelled with the Tarentines and seized Corcyra, where he met *Pyrrhus of Epirus, who saw Cleonymus as his entrée into the Peloponnese even as Cleonymus saw Pyrrhus as his means to the Spartan throne. After leading a Boeotian revolt against *Demetrius Poliorcetes in 293, and fighting various Peloponnesian cities in 279, Cleonymus marched on Sparta with Pyrrhus and a large army in 272. The city was barely rescued by Areus and *Antigonus Gonatas. Cleonymus' subsequent career is unknown.

BIBL. Forrest, *History of Sparta*; Jones, *Sparta*.

Cleopatra II Queen of Egypt, c. 175/4–116/15 BC and **Cleopatra III** Queen of Egypt, 142–101 BC.

Cleopatra (Kleopatra) II, the daughter of *Ptolemy V and Cleopatra I, married her full brother *Ptolemy VI and eventually ruled together with him and their mutual brother *Ptolemy VIII during the Sixth Syrian War (170–168 BC) against *Antiochus IV. Their children were *Cleopatra Thea (married to three Seleucid kings in succession), *Ptolemy VII, and Cleopatra III. Widowed in 145, Cleopatra claimed the regency for Ptolemy VII, but married Ptolemy VIII when he returned ostensibly to rule with the boy, whom he murdered on the wedding day.

Further outrages followed when Ptolemy VIII also married Cleopatra III in 142, keeping both queens but preferring daughter to mother. Cleopatra II revolted in 132, proclaiming king her son by Ptolemy VIII, Ptolemy Memphites. When the father hid the child, she proclaimed herself sole queen, and Ptolemy murdered Memphites. As civil war threatened, Cleopatra turned to her Seleucid son-

Marble portrait head, possibly of Cleopatra II or her daughter Cleopatra III, Ptolemaic queens of Egypt. Paris, Musée du Louvre.

Portrait head (the statue is of a different date) identified as the Ptolemaic queen Cleopatra VII from its resemblance to coin portraits. Vatican Museum.

in-law *Demetrius II, and offered him the Egyptian throne in return for his help. She fled to Asia, and Demetrius was killed with her husband's connivance.

Peace was somehow restored in 124, and the *ménage à trois* proclaimed a public reconciliation. Cleopatra II died in 116/15.

Ptolemy VIII (died 116) had willed his power to Cleopatra III and to whichever son she chose. She became hopelessly embroiled in the rivalries of her two sons, *Ptolemy IX and *Ptolemy X, and may have been murdered by the latter in 101.

BIBL. Otto and Bengtson, *Bayer. Abh.* n.f. xvii (1938); Will, *Hist. pol.* ii; Koenen, *ZPE* v (1970), 61 ff.

Cleopatra VII Ptolemaic queen, 51–30 BC.

The daughter of *Ptolemy XII Auletes, Cleopatra (Kleopatra) became joint ruler upon marriage to her younger brother *Ptolemy XIII in 51 BC. When Julius Caesar arrived in Alexandria, he ordered a reconciliation in the impending war between brother and sister, but, meeting Cleopatra (who, according to tradition, came wrapped in a carpet), he stayed and fought on her behalf the 'Alexandrian War', in which Ptolemy XIII was killed in 47. After Caesar and Cleopatra had taken their legendary Nile cruise, he left her in Alexandria, pregnant by him, supported by his legions, and married in haste to her other brother *Ptolemy XIV. When Ptolemy XV (Caesarion) was born, Cleopatra moved her court to

Caesar's villa in Rome, but she returned to Egypt after his death in 44, as the father's will made no provisions for the child. She poisoned her husband and declared her son joint ruler.

Summoned to Cilicia by Mark Antony in 41, Cleopatra sailed to him in her gold barge adorned as Aphrodite, a picture immortalized by Plutarch – and Shakespeare. Antony spent the winter of 41–40 with her in Alexandria, where their twins Alexander 'Sun' (Helios) and Cleopatra 'Moon' (Selene) were born. Their more permanent alliance after 37 involved Cleopatra in Antony's civil war against Octavian. His enthusiastic adoption of the trappings of Hellenistic monarchy and his vociferous support for Cleopatra and their children gave him a powerful base in the East, but Rome turned against him, and Octavian declared war on Cleopatra as the source of the evil in 32.

Antony was defeated at Actium in 31, and killed himself in Alexandria in 30. In order not to fall prey to Octavian, Cleopatra succumbed to the fatal bite of an asp, whereupon Egypt passed into Rome's control.

Caesarion was put to death, and 'Sun' and 'Moon' marched in Octavian's triumph in 29. The girl later married King Juba II of Mauretania, but the fates of 'Sun' and Cleopatra's other son by Antony, Ptolemy Philadelphus, are unknown.

Although as formidable as any of the Macedonian Ptolemaic queens, Cleopatra was perhaps the only one who at times considered herself an Egyptian. Although apparently not a conventional beauty, she used her considerable allure to her own political advantage. It is ultimately impossible to say whether she was ruled primarily by her head or by her heart.

BIBL. Will, *Hist. pol.* ii; W. W. Tarn and M. P. Charlesworth, *Octavian, Antony and Cleopatra* (1965); H. Volkmann, *Cleopatra* (1958); *Roman World* *Cleopatra, *Juba II, Gaius Julius *Caesar, *Octavian, *Plutarch.

Cleopatra Macedonian princess, died 309 BC.

Cleopatra (Kleopatra), daughter of *Philip II and *Olympias, was the wife of *Alexander of Epirus, though her marriage was marred by the assassination of Philip. She ruled Epirus as regent from *c*. 344 BC until *Olympias supplanted her. She returned to Macedonia in 325. After the death of her brother, *Alexander the Great, she represented a desirable match for several of the Diadochi (Successors), but their mutual hostilities kept her single and for many years an effective prisoner in Sardis. An attempt to travel to Egypt (to marry *Ptolemy I) caused *Antigonus to order her murder in 309.

BIBL. Berve, *Alexanderreich*, no. 433; Macurdy, *Hellenistic Queens* 33 ff.

Cleopatra (alias **Eurydice**) Wife of *Philip II of Macedonia, 337–336 BC.

Cleopatra (Kleopatra) was the niece of *Attalus whose marriage to *Philip II (337 BC) provoked a break with *Olympias and tension with *Alexander (the Great). After Philip's murder, and in Alexander's absence (335), Olympias forced Cleopatra to commit suicide. Alexander's displeasure did not prevent him from liquidating her male relatives.

BIBL. Berve, *Alexanderreich*, no. 434; W. Heckel, *Phoenix* xxxii (1978).

Cleopatra Berenice: see Later *Ptolemies

Cleopatra Thea Seleucid queen, floruit *c*. 150–120 BC.

The life of Cleopatra Thea (Kleopatra Thea), the daughter of *Ptolemy VI and *Cleopatra II, illustrates the lot of various Hellenistic princesses who were used as dynastic pawns. She was first married to the Seleucid pretender *Alexander Balas to cement his alliance with her father, and, when Ptolemy's alliance was switched to the legitimate king *Demetrius II, Cleopatra was

Coin portrait of Cleopatra Thea, Seleucid queen, with her first husband *Alexander Balas.

married to him. Her son by Balas, Antiochus VI, was proclaimed king, then deposed and murdered by *Diodotus Tryphon during his *coup* in 144 BC. While Demetrius was a Parthian prisoner (139–129), Cleopatra married his brother *Antiochus VII Sidetes, who claimed the throne. She was 'widowed' by Antiochus' death when Demetrius returned in 129; their relationship appears to have soured, since she did not help him when he was threatened and ultimately killed by the usurper Alexander II Zabinas in 127/6.

Cleopatra's next route to power lay through her sons. Her elder son by Demetrius, Seleucus V, claimed the throne on his father's death, but Cleopatra had him killed when he resisted her control. *Antiochus VIII Grypus, the younger, was established on the throne after 123; he yielded to his mother's precedence for a time, but poisoned her as she tried to poison him in 121–120.

BIBL. Macurdy, *Hellenistic Queens*; Will, *Hist. pol.*; Bellinger, 'End of the Seleucids'.

Cleophon Athenian politician, late 5th century BC.

Tendentious sources list Cleophon (Kleophōn) among the extreme democrats. On several occasions between 410 and 404 BC he led the opposition to peace with Sparta. He was responsible for introducing state subsidies for impoverished citizens (the *diobelia*). In 404 he was prosecuted, and he died in poverty. He was said to be a property-less lyre-maker.

BIBL. E. Vanderpool, *Hesperia* xxi (1952).

Clitomachus: see Cl(e)itomachus

Clonas Musician and poet, *c*. 660 BC (?).

Clonas (Klonas) of Tegea or Thebes systematized the seven aulodic nomes, himself writing those called *Apothetos* and *Schoinion*, and *prosodia*. A Sicyonian record attributed the *Three-part* nome to Clonas, not *Sacadas, and *Heracleides Ponticus made him a hexameter and elegiac poet.

BIBL. Pseudo-Plutarch, *On Music*, 1132C–1134B; PW xi. 875 f.

Colaeus Samian navigator, *c*. 638 BC.

Colaeus (Kōlaios) was captain of a Samian ship which was blown off course on a voyage to Egypt and carried through the Straits of Gibraltar to Tartessus (biblical Tarshish). This was the first contact the Greeks had with this rich Spanish silver-mining area and its friendly king Arganthonius, and Colaeus returned immensely rich.

BIBL. Herodotus iv. 152; Boardman, *Greeks Overseas* 213.

Colotes Epicurean philosopher, 4th–3rd centuries BC.

A pupil and admirer of *Epicurus, Colotes (Kolōtēs) of Lampsacus wrote polemical works on earlier philosophers, such as *Plato and *Democritus, to show that conformity with the doctrines of other philosophers would make life impossible. His work is mainly known from Plutarch's *Against Colotes*, in which he is criticized for misinterpreting his opponents. He was especially critical about those who doubted the trustworthiness of sense-perception.

BIBL. Plutarch, *Moralia* 1107–27; *Roman World* *Plutarch.

Conon Athenian leader, died 392 BC.

The family of Conon (Konōn) had been notable for several generations; his grandfather appears to have been the archon of 462 BC. He himself first appears as *strategos* in 414/13, commanding the Athenian fleet based at Naupactus. After the fall of *Alcibiades in 407, Conon became the main commander in the Aegean. In 406 a Spartan fleet blockaded him in Mytilene; he was freed by the destruction of the Spartans at Arginusae, and, because he had been unable to take part in that battle, he was not executed like six of the other *strategoi* (see *Theramenes). He was the only Athenian general to escape from the Spartans at Aegospotami in the following year. He fled to King *Evagoras, an old benefactor of Athens, who was trying to unite Cyprus under his rule (while remaining loyal to Persia). In 400, after the defeat of the pro-Spartan *Cyrus the Younger, Conon assisted the Persians against Sparta; in 397 *Artaxerxes II appointed him to command the Persian fleet provided by *Pharnabazus. He captured Rhodes, and after various engagements decisively destroyed the Spartans at the battle of Cnidos in 394. This put an end to the period of Spartan dominance in the Aegean. The Persian fleet attacked Laconia and occupied Cythera. Pharnabazus returned to Asia, leaving Conon to lead the Persian fleet to Athens, where he rebuilt the Long Walls, and settled cleruchs in the old Athenian colonies of Lemnos, Imbros, and Scyros.

The restoration of Athenian power forced Sparta to accept a cessation of hostilities. Pharnabazus' rival, the pro-Spartan Lydian satrap, *Tiribazus, convened a peace conference at Sardis (392), where he had Conon arrested. He managed to escape to Evagoras, but died soon after. His son was the general *Timotheus (2).

BIBL. Davies, *Athenian Families*, no. 13700; G. Barbieri, *Conone* (1955); R. Seager, *JHS* lxxxvii (1967).

Conon of Samos Astronomer and mathematician, 3rd century BC.

Conon (Konōn) was greatly admired by *Archimedes, but little is now known of his achievements. He was said to have discovered the constellation Coma Berenices (i.e. Lock of Berenice – see *Berenice II, *Callimachus), and to have worked on solar eclipses with the help of Egyptian records. Archimedes suggests that Conon would have anticipated his own work on spirals, if he had not died young.

BIBL. Archimedes, *On Spirals*; Callimachus, fr. 110 (*Coma Berenices*).

Corax Syracusan rhetorician, 5th century BC.

Corax's (Korax) name is associated with that of *T(e)isias (traditionally his pupil) as the first professional teacher of rhetoric. The rise of rhetoric took place in the aftermath of the replacement of the Deinomenid tyranny (see *Gelon, *Hieron I) in 467 BC by a democratic constitution which established popular courts (i.e. with large juries).

BIBL. Kennedy, *Art of Persuasion* 58–61; D. A. G. Hinks, *CQ* xxxiv (1940).

Corinna Lyric poetess, 6th–5th centuries BC (?).

A native of Tanagra in Boeotia, Corinna (Korinna) was believed by ancient scholars (of the first century BC onwards) to have been an older contemporary of *Pindar, and anecdotes were told of her rivalry with him. Some

Marble statuette of a young girl with the name 'Corinna' inscribed on the plinth. Probably a Roman copy of a 4th-century BC work. Compiègne, Musée Vivenel.

modern scholars, however, reject this evidence and place her as late as 200 BC.

Her poems were on mythical subjects, generally of local Boeotian interest; one of the papyrus fragments describes a singing contest between two personified Boeotian mountains. The fragments exhibit a literary dialect but a very simple and unaffected style.

BIBL. Lesky, *Greek Literature*; *Lyra Graeca* (Loeb) iii; D. L. Page, *Corinna* (1953).

Cotys King of Thrace, *c.* 383–360 BC.

Initially friendly to Athens (he was *Iphicrates' father-in-law and an Athenian citizen), Cotys (Kotus) later (365 BC) seized Sestos, inaugurating a war with Athens which lasted (with few Athenian successes) until Cotys' murder in a private vendetta. The united Thracian kingdom did not survive him.

BIBL. PW xi. 1551–2.

Crantor Philosopher, late 4th–early 3rd centuries BC.

Crantor (Krantōr) of Soli left his home in Cilicia for Athens, and studied under the Academic philosophers *Xenocrates and *Polemon. He wrote many works, of which only short fragments remain. The most famous was *On Grief*, which Cicero said was 'not a large book but golden, to be learnt word by word'. He lived with *Arcesilaus of Pitane, and bequeathed him his property.

BIBL. Diogenes Laertius iv. 24–7; *Roman World* *Cicero.

Craterus Macedonian general, died 321 BC.

Craterus (Krateros) commanded units of *Alexander the Great's army at the battles of the Granicus (334 BC) and Issus (333); at Gaugamela (331) he led the left flank of the Macedonian phalanx. He was given independent commands in Sogdiana and Bactria, and founded by the cities of Nicaea and Bucephala in the Punjab. He subsequently led the remainder of his army back to Persia by an inland route.

In 324 Craterus married the Persian princess Amastrine, *Darius III's niece, taking second place after *Hephaestion in the list of Macedonian chieftains involved in this mass wedding. Alexander ordered him to return to Macedonia to replace *Antipater as *strategus* in Europe, but he had progressed no further than Cilicia when Alexander died. Under the arrangements agreed by the Macedonian generals at Babylon, Craterus was given general responsibility for the government of King *Philip Arrhidaeus (*prostatēs tēs tou Arrhidaiou basileias*); just what this implied is disputed. He returned to Europe, and helped Antipater suppress an attempt by the Greeks to regain their independence in the Lamian War at the battle of Crannon (322). He married Antipater's daughter *Phila. In 321, threatened by the increasing power of *Perdiccas, he and Antipater joined *Antigonus, *Lysimachus, and *Ptolemy (I) against him, but he was defeated and killed by *Eumenes of Cardia in Asia Minor.

BIBL. Will, *Hist. pol.* i.

Craterus the Younger *Strategus* of Corinth, 321–c. 255 BC.

A trusted half-brother of *Antigonus Gonatas from the first marriage of their mother *Phila (a daughter of *Antipater the Regent) to *Craterus (a brilliant officer of *Alexander the Great), Craterus the Younger (Krateros) was appointed by Gonatas as *strategus* over the vital positions of Corinth and Euboea. He aided Gonatas against Aetolia, and in 264 BC stopped *Areus of Sparta at Corinth in his march to relieve Athens in the War of *Chremonides. He may have been the selector of, and author of a commentary on, a collection of Athenian decrees. His son, *Alexander of Corinth, succeeded him as *strategus*.

BIBL. Tarn, *Antigonos Gonatas*; *FGrH* 342; W. Fellmann,

Antigonos Gonatas, König der Makedonen, und die griechischen Staaten (1930).

Crates Comic poet from *c.* 450 BC.

According to *Aristotle, Crates (Kratēs) was the first poet of Attic comedy to 'abandon the invective form and write stories and plots of general interest'. What this meant in practice is not made clear either by the fragments or by *Aristophanes, *Knights* 537–40.

BIBL. Lesky, *Greek Literature*; Edmonds, *Attic Comedy* i.

Crates of Mallos Scholar, *c.* 175 BC.

Distinguished scholar and Stoic philosopher, Crates (Kratēs) was attracted to Pergamum by *Eumenes II to adorn the new library there. He wrote on the major Greek poets, probably in monograph form (evidence is poor), devoting his energies chiefly to the allegorizing exegesis perfected in the Stoic system – note his cosmic interpretation of **Achilles' Shield. This was surely anathema to the scientific procedure of his Alexandrian contemporary *Aristarchus of Samothrace. The two men came to represent the rival encampments of Stoic anomaly and Alexandrian analogy in grammatical studies – the recognition of idiosyncrasy in language versus the imposition of a principle of regularity and paradigmatic type (an enduring controversy which spread far beyond linguistics). While visiting Rome as an envoy (168 BC?) Crates broke his leg in a drain; the lectures he gave during convalescence made a profound impression on Roman scholarship.

BIBL. Pfeiffer, *Classical Scholarship* i.

Crates of Thebes Cynic philosopher, floruit 328–324 BC.

Crates (Kratēs) studied in Athens and was converted to

Idealized portrait bust of the philosopher Crates (an identification suggested by its resemblance to a wall-painting in Rome). Naples, Museo Nazionale.

the 'Cynic' philosophy of *Diogenes of Sinope. He disposed of his property and lived a life of poverty, wandering with his wife Hipparchia, who shared his philosophical beliefs. There are many anecdotes, some illustrating the general respect for him, others his austere manner. According to one, he was called 'Door-opener', because 'he used to enter every house and rebuke'. He wrote letters, poems, and tragedies, of which a few fragments survive.

BIBL. Diogenes Laertius vi. 85–98.

Crateuas Pharmacologist, early 1st century BC.

Botanist and physician to *Mithridates VI, Crateuas (Krateuas) produced a work on the pharmacological uses of plants and a fine illustrated herbal (fragments survive) to which Dioscorides was much indebted. The best drawings in the Juliana Anicia manuscript of Dioscorides apparently derive from Crateuan originals.

BIBL. PW xi. 2. 1644; *Roman World* *Dioscorides.

Cratinus Comic poet, active c. 450–c. 423 BC.

One of the leading poets of Old Comedy, Cratinus (Kratinos) is known to us from numerous fragments, including some that mock *Pericles. He was noted for his use of invective, uninhibited even by comparison with *Aristophanes; but at least one of his plays lacked invective altogether. Aristophanes praises his earlier work, but alleges that he has become a despised and senile drunkard.

BIBL. Aristophanes, *Knights* 526–36; Lesky, *Greek Literature*; Edmonds, *Attic Comedy* i.

Cratippus Historian, early 4th century BC (?).

Apparently an Athenian, Cratippus (Kratippos) composed a history which continued from where *Thucydides breaks off (410 BC) down to *Conon's victory at Cnidos (394). As in book viii of Thucydides, there appear to have been no formal set speeches.

Curiously, there are no references to Cratippus before the time of Augustus. This has led some scholars to suggest that he was actually a late Hellenistic writer. But it is more likely that he was a younger contemporary of Thucydides, whose death he mentions; some plausibly identify him with the *Oxyrhynchus Historian.

BIBL. *FGrH* ii. A, no. 64; H. D. Westlake, *CR* x (1960); *Roman World* *Augustus.

Cratylus Philosopher, late 5th century BC.

Cratylus (Kratulos) developed *Heracl(e)itus' theory of universal flux in an extreme form. Heracl(e)itus held that one cannot step in the same river twice, because 'different and different waters flow'. Cratylus claimed that one cannot do so even once. (Presumably the water changes even as one steps.) He believed that, since we can say nothing true about what is always changing, we should say nothing, and he 'merely waved a finger'. His scepticism about knowledge of the perceptible world greatly influenced *Plato.

BIBL. Plato, *Cratylus*.

Cresilas Sculptor, active c. 450–420 BC.

About a dozen works by Cresilas (Krēsilas) of Cydonia in Crete are known from literature and signed statue-bases. He seems to have worked mainly in Athens. We

Idealized portrait herm of *Pericles. Roman copy of an original by the sculptor Cresilas. Found in a villa near Tivoli. Vatican Museum.

have in good Roman copies his wounded Amazon – that is if we could tell it apart from those by *Pheidias and *Polycleitus made at the same time, supposedly for a competition at Ephesus – and probably his idealized portrait of *Pericles as general (*strategos*).

BIBL. P. Orlandini, *Kresilas* (1952); Richter, *Sculpture and Sculptors* 178–81; Robertson, *History of Greek Art* 333–7.

Critias (c. 460–403 BC) Leader of the 'Thirty Tyrants'.

Critias (Kritias) belonged to one of the wealthiest Athenian families. He had literary interests, writing plays and poems (one in praise of the constitution of Sparta) as well as philosophical and rhetorical treatises. He appears in several of the dialogues of his nephew *Plato.

Although implicated in the affair of the *Hermocopids, he seems not to have been involved in the oligarchic coup of 411 BC; he advocated the recall of *Alcibiades, and appears to have been exiled at *Cleophon's behest after Alcibiades' fall. He returned to Athens with the Spartan occupying forces in 404, and led the pro-Spartan oligarchy (which became known as the 'Thirty Tyrants'). The execution of his moderate rival *Theramenes alienated the population, and conflict within the Spartan leadership led to the withdrawal of military support;

Critias died fighting the democratic exiles under
*Thrasybulus.

BIBL. Diels and Kranz, *Vorsokratiker* ii. 371 ff., no. 88;
Guthrie, *Greek Philosophy* iii. 298.

Crito of Athens Disciple of Socrates, *c*. 400 BC.

Crito (Kritōn) was a devoted follower of *Socrates, and
being very wealthy was able to plan for Socrates to escape
his death sentence and go into exile. But Socrates could
not be persuaded. *Plato gives an account of his reasons
for refusing in his dialogue *Crito*. Some writings (now lost)
were attributed to Crito, but it is unlikely that he was a
distinguished thinker.

BIBL. Plato, *Crito*.

Critolaus Philosopher, 2nd century BC.

As head of the Peripatetic school of philosophy,
Critolaus (Kritolaos) of Phaselis in Lycia revived
philosophical and scientific work in the school, which had
flagged since the headship of *Lycon. He was chosen,
with the philosophers *Carneades and *Diogenes of
Seleucia, to form a delegation in 156/5 BC to plead with
the Romans for the remission of a fine imposed on Athens
for the destruction of Oropus. Their eloquence drew such
enthusiastic crowds that Cato, fearing the enfeebling effect
of philosophy on the Roman young, arranged for their
early departure.

BIBL. F. Wehrli, *Die Schule des Aristoteles* (1944–59);
Roman World *Cato the Elder.

Critolaus and **Diaeus** Achaean leaders, 146 BC.

Critolaus (Kritolaos) and Diaeus (Diaios) were two
popular Achaean leaders who, after the disappearance of
the restraining influence of *Callicrates of Leontium, were
largely responsible for the agitation which led in 146 BC to
the Achaean War with its disastrous consequences for
Greece. Sent as an envoy to Rome to argue against Sparta
in 149/8, Diaeus probably severely prejudiced the Senate
against the Achaean League. His misrepresentation of the
Senate's position led to war between the League and
Sparta. As the situation worsened, Critolaus and Diaeus
rashly emboldened the Achaeans to refuse to negotiate
with Rome. In 146 Critolaus raised a large force in the
Peloponnese and central Greece, despite the warning of
*Metellus Macedonicus. When rushing north to attack the
latter, Critolaus was severely defeated and probably
killed. Diaeus, desperately rallying a defence in the
Peloponnese, was defeated by *Mummius and committed
suicide.

BIBL. Will, *Hist. pol.* ii. 328 ff.

Croesus King of Lydia, 560–546 BC.

Croesus (Kroisos) succeeded his father *Alyattes, and
continued the conquest of the Ionian Greeks while
cultivating the friendship of those on the mainland,
especially the Delphic oracle. *Solon visited his court, but
offended Croesus by refusing to agree that he was the
happiest man in the world, explaining that he would not
call any man happy until he was dead, when it was
certain that his whole life had been fortunate. Croesus
brought about his own downfall by attacking *Cyrus,
who defeated him and captured Sardis. He decided to
have Croesus burned alive, but when Croesus was placed
on the pyre he remembered his conversation with Solon

An Athenian vase-painting of *c*. 470 BC showing Croesus on the
pyre. Paris, Musée du Louvre.

and called out his name. Cyrus asked for an explanation,
and was so impressed by what he heard that he saved
Croesus and kept him as a trusted adviser.

BIBL. Herodotus i. 26–56, 69–92, 153–6.

Ctesias Historian, early 4th century BC.

Ctesias (Ktēsias) of Cnidos belonged to a family of
physicians; as such, he was employed as court physician
by *Artaxerxes II from 405 BC. In 398 he acted as liaison
officer between the king and *Conon, subsequently
returning home and writing a history of Persia (*Persika*) in
23 volumes. Ctesias' style is highly rhetorical, aiming to
involve the emotions of his audience; consequently his
work is extremely unreliable in matters of fact, an
example of how fluid the boundaries are in antiquity
between the categories of romance and history.

BIBL. *FGrH* iii. C, no. 688; *Persika* fragments, ed. J.
Gilmore (1888); T. S. Brown, *Historia* xxvii (1978); J. M.
Bigwood, *Phoenix* xxx (1976).

Ctesibius Inventor, floruit *c*. 275–260 BC.

Ctesibius (Ktēsibios) was the most famous inventor of
his day, and probably worked under the patronage of the
*Ptolemies. Although some argue for two homonymous
inventors, the later with a second-century BC date, there

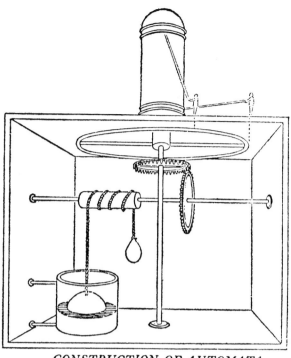

CONSTRUCTION OF AUTOMATA

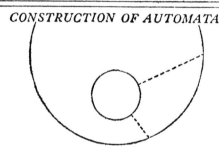

Hypothetical reconstructions of two automatic clocks invented by Ctesibius and described by Vitruvius (ix. 84 ff.).

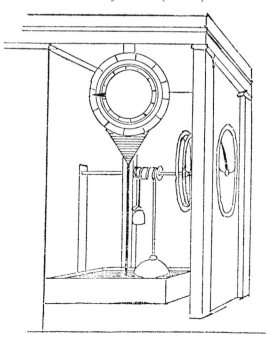

was probably only one Ctesibius, the son of a barber in Alexandria, who lived in the first half of the third century.

Ctesibius appears to have been a theorist (owing much to the theories of *Straton of Lampsacus) as well as an engineer: he discussed some of his theories (*Pneumatic Theorems*), and described some of his machines (*Commentaries*). He probably also taught in Alexandria, since *Philon of Byzantium considered himself his pupil. Some of his inventions are described by Philon, Vitruvius, and *Heron: a torsion catapult, the air-catapult, the water-organ, an accurate water-clock, and a force-pump with a cylinder and plunger. Apart from his interest in pneumatics, Ctesibius experimented with changing the direction of forces supplied by energy-sources (the water-clock had a rack and pinion mechanism), and also contrived ingenious toys such as self-moving statues and mechanically singing birds. He constructed a famous rhyton (a type of drinking-horn) which produced a musical tone as the wine flowed out; this was dedicated in a temple of *Arsinoe II as Aphrodite, and was commemorated in a neat epigram by *Hedylus.

BIBL. A. G. Drachmann, *Centaurus* ii (1951) 1 ff., and *Ktesibios, Philon and Heron: A Study in Ancient Pneumatics* (1948); Gow and Page, *Hellenistic Epigrams* 1843 ff.; Fraser, *Ptolemaic Alexandria* i. 425 ff.; *Roman World* *Vitruvius.

Cyclic Poets 7th–6th centuries BC.

A number of poets composed epics clearly intended to fill in the considerable areas of the Trojan legend not covered by *Homer's *Iliad* and *Odyssey*. Known chiefly from the *Chrestomathia* (*Handbook*) of Proclus, who already has them arranged to form a 'cycle', these poems were: (i) *Cypria*, in 11 books, starting with the Judgement of Paris, offering many incidents in the gathering of the expedition and landing at Troy, and many more in the Troad (including an inevitable union of **Achilles and Helen) until Briseis' capture and Achilles' quarrel with **Agamemnon. *Herodotus rejects its attribution to Homer, most ascribed it to Stasinus (Stasinos) of Cyprus (a conflict which legend resolved by making it a dowry from Homer to his son-in-law Stasinus), and Hegesias (Hegēsias) of Cypriot Salamis was also proposed. (ii) *Aethiopis*, in five books, dealing with the deaths of Troy's allies, Penthesilea the Amazon and Memnon the Ethiopian, and of Achilles himself. It was ascribed to Arctinus (Arktinos) of Miletus (see *Eumelus). (iii) *Little Iliad*, in four books, running from the award of Achilles' armour, which led to **Ajax's suicide, to the wooden horse and sack of Troy. It was most often ascribed to Lesches (Leskhēs) of Mytilene or Pyrrha, but Thestorides (Thestoridēs) of Phocaea, Diodorus (Diodōros) of Erythrae, and Cinaethon (Kinaithōn) of Lacedaemon were also proposed. (iv) *Sack of Troy*, in two books, overlapping the *Little Iliad*, and going from Trojan reactions to the wooden horse to the final departure of the Greeks. It was ascribed to Arctinus; the subject was also treated by *Sacadas and *Stesichorus. (v) *Returns of Heroes*, in five books, covering **Menelaus' wanderings and Agamemnon's murder and avenging by Orestes. It was usually ascribed to Agias (or Hegias (Hēgias)) of Troezen. (vi) *Telegony*, in two books to follow on from the *Odyssey*. It told of **Odysseus' death at the hands of a son by Circe, Telegonus, who then married

Penelope, while Telemachus married Circe. Another son, Arcesilaus, suggests sixth-century dating for the author, Eugammon (Eugammōn) of Cyrene, whose king was so named (see *Battiads).

Some non-Trojan epics were also included in the 'cycle': a *Theogony*, a *Titanomachy* (by Arctinus or *Eumelus), an *Oedipodeia* by Cinaethon of Lacedaemon, a *Thebais* (often, as perhaps by *Callinus, given to Homer), and an *Epigoni* (*Sons of Heroes*).

BIBL. Kinkel *EGF*; *Homeri Opera*, ed. T. W. Allen, v. (1912); Huxley, *Epic Poetry*; *Roman World* *Proclus.

Cylon Would-be tyrant of Athens, c. 630 BC.

An Athenian aristocrat, Cylon (Kulōn) first distinguished himself by winning an Olympic victory. With the support of his father-in-law, *Theagenes of Megara, he planned to make himself tyrant of Athens, and seized the Acropolis. He was besieged there by the archons, led by Megacles the *Alcmaeonid, and fled when he found his position hopeless. His followers sought sanctuary at an altar, but were dragged away and executed. This impious act was believed to have brought a hereditary curse upon the Alcmaeonids.

BIBL. Herodotus v. 71; Thucydides i. 126; *Epitome of Heracleides* 2 (part of the Aristotelean *Constitution of Athens*).

Cynisca Spartan princess, late 5th century BC.

Cynisca (Kuniska) was the daughter of the Eurypontid king *Archidamus I. She was the first woman to enter a chariot at the Olympics, winning the Games twice. The base of a statue-group dedicated by her has been found at Olympia.

BIBL. Xenophon, *Agesilaus* ix. 6; *Sammlung der griechischen Dialektinschriften* iii. 2 (1898), no. 4418.

Cypselus Tyrant of Corinth, c. 657–627 BC.

Cypselus (Kupselos) became tyrant by overthrowing the Bacchiad dynasty. The Bacchiads intermarried as a means of keeping their power within the family, but one of their women, Labda, was so deformed that none of them wanted her, and she was allowed to marry an outsider. When she produced a son, the Bacchiads realized that he might be a danger to them, and tried to have him killed, but Labda saved him by hiding him in a chest (*kupselē*), after which he was named. The 'Chest of Cypselus' which Pausanias saw at Olympia was said to have been dedicated in memory of this event. Little is known about Cypselus' policies, but he is said to have held the office of polemarch on his way to power, and he was encouraged by the Delphic oracle. He ruled for 30 years, and is said to have been so popular that he survived without a bodyguard.

BIBL. Herodotus iii. 48–53, v. 92; Aristotle, *Politics* 1315b; Andrewes, *Greek Tyrants*, ch. 4.

Cypselus, Athenian: see Philaids

Cyrus King of Persia, 559–529 BC.

Cyrus (Kuros, Persian Kurash) was the first Persian king. According to *Herodotus, he was the grandson of the Median king Astyages, whom he overthrew. When *Croesus, as Astyages' ally, attacked Cyrus, he was defeated, and Lydia, including the Ionian Greek states which were subject to it, became part of the Persian empire. Cyrus was killed in battle on his northern frontier, and his tomb can still be seen at Pasargadae. The Greeks came to regard him as a model ruler, a view expressed in *Xenophon's *Cyropaedia*.

BIBL. Herodotus i. 75–84, 95–130, 141, 152–7, 188–91, 201–14, ii. 89.

Cyrus the Younger (c. 423–401 BC) Persian satrap and usurper.

Arriving in western Asia Minor in 407 BC as satrap of Lydia, Greater Phrygia, and Cappadocia and commander of the 'troops who muster in the plain of Castolus', the 16-year-old Cyrus (Kuros), son of *Darius II, gave energetic financial support to *Lysander (as well as campaigning against the Pisidians and Mysians). His relations with Lysander's successor, *Callicratidas, were less good, and Cyrus joined in the successful request of the Greeks for Lysander's return to the naval war. In 405 he was recalled to Darius' sick-bed. (Some said that this was a pretext, the real reason being that Cyrus had executed his cousins for not deporting themselves in his presence as though he were king.) After Darius' death (405/4) Cyrus' elder brother succeeded as *Artaxerxes II, and Cyrus was accused of having planned his murder. His mother's importunities secured his release from prison, and he returned to Asia Minor, where he amassed a large mercenary force, ostensibly for a final solution of the Pisidian problem. In 401 he marched inland, met Artaxerxes' army at Cunaxa, and was killed in the ensuing battle. He was idolized by *Xenophon (q.v.), who wrote, *inter alia*, that there had 'never been anyone, Greek or barbarian, more generally beloved'.

BIBL. Xenophon, *Anabasis* i; D. M. Lewis, *Sparta and Persia* (1977); PW Suppl. iv. 1166–77.

Daedalus Sculptor.

The Greeks regarded Daedalus (Daidalos) as the original artist and craftsman. It is hard to say whether he was a real person; some sculptors active in the sixth century BC were called his pupils, but the story that he worked for King **Minos in Crete puts him back in the Bronze Age. It seems that his name came to be associated with any very ancient statue, and more recently the term 'daedalic' has been applied to seventh-century Greek sculpture.

BIBL. Stuart Jones, *Select Passages*, nos. 1–6; Robertson, *History of Greek Art* i. 34–44.

Damaratus: see Demaratus

Damarete: see Demarete

Damocles Courtier, floruit after 367 BC.

A notorious flatterer of *Dionysius II of Syracuse, Damocles (Damoklēs) unwisely expressed envy of the pleasures of a tyrant's life. Dionysius invited him to a banquet at which he had to sit beneath a sword suspended by a fine thread, to make the point that a tyrant is too frightened to enjoy the pleasures that his position affords.

BIBL. PW iv. 2068.

Damon of Athens Musical theorist, 5th century BC.

An Athenian sophist, Damon (Damōn) is best known for his theory about the moral effects of different kinds of music. *Plato borrowed the theory in the *Republic*, and allowed in his ideal State only music with rhythms and modes that are beneficial to the character.

BIBL. Plato, *Republic* 399e–400c.

Damon of Syracuse Pythagorean, 4th century BC.

Legend said that two *Pythagoreans, Damon (Damōn) and Phintias, had so fine a friendship that, when Phintias was condemned to death for a plot against the tyrant *Dionysius (I or II), Damon took his place while Phintias went away to arrange his affairs. Dionysius was so astonished when Phintias returned that he released both and asked to join the friendship. It is not recorded whether they agreed.

BIBL. Diodorus Siculus x. iv. 3.

Damophanes: see **Demophanes**

Damophon Sculptor, active *c.* 200–150 BC.

All the recorded works of Damophon (Damophōn) were in the Peloponnese, and were mostly temple cult-statues or cult-groups of marble. He carried out repairs on the ivory of *Pheidias' Zeus at Olympia, and received honours there. Substantial remains of the large cult-group of the temple of Despoina (i.e. Persephone) at Lycosura in Arcadia have been excavated, and its composition can be largely reconstructed. Damophon attempts a return to the restrained grandeur of the Pheidian period, but his classicizing employs obvious elements of advanced Hellenistic style and technique. A new head of Apollo, almost certainly by him, was found quite recently at Messene.

BIBL. Dickins, *BSA* xii (1905–6), xiii (1906–7); Despinis, *AA* 1966, 378 ff.; Robertson, *History of Greek Art* 555.

Marble head of Anytus by Damophon, from the temple at Lycosura. 2nd century BC. Athens, National Museum.

Darius I King of Persia, 521–486 BC.

Darius (Dareios, Persian Darayavaush) was one of seven Persian nobles who detected and overthrew the 'pseudo-Smerdis' who had rebelled against *Cambyses. Since *Cyrus' dynasty was now extinct, they decided to choose one of their number as king, and Darius was successful with the aid of his horse, which he and his groom contrived to make neigh first when the sun rose. He reorganized the administration and finances of the Persian empire, and carried out various campaigns, including one against the Scythians in Europe (513 BC). After the suppression of the Ionian Revolt (499–494; see *Aristagoras, *Histiaeus), he sent a punitive expedition against Athens, which had supported the Ionians; this expedition was defeated at Marathon (490). Darius became all the more anxious to punish the Athenians, but died before he could organize another expedition, leaving the task to his son *Xerxes.

BIBL. Herodotus iii. 68–96, iv. 83–98, 121–43, v. 105, vi. 94–119, vii. 1–4.

Darius II Ochus (or **Nothus**) King of Persia, 424–405 BC.

One of the 17 illegitimate sons of *Artaxerxes I (Nothus means 'bastard'), Darius (Dareios) was satrap of Hyrcania before coming to the throne. The misgovernment of his queen Parysatis led to rebellions in Syria and Lydia (413 BC), Egypt and Media (410). During much of his reign the rival satraps *Pharnabazus and *Tissaphernes were involved in supporting Sparta against Athens, in order to regain control of the Greek cities of Asia Minor. Darius was the father of *Cyrus the Younger, whom he appointed to command in Ionia in 408. He was succeeded by his eldest son, *Artaxerxes II.

BIBL. Olmstead, *Persian Empire*, ch. 26.

Darius III King of Persia, 336–330 BC.

A great-nephew of *Artaxerxes II and one-time satrap of Armenia, Darius (Dareios) was made king in 336 BC by *Bagoas. In 336/5 he suppressed an Egyptian insurrection, but the Macedonian threat (see *Philip II, *Alexander the Great), about which he was initially rather unconcerned, proved another matter. Personal defeat at Issus (333) led to an unsuccessful attempt at a negotiated settlement with Alexander. After Gaugamela (331) he fled eastwards, perhaps hoping to organize further resistance, but was murdered by *Bessus.

BIBL. Berve, *Alexanderreich*, no. 244.

Datames Persian satrap and rebel, died *c.* 362 BC.

Beginning as a member of the palace guard, Datames (Datamēs) rose to governorship of Cappadocia, but, despite – or because of – his military successes in Paphlagonia and Cataonia, court intrigue undermined his position, and he became a leading rebel in the 360s BC. He was the subject of a *Life* by Nepos, who called him the bravest and wisest of the barbarians after Hamilcar and Hannibal.

BIBL. Nepos, *Datames*; PW iv. 2224–5; Judeich, *Kleinasiatische Studien*; *Roman World* *Hamilcar, *Hannibal, Cornelius *Nepos.

Datis Persian commander, floruit 490s BC.

In the 490s BC Datis was involved in the suppression of the Ionian Revolt: a clay tablet from Persepolis shows that he returned from Sardis in January or February 494 to present a report to *Darius (I). In 490 he was put in command of the expeditionary force sent to punish Eretria and Athens for their support of the Revolt; Eretria was sacked, and the population transferred to Cissia (Persia); but the Athenians repulsed the Persians at Marathon (see *Miltiades).

BIBL. Burn, *Persia and the Greeks*; D. M. Lewis, *JHS* c (1980).

D(e)inarchus 'Attic orator', floruit late 4th century BC.

D(e)inarchus (Deinarkhos) was born at Corinth; at Athens, he associated with the Peripatetics *Theophrastus and *Demetrius of Phalerum. After Demetrius' regime fell (308/7 BC), he was exiled to Chalcis in Euboea for 15 years; on his return he prosecuted his former friend Proxenus for embezzling his money. The lost speech *Against Proxenus* is the basis for later biographies.

As a metic, he wrote professionally for others (like *Lysias); 60 or 64 speeches were known in the Augustan period. Three speeches dealing with the *Harpalus scandal survive, against *Demosthenes, Aristogeiton, and Philocles; they may or may not be genuine. These speeches frequently imitate Demosthenes and other earlier orators. The large number of participial clauses makes the syntax difficult to unravel, and the speeches tend to break up into a series of vignettes without logical coherence. D(e)inarchus is not just chronologically the last of the 'Ten *Attic Orators'.

BIBL. *Minor Attic Orators* (Loeb) ii. 161 ff.; Dionysius of Halicarnassus, *On Dinarchus*; Kennedy, *Art of Persuasion* 255–7; *Roman World* *Augustus.

Demades (c. 380–319 BC) Athenian politician.

Although initially a supporter of *Demosthenes, Demades (Demades) was persuaded by *Philip II of Macedon to arrange the peace agreement between Athens and Macedon after the battle of Chaeronea (338 BC), in which Demades had been taken prisoner. He subsequently led the pro-Macedonian group at Athens, and persuaded *Alexander (the Great) to act leniently towards Athens after the destruction of Thebes in 335. He was prosecuted by *Hyper(e)ides, but acquitted. In 323 he proposed that divine honours be paid to Alexander; this, together with his involvement in the distribution of bribes by *Harpalus, led to his exile. After the battle of Crannon (322) he was recalled to lead the peace negotiations with *Antipater; this resulted in the deaths of Demosthenes and Hyper(e)ides. In 319 he himself was executed together with his son Demeas by *Cassander, for supporting the Macedonian regent *Perdiccas.

Demades' involvement in the Harpalus affair and his responsibility for the deaths of his rivals made him a morally dubious character, and thus a favourite theme for declamatory exercises, fragments of which survive on papyrus. No genuine speeches survive. In contrast to *Isocrates and Demosthenes, Demades' rhetoric was extempore, including many witty apophthegms ('Demadeia').

BIBL. *FGrH* iiB, no. 227; Davies, *Athenian Families* no. 3263; Plutarch's lives of *Phocion* and *Demosthenes*; P. Treves, *Athenaeum*, n.s. xi (1933).

Demaratus Eurypontid king of Sparta, c. 515–491 BC.

Demaratus (Demaratos; or Damaratos) was the son of King Ariston by his third marriage; there were no heirs from the previous two. In 506 BC he and King *Cleomenes (I) led a Spartan army against Athens to reinstate *Isagoras; the kings quarrelled, and the expedition achieved nothing. After Demaratus attacked Cleomenes' expedition against Aegina (c. 492), Cleomenes had him deposed as illegitimate; soon after, Demaratus fled to the Persians. *Darius (I) granted him lands in Mysia, and he accompanied *Xerxes as an adviser during the invasion of Greece.

BIBL. Forrest, *History of Sparta*, chs. 8–9; Parke, *CQ* xxxix (1945).

Demarete Sicilian princess, early 5th century BC.

Daughter of *Theron of Acragas, Demarete (Demarete; or Damarete) was married to *Gelon of Syracuse. After his death in 478 BC, she passed to his brother Polyzalus, together with the lordship of Gela. According to *Diodorus Siculus, Demarete was responsible for the peace treaty with the Carthaginians agreed after Gelon's victory at Himera in 480; the indemnity was so substantial that Syracuse was able to issue a run of 10-drachma (about 44 g.) silver coins called Damareteion in her honour.

BIBL. Diodorus Siculus XI. xxvi. 3; C. M. Kraay, *Greek Coins and History* (1969) ch. 2.

Demetrius I Poliorcetes (336–283 BC) King of Macedon, 294–288 BC.

Son of *Antigonus Monophthalmus, Demetrius (Demetrios) was a brilliant military and naval commander who frequently led his father's forces against rivals among the Diadochi (Successors). To cement an alliance between Antigonus and *Antipater the Regent, Demetrius was married in 321 BC to the latter's daughter *Phila, the widow of *Craterus the Marshal, who bore him *Antigonus Gonatas and *Stratonice I. Demetrius fought against *Eumenes of Cardia in 317–16, but was defeated by *Ptolemy I at Gaza in 312. In 307 he was lauded as the liberator of Athens from *Cassander, and in 306 he soundly defeated Ptolemy's fleet off Cyprus, after which Demetrius and his father gave themselves the title of king. An unsuccessful year-long siege of Rhodes in 305 led to the bestowal of his nickname 'Poliorcetes' (the 'Besieger') because of his extensive use of advanced siege machinery.

Although Demetrius revived the League of Corinth, which duly acknowledged him as leader in Greece against Cassander, and wisely married a sister of *Pyrrhus of Epirus, he and his father (who was killed) were defeated by *Seleucus I and *Lysimachus at Ipsus in 301. A hasty alliance with Seleucus, to whom Demetrius married Stratonice, did not deter the Besieger from triumphantly reducing Athens in 294. His opportunity to enter Macedonia arose when he was summoned on one side of the quarrel between the sons of Cassander. Demetrius probably engineered the death of the claimant *Alexander V, and was proclaimed king by the Macedonian army in the autumn of 294.

Demetrius maintained his interest in Greece largely through his son Gonatas. In 293 he had founded a new capital near Volos, Demetrias-Pagasae, and in 291 he subdued Boeotia while still in control of Athens. To repay Pyrrhus for moves against him in Boeotia, Demetrius married the former's estranged wife, Lanassa, the daughter of *Agathocles of Syracuse, which led to the

Marble head from Herculaneum, thought to represent the Macedonian king Demetrius I Poliorcetes. Naples, Museo Nazionale.

alliance of Pyrrhus with the Aetolians and hostilities lasting until 289. His thirst for empire unquenched, Demetrius prepared to recover his father's Asian possessions, which had been lost at Ipsus: this frightened all rivals into a coalition to block him on every side. Macedonia was lost in 288 through the combined attack of Lysimachus and Pyrrhus, and Athens, helped by an Egyptian fleet, revolted in 287. Demetrius' remaining forces sailed to Caria in 286 to contest the Asian territories of Lysimachus, and his marriage at about this time to a daughter of Ptolemy I may indicate Ptolemaic neutrality at this point. (A son, *Demetrius the Fair, was the result of this union.)

During 285 Demetrius was hunted throughout Asia Minor by Lysimachus' son, *Agathocles, yet he had nearly defeated Seleucus when illness and the failure of a desperate attempt to reach his ships forced his surrender. To his credit, Seleucus treated a worthy enemy in a worthy manner, though it is true that as a captive (the threat of whose release was anathema to Seleucid rivals) Demetrius was more valuable alive than dead. Fate intervened: where even dramatic reversals of fortune had failed to subdue the quixotically brilliant Poliorcetes, drink succeeded. He died in captivity in 283.

BIBL. Tarn, *Antigonos Gonatas*; G. Elkeles, *Demetrios der Städtebelagerer* (1941); C. Wehrli, *Antigone et Demetrios* (1969); Will, *Hist. pol.* i; E. Manni, *Demetrio Poliorcete* (1951).

Demetrius II King of Macedon, 239–229 BC.

The son of *Antigonus Gonatas and Phila the younger, Demetrius (Dēmētrios) was probably joint ruler for many years of his father's long reign, but one episode in the War of *Chremonides is his only known action on the king's behalf. When Antigonus was besieging Athens before c. 263 BC, Demetrius defeated an invasion of Macedonia by *Alexander of Molossia, and unseated him from the throne of Epirus. He married his mother's half-sister Stratonice II (the daughter of *Stratonice I and *Antiochus I) c. 253, but she had been repudiated in uncertain circumstances by c. 245, when Gonatas arranged his son's betrothal to the widow of *Alexander of Corinth in a deceitful ploy to regain Corinth. (The marriage did not take place.)

After acceding to the throne, Demetrius married the daughter of the Epirote Alexander, Phthia-Chryseis, whose mother sought Macedonian aid for Epirus against Aetolia. This alliance involved him in the 'Demetrian War' with Aetolia and the Achaeans c. 238. Various engagements were fought in Acarnania, Argos, and Boeotia, but Demetrius' general finally defeated *Aratus of Sicyon possibly in 237–6, or perhaps as late as c. 233. When Acarnania asked Demetrius to intervene against Aetolia in 231, he was too pressed by the Illyrian Dardani in Macedonia; he was killed fighting them on his frontier in 229, leaving a young son *Philip (later V) to face the barbarian tribe and the resulting consequences in Greece of a weakened Macedonia.

BIBL. Will, *Hist. pol.* i; E. Manni, *Athenaeum*, n.s. xxxiv (1956) 249 ff.; P. Treves, *Rend. Linc.* 1932, 167 ff.

Demetrius I Soter Seleucid king, 162–150 BC.

The elder son of Seleucus IV, Demetrius (Dēmētrios) was sent as a hostage to Rome to replace his uncle

Head of a bronze statue, possibly depicting the Seleucid king Demetrius I Soter. Rome, Museo delle Terme.

*Antiochus IV, who thereby succeeded to the throne in his place in 175 BC. When, after Antiochus' death, his infant son was proclaimed Antiochus V under the regency of a minister in 165/4, Demetrius escaped from Rome. He regained the throne, killed the child, suppressed a revolt by the latter's partisans, and was recognized as the legitimate king by Rome in 160. Demetrius' measures to quell the Jewish civil war led to the death of *Judas Maccabaeus in 160. His anger over the Cappadocian king's refusal to marry his sister Laodice (the widow of *Perseus) led him to support the claims of a pretender against *Ariarathes V in 158. Ariarathes' ally *Attalus II therefore recognized and supported a pretender to the Seleucid throne, *Alexander Balas, who constituted a threat because of Demetrius' unpopularity. The king sent his son *Demetrius II to Rome (and possibly also *Andriscus, the Macedonian pretender who proved dangerous to Rome) in an unsuccessful attempt to prevent her recognition of Balas. Demetrius was killed in 150 after a short war against Balas and his numerous allies.

BIBL. Bevan, *House of Seleucus* ii; Will, *Hist. pol.* ii.

Demetrius II Nicator Seleucid king, 145–139 and 129–125 BC.

Deprived of the throne by the usurpation of his father *Demetrius I Soter by *Alexander Balas, Demetrius (Dēmētrios) was eclipsed for three years before attacking Balas in 147 BC. He defeated the usurper with the help of the turncoat *Ptolemy VI, whose daughter *Cleopatra Thea (Balas' wife) Demetrius had married. The deaths of Balas and Ptolemy in battle in 145 placed Demetrius on the throne. Disturbances in Antioch by the Jews increased the king's unpopularity and caused Demetrius to flee in 144 in the face of another pretender, *Diodotus Tryphon, with whom the empire was divided. In a campaign on behalf of the Greeks against Parthia, Demetrius was captured in 139 and not freed until 129, when the Parthians hoped to foment a dynastic quarrel between him and his younger brother *Antiochus VII Sidetes, who claimed the throne. Antiochus was killed in battle against those same Parthians, and Demetrius regained his throne. He was offered the throne of Egypt in a plot of his mother-in-law *Cleopatra II against her husband *Ptolemy VIII. His favourable reception of the plan caused Ptolemy, at war with his wife, to raise up yet another pretender against Demetrius, Alexander II Zabinas (the supposed adopted son of Antiochus VII). Demetrius fought, but lost his kingdom to Zabinas, and was murdered in 125.

BIBL. Will, *Hist. pol.* i; Bevan, *House of Seleucus.*

Coin portraits from the first and second reigns of the Seleucid king Demetrius II Nicator, showing him as a youth and as a mature man (enlarged).

Demetrius III: see Later *Seleucids

Demetrius I of Bactria King, *c.* 200/190–before *c.* 171 BC.

The son of *Euthydemus I, Demetrius (Dēmētrios) succeeded to the throne perhaps with one or more brothers at his side. He had been promised a marriage with a Seleucid princess after his father's peace with *Antiochus III, but it is not known if this took place. In a reign shrouded in mystery, Demetrius appears to have followed a plan of expansion – in Aria, Arachosia, possibly even Gedrosia and Carmania – although Greek expansion into India probably came later. This expansion into satrapies reconquered by Antiochus III (q.v.) was probably related to the defeat of the Seleucids by the Romans at Magnesia in 189 BC.

There is numismatic evidence for a Euthydemus II, who may be a son or younger brother of Demetrius. Also at about this time an independent Greek prince, Antimachus Theos, arose to challenge the Euthydemids. It has been suggested that he was a brother of Demetrius and a successor of Euthydemus II, but he may have been unrelated to them.

Coin portrait of Demetrius I, king of Bactria, wearing an elephant-scalp head-dress (enlarged).

A second Demetrius has been conjectured from coin types; it has been suggested that he was the son or grandson of Demetrius I, or perhaps of Antimachus Theos. It may be this second Demetrius who is called 'King of India' in western classical sources, and who was deposed by *Eucratides, but there may have been only one Demetrius to whom all the evidence pertains.

BIBL. Tarn, *Greeks in Bactria . . .*; Narain, *Indo-Greeks*; Will, *Hist. pol.* ii.

Demetrius the Fair (*c.* 286–*c.* 248 BC) Prince of Macedon.

Demetrius (Dēmētrios), whose appearance gave him the nickname 'the Fair' (ho Kalos), was the son of *Demetrius Poliorcetes and Ptolemais (a daughter of *Ptolemy I), whose marriage had resulted from a temporary alliance between Ptolemy and Poliorcetes. Demetrius studied philosophy in Athens with *Arcesilaus, and was the father of *Antigonus Doson. After the death of *Magas of Cyrene, his widow Apama, perhaps wishing to preserve Cyrene's independence from Egypt now that she was regent, summoned Demetrius and offered him the kingdom and her daughter *Berenice (later II), who was to marry *Ptolemy III. When Demetrius' amorous intentions focused on mother rather than daughter, he was slain in the former's bed on the latter's orders. The date of his death is uncertain (*c.* 249/8?), but afterwards *Demophanes and *Ecdelus were summoned to Cyrene to set up a new constitution.

BIBL. *CAH* vii. 712–13; Will, *Hist. pol.* i.

Demetrius of Phalerum Philosopher and politician, 4th–3rd centuries BC.

Demetrius (Dēmētrios) entered Athenian politics in 325/4 BC, and was an ambassador to *Antipater in 322. Condemned to death *in absentia* in 318, he was later installed as ruler of oligarchic Athens by *Cassander (318/17) and instituted sumptuary and judiciary laws (the former allegedly out of keeping with his own habits), abolished agonistic liturgies, and held a census. His period of rule, which was undisturbed by effective political opposition, ended with *Demetrius Poliorcetes' capture of Athens in 308/7. He fled *via* Thebes to Macedonia and then, on *Cassander's death, to Alexandria, where he acted as adviser to *Ptolemy I, and died in mysterious circumstances under *Ptolemy II. A pupil of *Theophrastus, he wrote prolifically (political speeches, autobiography, philosophical, philological, historical, and rhetorical works), and was undoubtedly the most accomplished philosopher-ruler of antiquity.

BIBL. Davies, *Athenian Families* 107 ff.; F. Wehrli, *Demetrios von Phaleron* (2nd ed., 1968); H.-J. Gehrke, *Chiron* viii (1978).

Demetrius of Pharos Illyrian dynast, floruit 229–214 BC.

When Demetrius (Dēmētrios) betrayed the Illyrians and handed Corcyra over to Rome in 229 BC, his reward was the rule of a petty state centred on Pharos in the Ionian Sea. Evincing the political recklessness which characterized his career, Demetrius was soon allied to *Antigonus Doson, and fought with him against *Cleomenes III at Sellasia in 222; he continued his Macedonian alliance with *Philip V. He openly contravened his treaty with Rome in 220 by ravaging the Aegean islands (in the company of *Scerdilaidas) until beaten by Rhodes. A Roman invasion of Illyria in 219 chased Demetrius from Pharos, but he escaped to Philip as a welcome friend and counsellor, who was always inciting Philip against Rome. He advised him to intervene in Messene in 215, which enraged *Aratus of Sicyon and the Achaean League. Philip withdrew, but sent Demetrius back in 214 in a night attack. The invaders were driven back, and Demetrius was killed.

BIBL. *Roman World*; *CAH* vii; Holleaux, *Études d'Épigraphie et d'Histoire Grecques* (1968) vi, index.

Democedes Doctor, *c.* 520 BC.

A distinguished doctor from Croton in southern Italy, Democedes (Dēmokēdēs) worked for *Polycrates, and accompanied him on his fatal journey to Magnesia. He was taken by the Persians to Susa, where he successfully treated King *Darius I and his favourite wife, and became court physician. However, he wished to return home, and did so after persuading Darius to send him to Greece as a spy.

BIBL. Herodotus iii. 125, 129–37.

Demochares (*c.* 360–275 BC) Athenian statesman.

A nephew of *Demosthenes the orator, Demochares (Dēmokharēs) of Leuconoe had a long civic career fighting for the maintenance of democratic government in Athens. He was thus a confirmed enemy of *Demetrius of Phalerum, even trying to ban philosophy from Athens, and was instrumental in defending the city from the attacks of *Cassander in 306 BC. When the partisans of *Demetrius Poliorcetes gained influence in 303, Demochares left Athens, probably living with *Lysimachus of Thrace, and returned to his native city only in 286/5, when Athens had successfully revolted from Poliorcetes. With the help of *Olympiodorus he repulsed an attack on Eleusis by *Antigonus Gonatas. Demochares took an active part in the administration of the city by settling the finances and soliciting funds from Macedon's enemies. He asked for, and received, public vindication for his uncle Demosthenes, who had always espoused anti-Macedonian policies. Retiring from political life, he devoted himself to scholarly work: orations, and a history which earned him the abuse of *Timaeus.

BIBL. Ferguson, *Hellenistic Athens*; *FGrH* 75; Habicht, *Untersuchungen*.

Democritus Philosopher, born *c.* 460 BC.

Born at Abdera in Thrace, Democritus (Dēmokritos) travelled widely in search of instruction and scientific data, and was said to have visited Persia, Egypt, Babylon, and even (implausibly) Ethiopia and India. Over 60 books were attributed to him, on ethics, natural philosophy, music, mathematics, and other subjects. About 300 fragments survive, mostly on ethics.

A pupil of *Leucippus, Democritus developed the theory of atomism, but his own contributions cannot be separated from those of his predecessor. According to the theory, 'there are in the universe just 'the full' or 'that which *is*', and 'the empty' or 'that which *is not*'. 'The full' consists of atoms, solid, ungenerated, and eternal; 'the empty' is the gaps between the atoms. There are infinitely many atoms, differing in size and shape and perhaps weight, but not in any other respect. The atoms move around in the void, sometimes colliding, and combining to form objects. That is how the world we know, and innumerable other worlds, were formed. The *apparent* differences between things, such as colours, tastes, and smells, are explained by the different shapes, sizes, positions, and arrangements of the constituent atoms, and their action on our sense-organs. The soul is fire, and consists of spherical atoms, because (according to *Aristotle) 'such shapes can most easily slip through everything and, being in motion themselves, set other things in motion'.

Although strikingly similar to the corpuscular physics of the seventeenth century, the theory had very different origins. It was largely an attempt to rescue the possibility of motion and change from *Parmenides' arguments, by reintroducing plurality and 'that which is not', while conceding that there is no real generation or destruction.

Democritus' ethical maxims (many of which may not be genuine) form no obvious system. Their emphasis is on cheerfulness achieved through moderation and pleasures of the right kind.

BIBL. Guthrie, *Greek Philosophy* ii. 8; C. Bailey, *The Greek Atomists and Epicurus* (1928).

Demodocus Elegiac poet, 6th century BC (?).

From Leros, a dependency of Miletus, Demodocus (Dēmodokos) was remembered for an elegiac couplet (fr. 1: 'Milesians are not fools, but they act like fools') and credited with others (plausibly fr. 2: '*All* Lerians are scoundrels – except Procles – Procles too is Lerian', also attributed to *Phocylides).

BIBL. West, *IEG* and *Studies*.

Demophanes and **Ecdelus** Megalopolitan liberators, mid-3rd century BC.

Two Megalopolitans whose very names are variously attested, Demophanes (Dēmophanēs; or Damophanēs) and Ecdelus (Ekdēlos) were exiled from their city and studied with *Arcesilaus of the Academy in Athens. They achieved a legendary reputation as liberators: they were responsible for the fall of Aristodemus 'the Good', the tyrant of Megalopolis, and – though it is not known which deed came first – they aided *Aratus in the liberation of Sicyon in 251 BC. These liberations combined with the revolt of *Alexander of Corinth to threaten the hold of *Antigonus Gonatas of Macedon in Greece. Shortly afterwards they were invited to Cyrene to reorganize the constitution, probably after the death of *Demetrius the Fair.

BIBL. Tarn, *Antigonos Gonatas*; Polybius X. xxii. 2; Plutarch, *Philopoemen* i; Pausanias VIII. xlix. 2.

Demosthenes (384–322 BC) Athenian orator.

Demosthenes (Dēmosthenēs) of Paeania was regarded in antiquity as the greatest of the Attic orators. His speeches are excellently structured, so that the arguments can be clearly followed, and thanks to his fine sense of rhythm and balance the audience hardly notices the sophistication of his 'periodic' sentences. Opinion has been divided about his political contribution. Some scholars have applauded his anti-Macedonian rhetoric as a symbol of the struggle for autonomy; others condemn it as based on an out-of-date belief in the viability of the city-state.

Demosthenes' father died when he was seven; his guardians wasted the family property, and he studied rhetoric under *Isaeus in order to prosecute them when he came of age (he made three speeches *Against Aphobus*, two *Against Onetor*; 361 BC). He became a professional speech-writer, providing texts on both commercial and criminal cases for his clients (*Orations* xxvii–lix, of which at least 15 are genuine). On occasion he would compose speeches for both sides.

In 355/4 he first wrote and then himself delivered speeches on issues of state finance, possibly supporting the policies of *Eubulus (*Against *Androtion*; *Against *Timocrates* (of Athens); *Against *Leptines*). His first public speech before the Assembly, *On the Symmories* (354/3), argues for reforms in the administration of the fleet.

From 352 *Philip II of Macedon's activities in Chalcidice, Thrace, and the Chersonese led Demosthenes to develop a consistent policy of hostility to Macedon. The first *Philippic* was delivered in 349; there followed the three *Olynthiacs*, advocating military intervention (which failed to save Olynthus). The failure of Eubulus'

Statue of Demosthenes (the hands, toes, and nose are restored). Copenhagen, Ny Carlsberg Glyptotek.

attempt to arrange a common peace-treaty among all Greek states, and thus exclude Macedonia from central Greece, forced Athens to seek a separate peace with Philip (346). Demosthenes was one of the ambassadors, and strongly recommended the 'Peace of *Philocrates'. When it became clear that Philip had only used the period of the diplomatic negotiations in order to strengthen his military position, Demosthenes again proposed war; but by the day of the Assembly debate news had come that Philip had occupied Thermopylae and that resistance was pointless. Demosthenes was shouted down in the Assembly, while *Aeschines' proposals were accepted. His bitter personal hatred of Aeschines was probably as important a factor for his subsequent behaviour as his theoretical opposition to Macedon. His supporter Timarchus unsuccessfully prosecuted Aeschines in 346, and Demosthenes himself attacked him in *On the Embassy* (343).

The years after 344 saw a series of anti-Macedonian speeches and pamphlets (*Philippics* ii–iv, *On the Chersonese*). An alliance with Byzantium resulted in war with Philip in late 340; Demosthenes proposed the alliance with Thebes which led to the crushing defeat at Chaeronea in 338. Nevertheless he continued to hold office. In 336 his supporter Ctesiphon proposed that he should be publicly crowned in recognition of his services to Athens, and although Aeschines indicted Ctesiphon for making an illegal proposal, he did not feel strong enough to proceed with the prosecution immediately. When he did, in 330, Demosthenes replied with the *On the Crown*; he won the case decisively, and Aeschines had to leave Athens.

Opposition to Macedon was pointless until news arrived in 324 of *Nicanor's plans to order the restoration of all Greek exiles. Subsequent diplomatic activity resulted in the *Harpalus affair. Demosthenes was implicated, was convicted of having taken bribes, and had to retire to Aegina (323). His supporter *Hyper(e)ides recalled him to Athens to participate in the Lamian War; after the Macedonian victory at Crannon (322), *Demades had him condemned to death. He fled to the temple of Poseidon on Calauria, where he took poison.

BIBL. Plutarch, *Life of Demosthenes*; G. Cawkwell, *CQ* xii (1962), xiii (1963), and *JHS* lxxxiii (1963); Kennedy, *Art of Persuasion* 206–35; L. Pearson, *The Art of Demosthenes* (1976).

Demosthenes, son of Alcisthenes Athenian general, died 413 BC.

Demosthenes' (Dēmosthenēs) activities during the *Archidamian War (431–421 BC) suggest a consistent attempt to seek victory through a decisive military operation on the Greek mainland, rather than through *Pericles' policy of defeating Sparta by maintaining the status quo.

He first operated with varying success in Aetolia in 427–426, saving Naupactus for Athens. *Strategos* again in 425, he stopped at Pylos on his way back to north-west Greece; a Spartan force which came to eject him was cut off on the island of Sphacteria, and their subsequent capture by Demosthenes and *Cleon gave the Athenians an important bargaining counter.

In 424 Demosthenes tried to occupy Megara, but was foiled by the fortuitous presence of *Brasidas with a

Peloponnesian force on its way north. He next seems to have been responsible for a disastrous plan for a double invasion of Boeotia: lack of co-ordination between his own force, attacking from Naupactus with Acarnanian support, and the main Athenian hoplite army resulted in the rout of that force at Delium.

He then disappears from the record until 418/17, when he was active in the Argolid; and then in 413 he was appointed to lead the Athenian fleet of 73 ships and 5,000 hoplites sent to assist *Nicias at Syracuse. He arrived in July; the failure of an immediate attack on the heights of Epipolae made him urge withdrawal. Delay led to the Athenians' defeat at sea; the retreat overland (October) resulted in the total destruction of the expedition. Demosthenes surrendered and was executed by the Syracusans.

BIBL. A. J. Holladay, *Historia* xxvii (1978); J. B. Wilson, *Pylos 425 B.C.* (1979); Westlake, *Individuals in Thucydides*, chs. 7, 13; D. Kagan, *The Archidamian War* (1974).

Dercyllidas Spartan general, floruit 411–389 BC.

Dercyllidas (Derkulidas), who as a bachelor suffered civic disabilities at home and preferred overseas service, was for over 20 years one of the leading Spartan commanders in the coastlands of Asia Minor. In 411 BC he occupied Abydos and Lampsacus on the Hellespont. From 399 to 397 he commanded the Spartan army in Asia, and forced the Persians to the point of negotiating about the Asiatic Greeks before being replaced by King *Agesilaus. After *Conon's victory at Cnidos in 394, Dercyllidas defended Spartan interests in the Hellespont until 390/89.

BIBL. Thucydides viii. 61 f.; Xenophon, *Hellenica* iii–iv; Hamilton, *Sparta's Bitter Victories*.

Diaeus: see **Critolaus**

Diagoras of Melos Lyric poet, late 5th century BC.

Diagoras was remembered more as a notorious atheist than as a poet. The brief surviving fragments of his poetry, however, display a conventional piety.

BIBL. *Lyra Graeca* (Loeb) iii; Pickard-Cambridge, *Dithyramb* . . .; L. Woodbury, *Phoenix* xix (1965).

Dicaearchus Philosopher and polymath, late 4th century BC.

Although little is known about his life, Dicaearchus (Dikaiarkhos) of Messana was believed to have been a pupil of *Aristotle and *Theophrastus. Like other Peripatetic philosophers, he had an enormous range of interests, making his works a major source for later Greek and Roman writers.

He wrote about the nature of the soul, oracles, and prophecy; on the constitutions of different Greek states, and on geography (a major enterprise was measuring the heights of mountains throughout Greece). His belief – in opposition to Theophrastus – that the practical life was superior to the theoretical led him to collect empirical information in the form of *bioi* ('lives') (collections of anecdotes about philosophers and literary figures, rather than systematic biographies in our sense of the word). His discussions of literature, including *Homer, tragedy, and comedy, were used by the Alexandrian critics.

BIBL. F. Wehrli, *Die Schule des Aristoteles i: Dikaiarchos* (1944).

Didymus Scholar, *c.* 40 BC.

Didymus (Didumos), a native Alexandrian, earned his nickname 'Chalcenterus' ('Brazen-guts') through his prodigious capacity for work. Coming at the end of the line of great Alexandrian scholars, he preserved their labours with dogged and loving care in his innumerable commentaries and lexicographical writings. By no means stupid, though occasionally gripped by silly opinions, Didymus excerpted and organized judiciously, and assembled much valuable supplementary information: papyrus fragments of a commentary on *Demosthenes' *Philippics* attest his merits. His compilations were eagerly cannibalized by later scholiasts.

BIBL. Pfeiffer, *Classical Scholarship* i.

Dinarchus: see D(e)inarchus

Diocles Syracusan leader, late 5th century BC.

In 412 BC Diocles (Dioklēs) was responsible for constitutional changes which made Syracuse a radical democracy on Athenian lines; there appears to have been a hero-cult in his honour. In 409/8 he led the Syracusan army against *Hannibal, who was besieging Himera; Diocles evacuated the town, and was consequently exiled by supporters of *Hermocrates.

BIBL. Diodorus Siculus xiii.

Diocles of Carystus Physician, 4th century BC.

Diocles (Dioklēs), who worked in Athens, was highly renowned for his medical writings. The fragments that remain do not show what innovations, if any, he made in medical practice or theory. He seems to have been an eclectic, borrowing from, among others, *Aristotle, *Empedocles, and the *Hippocratic school of Cos.

BIBL. W. Jaeger, *Diokles von Karystos* (1938).

Diodorus Cronus Philosopher, *c.* 300 BC.

A member of the Megarian school of philosophy (though he came from Iasus in Caria), Diodorus (Diodōros) was a skilled logician and devised several influential arguments. The most famous was the 'Master argument', intended to prove that nothing is possible except what is true or what will be true. The later belief of the Stoic philosophers that the future is predetermined was partly due to this argument.

BIBL. B. Mates, *Stoic Logic* (1953).

Diodorus of Erythrae: see Cyclic Poets

Diodorus Siculus Historian, floruit mid-1st century BC.

Only the briefest biography can be compiled for the historian Diodorus (Diodōros). Called 'Siculus' ('the Sicilian') because his home was Agyrium in Sicily, he lived during the age of Caesar and Augustus, but his exact dates are unknown and it is disputed whether the latest date mentioned in his writings is 36 or 21 BC. He travelled at least to Rome and Egypt. Diodorus wrote a World History which dealt in 40 books with historical events known to him from the earliest times until his own. The style of the work is directly reflected in its title, *Historical Library*, since it consists of excerpts from the works of other writers, with no historical analysis by Diodorus himself. Since the work can in this case be only as good as the works it depends on, the study of Diodorus must be

primarily a study of his sources. Various problems arise from this: many of the sources cannot be identified for certain, and, although many authors are quoted in long, apparently uninterrupted passages, other sections of the history draw primarily upon a single source but incorporate extracts from other writers. Books i–v and xi–xx exist in full, with the others in fragments, but the organization of the entire work is known: book i Egypt; ii Mesopotamia, India, Scythia, and Arabia; iii North Africa; iv–vi Greece and Europe; vii–xvii the Trojan War down to *Alexander the Great; xviii–xl the Diadochi down to Caesar. Some of his most important main sources included *Timaeus, *Agatharchides, *Hecataeus, *Ctesias, *Megasthenes, Dionysius Scytobrachium, *Ephorus, *Theopompus, *Cleitarchus, *Duris of Samos, *Hieronymus of Cardia, Philinus of Acragas, a Roman annalist, *Polybius, and *Pos(e)idonius. The narrative is clearly written despite the inevitable confusion arising from the various sources, but the real worth of Diodorus' history lies in its preservation of the work of better historians, much of which would be otherwise lost.

BIBL. PW v. 663 ff. (Diodoros 38); *Encicl. Ital.* xii, s.v. Diodoro Siculo; Will, *Hist. pol.* ii. 472–3; *Roman World* *Augustus, Gaius Julius *Caesar, *Diodorus.

Diodotus I Soter King of Bactria, *c.* 239/8–before *c.* 230(?) BC.

A Seleucid satrap of Bactria, Diodotus (Diodotos) perhaps entertained ideas of independence during the Third Syrian War (after 246 BC); these were reflected in his issues of coinage, which gradually replaced Seleucid motifs with his own. Although the chronology is extremely uncertain, it seems that Diodotus finally declared independence in 239–8 when the coinage was completely his own type. He styled himself king and took the title 'Soter' (Saviour). Not much is known about the king's career and achievements, although he probably did not marry a Seleucid princess, as some have asserted, and the territory he controlled is disputed. In view of his growing power, Diodotus was feared by another emerging dynast, *Arsaces I of Parthia.

Coin portrait of Diodotus I Soter, king of Bactria (enlarged).

Diodotus died before the expedition of *Seleucus II against Parthia (*c.* 230(?)–*c.* 227(?)), and was succeeded by his son Diodotus II, who concluded a peace and alliance with Arsaces. The younger Diodotus was replaced on the throne, and perhaps killed, by *Euthydemus at an unknown time after *c.* 227(?).

It has not yet proved possible to distinguish the coinage of father and son, or to fix their chronology.

BIBL. Tarn, *Greeks in Bactria . . .*; Narain, *Indo-Greeks*; Will, *Hist. pol.* i.

Diodotus Athenian leader, late 5th century BC.

In book iii of his history *Thucydides describes a debate at Athens in 427 BC on how to treat the allied city of Mytilene on Lesbos, which had revolted from Athens and been recaptured. The Athenians are first convinced by *Cleon's arguments advocating the execution of the entire population, and send orders accordingly; but, at a second debate, Diodotus, son of Eucrates, points out that the Mytilenean *demos* should be pardoned, so as to encourage the democrats in other subject states to remain loyal to Athens. A second ship is sent out to countermand the original orders, and arrives just in time to save the *demos* (while the wealthy are executed none the less).

BIBL. Thucydides iii. 36–49; A. Andrews, *Phoenix* xvi (1962); M. Ostwald, *GRBS* xx (1979).

Diodotus Tryphon Seleucid king, 142–137 BC.

A pretender to the Seleucid throne, Diodotus Tryphon (Diodotos Truphōn) saw his route to power in the growing unpopularity of *Demetrius II (q.v.) due to increasing Jewish disturbances in 145 BC. As a military commander in Apamea, Diodotus proclaimed as king Antiochus VI, the son of *Alexander Balas and *Cleopatra Thea, whose triumphant entry into Antioch caused Demetrius' flight in 144. Diodotus deposed and later killed the child, ruling in his own right as 'Tryphon' (the 'Magnificent') from 142.

Coin portrait of Diodotus Tryphon, Seleucid pretender and king.

To gain ground against Demetrius' considerable possessions, Diodotus conspired in the internal conflicts of Judaea, which yielded him certain territories but led to the establishment of the independent Hasmonean state in 143/2. Although Demetrius was conveniently a prisoner in Parthia in 139, Diodotus faced the king's brother *Antiochus VII Sidetes, who rose to power in 138. He easily defeated and captured Diodotus, who killed himself in 137.

BIBL. Bellinger, 'The End of the Seleucids'; Will, *Hist. pol.* ii.

Diogenes of Apollonia Eclectic philosopher, floruit 440/425 BC.

Diogenes (Diogenēs), probably from the Phrygian Apollonia, was an unoriginal thinker, who elaborated *Anaximenes' theory that air is the stuff of which things are made. More interesting is his physiological work, which includes an account of the arrangement of veins in the body, and explanations of how the sense-organs work. He held that thought was due to pure dry air, and it was almost certainly he who was parodied by *Aristophanes for having his head in the clouds: 'I would never have correctly discovered lofty things, if I had not hung up my intellect and mingled my subtle thought with the similar air.'

BIBL. Aristophanes, *Clouds* 227–30; Guthrie, *Greek Philosophy*, ii.

Diogenes of Seleucia Stoic philosopher, 2nd century BC.

A pupil of *Chrysippus, Diogenes (Diogenēs) 'the Babylonian' was head of the Stoic school of philosophy in the mid-second century BC. With *Carneades and *Critolaus, he was appointed to an Athenian delegation of philosophers to go to Rome in 156/5. Through his pupil *Panaetius he was influential in the growth of Stoicism in the Roman world.

BIBL. M. Pohlenz, *Die Stoa* (1948).

Diogenes of Sinope (c. 400–323 BC) Cynic philosopher.

Diogenes (Diogenēs) went to Athens after either he or his father was charged with adulterating the coinage at his native town on the Black Sea. From his manners and style of life he became known as 'dog' (*kuon*), thus giving the Cynic philosophers (*kunikoi*) their name. He probably learnt much from *Antisthenes, but developed no comprehensive system of philosophy. He despised studies that were of no practical use. He may have advocated a world State or 'cosmopolis', but his contempt for rules and conventions is more suggestive of anarchism. He lived

Idealized portrait of the philosopher Diogenes of Sinope, from a late 2nd-century mosaic from Cologne. Cologne, Römisch-Germanisches Museum.

what he took to be a life according to nature, one of extreme simplicity, sleeping in public places and trying (unsuccessfully) to eat raw meat (he seems, rather surprisingly, to have opposed vegetarianism).

Many legends grew quickly about him, and it is hard to be sure of any facts about his life. Hundreds of abusive remarks are attributed to him, mostly directed against hypocrisy, effeminacy, and wealth. According to a much illustrated story, he was asked by *Alexander the Great, while living in a tub, what he could do for him, and in reply asked Alexander to move out of the sunlight.

Others, beginning with *Crates of Thebes, spread his teaching, but there was never a formal Cynic school of philosophy.

BIBL. Diogenes Laertius vi. 20–81.

Dion 'Liberator' of Syracuse, died 354 BC.

A prominent courtier of his kinsman *Dionysius I, whose favour he kept despite differences of opinion during *Plato's visit *c.* 388 BC, Dion (Diōn) became an object of jealousy to other courtiers under *Dionysius II, and was expelled from Syracuse at the time of Plato's second visit (366). At first he lived comfortably in Academic circles in Athens, but Plato's attempt to secure his recall in 361 caused Dionysius to confiscate his property and give his wife to another husband. Dion prepared a *coup*: in 357 Syracuse was captured, and Ortygia fell two years later. But bad relations between Dion, intent on practical Platonism (effectively, reactionary tyranny), and his populist colleague Heracleides culminated in the latter's murder (355), and in 354 Dion himself duly fell victim to a fellow-Academic Callippus. Plutarch's best efforts cannot make Dion seem in any way a sympathetic figure.

BIBL. Plutarch, *Dion*; Stroheker, *Dionysios I*; Finley, *Ancient Sicily*; H. Berve, *Dion* (1956); *Roman World* *Plutarch.

Dionysius I Tyrant of Syracuse, 405–367 BC.

Effective demagogy in winter 406–5 BC enabled Dionysius (Dionusios) to secure election as general amidst popular discontent with the conduct of war with Carthage, and he soon became *strategos autokrator* and acquired a personal bodyguard. An oligarchic counter-revolution was put down and, when the Carthaginians accepted a favourable peace, Dionysius turned to securing his position by constructing a massive private fortress on Ortygia (an island in Syracuse), enfranchising numerous slaves and aliens and neutralizing the major cities of eastern Sicily (his methods included mass population-transfers). In 398 he started a new Carthaginian war, capturing Motya, and, despite a successful Carthaginian counter-attack in 396, was eventually able to confine the Carthaginians to western Sicily (392). Thereafter his interest turned to Italy (where Croton (388) and Rhegium (386) were defeated and Pyrgi (Etruria) looted (*c.* 384)), the Adriatic (colonies in the Dalmatian islands, Ancona, and at the mouth of the Po), and Greece (Syracusan ships fought for Sparta in 387/6). A second Carthaginian war began in 383–2 but ended with Dionysius' defeat at Cronium (375?) and a redivision of Sicily at the river Halycus. In 368 he returned to the attack, but died in 367 after over-indulgent celebration of a victory at the Lenaean tragic festival at Athens (which perhaps owed more to political

considerations than to his literary skill). A tyrant on the grand scale, Dionysius had a poor reputation during and after his lifetime, and a proper estimation of him is hindered by the later literature's extravagant application to him of *topoi* (rhetorical commonplaces) of tyrannical behaviour.

BIBL. K. F. Stroheker, *Dionysios I* (1958).

Dionysius II Tyrant of Syracuse, 367–343/2 BC.

On succeeding his father, *Dionysius I, Dionysius (Dionusios) made peace with Carthage and enjoyed ten quiet years of rule devoted to the pleasures of court intrigue, philosophy, and self-indulgence (the first two themes combine in *Plato's visit and *Dion's expulsion in 366). In 357–355 he lost control of Syracuse and Ortygia, but retained Locri until 347/6, when he returned to Syracuse only to be driven out again by Hicetas and *Timoleon. His later years were spent in exile at Corinth.

BIBL. Berve, *Tyrannis* 260 ff.

Dionysius Chalcus Elegiac poet, 5th century BC.

Dionysius (Dionusios) of Athens acquired the nickname Chalcus (Khalkous, 'of bronze') after advising the Athenians to adopt bronze coinage. Some fragments survive of his poems written for, and concerning, drinking-parties (symposia).

BIBL. Lesky, *Greek Literature*; *Greek Elegy and Iambus* (Loeb) i.

Dionysius of Heraclea (*c.* 330–250 BC) Philosopher.

A pupil of *Zeno of Citium and friend of *Aratus of Soli, Dionysius (Dionusios) of Heraclea Pontica accepted Stoicism for a time, but, when suffering from a severe eye disease, found that he could no longer accept that pain was 'indifferent'. He joined the hedonistic school of Cyrene and, according to late sources, indulged openly in carnal excesses. He starved himself to death at the age of 80.

BIBL. Diogenes Laertius vii. 166–7.

Dionysius Thrax Scholar, 2nd century BC.

Dionysius (Dionusios) was actually an Alexandrian, his identifying name deriving from his father's Thracian origin. A prominent pupil of *Aristarchus of Samothrace, he later migrated to Rhodes (in the dispersal of 145 BC?), where he was a successful teacher. His scholarly writings were numerous (they include polemic against *Crates of Mallos), but overshadowed by the fame of his grammatical handbook, probably the work extant under his name. This exceedingly spare Alexandrian classification of the parts of grammar, pirating much from Stoic linguistic theory, had a tremendous impact as the first systematization of the subject: it was widely translated and attracted copious commentary. Influential at an early date on Latin grammar through Dionysius' pupil *Tyrannio, it continued in use until the Renaissance.

BIBL. Edition: G. Uhlig, *Grammatici Graeci* i (1883); Pfeiffer, *Classical Scholarship* i.

Diopeithes (1) Athenian soothsayer, late 5th century BC.

Diopeithes (Diopeithēs) was responsible for the decree under which *Anaxagoras was prosecuted for impiety in the 430s BC, when other associates of *Pericles like *Pheidias and (?) *Aspasia were also prosecuted. Some identify him with the Diopeithes who published an oracle warning the Spartans against the rule of *Agesilaus in 399.

BIBL. Plutarch, *Pericles* 32; Diodorus Siculus XII. xxxix. 2; Xenophon, *Hellenica* III. iii. 3.

Diopeithes (2) Athenian general, mid-4th century BC.

Diopeithes (Diopeithēs) conducted cleruchs to the Thracian Chersonese in 343/2 BC (?) and, during fighting against Cardia, trespassed on Macedonian territory, provoking complaints from *Philip II to which *Demosthenes, *Oration* viii is a reply. Diopeithes was not recalled, but died soon afterwards before receiving gifts sent by *Artaxerxes III in recognition of his anti-Macedonian activities.

BIBL. Kirchner, *PA*, no. 4327; Davies, *Athenian Families* 168; Hammond and Griffith, *Macedonia* ii.

Diophantus Mathematician.

Diophantus (Diophantos) of Alexandria was the first known Greek to use methods of algebra, which he probably learnt from the Egyptians. He applied them mainly to various forms of indeterminate equations. He may have lived at any time between 150 BC and AD 250, though a later date seems the more probable.

BIBL. Heath, *Greek Mathematics* ii. 440–517.

Dioscorides Epigrammatist, later 3rd century BC.

Dioscorides (Dioskouridēs), who apparently lived in Alexandria, allows us vivid glimpses in his epigrams of life in Egypt (e.g. Nile floods (33, 34); popular entertainment (2, 26)) and treats erotic themes with frank gusto, but also shows a more cerebral interest in cult and literary history in some picturesquely learned pieces. Sositheus (*Pleiad) and *Machon are commended alongside great dramatists of the past.

BIBL. Gow and Page, *Hellenistic Epigrams*; Fraser, *Ptolemaic Alexandria*.

Diphilus New Comedy poet, born c. 355 BC.

With *Menander and *Philemon Diphilus (Diphilos) made up the canonized triad of New Comedy. Originally from Sinope on the Black Sea, he spent most of his life in Athens, where – although he died at Smyrna – he shared a tombstone with his father Dion and brother Diodorus, also a comic poet. Of some 100 plays we know about 60 titles; three victories at the Lenaea are recorded, the first no earlier than 318 BC. Titles and fragments are mainly typical of New Comedy, though certain features of Middle Comedy seem to have persisted in Diphilus: some titles for instance (*Danaids, Peliads*) suggest mythological burlesques; the play *Sappho* cast *Archilochus and *Hipponax as her improbable lovers. Diphilus' strongly delineated comedy, like Philemon's, attracted Plautus to adapt him in at least three plays, including the boisterous *Casina* and lively seaside *Rudens*. Terence incorporated into his Menandrian *Adelphi* – word for word, he asserts – a violent kidnap-scene from Diphilus' *Synapothnescontes* (*Comrades in Death*). Adaptations and fragments together suggest that well-organized, theatrically effective plots, a full-blooded realism, and a rapid, vivid style were Diphilean characteristics.

BIBL. Webster, *Later Comedy*; *IG* ii (2nd edn.) 10321 (tombstone); *Roman World* *Plautus, *Terence.

Dorieus Spartan colonist, c. 520 BC.

As the eldest son of *Anaxandridas by his first wife, Dorieus (Dōrieus) considered that he had a better claim to the Spartan throne than his half-brother *Cleomenes (I), although Cleomenes was the elder. When his claim was rejected, Dorieus and his supporters resolved to leave Sparta and found a colony. They went first to Libya, but were driven out by the Carthaginians, and then to western Sicily near Heraclea Minoa, where they again came into conflict with the Carthaginians, and Dorieus was killed.

BIBL. Herodotus v. 42–8; Forrest, *History of Sparta* 85–6.

Dorieus of Rhodes Athlete and politician, died 395 BC.

Dorieus' (Dōrieus) athletic fame was such that, despite his fierce anti-Athenian sentiments, the Athenians would not hold him as a prisoner of war on his capture in 407 BC. Twelve years later the Spartans captured him after Rhodes had joined *Conon, and killed him out of hand.

BIBL. PW v. 1560–1.

Dracon Athenian law-giver, c. 620 BC.

Dracon (Drakōn) was said to have given Athens its first written law-code, and also a constitution based on the hoplite franchise. He prescribed very severe ('draconian') penalties, and *Solon repealed all his laws except that dealing with homicide. The homicide law (or what was then believed to be it) is preserved in a late fifth-century BC inscription.

BIBL. Aristotelean *Constitution of Athens* 4, 7; Aristotle, *Politics* 1274b; Meiggs and Lewis, *Inscriptions*, no. 86; Forrest, *Greek Democracy* 146–7.

Ducetius Sicel leader, died 440 BC.

After the collapse of Deinomenid rule in Sicily (see *Hieron I), the Syracusan democracy was unable to control Hieron's immigrant settlers and mercenaries. Ducetius (Douketios) helped Syracuse expel the mercenaries from Aetna in c. 460 BC; in the following year, as 'King of the Sicels', he founded Menaion (Menaenum) as his capital. He later resided at Palice, the chief Sicel shrine of the earth-spirits. Conflict with Acragas led to Ducetius' defeat at Nomae in 450; he surrendered to the Syracusans, who sent him into exile at Corinth, but he soon returned to Sicily, on the grounds that Apollo had ordered him to found a new city at Caleacte. He died in 440, while trying to impose his rule on the Sicels of northern Sicily.

BIBL. Diodorus Siculus xi–xii; Woodhead, *Greeks in the West* 82 f.

Duris of Samos (c. 340–270 BC) Historian, and tyrant of Samos, after 322–after c. 300 BC.

Very little biographical information is known about Duris (Douris), a pupil of *Theophrastus who became tyrant of Samos. He probably followed his father in this role, and was a nationalist leader. Duris was also a prolific historiographical writer, whose variety of subjects reveals a basically antiquarian approach which reflected the aims of Peripatetic research. Only small fragments of his works survive, but he wrote a *Chronicle of Samos*, a Greek and Macedonian history (covering the years 370–281 BC), a life of *Agathocles of Syracuse, a history of art, and works on Law and athletics contests. The last three works were anecdotal in character. Duris' historical works were criticized in antiquity: he was an important figure in the development of sensational historiography (so-called 'tragic history'), which was characterized by an emotional, dramatic style and may have derived from the Peripatetics. He also aimed for realism through compilation and exactitude of detail, whether relevant or not. Duris criticized the historians *Ephorus and *Theopompus (perhaps, in the latter case, for excessive rhetorical display), and his *Life* of Agathocles was used by Plutarch and possibly also by *Diodorus Siculus.

BIBL. *FGrH* 76; Barron, *CR* xii (1962) 189 ff.; Kebric, *CPhil.* lxix (1974) 286 ff.; Walbank, *BICS* ii (1955) 4 ff., and *Historia* ix (1960) 216 ff.; *Roman World* *Plutarch.

Ecdelus: see **Demophanes**

Echecrates Pythagorean philosopher, 4th century BC.

Echecrates (Ekhekratēs) was a *Pythagorean from Phlius in the Peloponnese, where the movement seems to have flourished. He was probably associated with *Archytas of Tarentum and *Socrates. The account of Socrates' death in *Plato's *Phaedo* is addressed to him.

BIBL. Plato, *Phaedo*.

Echembrotus Elegiac poet, *c.* 586 BC.

Pausanias reports a dedication commemorating a Pythian victory for 'songs and elegies' of an Arcadian Echembrotus (Ekhembrotos), presumably in 586 BC, since (he says) the aulodic competition was abolished in 582. (The suggested reason, that *aulodia* was lugubrious, is guesswork, and insecure ground for supposing that lament characterized Peloponnesian elegy.)

BIBL. Pausanias X. vii. 5–6; West, *Studies*, 4 ff.; *Roman World* *Pausanias.

Empedocles Poet and philosopher, *c.* 492–432 BC.

An aristocrat from Acragas (Agrigento) in Sicily, Empedocles (Empedoklēs) supported democracy, and is said to have refused the kingship. But he was no egalitarian: 'I go among you all as an immortal god, no longer mortal, honoured as is fitting, crowned with ribbons and rich garlands.' There were stories of his healing the sick and even raising the dead.

Many fragments survive of his two books, written in verse, *On Nature* and *Purifications*. The former sets out to explain the universe. Agreeing with *Parmenides that nothing can come into existence or perish, he explains apparent generation and destruction as the mixing and separating of four eternal 'roots' or elements – earth, air, fire, and water. These elements come under the alternating rule of Love and Strife, in an eternal cosmic cycle. Details of the cycle are much disputed, but the following is a simple interpretation. Under Love, the elements are entirely blended in a sphere. Under Strife, they are entirely separated in concentric spheres. In between, when either Love or (as in the present era) Strife is gradually gaining control, the elements mingle and separate to form the world as we know it. 'There are these alone [i.e. the elements], but running through one another they become men and tribes of beasts.'

Purifications is concerned with the transmigration of souls and is influenced by *Pythagoreanism. A long cycle of reincarnations evidently results from the committing of

an offence, in Empedocles' case bloodshed. He has already, he says, been 'a boy, a girl, a bush, a bird, and a dumb fish of the sea'. But he is near the end of his cycle (hence the claim to be an immortal god).

Some scholars see the poems as inconsistent, as it is hard to see how an immortal god or soul can persist through all stages of the cosmic cycle. Others see the cycles as consistent and connected.

BIBL. Guthrie, *Greek Philosophy* ii; D. O'Brien, *Empedocles' Cosmic Cycle* (1969).

Marble head of a 'kouros' (youth) from Athens (?), attributed to the sculptor Endoios. Copenhagen, Ny Carlsberg Glyptotek.

Endoios Sculptor, active *c.* 530–500 BC.

Endoios worked mainly in Athens, whence come three or four of his signatures, and he was almost certainly Athenian. We have the sad remnant of what is probably his seated Athena, mentioned by Pausanias, in a battered marble statue from the Acropolis. He signed a column on the Acropolis with another sculptor, Philergus, which was perhaps the base for a surviving statue of a girl (now headless). Again from the Acropolis is a fine but fragmentary relief of a seated potter, with a signature almost certainly to be restored as Endoios. On the grounds of the potter's distinctive hair-style two fine works have been attributed to Endoios or his workshop: the well-known ball-player base in Athens and the Rayet head in Copenhagen. He has also been tentatively associated with architectural sculpture in Athens and Delphi.

BIBL. Deyhle, *AM* lxxxiv (1969); Robertson, *History of Greek Art* 106–8; Boardman, *Sculpture Archaic* 82–3; *Roman World* *Pausanias.

Epaminondas Theban politician and general, died 362 BC.

Epaminondas (Epameinōndas) escaped exile after the pro-Spartan coup of 382 BC (perhaps because an impoverished aristocrat of *Pythagorean interests did not seem politically dangerous), and, although he played some part in the liberation of Thebes in 379/8, his emergence as a leading ambassador at Sparta in 372/1 and as Boeotarch at the battle of Leuctra (371) is somewhat startling, the

Monument on the site of the battle of Leuctra (371 BC) commemorating the defeat of the Spartans by Epaminondas.

more so given the novel tactics which won that battle and which were doubtless of his devising. Leuctra, which showed that the hitherto invincible Spartan army could be defeated, certainly made him Thebes' leading political figure (though he did not lack opponents). He led four invasions of the Peloponnese, and persuaded the Thebans to make a bid for naval hegemony (364), but, apart from the foundation of Messene (369), his enterprises failed to produce permanent advantage for Thebes. He died at Mantinea in 362 after a campaign of singular ill-fortune. In later literature he is an almost mythic figure, famous for noble frugality, but sober reality hardly justifies Cicero's view that he was the greatest of the Greeks.
BIBL. Buckler, *Theban Hegemony*; G. Shrimpton, *Phoenix* xxv (1971); *Roman World* *Cicero.

Ephialtes Athenian leader, died 461 BC.
Ephialtes (Ephialtēs) was traditionally the 'democratic' opponent of *Cimon. During Cimon's absence in Messenia in support of the Spartans in 462/1 BC, he prosecuted various members of the aristocratic council, the Areopagus. His policies appear to have included an alliance with Argos and a *rapprochement* with Persia (see *Callias, son of Hipponicus (1)). Cimon's attempt to rescind these developments on his return led to his ostracism; but Ephialtes was assassinated soon after.
(This Ephialtes is not to be confused with the Trachinian who in 480 BC enabled the Persians to turn the pass at Thermopylae (see *Leonidas).)
BIBL. R. Sealey, *CPhil.* lxix (1964); E. Ruschenbusch, *Historia* xv (1966).

Ephippus of Olynthus Alexander historian.
Ephippus' (Ephippos) work *On the Funeral of *Alexander and *Hephaestion* is known only from Athenaeus, who quotes it for hostile accounts of Alexander the Great's court (e.g. the king's habit of dressing up as a god). Nothing is known about the author,

who need not be identified with an officer in Egypt in 331 BC.
BIBL. Pearson, *Lost Histories* 61–8; Bosworth, *Arrian* 276; *Roman World* *Athenaeus.

Ephorus Historian, 4th century BC.
Little is known about Ephorus' (Ephoros) life, except that he came from Cyme in Asia Minor. His son Demophilus edited and completed his 30-volume history, which covered the period from the Return of the **Heracleidae to the sack of Perinthus in 341. The treatment was by subject, not year by year. Ephorus is approved of by *Polybius and used by *Diodorus Siculus (books xi–xv), Nicolaus of Damascus, and *Strabo. Some other writings are attested, including an encomium on his native city. The tradition that he studied oratory under *Isocrates is probably based on his strong taste for rhetoric; pre-battle speeches by generals are a speciality.
BIBL. G. L. Barber, *The Historian Ephorus* (1935); R. Drews, *AJP* lxxxiv (1963); *Roman World* *Nicolaus of Damascus.

Epicharmus Comic poet, 6th–5th centuries BC.
The Sicilian (Syracusan?) dramatist Epicharmus (Epikharmos) was active in the reign of *Hieron I and probably earlier; *Aristotle thought of him as 'much earlier' than *Chionides and Magnes. The numerous brief fragments show a fondness for burlesque treatment of myth, as well as scenes from contemporary life; but there is still much uncertainty as to the nature of this Dorian comedy (e.g. the number of actors, the existence of a chorus) and its relation to Attic comedy.
Later writers oddly thought of Epicharmus as a *Pythagorean sage, and treatises on various subjects were incongruously fathered on him.
BIBL. Lesky, *Greek Literature*; Pickard-Cambridge, *Dithyramb* . . .

Epicrates Athenian politician, floruit 390s BC.
Epicrates (Epikratēs) received money from *Timocrates of Rhodes (395 BC), and service on an embassy to Persia greatly enriched him. He escaped charges of bribery and theft (see *Lysias xxvii) only to be condemned to death *in absentia* after an embassy to Sparta (392/1), when he supported peace. He was nicknamed 'Shield-bearer' because of his remarkable beard.
BIBL. Kirchner, *PA*, no. 4859; Davies, *Athenian Families* 181; Seager, *JHS* lxxxvii (1967).

Epicurus (341–270 BC) Philosopher.
Epicurus (Epikouros) was born in Samos, where his parents lived for a time as Athenian colonists. He went to Athens at eighteen, and later rejoined his parents at Colophon, where he was probably introduced by *Nausiphanes to *Democritus' atomism. He insisted, however, that he was self-taught, and spoke with contempt of Nausiphanes and other philosophers. He taught philosophy at Mytilene, Lampsacus, and finally at Athens, where his 'garden' became the secluded home of a school of reverent followers, including his brothers, and slaves, and at least one courtesan, *Leontion. Many stories were told of his gastronomic and sexual excesses, but it is more likely that life in the school was austere. Of his many writings three letters survive, which express the outlines

Small bronze bust of Epicurus, from the villa of the Pisones, Herculaneum. Naples, Museo Nazionale.

of his philosophy, some maxims and fragments, and his will. More details of his work can be learnt from Lucretius.

The criterion of good for Epicurus was pleasure, but men should aim not for carnal delights but freedom from trouble (*ataraxia*). The pursuit of this end is helped by acceptance of the atomist theory of the universe, according to which men are mortal and the gods have better things to do than interfere with men. Epicurus' atomism differs only in some details from Democritus'. He held a limited empiricist theory of knowledge: sense-perceptions were never wrong, and were the only foundation of knowledge.

His will entrusted the garden to *Hermarchus for the use of the school. It also provided for an annual celebration of his birthday, and a monthly commemoration of himself and his favourite pupil *Metrodorus.

BIBL. Diogenes Laertius x; C. Bailey, *Epicurus* (1926); Lucretius, *De rerum natura*; *Roman World* *Lucretius.

Epimenides Seer.

If he existed at all, Epimenides (Epimenidēs) was born at Knossos in Crete. He was said to have purged Athens of the plague that occurred after the killing of *Cylon's followers, and also to have visited Athens ten years before the Persian Wars, occasions more than a hundred years apart. Various authorities report his life-span as 154, 157, and 299 years. He claimed to have travelled independently of his body, and (perhaps) to have lived previous lives. A story tells that one day, when chasing lost sheep, he fell asleep in a cave for 57 years.

BIBL. E. R. Dodds, *The Greeks and the Irrational* (1951).

Epitadeus Spartan lawgiver, after 404 BC (?).

Epitadeus promulgated a *rhetra* permitting a man to give his household and *kleros* (lot of land) to anyone he wished, either in his lifetime or by testament. This was probably after the Peloponnesian War (431–404 BC), but the precise date and interpretation of this major revolution in Spartan property-law are contested.

BIBL. D. Asheri, *Athenaeum* xxxix (1961); G. Marasco, *Ant.Class.* xlix (1980).

Erasistratus Physician, early to mid-3rd century BC.

The boldest surgeon and medical scientist of the Hellenistic period, Erasistratus (Erasistratos), from Iulis on Ceos, probably studied philosophy in Athens before medicine in the Coan and Cnidian schools. He then worked in Alexandria (this has been disputed – tradition connects him also with Antioch), where his anatomical discoveries refined those of *Herophilus (q.v.). Erasistratus embraced *Democritean atomism and abandoned *Hippocratic humour-theory: his work, known mainly through Galen's critical assessment, was characterized by physiological explanations exploiting contemporary physics (e.g. *Ctesibius' mechanics). Thus he comprehended the valves and pump action of the heart – though he still failed to tumble to the circulation of the blood, retaining the current idea that arteries carried *pneuma*, vital air (he was blinded by the brilliance of his explanation, applying *Straton's *horror vacui* principle, of why severed arteries spurt blood). He seems to have made the first clear distinction between sensory and motor nerves, again advancing on Herophilus' discovery. While his absorption in experiment and theory left little time for practical doctoring, Erasistratus emphasized dietetics and a healthy regimen, opposing drastic therapies like purges and copious blood-letting.

BIBL. J. F. Dobson, *Proc. Roy. Soc. Med.* xx (1927) 825 ff.; Phillips, *Greek Medicine*; C. R. S. Harris, *The Heart and the Vascular System in Ancient Greek Medicine* (1973); *Roman World* *Galen.

Eratosthenes Scholar and scientist, born *c.* 280 BC.

Eratosthenes (Eratosthenēs), the first to call himself *philologos* to express his wide interests, was nicknamed 'Pentathlete' for his all-round excellence, and 'Beta' (i.e. 'Number Two' in every field – perhaps not so complimentary). From his native Cyrene he moved to Athens, where he established a high reputation before being invited to Alexandria to be head of the library (*c.* 246 BC, perhaps thanks to string-pulling by *Ptolemy III's Cyrenaean queen *Berenice II). He lived to be eighty. As a literary scholar he wrote authoritatively on Old Comedy, also on the mythology of the constellations, a work he echoed in his own well-turned poetry: an epyllion *Hermes* ended with a vision of the harmony of the cosmos, an aetiological narrative elegy *Erigone* transferred the heroine plus father and dog to the skies – the influence of his countryman *Callimachus is clear throughout. As a chronographer Eratosthenes made the first attempt to establish a systematic dating for Greek history (work taken up by *Apollodorus of Athens) in his *Chronographiai*. His work in mathematics was admired by *Archimedes, perhaps his greatest achievement lying in the application of geometry: he calculated the circumference of the earth with astonishing accuracy. He pioneered scientific geography in his *Geographica*, known through *Strabo. In this work he insisted that *Homer's geography was fiction, not fact, and that poetry should entertain, not teach. Throughout the scattered fragments of his interconnecting studies we perceive the rational independence of the highest intelligence.

BIBL. *FGrH* iiB. 241; Pfeiffer, *Classical Scholarship* i.

Eratosthenes (of Athens) Oligarch, floruit late 5th
century BC.

An active oligarch in 411 BC, Eratosthenes
(Eratosthenēs) later became one of the Thirty Tyrants (see
*Critias). He remained in Athens after their fall (403), and
was tried for the murder of Polemarchus (see *Lysias xii)
but apparently acquitted. He was later killed by a
cuckolded husband (see Lysias i).

BIBL. Kirchner, *PA*, no. 5035.

'Ergamenes' King of Meroe, 3rd century BC.

'Ergamenes' (Ergamenēs), the hellenized form of a
native name, was, according to *Diodorus Siculus, a king
of Meroe in the Sudan who was a contemporary of
*Ptolemy II and had some Greek education and
philosophical training. He ended the custom of the ritual
murder of the Meroitic kings by the powerful priesthood,
and is thus often praised, without foundation, as an
enlightened, hellenized monarch.

It is usually assumed that 'Ergamenes' is Arqamani, whose
contact with Ptolemaic Egypt is known through the joint
temples which he built with *Ptolemy IV at Philae and
Dakka, even though a long reign has to be assumed to
make him contemporary with *Ptolemies II and IV. The
hypothetical chronology of the Meroitic king list has
generated attempts to identify 'Ergamenes' with other
fourth-century kings with names suited to the
transliteration (Arqaqamani, Arnekhamani), who may be
contemporary with Ptolemy II. The possibility exists that
'Ergamenes' is only a name representing various conflated
traditions of Meroitic kings which filtered into Greek
historical tradition after the first Greek contacts were
made.

BIBL. Diodorus Siculus iii. 6; P. L. Shinnie, *Meroe: A
Civilization of the Sudan* (1967); B. Haycock, *Kush* xiii
(1965), 264 ff.; F. Hintze, *Die Inschriften des Löwentempels
von Musawwarat es Sofra* (1962) 16–17.

Erinna Poetess, late fourth century BC (?).

Erinna's (Ērinna) brief tragic life (she died at nineteen
(?)) belongs to the early Hellenistic period or shortly
before it (though one tradition claims her, like all women
poets, as friend of *Sappho). For homeland we choose
between Teos, Tenos, and Telos, the last usually
preferred, as she writes in Doric dialect sprinkled with
Aeolicisms. A first-century BC papyrus discovered in 1928
offers the mutilated remains of *The Distaff* (originally 300
hexameters, according to *Suda*), which lament her young
friend Baucis, dead soon after marriage, with poignant
evocation of shared childhood scenes (games of catch,
wool-working chores) burst through by grief. Two of three
surviving epigrams are epitaphs for the same girl.
*Asclepiades endorsed the impressive talent so
prematurely extinguished, and Erinna became a theme for
literary epigram. Her poetry, released by personal pain
and hauntingly vivid, is none the less highly skilful. There
are striking connections with *Theocritus.

BIBL. Bowra, *Poetry and Life* 325 ff. (i.e. *Problems*
151 ff.); Gow and Page, *Hellenistic Epigrams*; D. W. Levin,
HSCP lxvi (1962).

Eubulides of Miletus Philosopher, 3rd century BC.

A philosopher of the Megarian school, Eubulides
(Euboulidēs) devised ingenious arguments and paradoxes,
of which the most famous is the 'Liar': if a man says 'I am
lying', is he telling the truth? The puzzle has greatly
interested modern logicians. Eubulides' strong criticisms
of *Aristotle probably initiated the hostility that
developed between the Stoics, who adopted much of the
Megarian philosophers' logic, and Aristotle's school, the
Peripatos.

BIBL. Diogenes Laertius ii. 109–12.

Eubulides the Younger Sculptor, active c. 140–120 BC.

Eubulides (Euboulidēs) the Younger was from a

Pyramids at Meroe in the Sudan, the burial place of the kings with whom 'Ergamenes' may be identified.

Marble head of Athena from Athens, by Eubulides. Mid- or later 2nd century BC. Athens, National Museum.

prestigious Athenian family of sculptors which, like that of *Polycles, came to prominence in the second century BC, but, unlike them, not through Roman patronage (as far as we know, anyway). He was the son of the sculptor, Eucheir, with whom he often collaborated: we have about ten joint signatures. From inscriptions we know that his father was the Athenian sacred ambassador to Delphi c. 175/150 BC, and that he was an official at the Piraeus c. 120. His grandfather, the sculptor Eubulides the Elder, was Delphian *proxenos* in 191/90, and also probably created the remarkable portrait of *Chrysippus c. 200, which we know in Roman copies.

Pausanias saw near the Cerameicus in Athens a colossal group of Athena, Zeus, Memory, the Muses, and Apollo, which was both made and dedicated by Eubulides. Parts of this monument have been recovered – a head of Athena and a torso and head of a Nike (Victory) – along with a fragmentary signature of his father Eucheir. As often, both father and son must have collaborated on this work, which attempts to re-create a pure fifth-century style – they seem to have favoured a stricter neoclassicism than that of *Damophon or *Polycles.

BIBL. Becatti, *RIA* vii (1940); Stewart, *Attika*, ch. 2; *Roman World* *Pausanias.

Eubulus　Athenian politician, floruit 340s BC.

References in *Demosthenes show Eubulus (Euboulos)

to have been a major figure in Athenian politics after the Social War (357–355 BC), especially in the 340s. In 343 *Aeschines could claim that he was standing trial on behalf of Eubulus' policies, and *Theopompus later classed him among the major Athenian demagogues. Membership of, or influence over, the Theoric Commission gave Eubulus, who was perhaps partly responsible for its creation, considerable control over Athenian finances, a fact of increasing significance when fiscal measures caused public revenue to treble between 355 and 346. Under his leadership money was spent on public works and shipbuilding rather than on meeting passing military crises, much to *Demosthenes' disgust. Eubulus' aim was perhaps not peace at any price (note his sponsorship of a Greek front against *Philip II in 348/7) but the conservation of resources against the eventuality of a major direct threat to Athens. It is a great misfortune that his career is not better documented.

BIBL. Kirchner, *PA*, no. 5369; G. Cawkwell, *JHS* lxxxiii (1963); H.-J. Gehrke, *Phokion* (1976) 25 ff.

Eucl(e)ides of Megara　Philosopher, c. 450–380 BC.

Eucl(e)ides (Eukleidēs) founded the Megarian school of philosophy, where logic, and especially logical paradoxes, were a central interest. His friend *Socrates is said to have criticized his hair-splitting arguments. His only recorded positive doctrine is that 'the good' is just *one* thing, but called by different names such as 'God', 'wisdom', and 'intellect'. *Plato and other philosophers from Athens took refuge with him in Megara after *Socrates' execution (399 BC).

BIBL. Diogenes Laertius ii. 106–12.

Euclid　Geometer, c. 300 BC.

Scarcely anything is known of the life of Euclid (Eukleidēs) except that he lived in Alexandria under *Ptolemy I, to whom he said, when Ptolemy complained of the length of Euclid's proofs, 'There is no royal road to geometry.' More recent thinkers have also complained of Euclid's long-windedness. His *Elements* largely eclipsed earlier Greek geometers' work, and remained a standard introduction to the subject until the rigour of his proofs began to be challenged in the nineteenth century. It is uncertain how much of the work was original. Possibly Euclid's success lay in his organization more than in the discovery of new theorems.

BIBL. T. L. Heath, *The Thirteen Books of Euclid's Elements* (1956).

Eucratides I　King of Bactria, c. 171–c. 154 (?) BC.

The origins of Eucratides (Eukratidēs) are unknown, but the suggestion that he was related to the Seleucids has not been substantiated. He attained power at roughly the same time as Mithradates I of Parthia; his rule ended the succession of the Euthydemids, although it is uncertain whether his few soldiers defeated *Demetrius I (of Bactria) or a Demetrius II in successive encounters. Apparently consolidating his control over the regions held by the Greeks, Eucratides conceived a large plan of conquest in India with himself as the great conqueror. He was one of the few Bactrian kings to strike gold coinage (including the largest gold medallion known from antiquity), on which he was styled 'the Great'. He founded the Bactrian city Eucratideia. On his return from India he was murdered by one of his sons, and his death marked the end of the Bactrian empire, which passed to Mithradates, except for Bactria itself which was ruled by Eucratides' son Heliocles, perhaps until *c.* 135.

BIBL. Tarn, *Greeks in Bactria . . .*; Narain, *Indo-Greeks*; Will, *Hist. pol.* ii.

Eudemus of Rhodes Philosopher, late 4th century BC.

Although he wrote widely on science, philosophy, and mathematics, little is known of the work of Eudemus (Eudēmos), a pupil of *Aristotle. Probably he was mainly concerned with organizing and clarifying Aristotle's philosophy. Aristotle's *Eudemian Ethics* were once thought to be his.

BIBL. F. Wehrli, *Eudemos von Rhodos* (1955).

Eudoxus of Cnidos Mathematician and philosopher, traditionally 408–355 BC.

The (highly unreliable) ancient biographical tradition says that Eudoxus (Eudoxos) was a pupil of *Archytas and *Plato, and worked at the courts of *Nectanebon in Egypt and *Mausolus in Caria before setting up a school at Athens.

Some of his geometrical speculations on conic sections, the volume of spheres, and the doubling of the cube were used in books v and xii of *Euclid's *Elements*. Following the *Pythagorean and Platonic view that only circular motion could be continuous, Eudoxus' astronomical speculations led him to explain the movements of the stars and the retrogradations of planets as due to combinations of homocentric revolving spheres (later Greek astronomers abandoned this theory in favour of one in terms of epicycles). He also calculated the circumference of the earth. His description of the constellations was used by *Aratus for his poem *Phaenomena*.

BIBL. Diogenes Laertius viii. 86–91; Heath, *Greek Mathematics* i. 249, 320 ff.; G. Huxley, *GRBS* iv (1963).

Eudoxus of Cyzicus Explorer, floruit *c.* 125–100 BC.

Eudoxus (Eudoxos) is said to have gone to Alexandria during the reign of *Ptolemy VIII (146–116 BC) to announce at court a festival at Cyzicus. His visit coincided with that of a mariner who had been shipwrecked·while returning from India; the mariner led an expedition back, under royal auspices, and took Eudoxus aboard. The king confiscated their cargo on return. Eudoxus made a second journey to India after 116 under the patronage of *Cleopatra (either II or III), but on his return voyage he was blown off course down the coast of East Africa. He got back to Egypt some years later, only to have *Ptolemy IX confiscate his cargo. Undeterred, he set out to circumnavigate Africa from west to east to find a route to India with favourable winds. Forced to return overland from south of Morocco, he set out again on the same route. Eudoxus disappeared in the course of this fourth journey.

Eudoxus' voyages reflect increased Ptolemaic interest in the route to India at the end of the second century. He was probably one of the first explorers to make a limited use of the monsoon winds.

BIBL. *FGrH* 87 (Posidonius) F 28; J. Thiel, *Eudoxus of Cyzicus* (1968); M. Cary and E. H. Warmington, *The Ancient Explorers* (1929); Otto and Bengtson, *Bayer. Abh.*, n.F. xvii (1938).

Eugammon: see Cyclic Poets

Euhemerus Philosophical fabulist, *c.* 300 BC.

In his influential *Hiera Anagraphe* (*Sacred Record*), known through *Diodorus Siculus and an adaptation by Ennius, Euhemerus of Messene (Euēmeros) narrated how, in *Cassander's service (this is presumably autobiographical fact), he journeyed to fabulous islands in the Indian Ocean. His account of luxuriant Panchaia with its collectivist, priest-dominated society draws on earlier Utopia writings (e.g. *Plato's Atlantis) but has at its heart a coherent and novel theology. The 'Sacred Record' inscribed on a golden pillar within Zeus' distinctly Egyptianizing temple (the influence of *Hecataeus of Abdera is apparent here), narrated the deeds of Uranus, Kronos, and Zeus as great kings of the past, deified for their benefactions to men. This rationalizing, 'euhemeristic' account is clearly influenced by, and endorses, Hellenistic ruler-cult, established by *Alexander the Great; a political motive is therefore likely. Later Euhemerus evidently lived in Alexandria: *Callimachus sharply attacked his blasphemy; *Eratosthenes simply dismissed his romancing.

BIBL. Diodorus v. 41–6, vi. 1; Callimachus, *Iambs* 1; *FGrH* 63; Fraser, *Ptolemaic Alexandria*; *Roman World* *Ennius.

Eumelus Epic poet, *c.* 700 BC (?).

From the ruling Bacchiad family in Corinth, Eumelus (Eumēlos) exploited epic to endow Corinth with a rich heroic past (Helios, Glaucus, Jason and Medea). Two hexameters (?) survive from a *prosodion* sung by Messenians to Apollo at Delos. A *Bougonia* (*Birth from an Ox*) and *Europia* are dubiously ascribed, and a *Titanomachy* is attributed variously to Eumelus and Arctinus (see *Cyclic Poets).

BIBL. Kinkel, *EGF* 185 ff.; Bowra, *Greek Margins*, 46 ff.; Huxley, *Epic Poetry* 60 ff.

Eumelus of Bosporus: see Spartocids

Eumenes I Ruler of Pergamum, 263–241 BC.

On the death of his uncle and adopted father *Philetaerus, Eumenes (Eumenēs) succeeded as semi-independent ruler under *Antiochus I. Dissatisfied with subordinate status, Eumenes probably allied himself with *Ptolemy II to defeat Antiochus in 262 BC near Sardis. The territory subject to Pergamum was enlarged considerably, and her new independence was reflected in issues of non-Seleucid coinage. Although Eumenes never took the title of king, he seems to have had monarchical powers. He succeeded in bribing the marauding Gauls to spare Pergamum, and he began the extensive building programme on the acropolis there. Eumenes was a generous patron to the local philosopher *Arcesilaus of Pitane, who dedicated some works to him.

BIBL. Hansen, *Attalids*.

Eumenes II Soter King of Pergamum, 197–159 BC.

The eldest son of *Attalus I of Pergamum, Eumenes (Eumenēs) 'Saviour' continued his father's policy of being Rome's helper. In 195 BC he joined *Flamininus to defeat *Nabis of Sparta, and he assisted against attacks by *Antiochus III and the Aetolians in Greece. The

Pergamene and Roman fleets fought the Seleucid admiral *Polyxenidas off Asia Minor, and an attack on Pergamum by Antiochus and his son Seleucus IV was narrowly defeated by Eumenes by 190. Helped by his brother *Attalus (later II), the decisive role played by Eumenes in the battle of Magnesia in 189 (see Antiochus III) made him, through the Peace of Apamea, the most powerful ruler in Asia Minor, with territories extending to the Maeander, and including a port in Pamphylia. His vast acquisitions, the gift of Rome, angered dispossessed local dynasts. The claims of *Prusias I of Bithynia were settled in Pergamum's favour, and the war with *Pharnaces I of Pontus was concluded in 179 by Eumenes and his father-in-law *Ariarathes IV of Cappadocia. During these years Eumenes began extensive building operations on the Pergamene acropolis.

Silver tetradrachm with the only known portrait of Eumenes II Soter, king of Pergamum (enlarged).

Eumenes' support of *Antiochus IV for the Seleucid throne in 175 gave him a useful ally against the aggressive *Perseus of Macedon, who made accusations about him to the Senate. When Eumenes was ambushed near Delphi and reported dead, Perseus was accused of the crime, which initiated the Third Macedonian War. During the Pydna campaign in 168, Eumenes was forced to stay at home to deal with another Gallic uprising; Rome may have believed that Eumenes had tried to conclude a secret peace with Perseus, since the Senate did not receive the next Pergamene embassy. The Gauls were finally defeated in Phrygia, perhaps with the help of Antiochus and Ariarathes, whose friendship with Eumenes further cooled Rome's feelings towards him. Plagued by illness, Eumenes entrusted the government to Attalus II in 161/60, and died in 159.

BIBL. Hansen, *Attalids*.

Eumenes of Cardia (c. 362–316 BC) 'Successor' of Alexander the Great.

Eumenes (Eumenēs) came from Cardia in the Chersonese (Dardanelles); the historian *Hieronymus was a member of his entourage, which is one reason why the historical tradition is favourable towards him. At the age of twenty he became secretary to *Philip II of Macedon; in this capacity he was responsible for the official records of *Alexander the Great. Alexander entrusted to Eumenes diplomatic duties in India and, later, charge of the Euphrates fleet and, after *Hephaestion's death in 324,

command of the Macedonian cavalry. He had already been singled out at the great mass-wedding in Susa, receiving as his bride Artonis, sister of Artacama, who was allocated to the commander of the Bodyguard, *Ptolemy (I).

Unlike all the other *Diadochoi* (Successors), Eumenes was not a Macedonian chieftain but a Greek administrator whose power was derived solely from the authority of the royal court. Consequently he strongly resisted the diffusion of power to the generals after Alexander's death. In 323 he was given Cappadocia and Paphlagonia to rule; he supported *Perdiccas, as representative of the central court, against the coalition of hostile generals including *Craterus, whom he destroyed in Cappadocia in 321.

After Perdiccas' death, the succesful generals outlawed Eumenes at the conference of Triparadeisus (320); he was besieged for a year at Nora in the Taurus mountains by *Antigonus, but escaped and carried on the war against Antigonus on behalf of the regent *Polyperchon. In 316 Antigonus defeated him in Gabiene; his army surrendered him to Antigonus and he was condemned to death.

BIBL. Diodorus Siculus xviii–xix (based on Hieronymus of Cardia); Westlake, *Essays*, ch. 18; Will, *Hist. pol.* i; A. B. Bosworth, *GRBS* xix (1978).

Euphorion Poet, born c. 270 BC.

Euphorion (Euphoriōn), from Euboean Chalcis, became rich through an affair with the widow of the local ruler, *Alexander of Corinth (died c. 245 BC), and studied at Athens before leaving mainland Greece for the post of librarian to *Antiochus (III) the Great at Antioch (where he probably wrote the few learned prose works attributed). Though he apparently never gravitated to Alexandria, his poetry operates on extreme *Callimachean principles: its material is recherché myth, narrated in a compressed, wilfully difficult, and highly decorated manner, probably influenced by his compatriot *Lycophron. Euphorion favoured the hexameter epyllion (numerous fragments survive – from *Hesiod, Mopsopia, Dionysus*, etc.), and made a speciality of curse poems (*Thrax* apparently hung a flamboyant series of mythological bad ends on the imprecation of an alleged murderer; compare *Curses on a Cup Thief*). Papyrus finds have added bewilderingly to our knowledge of the contents of his poems; but while we can appreciate a frightfully mannered yet lively style, aiming at euphonious sound effects, the overall éclat of a complete Euphorionic creation eludes us. All this 'art' clearly bewitched the brightest young poets at Rome, the 'cantores Euphorionis' despised by Cicero.

BIBL. Powell, *Coll. Alex.*, pp. 28 ff.; *SH* 413–54; B. A. van Groningen, *Euphorion* (1977); *Roman World* *Cicero.

Euphranor Painter and sculptor, active c. 360–330 BC.

Euphranor (Euphranōr) was unusual in being considered equally highly for his painting and his sculpture. His place of origin is obscure, but he seems to have worked mainly in Athens. A dozen sculptures by him are recorded, among which are a Paris, an Athena, a Heracles, colossal personifications of Arete (Virtue) and Hellas (i.e. Greece), and portraits of *Philip II and *Alexander the Great in a chariot. His best-known commission was three paintings for the interior of the Stoa (Portico) of Zeus in the Athenian Agora: a cavalry battle, the twelve gods, and **Theseus with personifications of

Democracy and the Athenian people. None of these works
survives. He wrote treatises on colours and on
proportions.

A few comments in the sources suggest that his artistic
outlook may have been reactionary or establishment: it
was a noted impossibility that he might paint lewd
subjects (*lascivia*); the grandeur of his heroes (*dignitates
heroum*) was especially remarked on; and he himself
boasted that his Theseus was fed on real meat, that of
*Parrhasius on roses. Also, none of the new subjects in
the fourth century – Satyrs, Erotes, naked Aphrodites –
appear among his recorded works. He probably preferred
a more muscular style in the fifth-century tradition, in
opposition to the secularizing of subjects and feminizing
of style by some of his progressive contemporaries, like
*Praxiteles. The only surviving work by him is a fine and
massive headless torso of a draped Apollo in the Athenian
Agora, almost certainly his cult-statue of Apollo Patroös.

BIBL. O. Palagia, *Euphranor* (1980).

Euphron Tyrant of Sicyon, 368–366/5 BC.

An influential citizen under Spartan hegemony,
Euphron (Euphrōn) engineered a populist *coup* with
Arcadian and Argive help which, amidst murder,
confiscations, and enfranchisement of slaves, made him
tyrant. The Arcadians soon turned against him,
whereupon he sought help first from Sparta and then from
the Thebans, but was murdered in Thebes by Sicyonian
exiles. Despite his apparently cynical opportunism he was
popular in Sicyon, and was honoured posthumously as
archegetes ('founder') of the city.

BIBL. Berve, *Tyrannis* 305 f.; D. Whitehead, *LCM* v
(1980), vi (1981); P. Cartledge, *LCM* v (1980).

Euphronius Vase-painter and potter, active
c. 520–500 BC.

Euphronius (Euphrōnios) was one of the finest red
figure vase-painters. With his rival Euthymides he was
the leader of the 'pioneers', a group of vase-painters of the
second generation of red figure, who explored the
possibilities of the new technique for the representation of
the human body in action. We have six vases signed by
him as painter and, from later in his career, ten signed as
potter, which were decorated by other painters. His

Cup signed by Euphronius as painter and Kachrylion as potter:
Heracles fighting triple-bodied Geryon. Late 6th century BC.
Munich, Antikensammlungen.

Marble statue of Apollo from the Athenian Agora, probably by
Euphranor, *c.* 330 BC. Athens, Agora Museum.

Krater (mixing-bowl for wine) painted by Euphronius, showing Sleep and Death carrying off Sarpedon's body. Late 6th century BC. New York, Metropolitan Museum of Art.

masterpiece is a mixing-bowl (calyx crater) in New York depicting the dead Sarpedon being removed from the battlefield by Sleep and Death.

BIBL. Beazley, *ARV* 13–17, and *Paralipomena* 321–2; Boardman, *Red Figure* 32–3; M. Wegner, *Euthymides und Euphronios* (1979).

Eupolis Comic poet, active *c.* 429–412 BC.

The name of Eupolis, one of the most prominent poets of Old Comedy, is often coupled with those of *Aristophanes and *Cratinus. Targets of his ridicule included *Cleon, *Hyperbolus, and *Alcibiades, but he seems not to have shared Aristophanes' opposition to war with Sparta. We have numerous fragments, especially from the *Demes*, in which great Athenians of the past return from the Underworld to aid the city.

BIBL. Lesky, *Greek Literature*; Edmonds, *Attic Comedy* i; *Literary Papyri* (Loeb).

Euripides (485/4 (?)–407/6 BC) Tragedian.

Conflicting dates of birth are given for Euripides (Euripidēs), but he must have been born during the 480s BC. His family came from Phlya in Attica, and was certainly respectable; no attention need be paid to the allegation of comic poets that his mother was a greengrocer. Most of the legends concerning his life derive from equally unreliable sources; it is doubtful, for instance, whether he was prosecuted by *Cleon for impiety. Unlike *Sophocles he seems to have taken little part in public life. In 408 or 407 he went to the court of *Archelaus of Macedon to produce plays for him, and it was there that he died. The claim made in late sources, that he left Athens embittered at his lack of success there, is untrustworthy.

He is said to have competed 22 times at the Great Dionysia (first in 455) and to have written 92 plays; we know the titles of about 80. He won first prize only four times in his life (first in 441) and once after his death with plays that he had left unperformed. Most of his plays were self-contained, not belonging to connected

tetralogies; those produced in 415 (*Alexander, Palamedes*, the surviving *Trojan Women*, and *Sisyphus*) were an exception, but even here the connection will have been looser than in the *Oresteia* of *Aeschylus. He is said to have also written an ode in honour of an Olympic victory of *Alcibiades.

Nineteen plays survive under his name. One of them, *Rhesus*, is generally reckoned spurious. Another, *Cyclops* (based on *Homer, *Odyssey* ix), is not a tragedy but a satyr play (the only one that survives in full), and cannot be reliably dated. Of the remaining 17 tragedies the dates of several are known, and progressive changes in Euripides' metrical practice enable the rest to be fitted into a fairly reliable chronological sequence, as follows.

Alcestis, 438 (a tragedy performed in the position normally occupied by a satyr play). *Medea*, 431. **Heracleidae* (*Sons of Heracles*), *c.* 430/428. *Hippolytus*, 428 (the second play which Euripides wrote on this subject). *Andromache*, *c.* 425. *Hecabe*, *c.* 424. *Suppliant Women*, *c.* 423 (concerning the burial of the 'Seven against Thebes'). *Electra*, *c.* 422/416. *Heracles*, close to 415. *Trojan Women*, 415. *Iphigeneia in Tauris* (*among the Taurians*), *c.* 414/3. *Ion*, *c.* 414/3. *Helen*, 412. *Phoenician Women*, *c.* 409 (concerning the sons of **Oedipus). *Orestes*, 408. *Bacchae*, posthumously produced (concerning the death of

Inscribed bust of Euripides. Roman copy of a 4th-century BC original. Naples, Museo Nazionale.

Relief showing Euripides receiving a mask from Skene, the personification of Theatre, who holds a scroll in her right hand; on the right is Dionysus, holding a cantharus. Istanbul, Archaeological Museum.

Medea contemplates the murder of her children. Pompeian wall-painting, inspired by Euripides' *Medea*. Naples, Museo Nazionale.

Pentheus). *Iphigeneia at Aulis*, posthumously produced (probably left unfinished by Euripides and completed by another hand). In addition the numerous fragments – some of them substantial – and allusions in later authors mean that we are well informed about many of the lost plays.

The plays tend to contain certain stereotyped structural units: an artificial expository prologue, at least one set-piece debate (*agon*), a detailed and vivid messenger-speech, and at the end a divine epiphany prophesying future events. While these devices can be used in many different ways, Euripides develops each for its own sake, making much less effort than Sophocles to integrate the parts into a harmonious whole. Indeed, elegance of plot-construction is not among Euripides' main concerns; and the most skilful plots (the best is that of *Iphigeneia in Tauris*) tend to come in the less serious plays. Similarly the chorus is seldom closely involved in the action, and in the later plays, especially, its songs often serve to contrast with the action rather than to shed light on it.

The general uniformity of style and dramatic technique makes all the more remarkable the wide variation in the plays' tone and quality. Few dramatists could range from such a bleak evocation of unremitting suffering as *Trojan Women* to such a cheerful romance as *Helen*, or from the profundity of *Bacchae* to the inanity of *Andromache*. Much of Euripides' work can fairly be called melodramatic, in that it turns on intrigues, narrow escapes, sudden reversals of fortune, noble acts of self-sacrifice, terrible acts of revenge, and, in general, extremes of passion and pathos intensely but rather self-consciously evoked. In late Euripides the plot tends to become fast-moving, sensational, and episodic (but *Bacchae* shows a reversion to a simpler and more unified structure). In characterization Euripides is particularly fond of paradox and ambivalence, creating conflicts of sympathy in the audience; in some cases this leads to abrupt shifts in a character's behaviour (e.g. Hecuba and Orestes in the plays named after them), in others to real psychological complexity (e.g. Medea, Phaedra in *Hippolytus*, Pentheus in *Bacchae*).

The influence of intellectual developments associated with the sophists can be seen in Euripides' pervasive love of rhetoric and in the sceptical and unconventional attitudes that his characters often express. It is even possible for a Euripidean character to question the subordinate position of women (*Medea* 230–51) or the connection between noble birth and noble conduct (*Electra* 367–85). This does not, however, make it easy to determine Euripides' own views, and his religious attitudes, in particular, have been much debated; expressions of conventional piety (e.g. *Heracleidae* 766–9) and bitter denunciations of the gods' injustice (e.g. *Bacchae* 1344–51) are equally justified by the plays in which they occur, and we also find expressions of faith in gods that differ from those of myth (*Heracles* 1340–6, *Trojan Women* 884–9, *Iphigeneia in Tauris* 386–91). His political views are clearer: democratic (*Suppliant Women* 429–55) and deeply patriotic (*Suppliant Women*, *Heracleidae*, *Heracles*, *Medea*), but with a strong sense of the pathos of war (*Trojan Women*). But none of the plays is written for the sake of a definable 'moral'.

Euripides is a favourite target of *Aristophanes' humour, appearing in person in his *Acharnians*, *Thesmophoriazusae*, and *Frogs*. He is mocked as a sophistic and atheistic intellectual and (surprisingly) a misogynist, and charged with degrading tragedy by depicting trivial and vulgar subjects. After his death he became by far the most popular of the tragedians, greatly influencing Hellenistic and Roman literature. *Aristotle criticizes his plots but calls him 'the most tragic of the poets'.

BIBL. Lesky, *Greek Literature*; C. Collard, *Euripides* (GRNSC xiv, 1981); D. J. Conacher, *Euripidean Drama* (1967).

Eurybiades Spartan admiral, 480 BC.

Eurybiades (Eurubiadēs) commanded the combined Greek fleet which opposed the Persians at the battles of Artemisium and Salamis in 480 BC. (See also *Themistocles.)

BIBL. Herodotus vii–viii; Hignett, *Xerxes' Invasion*.

Eurydice Mother of Philip II of Macedonia.

Eurydice (Eurudikē) was the wife of *Amyntas III of Macedonia, after whose death she had a liaison with *Ptolemy Alorites, the alleged murderer of her son *Alexander II (*Philip's eldest brother). The lurid tales told of her may admit of some scepticism, and she certainly helped to ensure that the kingship remained with her family rather than falling to usurpers.

BIBL. Hammond and Griffith, *Macedonia* ii.

Eurydice: see also *Adea, *Cleopatra

Euthydemus I King of Bactria, c. 227(?)–200/190 BC.

Euthydemus (Euthudēmos) came from an unspecified city named Magnesia, and took the throne of Bactria from Diodotus II. It is not known if he was a local noble, a satrap, or a royal officer, or why he revolted (beyond the desire for power); the date of his revolt is likewise unknown, except that it was later than the expedition of *Seleucus II against *Arsaces I of Parthia (c. 227 BC?). *Antiochus III marched against him on his great anabasis in 208 to subdue his former satrapy. Euthydemus was besieged for two years before a compromise was reached.

Coin portrait of Euthydemus I, king of Bactria (enlarged).

Antiochus recognized him as the legitimate king of an independent kingdom, and promised the hand of a daughter to Euthydemus' son *Demetrius I. (It is not known if the marriage took place.) In return Euthydemus provisioned the Seleucid army and supplied elephants. He died within the decade 200–190.

BIBL. Polybius X. xlix; XXIX. xii. 8; Tarn, *Greeks in Bactria. . .*; Narain, *Indo-Greeks*; Will, *Hist. pol.*

Evagoras King of Cypriot Salamis, 411–374/3 BC.

After regaining his family's traditional control of Salamis in an anti-Phoenician *coup* (411 BC), Evagoras (Euagoras) strengthened and hellenized the city. He had close relations with Athens, and it was to Salamis that *Conon and others fled in 405. Evagoras sponsored Conon's appointment as a Persian admiral in 398/7, but later rebelled against *Artaxerxes II when the latter became concerned at Evagoras' expansionist tendencies. The revolt lasted a decade, and eventual defeat still left Evagoras as king of Salamis. He was murdered by a eunuch as a result of a private quarrel. *Isocrates wrote a biographical encomium (the *Evagoras*), and offered political advice to his son and successor Nicocles.

BIBL. K. Spyridakis, *Evagoras I von Salamis* (1935); E. Costa, *Historia* xxiii (1974); Hofstetter, *Griechen*, no. 105.

The Evangelists

The four canonical gospels were compiled within two generations of the crucifixion of Jesus. Their authors were, by the close of the second century AD and thereafter, traditionally identified with disciples of Jesus or companions of Apostles. (Matthew was formerly a tax collector; John the brother of James and son of Zebedee a fisherman. Mark appears in the New Testament as an associate of Barnabas, *Paul, and Peter; Luke as a doctor and companion of Paul.) But these identifications have been much debated since 1800.

The gospel attributed to Mark was most probably the earliest of the four. It was compiled around AD 66–70, and its brief component stories sound like accounts constantly retold in oral transmission. The author depicts Jesus as healer, exorcist, Messiah, and above all as suffering Son of Man. His extended account of the arrest and crucifixion presents these events as fulfilling passages in the psalms and prophets. The climax is the acknowledgement of Jesus as son of God by a Roman centurion. The account of the Resurrection ends very abruptly at 16:8.

The gospel ascribed to Matthew most likely conflated material from Mark with at least one other source (Q). The author presents Jesus as giver of a new moral law, and is concerned for church order, as well as Christology. His work is more comprehensive than Mark, and more ordered. He tends to group ethical teaching, parables, and miracles in sections. He probably compiled the gospel for a Christian community in a Hellenistic city (perhaps Antioch) a decade or so after AD 70.

The author of the Third Gospel also wrote Acts. But was this author Luke the companion of Paul? His account of Paul's journeys usually matches Paul's letters, with one or two major exceptions. His portrait of Paul's views differs at significant points from Paul's letters. If he was a companion of the Apostle, he offers a perspective of his own. His gospel is generally considered to have used Mark, and the second source Q, and other material as well. (His birth and Resurrection narratives contain notably independent items.) His editorial policy differs from Matthew's, in that he follows first one source then another in lengthy sequences. His editorial vocabulary and technique can be traced by making comparisons with Mark and Acts. In reports of Jesus' teaching it is sometimes Matthew, but quite often Luke who preserves older wording. He is especially concerned to convince the Graeco-Roman world of the political innocence of Jesus and his followers.

The Fourth Gospel is in some ways close to and in others distant from the first three. Since the discoveries at Qumran and Nag Hammadi, scholars have more clearly recognized its affinities with Jewish gnosis (speculations about good and evil). The author probably wrote for a Christian community which had suffered a dramatic break with Judaism (16:2), and was itself somewhat disunited (see 1 John 2:19). The author is, even more than the other evangelists, an interpretative theologian. He selects fewer stories and themes and presents them in the form of extended discourses. The viewpoint and style are distinctive. The focus is almost always on motifs such as the unique Sonship of Jesus, or his existence since eternity. Neither theme is wholly absent from the Synoptic gospels, but it is significant that the latter is hardly found there and is pervasive in the Fourth Gospel.

Those who uphold a link with the disciple John, son of Zebedee, tend nowadays to speak of a 'school' of teachers deriving from John. The author's interpretation is mystical rather than apocalyptic.

BIBL. W. G. Kümmel, *Introduction to the New Testament* (1975); *Roman World* *Jesus Christ, St *Paul, St *Peter.

D.M.

Exekias Vase-painter and potter, active *c*. 550–530 BC.

Exekias (Exēkias) was the greatest Attic black figure

Amphora signed by Exekias as both potter and painter, showing **Achilles and **Ajax playing a game, *c*. 540 BC. Vatican Museum.

Drinking cup by Exekias, *c*. 540 BC. Munich, Antikensammlungen.

vase-painter. He seems to have started his career making vases for other painters, and later both made and painted vases. We have ten pieces signed by him as potter – seven decorated by other painters and mostly made early in his career – and two signed as both potter and painter. As a potter he invented, or played a large part in inventing, several new vase shapes (amphora type A, eye-cup, calyx crater) and as a painter his powerful draughtsmanship is unrivalled. Nearly 30 vases have been attributed to his hand, as well as some extremely fine terracotta plaques with funerary subjects from a grave monument.

BIBL. Beazley, *ABV* 143 ff., and *Paralipomena* 59 ff.; Boardman, *Black Figure* 56–8, and *AJA* lxxxii (1978), 12–25.

Flamininus Roman consul, and general in Greece, 198–189 BC.

Titus Quinctius Flamininus received the consulship of 198 BC and with it the command against *Philip V (q.v.) in the Second Macedonian War. *Attalus I of Pergamum was one of his allies in the political manœuvres in Greece. After Philip was defeated at Cynoscephalae in 197, Flamininus became personally involved with a new Roman policy towards Greece, which was 'philhellenic' and involved the championing of local Greek autonomy. This diplomatic advantage combined with his ability (for an inexperienced Roman) to hold his own in negotiations with Hellenistic powers. When at the Isthmian Games of 196 Flamininus staged a melodramatic announcement of the Senate's decree that all Greeks should be free, he became as the Roman proconsul in Greece the personal focus of enthusiastic gratitude; his honours included cult-worship and the issue of coins bearing his portrait.

Flamininus' command was prolonged amid fears that *Antiochus III would invade Greece. In 195 he led a campaign (with the help of *Eumenes II of Pergamum) against *Nabis of Sparta, who had been an ally but not a military supporter of Philip. In 194 he secured the complete evacuation of Roman forces against considerable senatorial opposition. His apparent idealism masked a shrewd appreciation of Rome's strategic interests, and behind the philhellenism stood a proud Roman aristocrat who expected the nominally free Greeks to recognize their obligations to their Roman benefactors.

Flamininus scored a notable diplomatic success over Antiochus' envoys at a conference in Rome in 193, but as

Coin portrait of Flamininus, struck in Macedonia, in which the
Roman general is depicted with markedly hellenized features.

ambassador in Greece in 192 he discovered that his
personal authority was insufficient to prevent the
defection of Aetolia or to curb Achaean expansion in the
Peloponnese. The war with Antiochus and the Aetolians
(191–189) wrecked his settlement of Greece, but
vindicated his stand on Greek autonomy.

*Polybius gives an unfavourable picture of Flamininus,
drawing attention to his devious and underhand dealings.

BIBL. *Roman World*; E. Badian, *Titus Quinctius
Flamininus: Philhellenism and Realpolitik* (1970); Walbank,
Philip V.

Gelon Tyrant of Syracuse, 491–478 BC.

The family of Gelon (Gelōn), son of Deinomenes, were
hereditary priests of the gods of the Underworld at Gela in
southern Sicily. Gelon played a crucial role in supporting
the previous tyrant, *Hippocrates, as cavalry commander.
After Hippocrates' death in 491, Gelon seized power as
protector of his sons (who soon disappeared). In 489/8 he
joined his father-in-law *Theron, tyrant of Acragas, in an
attempt to expel the Carthaginians from Heraclea in
western Sicily (see *Dorieus). In 485 the Syracusan

aristocracy invited him to intervene in a civil war against
the *demos* and the local serfs (the Cyllyrioi): he captured
Syracuse, and made it his capital. Efficient administration
enabled him to finance both a fleet and a powerful
mercenary army; he is said to have granted citizenship to
a 'myriad' of mainly Arcadian soldiers, and to have
transferred to Syracuse the populations of other Sicilian
cities. He was thus able to govern with the support of the
Syracusan popular Assembly.

In 480 Gelon was faced with a major Carthaginian
invasion in support of Terillus and *Anaxilas of Rhegium.
The Carthaginians under *Hamilcar were defeated at
Himera; Anaxilas recognized Gelon as the most important
of the Sicilian tyrants.

BIBL. Dunbabin, *Western Greeks* 410 ff.; Woodhead,
Greeks in the West 76 ff.

Gorgias (*c.* 480–380 BC) Rhetorician.

Gorgias of Leontini came to Athens in 427 with a
delegation asking for assistance against Syracuse; he
appears to have remained in Athens teaching rhetoric, and
to have travelled and given public addresses at Delphi,
Olympia, and elsewhere in Greece. Like other sophists, he
required payment for his teaching.

Gorgias was one of the first to analyse the emotional
effect on the audience of different rhetorical techniques –
hence the view, criticized by *Plato (*Gorgias*), that a good
speaker must be able to make the worse case seem to be
the better. He was thought to have been the first
systematically to use the *schemata Gorgeia* (rhyming
words and balancing antithetical clauses) to 'bewitch' an
audience; this is illustrated in the surviving speeches, *In
Praise of Helen* (arguing that Helen was 'persuaded' by
Paris and therefore not responsible for the disasters of the
Trojan War) and *In Defence of Palamedes* against
* *Odysseus' accusations. He also produced works of
philosophical and rhetorical theory.

BIBL. Diels and Kranz, *Vorsokratiker* ii, no. 82; E. R.

Model in cork of the Temple of Zeus at Agrigento built after 480 BC to commemorate the defeat of the Carthaginians. Rome.

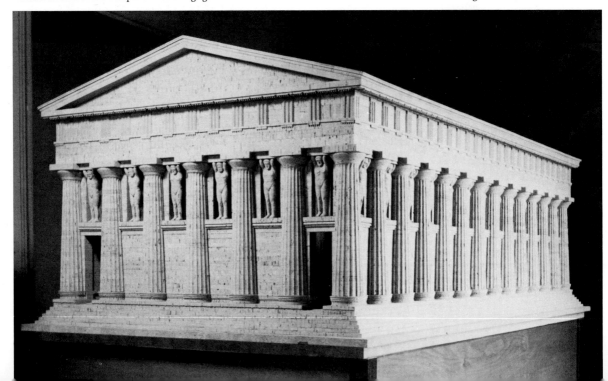

Dodds, edition of Plato, *Gorgias* (1959) 6 ff.; Kennedy, *Art of Persuasion* 61–9, 156 ff., 167 ff.; Guthrie, *Greek Philosophy* iii. 192 ff., 269 ff.

Gorgidas Theban general, 4th century BC.

Although not exiled in the pro-Spartan *coup* of 382 BC, Gorgidas played a part in the counter-revolution (379/8), and was reportedly elected Boeotarch immediately afterwards. Little is known of him, except that he created the 'Sacred Band', an élite battalion composed of pairs of male lovers who, the theory went, would never wish to disgrace themselves in the eyes of their beloved. The Sacred Band played a prominent role in the defeat of Sparta at Leuctra in 371 (see *Cleombrotus) and, in less happy circumstances, against the Macedonians at Chaeronea in 338 (see *Philip II, *Alexander the Great).
BIBL. Buckler, *Theban Hegemony*.

Gyges King of Lydia, c. 650 BC.

Gyges (Gugēs) rose from humble origins to seize the Lydian throne, founding the Mermnad dynasty. The spectacular fall of its last member, *Croesus, was seen by some as a divine punishment for his ancestor's crimes. Gyges began the Lydian conquest of Ionia, and also had more peaceful contacts with the Greeks, sending offerings to Delphi. *Archilochus called him 'tyrant' – the first use of the term in Greek.
BIBL. Herodotus i. 8–15; Plato, *Republic* 359c–360b; Andrewes, *Greek Tyrants* 21–2, 116.

Gylippus Spartan general, late 5th century BC.

When the Athenian expedition to Sicily attacked Syracuse in 415 BC, *Alcibiades (q.v.) advised the Spartans to send Gylippus (Gulippos) to assist them. He reached Syracuse with soldiers from other Sicilian cities, and was able to prevent the Athenians from enclosing the city. In 413 he won a decisive victory, destroying the Athenian fleet in the harbour of Syracuse: the Athenians attempted to withdraw and then capitulated. Their generals *Demosthenes (son of Alcisthenes) and *Nicias were killed by some Syracusans, in contravention of the terms agreed by Gylippus.

Gylippus is next heard of in 404, when he transported booty captured from the Athenians to Sparta; he was accused of peculation and exiled. One source says he committed suicide.
BIBL. Thucydides vi–vii.; Diodorus Siculus xiii. 106; Pos(e)idonius, *apud* Athenaeus vi. 234A; Westlake, *Individuals in Thucydides*, ch. 14.

Hagnon Athenian leader, second half of 5th century BC.

In 440 BC Hagnon (Hagnōn) was one of the *strategoi* who put down the Samian revolt. He is probably to be identified with the Athenian general sent out to found the colony at Amphipolis in Thrace in 437/6. Although he is said to have supported *Pericles when he was accused of embezzling public funds, he may have opposed Pericles' policy of restraint in 431/30, at the beginning of the Peloponnesian War. He served as *strategos* in 431 and 429, and was one of the oath-takers at the Peace of *Nicias in 421. In 413, together with *Sophocles, he was one of the ten *probouloi* appointed to consider public policy after the Sicilian disaster. His son was *Theramenes.
BIBL. Davies, *Athenian Families*, no. 7234.

Hamilcar King of Carthage, died 480 BC.

The father of Hamilcar (Amilkas; Punic Abd-Melkart) was the Carthaginian Magon, his mother a Syracusan. He was asked to Sicily by Terillus and *Anaxilas of Rhegium to expel *Theron of Acragas from Himera; it was widely believed that the expedition was planned to synchronize with *Xerxes' invasion of Greece. Hamilcar's army was destroyed at Himera by *Gelon of Syracuse; he was said to have immolated himself in a sacrificial fire.
BIBL. Dunbabin, *Western Greeks*, ch. 14.

Hannibal King of Carthage, died 406 BC.

Called the 'Greek-hater', Hannibal (Annibas) was the grandson of *Hamilcar. In 409 BC he invaded Sicily at the invitation of Segesta and plundered Selinus. *Diocles abandoned Himera to him; Hannibal then planned to conquer the whole of Sicily, making an alliance with Athens (407/6) which forced the Syracusans to withdraw their fleet from the Aegean. He died in 406 while besieging Acragas.
BIBL. Diodorus Siculus xiii. 43 ff., 54–62, 80, 85 ff.

Harmodius Athenian 'tyrannicide' 514 BC.

A handsome Athenian youth, Harmodius (Harmodios) was courted by *Hipparchus, but rejected him in favour of Aristogeiton. Fearing Hipparchus' vengeance,

A Roman copy of the monument to the 'tyrannicides' (Harmodius and Aristogeiton) which stood in the Agora at Athens. Naples, Museo Nazionale.

Harmodius and Aristogeiton conspired to kill him and his brother, the tyrant *Hippias. They planned to attack them at the Panathenaic procession, but succeeded only in killing Hipparchus before they were arrested and executed. Nevertheless, they were later glorified as 'tyrannicides'.

BIBL. Herodotus v. 55, vi. 109, 123; Thucydides i. 20, vi. 54–9.

Harpalus Paymaster to Alexander the Great, died 323 BC.

A boyhood friend of *Alexander, Harpalus (Harpalos) accompanied the Persian expedition as paymaster. In 333 BC he fled to Megara, but returned to his post in 331. During Alexander's absence in India, Harpalus lived a life of luxurious self-indulgence in Babylon (note the sumptuous funeral of his mistress Pythionice and the foundation of a sanctuary of Aphrodite Pythionice). In 324, fearing Alexander's displeasure, he fled again, taking money and troops, and attempted to install himself in Athens. Rebuffed, he took the army to Taenarum and returned to Athens alone. The Athenians imprisoned him, storing his money on the Acropolis, but Harpalus soon escaped to Crete (where *Thibron (2) murdered him), and half the deposited cash was discovered to have gone. The subsequent investigations ended *Demosthenes' political career.

BIBL. Berve, *Alexanderreich*, no. 143; E. Badian, *JHS* lxxxi (1961).

Hecataeus (c. 550–490 BC) 'Logographer'.

Although at first opposed to the Ionian revolt against Persia (499–494 BC), Hecataeus (Hekataios) of Miletus became one of its leaders. As part of the so-called 'Ionian Enlightenment' – the attempt by Greeks under Persian rule to assimilate elements of the other cultural traditions of the Persian empire – he was the first to write about the past in prose. His lost work, the *Genealogies*, was an attempt to rationalize the epic myths: the opening sentence includes the famous proposition that Greek traditions were numerous and absurd. He also wrote a *Periegesis*, a geography of the world as known to the Greeks and Persians, for which he produced a map.

BIBL. *FGrH* i, no. 1; Herodotus v. 36, 125; Pearson, *Ionian Historians*, ch. 2; T. S. Brown, *AJP* lxxxvi (1965).

Hecataeus of Abdera Historian, floruit c. 315–285 BC (?).

Probably from Abdera in Thrace, but living in Egypt during the time of *Ptolemy I, Hecataeus (Hekataios) was trained as a philosopher, but belongs to the Alexandrian historiographical tradition. He wrote on Egyptian antiquities, the Hyperboreans, and the poetry of *Homer and *Hesiod. Large sections of the Egyptian work are preserved in book i of *Diodorus Siculus; it included information on native kings, customs, geography, and religion, and it emphasized the comparison between Egypt and Greece, to the detriment of the latter in terms of antiquity and superiority. Hecataeus recorded his personal knowledge of Egypt (visits to monuments, interviews with priests, etc.), although he also used *Herodotus. His purpose may have been to praise the land now ruled by the Ptolemies, and he was one of the few Alexandrian historians to be interested in native aspects of Egypt.

BIBL. *FGrH* 264; PW vii. 2750 ff. (Hekataios 4); A. Burton, *Diodorus Siculus, Book I: A Commentary* (1972).

Hellanicus (trad. 490–405 BC) 'Logographer'.

Hedylus (Hēdulos) came from an Athenian family connected with Samos, with poetesses for mother and grandmother. He apparently gravitated to Alexandria in the 270s (see epigram 4 on a *Ctesibian mechanical toy dedicated to *Arsinoe II). His handful of epigrams show *joie de vivre* and close links with *Asclepiades and especially *Poseidippus (q.v.).

BIBL. Gow and Page, *Hellenistic Epigrams*; *SH* 457–9; Webster, *Hellenistic Poetry*.

Hegemon Parodist, 5th century BC.

*Aristotle calls Hegemon (Hēgēmōn) of Thasos the first writer of parodies (presumably meaning that he established this as a recognized genre). He parodied epic and perhaps tragedy, and is also said to have written a comedy.

BIBL. Lesky, *Greek Literature*; Athenaeus ix. 406 f., xv. 698 f.

Hegesias of Magnesia Orator, early 3rd century BC (?).

Fragments remain of Hegesias' (Hēgēsias) flowery *History of *Alexander (the Great), but virtually nothing of his speeches. Nevertheless he emerges from the shadows of Hellenistic oratory covered in the abuse of purists, e.g. *Agatharchides, and Cicero, who thought him altogether idiotic, the very type of 'Asianism'. Hegesias clearly developed to a high pitch the flamboyantly rhythmical and 'artistic' style which began with *Gorgias' jingling prose.

BIBL. *FGrH* 142; E. Norden, *Die antike Kunstprosa* (1909); D. A. Russell, *Criticism in Antiquity* (1981); *Roman World* *Cicero.

Hegesias of Salamis: see **Cyclic Poets**

Hegesippus Athenian politician, mid-4th century BC.

Hegesippus' (Hēgēsippos) public career stretched from at least 357/6 to 337 BC, and he was still alive in 325/4, but he is chiefly notable for his part in preventing renegotiation of the Peace of *Philocrates in 344–3 and 342; on the latter occasion he delivered *On Halonnesus* (= *Demosthenes vii), a *tour de force* of political obstructionism. Nicknamed 'Krobylos' ('Top-knot') from his hair-style, his ugly physical appearance provoked unkind comment from comic poets.

BIBL. Kirchner, *PA*, no. 6351; Davies, *Athenian Families* 209; Hammond and Griffith, *Macedonia* ii.

Hegias (or Agias): see **Cyclic Poets**

Hellanicus (trad. 490–405 BC), 'Logographer'.

Nothing reliable is known about the life of Hellanicus (Hellanikos) of Lesbos. He wrote on a wide range of subjects, including the genealogies of epic heroes (tracing some families down to his own time), and Greek and 'barbarian' ethnography; some of this was clearly earlier than *Herodotus. His most important achievement was to create a chronological system for dating past events based on the list of the priestesses of Hera at Argos. His history of Athens (*Atthis*) was in chronicle form, based on lists of kings and archons.

BIBL. *FGrH* iiiB, no. 323A; Pearson, *Ionian Historians*, ch. 5; Jacoby, *Atthis*; T. S. Brown, *Historia* xi (1962).

Hephaestion Macedonian general, died 324 BC.

A boyhood friend of *Alexander the Great, Hephaestion (Hēphaistiōn) was appointed joint commander of the Companion Cavalry after *Philotas' death (330 BC), and must be accounted one of the two or three senior marshals of the Macedonian army. Special intimacy with Alexander won him the status of chiliarch (vizier) and the hand of *Darius III's daughter Drypetis, but also made him self-important and unpopular with the Macedonians. In 324 he died of a sudden fever, aggravated by excessive eating and drinking. Alexander's grief was extravagant (10,000 talents were allegedly spent on a monument, while Ammon's oracle ordered the grant of heroic honours), and some have wondered if he ever regained proper self-control.

BIBL. Berve, *Alexanderreich*, no. 357.

Heracleides Lembus Civil servant and littérateur, mid-2nd century BC.

If identifications are correct, Heracleides (Hērakleidēs) ('Lembus' is obscure), a native of Callatis on the Black Sea and citizen of Alexandria, was an important official of *Ptolemy VI and a spare-time historian. He apparently lived at Oxyrhynchus and had *Agatharchides for amanuensis. His epitomes of *Hermippus of Smyrna, Sotion, and *Satyrus assisted an unreliable biographical tradition on its downward path. His extant selections from *Aristotle's *Politeiai* (*Constitutions*) show an irritating penchant for the anecdotal at the expense of significant information.

BIBL. *POxy.* 1367 (epitome of Hermippus); Fraser, *Ptolemaic Alexandria*; H. Bloch, *TAPA* lxxi (1940).

Heracleides Ponticus (*c.* 390–310 BC) Writer and philosopher.

Born at Heraclea on the Black Sea, Heracleides (Hērakleidēs) of Pontus studied with *Plato in Athens, and may have acted as head of the Academy when Plato visited Sicily in 361/60 BC. Later he joined *Aristotle's school, perhaps offended because *Speusippus had succeeded Plato. His many writings on music, literary criticism, mathematics, ethics, rhetoric, and physics were renowned for elegance, but are lost.

Two astronomical innovations are attributed to him: that the earth rotates, while the stars remain still, and that at least some of the planets revolve round the sun as a centre. But we know too little to tell quite how revolutionary an astronomer he was.

He adopted a form of atomism, but, unlike *Democritus, explained the happenings in the universe by divine purpose.

He was wealthy and fat, and wore 'soft clothes'.

BIBL. Diogenes Laertius v. 87–94; Heath, *Aristarchus of Samos*, ch. 18.

Heracl(e)itus Philosopher, early 5th century BC.

Heracl(e)itus (Hērakleitos) gave up his 'kingship' in Ephesus to his brother, out of 'pride'. Even this may be untrue, and all other information about his life consists of anecdotes built on his reputation for pride and misanthropy, and on perverse interpretations of his writings.

Over a hundred fragments of his work survive. They are mainly short, obscure, pregnant sentences, making

Marble statue of Heracleitus, as viewed by a sculptor of the Roman period. Crete, Heraclion Museum.

Gem of the Roman period inscribed with the name 'Heracleitus'. Athens, National Museum.

much use of puns, metaphor, and ambiguity. (He clearly thought that multiple meanings of words threw some light on reality.) He was fiercely contemptuous of other thinkers (e.g. *Homer, *Hesiod, *Pythagoras, *Xenophanes) and indeed of the majority of men for their ignorance. ('Other men do not notice what they do when awake, just as they forget what they do when asleep.') It is hard to extract a coherent account of what he believed to be the truth that others, in their stupidity, had missed, but the following are some of the clearer strands.

All things happen in accordance with the *logos*. *Logos* had many meanings, and may here mean a *rule* of nature, or perhaps simply an *account* of how things happen, or the *proportion* that is preserved through the various changes that occur in the world. Water, air, and earth constantly turn into one another (presumably in evaporation, freezing, silting, etc.), but always preserve the same proportions. This permanent stability through change was expressed by the image of a constantly burning fire (although the precise role of fire in Heracl(e)itus' system has been much disputed). A doctrine of eternal flux is attributed to him by later writers, e.g. *Plato, who summarizes the doctrine as 'Everything moves and nothing rests', and cites Heracl(e)itus' saying that one cannot step into the same river twice. It is uncertain whether the flux consisted just of familiar changes, or whether apparently stable things were supposed to undergo constant imperceptible change. His follower *Cratylus (q.v.) evidently held a more extreme version of the theory.

In many paradoxical sayings, Heracl(e)itus said that pairs of opposites were one ('The road up and down is one and the same.' 'The same thing is living and dead . . .'). No doubt the unity of opposites was connected with the preservation of stability through change.

His ethical maxims emphasize the importance of knowledge, moderation, and respect for law.

He influenced Plato's philosophy through the medium of Cratylus.

BIBL. Kirk and Raven, *Presocratic Philosophers*.

Herillus Stoic philosopher, 2nd century BC.

Herillus (Hērillos) of Carthage, a pupil of *Zeno of Citium, differed from other Stoics in holding that knowledge, and not virtue, was the greatest good. (His view is often mentioned by Cicero as 'long ago refuted'.) He wrote short books 'full of power', but none survives.

BIBL. Diogenes Laertius vii. 165–6; *Roman World* *Cicero.

Herippidas Spartan general, died 379/8 BC.

After the brutal suppression of civil discord at Heraclea Trachinia (395 BC), Herippidas (Hērippidas) served as one of *Agesilaus' subordinates in Asia Minor (commanding, among others, the remnants of *Cyrus the Younger's mercenaries) and as navarch (admiral; 393/2). In 382–379/8 he was one of the garrison-commanders in Thebes, and was ultimately executed for over-hastily surrendering the Cadmea.

BIBL. Poralla, *Prosopographie*, no. 349; H. Parke, *CQ* xxi (1927).

Hermagoras of Temnos Rhetorician, *c.* 150 BC.

Hermagoras, the only really important rhetorician to emerge from the Hellenistic period, is nevertheless a shadowy figure. The system of his vanished handbook can be reasonably well reconstructed, for it was persistently influential at Rome, e.g. on Quintilian and Hermogenes. 'Stasis'-theory was its real contribution – a method for analysing the basic issues of a case (he distinguished four classes). He apparently had little to say on style.

BIBL. Fragments, ed. D. Matthes (1962); Kennedy, *Art of Persuasion*; *Roman World* *Quintilian.

Hermarchus Epicurean philosopher, 3rd century BC.

Hermarchus (Hermarkhos) of Mytilene became head of

Small bronze bust, inscribed 'Hermarchus', found in the Villa dei Pisoni, Herculaneum. Naples, Museo Nazionale.

the Epicurean school on *Epicurus' death in 270 BC, inheriting his books and the use of his 'garden'. Only titles of his writings survive. Epicurus, when dying in pain, wrote to him, '. . . All these [sufferings] are compensated for by the joy that I receive from remembering our reasonings and discoveries' (a remark which Cicero found hard to square with Epicurean hedonism).

BIBL. Diogenes Laertius x. 15–25; *Roman World* *Cicero.

Hermesianax Poet, early 3rd century BC.

A minor but interesting Hellenistic poet, Hermesianax (Hermēsianax) published three books of erotic elegiac narrative named after his mistress *Leontion*. In this he purports to follow his fellow-Colophonians *Mimnermus (with his *Nanno*) and *Antimachus (*Lyde*), who both appear, with girl-friends, in a curious catalogue, preserved by Athenaeus, of poets and their lovers, running from Orpheus to Hermesianax's mentor *Philitas, with an appendix on philosophers. *Homer is enamoured of Penelope, *Alcaeus and *Anacreon jealous rivals for *Sappho: though the ancients always *were* ready to extract biographical fact from poetry, we must read this as a cumbrously handled joke. Other fragments from *Leontion* attest pastoral themes anticipating *Theocritus, and the learnedly aberrant mythological love-stories (preoccupied with metamorphosis, incest, etc.) so beloved of Hellenistic poets.

BIBL. Athenaeus 597b; Powell, *Coll. Alex.*; *Roman World* *Athenaeus.

Hermias Tyrant of Atarneus, died 341 BC.

An ex-slave, Hermias seized power in Atarneus (Asia Minor) after murdering Eubulus, his erstwhile owner and co-ruler. His court was frequented by *Aristotle (who married his niece) and other Academic philosophers. Reports of his communications with *Philip II of Macedon led to his arrest by *Mentor, who sent him to *Artaxerxes III. He died under torture and his failure to reveal any secrets was praised by some (though *Theopompus vilified him); but he may have had little to reveal, and his fate was that of a Persian vassel who affected a greater independence than his actual resources warranted.

BIBL. Berve, *Tyrannis* 332 f.; Hammond and Griffith, *Macedonia* ii. 518 ff.; Hofstetter, *Griechen*, no. 143.

Hermippus Comic and iambic poet, active c. 435–c. 415 BC.

The comedies of Hermippus (Hermippos), one of *Aristophanes' rivals, included the *Baker Women*, which ridiculed *Hyperbolus. A fragment from another play (fr. 46) urges *Pericles to resist attacks by *Cleon. He also wrote some non-dramatic verse. Plutarch claims that he unsuccessfully prosecuted *Aspasia for impiety, but this may rest on a misunderstanding.

BIBL. Edmonds, *Attic Comedy* i; *Greek Elegy and Iambus* (Loeb) ii; *Roman World* *Plutarch.

Hermippus of Smyrna Biographer, late 3rd century BC.

Hermippus (Hermippos) wrote his biographies of law-givers, philosophers, and others in Alexandria, where he had access to the scholarly information of his master *Callimachus' *Pinakes*. He was, however, easily tempted to fill gaps with anecdotal material and from his fertile

imagination (to particularly good effect in death scenes). With his specious authority and sensational appeal he regrettably displaced the sounder biographical tradition as a source for Diogenes Laertius and others.

BIBL. F. Wehrli, *Hermippos der Kallimacheer* (1974); *Roman World* *Diogenes Laertius.

Hermocopids ('herm-cutters') at Athens, 415 BC.

Just before the Athenian expeditionary force set sail for Sicily in 415 BC, vandals mutilated many of the *Hermae*, square pillars with busts representing the god Hermes, which stood at street corners. This ominous event resulted in mass hysteria explained by *Thucydides as due to the Athenians' fear of a tyrannical *coup d'état*. Large numbers of wealthy or aristocratic young Athenians were accused of involvement in this or in parodying the Eleusinian Mysteries; an inscription records the public sale of their sequestered property.

See also *Adeimantus, *Alcibiades, *Andocides.

BIBL. Thucydides vi. 27, 53; Lysias vi; Andocides, *On the Mysteries*; Meiggs and Lewis, *Inscriptions* 79.

Hermocrates Syracusan leader, died 407 BC.

In 424 BC Hermocrates (Hermokratēs) called on all the Sicilian Greeks to unite to resist Athenian interference. In 415 he was one of the three Syracusan generals given absolute authority to oppose the Athenian invasion, but he was deposed in the following year. In 412 he was sent to the Aegean with a fleet of 20 ships to support Sparta. He was banished from Syracuse after he lost his ships at the battle of Cyzicus (410). He returned to Sicily to fight the Carthaginians, but was not recalled; in 407 he and his supporters (including his son-in-law *Dionysius I) attempted to gain control of Syracuse by force, but he was killed in the fighting.

BIBL. Westlake, *Essays*, ch. 12.

Hermogenes Architect, 2nd century BC.

Perhaps from Priene, Hermogenes (Hermogenēs) strongly favoured the Ionic style rather than the Doric style for temple architecture. His dates are disputed: he was active either c. 200 BC or c. 130 BC, more probably the latter. Two temples by him are recorded, those of Dionysus on Teos and of Artemis Leucophryene at Magnesia on the Maeander, and there are substantial remains of both. He wrote treatises on them and provided extensive rules for a series of ideal proportions for Ionic temples. These prescriptions appear in Vitruvius, and consequently they influenced Renaissance and later architects.

BIBL. Vitruvius III. ii. 6, iii. 7 ff., IV. iii. 1 f., VII *praef.* 12; W. G. Dinsmoor, *The Architecture of Ancient Greece* (4th ed., 1950), 273–6; *Roman World* *Vitruvius.

Herodas Mime poet, c. 270 BC (?).

Herodas (Herōdas) (Herōndas in Athenaeus) was just an obscure name before a major papyrus (published in 1891), supplemented by later fragments, presented eight mimes almost complete and the beginning of a ninth. Each about 100 lines long and intended for virtuoso solo rendition, these *mimiamboi* are highly effective dramatic realizations of scenes from the seamier side of lower-middle-class life, which aim at capturing realistic character (mostly female) through apt observation of detail. Herodas' name seems

Athens, and Thurii, and had personally visited Egypt, the Black Sea (including Scythia), Babylonia, and Cyrene.

The need to come to terms with the Persian presence in Asia Minor was one root of both Ionian philosophy and history (see *Xanthus, *Hecataeus). Another was *Homeric epic. Like the *Iliad*, Herodotus' history is about a great war between the Greek world and a barbarian kingdom, composed 'in order that the glorious deeds on both sides should not be forgotten'; and, like Homer, Herodotus feels he must begin by recounting, in chronological order, the series of events which led up to and therefore 'caused' the main conflict.

Thus the first 4 of the 9 books into which his text was divided in the Hellenistic period are not about the Greek conflict with Persia at all. Book i contains the history of Lydia up to the defeat of *Croesus by *Cyrus in 546, and an account of the rise of Persia up to that moment, with Cyrus' victories over the Medes and Babylonians. Book ii is a long digression on the geography and ethnography of Egypt, introducing the conquest of Egypt by *Cambyses in iii, which also tells of the brief rule of Smerdis, and *Darius' (I) seizure of power. Book iv begins with a digression on Scythia, and then relates Persian operations against Thrace and Scythia under Darius, and in North Africa. With book v Herodotus comes on to the revolt of the Ionian Greeks against Persia (499–494), leading on to the final suppression of that revolt and the Persian expedition sent to punish Eretria and Athens (490) in book vi; these 2 books include much material about the earlier history of mainland Greece, in order to explain why particular states reacted as they did to the Persian threat. The final 3 books give an account of *Xerxes' expedition in 480/79; the Greek and Persian preparations, and the Persian advance with the battles at Artemisium and Thermopylae in book vii, Salamis in viii, and Plataea and Mycale in ix; an epilogue stresses that the Persians are no longer a threat to Greece.

In antiquity Herodotus was widely read for his wealth of entertaining and varied episodes, and his ethnographical material; critics claimed that he was insufficiently hostile to the 'barbarians'. In the nineteenth century he was criticized for lack of originality and unreliability, especially with regard to statistics and accounts of military operations. He was also accused of believing in the miraculous and being insufficiently 'scientific'; in fact, however, he shares many of the attitudes of Ionian philosophy, e.g. on the causes of earthquakes (vii. 128–30). He also provides a rational explanation for the intervention of the gods in the human world: those individuals who rise above their proper station provoke the envy of the gods, who destroy them (*hubris* leads to divine envy (*phthonos*), which leads to *nemesis*). Moral guilt may or may not be involved (*Polycrates tries to do what he can to assuage the anger of the gods, but to no avail: iii. 39–43). Herodotus was also keenly aware of the limitations of a historical enquiry which depended largely on oral sources. Where he is unable to choose between different versions or explanations, he frequently gives alternative accounts, even if he does not believe them himself (e.g. on the death of *Cleomenes (I): vi. 84). Some of the 'fables' which he himself discounted – such as that the sun appears in the north in the southern hemisphere (iv. 42) – show that he generally reported his sources accurately and reliably.

Part of the 2nd-century AD papyrus which preserves Herodas' *Mimes* (iii. 26–42). London, British Museum.

Dorian; evidence extractable from the poems (*Mime* i mentioning the wonders of Egypt, including the Museum, date after 272/1 BC (?); *Mime* ii set on Cos, date before 266(?)) suggests a circuit and period similar to *Theocritus'. Both writers contrive a piquant tension between realism and artificiality by elevating the highly popular sub-literary mime to the status of sophisticated poetry (compare especially Herodas iv and Theocritus xv, where two distinctly characterized women admire works of art). Herodas, however, takes his vocabulary, dialect, and metre (choliambic), together with his unsavoury emphasis, from the Ionian tradition of *Hipponax (*Mimes* vi and vii, a fascinating pair about women buying dildos, are localized in Ionia). His serious literary aspirations are defended in the mutilated eighth mime, 'The Dream'.

BIBL. I. C. Cunningham, *Herodas Mimiambi* (1971); W. G. Arnott, *Greece and Rome* xviii (1971); *Roman World* *Athenaeus.

Herodotus (traditionally 484–420 BC) 'Father of History'.

Ancient biographies of Herodotus (Hērodotos) are largely based on speculation; but it seems that he was related to the ruling dynasty of Halicarnassus (see *Artemisia), and that he had to leave his home, perhaps *c.* 460 BC, as a result of civil strife. He lived at Samos,

Head of Herodotus (the bust is modern). Roman copy of a 4th-century original. Dresden, Skulpturensammlung.

BIBL. Translations include that of A. de Selincourt (Penguin Classics, 1954); the commentary by W. W. How and J. Wells (2nd ed., 1928) remains standard; J. L. Myres, *Herodotus the Father of History* (1953); G. E. M. de Ste Croix, *Greece and Rome* xxiv (1977).

Heron of Alexandria Mathematician and inventor, probably *c.* 100 AD.

Virtually nothing is known of Heron's (Hērōn) life, and his floruit date has been placed as far apart as 200 BC and AD 200. His surviving works are most striking for the inventions they describe. Many of these are mere toys (e.g. a wind-powered organ, a coin-in-the-slot machine for supplying measures of purifying water, a steam-engine that causes a sphere to rotate at high speed, and an 'automatic' puppet-theatre operated by weights). But he also describes workable cranes and hoists using worm gears as well as pulleys, and discusses in detail the mathematics of the various systems. Similarly, his account of the *dioptra*, an elaborate surveying instrument, combines mathematical techniques with inventive ingenuity.

BIBL. J. L. Landels, *Engineering in the Ancient World* (1978).

Herophilus Physician, early 3rd century BC.

The great Alexandrian doctor Herophilus (Hērophilos) came from Chalcedon, was possibly of humble origin, and learnt his medicine under Praxagoras on Cos. Knowledge of his work derives chiefly from Galen, who recognized his achievements. Together with his younger contemporary *Erasistratus, Herophilus made tremendous advances in anatomy – progress which petered out after them – establishing human dissection as regular practice. Reports that they were also vivisectionists, the *Ptolemies being ready to further science with a supply of criminals, should probably be credited. Herophilus' famous anatomical writings included works on the brain (recognized as the centre of the nervous system (and seat of the soul – unlike *Aristotle's view)), eye, liver, and reproductive organs. He clearly distinguished veins and arteries and 'discovered' the nerves. Many of his colourful coinages have persisted in technical vocabulary. Clinically his most important work was on the pulse: he devised an (over-)elaborate system for analysing its rhythm. He was also a famous obstetrician. He softened his dogmatic medicine in the light of experience. His powerful personality was influential on contemporary intellectuals.

BIBL. J. F. Dobson, *Proc. Roy. Soc. Med.* xviii (1925), 19 ff.; Phillips, *Greek Medicine*; Solmsen, *MusHelv* xviii (1961); *Roman World* *Galen.

Hesiod Epic poet, *c.* 700 BC.

Our earliest palpable literary personality, Hesiod (Hēsiodos) presents his father as an immigrant from Aeolian Cyme settled in the 'wretched village Ascra' near mount Helicon in Boeotia (*Works* 633–40). Hesiod's only previous travel was when he won a tripod at the funeral games of Amphidamas in Chalcis (Euboea) with a hymn. This hymn is taken by some to be the *Theogony*, and ancient ascriptions of the *Theogony* and the *Works and Days* to the same poet are widely accepted. Disagreement persists on how much of the *Works'* scenario is real: it begins as a diatribe on the rewards of justice and hard work, reinforced by mythology (Prometheus and Pandora (47–105)), history (the Five Ages (109 ff.)), fable (the hawk

'Portrait' of the poet Hesiod in a mosaic from Trier by Monnus. 4th century AD. Trier, Rheinisches Landesmuseum.

and the nightingale (202 ff.)) and maxims, addressed now to Hesiod's brother, Perses, now to kings whose corrupt judgements favoured Perses in the division of their father's land. But Perses' situation changes to suit Hesiod's theme (which becomes (360 ff.) specific advice on farming, seafaring, and propitious days, though moral maxims recur throughout) and he is probably fictitious. Manifestly related to and possibly influenced by Near Eastern wisdom literature, the *Works and Days* was seen as the fountainhead of didactic poetry. Many vivid pictures and sympathetic perceptions contribute to the appeal of a poem in which even the bluntness of agricultural and social advice has certain attractions.

The *Theogony* was equally important in establishing Hesiod (named in i.22 as inspired and ordered by the Muses on Helicon to sing it) as the father of catalogue poetry and, with *Homer, of the Olympian hierarchy, whose installation, *via* the succession Uranus–Kronos–Zeus, and genealogies it narrates. Its last section, on goddesses' unions with mortals, is of a later date, as is the *Catalogue of Women* (or *Ehoiai*, 'Or such as' . . .) which continued it in five books (well represented in papyri) and which most ancients thought Hesiodic. The *Shield*, narrating in 480 lines Heracles' fight with Cycnus, and so called from the description of Heracles' shield (139–320) based on Homer's description of **Achilles', was apparently thought Hesiodic by *Stesichorus, but *Aristophanes of Byzantium contested the ascription, and artistic motifs suggest an early sixth-century date.

Other poems sometimes ascribed and now lost are: *Great Ehoiai* (more genealogy); *Marriage of Ceyx*; *Melampodia* (Melampus and other seers); *Peirithous' Descent* (to the Underworld; *Idaean Dactyls*; *Precepts of Cheiron* (to Achilles – another wisdom poem); *Great Works* (modelled on *Works*); *Astronomy* (imitated by *Aratus); *Aegimius* (also attributed to Cercops of Miletus); *Kiln* or *Potters*; and *Prophecy from Birds*.

Knowledge of Hesiod's poetry spread as early as *Semonides (fr. 6), *Tyrtaeus (fr. 12.43), *Mimnermus (fr. 6), and *Alcaeus (fr. 347), and he remained central throughout antiquity. In the fifth century he was said to have died at Ozolian Locri (*Thucydides) but later, in Pausanias' time, his tomb was shown in Orchomenus.

BIBL. M. L. West (ed.), *Theogony* (1965), *Works and Days* (1978); R. Merkelbach and M. L. West (ed.), *Fragmenta Hesiodea* (1967); H. Fraenkel, *Early Greek Poetry and Philosophy* (1975); *Roman World* *Pausanias.

Hieron I Tyrant of Syracuse, 478–467/6 BC.
Hieron (Hierōn) was the second son of Deinomenes of Gela; in 485 BC he was appointed ruler of Gela on behalf of his elder brother *Gelon. On Gelon's death (478) he succeeded him as tyrant of Syracuse. Despite initial conflict with his brother Polyzalus, who fled for support to *Theron of Acragas, his rule was remarkably successful. He intervened in southern Italy against *Anaxilas of Rhegium and against Croton, and won a decisive naval victory against the Etruscans at Cumae (Cyme) in 474. He founded a Syracusan colony on Ischia, and in 475 re-founded Catana under the name Aetna. The lyric poets *Pindar and *Bacchylides wrote odes celebrating a series of victorious entries in the Olympic and Pythian Games by Hieron's chariots. *Simonides, *Aeschylus, and *Epicharmus also stayed at his court, which is the scene of *Xenophon's dialogue *Hieron*, on whether a tyrant can be really happy.

After Hieron's death the tyranny passed to his younger brother Thrasybulus (Thrasuboulos); his unpopularity resulted in an uprising in which the Syracusans were supported by other Sicilian cities, and, despite the loyalty of Hieron's new settlers at Aetna (see *Ducetius), Thrasybulus was defeated and retired to Locri in southern Italy.

BIBL. Diodorus Siculus xi; Pindar, *Olympian* i; *Pythians* i–iii (with Scholia); Woodhead, *Greeks in the West*; W. S. Barrett, *JHS* xciii (1973).

Hieron II King of Syracuse, *c.* 270–215 BC.
Originally a native lieutenant of *Pyrrhus of Epirus in Sicily, Hieron (Hierōn) was elected *strategos* in Syracuse after Pyrrhus' death in 272 BC. Although of non-royal origins, he grew powerful through military endeavours like many Greek tyrants, and was elected king *c.* 270. He initially opposed Roman intervention in Sicily in 264 when the Mamertines (resettled Campanian mercenaries who controlled Messina) requested Roman help against Carthage, but he wisely concluded alliances with Rome which kept Syracuse at peace throughout the Punic Wars.

Syracuse reached her zenith of wealth and prosperity during his long, peaceful reign (even his war-machines were given to Rhodes). With Roman payments for corn, Hieron beautified and enlarged Syracuse and encouraged Greek culture: the new, huge theatre attests the prevalence of drama, *Theocritus wrote an encomium

The Great Altar at Syracuse built during the reign of Hieron II (*c.* 270–215 BC).

Coin portrait of Hieron II, king of Syracuse (enlarged).

(*Idyll* xvi) on Hieron, and his friend *Archimedes was
a native of Syracuse. He maintained ties with the rest of
the Greek world also. His son Gelon was married to an
Epirote princess who may have been Pyrrhus' daughter.
Connections with the Alexandria of *Ptolemies II and III
may be suggested by the similarities between the
Syracusan and Ptolemaic standards in coinage, and
between Hieron's fiscal system (Lex Hieronica) and the
Revenue Codes of Ptolemy II. His mammoth merchant
ship, the *Syracusa*, was sent as a gift to Alexandria.
  BIBL. H. Berve, *König Hieron II* (1959), and *Tyrannis* i.
462 ff.; A. Schenk von Stauffenberg, *König Hieron II von
Syrakus* (1933); Athenaeus 206 D ff. (description of
merchant ship).

Hieronymus of Cardia (*c.* 364–260 BC) Administrator and
historian.
  The adult life of Hieronymus (Hierōnumos) spanned the
expedition of *Alexander the Great, the struggles among
the Diadochi (Successors), and the establishment of the
Hellenistic kingdoms; he participated in many of these
events, and recorded them in his writings. He was a friend
of *Eumenes of Cardia (q.v.), the principal secretary to
*Philip II and Alexander. After their deaths he shared
Eumenes' adventures on behalf of Alexander's heirs and
their regents. When Eumenes was killed in 316 BC at
Gabiene, the wounded Hieronymus was saved by
*Antigonus I (q.v.), whose family he served as
administrator and general for the rest of his life. He was a
commissioner of the Dead Sea in 312, was present at Ipsus
in 301, and was appointed governor of Boeotia by
*Demetrius Poliorcetes in 293. He took up residence at
Pella at the court of *Antigonus Gonatas.
  Despite his active political life, Hieronymus the man has
faded before Hieronymus the historian. Although we
know neither the name nor the scope of the work in
which he recorded the wars of the Successors (probably
from 323 until the death of *Pyrrhus of Epirus in 272), his
lost history has been called one of the best and most
important ever written. Perhaps lacking the stylistic
refinements which might have assisted his work's
preservation (Dionysius of Halicarnassus pronounced it
unreadable), Hieronymus was careful to tell the truth as
he knew it from his own experience. His importance lies
in the use made of him by later historians. He was an
important source (whether direct or indirect) for books
xviii–xx of *Diodorus Siculus, he was used by Arrian for
the *Events after Alexander* and by Plutarch for his *Lives* of
Eumenes, Pyrrhus, and Demetrius. He was known to
Trogus and Pausanias, among others. An 'obituary'
written by *Agatharchides records that he lived until the
age of 104, and preserved all his faculties until his last
day.

  BIBL. *FGrH* 86 F4 (Agatharchides), 154; PW viii. 1540 ff.;
Jane Hornblower, *Hieronymus of Cardia* (1981); *Roman
World* *Arrian, *Dionysius of Halicarnassus, *Pausanias,
*Plutarch, *Trogus.

Himilcon Carthaginian general, died 396 BC.
  Himilcon (Himilkōn) twice led Carthaginian expeditions
to Sicily (406–5, 397–6 BC), and twice failed to capture
Syracuse because of an outbreak of plague among his
troops. After the second failure he committed suicide.
  BIBL. Stroheker, *Dionysios I*.

Hipparchus Peisistratid, assassinated 514 BC.
  The second son of *Peisistratus, Hipparchus
(Hipparkhos) became known as a patron of the arts. His
advances to *Harmodius brought about his assassination
by Harmodius and Aristogeiton. The story that he was
tyrant along with or instead of his brother *Hippias seems
to have been fabricated by those who wished to glorify
Harmodius and Aristogeiton as 'tyrannicides'.
  BIBL. Herodotus v. 55–6, vi. 123, vii. 6; Thucydides
i. 20, vi. 54–9.

Bronze coin from Nicaea showing the astronomer Hipparchus
seated in front of a globe on a pillar (enlarged).

Hipparchus of Nicaea Astronomer, *c.* 150 BC.
  By combining mathematics (notably trigonometry) with
extensive observations and the use of old Babylonian
records, Hipparchus (Hipparkhos) achieved remarkable
results in scientific astronomy. Some of the best known of
these are the discovery of the precession of the equinoxes,
a fairly accurate calculation of the size and distance of the
moon, and an improvement of *Callippus' 'cycle'. (He
calculated the length of the mean lunar month correctly to
within a second.) His adherence to the geocentric theory
probably had an unfortunate long-term effect. His only
surviving work is a commentary on the *Phaenomena* of
*Eudoxus (of Cnidos) and *Aratus (qq.v.).
  BIBL. Tannery, *Histoire de l'astronomie ancienne* (1893).

Hippasus Philosopher, early 5th century BC (?).
  An early follower of *Pythagoras, Hippasus (Hippasos)
of Metapontum in southern Italy was said to have
published the secret of 'the sphere from twelve
pentagons', i.e. the regular dodecahedron, and to have
been lost at sea because of this impiety. Others connected
his breach of Pythagorean secrecy with the discovery of

irrational numbers (a problem for the school, which aimed to explain the world in terms of natural numbers).
BIBL. Burkert, *Pythagoreanism*.

Hippias Tyrant of Athens, 527–510 BC.

The eldest son of *Peisistratus, Hippias succeeded him as tyrant. He seems to have tried at first to conciliate the great Athenian familes by allowing their leading members to hold the archonship, but the aristocrats became increasingly hostile, and after the assassination of his brother *Hipparchus Hippias' fears for his own safety made his rule more oppresive. He was overthrown by the Spartans in 510 BC, and went into exile at Sigeum in the Troad. After the failure of a Spartan attempt to restore him, he turned to the Persians for help, and accompanied the expedition of 490. He is not heard of again after the defeat at Marathon.
BIBL. Herodotus v. 62, 91–6, vi. 102, 107; Thucydides i. 20, vi. 54–9; Andrewes, *Greek Tyrants* 109 ff.

Hippias of Elis Polymath, late 5th century BC.

Hippias held that a true 'sophist' (wise man, expert) should be able to turn his hand to any skill; he is said to have appeared at an Olympic festival wearing clothes and shoes he had made himself. His interests included mathematics, in which he discovered that there could be regular curves other than that of the circle (the 'quadratrix'), and ethics; he argued that laws are equivalent to tyrants, and therefore unnatural. A particularly important achievement was the production of a list of Olympic victors. *Plato wrote two dialogues named after him.
BIBL. Diels and Kranz, *Vorsokratiker* ii, no. 86; Guthrie, *Greek Philosophy* iii, 280 ff.

Hippocleides: see **Philaids**

Hippocrates of Chios Mathematician, 5th century BC.

Hippocrates (Hippokratēs) is said to have been a trader who lost all his wealth to pirates; while at Athens hoping to obtain redress at law, he frequented the sophists and became interested in *Pythagorean mathematics. He wrote a lost work on geometry, the *Elements*. Some of his astronomical theories are referred to by *Aristotle.
BIBL. Diels and Kranz, *Vorsokratiker* i, no. 42; Heath, *Greek Mathematics*, ch. 6.

Hippocrates of Cos (traditionally *c.* 460–380 BC) Physician.

Antiquity saw Hippocrates (Hippokratēs) as a semi-historical example of the ideal physician; hence the ascription to him of the Hippocratic Oath and of a collection of 53 works on medical topics. They are of various dates (some perhaps at late as 100 BC), but all written in the Ionian dialect. It has been suggested that at least some of this Corpus represents an Alexandrian edition of the contents of the library of the Asclepiad guild of priest-healers at Cos. Among the most interesting of these works are *On Ancient Medicine*, arguing in favour of an empirical attitude to dietary theory and against *a priori* categories such as hot and cold, wet and dry; *On the Sacred Disease*, arguing that just because epilepsy is said to be divine does not absolve physicians from looking for natural causes; *Airs, Waters, Places*, which examines the

Bust of the physician Hippocrates of Cos, probably a copy of a late 3rd-century original (?). Naples, Museo Nazionale.

effect of climate on character, and in particular contrasts Asia with Europe in a very *Herodtean fashion; and the *Epidemics*, accounts of 42 individual cases.

Unfortunately none of the works in the Corpus share the ideas ascribed to the historical Hippocrates, especially by *Plato (in the Phaedrus). Hippocrates believed that the human body had to be studied as a single organism, and that the function of each part could only be understood in the context of the whole. The ancient biographies say that he was the son of the physician Heracleides, and that he died at Larissa.
BIBL. G. E. R. Lloyd, *CQ* xxv (1975); G. E. R. Lloyd (ed.), *Hippocratic Writings* (Pelican Classics, 1978).

Hippocrates of Gela Tyrant, 498–491 BC.

Hippocrates (Hippokratēs) and his brother Cleander came from a wealthy landowning family (their father Pantores had won an Olympic chariot victory in 512 or 508 BC). Cleander ruled Gela (southern Sicily) from 505 until he was assassinated in 498 and succeeded by Hippocrates, developing a strong cavalry under the command of *Gelon. Hippocrates conquered Naxos, Leontini, and Zancle, which brought him into conflict with *Anaxilas of Rhegium. An attack on Syracuse failed; the mediation of Corinth granted him Camarina, which he re-founded (492), but he died the following year, fighting the Sicels.
BIBL. Dunbabin, *Western Greeks*, ch. 13.

Hippodamus City-planner, 5th century BC.

Son of Euryphon of Miletus, Hippodamus (Hippodamos)

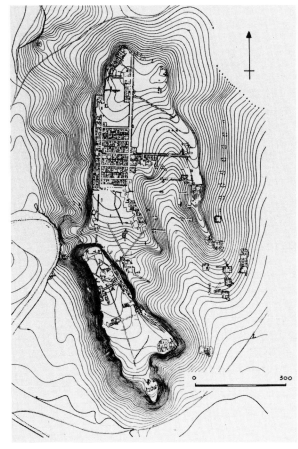

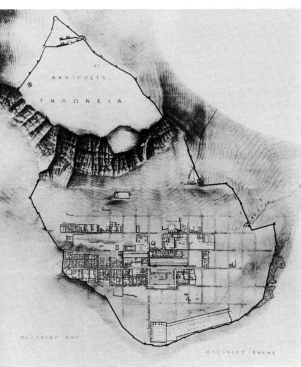

Plans of Olynthus (*above*) and Priene (*below*): two towns designed on 'Hippodamian' principles.

was the most famous ancient city-planner, and was also a noted political and social theorist. He was apparently rather eccentric in character and appearance. Miletus was destroyed in 494 BC in the Ionian Revolt (see *Histiaeus, *Aristagoras) and rebuilt soon after with a new layout based on a grid of straight, parallel roads intersecting at right angles; it is not known if this was due to Hippodamus or was carried out before his birth. The sources attribute to him the layouts of the Piraeus, of Thurii in southern Italy (444/3), and Rhodes (408/7); the last is obviously problematical chronologically if he planned Miletus. Boundary stones from the Piraeus show that, when the site was laid out sometime after the Persian Wars, detailed zoning arrangements were adhered to; this may well indicate Hippodamus' involvement, for he stressed that architects had to take into account the different functions performed by craftsmen, peasant smallholders, and other social groups. His main achievement seems to have been a considered and special application of the rectangular grid-sytem (which was already known) in residential quarters and perhaps in the placing of public buildings within the grid. The best excavated examples of such 'Hippodamian' planning are Olynthus (432 BC) and Priene (*c.* 350 BC).

BIBL. Aristotle, *Politics* ii. 8. 1267b, vii. 11. 1330b; A Burns, *Historia* xxv (1976); F. Castagnoli, *Orthogonal Town Planning in Antiquity* (1971); J. B. Ward-Perkins, *Cities of Ancient Greece and Italy* (1974), 14–17.

Hippon Eclectic philosopher, 5th century BC.
*Aristotle's judgement that Hippon (Hippōn) of Samos was not worth including in a list of philosophers because of the cheapness of his thought is consistent with the other evidence. Following *Thales, he held that things were generated from water, arguing from the fact that semen is moist. He was said to be an atheist.

BIBL. Guthrie, *Greek Philosophy* ii.

Hipponax Iambic poet, *c.* 540 BC.
Tradition (e.g. Pliny, confidently dating him to 540–537 BC) knew Hipponax (Hippōnax) as an Ephesian exiled to Clazomenae who, provoked by caricaturing and perhaps obscene statues, drove their sculptors, Bupalus and Athenis, to suicide by iambic abuse (compare *Archilochus). The choliambic fragments of his first iambus, addressed to Clazomenians, indeed attack Bupalus (frs. 1, 12), have him invoke Hermes, god of thieves (fr. 3), recall an orgy the poet had with Bupalus' girl Arete (frs. 13–17), and pray that Bupalus be beaten and cast out like a scapegoat (frs. 6–10). Other fragments, often coarse in incident and language, present Hipponax (frequently named) as a down-and-out involved in sordid escapades, one apparently a bizarre cure for impotence (fr. 92): most scenes defy reconstruction, and their vivid glimpses of Bohemian life in Greek cities should probably not be treated as windows on Hipponax's own personality.

A second book, including iambic trimeters, is attested (fr. 118a), as are iambic tetrameters catalectic (fr. 119), trochaic tetrameters (fr. 120, threatening Bupalus), hexameters parodying *Homer (frs. 128–9a), and epodes. One papyrus epode is a curse so direct and vigorous (fr. 115) as to have been ascribed to *Archilochus despite the name 'Hippona[——]' in the poem next but one (fr. 117). But Hipponax's reputation for invective was equally high:

he was remembered in *Aristophanes' Athens (compare *Ananius), imitated by *Phoenix and *Herodas, and echoed by *Callimachus.

BIBL. West, *IEG*, and *Studies* 22 ff., 140 ff.; Campbell, *Lyric Poetry*; *Roman World* *Pliny the Elder.

Histiaeus Tyrant of Miletus, died 493 BC.

After their conquest of Lydia (546 BC), the Persians found it convenient to rule the Greek cities of the Asian littoral through monarchies ('tyrants'). As ruler of Miletus, Histiaeus (Histiaios) led the Ionian fleet which participated in *Darius' (I) expedition against Scythia in 513. As a reward for his loyalty in thwarting a plan by some other Greeks to destroy the Persian army by cutting the bridge across the Danube, Darius granted him Myrcinus in Thrace. He subsequently accompanied Darius to Susa, leaving his relative *Aristagoras to rule Miletus, and was responsible for inciting Aristagoras to begin the Ionian Revolt (499). Although he supported the Revolt, he was unable to return to Miletus; in 493 he was captured and executed by *Artaphernes (1).

BIBL. J. A. S. Evans, *AJP* lxxxiv (1963); G. A. H. Chapman, *Historia* xxi (1972); P. B. Manville, *CQ* xxvii (1977).

Homer Epic poet, *c.* 700 BC (?).

Revered throughout classical antiquity as Greece's earliest and greatest poet, Homer (Homēros) was almost universally credited with the *Iliad* and *Odyssey*, and sometimes other early epics (*Cypria*, *Thebais* – see *Callinus, *Cyclic Poets – *Epigoni*, etc.).

Investigation of his life began early (see *Theagenes of

Herm of Homer (the so-called 'Apollonius of Tyana' type) based on an original of *c.* 300 BC. Rome, Capitoline Museum.

Rhegium), but epic narrative has no place for the poet's *persona*, and, despite the poems' early success (see *Terpander, *Semonides, *Tyrtaeus, suggesting widespread knowledge by 660–640 BC) and the establishment of a guild of reciters (*Homeridai*) at Chios, fiction and not memory is the likely basis of ancient attempts at biography. These disputed his origin (Chios, Smyrna, Cyme, and Colophon were strong candidates, Chios drawing support from the *Hymn to Apollo*'s presentation of its poet as a blind Chiote in line 172); paternity (Meles, Smyrna's river, was favoured); and date, ranging from the Trojan Wars to 500 years later, i.e. *c.* 675 BC (*Theopompus of Chios). That an important stage in the poems' composition took place in the eastern Aegean is suggested by their poetic language's blend of Ionic and Aeolic dialect, by references in similes to Ephesus' river Cayster (*Iliad* ii. 459 ff.) and to a Maeonian or Carian woman (*Iliad* iv. 141 f.), and by the *Iliad*'s interest in and knowledge of the Troad. The poems' picture of bards as craftsmen who could be retained by palaces may reflect the composer's status but cannot be unaffected by his image of a heroic past.

Antiquity already disputed the attribution of *Iliad* and *Odyssey* to the same poet and the authenticity of lines or whole sections: one view, not without modern followers, held that jumbled lays were only assembled to make the *Iliad* and *Odyssey* in *Peisistratus' Attica. Separatism has played a role of varying importance since F. Wolff made the first serious contribution to modern scholarship, but its form has been different since Milman Parry's demonstration that Homer's dependence on formulaic language and themes places him in a tradition of oral poetry. Comparative study of oral tradition has helped to elucidate techniques of narrative, to suggest that poems of great length can be orally composed and (though not without modification) transmitted, and to make acceptable many inconsistencies previously held against single authorship. Much remains in dispute: whether poems as long as 15,000 and 12,000 lines were or could be composed without writing; whether, if they were, their recording in writing was a subsequent process by the poet, by contemporary admirers, or by a later generation whose version had inevitably been modified by recitation; and, on this last hypothesis, whether the greatest credit (and name Homer?) should go to the last bard in the chain leading to writing. The arrival of writing in Greece by *c.* 750 BC, perhaps earlier, allows contemporary recording of poems some of whose content seems to relate to the late eighth or even early seventh century (perhaps hoplites (*Iliad* xiii. 131 ff)): but only antiquity's tendency to make Homer early counts against a great composer as late as *c.* 680 (a date preferred by scholars who see links with *Hesiod as indicating Hesiodic priority).

However credit should be apportioned, the greatness of the *Iliad* and *Odyssey* is indisputable.

The *Iliad* sings the wrath of **Achilles, one episode in the Trojan War's tenth year which the poet makes a prism of the long, destructive struggle. Deprived by **Agamemnon of his prize Briseis, Achilles retires to his tents while Zeus promises his mother Thetis that the Greeks will be made to honour him. After initial successes, which introduce heroes and build up the tempo of battle, they are driven back to their ships and send a

The Trojan Horse: a relief depiction on the neck of a storage jar from Mykonos, c. 675 BC. Mykonos, Archaeological Museum.

fruitless embassy to seek Achilles' help. Further disasters persuade his friend Patroclus to obtain Achilles' consent to take the field in his armour: the Trojans fall back, but Patroclus pursues too far, against Achilles' instructions, and **Hector slays him. We already known enough of Achilles' all-or-nothing temperament to comprehend the magnitude of his grief and fury. In armour fashioned by Hephaestus he returns to battle: Hector's death is as sure as Achilles' own (which he knows will soon follow), and Achilles takes horrible vengeance on his corpse. But after the ceremonial burial of Patroclus, Achilles releases Hector's body at his father **Priam's pleas: their mingled tears round off our picture of Achilles, human as well as heroic, and close the concerto of war on a note of reconciliation.

The poet is a master. He rarely loses control over detail or structure of his long narrative, where tension is subtly modulated, incidents are built up with power and pathos to contribute to his wider canvas, and characters are progressively created by epithets, similes, speeches, and actions. Many heroes generate interest for their own qualities, but they and their often fatal duels are also a backcloth against which the principals' divergent embodiment of heroic ideals can be assessed – Achilles unstable and egotistic, Hector a loyal leader who knows but misconstrues his duty to Troy.

Little of the *Iliad*'s tension and tragic feeling comes over in the *Odyssey*, but its poet, too, deploys mastery of structure. After a vignette of **Odysseus weeping nostalgically on Calypso's isle, our image of him is built up by his son Telemachus' journeys to find him, journeys including visits to **Nestor and **Menelaus which are also designed to establish Iliadic links. Book v returns us to Odysseus: his voyage from Calypso's island to Phaeacia allows a brief encounter with the nubile princess Nausicaa and full narration, to the court of her father Alcinous, of his adventures since Troy's fall. Voyaging ends with his return by Phaeacians to Ithaca, but his cunning and endurance necessarily persist as, in beggar's guise, he encompasses the destruction of the loutish princelings who woo his wife Penelope and consume his produce. Their battles with Odysseus, Telemachus, and the swineherd Eumaeus attain Iliadic intensity, but overall the *Odyssey* is a poem of travel and peace, not of war, and its romantic elements are fittingly crowned by Odysseus' final return to his marriage-bed.

The two poems are shown by language and treatment to be in the same tradition, and difference of theme, not of date, accounts for some differences in outlook. To assign them to the same poet is perhaps easier than to postulate two contemporary and closely related masters.

Their influence on ancient literature, prose as well as poetry, was wide-ranging, persistent, and profound.

BIBL. Commentaries: W. B. Stanford, *Odyssey* (1947); M. M. Willcock, *Companion to the Iliad* (1978). Discussion: G. S. Kirk, *The Songs of Homer* (1962); M. Parry, *The Making of Homeric Verse* (1970); J. Griffin, *Homer on Life and Death* (1980).

Homerus of Byzantium: see **The Pleiad**

Hybrias Lyric poet, late 6th century BC (?).
Athenaeus reports as sometimes classified with skolia the ten-line song of a Cretan Hybrias (Hubrias, or Hybrios – compare Hesychius' Ibrios, composer of a Cretan marching song). It claims that weapons secure his wealth and power and that all kow-tow to him as Great King (indicating a date later than Greek knowledge of the Persian monarchy?).

BIBL. Athenaeus 695 F; Page, *PMG*, fr. 909; Bowra, *Lyric Poetry* 398 ff.; *Roman World* *Athenaeus.

Hyperbolus Athenian leader, died 411 BC.
Attacked as a *banausus* (artisan) by his political opponents on the grounds that he owned a lamp-factory, Hyperbolus (Huperbolos) has traditionally been seen as typical of the *nouveaux riches* demagogues who ousted the old aristocracy from political leadership after the death of *Pericles.

In 425/4 BC Hyperbolus appears as *strategos*; in 422 he was Athenian representative to the Amphictyonic Council at Delphi. His pre-eminence after *Cleon's death in 422 can be gauged from the references to him in *Aristophanes' *Peace*; he opposed the Peace of *Nicias (421), and competed with *Alcibiades as an anti-Spartan. After the collapse of Alcibiades' attempts to create an anti-Spartan front in the Peloponnese at the battle of Mantinea in 418, Hyperbolus proposed to revive the obsolete procedure of ostracism, assuming that Alcibiades would be removed. But Alcibiades came to an arrangement with Nicias which resulted in the ostracism of Hyperbolus himself (417); he retired to Samos, where he was murdered by oligarchs in 411.

BIBL. Davies, *Athenian Families*, no. 13910; ostraca: *Hesperia* viii (1939), 246; xvii (1948), 186 f.; xviii (1949), 78–83.

Hyper(e)ides (traditionally 390–322 BC)   '*Attic Orator'.
Hyper(e)ides (Hupereides) was believed to have been a pupil of both *Isocrates and *Plato; although a professional speech-writer, he acted as prosecutor in a number of political trials. His political stance was consistently hostile to Macedonia. In 343 BC he successfully prosecuted *Philocrates for corruption in connection with the negotiations for peace with *Philip II in 346. After the Macedonian victory at Chaeronea in 338, he proposed a series of extreme measures to enable Athens to resist, including the liberation of slaves to fight in the army; he was prosecuted for proposing unconstitutional decrees by the pro-Macedonian *Demades, and replied with a counter-accusation.

Herm from Ostia (?) ascribed to the orator Hypereides. Rome, Museo Torlonia.

In 324 he was one of the accusers of *Demosthenes in the *Harpalus scandal, but the two were later reconciled. Hypereides was primarily responsible for the uprising against Macedon called the Lamian War (323–322); he delivered a funeral speech in honour of the Athenian general *Leosthenes and the other casualties. After the defeat of the Greeks at Crannon (322), *Antipater required the surrender of Hypereides and Demosthenes; Hypereides was condemned and executed.

Fragments of six speeches survive on papyrus; his restrained, conversational tone, aiming to win the sympathy of his audience rather than to blacken his opponents, clearly made him very popular with Hellenistic readers.

BIBL. *Minor Attic Orators* (Loeb) ii; Davies, *Athenian Families*, no. 13912; Kennedy, *Art of Persuasion* 252 ff.

Iambulus travel-fabulist, 3rd/2nd century BC (?).

Iambulus (Iamboulos), whose name seems Syrian, is otherwise a mystery. *Diodorus Siculus excerpted his fabulous travel-story set in the third century, which takes the author to the paradisical islands of the Sun. The account of happy communistic life there draws on the Utopia tradition (compare *Euhemerus) and more heavily on the exuberant imagination of the traveller's tale (the natives boast flexible bones and double tongues). This popular form of literature, boosted by Hellenistic contact with the East, contributed to the Greek novel proper.

BIBL. Diodorus ii. 55–80; Rohde, *Der griechische Roman*.

Ibycus Lyric poet, *c.* 536 BC.

From Rhegium in southern Italy, where, a proverb implied, he could have become tyrant, Ibycus (Ibukos) was familiar with Sicily – an anecdote in Himerius has him visit Catana and Himera, fragments mention Leontini (*Suppl.* 220) and Syracuse (*PMG* 321). He perhaps visited Sicyon, and certainly Samos, whither he was invited by the father of the tyrant *Polycrates, probably *c.* 540 BC (the *Suda* improbably dates this *c.* 564–561). Polycrates is praised for beauty and promised renown in our longest piece (fr. 282/*Suppl.* 151), whose 48 surviving lines

dismiss at length traditional heroic themes. Such themes are prominent in the surviving fragments, but perhaps merely illustrated the love-poetry which established Ibycus' reputation (the remaining scraps of this offer vivid images for the onset of passion (frs. 286–8)) rather than forming the subjects of narrative poems like those of *Stesichorus. The two poets share features of metre, dialect, and vocabulary, and some ascribed Stesichorus' *Games for Pelias* (compare fr. 179) to Ibycus; but modern attributions of narrative (*Suppl.* 166, 176) are insecure, and the Alexandrian editors' arrangement in seven books (*Suda*) suggests that his poems were shorter and untitled. Love-poetry (probably monodic, not choral) suited *Polycrates' court (see *Anacreon), but need not be confined to a 'Samian period' (note fr. 289, a song to one Gorgias, perhaps from Leontini). Tradition had Ibycus invent a form of lyre and be murdered by robbers (who were caused by cranes to betray themselves).

BIBL. Page, *PMG* and *Suppl.*; Campbell, *Lyric Poetry*; Bowra, Lyric Poetry; Kirkwood, *Greek Monody*; *Roman World* *Himerius.

Ictinus Architect, active *c.* 450–420 BC.

Of unknown origin, Ictinus (Iktinos) is best known as the architect of the Parthenon, started in 448/7 BC and

The Parthenon, Athens, by Ictinus: general view from the east; 447–432 BC.

Left: plan of the Parthenon. *Centre and right*: plan and interior of the temple of Apollo at Bassae, designed by Ictinus.

substantially complete in 438/7, when the cult-statue by *Pheidias was dedicated. It was the first large temple in mainland Greece to be built entirely of marble, and in it Ictinus introduced an influential new set of proportions for Doric architecture. He also made discreet use of Ionic elements, and incorporated many extraordinarily subtle (and expensive) optical refinements. Callicrates is named once as co-architect, and one Carpion wrote a treatise on it with Ictinus.

He is also recorded as the architect of the Telesterion at Eleusis, a large covered hall for conducting the Mysteries, but one source gives it to three other architects. It is possible that an early phase of the new *Periclean hall, which entailed unusually wide spans later reduced, is to be attributed to him. Pausanias records him as the architect of the temple of Apollo at Bassae in the Arcadian mountains, begun *c.* 430, much of which is still standing today.

BIBL. W. B. Dinsmoor, *The Architecture of Ancient Greece* (4th ed., 1950), 154–69, 195–6; Becatti, *Enc. Art. Ant.* iv. 100–3; *Roman World* *Pausanias.

Inarus Egyptian leader, died *c.* 454 BC.

Inarus (Inaros), described by *Herodotus as a Libyan, exploited the confusion at the Persian court caused by the assassination of *Xerxes in 465 BC to overthrow Xerxes' brother Achaemenes, satrap of Egypt. He proclaimed himself pharaoh and controlled Egypt with a mercenary army. In 459 Athens sent its fleet to support him; after six years the expedition was cut off and destroyed at Prosopitis in the Nile Delta, with the near-total loss of 250 or 300 triremes. Inarus himself was captured and crucified. The ensuing feeling of insecurity led the Athenians to transfer the treasury of the Delian League to Athens.

BIBL. Westlake, *Essays*, ch. 3; J. M. Bigwood, *Phoenix* xxx (1976).

Ion of Chios (*c.* 480–*c.* 422 BC) Poet and prose writer.

The wealthy and genial Ion (Iōn) spent much of his life at Athens, and was active in an unusual variety of literary genres. In verse he was remembered chiefly for his tragedies, being admitted to a canon of tragedians with *Aeschylus, *Sophocles, *Euripides, and *Achaeus of Eretria; Longinus found his tragedies faultless but quite lacking in the 'sublimity' of Sophocles. He also wrote satyr plays, elegiac and lyric poetry (we have fragments from all these genres), and possibly comedies.

Prose writings included the *Founding of Chios*, the *Triagmos* (a book of *Pythagorean philosophy), and the *Epidemiae* (a book of reminiscences). Among the acquaintances mentioned in this last work were *Cimon (whom Ion admired), *Pericles (whom he disliked), Sophocles, Aeschylus, and *Socrates; some extant anecdotes concerning Cimon and Sophocles, in particular, derive from this source.

BIBL. Lesky, *Greek Literature*; F. Jacoby, *CQ* xli (1947); A. von Blumenthal, *Ion von Chios* (1939); *Roman World* *Longinus.

Iphicrates Athenian general, floruit 390–355 BC.

A self-made man of low birth, Iphicrates (Iphikratēs) shone early as a mercenary-commander when he severely mauled a Spartan hoplite battalion near Corinth (390 BC); but later successes in the Hellespontine area were neutralized by *Antalcidas' Persian alliance. After 387/6 Iphicrates served *Cotys of Thrace and was sent by Athens to fight for Persia against Egypt. On his return he supplanted *Timotheus (2) (373/2), but plans to attack the Peloponnese were forestalled by the peace of 372/1, and in 370/69 he found himself operating there in Sparta's favour. The 360s took him back north, first as Athenian *strategos* around Amphipolis and then in Thracian service. His career ended with failure against rebel allies at the battle of Embata (356), for which he was prosecuted but acquitted. He is credited with innovations in armament designed to create a compromise between the light-armed skirmisher or peltast and the hoplite.

BIBL. Kirchner, *PA*, no. 7737; Parke, *Mercenary Soldiers*; J. G. P. Best, *Thracian Peltasts and their Influence on Greek Warfare* (1969).

Isaeus *'Attic orator', 4th century BC.

Isaeus (Isaios) is said to have come from Chalcis on Euboea; as a metic at Athens, he wrote speeches to be delivered by others, on forensic rather than political subjects. Eleven of 50 genuine speeches known in antiquity survive; they appear to date between 389 and 353 BC (or 343, if *Oration* xii is genuine), and all concern some aspect of disputed inheritances. Isaeus shows great skill in explaining highly technical legal problems simply and clearly. He was remembered as a pupil of *Isocrates and teacher of *Demosthenes.

BIBL. Commentary: W. Wyse (1904); Jebb, *Attic Orators*, ii. 261 ff.; Kennedy, *Art of Persuasion* 140 ff.

Isagoras Athenian leader, end of 6th century BC.

Isagoras' family were hereditary priests of Zeus Carius; he himself was a *xenos* (guest-friend) of King *Cleomenes (I) of Sparta. After Cleomenes had expelled the tyrant *Hippias from Athens in 510 BC, Isagoras persuaded him to intervene again to expel the rival aristocratic leader *Cleisthenes. As archon for 508/7, Isagoras planned to rule through a Council of Three Hundred, and this provoked popular resistance; he and the Spartan garrison were besieged on the Acropolis and had to withdraw from Athens. An expedition led by the two Spartan kings Cleomenes and *Demaratus did not proceed further than Eleusis (506); Isagoras was condemned to death in his absence, and Cleisthenes was left in control of Athens.

BIBL. Herodotus v. 66–75; Aristotelean *Constitution of Athens* 20; Hignett, *Athenian Constitution*, ch. 6.

Ismenias Theban politician, died 382 BC.

Ismenias (perhaps more correctly Hismēnias) helped *Thrasybulus (q.v.) in 404 BC, and was a leading anti-Spartan at the outbreak of the Corinthian War (395–387/6). His political influence after 387/6 can be discerned in a decree forbidding Theban participation in Spartan operations against Olynthus and in plans for a Theban–Olynthian alliance. After *Phoebidas seized the Cadmea Ismenias was executed, ostensibly for medism (i.e. his role in causing the Corinthian War). His homonymous son was a diplomatic associate of *Pelopidas in Thessaly and at Susa (where he devised a method of performing *proskynesis* without compromising his conscience, viz. stooping to retrieve a deliberately dropped ring as he approached the Great King).

BIBL. Buckler, *Theban Hegemony*.

Isocrates (436–338 BC) Athenian rhetorician.

Isocrates (Isokratēs) more than any other literary figure except *Homer defined the culture of the Greek-speaking world during the Hellenistic and Roman periods. Although the close-knit community of the city-state was losing its political and military pre-eminence, it continued to be the arena in which most conflicts arose and were resolved. Hence rhetoric was by far the most important managerial skill required of the élite; and Isocrates, by

setting up a regular school, organized and justified a rhetorical system of education which was much more relevant to the needs of his world than that provided by philosophical institutes like *Plato's Academy. Among his immediate pupils were *Androtion, *Hyper(e)ides, *Isaeus, *Lycurgus, and *Timotheus (2); he greatly influenced *Ephorus and *Theopompus (of Chios). Isocrates' emphasis on the role of the Greek language led him to believe in Greek political unity as well as cultural superiority over 'barbarians', especially Persians; and to advocate monarchy as the only guarantee of internal order. Hence he argued that Greece should attack the Persian empire under the leadership of a king like *Agesilaus, *Dionysius of Syracuse, *Jason of Pherae, and finally *Philip II of Macedon.

Isocrates is said to have learnt his rhetoric from the sophists *Prodicus, *Gorgias, and *Protagoras. He suffered from a weak voice and considerable shyness; consequently he wrote speeches for others which he did not deliver himself. This allowed him to perfect a highly artificial style, with complex and elaborately balanced periodic sentences. He avoids any dissonant or harsh combinations of syllables or letters, as well as hiatus.

Surviving writings include six forensic speeches, expositions of his educational or rhetorical principles (*Or.* xiii, *Against the Sophists* (390 BC); *Or.* xv, the *Antidosis* 354)), and school exercises illustrating his technical

Small bust bearing the name 'Isocrates'. Roman copy, possibly descended from a statue by Leochares. Rome, Villa Albani.

ability (*Or.* x, *Helen*; *Or.* xi, *Busiris*). The *Panegyricus* (*Or.* iv, of 380), while on a conventional theme, contains the political message that Greece should unite under the joint hegemony of Athens and Sparta. The essays of advice on statecraft *To Nicocles* and *Nicocles*, and the panegyrical **Evagoras* (*Or.* ii, iii, and ix (*c.* 374–365)) also contain elements of conventional exercises.

There are many political speeches or pamphlets: the anti-Theban *Plataicus* (*Or.* xiv, of 373); the *On the Peace* (*Or.* viii, of 355), arguing against imperialism and in favour of a common peace covering all Greek states; the *Areopagiticus* (*Or.* vii, of 355), advocating the restoration of a strong supervisory function to the Council of the Areopagus. The *Philippus* (*Or.* v, of 346), written after the Peace of **Philocrates* but before it was learnt that Philip had moved to seize central Greece, called on Philip to become the leader of Greece and to expel the Persians from Asia Minor. The *Panathenaicus* (*Or.* xii), completed in 339, compares the achievements of Athens and Sparta, to the advantage of the former. There are also nine letters, at least some of them authentic; *Epistle* iii, addressed to Philip, illustrates the intellectual's incomprehension at the political leader's failure to adhere to the ideals of the *Philippus*. Soon after the battle of Chaeronea, Isocrates starved himself to death.

BIBL. Kennedy, *Art of Persuasion* 174 ff.; H. I. Marrou, *History of Education in Antiquity* (1956), ch. 7, p. 79 ff.

Ister Antiquarian, late 3rd century BC.

A protégé of **Callimachus* at Alexandria and possibly a fellow-Cyrenean, Ister (Istros) was a zealous researcher into local history, focusing not only on the old world – Argos, Elis – but also on Egypt. His chief work *Attika*, drawing on **Philochorus*, treated Athens' mythical pre-history with a scholarly disinterest not found in earlier Atthidographers.

BIBL. *FGrH* 334; Pfeiffer, *Classical Scholarship* i.

Jason of Pherae Tyrant, died 370 BC.

Tyrant of Pherae from before 379 BC, Jason's (Iasōn) high-quality mercenary force cowed the Thessalians and, with the submission of Pharsalus (375), he was elected *tagos*. The following years are ill-documented (though he started building a fleet), and his real power may not have been all that great. Summoned to Leuctra in 371, he persuaded his Theban allies to spare the Spartan survivors. The subsequent months saw further extensions of power, and he planned to lead a Thessalian federal army to Delphi in autumn 370 and to preside over the Pythian Games. His purpose may have been the proclamation of a Panhellenic crusade against Persia (**Isocrates* reports his interest in such ideas), though some said he meant to steal the Delphic treasure. His assassination in summer 370 by a group of young Thessalians (whose motive was and is disputed) supervened before all could become clear.

BIBL. Berve, *Tyrannis* 285 ff.

Judas Maccabaeus Jewish revolutionary, floruit 166–160 BC.

After various disturbances among the Jews had led to revolts and persecutions under **Antiochus IV*, a more serious revolt was led by Judas Maccabaeus (Ioudas Makkabaios) to break the polarized situation in 166 BC.

The second leader from the Hasmonaean family, Judas continued the policy of a more militant resistance against the Seleucid generals in charge of suppressing the revolt. He was successful in several encounters: he regained Jerusalem and re-purified its Temple in 164. He might have expelled the Seleucid garrison from the citadel in 163 but for the rivalries among the Greek generals, which led to concessions for the Jews and a temporary truce. Judas refused to accept these half measures, and the hellenized High Priest who was supported by the Seleucids. His complaints were ignored by **Demetrius I Soter*, who had to send troops to quell the war between the traditionalist and hellenized Jews. Judas was killed in 160 by a punitive force avenging the death of a Seleucid general, and the Hellenists temporarily triumphed at Jerusalem.

BIBL. 1 and 2 Maccabees; Abel, *Les Livres des Maccabées* (1949); A. Momigliano, *Prime Linee di Storia della Tradizione Maccabaica* (1931); E. Bickermann, *Der Gott der Maccabäer* (1937).

K. . . , Kh. . .: see C. . . , Ch. . .

Lacedaemonius Athenian general, mid-5th century BC.

Lacedaemonius' (Lakedaimonios) name indicates his father **Cimon's* close links with Sparta. At the battle of Oenophyta (457 BC) he served as hipparch (cavalry commander). In 433 he was one of the Athenian *strategoi* commanding the fleet sent to support Corcyra against Corinth.

BIBL. Davies, *Athenian Families*, no. 8429 XIII (A).

Lachares Athenian statesman, floruit *c.* 301–295 BC.

One of the Athenian politicians who were influential after **Demetrius Poliorcetes* left Athens for Ipsus in 301 BC (leaving **Cassander* free to threaten Greece again), Lachares (Lakharēs) became powerful in 298/7 (?) after a civil war in which he defeated Charias, the hoplite general. When Lachares' supporter Cassander died in 298/7 and left Greece open to renewed attacks by Poliorcetes, discontent against Lachares broke into open revolt. He suppressed the opposing faction, which withdrew to the Piraeus, making him in effect tyrant in the city in 295. Poliorcetes besieged the city and starved it into submission in 294. Lachares escaped to Boeotia, and his later career, like the name of his father and deme, is unknown.

BIBL. Habicht, *Untersuchungen*; Ferguson, *Hellenistic Athens*.

Lacydes Philosopher, 3rd century BC.

No original philosophy is attributed to Lacydes (Lakudēs) of Cyrene. He was said to be an earnest, hard-working man, but also to have died of excessive drinking. He became head of the Academy after **Arcesilaus of Pitane*, but retired several years before his death.

BIBL. Diogenes Laertius iv. 59–61.

Lamachus Athenian general, died 415 BC.

Lamachus (Lamakhos) served in the Black Sea with **Pericles* during the 430s BC; he lost his trireme in a storm off Heraclea Pontica in 433/2. He was one of the officials who swore to the Peace of **Nicias* in 421. In 415 he was chosen to lead the Sicilian expedition, together with Nicias and **Alcibiades*. He was killed in the initial attack on Syracuse in that year. His popularity can be judged from the references to him by *Aristophanes. He became the symbol of an honest (and therefore impoverished) general.

BIBL. Aristophanes, *Acharnians* 270, 614 ff., *Thesmophoriazusae* 841; P. Green, *Armada from Athens* (1971).

Lampon Soothsayer, 5th century BC.

Lampon (Lampōn) was a friend and political supporter of *Pericles; together with Xenocritus, he was sent to found Thurii in 444 BC. Plutarch relates how Lampon correctly interpreted the omen of a one-horned lamb to presage Pericles' supremacy. He was selected as one of the Athenian ambassadors who swore to the terms of the Peace of *Nicias in 421; he was formally consulted by the Assembly on religious questions, and made fun of by *Aristophanes. His position of importance shows that the 'Athenian enlightenment' should not be interpreted as widespread rationalist rejection of inherited religious belief.

BIBL. Diodorus Siculus XII. x. 3 ff. (Thurii); Plutarch, *Pericles* 6; Thucydides v. 19, 24 (ambassador); *IG* i. (2nd ed.) 76. 47 ff. (Assembly); Aristophanes, *Birds* 521, 988, *Clouds* 322; *Roman World* *Plutarch.

Laodice I Seleucid queen, 261–c. 253 BC.

Laodice (Laodikē) was the daughter of Achaeus (perhaps a brother of *Antiochus I, and the grandfather of *Achaeus the general), and was married to *Antiochus II. Their children were *Seleucus (later II), *Antiochus Hierax, and two daughters married to *Mithridates II of Pontus and *Ariarathes III of Cappadocia. When her husband married *Berenice Syra c. 253 BC, Laodice established a rival court at Ephesus. After the king's death in 246, the throne was claimed for Berenice's son and for Laodice's son Seleucus. The latter may have been renamed heir by Antiochus, was fiercely supported by his mother, and was proclaimed king in Asia Minor. In order to forestall Berenice's party and its Egyptian allies, Laodice had her rival and child murdered, and directed her son in the opening phase of the Third Syrian, or Laodicean, War against *Ptolemy III.

BIBL. Bevan, *House of Seleucus* i; Macurdy, *Hellenistic Queens*; PW xii. 701 (Laodice (13)).

Lasus Musician and poet, late 6th century BC.

Traditionally one of the *Seven Sages, the 'inventor' of quibbling arguments, and the first writer on music (*Suda*), Lasus (Lasos) of Hermione made important changes in the rhythms and scales of lyre music. An anecdote in *Aristophanes' *Wasps* has him competing with *Simonides, and one in *Herodotus tells of his exposing to *Hipparchus the forgery of an oracle of Musaeus by *Onomacritus. We know of *Dithyrambs* (fr. 703), and a poem *Centaurs* (fr. 704) which, like a *Hymn to Demeter* (fr. 702 has three lines), eschewed the letter *sigma*.

BIBL. Herodotus vii. 6; Pseudo-Plutarch, *On Music* 1141C; Page, *PMG*; G. A. Privitera, *Laso di Ermione* (1965); *New Grove Dictionary of Music* (1980) x. 502.

Leonidas Agiad king of Sparta, 488–480 BC.

Leonidas (Leōnidas), son of *Anaxandridas, succeeded his step-brother *Cleomenes I, whose daughter Gorgo he

Marble statue of a Spartan warrior, early 5th century BC. Athens, National Museum. (See *Leonidas.)

had married. His only memorable achievement was as commander at Thermopylae. In July to August 480 BC he occupied the pass with a force of 7,000 to prevent the Persians from entering central Greece. A Trachinian named Ephialtes helped the Persians to by-pass the Greek position: while most of the army managed to escape, Leonidas himself stayed behind, for unexplained reasons which may be connected with rivalry between kings and ephors inside Sparta. He died heroically with 700 Thespians and 300 Spartans (order of the day: 'Breakfast here, supper in Hades'). Forty years later a hero-cult was instituted for him at Sparta.

BIBL. Herodotus vii; E. Bradford, *The Year of Thermopylae* (1980).

Leonidas of Tarentum Epigrammatist, 3rd century BC.

Leonidas (Leōnidas), the most imitated Hellenistic epigrammatist, leaves us about one hundred poems but scant biographical information. He is usually put early in the third century BC, but Gow prefers a dating in the middle or later part of the century. His relation to other writers, e.g. *Anyte and *Theocritus, is notably hard to assess. Leonidas embraces a life of wandering poverty with gloomy joy (33, 36, 37, 93) – how authentically is not clear. He left southern Italy, possibly saw Athens, Cos, and Epirus (?); nothing suggests Alexandria. Leonidas steered epigram on a different tack from *Asclepiades of Samos, eschewing the sophisticated love-life of the symposium for themes from the working poor, though the realism of his genre pictures is in tension with his bizarre

and fanciful language. He has a particular penchant for
fictitious artisan dedications larded with technical
vocabulary (e.g. 8: the contents of a carpenter's tool-bag).
Leonidas' outlook on life appears to have been generally
miserable, despite some sunny rustic scenes: note epigram
85, his famous spring poem.
BIBL. Gow and Page, *Hellenistic Epigrams*.

Leonnatus Macedonian general and satrap, died 322 BC.
Companion and (from 332/1 BC) Bodyguard of
*Alexander the Great, Leonnatus (Leonnatos) was greatly
honoured for services in India and during the return west.
After Alexander's death he was guardian of
*Alexander IV and satrap of Lesser Phrygia. In 322 he
returned to mainland Greece to support *Antipater in the
Lamian War (see *Hyper(e)ides), but was killed in a
skirmish.
BIBL. Berve, *Alexanderreich*, no. 466.

Leontiades Theban politician, died 379/8 BC.
Grandson of the Leontiades who fought at Thermopylae
and son of the Eurymachus who seized Plataea in 431 BC,
Leontiades (Leontiadēs) was polemarch in 382 and
encouraged *Phoebidas to seize the Cadmea, sparking off a
pro-Spartan revolution from which he emerged as the
dominant figure in a strictly repressive regime. He was
killed by insurgents in winter 379/8.
BIBL. Buckler, *Theban Hegemony*.

Leontion Epicurean philosopher, early 3rd
century BC (?).
A rare example of a woman philosopher in Greece,
Leontion was a *hetaira* and pupil of *Epicurus. According
to Cicero, she 'dared to write against *Theophrastus, . . .
such was the licence in Epicurus' garden.'
BIBL. Diogenes Laertius x; *Roman World* *Cicero.

Leosthenes Athenian general, died 323/2 BC.
Leosthenes (Leōsthenēs) became the recognized leader
of large numbers of unemployed mercenaries who
congregated at Taenarum in 324 BC (some of whom he had
brought there from Asia Minor). The Exiles' Decree (323;
see *Alexander the Great) failed to disperse them and,
after Alexander's death, Leosthenes, who had secretly
contacted *Hyper(e)ides and was elected Athenian
strategos in 324/3, put 8,000 mercenaries at Athens'
disposal for rebellion. With central Greek allies he trapped
*Antipater in Lamia, but was killed during the ensuing
siege. His anti-Macedonian stance contrasts strikingly
with the long residence of his father (also named
Leosthenes) in Macedonia as an Athenian exile.
BIBL. Kirchner, *PA*, no. 9142; Davies, *Athenian Families*
342 ff.; Berve, *Alexanderreich*, no. 471.

Leotychidas Eurypontid king of Sparta, 491–476 BC.
Ostensibly a great-grandson of a sixth-century king of
the same name, Leotychidas (Leōtukhidas; or Latykhidas)
was installed by *Cleomenes I after *Demaratus had been
declared illegitimate. He accompanied Cleomenes in
operations against Aegina, which led to prosecution at
Sparta *c.* 488/7 BC. After the battle of Salamis (480) he led
the Greek fleet across the Aegean to destroy the Persian
navy at Mycale in 479; he then returned home, leaving
the Athenians under *Xanthippus free to lead the

remaining Greeks against Sestos. In 478/7 he led an
expedition against the pro-Persian *Aleuadae of Thessaly,
with little success: he was accused of having taken bribes,
and fled to Tegea.
BIBL. Herodotus vi. 65–87, viii. 131, ix. 90 ff., 98 ff.,
114; Diodorus Siculus xi. 34–7, 48.

Leptines Athenian politician, floruit 360s–350s BC.
Leptines (Leptinēs) supported the Athenian–Spartan
alliance of 369 BC, held a special financial office in 363/2
and, in 356/5, made a proposal for severe curtailment of
ateleiai (in the interests of public revenue) which was
attacked by *Demosthenes (*Or.* xx).
BIBL. Kirchner, *PA*, no. 9046; Davies, *Athenian Families*
340.

Leptines of Syracuse Admiral of Dionysius I, floruit first
half of 4th century BC.
Leptines (Leptinēs) served his brother, *Dionysius I of
Syracuse, as admiral in the first war with Carthage (during
which he assisted at the siege of Motya (397 BC), but failed
to prevent *Himilcon's landing in Sicily and was defeated
by *Magon at Catana (396)). Like his brother Thearidas
and brother-in-law Polyxenus, he appeared alongside
Dionysius in an Athenian honorific decree of 393. But his
reconciliation of warring Greeks and Lucanians (389 ?)
went against Dionysius' policy, and he was subsequently
exiled (386/5 ?), taking refuge at Thurii. Later recalled, he
was killed at Cronium (375 ?).
BIBL. Stroheker, *Dionysios I*.

Lesches: see **Cyclic Poets**

Leucippus Philosopher, mid- to late 5th century BC.
Leucippus (Leukippos) first devised the atomist theory
of matter, which was developed further by his follower
*Democritus. It is impossible to separate the contributions
which each made to the theory, but one sentence is firmly
attributed to Leucippus: 'Nothing happens in vain, but
everything from reason and by necessity.' He is variously
said to have been born at Abdera, Elea, and Miletus, but
these may be guesses based on his philosophical
connections with Democritus, *Parmenides,
*Anaximander, and *Anaximenes. *Epicurus, who
adopted the atomist theory, denied Leucippus' existence,
no doubt to promote his own reputation for originality.
BIBL. Guthrie, *Greek Philosophy* ii. 283–6.

Leucon I: see **Spartocids**

Lycomedes Arcadian politician, died 366 BC.
Lycomedes (Lukomēdēs) of Mantinea played a central,
though ill-documented, role in the formation of the
fourth-century Arcadian League after the Spartan defeat
at Leuctra (371 BC; see *Epaminondas), and encouraged
the Arcadians to resist Theban pretensions and pursue an
independent line. He was assassinated by exiles after
concluding an alliance with Athens.
BIBL. Buckler, *Theban Hegemony*; J. Roy, *Historia* xx
(1971).

Lycon (*c.* 300–226 BC) Philosopher.
By *Straton's will, the Peripatetic school of philosophy
was bequeathed to Lycon (Lukōn) of Troas, 'since, of the

others, some are too old and others have no time', and for 44 years he presided over its decline. 'Eloquent and skilled in the education of boys', he probably lacked philosophical ability, but very few fragments of his writings have survived.

BIBL. Diogenes Laertius v. 65–74.

Lycophron Tragic poet, c. 280 BC.

Lycophron (Lukophrōn), from Euboean Chalcis, was brought to Alexandria by *Ptolemy II to work in the library under *Zenodotus. He undertook the organization and basic editing of the comic poets, and as a by-product wrote a glossary later criticized by *Eratosthenes. Lycophron was himself a tragedian, a member of the *Pleiad, and author of 64 or 46 lost plays. Interesting among 20 titles in the *Suda* are *Cassandreis*, presumably prompted by recent history (see *Cassander), and a satyr play *Menedemus*, chaffing Lycophron's alleged teacher.

The ascription to this Lycophron of the famously obscure poem *Alexandra* provoked scholarly dissent even in antiquity. A kind of messenger-speech in 1,474 iambic trimeters, it reports the prophetic ravings of Cassandra (Alexandra) in wildly difficult and peculiar language. With cryptic allusions and the most recondite learning it moves from the fall of Troy to the compensatory sufferings of the Greeks, culminating in their defeat by Rome (Troy reborn) and the union of East and West. The poem's allusion (1446 ff.) to the conqueror of the Macedonians must be connected with Rome's defeat of *Pyrrhus if the authorship of our Lycophron and a date soon after 273 are maintained. Such early awareness of Rome's power is startling but perfectly possible, given the strong influence of *Timaeus. Some, however, seeing *Flamininus' victory over *Philip V (197 BC) as the only reasonable reference, propose a later Lycophron.

BIBL. G. W. Mooney, *The Alexandra of Lycophron* (1921); A. Momigliano, *JRS* xxxii (1942); *Roman World*.

Lycophron of Pherae Tyrant, floruit 404–395 BC.

Lycophron (Lukophrōn) attempted, with uncertain success, to control all of Thessaly (although he defeated Larissa and other States on 3 September 404 BC he was still, or again, at war with her in 395) and is sometimes thought to have been *Jason's father (though some other relationship is equally possible).

BIBL. Berve, *Tyrannis* 283 ff.

Lycurgus (c. 390–324 BC) *'Attic orator' and statesman.

Lycurgus (Lukourgos) belonged to the priestly clan of the Eteobutadae. In the 330s BC, when he was a strong supporter of *Demosthenes' policy of opposition to Macedonia, he played an important role in connection with a major building programme. He was particularly interested in restoring Athens' national cults and festivals, and several of his speeches appear to have been accusations of impiety. The only one which survives, *Against Leocrates*, was delivered in 331 against an Athenian who had abandoned the city with his property after the battle of Chaeronea (338). Lycurgus was responsible for the official edition of the texts of *Aeschylus, *Sophocles, and *Euripides.

BIBL. *Minor Attic Orators* (Loeb) ii; Davies, *Athenian Families*, no. 9251; E. M. Burke, *Phoenix* xxxi (1977); Kennedy, *Art of Persuasion*, 249.

'Portrait' of Lycurgus of Sparta on the reverse of a Roman coin of Lacedaemon (enlarged).

Lycurgus of Sparta Statesman, c. 650 BC (?).

Lycurgus (Lukourgos) was considered by the Spartans to have been the founder of their peculiar social and political system, but it is not at all clear when he lived, or even whether he was a real person at all. His political reforms were embodied in the 'Great Rhetra', a document said to have originated from Delphi, which provides for a council ('Gerousia') of 30 members including the kings, and a popular assembly ('Apella'), and defines their powers (though its exact meaning is much disputed). On the social side, he was said to have originated the 'Agoge', the system of education and military training for young Spartiates. At the age of seven the boy left home and began his training, which included such useful exercises as stealing his food (those who were caught were punished not for the theft but for inefficiency in carrying it out). Even adult Spartiates had much less private life than most Greeks, taking their meals in communal messes (*sussitia*). Severe sumptuary laws and the prohibition of coinage left little scope for private luxury, and the distribution of land in equal, inalienable lots gave all Spartiates a basic minimum to live on. The aim of all this was to promote public spirit and military effectiveness, which the Spartiates found even more necessary than other Greeks because they were holding down a large and potentially rebellious helot population, especially in Messenia. The occasion for the reforms may have been the need to improve Sparta's military position after defeats in the Second Messenian War (see *Aristomenes) and at Hysiae (see *Pheidon), but this is very uncertain.

BIBL. Herodotus i. 65–6; Plutarch, *Life of Lycurgus*; Forrest, *History of Sparta* 40–68; Andrewes, *Greek Tyrants*, ch. vi.

Lydiadas Megalopolitan statesman, 251–227 BC (tyrant, 244–235 BC).

Although a previous tyrant had been expelled by *Demophanes and *Ecdelus, Aetolian intervention in the Peloponnese in 244 BC prompted Lydiadas (Ludiadas) to declare himself tyrant in Megalopolis in 243 to protect his city. He kept his Megalopolitan hatred of Sparta throughout his career, but his originally pro-Macedonian stance wavered before the growing power of the anti-Macedonian Achaean League. Lydiadas obtained an amnesty from *Aratus of Sicyon, abdicated in 235, and joined Megalopolis to the League. This action was appreciative of political realities rather than altruistic.

Lydiadas was frequently elected *strategus* of the League after 234. He persuaded other tyrants to abdicate, and he was a rival to Aratus officially and personally. His support of a stronger anti-Spartan policy in the League was, ironically, blocked by Aratus, who soon desired war with Sparta himself. When Aratus elicited a promise of help from *Antigonus Doson against *Cleomenes III of Sparta, he was elected *strategus* of the League instead of Lydiadas in 227. As cavalry leader, Lydiadas led the Achaean horse in campaigns against Cleomenes. When Cleomenes marched on Megalopolis in 227, Aratus successfully drove him back from the walls, but refused to follow up his victory. This proved too much for Lydiadas: disobeying Aratus, he charged the Spartans with his cavalry, but was killed with many of his men. He saved Megalopolis but harmed the Achaean League.

BIBL. Walbank, *Aratos of Sicyon*.

Lysander Spartan leader, died 395 BC.

The ancient sources are largely unsympathetic to Lysander (Lusandros), despite his obvious military and organizational ability: like other outstanding Spartans, his successes led to resentment and hostility on the part of his peers.

Although not a member of either royal family, Lysander claimed descent from the **Heracleidae. In 408 BC he was appointed navarch (admiral) of the Spartan fleet in the Aegean, which had been heavily defeated by *Alcibiades at Cyzicus in 410. He won the friendship of *Cyrus the Younger, who had been sent by *Darius II to take general command of Asia Minor. With Persian support he defeated the Athenians at Notium, which led to the elimination of Alcibiades. When his successor *Callicratidas was defeated at Arginusae, Lysander was appointed as adviser (*epistoleus*) to the Spartan navarch for 405/4, Aracus. He blockaded the Hellespont, then caught the Athenian fleet unprepared at Aegospotami and destroyed it. During the winter of 405/4 he blockaded Athens, and, after the surrender negotiated by *Theramenes, he installed a pro-Spartan oligarchy, the 'Thirty Tyrants', under *Critias.

Lysander's installation of his friends as 'harmosts' ruling the member-states of the former Athenian empire through oligarchic committees of ten (decarchies), and the semi-divine honours he was accorded as a hero, provoked the opposition of the Spartan government. By late 403 the Spartans had allowed democracies to be re-established at Athens (see *Thrasybulus) and elsewhere. Lysander tried, but failed, to have the Spartan constitution amended so as to have an elective kingship; later (399) he had *Agesilaus installed as king in place of his brother Leotychidas. In 396 Lysander accompanied Agesilaus to Asia Minor, but found himself politically isolated. At the outbreak of the Corinthian War in the following year, he commanded a Lacedaemonian force operating against Boeotia, but was killed at Haliartus.

BIBL. W. K. Prentice, *AJA* xxxviii (1934); R. E. Smith, *CPhil.* xliii (1948).

Lysias (traditionally 459–380 BC) *'Attic orator'.

Lysias' (Lusias) father, the Cephalus of *Plato, *Republic* i, was a Syracusan metic resident in Athens. The family lived at Thurii for a time, and there Lysias learned his

Inscribed bust of Lysias, made for insertion in a statue. Roman period copy of an early 4th-century BC Greek original. Rome, Capitoline Museum.

rhetoric. When the Decelean War began in 413 BC, they returned to Athens, making a good living as arms manufacturers. The oligarchic regime of 404, wishing to raise funds, confiscated their property; Lysias' brother Polemarchus was executed, and he himself fled to Megara, supporting *Thrasybulus' invasion of Attica in the following year. Thrasybulus tried to have his metic supporters given full citizenship, but this was declared illegal.

As a metic, Lysias was not entitled to speak for himself on formal occasions; the 200 speeches he is said to have composed were almost all intended for delivery by others. 35 speeches survive, 23 in their entirety; sceptical scholars have argued that there is no evidence that any apart from *Or.* xii were actually written by him, and some (vi, viii, xx) are certainly spurious. The corpus includes political cases (embezzlement of public funds, sacrilege), as well as disputes about property. Three speeches may have been delivered by Lysias in person: *Against *Eratosthenes* (*Or.* xii), about the reign of terror under the Thirty (see *Critias); the *Epitaphios* (*Or.* ii), in honour of the dead of the Corinthian War (395–387/6); and the *Olympiacus* (*Or.* xxxiii of 388 BC), calling for Greek unity against Persia.

Together with *Antiphon, Lysias was later regarded as the exemplar of a simple 'Attic' prose style, with a clear and simple arrangement of material, and some vivid passages of narrative reporting.

BIBL. K. J. Dover, *Lysias and the Corpus Lysiacum* (1968); reviewed by S. Usher, *JHS* xci (1971); S. Usher, *GRBS* xvii (1976), and *Eranos* lxiii (1965).

Lysimachus (*c.* 361–281 BC) Macedonian dynast.

Lysimachus (Lusimakhos) came from Pella in Macedonia; his family may have been of Thessalian origin. He was a member of *Alexander the Great's Bodyguard and took part in his hunting expeditions; on one of them he killed a lion with his own hands.

After Alexander's death in 323 BC, he was allocated Thrace to govern on *Antipater's behalf; his first wife was Antipater's daughter Nicaea. He joined the successful coalitions against *Perdiccas (322–1), *Polyperchon (319) and *Antigonus (315–311). In 309 he founded Lysimachia on the Chersonese as his capital; in 305, together with the other surviving dynasts, he proclaimed himself king of the Macedonians. In 302/1, in association with *Seleucus I, a carefully prepared campaign was fought against Antigonus in Asia Minor, leading to Antigonus' defeat and death at the battle of Ipsus; subsequently Seleucus agreed to let Lysimachus rule Asia Minor west of the Taurus mountains. But Lysimachus was chiefly concerned to strengthen his position in the Aegean (re-founding Ephesus) and in Europe, with campaigns against the Getae north of the Danube (where he was taken prisoner for a time by their chieftain Dromichaites in 292), and in Macedonia and Thessaly, which he conquered from *Demetrius Poliorcetes in 287/6. There followed a struggle for the succession resulting in the execution of his son *Agathocles, whose wife Lysandra fled to Seleucus; Seleucus invaded Lysimachus' domain, and defeated and killed him at Corupedium (281). Lysimachus failed to establish a dynasty to succeed him; consequently his rule was considered harsh by a hostile historiographical tradition.

BIBL. Will, *Hist. pol.* i.

Lysippus Sculptor, active *c.* 360–315 BC.

Apparently starting work as a foundry-worker in his home town of Sicyon, Lysippus (Lusippos) was a younger contemporary of *Praxiteles and came to equal his fame and influence, specializing in different areas of sculpture. He seems to have worked exclusively in bronze and was very prolific, making in his life a reputed 1,500 statues. About 35 commissions – groups and individual statues – are recorded, mostly in Greece, especially at Olympia, but he travelled to Tarentum in the west and to Rhodes and Asia Minor in the east. He specialized in athletic statues, in statues of Zeus and Heracles, and in portraits. An Eros and a Satyr are mentioned, but apparently he made no Aphrodites. He made portraits of *Alexander the Great from boyhood onwards, and was often said (wrongly) to be Alexander's exclusive portrait-sculptor.

His style was noted for its fineness 'even in the smallest details', and it is said that he was heedful of *symmetria* but made changes in the old four-square conception of statues (*Polycleitus' canon is no doubt meant), making the heads smaller and the bodies leaner to make the figures look taller. He made a statue of a youth scraping himself clean ('Apoxyomenos'), which most probably is reproduced in a complete Roman copy in the Vatican; it shows just these alterations in the canon for nude males,

'Apoxyomenos', a young athlete scraping himself clean, by Lysippus. Roman period copy in marble of a bronze of the mid- or later 4th century BC. Vatican Museum.

and also a new interest in extending parts of the figure boldly into the third dimension and so creating more than the usual single, frontal viewpoint. From this developed the complex multi-view compositions of Lysippus' successors in the third century BC.

The new canon of proportions was very influential, and it is hard to distinguish the master's works from those of his followers. We have surviving the relief on the base for his statue of Poulydamas at Olympia, and a contemporary marble version at Delphi of his bronze statue of the athlete Agias, and in addition to the Apoxyomenos, we have in Roman copies his seated Heracles, and perhaps also his drunken flute-girl, Satyr, and Eros. Of the portraits there are copies of probably his *Socrates and several possible Alexanders. While clearly being very important for the subsequent development of Greek sculpture, Lysippus' artistic personality remains for us blurred. He left at least five pupils who became prominent sculptors (one of whom, *Chares of Mytilene, made the Colossus of Rhodes); this number reflects his very large workshop, which could take on commissions like the Battle of the Granicus Memorial at Dium (334 BC) consisting of portraits of Alexander and 25 of his fallen cavalry Companions.

BIBL. F. P. Johnson, *Lysippos* (1927); Richter, *Sculpture and Sculptors* 224–32; Robertson, *History of Greek Art* 463 ff.

Machon Comic poet, mid-3rd century BC.

Machon (Makhōn) moved from his native Corinth or Sicyon to Alexandria, where as a comic dramatist he was a fairly rare bird and highly esteemed: *Aristophanes of Byzantium was apparently his eager pupil. *Dioscorides' epitaph billing him as pungent (Attic) thyme growing by the Nile has been pressed to suggest a revival of *Aristophanic comedy in Machon, but the two certain fragments are too neutral to support this. His iambic *Chreiai* (*Quips*), salty anecdotes about famous prostitutes and their associates, extensively quoted by Athenaeus, are valuable as our main witness to an evidently popular literary form.

BIBL. Dioscorides 24 GP; A. S. F. Gow, *Machon* (1965); *Roman World* *Athenaeus.

Magas Dynast of Cyrene, floruit *c.* 300–*c.* 250 (?) BC.

Son of the Egyptian queen *Berenice I from her first marriage, Magas benefited from his mother's position when his step-father *Ptolemy I appointed him governor of an independent Cyrene *c.* 300 BC. He married Apama, the daughter of *Antiochus I and sister of *Antiochus II. He governed Cyrene loyally until Ptolemy's death, but, after the accession of *Ptolemy II, he declared himself king perhaps with the hope of Seleucid support. Hostilities broke out *c.* 275, but Ptolemy's First Syrian War took precedence: a truce was declared and sealed by the engagement of their children *Ptolemy (later III) and *Berenice (II), whose eventual marriage would unite the two countries. Relations were peaceful for the rest of Magas' reign, although he did make alliances with several Cretan cities. His death occurred within the decade 260–250, probably nearer to 250.

Magas' name is mentioned in Rock Edict xiii of the Mauryan king *Aśoka as one of several Greek monarchs with whom he had connections.

BIBL. Will, *Hist. pol.* i; Chamoux, *Revue Historique* ccxvi (1956), 18 ff.; P. M. Fraser, *Afghan Studies* ii (1979), 16, note 22.

Magon Carthaginian general, died 375 BC ?

Magon (Magōn) fought in two wars against *Dionysius I of Syracuse. In 397–392 BC he had a fleet and then took supreme command, but was eventually compelled to negotiate a treaty giving Dionysius most of Sicily. In 383/2 he took command again (as suffete), but was killed at Kabala (375 ?).

BIBL. Stroheker, *Dionysios I.*

Manethon Egyptian priest and historian, floruit *c.* 280–260 BC.

The first native Egyptian known to have written in Greek, Manethon (Manethōn) was a high priest from the northern Delta whose floruit probably coincided with the early reign of *Ptolemy II. (*Ptolemy I is said to have consulted him earlier about a statue of Sarapis.) He wrote a history of Egypt including the religious customs of the country from the earliest period until 323 BC. It could have been written, whether by royal request or not, to recount the history of the kingdom to the new rulers; there is some suggestion that it was addressed to Ptolemy II. Manethon used *Herodotus and *Hecataeus, but also the Egyptian priestly records to which he had access. Although in narrative form, the work emphasizes chronology. Manethon's framework of pharaonic regnal lists (apportioning the kings into dynasties and kingdoms) lies behind the system used by all later historians and chronographers of Egypt down to the Byzantine period, but little of the narrative of the original work survives.

BIBL. *FGrH* 609 (cf. *FHG* ii. 512 ff.); Loeb (ed. Waddell); Fraser, *Ptolemaic Alexandria* i. 505 ff.

Mardonius Persian general, died 479 BC.

Gobryas, the father of Mardonius (Mardonios, Persian Mardunija), had played an important role under *Cyrus (on whose behalf he had conquered Babylon), and was one of *Darius' (I) closest supporters, accompanying him on the Scythian expedition (513 BC). Mardonius' mother was a sister of Darius, and Darius in turn married one of Mardonius' sisters. After the Ionian Revolt, Darius instructed him to replace the 'tyrants' who had ruled the Greek cities in Ionia with democratic regimes. In 492 Mardonius restored Persian authority over Thrace. *Herodotus suggests that he was responsible for *Xerxes' plan to conquer Greece. When Xerxes left Greece after Salamis (480), Mardonius remained to command the Persian forces. In 479 he reoccupied and destroyed Athens; but at Plataea in Boeotia the superior skill and armour of *Pausanias' (I) hoplites led to his defeat and death.

BIBL. Hignett, *Xerxes' Invasion.*

Mausolus Carian satrap and dynast, died 353/2 BC.

Mausolus (Mausōlos) was nominally satrap of Caria (from *c.* 377 BC), but the disturbed state of Asia Minor at the time of *Ariobarzanes' rebellion (*c.* 367), which he opposed, and the Satraps' Revolt, which he joined, permitted his acquisition of an independent position. His political influence spread widely along the Asiatic seaboard, and he played a central role in fomenting the

Portrait statues of Mausolus and (?) Artemisia from the Mausoleum at Halicarnassus. London, British Museum.

Athenian allies' revolt in 357 (the 'Social War'). Originally from Mylasa, he made his capital at Halicarnassus, which he enlarged by synoecism and decorated with fine architecture, the greatest item being the Mausoleum, completed posthumously by his sister and consort Artemisia. Rule of Caria remained with his siblings into *Alexander the Great's time.

BIBL. PW xiv. 2414–16; N. S. R. Hornblower, *Mausolus* (1982).

Mazaeus Persian satrap, 4th century BC.

Satrap of Cilicia under *Artaxerxes III (died 338/7 BC) and of Coele-Syria with Mesopotamia under *Darius III, Mazaeus (Mazaios) surrendered Babylon to *Alexander the Great after Gaugamela (331), and was rewarded with the Babylonian satrapy (Alexander's first such appointment of an Iranian).

BIBL. Berve, *Alexanderreich*, no. 485; Bosworth, *Arrian* 314–15.

Medius: see **Aleuadae**

Megacles Athenian statesman, 6th century BC.

Megacles (Megaklēs) the *Alcmaeonid married *Agariste of Sicyon, and in the division of parties which followed *Solon's reforms he became leader of the Coast (Paralioi). When *Peisistratus became tyrant (c. 560 BC), the Coast and Plain (Pedieis) united to expel him, but Megacles was subsequently reconciled with Peisistratus, brought him back to Athens, and married him to his daughter. The marriage and the alliance soon broke up, however, and Peisistratus was exiled again.

BIBL. Herodotus i. 59–61, vi. 126–31.

Megacles, son of Hippocrates Alcmaeonid chieftain, early 5th century BC.

Megacles (Megaklēs) was the son of *Cleisthenes' brother Hippocrates and the maternal uncle of *Pericles. His chariot victory at the Pythian games was celebrated by *Pindar (*Pythian* vii). In 487 BC he was ostracized, in the wake of anti- *Alcmaeonid feeling associated with the story that the Alcmaeonids had supported the Persian-backed tyrant *Hippias at the time of Marathon (490).

BIBL. Davies, *Athenian Families*, no. 9688; J. Holladay, *Greece and Rome* xxv (1978).

Megacles: see also **Alcmaeonids**

Megasthenes (c. 350–290 BC) Seleucid ambassador to India.

An Ionian Greek who was Seleucid envoy first at the court of the satrap in Arachosia (southern Afghanistan), Megasthenes (Megasthenēs) was sent in 302 BC to the court of *Sandracottus (Chandragupta), the founder of the Mauryan kingdom of the Punjab, when the treaty concluded between him and *Seleucus I in 303 encouraged the exchange of ambassadors between their courts. He spent some ten years at the capital Pataliputra (the City of Lotus), which he described, and he travelled widely in northern India. He was the first Greek to write about India with firsthand knowledge, although his information about the South was based on hearsay and he was susceptible to many fantastic tales. His *Indica*, which dealt with geography, people, government, religion, history and legends, survives in later authors (e.g. *Strabo), to whom he was the principal source of information for over a century.

BIBL. *FGrH* 715, with E. A. Schwanbeck, *Megasthenis Indica* (1846); A. Dahlquist, *Megasthenes and Indian Religion* (1962); Fraser, *Ptolemaic Alexandria* ii. 768, note 125; *Cambridge History of India* (1922) i., ch. 16.

Meidias Athenian politician, floruit mid-4th century BC.

A man of wealth (partly derived from silver-mines), reflected in extensive liturgic activity, who also served in several public offices, Meidias is most famous for his bad relations with *Demosthenes (see *Demosthenes xxi). In 348 BC he assaulted Demosthenes at the Dionysia but, after Demosthenes had secured unanimous support in a preliminary Assembly meeting, he settled out of court, and *Against Meidias* (*Or.* xxi) was never delivered.

BIBL. Kirchner, *PA*, no. 9719; Davies, *Athenian Families* 385.

Melanippides (c. 520–after 450 BC) Dithyrambic poet.

Melanippides (Melanippidēs) of Melos died at the court of *Perdiccas II of Macedon. He introduced astrophic solo passages into the dithyramb, so starting the movement which led to the dithyrambs of *Timotheus (1) and *Philoxenus of Cythera. Little survives.

BIBL. Lesky, *Greek Literature*; *Lyra Graeca* (Loeb) iii; Pickard-Cambridge, *Dithyramb* . . .

Meleager Epigrammatist, c. 95 BC.

Three autobiographical 'epitaphs' affirm that Meleager (Meleagros) was born in Gadara, raised in Tyre, and retired in old age to Cos. His *Charites* (*Graces*: now lost) were satirical compositions in the manner of his compatriot *Menippus. More important for posterity was his compilation of an anthology of epigrams, the foundation of our Palatine Anthology. The original *Stephanos* (*Garland* – each poet tastefully linked with a flower) was apparently arranged thematically, and interwove earlier epigrams with Meleager's own, of which more are preserved (about 130) than of anyone else. We need not regret this self-regard: Meleager is complete master of the genre, varying and combining themes from his predecessors with his own fertile invention, in fastidiously lucid and versatile style. Most of the epigrams are erotic, picking up the tradition of *Asclepiades of Samos (contrast *Antipater from near-by Sidon). Profound emotion is not to be sought in this fundamentally intellectual poetry, but there is vitality and often poignancy in Meleager's condensed expression of susceptibility to love, for boys and girls alike: he was an important channel for the influence of Hellenistic epigram on Roman love-poetry.

BIBL. Gow and Page, *Hellenistic Epigrams*.

Melinno Poetess, early 2nd century BC (?).

Melinno (Melinnō), whose place of origin is unknown, was the authoress of a poem in Doric dialect and in Sapphic stanzas on the greatness of Rome.

BIBL. C. M. Bowra, *JRS* xlvii (1957). N.H.

Melissus of Samos Eleatic philosopher and general, mid-5th century BC.

Melissus (Melissos) was in command when the Samians defeated an Athenian fleet in 441 BC, during their unsuccessful revolt against Athens. In his philosophy he closely followed *Parmenides, but differed in holding that reality was infinite. If it were not, he argued, it would be limited by void, i.e. something that *is not*, which, on Parmenides' own principles, was inadmissible.

BIBL. Guthrie, *Greek Philosophy* ii.

Memnon of Rhodes Mercenary general, died 333 BC.

Memnon (Memnōn) fled with *Artabazus (son of *Pharnabazus) to Macedonia in *c.* 352 BC, but later succeeded to his brother *Mentor's Troad domains and played an important role in Persian resistance to Macedonian invasion both before and after the arrival of *Alexander the Great. As commander-in-chief in Asia Minor (334) he started a major counter-attack, and his early death was one of Alexander's more notable pieces of good fortune.

BIBL. Berve, *Alexanderreich*, no. 497; Hofstetter, *Griechen*, no. 215.

Menander (342/1–293/2 or 290/89 BC) New Comedy poet.

The supreme poet of New Comedy, Menander (Menandros) was a well-connected Athenian, reputed to have been a friend of *Demetrius of Phalerum and pupil of *Alexis and *Theophrastus (Peripatetic influence has been sought in his work), and to have done military service with *Epicurus. That he was long in love with one Glycera is probably fiction concocted from the existence of one or more heroines of his of that name; that he

Mosaic by Dioscorides of Samos showing musicians in a scene from New Comedy. Augustan period. Naples, Museo Nazionale.

drowned off the Piraeus could be fact. Of about 108 plays eight won victories, including *Dyscolus* (*The Bad-tempered Man*) in 317/16 BC. If his contemporaries esteemed him less highly than *Philemon, future generations soon asserted his peerless genius: *Aristophanes of Byzantium, with notable passion, ranked him second only to *Homer. Until early this century our only contact with this reputation was through upwards of 900 ancient quotations – chosen largely for their edifying content, showing that Menander was much read, but miserable evidence of his dramatic skills – and hypothetical reconstructions extracted from Latin adaptations. (The use of Menander by Plautus and especially Terence, in four plays each, it seems, is now better understood but still a frustrating study.) However, exciting papyrus discoveries began in 1905, and culminated almost miraculously in the publication in 1959 of a complete play, *Dyscolus*. We now have substantial portions of *Samia* (*The Samian Woman*), *Epitrepontes* (*The Arbitrants*), *Periceiromene* (*The Shorn Girl*), *Aspis* (*The Shield*), *Sicyonius* (*The Sicyonian*), and smaller but important pieces of many others. The texts are battered, but finds accrue continually: Menander's reputation has at last come alive.

The poet Menander: head from a double herm, paired with a portrait of *Homer. Rome, Museo delle Terme.

Poor evidence for dating the plays hampers discussion (according to Plutarch Menander got better all the time). *Dyscolus* is the work of a 25-year-old. The plot is simple, introduced by a detailed account of the story so far delivered by Pan. The misanthropic farmer Cnemon lives with his artless daughter, with whom wealthy young Sostratus falls in love at sight. Cnemon falls down a well between acts, and, rescued by his estranged stepson and Sostratus, is a softened man. Sostratus marries the girl, his

sister marries the stepson. The farcical persecution of Cnemon by the cook and slave closes the play. Much here is typical of the essentially middle-class New Comedy, which excludes the traumatic events of contemporary politics to focus on private relationships and family preoccupations – wealth, weddings, etc. *Dyscolus* is less a comedy of errors than other plays, e.g. *Epitrepontes*, *Periceiromene*, which turn characteristically on misunderstanding, remarkable coincidence, and the recognition of foundling babies, a favourite motif bequeathed to comedy by *Euripides. The happy end is obligatory and true love the dominant theme.

It is Menander's genius to accept the stock and conventions of earlier comedy and conceal their artificiality by his natural art. His plots, deftly managed and laid out with subtle symmetry, are perfectly harmonized with his finely tuned characterization. A great gift for individualizing standard characters is everywhere apparent (e.g. *Epitrepontes*' golden-hearted whore Habrotonon; *Periceiromene*'s silly but sympathetic hot-headed soldier Polemon). The dialogue, in trimeters of quite astonishing ease, is concise, significant on several levels, yet perfectly colloquial. It is above all the pervasive humanity and sympathetic irony with which Menander perceives the foolishness but essential goodness of most ordinary human beings which lends his plays the quality of universal truthfulness to which Aristophanes of Byzantium alluded, asking 'Menander and Life, which of you imitates the other?'

BIBL. Text: F. H. Sandbach (1972, reprinted with corrections 1976); Commentary: A. W. Gomme and F. H. Sandbach (1973); W. G. Arnott, *Menander*, *Plautus*, *Terence* (GRNSC, 1975); Sandbach, *The Comic Theatre of Greece and Rome* (1977); *Roman World* *Plautus, *Plutarch, *Terence.

Menander (Milinda) King of the Indo-Greeks, c. 130 (?)–c. 100 (?) BC.

The rule of various Greek kings in the East passed to that of the Indo-Greeks with the accession of Menander (Menandros). He is the Milinda of Indian legend, and Indian writings contain a dialogue between him and a Buddhist sage on various philosophical and religious questions. He was perhaps a Buddhist himself.

Menander's main base of power was the western Punjab and Gandhara, but classical sources universally attest his vast conquests in India. He advanced further east than any 'Greek' king, and reached Pataliputra, the old capital of the Mauryan empire (see *Sandracottus, *Aśoka). There is no trace of permanent occupation there, and tradition records a quarrel between Menander and his

Hellenized coin portrait of Menander (Milinda), king of the Indo-Greeks (enlarged).

allies, but it is questionable whether settlement so far east had ever been the intention.

Menander's abundant coinage and the achievements ascribed to him suggest that his reign was a long and prosperous one. In Buddhist tradition, he abdicated in favour of his son and retired from the world; Plutarch says that he died in camp.

BIBL. Narain, *Indo-Greeks*; Tarn, *Greeks in Bactria . . .*; J. W. Sedlar, *India and the Greek World* (1980); *Roman World* *Plutarch.

Menecleidas Theban politician, floruit 360s BC.

Exiled after the pro-Spartan *coup* of 382 BC, Menecleidas (Menekleidas) returned in 379/8. He was noted for political opposition to *Epaminondas and *Pelopidas in the earlier 360s (note their trial in early 369 and Epaminondas' eclipse in 369/8). He is reported to have plotted constitutional revolution but, unless this refers to disturbances in Orchomenus in 364, details are lacking.

BIBL. Buckler, *Theban Hegemony*.

Menedemus of Eretria (*c.* 339–265 BC) Philosopher.

Menedemus (Menedēmos) was renowned for his skill in argument, but nothing clear is known of his philosophy. He was said to have eliminated complex and negative propositions by translating them into simple affirmative propositions, but it is not known how he carried out this logical feat. His interest in logic was no doubt stimulated by his friendship with *Stilpon of the Megarian school, where logic flourished. He was an active politician, and his dealings with *Antigonus Gonatas led to his exile from his native town on the island of Euboea.

BIBL. Diogenes Laertius ii. 125–44.

Menippus Satirical philosopher, first half of 3rd century BC.

Menippus (Menippos) came from Gadara, near Galilee; further colour offered by Diogenes Laertius – that he was a slave at Sinope who became a citizen of Thebes, a prosperous money-lender who hanged himself – is hardly reliable. His combative, burlesquing writings in the funny–serious (*spoudogeloion*) style popularized the Cynic outlook on life, attacking common folly and the pretensions of philosophers in imaginative frameworks, e.g. *Descent to the Underworld*, *Wills*, and *Letters from Gods*. Surviving only in the scantiest fragments they are a sad loss. Lucian proclaims his debt to this 'barking, biting, laughing Cynic', uses him as a dramatic character, and, like Varro in his *Menippean Satires*, follows his lacing of prose with verse.

BIBL. D. R. Dudley, *A History of Cynicism* (1937), 69 ff.; R. Helm, *Lucian und Menipp* (1906, reprinted 1967); *Roman World* *Diogenes Laertius, *Lucian, *Varro.

Mentor of Rhodes Mercenary general, died after 342/1 BC.

Mentor (Mentōr) served his brother-in-law *Artabazus (son of *Pharnabazus) as a mercenary commander (receiving a principality in the Troad (see *Memnon) as a reward), and joined his rebellion (*c.* 356 BC). Regaining *Artaxerxes III's favour with the surrender of Sidon (344/3), he participated in the Egyptian reconquest, and died shortly after his arrest of *Hermias.

BIBL. Hofstetter, *Griechen*, no. 220.

Metellus, Quintus Caecilius Roman envoy, 185–183 BC.

A former consul, Quintus Caecilius Metellus came to Macedonia in 185 BC with an embassy to hear complaints against *Philip V. On a visit to Achaea, Metellus unofficially reproached the Achaeans for their harsh policy towards Sparta, which was defended by *Philopoemen and Lycortas, the father of *Polybius. He was refused access to a meeting of the full Achaean Assembly. Rome was forced into new activity in the old quarrel with Achaea over Sparta. In 184/3 Metellus was appointed with *Flamininus to a committee to settle the issue. From this point relations deteriorated, and this led to the Third Macedonian War (169).

BIBL. *Roman World*; R. M. Errington, *Philopoemen* (1969).

Metellus Macedonicus Roman governor of Macedonia, 148 BC.

Quintus Caecilius Metellus Macedonicus, the Roman praetor, went to Macedonia in 148 BC with a large army to suppress the revolt of *Andriscus, the pretended son of *Perseus and claimant to the throne of Macedon, who had already worsted one diplomatic and one military mission from Rome. Metellus defeated and captured Andriscus, and eventually put him to death. He remained in Greece as the first governor of the Roman province of Macedonia, and a statue was erected to him at Olympia for services to the province. Various warnings and envoys sent by him to the fractious Achaean League were ignored, which led to the outbreak of the Achaean War in 146. Marching south, Metellus defeated the Achaean agitator *Critolaus, and proceeded to Corinth, where he was relieved by *Mummius.

BIBL. *Roman World*; Will, *Hist. pol.* ii; *Sylloge* (3rd ed.) 680.

Meton Astronomer, *c.* 432 BC.

An Athenian astronomer, Meton (Metōn) tried to correlate the cycles of the moon and the sun, and devised a 6,940-day cycle, of 19 solar years or 235 lunar months. His calculations of the length of the year and the month were wrong by about thirty minutes and two minutes respectively, and were later improved on by *Callippus and *Hipparchus of Nicaea. It is uncertain whether his cycle was ever used as the basis of an official calendar in Athens.

BIBL. Heath, *Aristarchus of Samos* 293–6.

Metrodorus of Lampsacus (330–277 BC) Philosopher.

A favourite pupil of *Epicurus, Metrodorus (Metrodōros) died before him. In his will Epicurus provided for the care of Metrodorus' son and daughter. According to Cicero – a fierce opponent of Epicureanism – he advocated a particularly crude form of hedonism, and criticized his brother because he hesitated to 'measure by the belly everything that pertains to a happy life'.

BIBL. Diogenes Laertius x; *Roman World* *Cicero.

Micythus Ruler of Rhegium 476–467 BC.

Micythus (Mikuthos) was a supporter of *Anaxilas, tyrant of Rhegium; a widespread fable made him a slave. Anaxilas, at his death in 476 BC, appointed Micythus as tutor to his children and ruler of Rhegium and Messana; in this capacity he supported Tarentum against Iapygian attacks. In 467, he either handed over the two cities to Anaxilas' sons, or else was expelled on the suggestion of *Hieron I; he retired to Tegea (or alternatively Olympia). He thus became an exemplar of the dutiful slave.

BIBL. Herodotus vii. 170–4.

Milon Athlete, floruit 532–512 BC.

Milon (Milōn) of Croton was a famous wrestler who won six Olympic and seven Pythian victories. Many stories were told about his feats of strength, the last of which proved fatal: he tried to split open a tree-trunk with his bare hands, but became trapped and was eaten by wolves.

BIBL. Pausanias vi. 14; Strabo vi. 263.

Miltiades (c. 550–489 BC) Athenian general.

Miltiades (Miltiadēs), son of Cimon, belonged to the powerful *Philaid clan. He was archon in 524/3 BC; soon

Bronze helmet found at Olympia, inscribed 'Miltiades dedicated me'. Olympia, Museum.

after, the tyrant *Hippias sent him to the Chersonese to ensure Athenian control over the sea-route from the Black Sea, vital for Athenian grain imports (see *Spartocids). He established an Athenian cleruchy on Lemnos. In about 515 he married Hegesipyle, daughter of the Thracian king Olorus. In 513 he took part in *Darius' (I) campaign against the Scythians; it was later claimed that he had advocated dismantling the bridge over the Danube in order to destroy Darius, but in fact he seems to have been a loyal Persian supporter up to the time of the Ionian Revolt (began 499: see *Histiaeus, *Aristagoras). With the defeat of that rebellion in 494/3, he fled to Athens, where he was prosecuted for having ruled the Chersonese as a 'tyrant', but acquitted. His personal fear of the Persians led him to advocate resistance to Darius' attempt to punish Athens for its part in the Ionian rebellion; in 490 it was Miltiades who led the Athenian army out to its victory over *Datis' expeditionary force at Marathon, despite the pro-Persian sentiments of some Athenians (see *Alcmaeonids). In the following year he led an Athenian fleet against Paros, but he was wounded and the expedition was a failure; on his return he was put on trial and fined 50 talents, but died immediately after from his wounds. His son *Cimon continued Miltiades' imperialist and anti-Persian policies.

BIBL. Herodotus vi; Burn, *Persia and the Greeks*.

Miltiades the Elder, Miltiades of Laciadae: see **Philaids**

Mimnermus Elegiac poet, c. 630 BC.

From Colophon or Smyrna in Ionia, Mimnermus (Mimnermos) was, like *Archilochus and *Callinus, labelled 'inventor of elegy': the *Suda* dates him

The Treasury of the Athenians (restored) at Delphi, built after the battle of Marathon (490 BC, see *Miltiades) and dedicated to Apollo.

632–629 BC, and he is certainly no later than *Solon, whose fragment 20 corrects Mimnermus' wish (fr. 6) to die at sixty.

Of the two books known to Alexandrians, *Nanno* (whence seven pieces are quoted, at least one wrongly, and most others doubtless derive) was apparently a collection of short poems, rated higher by *Callimachus than a long poem, now known to have been entitled *Smyrneis* (fr. 13a), probably a history of Smyrna from mythical foundation by an Amazon Smyrna down to historical struggles with Lydia (perhaps fr. 14). *Hermesianax presents Mimnermus in love with Nanno, but no fragment mentions her: she may have been his *aulos*-player, conveniently available for formal address that could mark the song as his (compare *Theognis). His appeal as a love-poet comes across in fragment 1, in praise of love-making, destined for extinction by painful old age, and fragment 2, which moves on from *Homer's comparison of man with the leaves of a tree to argue that death is a better fate than senility (cleverly transposing themes of exhortations to die fighting – see *Tyrtaeus). Myths were told (fr. 12: the Sun sails overnight from west to east in a golden bed), but perhaps just to illustrate the brevity of youth and nastiness of age (see fr. 4 on Tithonus). This theme dominates the impression we gain from quotations, but inferences about his personality or society would be unwise (note the Tyrtaeus-like exhortation in fr. 14).

BIBL. West, *IEG*; Campbell, *Lyric Poetry*; Bowra, *Greek Elegists*.

Mithridates II King of Pontus, c. 250–c. 185 BC.

Although his grandfather Mithridates Ktistes (the 'Founder' – an independent dynast of Pontus) had joined the Northern League with *Nicomedes I of Bithynia against *Antiochus I, Mithridates (Mithridatēs) II – whose long reign is probably to be divided between two homonymous kings ruling c. 250–c. 220 BC and c. 220–c. 185 – formed an alliance with the Seleucids by marrying Laodice, a sister of *Seleucus II. Seleucus may have hoped that this ally would support him in his fraternal war against *Antiochus Hierax, but Mithridates supported Hierax, perhaps hoping to benefit more from the rival who hoped to divide, and therefore weaken, the Seleucid empire. Along with other kings, Mithridates made a contribution to Rhodes after the earthquake in 224.

BIBL. PW xv. 2160; Will, *Hist. pol.* i.

Mithridates VI Eupator King of Pontus, 120–63 BC.

Mithridates (Mithridatēs; the title Eupator means 'Born of a Noble Father') was Rome's arch-enemy who was conquered only after three 'Mithridatic' Wars against him (88–63 BC), and his early adventures proved costly to Hellenism. In the first war with Rome (88), he occupied large areas of the Greek mainland, the islands, and Asia Minor. The goodwill of Greeks who hated Rome, her governors, and her tax-collectors, focused on Mithridates as Rome's eastern challenger and Greece's liberator. This idealism did not last. His Greek general Archelaus (from Amisus or Sinope) was defeated on the mainland in 87 by Sulla, whose consequent treatment of Greece was cruel and costly. Mithridates' straitened circumstances changed him from philhellene to oriental despot in Asia. Greece was obliged to produce money, men, and supplies, and his arbitrary cruelties (like the deportation of Chiots)

Coin portrait of Mithridates VI Eupator, king of Pontus (enlarged).

alienated the population. Revolts led to reprisals, and continuing Greek discontent with economic reforms prompted more punitive measures.

When Archelaus was forced to negotiate with Sulla in 86, Rome replaced Mithridates as the protector of Hellenism. Greece was, however, caught between the two, and suffered exactions and atrocities from both sides. Recovery was limited before the further disturbances of the Roman civil wars, and desolation throughout Greece was widespread.

BIBL. *Roman World* (for his later career), *Sulla; Reinach-Goetz, *Mithridates Eupator König von Pontus* (1895); *CAH* ix; M. I. Rostovtzeff, *SEHHW*, index.

Moschus Poet, c. 150 BC (?).

A rare talent in the poetic doldrums of the second century BC, Moschus (Moskhos) was, according to the *Suda*, a Syracusan, a pupil of *Aristarchus of Samothrace, and a grammarian (he perhaps wrote on the Rhodian dialect); he was also the successor to *Theocritus in pastoral poetry. Five short epigrammatically-flavoured hexameter pieces, three allegedly from the *Bucolica*, show a preoccupation with Eros and a charm founded on simple style and sentimental treatment. Since Moschus did not write the *Lament for *Bion* commonly ascribed to him, his reputation must rest on the *Europa*, a valuable survival in 166 hexameters of the 'epyllion' form presumed to be characteristic of Hellenistic poetry. Zeus in bull disguise abducts Europa; a description of the pictures on her flower-basket insets the parallel story of Zeus and Io. The whole draws heavily on earlier poetry, but is finished with nice touches: the heroine rides decoratively across the sea, gathering up her skirts, accompanied by a rococo cavalcade of dolphins, Nereids, and Tritons – a scene which may copy contemporary art.

BIBL. Gow, *Bucolici Graeci*, and *Bucolic Poets*; H. Bühler, *Hermes Einzelschriften* xiii (1960).

Mummius Roman consul and general, 146 BC.

Lucius Mummius was sent to take charge of the Achaean War in 146 BC, and relieved the temporary commander there, *Metellus Macedonicus. He defeated the Achaean leader *Diaeus, and, with the help of a Pergamene force sent by *Attalus II, attacked and totally sacked Corinth, which ceased to exist for over a century, while her valuable works of art were widely dispersed amid the booty. Rome's unduly severe treatment served as a lesson to the mainland Greeks that similar trouble in Achaea could not be tolerated.

BIBL. *Roman World*; Will, *Hist. pol.* ii. 332 ff.

Myron Sculptor, active *c.* 460–430 BC.

From Eleutherae in Attica, Myron (Murōn) was one of the most famous sculptors of the mid-fifth century BC. He worked primarily or only in bronze. Contemporary with *Polycleitus of Argos, he was said to be his equal and 'fellow-learner' under Ageladas of Argos; however, his system of design and proportions for statues of the human figure was held to be the more complex ('numerosior in arte . . . in symmetria diligentior' (Pliny)). He apparently made great advances in the faithful rendering of nature, concentrating on bodily forms rather than emotions, and was criticized for his archaic treatment of head and pubic hair.

Such remarks in the literary sources are well supported by the famous statue of the discus-thrower (Discobolus), known in several Roman copies, which can be ascribed to him with certainty. It is a masterpiece combining sustained observation of nature with design and *symmetria*; it showed the potential of bronze for free-standing action sculpture. His only other work recognized in Roman copies with any certainty is the group of Athena and Marsyas. Literature records about 17 other commissions for statues of gods, athletes, and animals. His best-known work was his bronze cow on the Acropolis at Athens.

BIBL. P. E. Arias, *Mirone* (1940); Robertson, *History of Greek Art* 339–44; G. Daltrop, *Il gruppo mironiano di Atena e Marsia* (1980); *Roman World* *Pliny the Elder.

Marsyas, by Myron. Roman period copy, in marble, of a bronze of the mid-5th century BC. Vatican Museum.

Discus-thrower (Discobolus) by Myron. Roman period copy, in marble, of a bronze of the mid-5th century BC. Rome, Museo delle Terme.

Myronides Athenian general, 5th century BC.

Myronides (Muronidēs) defeated the Corinthians at Megara with an army of 'the oldest and the youngest' as *strategos* in 458 BC, and the Thebans at Oenophyta in 457/6; he went on to destroy Tanagra, giving Athens control over Boeotia for a time. In 454 he led an unsuccessful expedition into Thessaly. It is conceivable that he is identical with the Myronides who in 479 was chosen to accompany *Cimon and *Xanthippus on an embassy which successfully persuaded the Spartans to continue to resist Persia, and that he was one of the Athenian generals at Plataea. Myronides has been seen as a representative of hoplite interests as against those of the navy. His reputation can be judged from his appearance as the leader of a delegation of dead Athenian statesmen in a fragment of *Eupolis' comedy *The Demes* (412 BC).

BIBL. Thucydides i. 105 ff.; Diodorus Siculus xi. 79–83; *Literary Papyri* (Loeb) 202.

Nabis King of Sparta, 207–192 BC.

After some 15 years of unrest following the exile of *Cleomenes III, Nabis succeeded Machanidas as regent to the king, a minor; Machanidas, as an ally of Rome in the First Macedonian War, had been killed in 207 BC by the Achaeans under *Philopoemen. Nabis killed his charge and declared himself king, carrying out revolutionary reforms such as the redistribution of land and the liberation of slaves, which earned him a large following. When the Achaeans turned to Rome after 200, Nabis agitated against Achaea and was drawn to *Philip V.

Coin portrait of Nabis, king of Sparta (enlarged).

Although he took no overt action in the Second Macedonian War, he none the less shared in Rome's punishment of Macedon. *Flamininus besieged Sparta with *Attalus I of Pergamum, and forced a harsh truce on her, although Nabis was allowed to remain in power. With the apparent support of the Aetolian League, Nabis tried to regain his losses, which prompted Achaean reprisals under Philopoemen. Aetolian troops killed Nabis in 192, but were massacred by the populace as they tried to secure Sparta. After Nabis' death, Sparta lost her independence and was included in the Achaean League.

BIBL. *Roman World*; R. M. Errington, *Philopoemen* (1969); Forrest, *History of Sparta*; Jones, *Sparta*.

Nausiphanes Atomist philosopher, late 4th century BC.

A pupil of *Pyrrhon, Nausiphanes (Nausiphanēs) of

Teos was said to have taught *Epicurus philosophy and introduced him to *Democritus' atomism. Epicurus, unwilling to acknowledge the debt, called Nausiphanes 'a cheat, a jelly-fish, an illiterate, and a prostitute'.

BIBL. Diels and Kranz, *Vorsokratiker* ii. 246–50.

Neaera Corinthian *hetaira*, 4th century BC.

As an ex-*hetaira*, Neaera (Neaira) married the Athenian Stephanus, who passed off her illegitimate children as his own by an earlier marriage and therefore of Athenian citizen birth. This exposed her to virulent attack by *Apollodorus, son of *Pasion (i.e. *Demosthenes, *Or.* lix), a political enemy of Stephanus.

BIBL. U. E. Paoli, *Die Geschichte der Neaira* (1953).

Neanthes of Cyzicus Writer and historian, 3rd (?)–2nd century BC.

Confusion exists between two writers named Neanthes (Neanthēs). Neanthes the rhetorician lived in the third century BC (a pupil of Philiscus of Athens who was honoured at Delphi early in that century); a younger Neanthes was a Pergamene scholar who wrote a long history of the reign of *Attalus I. Literary works of a Neanthes are attributed to one or the other: a history of Greece, works on the annals and legends of Cyzicus, and pinacographical (tabular) biographies of notable philosophers and poets (among them the famous misanthrope *Timon of Athens). This work was sprinkled with fantastic details, and *Polemon of Ilium criticized Neanthes for unreliability. The historical preferences of this author and the close ties between Cyzicus and Pergamum, plus the possibility that the author of the legends of Cyzicus refers to an event of 200 BC, suggest that the younger Neanthes may have been responsible for all the works, although this is not certain.

BIBL. *FGrH* 84 and 171; Hansen, *Attalids* 403–4; Lesky, *Greek Literature*; PW xvi. 2108.

Nearchus of Crete Alexander's admiral, floruit 320s BC.

*Alexander the Great's friend from youth and satrap of Lycia and Pamphylia in 334/3 BC, Nearchus (Nearkhos) is chiefly notable for his voyage from the Hydaspes (Jhelum) to the Tigris in 326–324. This enterprise, plus a description of India, formed the subject of a *Herodotean treatise, which is a major source of Arrian's *Indica*. He subsequently served *Antigonus and *Demetrius Poliorcetes, but his eventual fate is unknown.

BIBL. Pearson, *Lost Histories* 112–49; E. Badian, *YCS* xxiv (1975); *Roman World* *Arrian.

Nectanebon Kings of Egypt, 381–343 BC.

Two 30th dynasty Egyptian kings were called Nectanebon (Nektanēbōn) or Nectanebus by the Greeks (their Egyptian names differ). The first ruled c. 381–363 BC, and successfully weathered *Artaxerxes II's attempts at reconquest. His homonymous grandson, on the other hand, was the last native king of Egypt, being driven out by the Persians in 343.

BIBL. PW xvi. 2234–40; Kienitz, *Geschichte Ägyptens*.

Nicander Didactic poet, mid-2nd century BC (?).

Nicander (Nikandros) says that he lived at the shrine of Apollo at Claros near Colophon. Ancient confusion about his date is explicable by reference to an urge to link him with *Aratus, his eminent predecessor in the versification of science, and the existence of another Nicander of Colophon, a mid-third-century epic poet. The second-century date offered in some sources is much more likely: the Attalus addressed in fragment 104 will then be *Attalus III (138–133 BC). Assertions that Nicander lived in Aetolia are likely to derive from his prose *Aetolica*. Two poems, relished by ancient readers, survive in unappealing entirety: *Theriaca* (*On Poisonous Creatures*, with remedies for their bites) and *Alexipharmaca* (*Antidotes*, on miscellaneous poisons), both rendering into hexameters the early third-century treatise(s) of Apollodorus Iologus. Nicander's own competence in toxicology is non-existent. He preserves some detailed descriptions but regularly garbles his material, labouring chiefly to rarefy his diction with recondite words; a metrically intractable plant may be replaced with another – woe betide anyone fool enough to make practical use of Nicander's advice! Among numerous other compositions lost but for fragments, epics (*Oetaica*, *Thebaica*, etc.) could well be by the other Nicander. Didactic works securely attributable to ours include a versification of the *Hippocratic *Prognostics*, and *Georgics* (substantial fragments on vegetable recipes and flowers survive) which were not apparently an influence on Virgil. *Heteroeoumena*, mythological *Transformations*, provided material but hardly inspiration for the *Metamorphoses* of Ovid.

BIBL. A. S. F. Gow and A. F. Scholfield, *Nicander* (1953; reprinted 1979); *Roman World* *Ovid, *Virgil.

Nicanor of Stagira Ambassador and general, late 4th century BC.

Nicanor (Nikanōr), a pupil and son-in-law of *Aristotle, was sent to Greece by *Alexander the Great in 324 BC to implement the Exiles' Decree (ordering repatriation of most Greek exiles) and other measures. Later he was *Cassander's garrison-commander in Athens (319) and admiral in the Bosporus (318), but a quarrel led to his execution for treason.

BIBL. Berve, *Alexanderreich*, no. 557.

Nicias Athenian leader, died 413 BC.

Nicias (Nikias), son of Niceratus, was remembered in antiquity for his enormous wealth, which included (but was not necessarily based on) a thousand slaves working in the silver mines at Laureum, and for the emphasis on religious observance which led to his downfall. His lavish arrangements for the festival at Delos (probably in 417 BC rather than 426/5) were famous.

In 427 he commanded a force which occupied the Megarian island of Minoa. In the following year he fought against Tanagra in Boeotia. In 425/4 he defeated the Corinthians and occupied the island of Cythera. While *Cleon worked for a military victory over Sparta, Nicias appears to have recognized the effectiveness of diplomacy: in 423 he helped arrange a year's truce with Sparta, which he used to reconquer Mende in Thrace and to persuade *Perdiccas II of Macedon to become an ally of Athens. This nullified the effects of *Brasidas' intervention in Chalcidice, so that both Athens and Sparta were prepared to accept the 50 years' alliance called the 'Peace of Nicias' (421).

The rise of *Alcibiades in the following years forced Nicias to oppose his adventurist schemes (although Alcibiades persuaded him to support him against *Hyperbolus in 417). In 415 Nicias was appointed to command the expedition to Sicily, together with *Lamachus and Alcibiades, its principal advocate. Alcibiades' recall and Lamachus' death left him responsible for a strategy he had not wanted and could not put into effect. Syracuse could not be captured, even with the help of the relief expedition under *Demosthenes (son of Alcisthenes). An eclipse (27 August 413) made Nicias reject Demosthenes' advice to withdraw immediately; the Athenian fleet was destroyed in a battle in the harbour of Syracuse, and the attempt to withdraw overland resulted in the total destruction of the Athenians near the river Assinarus. Nicias was captured and then killed by some Syracusans who had previously hoped for his help in staging an oligarchic *coup* in their city.

BIBL. Davies, *Athenian Families*, no. 10808; A. W. H. Adkins, *GRBS* xvi (1975); Westlake, *Individuals in Thucydides*, chs. 6, 11; P. Green, *Armanda from Athens* (1971).

Nicias, son of Nicomedes Painter, active c. 360–340 BC.

We know of about a dozen paintings by Nicias (Nikias) of Athens, son of Nicomedes: all are lost, but his 'Andromeda', 'Io', and 'Calypso' may be copied in wall-paintings from Pompeii. The sculptor *Praxiteles preferred his marble statues to be coloured by Nicias. He

Andromeda freed by Perseus. Wall-painting from Pompeii, probably after Nicias. Naples, Museo Nazionale.

was especially known for his painting of women, to whose formerly pure white figures he perhaps introduced shading. He invented or experimented with the encaustic technique. He is reported as saying that painters should choose large and whole subjects like cavalry or naval battles, not merely small sections of life, like birds or flowers – the beginnings of a controversy with a great future.

BIBL. Becatti, *Enc. Art. Ant.* v. 476–82; Robertson, *History of Greek Art* 436–9.

Nicobule Alexander historian.

Nicobule (Nikoboulē) is quoted by Athenaeus as the (perhaps pseudonymous) author of a work describing *Alexander the Great's last banquet, and is named by Pliny as an authority on trees. Neither her date nor anything else is known of her.

BIBL. Pearson, *Lost Histories* 61–7; *Roman World* *Athenaeus, *Pliny the Elder.

Nicomachus Philosopher, 4th century BC.

*Aristotle's best-known work on moral philosophy, the *Nicomachean Ethics*, was named after his son Nicomachus (Nikomakhos), and was thought by some ancient authors to have been written by him. Nothing is known of his life. His mother was said to be a concubine called Herpyllis.

BIBL. Diogenes Laertius v.

Nicomedes I King of Bithynia, c. 279–c. 250 BC.

Nicomedes (Nikomēdēs) succeeded to the throne of his father Zipoetes, but struggled with his brother for sole control. He allied himself with Heraclea Pontica and the cities of the Northern League, and temporarily with *Antigonus Gonatas of Macedon, against the Seleucids. To suppress his brother, and to obtain additional allies when Gonatas withdrew, Nicomedes made the fatal error of inviting the Gauls into Asia Minor, and these soon broke loose from his control. After their defeat an uneasy peace was maintained between Bithynia and *Antiochus I.

Coin portrait of Nicomedes I, king of Bithynia (enlarged).

Nicomedes hellenized his kingdom, struck Greek coinage, and founded a capital at Nicomedia c. 260 BC. He was succeeded by his son Ziaelas (father of *Prusias I), despite his own preference for his younger sons, whom, as an anti-Seleucid gesture, he had entrusted to the care of Gonatas and *Ptolemy II.

BIBL. PW xvii. 493 (Nikomedes (3)).

Nicomedes II King of Bithynia, 149–c. 127 BC.

Originally a trusted envoy of his father *Prusias II, Nicomedes' (Nikomēdēs) increasing popularity at home and at Rome (where he had been sent) threatened the old king's throne. When a paternally-contrived test of his loyalty failed before the Senate (he had been required to effect a reduction of the Bithynian indemnity after the peace with *Attalus II of Pergamum in 154 BC), the ambassador who was to slay the prince joined him, and persuaded Attalus to replace his old enemy Prusias with the more docile Nicomedes. The prince was acclaimed king by some Bithynian soldiers, and, when Prusias refused to abdicate, an ineffective Roman embassy did not prevent Attalus and Nicomedes from entering the country. The unpopular king was betrayed by the inhabitants of Nicomedia and killed. Nicomedes later sent troops to aid Rome against the Macedonian pretender *Aristonicus in 131, and received in return the northernmost part of Greater Phrygia, known as Phrygia Epictetus.

BIBL. PW xvii. 494 (Nikomedes (4)).

Nossis Poetess, early 3rd century BC.

Nossis from Locri saw herself as the *Sappho of southern Italy (epigram 11). Lost lyric poetry possibly justified her boast better than the eleven slight epigrams preserved through *Meleager, one a fresh little celebration of love, the rest mostly dedicatory and to do with women.

BIBL. Gow and Page, *Hellenistic Epigrams*; Luck, *MusHelv* xi (1954).

Oenopides Astronomer, mid-5th century BC.

Achievements that may be attributed to Oenopides (Oinopidēs) of Chios with some confidence are (i) the discovery of the obliquity of the ecliptic (perhaps learnt from the Egyptians); (ii) a calculation which set the solar year as $365\frac{22}{59}$ days.

BIBL. Heath, *Greek Mathematics* i. 174–6.

The 'Old Oligarch' 5th century BC.

The 'Old Oligarch' is the title given in the English-speaking world to a short essay on the Athenian constitution which already in antiquity was ascribed to *Xenophon; recent speculation has implausibly suggested it might have been composed by *Cleon. The writer bemoans the lack of respect for the aristocracy at Athens, and explains this as due to the importance of the navy in a maritime empire. The work must date to the period of the *Archidamian War (431–421 BC) if not earlier, and is thus one of the earliest examples of Attic prose.

BIBL. Loeb ed. with Xenophon, vol. vii (1968), 459 ff.; comm. L. Stecchini (1950); M. L. Lang, *CPhil* lxvii (1972).

Olympias Mother of Alexander the Great, died 316 BC.

An Epirote princess who was a devotee of Orphic and Dionysiac cults, Olympias (Olumpias, alias Polyxena, Myrtale, Stratonice) met *Philip II of Macedonia at the Samothracian Mysteries and became his principal wife in 357 BC. Twenty years later Philip's marriage to *Cleopatra (Eurydice) led to Olympias' withdrawal to Epirus, whence she returned only after Philip's murder (336). *Alexander's firm support of his viceroy, *Antipater, kept her away from real power, and in 331 she retired again to Epirus. After Alexander's death

Gold medallion of the Roman period with a portrait of a lady with diadem and veil, perhaps Olympias, the mother of *Alexander the Great. Thessaloniki, Archaeological Museum.

(323) she failed in an attempt to woo the support of *Leonnatus and then *Perdiccas against *Antipater, but on the latter's death (319) joined forces with *Polyperchon, invaded Macedonia, and killed *Philip III Arrhidaeus and *Adea (Eurydice), leaving *Alexander IV as nominal king and herself (at last) in power (317). She celebrated with an orgy of murders, but *Cassander soon trapped her in Pydna (316) and organized her murder by some of her victims' relatives. Her status as Philip's queen and Alexander's mother meant that Macedonian troops were prepared to desert to her and that it was difficult to find assassins prepared to strike her down; but few can have genuinely mourned this singularly unappealing character.

BIBL. Berve, *Alexanderreich,* no. 581; Hammond and Griffith, *Macedonia* ii; Will, *Hist. pol.*

Olympiodorus Athenian leader, floruit *c.* 307–280 BC.
  Frequently holding the office of *strategos,*

Inscribed portrait herm of Olympiodorus of Athens. Oslo, National Museum.

Olympiodorus (Olympiodōros) accomplished much for the democratic cause of Athens. His alliance with the Aetolians in 306 BC enabled *Cassander's attack on Athens to be repulsed, and, later, his co-operation with the Elataeans of Phocis forced Cassander to retreat beyond Thermopylae. He was elected archon in the years following the submission of Athens to *Demetrius Poliorcetes, and was instrumental in fomenting the city's revolt in 287. He led the successful attack on the Macedonian garrison on the Museum Hill which freed the city proper, and, with *Demochares, repulsed a later attack by *Antigonus Gonatas at Eleusis. Pausanias states that Olympiodorus freed the Piraeus from its Macedonian garrison, but the date of this, and indeed the event, is still questioned.

BIBL. T. L. Shear, Jr., *Hesperia* Suppl. xvii; Osborne, *ZPE* xxxv (1979), 181 ff.; Habicht, *Untersuchungen*; Ferguson, *Hellenistic Athens*; *Roman World* *Pausanias.

Olympus Musician, *c.* 700 BC.
  With the name Olympus (Olumpos) tradition associated the transmission to Greece of Phrygian *aulos* music, and developments in music including the composition of certain nomes (e.g. the *harmateios,* taken over by *Stesichorus). But it is obscure what should be credited to which of two discernible figures called Olympus, one a semi-mythical pupil and boy-friend of Marsyas, the other perhaps a historical musician from Phrygia, to whom lyric and elegiac poems were attributed (*Suda*).

BIBL. Pseudo-Plutarch, *On Music,* 1132F ff.; *New Grove Dictionary of Music* (1980) xiii. 589.

Onesicritus Alexander historian, floruit 320s BC.
  A pupil of *Diogenes of Sinope, Onesicritus (Onēsikritos) of Astypalaea in the Cyclades served under *Nearchus on the voyage to the Tigris and later wrote a work entitled *On the Education of *Alexander* (or perhaps *On the Anabasis of Alexander*). Although his treatment of the Far East, especially India, which he described from both autopsy and hearsay, was not innocent of imagination and philosophic 'improvement' and could be criticized for flattery and over-credulity, he was not a totally contemptible authority. The tendency to stress his work's *Xenophontic and/or philosophic (Cynic) character ought not to be accepted without question.

BIBL. Pearson, *Lost Histories* 83–111; T. S. Brown, *Onesicritus* (1949).

Onomacritus Oracle-monger and poet, *c.* 520 BC.
  Editor of Musaeus' oracles, the interpolation of which (exposed by *Lasus) lost him *Hipparchus' favour, Onomacritus (Onomakritos) of Athens was later credited with Orphic *Oracles* and *Rites* (*Teletai*), with an *Orphica* (Cosmogony/Theogony), and with interpolations in the *Odyssey* (xi. 601–4) and perhaps in *Hesiod (*Theogony* 947 ff.). On their expulsion the Peisistratids (see *Hippias) took Onomacritus to Susa, where by careful selection of oracles he encouraged *Xerxes to invade Greece.

BIBL. Herodotus vii. 6; Kinkel, *EGF* 238 ff.; 53 ff.; T. W. Allen, *CQ* xxii (1928).

Onomarchus Phocian general, died 352 BC.
  Succeeding *Philomelus as *strategos autokrator* (354 BC),

Phocis-Locris in central Greece (see *Onomarchus).

Onomarchus (Onomarkhos) successfully repaired Phocian fortunes in the Third Sacred War, acquiring part of Boeotia and defeating *Philip II of Macedon twice in Thessaly (353). But a third encounter in Thessaly ended with his death at the Crocus Field (352). His body was crucified as a gesture against temple-robbers.

BIBL. Parke, *Mercenary Soldiers*; Hammond and Griffith, *Macedonia* ii.

Ophellas Ruler of Cyrene, died 310/309 BC.

Despatched to suppress *Thibron (2) in Cyrene (322 BC), Ophellas became the region's *Ptolemaic governor and seems in due course to have acquired a fairly independent position, despite or because of the disturbances there in 313/12. In 310/309 he crossed the desert to join *Agathocles' attack on Carthage, only to be murdered by his host. A so-called '*Periplous* of Ophellas' (describing West Africa) existed in antiquity.

BIBL. V. Ehrenberg, *Polis und Imperium* (1965), 539–47; PW xviii. 1. 632–5.

Orontes Persian satrap, floruit first half of 4th century BC.

Already satrap of Armenia in 400 BC, Orontes (Orontēs)

shared command of the war against *Evagoras of Cyprus with *Tiribazus, whom he ousted with accusations of collusion with the enemy. Tiribazus' later restoration to favour meant disgrace for Orontes, who disappears until c. 362 when, as satrap of Mysia, he led the 'Satraps' Revolt' and then deserted it. The general supposition that he rebelled again in the 350s may be inaccurate.

BIBL. M. J. Osborne, *BSA* lxvi (1971), *Historia* xxii (1973), and *Grazer Beiträge* iii (1975).

Orsippus Olympic victor, 720 BC (?).

Orsippus (Orsippos) of Megara originated the classical Greek practice of doing athletics in the nude. While running in an Olympic race he found his loin-cloth (then the customary athletic costume) cumbersome, threw it away, and went on to win. Obviously a man of more resource than scruple, he later became a successful general in a boundary-war between Megara and Corinth.

BIBL. Pausanias i. 44; Andrewes, *Greek Tyrants* 44.

Orthagoras Tyrant of Sicyon, c. 650 BC.

Andreas, Orthagoras' father, is said to have visited Delphi as cook to a party of Sicyonian noblemen. The oracle told them that whichever of them first had a son born to him after returning home would become tyrant of Sicyon. This son was Orthagoras, and it was he rather than his father who rose to power by way of a distinguished military career.

BIBL. Diodorus Siculus viii. 24 + *POxy*. 1365; Andrewes, *Greek Tyrants* 57.

'Oxyrhynchus Historian'

A papyrus containing a fragment of a detailed history of Greece (hence also called the *Hellenica Oxyrhynchia*) during 396–395 BC was discovered at Oxyrhynchus in Egypt in 1906. The writer appears to have continued from where *Thucydides leaves off. Various suggestions have been made as to authorship; the present consensus is in favour of *Cratippus (q.v.).

BIBL. I. A. F. Bruce, *Historical Commentary on the Hellenica Oxyrhynchia* (1967).

Paches Athenian general, died 427 BC.

In 428 Paches (Pakhēs) was sent to put down the rebellion of Mytilene (Lesbos): he besieged the city and forced it to surrender in the following year. The story has it that on his return to Athens he was accused of having dishonoured two aristocratic Lesbian ladies, and committed suicide in open court.

BIBL. H. D. Westlake, *Phoenix* xxix (1975).

Paeonius Sculptor, active *c*. 430–410 BC.

Paeonius (Paiōnios) of Mende in Thrace made a fine statue in Parian marble of a winged Nike (Victory) landing on a 30-foot high triangular pillar, which stood near the

Marble statue of Nike (Victory) by Paeonius, from Olympia, *c*. 425/420 BC. Olympia Museum.

front of the temple of Zeus at Olympia and was excavated there in 1875. The inscription on the pillar says it was dedicated by the Messenians and Naupactians as a tithe of the spoils of their enemies (i.e. the Spartans, whom they helped the Athenians to defeat at Pylos in 424 BC) and that Paeonius, its sculptor, also won the commission to make the acroteria of the temple (of Zeus, presumably). This might explain Pausanias' error in attributing to him the sculpture of the temple's east pediment.

BIBL. G. Treu, *Olympia* iii (1892), 182 ff.; Richter, *Sculpture* 186–8; Robertson, *History of Greek Art* 284 ff.; *Roman World* *Pausanias.

Paerisades I and V: see Spartocids

Pammenes Theban general, mid-4th century BC.

Pammenes (Pammenēs) was a notable figure both during the 'Theban hegemony' (371–362 BC) and afterwards (when he supported *Artabazus (son of *Pharnabazus), twice defeating armies loyal to *Artaxerxes III (*c*. 354), and fought against the Phocians in the Third Sacred War of 355–346). The young *Philip II of Macedon stayed at his house as a hostage in the early 360s, an acquaintance renewed at Maronea in 353/2. Tactics attributed to Pammenes and Philip show certain mutual resemblances.

BIBL. Buckler, *Theban Hegemony*; Hammond and Griffith, *Macedonia* ii.

Panaetius (*c*. 185–109 BC) Stoic philosopher.

Panaetius (Panaitios) went to Rome in 144 BC, and was associated with *Scipio Aemilianus and his friends. In 140/39 he accompanied Scipio on an embassy to the eastern Mediterranean, but, though the two men were associated long and closely, there is no proof of philosophical influence on Scipio's policy.

BIBL. Strasburger, *JRS* lv (1965), 44 ff.; A. E. Astin, *Scipio Aemilianus* (1967), 296 ff.   N.H.

Panyassis Epic poet, died *c*. 460/450 BC.

A native of Halicarnassus and uncle or cousin of *Herodotus (?), Panyassis (Panuas(s)is) was the author of a *Heracleia* (which was praised by ancient critics and from which some fragments survive) and an *Ionica* (on the foundation of the Ionian cities).

BIBL. Lesky, *Greek Literature*; Huxley, *Epic Poetry*; V. J. Matthews, *Panyassis of Halikarnassos* (1974).

Parmenides Eleatic philosopher, born 515/510 BC.

Little is known of the life of Parmenides (Parmenidēs), but large parts of his work survive. He was the first Greek philosopher to produce rigorous and sustained arguments. With their conclusions radically opposed to 'common sense', his arguments greatly influenced later philosophers. The systems of *Empedocles, *Anaxagoras, and *Democritus were all partly devised to evade his conclusions, and *Plato respected him highly.

His work was a poem in hexameters. His extreme terseness makes the arguments hard to follow. The poem begins with an allegorical introduction, in which the author is led in a chariot from night to day, where a goddess welcomes him, and promises to tell him of 'well-rounded truth', and then of mere mortal opinions, 'in which is no true belief'. This takes up the rest of the work.

He (she?) first argues that 'It is', by rejecting the alternatives 'It is not' and the muddled popular view that is a confusion of the other two. He then proves that 'it' is without birth or destruction, single, continuous, motionless, and limited 'like a ball'. As these arguments are apparently applicable to *any* subject, it follows that the universe has these characteristics, and that diversity and change are an illusion.

There follows an account of 'mortal opinions', which explains the origins and nature of the familiar world, and is clearly inconsistent with the earlier part of the poem. It was probably intended to show that Parmenides was as good at natural science as anyone, even though it was all wrong.

BIBL. L. Taran, *Parmenides* (1965); Guthrie, *Greek Philosophy* ii.

Parmenion Macedonian general, died 330 BC.

*Philip II's finest general and joint commander of his invasion of Asia Minor (336 BC), Parmenion (Parmeniōn) became *Alexander the Great's second-in-command, fought at Granicus, Issus, and Gaugamela (generally on the defensive wing), and carried out independent operations. The tradition records many cases of Alexander's refusal to accept advice from Parmenion, and Philip's old general may have been unsympathetic to the style and ambitions of Philip's son. But he was left at Ecbatana in 331/30 to guard the royal treasure, which hardly suggests manifest unreliability, and his hasty murder after the execution of his son *Philotas says more about the dubiety of Philotas' guilt than about Parmenion's involvement in conspiracy.

BIBL. Berve, *Alexanderreich*, no. 606; Hammond and Griffith, *Macedonia* ii.

Parrhasius Painter, active *c.* 430–390 BC.

Son and pupil of Euenor of Ephesus, Parrhasius (Parrhasios) was the great contemporary and rival of *Zeuxis. Works of his are recorded on Rhodes, but he perhaps worked mainly at Athens. Some later sources call him an Athenian. He was apparently very arrogant, claiming descent from Apollo and calling himself the lord of art ('princeps artis'). He dressed extravagantly and nicknamed himself 'luxurious' (*habrodiaitos*). We know of over 20 paintings by him, all lost, many of which seem to have been of single figures; the majority were mythological, but there were also priests, hoplites, a naval captain, and a Thracian nurse with an infant. His Hermes was thought to be a self-portrait. He also painted small erotic pictures 'to refresh himself'; we hear of one, later in the possession of the Emperor Tiberius, of Meleager having sexual intercourse with Atalanta – a theme, hitherto confined to vase-painting, later popular at Pompeii and elsewhere. He drew designs for the famous metal-chaser Mys, and left master drawings on panel or parchment for later artists to study – a new artistic self-consciousness.

Parrhasius was the acknowledged master of line, and was contrasted with Zeuxis, the early master of chiaroscuro. A very reliable source describes as Parrhasius' achievement the subtle use of contour line to express and suggest the hidden three-dimensional volume of his figures. The precise description also well characterizes the masterful drawing (on a white background) on a certain class of contemporary Athenian

A dead soldier seated at his tomb: scene on a white grave-lekythos (oil bottle) of 'Group R', probably reflecting the style of Parrhasius. Athens, National Museum.

funerary vases (lekythoi of 'Group R') and they probably reflect something of Parrhasian style. His **Theseus was said to be fed not on meat but roses, and his style was no doubt often rather willowy and effeminate, as is the drawing of one major contemporary Athenian red figure vase-painting workshop (that of the Eretria and Meidias painters), which cultivated a luxurious and often affected style, no doubt influenced by major painters of the day.

BIBL. Pliny, *Natural History* xxxv. 67; Robertson, *History of Greek Art* 411 ff; *Roman World* *Tiberius.

Pasion (*c.* 430–370/69 BC) Athenian banker.

A manumitted slave, Pasion (Pasiōn) ran Athens' best-documented bank, having received control before 394 BC from its (and his) erstwhile owners. By 386 notable civic benefactions had earned citizenship for him and his descendants (notably his son *Apollodorus). Between 372/1 and his death he leased his interest in the bank to another ex-slave, Phormion, who retained control until 362. Pasion's clients and associates included *Agyrrius, *Timotheus (2), and *Demosthenes' father, and many non-Athenians (his credit being good throughout Greece and beyond).

BIBL. Kirchner, *PA*, no. 11672; Davies, *Athenian*

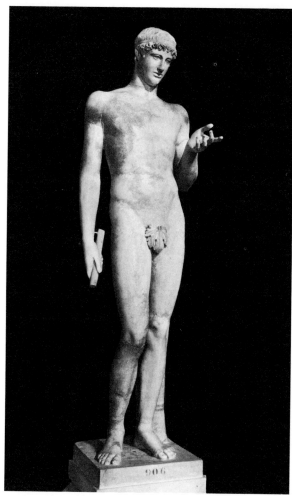

Marble statue of a classical athlete, signed by Stephanus, a pupil of Pasiteles. Mid-1st century BC. Rome, Villa Albani.

against *Demetrius Poliorcetes in 286. When Antiochus was entrusted with the Upper Satrapies c. 294/3, Patrocles served as the governor of the Caspian and Bactrian areas. Probably c. 285 he undertook a naval expedition of two voyages in the Caspian Sea for reconnaissance and exploration. His book, the *Periplous* (*Circumnavigation*), was the standard authority for this region, although, curiously, Patrocles thought that the Caspian Sea communicated with the Ocean via India. He also included much accurate information about India, which was probably taken from merchants rather than from personal knowledge. In about 279 Antiochus entrusted him with the job of keeping Bithynia pro-Seleucid, but his lieutenant was defeated there by the father of *Nicomedes I.

BIBL. *FGrH* 712; Tarn, *Greeks in Bactria. . . .*; PW xviii. 4. 2263 ff. (Patrokles (5)).

St Paul 'Apostle of the Gentiles', died c. AD 64.

The main sources are the authentic letters. Acts contains apologetic and legendary elements. The sources mostly agree on the broad historical outline, but differ on significant details, notably Paul's relations with the Jerusalem Church leaders and attitude to the Jewish law. Paul was at first a zealous Jewish opponent of Christianity, then a convert to it (c. AD 34) as a result of visionary experience (1 Cor. 15 : 8). After travels to Arabia and Jerusalem, Paul worked with the Hellenistic Christians in Antioch, preaching in Syria and Cilicia. His religion of salvation, free of the ritual demands of the Jewish law, made headway in the Hellenistic world, especially amongst those already attracted by Jewish monotheism and morality. But controversy over his Gentile mission continued for years after the Apostolic council in Jerusalem (c. AD 48), about which our sources differ. By 51 he had established congregations in Asia Minor and in Greece. But some thought he gave too much emphasis to moral norms, others too little. In letters to Corinth, Galatia, and Rome (c. 54–6) he contests various opposing views, using Jewish and Hellenistic ideas to new ends in developing Christian doctrines. He planned to

The theatre at Ephesus, built in the first half of the 3rd century BC; scene of the riot of the silversmiths in opposition to St Paul (Acts 19).

Families 427 ff.; R. Bogaert, *Banques et Banquiers dans les Cités grecques* (1968).

Pasiteles Sculptor, active c. 90–50 BC.

A Greek from southern Italy, Pasiteles (Pasitelēs) was a contemporary of Pompey and one of the very few artists to achieve prominence in Italy under the Romans. He received Roman citizenship in 89 BC and worked in Rome, where he made an ivory statue of Jupiter for the temple built by *Metellus Macedonicus. He wrote a book in five volumes on famous works of art of the past ('nobilia opera'). None of his works is preserved, but a classicizing statue of an athlete in Rome, pretending to be a work of the early fifth century BC, is signed by his pupil Stephanus.

BIBL. M. Borda, *La Scuola di Pasiteles* (1953); Wedeking, *Enc. Art. Ant.* v. 984–5; *Roman World* *Pompey.

Patrocles (c. 230 (?)–c. 275 BC) Seleucid general.

Patrocles (Patroklēs) served in various capacities in a long career as *strategus* to *Seleucus I and *Antiochus I. He was left by Seleucus in 312 BC as the commander in Babylon, and he counselled Seleucus in the final battle take financial aid from Greece to Jerusalem, then travel to Rome and Spain. But he was arrested and imprisoned, not for the first time, soon after arrival in Judaea. Acts says Festus sent him to Rome on appeal (c. 60–2). He probably died there as a martyr (1 Clem. 5) under Nero (c. 64).

BIBL. G. Bornkamm, *Paul* (1971); *Roman World* *Festus, *Nero, St *Paul.   D.M.

Paullus, Lucius Aemilius Roman consul, and general in Greece 168–167 BC.

Elected to a second consulship in 168 BC, Lucius Aemilius Paullus reversed the disappointing record of previous Roman generals in the war against *Perseus of Macedon (q.v.). Restoring discipline to the army in Macedonia, he proceeded within weeks to inflict the final defeat on Perseus at Pydna, helped by allied Pergamene troops under the command of *Attalus (later II). Paullus was not immune to the attractions of Greek culture. As proconsul in 167 he toured the sights of Greece and had Perseus' library shipped to Italy. At Delphi he used the victory monument commissioned by Perseus to carry his own equestrian statue. It is claimed that Paullus disagreed with the harsher aspects of Rome's policy towards Greece, such as the enslavement of the Epirotes and the demand for prominent Greek hostages in Italy. This favourable historical tradition about him may partly reflect the bias of *Polybius, who was closely attached to his family.

Artist's reconstruction of the equestrian statue set up at Delphi by Lucius Aemilius Paullus to commemorate his victory over Perseus at Pydna in 168 BC.

Paullus returned to Italy to celebrate a magnificent triumph, in which Perseus was led in chains.

BIBL. *Roman World*; Plutarch, *Life of Aemilius Paullus*; Walbank, *HCP* iii.

Pausanias (1) Spartan regent, died c. 467/6 BC.

Pausanias, son of Cleombrotus, was a member of the Spartan royal family of the Agiads. After *Leonidas' death at Thermopylae (480 BC), he became regent on behalf of his cousin, Leonidas' son Pleistarchus (died 458). As regent, he commanded the Greek land forces at the battle of Plataea in 479, where – despite considerable confusion and the attempt by some of the Greek contingents to desert – the Spartans successfully resisted the Persian attack. *Mardonius' death meant the end of the Persian threat to Greece.

Portrait herm possibly of the Spartan regent Pausanias. Rome, Capitoline Museum.

Pausanias dedicated a bronze serpent-column bearing his name at Delphi to commemorate the victory. The Spartans had his name erased and replaced by those of the 31 Greek states that had fought in the battle. Nor could they tolerate Pausanias' individualistic behaviour when, as commander of the combined Greek fleet, he captured Byzantium from the Persians in 478: he was replaced by another Spartan, Dorieus, recalled, and accused of having been in contact by letter with *Xerxes. He was acquitted, however, and returned on his own initiative to Byzantium, where he ruled until *Cimon expelled him sometime between 475 and 470. While in exile at Colonae, he was ordered to return to Sparta; here he was accused of having tried to negotiate a peace agreement through a Persian general, *Artabazus, together with *Themistocles, and then of instigating the helots to rebel. He fled to the temple of Athena Chalcioecus (Athena of the Bronze House) for sanctuary: unwilling to commit sacrilege, the Spartan authorities starved him to death by bricking up the temple door, apparently on the advice of his mother (c. 467/6). His career is one of many examples of the Spartans' inability to resolve the conflict between their leaders' desire for honour and the imperative that all citizens be *homoioi*, equals.

BIBL. Forrest, *History of Sparta*, ch. 9; P. J. Rhodes, *Historia* xix (1970).

Pausanius (2) Agiad king of Sparta, c. 445/4–427/6 and 408/7–394 BC.

Grandson of *Pausanias (1), Pausanias first reigned as king during the exile of his father *Pleistoanax, under the guardianship of his uncle Cleomenes. After his father's death, Pausanias led the Spartan blockade of Athens (405 BC). In 403, in opposition to *Lysander, he withdrew Spartan support from the regime of the 'Thirty Tyrants', which led to the restoration of democracy at Athens. In 394 Pausanias failed to prevent the death of Lysander at the battle of Haliartus in Boeotia: he was condemned to death, and fled into exile at Tegea.

BIBL. Diodorus Siculus xiii–xiv; Xenophon, *Hellenica* ii–iii.

Pausanias (3) Murderer of Philip II, died 336 BC.

It is certain that Pausanias killed *Philip II of Macedonia during the celebrations surrounding the marriage of Princess *Cleopatra (336 BC), but his motive for so doing remains controversial. One ancient version involved a squalid tale of sexual assault and revenge (not without parallels among Greek 'political' murders); another suspected the complicity of the children of Aeropus (two of whom were executed). Perhaps predictably suspicion has also occasionally been thrown on *Olympias and/or *Alexander (the Great). Pausanias did not survive long enough to have his version elicited from him, and the matter must remain obscure.

BIBL. E. Badian, *Phoenix* xvii (1963); A. B. Bosworth, *CQ* n.s. xxi (1971); Hammond and Griffith, *Macedonia* 675 ff.

Peisander Athenian politician, late 5th century BC.

As a councillor in 415 BC, Peisander (Peisandros) was a member of the commission which investigated the affair of the *Hermocopids. In 411 he was leader of the pro-Spartan wing of the oligarchic regime of the Four Hundred; opposed by *Theramenes, he fled to the Spartans at Decelea. *Plato Comicus named a play after him.

BIBL. Thucydides viii. 65 ff., 98; Andocides, *On the Mysteries* 27.

Peisistratus Tyrant of Athens, c. 560–527 BC.

A relative of *Solon, Peisistratus (Peisistratos) first became prominent as a general in the war with Megara and leader of the Hillmen (Hyperakrioi) party. He made himself tyrant by pretending to have been the victim of an assassination attempt, as a result of which he was allowed to keep a bodyguard, which he used to seize the Acropolis. He was soon driven out, returned briefly, thanks to a reconciliation with *Megacles, but then went into exile for a longer period. This time he returned with an army, won a battle at Pallene, and remained in power from then until his death in 527. He was on the whole a humane ruler and a patron of the arts, and carried out many public works such as the building of the Enneakrounos ('Nine-spouted') fountain-house. He levied a ten per cent tax on agricultural produce, but helped the poorer farmers with loans. One story tells how, while travelling incognito in the Attic countryside, he came upon a farmer working a very poor and stony field, and got into conversation with him. The farmer grumbled lengthily about the hardships of his life, and then said:

'And even of my backache Peisistratus must have one-tenth!' Peisistratus laughed and remitted the man's taxes.

BIBL. Herodotus i. 59–64; Aristotelean *Constitution of Athens* 13–17; Forrest, *Greek Democracy*, ch. 7; Andrewes, *Greek Tyrants*, ch. ix.

Pelopidas Theban general, died 364 BC.

One of the counter-revolutionaries of 379/8 BC (his part is perhaps overstated in the tradition), Pelopidas was elected Boeotarch after the liberation of Thebes from the pro-Spartan junta whose *coup* in 382 had driven him into exile. He led the Sacred Band victoriously at Tegyra (375) and at Leuctra (371) he was outshone by *Epaminondas and, except for the Peloponnesian campaign of 370/69, the two operated separately (though their friendship was much stressed in later literature). Pelopidas' special interest was northern Greece, where he intervened against Pherae (on one occasion being imprisoned by *Alexander of Pherae) and checked Macedonian aspirations, and it was in Thessaly that he died fighting against Alexander (at Cynoscephalae in 364), after which the Thessalians erected a monument to him at Delphi. In 367 he had persuaded *Artaxerxes II to issue a pro-Theban rescript, but its enforcement in Greece proved difficult. The tendency to belittle Pelopidas by comparison with Epaminondas is unfair to the former and over-generous to the latter.

BIBL. Plutarch, *Pelopidas*; Buckler, *Theban Hegemony*.

Perdiccas II King of Macedon, c. 450/440–413 BC.

Perdiccas (Perdikkas) was the son of *Alexander I; he fought a series of civil wars against his brothers Alcetas and Philip during the 440s and 430s BC. Athens' support for his brother Philip led him to support the rebellion of Potidaea before he made his peace with Athens in 431. He repulsed an invasion by the Thracian king *Sitalces in 429, and supported *Brasidas in 424; another treaty with Athens followed in 423/2.

BIBL. Hammond and Griffith, *Macedonia* ii. 115–36; J. W. Cole, *Phoenix* xxviii (1974); R. J. Hoffman, *GRBS* xvi (1975).

Perdiccas III King of Macedon, 368–359 BC.

Shortly after the removal of *Ptolemy Alorites (q.v.), Perdiccas (Perdikkas) lost Methone and Pydna to *Timotheus (2) and had to help him against Amphipolis. An attempt to break away brought military defeat, but Perdiccas none the less sent secret help to the Amphipolitans. After 361 BC Macedonia benefited from the financial expertise of *Callistratus, whom Perdiccas received during his exile from Athens, but Perdiccas' death fighting the Illyrians (perhaps the result of over-ambitious aggression) threw the kingdom into turmoil.

BIBL. Hammond and Griffith, *Macedonia* ii.

Perdiccas Macedonian general and regent, died 321/320 BC.

Perdiccas (Perdikkas) was the son of Orontes, a chieftain in Orestis on the western borders of Macedon. He participated in *Alexander the Great's campaigns as a captain, joined the élite royal bodyguard, and served as cavalry commander. After the death of *Hephaestion in 324, Perdiccas succeeded him as chiliarch. When Alexander died in 323, he gave his seal-ring to Perdiccas, who took over the administration of the Asian empire on behalf of Alexander's half-brother (*Philip Arrhidaeus) and his posthumous son (*Alexander IV). He suppressed a rebellion by Greek settlers in Bactria, and campaigned successfully in Cappadocia; but his increasing authority was resented by the other generals – *Antigonus, *Craterus, *Lysimachus, and *Antipater (whose daughter Nicaea he repudiated as his wife in favour of *Cleopatra, daughter of the queen-mother *Olympias). While *Eumenes of Cardia successfully resisted the other Macedonian generals in Asia Minor, Perdiccas invaded Egypt to eliminate *Ptolemy (I); here he was assassinated by his army officers.

BIBL. R. M. Errington, *JHS* xc (1970); Will, *Hist. pol.* i.

Periander Tyrant of Corinth, *c.* 627–585 BC.

The son and successor of *Cypselus, Periander (Periandros) was one of the most famous of the early Greek tyrants, but also allegedly one of the most bloodthirsty. He killed his wife, and avenged the death of his son in Corcyra by sending 300 Corcyrean boys to Lydia to be made into eunuchs (they escaped on the way).

'Portrait' herm of Periander, inscribed with his most famous saying: 'Practice is everything'. Vatican Museum.

However, Corinth prospered under his rule – he was apparently responsible for building the Diolkos by which ships could be carried across the Isthmus. He also had a reputation as a wise man, and appeared in some lists of the *Seven Sages.

BIBL. Herodotus iii. 48–53, v. 92; Diogenes Laertius i. 94 ff.; Andrewes, *Greek Tyrants* 50–3.

Pericles Athenian statesman, died 429 BC.

Pericles (Periklēs), son of *Xanthippus, was effectively the ruler of Athens at the peak of her power in the 440s and 430s BC. He was directly responsible for the rebuilding of the Parthenon and of other temples after the end of the war with Persia in 449, and, together with his second wife *Aspasia, he was at the centre of the Athenian intellectual life of his time. It is not surprising that his period of pre-eminence should be known as the 'Periclean Age': his conquests no less than his building programme made Athens an 'example to all Greece', as Pericles put it in the famous funeral speech of 431/30 (*Thucydides ii. 41).

Herm bearing the name 'Pericles', from Tivoli. Roman copy of a contemporary Greek original. London, British Museum.

He appears first in 472, when he provided the chorus for *Aeschylus' trilogy (including the *Persians*). In 463, as a young man, he tried to prosecute *Cimon for receiving bribes from *Alexander I not to invade Macedonia; the feud against the Cimonids was hereditary (Cimon's father *Miltiades had been prosecuted by Xanthippus in 489). Pericles' opposition to Cimon aligned him with *Ephialtes and the other opponents of the Areopagus; the reform of 457, giving all hoplites access to the archonship and other offices, was ascribed to him. But he was by no means the only prominent leader in this period: responsibility for the costly expansionism of the next ten years lay with the generals Leocrates, *Myronides, and *Tolmides, who all appear to have been Pericles' seniors (Leocrates had already been a *strategos* at Plataea) and by no means merely his supporters. One by one these rival leaders were discredited or died. Although Pericles was present at Athenian defeats like Tanagra (457), he was not associated with the disaster of the Egyptian expedition in support of *Inarus during 454; he appears to have commanded a flotilla in the Corinthian gulf in that year. The atmosphere of crisis following that disaster is probably the context of his personal proposal to recall Cimon. It is not clear what Pericles' role was in the negotiations which led to the so-called 'Peace of *Callias' (son of Hipponicus (1)) with Persia; there is some evidence that in 448 he proposed a general peace congress for all the states which had fought Persia. Peace led to the reconstruction of Athenian shrines (largely at the allies' expense), under Pericles' supervision.

The following years saw the elimination of the rival leaders Tolmides, killed at Coronea in 447, and *Thucydides, son of Melesias, ostracized in 443. In 446 Pericles distinguished himself by harshly suppressing a revolt in Euboea, and by preventing the devastation of Attica by the Spartans through persuasion or bribery; a 30 years' peace gave Athens a free hand to concentrate on putting down further revolts among her allies (Samos–see *Melissus–and Byzantium, 441–439).

It has been suggested that Pericles supported a consistent policy of westward expansion, leaving the Greek mainland to Sparta. But the alliances with Sicilian cities such as Segesta, and especially the support given to Sybaris in 447, leading to the new foundation of Thurii in 444, and the Athenian alliance with Corcyra (433), one of the immediate causes of the Peloponnesian War, need not be seen as part of such a strategy. It has often been assumed that Pericles wanted war with Sparta, although few nowadays would explain this in terms of the need to eliminate Corinth from western export markets, or to restore the moral fibre of the citizenry; he may merely have seen that Sparta would not tolerate Athenian imperialism for ever. But it does seem that in the late 430s there was increasing resentment on the part of younger potential leaders like *Cleon that Pericles' predominance prevented them coming to the fore. Several of Pericles' associates, including Aspasia and *Pheidias, were prosecuted; one story said that *Alcibiades advised him to go to war in order to avoid an investigation by his opponents into his malversation of public funds.

Pericles believed that Athens would achieve its aims in a war with Sparta by simply avoiding defeat and demonstrating that Sparta did not have the power to destroy Athenian hegemony over the Aegean. Consequently he saw to it that adequate funds for the navy were prepared long before the war actually began in 431 (see *Callias, son of Calliades); and he avoided any major confrontation with the enemy by land. This led to increasing unpopularity, and, when the plague then struck Athens (in 430), Pericles was removed from office; although re-elected the following year, he died of the plague soon after.

BIBL. Davies, *Athenian Families*, no. 11811; A. R. Burn, *Pericles and Athens* (1948); C. M. Bowra, *The Periclean Age* (1971); A. Andrewes, *JHS* xcviii (1978); A. J. Holladay, *Historia* xxvii (1978).

Persaeus Stoic philosopher, c. 260 BC.

Persaeus (Persaios) was a pupil, and in some accounts a slave, of *Zeno of Citium. When *Antigonus Gonatas invited Zeno to visit him, Zeno, excusing himself because of great age, sent Persaeus instead, and assured Antigonus that he would be no less help than himself in guiding him to happiness. He acquired political influence, and was put in command of Corinth, which he failed to defend against an attack by *Aratus of Sicyon.

BIBL. Long, *Hellenistic Philosophy*; Rist, *Stoic Philosophy*.

Perseus King of Macedon, 179–168 BC.

The elder son of *Philip V, Perseus attained the throne despite insinuations of illegitimacy brought by the supporters of his younger brother Demetrius, who wished the latter's pro-Roman policy to prevail over the imperialist tendencies shared by Perseus and his father. He intrigued against Demetrius, whom Philip proceeded to have murdered in 181 BC. Succeeding in 179, Perseus ameliorated Macedon's position at home and abroad. He renewed an old alliance with Rome, secured rival factions in Macedon, and repaired foreign relations: c. 177 he married Laodice, the daughter of Seleucus IV, who was escorted to her bridegroom by an impressive Rhodian armada, and he married his half-sister Apama (a daughter of Philip V) to *Prusias II of Bithynia. His policy of kindness won him friends in Greece, where he now appeared preferable to Rome. He consulted the oracle at Delphi in 174 in the presence of his army.

Coin portrait of Perseus, king of Macedon (enlarged).

*Eumenes II of Pergamum feared the growing power of Perseus, which he complained about in an embassy to Rome in 172. Although the warning was heard, no pretext for Roman intervention was afforded until Eumenes was ambushed near Delphi and nearly killed on his way home. Perseus was accused of the crime against Rome's friend, and war was declared in 171. Although outnumbered by Rome and her allies, Perseus managed to protract the war until L. Aemilius *Paullus was given the command. Aided by Pergamene troops, he totally defeated Perseus at Pydna in 168. Perseus was taken to Rome to march in Paullus' triumph, and Rome thought herself rid of the problem of Macedon when he died shortly afterwards in a Roman jail (but see *Andriscus).

BIBL. P. Meloni, *Perseo e la Fine della Monarchia macedone* (1953); Walbank, *Philip V*; Will, *Hist. pol.* ii; *Roman World*.

Peucestas Macedonian general and satrap, died after 317/16 BC.

After saving *Alexander the Great's life at the city of the Malloi (326/5 BC), Peucestas (Peukestas) became satrap of Persis and a Bodyguard. In furtherance of the orientalizing policy, he took to wearing Iranian clothes and learned Persian, and in 323 he collected 20,000 Iranian troops for incorporation in the Macedonian army. After Alexander's death he retained Persis, and in the war between *Antigonus and *Eumenes of Cardia initially supported the latter. His desertion at Gabiene (317/16) sealed Eumenes' fate, but his only reward was removal from his satrapy and disappearance into obscurity.

BIBL. Berve, *Alexanderreich*, no. 634; Will, *Hist. pol.*

Phaedo Philosopher, 5th century BC.

An Elean of high birth and great beauty, Phaedo (Phaidōn) was taken as a slave to Athens, and forced into prostitution. He was released by ransom and became a pupil of *Socrates. In *Plato's *Phaedo* it is he who recounts the last hours of Socrates' life. He later returned to Elis and founded a school of philosophy. He wrote several Socratic dialogues, of which nothing survives but titles.

BIBL. Plato, *Phaedo*.

Phaedrus of Sphettus Athenian leader, floruit *c.* 300–*c.* 270 BC.

A son of Thymochares of the Attic deme of Sphettus and a member of a well-known Athenian family, Phaedrus (Phaidros) adopted a politically 'moderate' stance in public affairs. Both in 296/5 BC during the tyranny of *Lachares and during the Macedonian occupation after 294, he held various offices in the *strategia*: hoplite general, mercenary commander, general for home defence, and general for the preparation of military machines and stores. Phaedrus also went as an ambassador to *Ptolemy I. His complex role in Athens' revolt from *Demetrius Poliorcetes in 287, which had been considered pro-Macedonian, has been clarified in a decree for his brother *Callias (of Sphettus – q.v.), a supporter of the democratic cause. The brothers collaborated in helping Athens: both helped to gather the harvest of 287 in preparation for the expected siege. After the revolt Phaedrus may well have urged caution, if not accommodation, towards Demetrius, and he was perhaps involved (along with Callias) in the peace negotiations between Demetrius and Sostratus, the representative of Ptolemy I. During the following years of independence, Phaedrus ceased to be active in political affairs, which perhaps reflects an incomplete agreement with the democratic government, although he still supported public causes, and sacred and athletic occasions.

BIBL. *IG* ii (2nd ed.) 682; Habicht, *Untersuchungen*; T. L. Shear, Jr., *Hesperia*, Suppl. xvii; Osborne, *ZPE* xxxv (1979), 181 ff.

Phalaecus Phocian general, died *c.* 342 BC.

Strategos autokrator from 351 BC, Phalaecus (Phalaikos) was deposed in 347, regained power in 346, and refused Athenian and Spartan assistance in holding Thermopylae against the Thessalians and Macedonians. In summer 346 he secured a safe-conduct for his army and let the Macedonians enter central Greece to crush Phocis and end the Sacred War. Thereafter he fought as a mercenary in Italy and Crete, where he was killed.

BIBL. Hammond and Griffith, *Macedonia* ii; Parke, *Mercenary Soldiers*.

Phalaris Tyrant of Acragas, *c.* 550 BC.

Phalaris is said to have become tyrant by way of holding high office at Acragas (Agrigento). He is chiefly renowned for his cruelty and its punishment: he allegedly roasted his enemies in a hollow bronze bull, and finally

suffered this fate himself. The seventeenth-century scholar Bentley showed that his supposed letters were forgeries.

BIBL. Pindar, *Pythian Odes* i. 95–8; Aristotle, *Politics* 1310b; Andrewes, *Greek Tyrants* 129.

Phanocles Poet, 3rd century BC (?).

Nothing is known of Phanocles (Phanoklēs), though his '*Hesiodic' catalogue, in easy elegiacs, of the paederastic amours of gods and heroes (*The Loves, or Beautiful Boys*), shows similarities with *Hermesianax. The aetiological colour and perverse angle on myth in a fragment narrating the murder of Orpheus for homosexuality also suggest the high Hellenistic period.

BIBL. Powell, *Coll.Alex.*

Phanodemus Historian, 4th century BC.

Phanodemus (Phanodēmos) wrote a history of Athens (*Atthis*) in at least nine volumes, as well as a history of the island of Icus in the Sporades. Surviving inscriptions show that he was a member of the Athenian Council in 343/2 BC, when he was awarded an honorific wreath. Between 332 and 328 he was connected with the restoration of the cult of Amphiaraus, as a political supporter of *Lycurgus.

BIBL. *IG* ii (2nd ed.) 223; vii. 4252–4; *FGrH* iiiB, no. 325; Jacoby, *Atthis*.

Pharax Spartan general, died after 370/69 BC.

A junior officer at Aegospotami (405 BC, the last battle of the Peloponnesian War) and navarch (admiral) in 398/7 (operating in the eastern Aegean), Pharax was then sent to Sicily to help *Dionysius I. He last appears as ambassador to Athens in 370/69. His homonymous grandson also served the cause of Sicilian tyranny in the days of *Dionysius II.

BIBL. D. J. Mosley, *Historia* xii (1963); Stroheker, *Dionysius I.*

Pharnabazus Persian commander, died *c.* 370 BC.

Pharnabazus (Pharnabazos) was hereditary satrap of Phrygia. His rivalry with the Lydian satrap *Tissaphernes was one reason for the alternation between Persian support for and hostility towards Sparta during the last phase of the Peloponnesian War. In 409 BC Pharnabazus made an agreement with Athens at *Alcibiades' behest, but the arrival of *Cyrus the Younger in Ionia in 408 made this policy inoperative. Between 400 and 395, Spartan armies ravaged his satrapy; *Xenophon describes a famous interview in which he complained about this to *Agesilaus. The war with Sparta ended in 394 with the victory by a Persian fleet commanded by *Conon at Cnidos. In 392 Pharnabazus joined the court at Susa, where he married a daughter of *Artaxerxes II. In *c.* 388–386 and again in 373, he attempted unsuccessfully to put down a rebellion in Egypt with the support of the Athenian mercenary commander *Iphicrates. He was father of *Artabazus.

BIBL. Xenophon, *Hellenica* iv. i. 29; Olmstead, *Persian Empire*, chs. 26–8.

Pharnaces I King of Pontus, *c.* 185–*c.* 159/156 BC.

Succeeding to the throne in *c.* 185 BC, Pharnaces' (Pharnakēs) ambitions to extend his kingdom soon

Coin portrait of Pharnaces I, king of Pontus (enlarged).

involved him in a war with most of the other dynasts in Asia Minor (183). When he seized the Greek city of Sinope on the Black Sea, and invaded Cappadocia, the complaints of *Eumenes II, *Ariarathes IV, and Rhodes (whose commercial interests were threatened) were ignored by Rome. Pharnaces' attacks moved westwards through Paphlagonia to Tieum, which Eumenes had taken from *Prusias I of Bithynia. Pergamum, Cappadocia, and Bithynia formed an alliance against Pontus and various Gallic chiefs. Roman embassies did not prevent Pharnaces from ravaging parts of Galatia which were still loyal to Eumenes, nor from again attacking Cappadocia; the Romans eventually departed without arranging a truce. Since Rhodes would not agree to a blockade of the Hellespont, the allies resorted to further land campaigns and finally forced peace on Pharnaces in 179. The numerous rulers who signed the treaty reveal the extent of the struggle throughout Asia. The allies demanded extensive reparations of territory and money from Pharnaces, but he kept Sinope as his capital and founded Pharnaceia on the coast further east.

BIBL. PW xix. 1849; Will, *Hist. pol.* ii; Hansen, *Attalids* 101 ff.

Phayllus Phocian general, died 351 BC.

Phayllus (Phaüllos) succeeded *Onomarchus on the latter's death at the battle of the Crocus Field, doubled his mercenaries' pay and, with Athenian and Spartan help, prevented *Philip II of Macedon from penetrating south of Thermopylae (352 BC). But his subsequent career was less successful (he captured Locrian Naryx but suffered several reverses in Boeotia), and he soon died of illness.

BIBL. Berve, *Tyrannis* 297.

Pheidias Sculptor, active *c.* 450–430 BC.

The son of Charmides of Athens, Pheidias was the most famous sculptor of antiquity, and one of his works, the Zeus at Olympia, was one of the seven wonders of the ancient world. Apparently starting his career as a painter, he seems to have worked mainly in bronze, but was especially noted for his great chryselephantine cult-statues; statues in marble are also recorded. His recorded works were all in mainland Greece, except his Amazon at Ephesus (see *Polycleitus).

Among his earlier works were probably two large Athenian state commissions, both paid for from the spoils of Marathon: one at Delphi for a bronze group of Athena, Apollo, the general *Miltiades, and seven Attic heroes, the other on the Athenian Acropolis for a vast bronze statue of Athena 'Promachos' (the 'Champion') armed with helmet and spear. When *Pericles initiated the great Athenian rebuilding programme in the early 440s BC, Pheidias, who was a close friend of Pericles, was appointed artistic overseer of all the architects and sculptors ('panton episkopos'). He was also commissioned to make the new chryselephantine cult-statue of Athena Parthenos (the 'Maiden'), which was finished and dedicated in 438/7.

Soon after this Pheidias became one of the prime targets for the attacks launched against Pericles and his circle in the 430s. Two of the Greeks in the Amazonomachy reliefs on the shield of the Parthenos were said to be portraits of himself and Pericles; he was said to be procuring free women at the building-site for Pericles; and formal charges were brought against him of embezzling gold intended for the statue, but these were refuted by the weighing of the gold which had been designed in sections for easy removal. He subsequently left, escaped, or was exiled from Athens and went to Olympia, where he made the great chryselephantine cult-statue of Zeus. His workshop there, a noted tourist attraction in antiquity, has been excavated, and a mug, inscribed 'I am Pheidias's', was found along with various bits of

Head of Athena: marble copy of the Roman period of a statue of *c.* 440 BC, perhaps by Pheidias. Bologna, Museo Civico.

Marble relief of the Roman period copying scenes from the Amazonomachy depicted by Pheidias on the shield of the Athena Parthenos, 447–438 BC. Piraeus Museum.

sculptural equipment. He seems to have come to a sad end in prison at either Athens or Olympia, perhaps executed in 432 on further or the same charges of embezzlement. He left in Athens two famous rival pupils, *Agoracritus and *Alcamenes.

Pheidias' name tended to attract false attributions, of which we can detect several; there remain about 18 certain commissions recorded. Of these we have only the general appearance of the Athena Parthenos and the Olympian Zeus on coins and gems, and some small-scale and unpleasant reproductions of the Parthenos. Inspired guesses have been made to locate among Roman copies his Amazon at Ephesus and his Athena Lemnia and Apollo Parnopios on the Acropolis at Athens; but they are only guesses. His connection with the architectural sculpture of the Parthenon is at best uncertain. Although he had probably already left Athens when most of the frieze and pediments were being carved, his style and perhaps design are often considered to have moulded the very distinctive and highly restrained classical idealism of the frieze. Some reliefs of the Roman period survive, however, which certainly copy parts of the relief decoration of the Parthenos' shield and of the throne of the Olympian Zeus. They are the safest and closest evidence of the master's style, and have a rather different, more violent character.

BIBL. G. Becatti, *Problemi fidiaci* (1951); Richter, *Sculpture and Sculptors* 167–78; Robertson, *History of Greek Art* 292–322.

Pheidippides (or **Philippides**) Marathon runner 490 BC.

Pheidippides (Pheidippidēs; or, according to some manuscripts, Philippidēs) was an Athenian messenger sent to Sparta before the battle of Marathon in 490 BC to summon the Spartan army to come to Athens' help. He completed the 120-mile journey in two days, enjoying a vision of the god Pan en route, and gave us the name 'marathon' for a long race.

BIBL. Herodotus vi. 105 f.

Pheidon King of Argos, 7th century BC (?).

Pheidon (Pheidōn) is an important but shadowy figure,

even his date being uncertain. As king of Argos, he claimed descent from Temenus, the original Dorian conqueror (see **Heracleidae), and he tried to extend Argive domination over all of the north-east Peloponnese, the traditional 'lot of Temenus'. He came into conflict with Sparta, and won a battle at Hysiae near the Argive– Spartan border. He is also said to have marched across the Peloponnese to Olympia and taken over control of the Games there. The other major act attributed to him is the introduction of silver coinage and a new system of weights and measures.

BIBL. Herodotus vi. 127; Andrewes, *Greek Tyrants*, ch. iii.

Pherecrates Comic poet, from *c.* 438 BC.

The fragments of Pherecrates (Pherekratēs), one of *Aristophanes' rivals, include a passage (doubtfully ascribed) attacking the 'New Music' of *Melanippides, Phrynis, *Cinesias, *Timotheus (1), and (?) *Philoxenus of Cythera.

BIBL. Lesky, *Greek Literature*; Edmonds, *Attic Comedy* i.

Phila I Queen of Demetrius Poliorcetes, 321–288 BC.

Already the widow of *Craterus the marshal and the mother of *Craterus the Younger, Phila was married in 321 BC to *Demetrius Poliorcetes (many years her junior) to confirm the alliance between their fathers (*Antipater and *Antigonus (I), respectively). Their children were *Antigonus Gonatas and *Stratonice I. Phila was renowned for her generosity, fairness, and tact as well as ability in political matters; enduring alike Demetrius' military vicissitudes and his numerous other marriages, she always returned to him when he needed her. Her long-suffering nature reached its breaking-point when Macedonia was lost to Demetrius for ever in 288, and she poisoned herself at Cassandreia.

BIBL. Diodorus Siculus XIX. lix. 3–6; Macurdy, *Hellenistic Queens*; PW xix. 2087 (Phila (2)).

Philaids Athenian family.

One of the most distinguished Athenian aristocratic

families, the Philaids (Philaidai) claimed descent from the hero **Ajax. A daughter of the Corinthian tyrant *Cypselus married into the family, and her son, also called Cypselus (Kupselos), was archon early in the sixth century. His nephew(?) Hippocleides (Hippokleidēs) was an unsuccessful suitor for *Agariste, being rejected by her father when he got drunk at a banquet and 'danced away his marriage'. His reply, 'Hippocleides doesn't care!' became proverbial. Hippocleides was archon in the year (566/5?) when the Great Panathenaea was first celebrated.

Cypselus' son Miltiades (Miltiadēs) became a rival of *Peisistratus, and in order to avoid living in Athens under the tyranny went to Thrace, where he made himself ruler of the Chersonese, and was succeeded by the sons of his half-brother Cimon (Kimōn), first Stesagoras (Stēsagoras) and then *Miltiades. Cimon was alleged to have been murdered by the Peisistratids (see *Hippias, *Hipparchus) after winning three Olympic chariot-victories, a remarkable record which they saw as making him a dangerous rival. The younger Miltiades fell foul of the Persians, returned to Athens, and was largely responsible for persuading Athens to resist Persia in 490; his son *Cimon inherited an anti-Persian, pro-Spartan policy (one of his sons, *strategos* in 433, was called *Lacedaemonius). Certainly or probably related to the family were *Thucydides the historian and *Pericles' opponent *Thucydides, son of Melesias; a Cimon who was sent on an embassy to *Philip II in 346; Miltiades of Laciadae, sent to found a colony in the Adriatic in 325/4, whose daughter became one of the many wives of *Demetrius Poliorcetes; and the philosopher *Epicurus.

BIBL. Herodotus vi. 34–41, 103–4, 126–31, etc.; Davies, *Athenian Families*, no. 8429, cf. no. 7268 III–VII.

Phileas Geographical writer, 5th century BC.

Phileas was an Athenian. The sparse fragments of his *Ges periodos* (*Circuit of the Earth*) suggest a list of geographical features with antiquarian notes on cities and shrines. He is already quoted in the *Periplous* of Pseudo-*Scylax (q.v).

BIBL. PW xix. 2. 2133–6.

Philemon (*c*. 363–*c*. 264 BC) New Comedy poet.

By all accounts Philemon (Philēmōn) lived for roughly a century, alert to the end. Probably from Syracuse (*Suda*), he acquired citizenship before 307 BC in Athens, home of comedy, where he won his first victory at the Dionysia in 327. Three Lenaean victories are recorded, none earlier than 320. Alciphron's suggestion that he visited Egypt, itself unreliable, derives support from the Alexandrian setting of Philemon's *Panegyris* (*Festival*), and the anecdote which puts him, shipwrecked, at the mercy of *Magas of Cyrene, whose boorishness he had unfortunately mocked on stage. Of his 97 comedies over 60 titles are known, including a few (e.g. *Myrmidons*) hinting at the mythological plots characteristic of Middle Comedy (compare *Diphilus). Philemon was frequently preferred by his contemporaries to *Menander, though posterity soon made him the runner-up: he is much less often quoted, and no papyri are securely attributed. However, his robust comedy appealed, like Diphilus', to Plautus, who states that his *Mercator* derives from Philemon's *Emporos* (*Merchant*) and *Trinummus* from *Thesauros* (*Treasure*); *Mostellaria* very probably adapts *Phasma* (*Ghost*). Fair assessment of Philemon's work is difficult: typical features perhaps include a well-contrived action focusing on witty individual scenes, dialogue laced with platitudinous moralizing and enlivened with lines of tragic parody, and characterization tending to caricature.

BIBL. Apuleius, *Florida* 16; Webster, *Later Comedy*; *Roman World* *Plautus.

Philetaerus (*c*. 343–263 BC) Founder of the Attalid dynasty at Pergamum.

Born of mixed Macedonian and Paphlagonian parentage at Tios (on the Black Sea), Philetaerus (Philhetairos), son of one Attalus, first appears in the service of *Antigonus. In 302 BC he deserted him for *Lysimachus and was put in charge of Pergamum, where Lysimachus had deposited a treasure of some 9,000 talents. In 282 he rebelled and offered his services to *Seleucus (I) when the latter mobilized to exploit the unrest caused by Lysimachus'

Pergamum in Asia Minor, capital of the Attalid dynasty (founded by Philetaerus).

execution of his own eldest son *Agathocles. Lysimachus'
death at Corupedium (281) and Seleucus' murder shortly
afterwards left Philetaerus a fairly free agent, but he
showed his continuing goodwill to the Seleucids by
purchasing Seleucus' corpse from *Ptolemy Ceraunus and
sending the ashes to *Antiochus I, and the presence of
Seleucus' portrait on Pergamene coins expressed a nominal
subservience to his successor, which persisted until the
accession of Philetaerus' nephew and adopted son
*Eumenes I. Philetaerus' long rule was notable for his
defence of Pergamum from the Celtic Galatians (278–276),
for the building of temples and defences in the city, and
for generous donations to cities and sanctuaries in Asia
Minor and Greece.

BIBL. Hansen, *Attalids*; R. B. McShane, *The Foreign
Policy of the Attalids of Pergamum* (1964).

Philetas: see Philitas

Philicus Poet, c. 275 BC.

Philicus (Philikos) (not Philiscus) came from Corcyra but
rooted himself at Alexandria, where he was priest of
Dionysus and one of the *Pleiad. Of 42 tragedies (*Suda*)
not even a title is known, unless we accept some
conflation with 'Philiscus the comic poet' whose works
are named in *Suda*. However, a papyrus fragment of a
Hymn to Demeter, a literary not a cult creation (compare
*Callimachus), has been securely attributed to Philicus: it
is in the exacting choriambic hexameter metre he claimed
elsewhere to have invented.

BIBL. *Literary Papyri* (Loeb), no. 90; *SH* 676–80, 980;
Webster, *Hellenistic Poetry*; Fraser, *Ptolemaic Alexandria*.

Philidas Theban politician, floruit 379/8 BC.

After the pro-Spartan *coup* at Thebes in 382 BC, Philidas
participated in the counter-revolution of 379/8, his role
being to provide access to the polemarchs, whom he
served as secretary. According to *Xenophon, but not
other sources, he was virtually the author of the whole
coup.

BIBL. Buckler, *Theban Hegemony*.

Philinus of Cos Physician, c. 250 BC.

Influenced by the sceptic philosophy of *Pyrrhon,
Philinus (Philinos) broke with his master *Herophilus to
found, according to Galen – Serapion is also given this
credit – the empiric school of medicine influential at
Alexandria. Perpetually at war with the dogmatists,
empiricists rejected all scientific theory to rely on
experience and observation of symptoms in the treatment
of disease.

BIBL. Phillips, *Greek Medicine*; L. Edelstein, *Ancient
Medicine* (1967); *Roman World* *Galen.

Philip II (c. 382–336 BC) King of Macedon 359–336 BC,
father of Alexander the Great.

Philip (Philippos) first appears as a hostage at Thebes
(368–365 BC), where he perhaps learned at first hand
something of the military innovations of *Epaminondas'
Thebes (see *Pammenes). After the removal of *Ptolemy
Alorites, *Perdiccas III accepted the advice of Euphraeus
(an emissary of *Plato) and granted Philip some territory
in Macedonia (though the precise nature of this grant is
disputed). On Perdiccas' death Philip became king (not

merely regent for Perdiccas' infant son Amyntas), but was
faced by hostile Illyrians and Paeonians and by two
pretenders, Pausanias (supported by Berisades of Thrace)
and Argaeus (supported by Athens). Argaeus was defeated
at Methone (Athens being kept sweet by the free release
of Athenian prisoners-of-war), while money and promises
kept other threats at bay (Pausanias disappears from sight
altogether). After energetic military preparations the
Paeonians were chastened and the Illyrians heavily
defeated near Monastir (358), an encounter showing
certain post-Epaminondean features. Philip's kingdom was
now (relatively) safe, and he may have intervened briefly
in Thessaly.

With Athenian involvement in the Social War
(357–355) a new phase opened. Abandoning friendship
with Athens, Philip sought greater security with the
capture of Amphipolis and Pydna (357), which became
(effectively) provincial Macedonian towns; an alliance
with the Olynthians (who were given Potidaea, captured
in 356); the colonization of Crenides, in the gold- and
silver-rich Pangaeum area, as Philippi (the first Greek city
named after its oecist); and the capture of Methone
(355/4), whose territory was given to Macedonian settlers.
A short exploratory thrust into Thrace (353) was followed
by major intervention in Thessaly against Pherae and her
Phocian allies, but for once Philip was worsted in battle,
suffering two defeats at the hands of *Onomarchus. (The
part played by catapults may have encouraged Philip to
devote thought to ballistic weaponry: the torsion-catapult
was the invention of his engineers.) Undeterred he
returned in 352, dealt with Onomarchus at the Crocus
Field (near Pagasae) and became archon of the Thessalian
league (an extraordinary development, which effectively
made Thessaly part of the Macedonian kingdom). Finding
Thermopylae blocked by Athens and Sparta he
characteristically took his winnings, retired north, and
immediately struck deep into Thrace, reaching Heraion

Philip II, *Olympias, and *Alexander the Great (as a new-born
infant) on a 4th-century AD mosaic from Baalbek. Beirut Museum.

Teichos (near Perinthus) and provoking panic at Athens. Illness, however, interrupted the campaign. After a warning move against Olynthus, by now a rather unhappy ally, Philip attended to Illyria (again) and to Epirus (where Arrybas became a mere vassal). A lull follows until the final show-down with Olynthus (349–348). Despite some Athenian help the city was razed to the ground, releasing more land for Macedonian settlement. (A similar fate befell *Aristotle's home-town (Stagira), but perhaps not 30 other cities, *pace* *Demosthenes.)

Silver tetradrachm of the time of Philip II with a presumed portrait of the king (enlarged).

From before the fall of Olynthus Philip had mooted peace with Athens. This (and an alliance) was achieved in 346 (the Peace of *Philocrates) in circumstances which permitted Philip to enter central Greece and, with Thessalian and Theban help and Athenian inaction, crush Phocis – though her punishment for desecrating Delphi would have been more dire but for Philip's influence. (The precise mechanics of all this and the question of Philip's motives are highly controversial, but the suggestion that he would have preferred to crush *Thebes* is unconvincing, and one should not over-confidently assert that he was already planning for war with Persia.)

In the subsequent period Philip attended to the security of his immediate borders, with intervention in Illyria (345), Thessaly (344, 342), and Epirus (343/2: the installation of *Alexander of Epirus). More importantly (to outsiders) he meddled in the affairs of southern Greek cities (e.g. in Euboea and at Megara and Elis), a circumstance much stressed, but not wholly invented, by Demosthenes and the anti-Macedonian party, which also contrived to thwart negotiation of a Common Peace (344/3, 343/2). In summer 342 Philip returned to eastern Thrace. Formal peace with Athens survived his expulsion of *Cersobleptes and even his attacks on Perinthus and Byzantium (340), but the seizure of Athenian corn-ships (September 340) caused Athens to declare war. Unmoved, Philip went off to campaign in the Dobruja, but in late 339 he entered central Greece to lead the Amphictyonic states against Amphissa (the Fourth Sacred War), and in due course defeated the Athenians, Thebans, and others at Chaeronea (August 338). Individual peace-treaties and

local settlements in central Greece and the Peloponnese were followed by the establishment of a Common Peace and of the 'League of Corinth'. Behind a smoke-screen of autonomy, freedom from garrisons and tribute, protection from internal revolution, and the right of deliberation in league synods, this organization was the instrument for the control of Greece by its elected *hegemon*, 'leader' (Philip) and for the extraction of military support for a projected Panhellenic war against Persia, for which Philip was duly appointed *strategos autokrator*. In 337 Philip, perhaps unwisely, married *Cleopatra (Eurydice), provoking a break with *Olympias and bad feeling with his son *Alexander. In 336 the invasion of Asia Minor started, but before he could take personal command Philip was assassinated by *Pausanias (3). He was buried at Aegae, but the identification of a rich tomb unearthed there in 1977 as his remains controversial.

Philip's achievement was quite as remarkable as Alexander the Great's, though perhaps less romantic. It is also less well-documented. None of his battles is properly recorded (Monastir and Chaeronea are but partial exceptions), and most are not recorded at all. The creation of the Macedonian army familiar from the early days of Alexander's reign, the socio-economic transformation of Macedonia from transhumance to settled agriculture, or the internal colonization of Greater Macedonia are all, for us, *faits accomplis*, not traceable processes. A detailed description of the administration of the Macedonian domains (at least north of Thermopylae) is scarcely possible. There are tantalizing hints, but no more, of the first steps on the path to ruler-cult. Even Philip's diplomatic actions must be seen through the distorting lens of Athenian forensic mendacity. Of Philip the man one can say that his successes in war and diplomacy presuppose remarkable political intelligence, strategic and tactical skill, charm, and energy, and that, though a hard fighter (he was wounded three times in battle) and a devotee of the boisterous Macedonian life-style, he was not devoid of cultural interests (especially in drama), and did appoint *Aristotle as his heir's tutor. But it remains difficult to get him properly in focus. However, *Theopompus' observation that Europe had never known his like hardly seems absurdly extravagant (though Theopompus seems, characteristically, to have thought of him as unprecedentedly appalling!).

BIBL. J. R. Ellis, *Philip II and Macedonian Imperialism* (1976); G. Cawkwell, *Philip of Macedon* (1978); Hammond and Griffith, *Macedonia* 203–726; G. S. Shrimpton, *Phoenix* xxxi (1977); M. B. Hatzopoulos and L. D. Loukopoulos (ed.), *Philip of Macedon* (1981).

Philip III Arrhidaeus King of Macedonia, 323–317 BC.

Son of *Philip II and Philinna, and elder half-brother of *Alexander the Great, Philip Arrhidaeus (Philippos Arrhidaios) was mentally subnormal (some attributed this to drugs administered by *Olympias), but eventually became joint king (with *Alexander IV) in 323 BC, a position he retained under self-interested regents until his capture and murder by Olympias in 317.

BIBL. Berve, *Alexanderreich*, no. 781; Will, *Hist. pol.*, index; R. M. Errington, *JHS* xc (1970).

Philip V King of Macedon, 221–179 BC.

Philip (Philippos), the son of *Demetrius II and Phthia-

Chryseis, was only a boy of eight when his father was killed. He was adopted by his father's cousin *Antigonus Doson, who ruled as regent until 221 BC. Part of the prince's education had included a visit to *Aratus of Sicyon to learn about the Greeks and the Achaean League. The so-called 'Social War' (220–217), which pitted Philip and the Hellenic League against Aetolia and her allies, marked his growth into a mature king. Philip turned gradually away from his mentor Aratus (finally breaking with him completely by marrying his daughter-in-law) towards *Demetrius of Pharos, who had been chased out of his kingdom by Rome. Demetrius incited Philip against the Romans in Illyria, to the dismay of most Greeks, and a treaty with Hannibal in 215 meant the end of any friendship between Philip and Rome. The war began badly for Philip: he lost a naval battle to the Romans and *Scerdilaidas in 216, he invaded Messene in 215 but was persuaded to withdraw by Aratus, he was ignominiously forced to burn his fleet in 214, and he attacked Messene again in 214, taking the town with such savagery that the Greeks were repelled and the Achaean League enraged. Although Rome was joined by *Scopas of Aetolia in 211, and by *Attalus I of Pergamum, Philip's superior forces on land (combined with Roman inactivity in 207) led to the sack of Thermum and terms forced upon Aetolia in 206. The First Macedonian War was ended by the Peace of Phoenice, proposed by Rome in 205 and favourable to Philip.

Coin portrait of Philip V, king of Macedon (enlarged).

Philip's ambitions turned eastward. In 203/2 he colluded with *Antiochus III to divide Egypt, but in 201 his fleet was defeated off Chios by Attalus and the Rhodians who both feared his expansion. Rome declared the Second Macedonian War in 200. Campaigns were fought in Greece, Thrace, Macedon, and Thessaly for three years, sometimes with notable success for Philip, until Rome in desperation appointed *Flamininus to the command. He defeated Philip decisively at Cynoscephalae in 197, and imposed harsh military and financial terms on Macedon. Philip's son Demetrius was taken as a hostage to Rome.

Confined to Macedon, Philip concentrated on rebuilding his country. He was now an uneasy ally of Rome, and had to be seen to support her; he helped Rome against *Nabis of Sparta in 195, and against Antiochus and Aetolia (192–189). Rome's continuing suspicions about him were fuelled by complaints from his neighbours. Bridling at his treatment, Philip adopted an aggressive Balkan policy after 185, defeating some Thracian tribes, resettling others, and making alliances

with others. This activity was regarded in the worst possible light by Rome. Philip finally killed his pro-Roman son Demetrius and secured the succession for *Perseus, who shared his imperialist tendencies. While touring his kingdom, he died of sickness at Amphipolis in 179.

Philip's brilliance as a military commander often got him further than the odds against him should have allowed, but this must be contrasted with his violent temper, perhaps inherited from Epirote ancestors. The responsibility for Rome's eventual domination of Greece must be laid at least partly at his door.

BIBL. M. Holleaux, *Rome, la Grèce, et les Monarchies hellénistiques* (1921); F. W. Walbank, *Philip V of Macedon* (1940), and *HCP*; *Roman World* *Hannibal.

Philip I and II (Seleucids): see Later *Seleucids

Philiscus: see **Philicus**

Philistion Physician, early 4th century BC.
Born at Locri in southern Italy, Philistion (Philistiōn) based his physiology on *Empedocles' theory of matter. Health depended on the proper balance of the elements earth, water, air, and fire in the body. There is some unreliable evidence that he was a friend of *Plato.
BIBL. Phillips, *Greek Medicine*.

Philistus (*c.* 430–356 BC) Sicilian historian and statesman.
Philistus (Philistos) of Syracuse helped *Dionysius I to establish himself as tyrant of Syracuse in 405 BC, and was appointed to rule the city on his behalf. He was later exiled by Dionysius, but recalled by his son *Dionysius II. In 366 he was responsible for exiling Dionysius' republican-minded uncle *Dion, who had invited *Plato to Sicily. In 357/6, during the absence of Dionysius in Italy, Philistus was defeated by a naval expedition led by Dion, and he committed suicide.

Philistus is primarily significant for writing an unfinished history of Sicily in about 11 to 13 books; via *Timaeus and *Ephorus he is a major source of *Diodorus Siculus. He was highly regarded by Cicero (who called him 'almost a little *Thucydides'), Dionysius of Halicarnassus, Quintilian, and other critics as an outstanding example of pure Attic prose-writing.
BIBL. *FGrH* iiiB, no. 556; *Roman World* *Cicero, *Dionysius of Halicarnassus, *Quintilian.

Philitas Poet and scholar, born *c.* 330 BC (?).
Philitas (this is attested by inscriptions as the Coan form; manuscripts offer Philētas) is a key figure of ancient literature known only through tantalizing scraps and allusions. *Ptolemy I chose him as tutor to his son (later *Ptolemy II Philadelphus), born on Philitas' own island, Cos, in 309/8 BC. He also taught *Zenodotus. Dubbed 'poet and scholar in one' (*Strabo), he pioneered the Alexandrian tradition of learned poetry inherited by *Callimachus (q.v.), and moulded his royal pupil into its greatest patron. His *Miscellaneous Glosses*, a lexicon of rare and obscure words, was an immediately influential piece of scholarship, but also a working-tool in the creation of his own choice poetry. Among known works are the hexameter epyllion *Hermes*, which gave a characteristically novel angle on traditional myth, creating

an amorous encounter between **Odysseus and Aeolus' daughter Polymele; *Demeter*, a narrative elegy, widely admired; and *Paignia* (*Playful Poems*) and *Epigrammata*, possibly alternative titles for miscellaneous short poems. It was as an elegist that Philitas was canonized, and as a love elegist in particular that his name became significant in Roman poetry (Propertius, Ovid); but here our knowledge is wretchedly defective. *Hermesianax describes a Coan statue of Philitas 'singing of swift Bittis under a plane-tree': was she nymph or live mistress? Did Philitas' erotic elegy treat 'objectively' of mythological amours, or 'subjectively' of what purported to be personal experience? A mixture is perhaps most likely. Several clues encourage speculation that Philitas used pastoral settings in this poetry; *Theocritus certainly pays tribute to him in his mysterious seventh idyll set on Cos.

BIBL. Pfeiffer, *Classical Scholarship* i; F. Cairns, *Tibullus* (1979); E. L. Bowie, forthcoming article in *CQ*; *Roman World* *Ovid, *Propertius.

Philochorus Antiquarian, died *c.* 263/2 BC.

Philochorus (Philokhoros) was of good Athenian family and held the office of seer and interpreter of sacrifices (fr. 67: 306/5 BC): he was murdered by *Antigonus Gonatas for political activity at Athens on behalf of *Ptolemy II. 27 titles display the varied interests of a dedicated antiquarian: overshadowing his monographs on religious practices, literature, etc. is his great annalistic *Atthis* (*Attic History*), to which most fragments belong. This passed swiftly but effectively over the early period dwelt on by his predecessors (the section used by *Callimachus in the *Hecale*, and by *Ister) to concentrate on contemporary history: 11 of 17 books were probably allotted to the half-century from *Demetrius of Phalerum to the *Chremonidean War (c. 317–267 BC). Philochorus' mature research techniques (note his collection of Attic inscriptions) and eye-witness knowledge, combined with intelligence and a no-nonsense style, make him a serious historiographer as well as last and best of the Atthidographers.

BIBL. *FGrH* 328, iiiB suppl. i (1954), 220 ff.; Jacoby, *Atthis*.

Philocrates Athenian politician, floruit 340s BC.

Philocrates' (Philokratēs) first proposal that *Philip II of Macedon be invited to discuss peace (348 BC) lapsed after a *graphe paranomon* (though *Demosthenes secured his acquittal). In 346 he proposed an embassy to Macedonia to discuss peace and alliance, drafted the decree by which Athens accepted the resulting terms, and later secured extension of the peace and alliance to Philip's descendants and official praise of Philip's promises of just dealing. This formal role, which is responsible for the modern term 'Peace of Philocrates', made him a target for later Athenian disillusion, and in 343 he was condemned to death *in absentia* on the (questionable) charge of taking bribes.

BIBL. Kirchner, *PA*, no. 14599; Hammond and Griffith, *Macedonia* ii. 329–47; Cawkwell, *Philip* 91–113.

Philolaus Pythagorean philosopher, 5th century BC.

Born in southern Italy, probably at Croton, Philolaus (Philolaos) went to Thebes in about 450 BC, when the *Pythagorean clubs were broken up, and probably contributed much to the propagation of Pythagoreanism in mainland Greece. Surviving fragments of his works may be forgeries, and other evidence about him is late and suspect. The following theories may be attributed to him with only moderate confidence: that the earth is not at the centre of things, but, like the sun, moon, and planets, moves round a central mass of fire; that the moon is inhabited; and that the soul is an 'attunement' (*harmonia*) of the parts of the body (a belief hard to reconcile with the Pythagorean theory of reincarnation).

BIBL. Burkert, *Pythagoreanism*.

Philomelus Phocian general, died 354 BC.

Provoked by Theban hostility, Philomelus (Philomelos) seized Delphi and reasserted ancient Phocian control of the sanctuary. On the declaration of a Sacred War (355 BC) he used sacred funds to hire mercenaries, but committed suicide after defeat at Neon (354), and was succeeded by his brother *Onomarchus.

BIBL. Parke, *Mercenary Soldiers*; Hammond, *Studies* 486 ff.

Philon of Byzantium Writer on technology, second half of 2nd century BC.

Philon (Philōn), a student of applied mechanics although not himself a great inventor, was a pupil of *Ctesibius (q.v.), and apparently heard his lectures and observed some of his machines. He tells us that he spent a considerable time in Alexandria, and also in Rhodes, but was in neither when he wrote his *Mechanical Handbook*, parts of which survive. This work, originally in several books, describes various techniques of siege warfare (catapults, siege engines, pneumatic devices, and defensive works); in addition to recording this information, Philon discusses the development of the technology, and from this it emerges that Alexandria must have been a centre of ballistics research. The work is written in the form of a literary epistle, addressed to an unidentifiable Ariston. Much of the handbook was later used by *Heron of Alexandria.

BIBL. Fraser, *Ptolemaic Alexandria* i. 428 ff.; A. G. Drachmann, *Ktesibios, Philon and Heron: A Study in Ancient Pneumatics* (1948); E. W. Marsden, *Greek and Roman Artillery: Technical Treatises* (1971), and *Greek and Roman Artillery, Historical Development* (1969).

Philon of Larissa (159–*c.* 80 BC) Philosopher.

Philon's (Philōn) philosophy was moderately sceptical, like that of *Carneades: true knowledge was impossible, but some beliefs were more probable than others. He defended this position by appeals to authorities, trying to show that earlier philosophers such as *Socrates and *Plato were sceptics. He became head of the Academy in Athens, but in 88 BC, at the time of the *Mithridatic Wars, went to Rome, where he lectured on philosophy and rhetoric, and had much influence on Cicero.

BIBL. Dillon, *Middle Platonists*; *Roman World* *Cicero.

Philopoemen (252–182 BC) Achaean statesman.

Born into an aristocratic Megalopolitan family, Philopoemen (Philopoimēn) was educated after his father's death by *Demophanes and *Ecdelus. He fought in the unsuccessful defence of Megalopolis against *Cleomenes III of Sparta (q.v.) in 223 BC, and refused to join those citizens wishing to treat with the Spartan. At the battle of Sellasia in 222 Philopoemen made an independent attack (against orders), which *Polybius glorified to excess. He went to Crete after Sellasia, rejecting an offer of service with *Antigonus Doson of Macedon; whether he went with an Achaean expedition arranged by *Aratus of Sicyon, or independently, he collaborated with Macedonian interests there. Returning in 211 (which coincided not only with the power vacuum left by the death of Aratus but with Rome's alliance with Aetolia and Sparta against *Philip V of Macedon), he was elected hipparch of the League in 210/209. He reorganized the cavalry and, as *strategus* in 208/7, the infantry. Fighting on Philip's behalf, he defeated the Spartan regent Machanidas in 207.

The League's improved military position now made independence from Macedon possible. By 200, Philip had turned to the new Spartan king *Nabis, and Achaea to Rome. Philopoemen returned to Crete when a pro-Macedonian party came to power in 201, and fought Nabis by opposing his side in a Cretan civil war. When *Flamininus deprived Nabis of his Cretan possessions, Philopoemen returned to Achaea in 194. When Nabis died in 192, Sparta came into the League, along with Messene (on Flamininus' orders). When Sparta was torn by faction, Philopoemen believed that it was an internal problem of the League, not a matter for Rome. He interpreted an ambiguous ruling by the Senate on this in 188 as a mandate to deal with Sparta; he massacred several Spartans at Compasion and imposed harsh terms. This led to an unofficial reprimand by Q. Caecilius *Metellus, but Philopoemen's party stayed in power.

Messene rebelled in 183/2, and Philopoemen was summoned from his sick-bed to defend Corone from the Messenians in 182. Ambushed and captured, he died in prison perhaps from natural causes, although poison was claimed by his political heirs. His dramatic State funeral completed his transformation into a great folk-hero of the Achaean League.

Philopoemen was a great soldier and patriot, but his outlook was narrow and his policies often short-sighted. Hindsight shows that it was a fundamental error to think that the Achaean League could resist Rome. The meaning of his accolade 'the last of the Greeks' has been disputed in ancient and modern times.

BIBL. R. M. Errington, *Philopoemen* (1969); *Roman World*.

Philotas Macedonian general, died 330 BC.

A distinguished commander of *Alexander the Great's Companion Cavalry, Philotas (Philōtas), son of *Parmenion (q.v.), was executed for treason in 330 BC. His mistress had allegedly made regular reports of his private criticisms of Alexander, but the immediate occasion of his fall was his failure to pass on information of a conspiracy against Alexander. Although he was condemned not *in camera* but by the army assembly, doubt must remain about his guilt, and it looks as though Alexander or some of his entourage were delighted at finding an excuse for removing a prominent figure who was not actually disloyal.

BIBL. Berve, *Alexanderreich*, no. 802; E. Badian, *TAPA* xci (1960); W. Heckel, *Phoenix* xxxi (1977); Bosworth, *Arrian* 359 ff.

Philoxenus of Cythera (435/4–380/79 BC) Dithyrambic poet.

Various anecdotes are told of the life of Philoxenus (Philoxenos) at the court of *Dionysius I of Syracuse; at one time the tyrant is said to have imprisoned him in a stone-quarry. He wrote the same type of dithyrambs as *Timotheus (1); the most famous was the *Cyclops*, which portrayed the Cyclops in love, was parodied by *Aristophanes (*Plutus* 290–301), and influenced *Theocritus (poems vi and xi).

This Philoxenus is often confused in our sources with Philoxenus of Leucas, the probable author of a lyric poem describing a banquet (*Deipnon*), much of which survives.

BIBL. Lesky, *Greek Literature*; *Lyra Graeca* (Loeb) iii; Pickard-Cambridge, *Dithyramb* . . .

Phocion (402/1–319/18 BC) Athenian politician.

One tradition claimed that Phocion (Phōkiōn) was a pestle-maker's son, but his family was actually of the liturgic class, and in his youth he frequented *Plato's Academy. A skilled orator, who was also elected *strategos* 45 times 371–319/18 BC, Phocion became important in the 340s. At first moderately anti-Macedonian (though he defended *Aeschines in 343), from 338 on he largely favoured complaisance to Macedonia, although he was cautious about the League of Corinth (see *Philip II) and mitigated *Alexander the Great's and *Antipater's

Portrait of a general often identified as the Athenian politician Phocion. Vatican Museum.

hostility in 335 and 322. After the constitutional changes of 322 he dominated Athenian politics, but Antipater's death and *Polyperchon's restoration of the pre-322 constitution undermined his position (especially since he was suspected of collusion with *Nicanor), and he was soon executed at Polyperchon's behest. A man of austere life-style, who had his son 'educated' at Sparta, Phocion was heroized in later tradition as a (sanctimonious) opponent of democratic extremism, and his execution was almost put on a par with that of *Socrates.

BIBL. Kirchner, *PA*, no. 15076; Davies, *Athenian Families* 559 ff.; H.-J. Gercke, *Phokion* (1976).

Phocylides Hexameter poet, c. 550 BC (?).

To Phocylides (Phōkulidēs) of Miletus are attributed some 15 hexameter maxims, four beginning 'This too is Phocylides'' (probably all were so marked originally). Only fragment 2, comparing women to bitch, bee, sow, and mare (influenced by *Semonides?) exceeds two lines. Fragment 1 (elegiac) is probably (from its wit) by *Demodocus.

BIBL. B. Gentili and C. Prato, *Poetae Elegiaci* (1979); M. L. West, *JHS* xcviii (1978).

Phoebidas Spartan general, died 378/7 BC.

While leading an army to Olynthus, Phoebidas (Phoibidas) occupied the Theban Cadmea (acropolis) at the instigation of *Leontiades and perhaps with the foreknowledge of *Agesilaus (382 BC). Phoebidas was possibly fined for this officially unauthorized action, but Sparta retained the Cadmea. He died fighting as harmost of Thespiae, evidently no longer even theoretically in disgrace.

BIBL. Poralla, *Prosopographie*, no. 734.

Phoenix of Colophon Iambic poet, c. 285 BC.

Pausanias asserts that Phoenix (Phoinix) lamented the destruction of his home-town Colophon by *Lysimachus (287/1 (?), after which he possibly moved to Ephesus). Fragments of his moralizing choliambics attacking gluttony, the foolishness of the rich, etc. revive the local tradition of *Hipponax. Of folkloric interest is a version of a begging-song, *Coronistae*, performed from house to house with a crow (korōnē).

BIBL. Loeb: Herodes etc. (with Theophrastus, *Characters*) (1929) 242 ff.; Wills, *CQ* xx (1970); *Roman World* *Pausanias.

Phormion Athenian commander, 5th century BC.

In 440/39 BC Phormion (Phormiōn) was involved in suppressing the revolt of Samos (see *Melissus); in 432 he persuaded the Acarnanians to become allies of Athens. He fought at Potidaea, and commanded the Athenian fleet based on Naupactus which blockaded the Gulf of Corinth. He won two significant naval battles over the Peloponnesians in 429, and campaigned successfully in Acarnania. Soon after this he died, probably of the plague.

BIBL. Westlake, *Individuals in Thucydides*, ch. 4.

Phrynichus (1) Tragedian, 6th–5th century BC.

The most prominent of *Aeschylus' rivals, Phrynichus (Phrunikhos) won his first victory between 511 and 508 BC. He is chiefly remembered for two plays on historical subjects: the *Capture of Miletus* (concerning the suppression of the Ionian Revolt (see *Histiaeus, *Aristagoras) in 494), which, according to *Herodotus, so upset the Athenians that Phrynichus was heavily fined; and the *Phoenician Women* (?), which influenced Aeschylus' *Persians*, and may have been among the plays sponsored by *Themistocles, Phrynichus' choregus in 476. Not many fragments survive.

Phrynichus is also the name of a comic poet contemporary with *Aristophanes.

BIBL. Lesky, *Greek Literature*; Pickard-Cambridge, *Dithyramb* . . .; H. Lloyd-Jones (in English), *Estudios sobre la Tragedia griega* (1966) 19 ff.

Phrynichus (2) Athenian politician, died 411 BC.

In 412/11 BC, as one of the generals commanding the Athenian fleet at Samos, Phrynichus (Phrunikhos) opposed the recall of *Alcibiades. He then became a leading member of the oligarchic regime of the Four Hundred at Athens; he attempted to negotiate peace-terms with Sparta, but returned without success, and was assassinated in the Agora.

BIBL. Thucydides viii. 25, 47–50, 68, 90 ff.

Phylarchus Historian, second half of 3rd century BC.

Although Phylarchus (Phularkhos) wrote several other works known only by their titles, he is best known for his *History*, a work in 28 books which dealt with the period between the deaths of *Pyrrhus of Epirus in 272 BC and *Cleomenes III of Sparta in 220. He wrote his history in Athens, although various cities are given as his home, and was a contemporary of some of the events he described. His own political beliefs as a supporter of the social reforms of Cleomenes prejudiced him against the anti-Cleomenes faction at Sparta, Macedon, and the Achaean League and *Aratus of Sicyon. These views inevitably coloured his reconstruction of the period.

Phylarchus' work survives only in quotation. He was the main source of Plutarch in his *Lives* of Cleomenes and *Agis IV, and a subsidiary source for those of Aratus and Pyrrhus. The greatest amount of information about Phylarchus is preserved in *Polybius, who discusses his merits as one of his own sources for the period before 220. Polybius hated him (being himself in favour of Aratus and the Achaean League), but his criticism of Phylarchus' carelessness, inaccuracy, and sensationalism seems to be a substantially correct picture of the work of this 'rhetorical historian'.

BIBL. *FGrH* 81; PW Suppl. viii. 471 ff.; Walbank, *Aratos of Sicyon* 3 ff.; *Roman World* *Plutarch.

Phyromachus Sculptor, active c. 250–220 BC.

In the bleak record left us of the very creative third century BC, Phyromachus (Phuromakhos) of Athens is one of the few famous sculptors whose name has survived and of whose work we have some idea. He signed two bases, at Cyzicus and at Delos, with an older fellow-Athenian sculptor, Niceratus, and like him seems to have worked mainly for the Attalid kings of Pergamum; he collaborated on the Gallic monuments of *Attalus I and made the famous cult-statue for the Pergamene Asclepieium. In 1969 an inscribed base was found at Ostia naming him as the sculptor of a portrait of the Cynic philosopher *Antisthenes, no doubt the one known to us in several copies. Its style is close to some figures of Attalus' 'Small

Dedication' and shows Phyromachus to have been one of
the leading exponents of third-century baroque sculpture.
BIBL. F. Zevi, *Rend. Pont. Acc.* xlii (1969–70), 110–14;
Stewart, *Attika* 8–16; B. Andreae, *Eikones*; *Festschrift H.
Jucker* (1980), 40–8.

Pindar (518 (?)–after 446 BC) Lyric poet.

The Theban poet Pindar (Pindaros) brought the
tradition of Doric choral song to its highest point of
development and elaboration. He was born either in
518 BC or possibly in 522. Most of the traditions
concerning his life are quite unreliable, but we know that
he was receiving commissions by 498 (the date of the
victory celebrated in the earliest surviving ode,
Pythian x), and his work provides evidence of visits to
various parts of the Greek world, notably to Sicily in the
470s. The last datable ode, *Pythian* viii, celebrates a
victory won in 446.

Ancient scholars collected Pindar's work into 17 books,
and divided these into Hymns, Paeans, Dithyrambs,
Processional Songs, Maidens' Songs, Dance Songs
(Hyporchemes), Encomia, Dirges, and Victory Songs
(Epinicians). The four books of Victory Songs survive (45
authentic odes), together with a number of fragments,
notably of Paeans.

The Victory Songs were composed (with a few
exceptions) in honour of victors in the four major athletic
festivals, the Olympic, Pythian, Nemean, and Isthmian
Games. They are written in a highly artificial and often
very difficult style: rich mixtures of metaphors, abrupt
and unexplained transitions, and a habit of hanging great
tangled masses of nouns and adjectives on every verb,
ensure that the reader or hearer must concentrate to the
full upon each individual word. Though certain structural
principles can be discerned, Pindar takes pains to vary
and disguise formal divisions and to make them conflict
with the metrical pattern.

Several of Pindar's finest odes were written for the
tyrants *Hieron I of Syracuse and *Theron of Acragas;
others were written for aristocratic patrons from various
cities, notably Aegina. Each is designed as a public
celebration of the patron's achievements; so, while
Pindar's distinctive style certainly conveys a distinctive
vision of the world, we cannot expect him to express
personal and controversial opinions.

The actual victory, however, generally occupies only a
small part of the poem, since Pindar's purpose is to relate
it to a wider context. Competition in the games depended
on wealth and high social status, and provided an
opportunity to display these qualities to all Greece;
victory revealed the favour of the gods and an innate
talent derived from noble birth; and the victor could be
seen as the successful champion of his city, like the heroes
of myth and epic from whom he often claimed descent.
Pindar celebrates all these things, using imagery and
juxtaposition to link them together, and using the baroque
grandeur and richness of his language to impress us with
the immense worth and splendour of the aristocratic ideal.

At the centre of all but the shortest odes stands an
allusive account of a myth, often developed at length, but
often introduced on a very slender pretext. There has
been much dispute as to the relevance of these myths and
the unity of Pindar's poems in general; attempts to find
underlying thematic unity work better for some poems

Bronze charioteer dedicated at Delphi by Polyzalus, brother of
Pindar's patron *Hieron I, in celebration of a victory in the
Pythian Games of 478 or 474 BC. Delphi Museum.

than for others, and Pindar may sometimes have thought it sufficient to associate *any* patron with *any* myth.

Another constant element is the expression of proverbial wisdom, often concerning the danger of excessive prosperity and the need to remember that one is mortal. This moralizing should be seen, not as an impertinent attempt to reform the patron's character, but as serving much the same purpose as a *memento mori* in a portrait of a Renaissance nobleman: it guarantees the moral earnestness of Pindar's work as a whole, and, by showing that he is fully aware of the gods' laws, removes any danger that his extravagant praise of his patron might be thought to contravene them. Again, it is in keeping with the tone of high moral seriousness that Pindar should often express pride in his own work and his poetic calling; he is disdainful of rivals, though it is uncertain whether some passages specifically attack *Simonides and *Bacchylides.

BIBL. Lesky, *Greek Literature*; H. Fränkel, *Early Greek Poetry and Philosophy* (1975); C. M. Bowra, *Pindar* (1964).

Pittacus Tyrant of Mytilene, *c.* 600 BC.

Pittacus (Pittakos) became ruler of Mytilene after overthrowing a tyrant. He is said to have held power for ten years and then retired, in this respect differing from other tyrants (*Aristotle gives him the special title

'Portrait' of the tyrant Pittacus, found at Pompeii, which owes much to *Alcaeus' description of him as pot-bellied and unwashed. Pompeii, Museum.

aisumnetes – 'elective monarch'). He was not a constitutional reformer, but passed sumptuary laws, and imposed double fines for offences committed when drunk. His physical ugliness and low birth were attacked in the poems of his enemy *Alcaeus.

BIBL. Aristotle, *Politics* 1274b, 1285a; Diogenes Laertius i. 74 ff.; Andrewes, *Greek Tyrants*, ch. 8.

Plato (*c.* 429–347 BC) Philosopher.

Born of an aristocratic Athenian family (*Critias was his mother's cousin), Plato (Platōn) became one of the circle of *Socrates' friends and devotees. After Socrates' death in 399 BC, he took refuge with *Eucl(e)ides in Megara, and then travelled for some years, during which he met *Dionysius I, the ruler of Syracuse. He visited Syracuse twice more after Dionysius' death, and was said to have helped *Dion (q.v.) in an attempt to model *Dionysius II's (q.v.) rule on that of the 'philosopher-kings' in Plato's *Republic*. If the story is true, the attempt failed. But Plato may have been little more than a court philosopher. He set up a 'school', the Academy, in a grove of that name on the outskirts of Athens. The range of studies pursued there is uncertain, but included mathematics and astronomy. His nephew *Speusippus succeeded him as its head, and the school survived, probably with intermissions, until closed by Justinian in AD 529.

Plato's philosophy is known mainly from his published dialogues – philosophical discussions in dramatic form, in which Socrates often plays a leading part. (About 25 of the dialogues attributed to him are probably genuine.) There also survive 13 letters, some or all of which may not be genuine, and the *Apology*, a reply placed in Socrates' mouth to the charges for which he was condemned to death. A common division of Plato's philosophy into three periods provides a good framework for an account of how his thought developed, although the changes were not abrupt.

The early dialogues are generally inconclusive. They were probably intended to leave the reader in perplexity about matters on which he had previously held unquestioned convictions. (It is better to know one's ignorance than to be wrong.) Typically, Socrates asks for a definition, usually of an ethical notion such as virtue (*Meno*), courage (*Laches*), or piety (*Euthyphro*). He does not want a list of virtues or virtuous acts, but an account of the 'being' of virtue: what all virtues have in common that *makes* them virtues. Then, by a series of 'yes or no' answers, he leads his interlocutor into self-contradiction. A question often raised is 'Can virtue be taught?' (e.g. in *Meno*, *Protagoras*). Consideration of this prompted Plato to argue that virtue is knowledge (and hence can be taught), and that all wrong action is due to ignorance. But, even on the teachability of virtue, the conclusions of the early dialogues are not unanimous.

Plato's middle period saw the development of his theory of Forms. He never offers a proof of the theory, but introduces it as a hypothesis, or as already agreed upon; but it is fairly clear what sort of considerations led him to it. Familiar things such as men, sticks, animals, and men's actions have various paradoxical features. An elephant is both large and small (a small elephant, a large animal); two sticks appear both equal and unequal (depending on how we look at them); hitting someone is both good and bad (good when it is a just punishment, bad when an assault). We cannot therefore, Plato holds, explain the *meaning* of 'large', 'equal', or 'good' by reference to these things. There must be some stable and unambiguous standard of 'large', 'equal', and 'good', to explain how we know what they mean. Thus Socrates' demands for definitions led Plato to postulate entities quite distinct from the things to which we normally apply the words. To define 'just', for example, we must grasp the 'Form of the just', an unchanging thing which (unlike men's 'just' actions) is in no way unjust, and is known by intellect, not by sense-perception; and this Form is the standard by which all other things are judged just or not.

For similar reasons, we cannot have *knowledge* about things in the familiar world. We cannot know that an elephant is small, for it is equally true that it is large; nor that hitting people is wrong, because sometimes it is right; and so on. Genuine knowledge can only be of the Forms, since only they lack the paradoxical features of things we see, hear, and feel. The Forms also have a role in explaining the world. If something is large, that is *because* it resembles, or shares in, the Form of the large. Even the Forms themselves are to be explained by the supreme Form, that of the Good. (No doubt such explanations were intended to show that all is for the best in both the perceptible world and the world of Forms.) But Plato talks of the Forms and their relations with other things mainly in similes and metaphors, and sometimes inconsistently. Probably he never settled on a version of the theory as wholly satisfactory.

The Forms dominated Plato's thought for a time on subjects as diverse as politics, education, literary criticism, and the nature of the soul. For example, since issues of justice and injustice can only be correctly judged by the Forms, and only philosophers understand the Forms, philosophers should be rulers. In the *Republic*, Plato proposes an ideal State with a caste system that would ensure this, and outlines the education that such philosopher-rulers would need to undergo. He also criticizes poets, largely because they had a false and dangerous reputation as authorities on morality, a role that only philosophers were fit for. In the **Phaedo*, arguments for the immortality of the soul are based on the theory of Forms, together with the thesis that we know the Forms, in some sense, even before we are born. In the *Symposium*, the highest kind of love is apparently supposed to lead to knowledge of the Form of beauty.

In the last period, strong objections are brought against the theory. Although it is unclear whether Plato abandoned it altogether, it was no longer central to his philosophy. Instead, he investigated various philosophical issues separately and with considerable subtlety. The discussions were more technical and often inconclusive. A short summary of his late work is impossible, but a few examples may be mentioned. In the **Theaetetus*, he assesses a series of definitions of knowledge (some very like theories that have had recent currency), and rejects them all. The *Sophist* explores problems of meaning. Picking up **Parmenides'* challenge, 'How can we speak of what is not?', he tries to develop a theory of meaning that works for negative judgements. In the *Laws*, he presents more detailed and realistic political recommendations than in the *Republic*. Probably also in this period he wrote the *Timaeus*, his only work on natural science, in which Timaeus of Locri explains how a creator made the perceptible world on the model of 'what truly is', and the *Philebus*, in which it is argued that knowledge is a more important element in 'the good' than pleasure.

Plato's prose style has been much admired for its richness and variety. These are most evident in the more dramatic early and middle dialogues. The language of the late works grew more technical and austere.

BIBL. P. Shorey, *What Plato Said* (1933); I. M. Crombie, *An Examination of Plato's Doctrines* (1962–3); G. Ryle, 'Plato', *The Encyclopedia of Philosophy* (ed. P. Edwards, 1967).

Plato Comicus Comic poet, active *c.* 420–*c.* 390 BC.

This Plato (Platōn), known to us from a number of fragments, was one of **Aristophanes'* rivals. His work seems to have been strongly political, three of the plays being named after *Cleophon, *Hyperbolus, and *Peisander.

BIBL. Lesky, *Greek Literature*; Edmonds, *Attic Comedy* i.

The Pleiad Group of poets, 3rd century BC.

Seven 'stars' of contemporary tragedy composed the so-called Pleiad (Pleias) at Alexandria, supported by *Ptolemy II in rivalry of Athens' tradition of comedy. Five members are agreed: *Alexander Aetolus, Homerus (Homēros) of Byzantium, *Lycophron, *Philicus, and Sositheus (Sōsitheos). Front-runners for the remaining places are Sosiphanes, Dionysiades, and Aiantides. Titles and fragments of all are nugatory.

BIBL. Fraser, *Ptolemaic Alexandria*.

Head of Plato. Fitzwilliam Museum, Cambridge.

Pleistoanax Agiad king of Sparta, 458–408 BC.

Son of *Pausanias (1), Pleistoanax invaded Attica in
446 BC, after Boeotia and Euboea had revolted from
Athens, but withdrew without a battle, probably after
coming to an arrangement with *Pericles. He was
condemned for taking bribes, and went into exile; in 427
he was recalled at the behest of a Pythian oracle. He
supported peace with Athens in 421, but subsequently
played only a minor political role.

BIBL. Thucydides i. 107, 114, ii. 21, v. 16 ff., 19 ff.,
23 ff., 33, 75; Diodorus Siculus XI. lxxix. 6, XIII. lxxv. 1.

Polemon of Athens Head of the Academy, died
c. 270 BC.

A dissipated son of wealthy parents, Polemon (Polemōn)
was said to have burst into a lecture by *Xenocrates while
drunk, and to have been so impressed that he stayed as a
pupil. He became a man of strong and imperturbable
character, and succeeded as head of the school in 314 BC.
If he made original contributions to philosophy, they are
lost, but he valued good conduct more than theory.

BIBL. Diogenes Laertius iv. 16–20.

Polemon of Ilium Antiquarian, c. 180 BC.

An impressive scholar of antiquities, Polemon
(Polemōn) 'the Periegete', though connected with the
*Attalids at Pergamum, travelled throughout the Greek
world hunting monuments and avidly copying
inscriptions. He was honoured at Delphi (decree extant,
177/6 BC), perhaps in recognition of work on its treasures.
He wrote many learned books in the travel-guide genre,
and often had the pleasure of correcting his predecessors,
e.g. *Eratosthenes.

BIBL. Pfeiffer, Classical Scholarship i.

Pollis Spartan admiral, died after 376 BC.

After service as a naval commander in the 390s BC
(navarch in 396/5, epistoleus in (?) 393/2), Pollis visited
*Dionysius I of Syracuse as an ambassador, and on his
return journey allegedly sold *Plato as a slave at Aegina
(c. 388). In 376 he was defeated by *Chabrias at Naxos.

BIBL. Poralla, Prosopographie, no. 621.

Polyaenus of Lampsacus Epicurean philosopher, early
3rd century BC.

Once a distinguished geometer, Polyaenus (Poluainos)
was persuaded by *Epicurus to devote himself to
philosophy, and, according to Cicero, came to believe that
'all geometry was false'.

BIBL. E. Zeller, Die Philosophie der Griechen III. i (1923),
379–80; Roman World *Cicero.

Polybius (c. 200–after 118 (?) BC) Historian.

Son of the prominent Megalopolitan politician Lycortas,
Polybius (Polubios) was brought up against the
background of the Achaean League's uncomfortable
alliance with Rome. Sent to Rome in 167 BC with the
political hostages after Pydna (see *Perseus), Polybius
(who had held a League office and had carried the ashes of
*Philopoemen (q.v.) to burial) became friendly with L.
Aemilius *Paullus and *Scipio Aemilianus. In touch with
the community of Greek exiles, he was probably
instrumental in the escape from Rome of the future
Seleucid king *Demetrius I in 162. He travelled in Italy

and accompanied Scipio to Africa and Spain in 151,
whence he returned via Hannibal's route across the Alps.
Free to return to Greece in 150, he avoided Achaea, which
was on the brink of war with Rome. He witnessed the
sack of Carthage with Scipio in 146, and journeyed to the
African and Portuguese coasts beyond Gibraltar.

Polybius returned home in 146, and, although he
visited Sardis and the Alexandria of *Ptolemy VIII, he
devoted himself to the internal problems of Achaea and to
his Histories. Remarks about an event of 118 may have
been inserted into the work by him; he is said to have
died falling from a horse at the age of 82.

Although Polybius wrote various historical works
(Tactics, a history of the Numantine War in Spain, a

Grave stele of a warrior, possibly Polybius, found at Kleitor in
Arcadia. This cast (once in Berlin, now lost) shows more detail
than the surviving stele. Mazeïka.

geographical work on equatorial regions, and an encomium of Philopoemen – all lost), he is justly famous for his *Histories*. The work focused on the period 220–168 when Rome established her control over most of the inhabited world, which Polybius saw as a unique event, but it also covered the years 264–220 and 168–146. Parts of the 40 books exist in their entirety, parts in excerpts.

Polybius saw history as an instruction in practical life, one reason why he, as a man versed in political affairs, could write it. Facts and events, and the accuracy of reporting them, were vitally important, and Polybius criticized contemporary 'rhetorical' historians (like *Phylarchus) whose sensationalism distorted truth. Although he was careful to ascertain truth as he saw it, and did attain a high standard, he was susceptible to prejudice: he had a political bias in favour of the Achaean League, *Aratus of Sicyon, and Philopoemen, but against *Callicrates of Leontium, and a personal bias in favour of Scipio and Paullus, but against *Timaeus. He was subject also to inherent distortions in his literary sources (Aratus, Phylarchus, the Roman Fabius Pictor, and others). In addition he used direct sources such as personal experience and travel, eyewitness accounts and interrogation, documents, letters, and inscriptions. He stressed historical causality, but attributed a certain role to Fortune (Tyche). Despite a moralizing tendency and an inelegant literary style, Polybius' lucid narrative remains the main historical source for this important period.

BIBL. Text: ed. Th. Büttner-Wobst (1889–1905); P. Pédech, *La Méthode historique de Polybe* (1964); Walbank, *HCP* i–iii, and *Polybius* (1972); *Roman World* *Hannibal, *Polybius; PW xxi. 2. 1440 ff.

Polycleitus Sculptor, active *c.* 450–420 BC.

The great contemporary and rival for fame of *Pheidias, Polycleitus (Polukleitos) came from Argos and was a pupil (with *Myron) of the Argive sculptor, Ageladas. He worked mainly in the Peloponnese, and specialized in statues of naked male athletes, working almost exclusively in bronze; the chryselephantine cult-statue of Hera at Argos (after 423 BC) was commonly attributed to him, but may have been by a younger Polycleitus. About 20 of his works are recorded, of which we have certainly two in marble copies of the Roman period: the Doryphoros or youth with a spear (*c.* 440s BC) and the Diadoumenos or youth tying a band round his head (*c.* 430s). The Doryphoros was his most famous and influential work, called also his Canon, since it was made to embody his theories and rules of the ideal proportions of the human (male) body. Beauty for him, we are told by later writers, consisted in the precise proportional relationship (*symmetria*) of the various parts to each other and to the whole, 'of finger to finger and of all these to hand and wrist and of those to forearm, or forearm to arm and of all to all'. He seems to have been the first who set out this idea, that there existed ideal human proportions, which could be ascertained and expressed in mathematical rules; the idea was very influential in Greece, and re-appears in Vitruvius, from there to bewitch Renaissance artists.

The Doryphoros and Diadoumenos are very distinctive in the composition and design of their musculature, faces, and hair-styles and enable us to recognize many other naked athletic statues as 'Polycleitan'. This confirms the literary record of his large and active school following.

Doryphoros (Spear-carrier), by Polycleitus. Marble copy from Pompeii of a bronze of the mid-5th century BC. Naples, Museo Nazionale.

Varro criticized his statues for being 'four-square [i.e. rather stocky] and almost all made to one design'. Also he perhaps suffered from frequent comparison with Pheidias, who was known as the sculptor of gods, but he, Polycleitus, of men, since he was reckoned unable to achieve in sculpture the full dignity of the gods. However, his Amazon at Ephesus, made supposedly for a competition with Amazons by Pheidias and *Cresilas and Phradmon, was judged to be the finest, Pheidias' statue coming second.

BIBL. P. E. Arias, *Policleto* (1964); Robertson, *History of Greek Art* 328 ff.; A. F. Stewart, *JHS* xcii (1978); *Roman World* *Varro, *Vitruvius.

Polycleitus of Larissa Alexander historian, floruit 320s BC.

Polycleitus (Polukleitos), who probably accompanied *Alexander the Great's army, wrote a work entitled *Historiai*, which is quoted for romantic gossip about Alexander and for descriptions of places and customs (*Strabo's account of Persis and Susiana contains several fragments).

BIBL. Pearson, *Lost Histories* 70–7.

Polycles Sculptor, active *c.* 160–120 BC.

This Polycles (Poluklēs) came from a prestigious family of Athenian sculptors, which could trace its origins in the business back probably to the fourth century BC. He was, as far as we know, the fourth to bear the name Polycles, and the most famous and successful of them all. The family came into special prominence in the second century BC under Roman patrons who favoured its strongly classicizing work. He was probably based in Athens, being mint magistrate there in 149/8 and 130/29 BC, but executed important commissions in Rome: a Hercules for the temple of Ops, and a Juno and a Jupiter for their temples in the Porticus Octavia, on which he collaborated with his brother Dionysius. Parts of the original Hercules and Juno have been recently and perhaps correctly recognized in marble heads in the Capitoline Museum in Rome. A 'noble hermaphrodite' by him is recorded, and is probably to be recognized in a number of good copies of a moving figure of a sleeping but restless hermaphrodite (though it might have been by his grandfather, Polycles III, *c.* 200 BC).

Other works by members of his family fill out the picture of their eclectic use of models of the classical period: we have copies of the Apollo with a cithara at Rome by his father Timarchides (I), *c.* 170 BC, and the original torso of a naked portrait-statue of a Roman at Delos signed by his brother Dionysius and his son Timarchides (II), *c.* 110 BC. These and the Hercules and Juno heads draw freely on fourth-century models, while Polycles' Athenian contemporaries, *Eubulides and Eucheir, favoured a purer fifth-century style.

BIBL. Coarelli, *Studi Miscellanei* xv (1970); Stewart, *Attika* 42 ff.; *Roman World* s.v. Gnaeus *Octavius.

Polycrates Tyrant of Samos, died *c.* 523 BC.

As tyrant of Samos, Polycrates (Polukratēs) commanded a powerful navy which controlled the eastern Aegean. He was famous for his public works, especially the building of the harbour at Samos, the great temple of Hera, and the tunnel (designed by Eupalinus) which brought water to his capital. His power and wealth attracted the envy of the Persian satrap Oroetes, who lured him to Magnesia-on-the-Maeander and put him to death. The contrast between his prosperous life and miserable end gave much scope for moralizing, as can be seen in the story of his attempt to break his too-good luck by throwing his ring into the sea – only to have it returned to him in the belly of a fish.

BIBL. Herodotus iii. 39–46, 54–60, 120–6; Andrewes, *Greek Tyrants* 117–22.

Polygnotus Painter, active *c.* 490–460 BC.

One of the most famous and admired painters of antiquity, Polygnotus (Polugnōtos), son of Aglaophon of Thasos, was the chief exponent of the new early classical style in the years after the Persian Wars. He and his brother Aristophon were taught by their father, also a painter. He worked mainly in Athens, where he received citizenship, although his most famous wall-paintings were

Sleeping Hermaphrodite, probably by Polycles. Marble copy of the Roman period. Rome, Museo delle Terme.

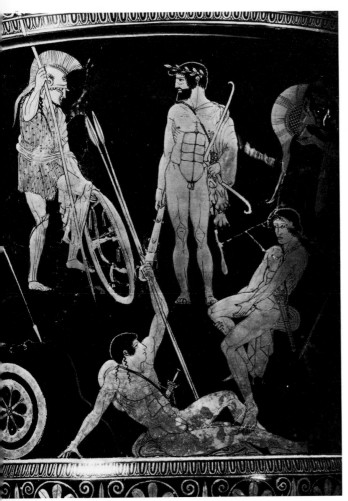

Krater depicting Heracles, **Theseus, and Peirithous, c. 460 BC.
The style of figure painting probably owes much to the works of
Polygnotus (now lost). Paris, Musée du Louvre.

done for the Cnidians in their club-house ('Lesche') at
Delphi, depicting the Sack of Troy and the Underworld.
At Athens, often collaborating with Micon, he did wall-
paintings in the Stoa Poikile, Theseum and Anakeion, all
perhaps built under the patronage of *Cimon, whose
sister, Elpinice, he featured in a crypto-portrait as one of
the Trojan women in his other Sack of Troy in the Stoa
Poikile. He was reportedly her lover (along with others).

All his works are now lost, but from extensive literary
descriptions it is clear that his paintings abandoned the
customary single-level ground-line, and that he placed his
figures up and down the picture plane in a schematic sort
of perspective without recession or diminution, which
seems to be reflected in the work of a group of
contemporary vase-painters (the Niobid painter and his
circle). Polygnotus' figures seem typically to have been
isolated from each other and in quiet reflective repose,
expressive, *Aristotle tells us, of their inner character
(ethos), which was contrasted with the outer emotion
(pathos) shown by the figures of later painters like *Zeuxis
and *Parrhasius.

BIBL. Rumpf, Enc. Art. Ant. vi. 292–6; Barron, JHS xcii
(1972); Robertson, History of Greek Art 242–70.

Polymnestus Musician and poet, 660/600 BC.

A citharode from Colophon, Polymnestus (Polumnēstos)
is associated by Pseudo-Plutarch, On Music, with the
Second School of music at Sparta and the composition of
aulodic nomes, particularly those called Orthioi (High-
pitched). He wrote elegiac and hexameter poems, the latter
including one on *Thaletas mentioned by Pausanias. This
and mention by *Alcman limit his dates.

His songs seem, from a line of *Cratinus, to have been
in Athenian musical curricula, and are unlikely to have
been lewd (as suggested by ancient interpretations of
Aristophanes, Knights 1287).

BIBL. Pseudo-Plutarch, On Music 1132C–1134B;
Pausanias I. xiv. 4; W. Schmid and O. Stählin, Geschichte
der griechischen Literatur (1929–) I. i. 429 f.; New Grove
Dictionary of Music (1980) xv. 54; Roman World
*Pausanias.

Polyperchon Macedonian general, died c. 303 BC.

Polyperchon (Poluperkhōn) was the son of Simmias,
and chieftain of Tymphaea, an area on the borders
between Macedonia and Epirus. From 333 BC on he
commanded units from Tymphaea with distinction in
*Alexander the Great's invasion of Asia. In 324 he was
sent back to Europe as *Craterus' second-in-command,
either because of his age or possibly because of his
opposition to Alexander's pro-Iranian policy.

Before his death in 319 *Antipater appointed him his
successor as strategus or supreme commander over the
European part of the empire; this threatened the position
of Antipater's son *Cassander, who engineered a coalition
of the generals *Antigonus, *Lysimachus, and *Ptolemy
(I) against him. Polyperchon was supported by the royal
court of *Olympias and by *Eumenes of Cardia, as well as
by the Greek cities which he allowed to revert to a
democratic form of government. Nevertheless he was
unable to maintain his position outside the Peloponnese.
He was excluded by the other generals in the redivision of
the empire in 311. In 309, in agreement with Cassander,
he put to death Alexander's bastard son Heracles. He lost
his last bases in the Peloponnese to Ptolemy and
*Demetrius Poliorcetes during the 'Four Years' War'
(307–304), and disappears from the historical record.

BIBL. Diodorus Siculus xviii–xix (based on *Hieronymus
of Cardia); C. Wehrli, Antigone et Demetrios (1969); Will,
Hist. pol. i.

Polyxenidas Seleucid admiral, floruit c. 200–185 BC.

A Rhodian exile, Polyxenidas (Poluxenidas) commanded
the Seleucid fleet for *Antiochus III (q.v.) against Rome.
Off Samos in 190 BC he nearly destroyed through
treachery a Rhodian fleet sailing north to join the Romans,
but did not press his advantage over the nearby Roman
fleet. Although the Romans were later forced to divide
their fleet, when Polyxenidas faced them between
Myonessus and Corycus, his greater numbers were
neutralized in an outflanking manœuvre by the
exceptional speed of the Rhodian contingent. Antiochus,
watching the decisive defeat from the shore, thus lost his
mastery of the sea. When the disastrous news of his defeat
at Magnesia came to Polyxenidas in Ephesus, he
abandoned his fleet in Lycia and journeyed overland to
Syria.

BIBL. CAH viii; Bevan, House of Seleucus ii.

Porus Indian king, died 317 BC.

Defeated by *Alexander the Great in 326 BC at the river Hydaspes (Jhelum), Porus (Pōros) was permitted to retain his extensive domains between that river and the Acesines (Chenab), was given extra land, and was later declared king of the conquered parts of India. He was murdered in 317 by the Macedonian satrap Eudamus.

BIBL. Berve, *Alexanderreich*, no. 683.

Papyrus of the 2nd century BC, rather badly written, preserving two epigrams by Poseidippus. Paris, Musée du Louvre.

Poseidippus Epigrammatist, *c.* 275 BC.

Poseidippus (Poseidippos) came from Macedonian Pella, but epigrams on the Pharos (11) and the temple of *Arsinoe II as Aphrodite at Zephyrium (12, 13) attest an Alexandrian period of at least 280–270 BC. His erotic and symposiac epigrams, robust in style and attitude, show him to be a talented acolyte of *Asclepiades of Samos, whom he probably knew at Alexandria. Reitzenstein's hypothesis that Asclepiades, Poseidippus, and *Hedylus published from Samos a joint anthology called *Soros* (the *Heap*), is too often treated as fact, though the three were evidently closely associated. A third-century papyrus entitled *Mixed Epigrams*, bearing Poseidippus' name together with others less decipherable, does indicate a contribution to a presentation anthology in honour of the marriage of *Arsinoe I (?). Poseidippus was clearly a man of parts, honoured with Aetolian *proxenia* in 264/3. He probably ended his days back in mainland Greece.

BIBL. Gow and Page, *Hellenistic Epigrams*; *SH* 698–708; Fraser, *Ptolemaic Alexandria*; Lasserre, *RhM* cii (1959).

Pos(e)idonius (*c.* 135–51 BC) Polymath.

A native of Apamea in Syria, Pos(e)idonius (Poseidōnios) was a pupil of the Stoic philosopher *Panaetius. He settled in Rhodes, visited Rome, travelled the western provinces, hated Marius, taught Cicero, deeply admired Pompey, and recorded his deeds. Copious fragments of his numerous historical works survive, as do fragments scientific and philosophical, and his influence

on historical narrative and geographical excursuses in, for example, Caesar, Sallust, Tacitus, and Plutarch was profound. He provided a narrative of events from 136 to *c.* 85 BC (severely critical, at times, of Roman degeneration and brutality, but with an aristocratic tinge), and furnished the Romans with the means towards a philosophical justification of the existence of their Empire.

BIBL. Fragments, ed. Edelstein and Kidd (1972); Strasburger, *JRS* lv (1965); *Roman World* Gaius Julius *Caesar, *Cicero, *Marius, *Plutarch, *Pompey, *Sallust, *Tacitus. N.H.

Chorusmen of a satyr play on an Apulian red figure bell-krater of *c.* 400–380 BC. Sydney, Nicholson Museum.

Pratinas Tragedian, 6th–5th century BC.

A native of Phlius near Corinth, though he made his career at Athens, Pratinas is said by the *Suda* to have been the first writer of satyr plays and to have written 50 plays of which 32 were satyric; this information is variously interpreted by scholars. Equally controversial is the one substantial fragment, said to be from a hyporcheme (part of a satyr play, or an independent composition?), in which a chorus attacks *aulos*-players who let the music drown the words that it accompanies.

BIBL. Lesky, *Greek Literature*; Pickard-Cambridge, *Dithyramb* . . .; D. F. Sutton, *The Greek Satyr Play* (1980).

Praxilla Lyric poetess, 5th century BC.

Praxilla of Sicyon wrote hymns, dithyrambs, and drinking-songs. In her *Hymn to Adonis* she portrayed Adonis in the Underworld being asked what were the fairest things he had left on earth; he replied, the light of the sun, the stars, the moon, 'and ripe cucumbers, apples, and pears'. The line became proverbial for its silliness; little else survives.

BIBL. Lesky, *Greek Literature*; *Lyra Graeca* (Loeb) iii; Kirkwood, *Greek Monody*.

Praxiteles Sculptor, active *c.* 370–330 BC.

The son, probably, of the well-established Athenian

Sculptures by Praxiteles: (*left*) Apollo Sauroctonus (Lizard-slayer), marble copy of the Roman period of a mid-4th century bronze; (*right*) Aphrodite of Cnidos, marble copy of the Roman period of a mid-4th century marble original. Vatican Museum.

sculptor Cephisodotus, Praxiteles (Praxitelēs) was one of the greatest and most influential of Greek sculptors. His family's involvement in the business can be traced down to the first century BC; at least seven of them were called Praxiteles. He worked mostly in mainland Greece – Athens and the Peloponnese – but travelled for some commissions to the islands and Asia Minor. Literary sources record over 50 commissions comprising well over 75 statues. He was much in demand for cult-statues and cult-groups, and especially for goddesses and gods with feminine interests or appearance: Dionysus, Eros, Apollo. Athletic statuary, portraiture, and architectural sculpture seem to have interested him hardly at all. Marble was his preferred medium, but he was proficient in bronze as well; he liked to have his marble statues coloured by the painter *Nicias (son of Nicomedes).

His naked marble Aphrodite of Cnidos, bought by the Cnidians apparently after being rejected by the Coans in favour of a more modest, clothed version, was one of the most famous sculptures of antiquity, during which it remained an object of pilgrimage, critical appreciation,

and lust. It was probably the first monumental independent free-standing statue of a nude woman. Many Roman copies of the lost original can be identified by the representation of the statue on Roman coins of Cnidos. The statue seems immediately to have canonized a new ideal for feminine beauty, both of face and body, whose influence it would be hard to overestimate.

His other most famous works, now lost, were an Eros in Thespiae and a gilded statue of his favourite courtesan, Phryne of Thespiae, which she set up on a column at Delphi, provoking some conservative indignation. At Thespiae he made another statue of Phryne, which was set up beside the Eros and his Aphrodite there; all three were of marble. Phryne was also said, no doubt correctly, to have been the model for the Cnidian Aphrodite.

His lizard-slaying Apollo ('Sauroktonos') is certainly to be recognized in Roman copies of an effeminate adolescent boy leaning in a sinuous S-curve on a tree on which is a lizard tethered to his hand by a string; almost certainly, too, one of his well-known Satyrs, in a multitude of copies of a youthful and fleshy Satyr leaning in a similar S-Curve on a tree-stump. The famous statue of Hermes with the child Dionysus at Olympia, attributed by Pausanias to Praxiteles, is still controversial, but on technical grounds seems to have been carved later than the fourth century BC. Probably from Praxiteles' workshop are three large and dull reliefs from Mantinea, which almost certainly adorned the base of his cult-group there of Leto, Apollo, and Artemis.

BIBL. G. E. Rizzo, *Prassitele* (1932); Richter, *Sculpture and Sculptors* 199–206; Robertson, *History of Greek Art* 386–96; *Roman World* *Pausanias.

Prodicus (*c.* 470/60–early 4th century BC) Sophist.

Prodicus (Prodikos) of Ceos travelled widely on diplomatic missions, and earned large fees from his teaching. *Plato often represents him as insisting on fine distinctions between the meanings of words. This was no doubt important in his teaching of rhetoric, but probably also had philosophical significance and helped to foster an interest in definitions in his 'friend and pupil' *Socrates (though Socrates could not afford the '50-drachma lecture', according to Plato, and heard only the drachma one).

Prodicus was said to be an atheist, and held that men first considered as gods 'things useful to human life' such as sun, moon, rivers, and springs. He was much admired for a discourse on Heracles' choice between virtue and vice, personified as two women. From *Xenophon's paraphrase, the moral lessons seem to have been conventional.

BIBL. Guthrie, *Greek Philosophy* iii.

Protagoras (*c.* 490–*c.* 420 BC) Sophist and philosopher.

A sophist of high reputation, Protagoras (Prōtagoras) of Abdera earned a considerable fortune from teaching. At Athens he became a friend of *Pericles, who was said to have invited him to draft laws for the new colony at Thurii. According to late sources, he was charged with impiety and expelled from Athens.

Our knowledge of his philosophy depends largely on a few fragments and discussions of it by *Plato, who evidently respected him more than other sophists. His work *Truth* began, 'Man is the measure of all things, of those that are, that they are, and of those that are not, that they are not.' Plato interprets this as 'Whatever *seems* to anyone *is* to that person', and cites as examples perceived qualities (a wind that feels cold to you and warm to me *is* cold for you and warm for me) and moral beliefs (whatever seems just and good to each State *is* just and good to it). It is unclear whether the thesis applied to all beliefs, but Plato suggests that it can be turned against itself (if the thesis were true, it would be false for the majority who believed it false).

Protagoras' claim to teach 'virtue' is hard to square with his thesis that any moral belief is true for those who hold it. Plato suggests that his professed 'wisdom' lay, like a doctor's, in his ability to *change* the way things seem to people. In the *Protagoras*, Plato attributes to him a less obviously subjective, but equally democratic, theory of virtue: men could survive only in societies, and a society could exist only if all its members shared in justice and other virtues; all citizens, not just a few specialists, taught virtue (just as they all taught Greek).

Protagoras' theology is expressed in a famous fragment,

'About the gods I cannot know either that they are or that they are not, or what they are like in form; for there are many things preventing knowledge, obscurity and the shortness of man's life.'

BIBL. Plato, *Protagoras, Theaetetus* 151–79; Guthrie, *Greek Philosophy* iii; G. B. Kerferd, *The Sophistic Movement* (1981).

Prusias I King of Bithynia, *c.* 230–*c.* 182 BC.

Prusias, the son of Ziaelas, spent much of his reign in ambitious military adventures to increase his kingdom. He campaigned against Byzantium in 220/19 BC and against the Gauls (Galatians) in 217. During the First Macedonian War (214–205), he harried lands of *Attalus I of Pergamum, perhaps incited by *Philip V (whose daughter may at this time have been betrothed to Prusias' son, later *Prusias II). He also supplied Philip with ships, and was included as a Macedonian ally in the Peace of Phoenice in 205. In 203–202 he received Cius and Myrleia on the Propontis as a reward from Philip.

Coin portrait of Prusias I, king of Bithynia.

Counselled by the *Scipios (Africanus and Asiagenus), Prusias remained neutral at Magnesia, but the Treaty of Apamea gave to *Eumenes II of Pergamum land once belonging to Bithynia, and hostilities erupted before 184. Prusias was supported by the Gauls and Philip, Eumenes by Heraclea Pontica (much of whose territory Prusias had once seized). Prusias' trump card was the Carthaginian Hannibal, who had fled the Seleucid court to escape Rome, and under whose guidance the war fared better. One naval battle was won decisively against the odds, albeit by an unorthodox stratagem: jars of poisonous serpents were lobbed on to the enemy ships, the crews fled in confusion, and Hannibal carried the day. Terms were agreed, and, although self-administered poison robbed Rome of Hannibal, Prusias relinquished the disputed territory and died about 182.

BIBL. PW xxxiii. 1. 1086 ff.; Habicht, *Hermes* lxxxiv (1956), 90 ff.; *Roman World* *Hannibal.

Prusias II King of Bithynia, *c.* 182–149 BC.

Prusias II inherited the antipathy of his father *Prusias I towards Pergamum, but fought with *Eumenes II against *Pharnaces I of Pontus in 183–179 BC. He received Tieum in return, which Eumenes may have taken from Bithynia in 184. While *Perseus of Macedon was forging alliances after his accession in 179, his sister Apama was married to Prusias (although the betrothal may date from the time of *Philip V). In 166 Rome nullified Eumenes' victory over the Gauls; Prusias reverted to his anti-Pergamene stance by complaining that Eumenes had not evacuated Galatia, had occupied parts of Bithynia, and had conspired with *Antiochus IV. War broke out with *Attalus II in 156. Rome ordered Prusias to negotiate, but he betrayed a truce and attacked Attalus with his whole army, later ravaging Pergamene territory up to the citadel itself. Peace was finally arranged in 154, with Prusias paying a substantial indemnity.

Attalus had the last word against Prusias when in 149 he supported the attempt of the latter's son *Nicomedes (II) to seize the throne. Ignoring Rome, Attalus and Nicomedes invaded Bithynia; their presence and Prusias' unpopularity made troops provided by Diegylis of Thrace ineffective in protecting the king. Betrayed by the inhabitants of Nicomedia, he was murdered in the temple of Zeus by his son's emissaries.

BIBL. *Roman World*; PW xxiii. 1. 1107 ff.; Habicht, *Hermes* lxxxiv (1956), 101 ff.

Psammetichus Egyptian pharaoh, 660–609 BC.

An oracle told Psammetichus (Psammētikhos; Egyptian Psamtik) that he would become pharaoh with the help of 'bronze men from the sea'. These proved to be Ionian and Carian pirates with their bronze armour, whom Psammetichus recruited as mercenaries. During his reign large numbers of Greeks settled in Egypt, and Naucratis was founded.

BIBL. Herodotus ii. 151–4; Strabo xvii. 801.

Ptolemy I Soter Founder of the Ptolemaic dynasty, died 283/2 BC.

Ptolemy (Ptolemaios) (whom some, mendaciously, claimed to have been *Philip II's natural son) was a friend of *Alexander the Great in youth, and was exiled as such

Marble head of Ptolemy I Soter, king of Egypt. Paris, Louvre.

c. 337–6 BC. Returning to Macedonia after Philip's murder (336), he joined the Persian expedition as a junior officer. In 330 he became a Bodyguard and is thereafter prominent in the military narrative (an early achievement was the arrest of *Bessus) and at court (he appears in the *Cleitus incident and the Pages' Conspiracy). In 324 he received a daughter of *Artabazus (son of *Pharnabazus) at the Susa marriages.

After Alexander's death (323), by luck or judgement, Ptolemy received the Egyptian satrapy, and in 322 directly challenged *Perdiccas' authority by stealing the body of Alexander (on its way to burial at Aegae) and taking it to Alexandria on the plea that Alexander had wished to be buried at Siwah. (The corpse never actually got further than Ptolemy's capital.) A consequent alliance with the anti-Perdiccas coalition was sealed by marriage to *Antipater's daughter Eurydice. After Perdiccas' abortive invasion of Egypt Ptolemy wisely refused the regency, which passed at Triparadeisus to Antipater. On the latter's death (319) Ptolemy defied *Polyperchon by seizing Palestine and Coele-Syria; but he lost them again to *Eumenes of Cardia and (after entering a coalition with *Cassander, *Seleucus (I), and *Lysimachus in 315) to *Antigonus. In 314 he answered Antigonus' proclamation of Greek autonomy with a similar one of his own, but troubles in Cyrene and Cyprus prevented operations against Antigonus until 312, when he defeated *Demetrius Poliorcetes at Gaza (permitting Seleucus to return to Babylon), only to retire again to Egypt. Accession to the Peace of 311 afforded a temporary protection to his position. In 310–309 he installed his brother Menelaus as governor of Cyprus and occupied Cos, and in 309–8, after a reconciliation with Demetrius, briefly irrupted into mainland Greek affairs, where, however, his talk of freedom was belied by the garrisoning of Sicyon and Corinth. In 306 open war with Antigonus was renewed: utterly defeated off (Cypriot) Salamis, Ptolemy lost all his extra-Egyptian possessions, and Antigonus was only prevented from entering Egypt by adverse weather. Fortunately for Ptolemy (who took the title 'King' in 305/4 (the later title Soter means 'Saviour')) Antigonus did not return to the attack, and after Ipsus (301, at which he was not present) Ptolemy retook Palestine and Coele-Syria (laying the ground for five Syrian Wars between Egypt and the Seleucids in the following century). Demetrius' attack on Greece (296) permitted repossession of Cyprus and parts of southern Asia Minor, though a Ptolemaic squadron failed to save Athens from Demetrius in 294. Six years later, however, his ships were in at the liberation of Athens, and he had in the meantime extended his overseas control into the Cyclades. (Some date this to 286–285.) In 285 he abdicated in favour of *Ptolemy II, his son by *Berenice I (*Ptolemy Ceraunus, a son by Eurydice, having been displaced).

Ptolemy's reign probably saw the establishment of all the main features of the military and administrative organization of Ptolemaic Egypt. He also founded the cult of Sarapis (derived from Osor-Hapi, the Apis-bull deified as Osiris) to provide a new and local focus for the Greeks of his realm, and (perhaps with advice from *Demetrius of Phalerum) established the Museum (a sort of cross between temple and Oxbridge college) and the Library, which came to dominate the cultural and scientific life of the Hellenistic world.

Ptolemy himself wrote a history of Alexander's reign, which languished almost unnoticed until Arrian, impressed by its truthfulness ('as he himself was a king, mendacity would have been more dishonourable than for anyone else'), used it as a major source. The work is generally supposed to have been composed late in life, with the purpose of countering the mythologizing of Alexander and with a soldier's emphasis on military matters; but all these suppositions may be false, and Ptolemy's 'truthfulness' may be less a matter of telling the whole truth than of not actually uttering falsehoods.

BIBL. Will, *Hist. pol.* i; Pearson, *Lost Histories* 188–211; Badian, *Studies* 250 ff.; R. M. Errington, *CQ*, n.s. xix (1969); *Roman World* *Arrian.

Ptolemy II Philadelphus King of Egypt, 283–246 BC.

Ptolemy (Ptolemaios) was born on Cos in 308 BC, and was chosen as heir by his father *Ptolemy I, who married the boy's mother *Berenice I and disinherited an elder son, *Ptolemy Ceraunus. Sometime in the 280s Ptolemy (II) married *Arsinoe I, daughter of *Lysimachus, whom he divorced probably before c. 279. He was associated on the throne in 285 before succeeding two years later. An initial encounter with *Antiochus I (the 'Carian War') was concluded in 279, and a revolt by *Magas of Cyrene c. 275 was also settled. The First Syrian War developed c. 274 with Ptolemy's invasion of Syria. At about this time (before 274/3) Ptolemy married his full sister *Arsinoe II and made her joint ruler. (Although the custom of brother–sister marriage had been standard among the dynastic Egyptian pharaohs, this was the first instance among Greek royalty, and the marriage scandalized the Greek population (see *Sotades).) To this clever woman is attributed the conduct of the war, which ended in a glorious victory for Egypt in 271. Ptolemy proclaimed his own and his wife's deification in 272/1, and later adopted her title and cult-title, Philadelphus ('Loving One's

Brother/Sister'). Ptolemy supported Athens in the War of *Chremonides (266–261), but did not supply enough military aid for the control of *Antigonus Gonatas of Macedon to be shaken. The details of the Second Syrian War against *Antiochus II (c. 260–c. 253) are obscure, but Egypt lost large areas of Asia Minor, and Ptolemy married his daughter *Berenice Syra to Antiochus.

Ptolemy is credited with extensive 'hellenization' of Egypt. He established strict royal control over the economy (which blossomed), made many Greek settlements and supported exploration along the Red Sea and in the south, and drew many prominent Greeks to Alexandria with its famous Library and Museum. These 'golden years' of Alexandria saw *Callimachus, *Theocritus, and *Apollonius Rhodius, to name but a few. Although Ptolemy had intellectual interests and encouraged scholarship, he had an undeniable penchant for luxury (note his mistresses, his extreme wealth, and the vulgar extravagance shown in the procession described by Callixeinus). Not always successful in war, he yet left an empire which was prosperous and powerful, and a capital city which was the cultural and intellectual capital of the Greek world.

BIBL. Fraser, *Ptolemaic Alexandria*; Theocritus xvii; PW xxiii. 2. 1645 ff. (Ptolemaios (19)); *FGrH* 627 F 2 (procession).

Coin portrait of Ptolemy III Euergetes, king of Egypt (enlarged).

Left: head of an Egyptianizing statue of Ptolemy II Philadelphus, king of Egypt. Paris, Musée du Louvre. *Right*: bronze bust from Herculaneum, probably depicting Ptolemy II. Naples, Museo Nazionale.

Ptolemy III Euergetes King of Egypt, 246–222/1 BC.

The son of *Ptolemy II and *Arsinoe I, Ptolemy (Ptolemaios) the 'Benefactor' acceded to the throne in 246 BC, and married *Berenice II, the daughter of *Magas of Cyrene. He invaded Syria in the Third Syrian War in 246 to support the claims of the son of his sister *Berenice Syra to the Seleucid throne, but this turned into a war of vengeance after they were murdered by rivals. Ptolemy is said to have marched through the Seleucid empire as far as Bactria, although extensive military conquests there are doubtful. He returned to Egypt to deal with an uprising in the Delta, but defeated an attack by *Seleucus II in Coele-Syria. The Seleucid's coalition with his brother *Antiochus Hierax forced Ptolemy to make peace on terms which are not certain, but Ptolemy received some territory in Asia Minor and Thrace.

Egypt remained at peace for the rest of Ptolemy's reign (which led to a dangerous weakening of military strength), but the king did intervene in Greece. He had allied himself with *Aratus of Sicyon, who opposed Macedonian rule in Greece, and, when the latter had expelled *Antigonus Gonatas from Corinth in 243, Ptolemy was elected *strategus* of the Achaean League. He was generous to Athens, after her liberation from Macedon in 228, with benefactions and dedications. When Aratus began to court *Antigonus Doson for help against *Cleomenes III of Sparta, Ptolemy transferred his financial support to Cleomenes *c.* 225, and also negotiated with the latter's ally, Aetolia. He abandoned Cleomenes to his fate at Sellasia in 222, apparently negotiating secretly with Doson, but received him as a refugee in Egypt later. Ptolemy may have thought that the considerable military support needed by Cleomenes would have led to war between Egypt and Macedon, and he may have wanted all his available resources in Asia, since *Antiochus III was beginning to reconquer Asia Minor and threaten Coele-Syria. Ptolemy died either at the end of 222, or at the beginning of 221.

BIBL. PW xxiii. 2. 1667 ff. (Ptolemaios (21)); Will, *Hist. pol.* i.

Ptolemy IV Philopator King of Egypt, 221–204 BC.

Ptolemy (Ptolemaios) the 'Father-loving' was probably a minor when he succeeded his father *Ptolemy III. A pupil of the Alexandrian scholar *Eratosthenes, Ptolemy's predilections were intellectual and dilettante rather than for public affairs, and he gladly succumbed to the control

of his ministers *Sosibius and *Agathocles (q.v.).

The Fourth Syrian War against *Antiochus III ended with Egypt's decisive victory at Raphia in 217. Ptolemy pressed for no concessions in the peace-treaty, an example of his lack of positive foreign policy. After Raphia Egypt was shaken by severe internal riots, and, in 207, by the secession of Upper Egypt. Ptolemy nevertheless spent the rest of his life in a self-indulgent neglect of public affairs: he wrote a tragedy on Adonis, was fanatically devoted to the cult of Dionysus, and experimented in the construction of huge warships and luxury barges. He allowed his wife, his full sister *Arsinoe III, to be sent away by his ministers. A ruler of only mediocre talents, Ptolemy died suddenly in 204 (though *Polybius says 203), but his death was concealed for some time to further his ministers' designs.

BIBL. A. Bouché-Leclercq, *Histoire des Lagides* (1903); Will, *Hist. pol.*

Coin portrait of Ptolemy V Epiphanes, king of Egypt (enlarged).

Ptolemy V Epiphanes King of Egypt, 204–180 BC.

The child of *Ptolemy IV and *Arsinoe III, Ptolemy (Ptolemaios) 'God Made Manifest' was associated on the throne at birth, but after his father's death was the young pawn of *Agathocles and *Sosibius, his ministers. Egypt faced serious problems: *Philip V of Macedon and the Seleucid *Antiochus III colluded to divide Egypt in 203–2 BC, and Antiochus invaded Coele-Syria in 202 and was victorious despite a counter-offensive by *Scopas of Aetolia. Roman embassies in 200 and 196 proved ineffective in protecting Ptolemy from Antiochus. In 197, Ptolemy was declared of age, and was crowned at Memphis according to ancient Egyptian rites, which the decree carved on the Rosetta Stone commemorates. Peace with Antiochus concluded, Ptolemy married the latter's daughter Cleopatra I in 193. The rest of his reign was relatively stable: although Coele-Syria was renounced and some overseas possessions were lost, Upper Egypt was reunited in 186 and disturbances in Lower Egypt were quelled. Ptolemy died in 180, by poison according to ancient tradition.

BIBL. *OGIS* 90; Will, *Hist. pol.* ii.

Ptolemy VI Philomator King of Egypt, 180–145 BC.
Ptolemy VII Neos Philopator Joint ruler in Egypt, 145–144 BC.
Ptolemy VIII Euergetes II (Physkon) King of Egypt, 170–116 BC.

Ptolemy VI (Ptolemaios) the 'Mother-loving' was the son of *Ptolemy V and Cleopatra I, and ruled jointly with

Marble head of Ptolemy IV Philopator, king of Egypt. Courtesy, Museum of Fine Arts, Boston.

his mother until her death in 176 BC. Claims that Coele-Syria had been her dowry led to the Sixth Syrian War with *Antiochus IV in 170. Ptolemy, in flight, fell into his uncle Antiochus' hands, and was used as a pawn against his brother Ptolemy VIII (whom the Alexandrians had declared king) to further the Seleucid's plans. The brothers reunited in 168 and ruled jointly with their mutual sister *Cleopatra II (Philometor's wife).

Constant hostility prevailed between the brothers, and they finally agreed to divide the empire, after Philometor had abandoned Alexandria for the year 164–3. The latter was content with Egypt and Cyprus, but Physkon complained to Rome for a decade over his portion of Cyrene and demanded Cyprus also. In 155 Physkon dramatically willed his kingdom to Rome, and Philometor installed his son Ptolemy VII (the 'New Father-loving') as governor in Cyprus to forestall his brother's invasion.

Philometor supported the cause of the Seleucid pretender *Alexander Balas, to whom he married his daughter *Cleopatra Thea. When Balas tried to kill him, Philometor transferred his allegiance and his daughter to *Demetrius II. He appears to have been offered the throne of Antioch, but preferred to be the power behind Demetrius. He helped to defeat Balas, but died in the attempt in 145.

Coin portraits of Ptolemy VI Philometor and Ptolemy VIII Euergetes II (Physkon), kings of Egypt (enlarged).

After his brother's death, Physkon was recalled to Alexandria, and dealt with Ptolemy VII and Cleopatra II (who had declared themselves joint rulers) by murdering the former and marrying the latter. As well as for his obesity (the nickname 'Physkon' means 'Pot-belly'), Physkon is notorious for expelling the remaining scholars from Alexandria, and, in 142, for seducing and marrying *Cleopatra III (the daughter of his brother and sister) while still keeping as wife Cleopatra II (his own sister and his bride's mother). He was, however, by no means incapable of competent administration or of magnanimous gestures (such as his reception of the embassy of *Scipio Aemilianus in 140/39).

When Cleopatra II revolted from the *ménage à trois* in 132 and declared first her son by Physkon, Ptolemy Memphites, king and then herself queen, Physkon murdered the child, sent the dismembered corpse to the mother, and subdued an Alexandria sickened by these atrocities in 127/6. In answer to Cleopatra II's plan of offering Egypt to the Seleucid Demetrius II, Physkon supported the pretender Alexander Zabinas to unseat him in 126/5, and allied himself to the rightful king *Antiochus VIII Grypus by giving him in marriage Cleopatra Tryphaena, his daughter by Cleopatra III. An

official reconciliation was proclaimed between the king and his two queens in 124; Physkon died in 116, bequeathing the throne to Cleopatra III and her children.

BIBL. Otto and Bengtson, *Bayer. Abh.*, n. F. xvii (1938); Will, *Hist. pol.* ii.

Ptolemy IX Soter II (Lathyrus) King of Egypt, 116–81 BC.
Ptolemy X Alexander I King of Egypt, 116–88 BC.
Ptolemy Apion Ruler of Cyrene, died 96 BC.

On the death of *Ptolemy VIII (q.v.), his throne was willed to *Cleopatra III and to her choice of their two sons. The elder, Ptolemy (Ptolemaios) IX, was governing Cyprus, and the younger, Ptolemy X (his mother's favourite), was proclaimed king until popular demand recalled Ptolemy Lathyrus to Alexandria and sent Ptolemy Alexander to Cyprus. Lathyrus (this popular nickname means 'Chick-pea'; his official title was 'Saviour') had been married to his full sister Cleopatra IV; he was forced to divorce her and marry another sister, Cleopatra Selene, who ultimately divorced him. (Both subsequently married various Seleucid kings.) Constant strife between the brothers admitted two periods of joint rule in 110 and 108 BC, but in 107 Lathyrus, forced from Alexandria, reconquered Cyprus from Syria and became an independent king. Both brothers were embroiled in the conflicts between the Seleucids *Antiochus VIII and *Antiochus IX, and with the Jewish state. Alexander is said to have murdered his mother in 101, and he married his brother's daughter Cleopatra Berenice (see later *Ptolemies). Cyprus and Egypt remained separate until 88, when Lathyrus returned to defeat Alexander and reunite the kingdom. He ruled jointly with his daughter until 81.

Ptolemy Apion (Ptolemaios Apiōn) was an illegitimate son of Ptolemy VIII, and through obscure means became the governor of Cyrene at least by 101. He bequeathed the country to Rome in 96, ending the tripartite division of his father's realm.

BIBL. Will, *Hist. pol.*; Otto and Bengtson, *Bayer. Abh.* n. F. xvii (1938).

The Later Ptolemies
Cleopatra Berenice Queen of Egypt, 81–80 BC.
Ptolemy XI Alexander II King of Egypt, 80 BC.
Ptolemy XII Auletes King of Egypt, 80–51 BC.
Ptolemy XIII King of Egypt, 51–47 BC.
Ptolemy XIV King of Egypt, 47–44 BC.

The legitimate descendants of the Ptolemies died with the daughter of *Ptolemy IX, Cleopatra Berenice (Kleopatra Berenikē), and with *Ptolemy X's son, Ptolemy (Ptolemaios) XI: the latter murdered Cleopatra and was in turn murdered by the Alexandrians in 80 BC. The throne

Coin portrait of Ptolemy XII Auletes, king of Egypt (enlarged).

passed to an illegitimate son of Ptolemy IX, Ptolemy XII, known as 'Auletes' ('Flute-player') because of his frivolous tendencies. He married his full sister and managed to rule until 51, with Roman financial support and numerous vicissitudes, though he ceded Cyprus to Rome in 58 and was temporarily deposed in 55. Auletes' children included Ptolemy XIII, Ptolemy XIV, and *Cleopatra VII. Both brothers married their famous sister; the elder was killed fighting Julius Caesar in 47, and the younger was killed on his sister's orders in 44.

BIBL. *Roman World* Gaius Julius *Caesar, *Ptolemy XII Auletes; Will, *Hist. pol.* ii.

Ptolemy Alorites Macedonian regent, 368–365 BC.

Son-in-law of *Amyntas III (during whose reign he visited Athens as ambassador) and (perhaps) son of another Amyntas who was briefly king in the 390s, Ptolemy (Ptolemaios Aloritēs) emerged as regent for *Perdiccas III, having allegedly connived at the murder of *Alexander II. He successfully resisted the pretender Pausanias, but fell victim eventually to Perdiccas' machinations.

BIBL. Hammond and Griffith, *Macedonia* ii.

Ptolemy Apion: see **Ptolemy IX and X**

Ptolemy Ceraunus King of Macedon, 281–279 BC.

Ptolemy (Ptolemaios) was the eldest son of *Ptolemy I: angry over his disinheritance in favour of his half-brother *Ptolemy II, he lived in exile at rival courts whose kings might restore him to his throne. At the court of *Lysimachus, Ptolemy's role in the death of Lysimachus' son *Agathocles is obscure, but he fled with the latter's widow Lysandra (his own full sister) to the court of *Seleucus I to seek refuge and, probably, to incite revenge against Lysimachus. When Seleucus defeated Lysimachus at Corupedium and crossed to Europe to invade Macedonia (dashing Ptolemy's own hopes for that throne), Ptolemy killed Seleucus ostensibly to avenge Lysimachus. He was acclaimed king by the Macedonian army as 'Ceraunus' (Thunderbolt), a tribute to his dynamic energy no less than to his violent, quixotic temper. Consolidating his position by defeating the navy of *Antigonus Gonatas and by marrying Lysimachus' widow (his own half-sister *Arsinoe – later II), he ruled for 17 months until killed in a rash attack on invading Gauls.

BIBL. Tarn, *Antigonos Gonatas*.

Pyrrhon (c. 360–270 BC) Philosopher.

Pyrrhon (Purrhōn) of Elis was regarded as the first of the Greek sceptical philosophers. Born poor, and at first a painter, he studied under *Anaxarchus. A central aim of the sceptics was the pursuit of freedom from trouble (*ataraxia*) by avoiding dogmatism. This may partly explain why Pyrrhon left no written works. His pupil *Timon of Phlius wrote various works, but it is hard to distinguish Pyrrhon's thought from that of other sceptics, and it is unclear on what arguments his scepticism was based. With *Anaxarchus, he accompanied *Alexander the Great's eastern campaigns, and was said to have been influenced by Persian magi and Indian gymnosophists (naked philosophers).

BIBL. Diogenes Laertius ix. 61–108; Long, *Hellenistic Philosophy*.

Pyrrhus (319–272 BC) King of Epirus.

A cousin of *Alexander the Great, Pyrrhus (Purrhos) was heir to a throne caught in dynastic trouble, and was first exiled in 317 BC. (His rival, Neoptolemus, was supported by the general *Cassander.) The marriage of his sister to *Demetrius Poliorcetes in 303 marked the latter's alliance with Epirus, and Pyrrhus fled to Demetrius when exiled again in 302. After Ipsus (301), Demetrius sent Pyrrhus as a hostage to *Ptolemy I; he impressed the Ptolemaic court, and married the daughter of *Berenice I. When Cassander died, Ptolemy gave Pyrrhus money and troops to regain his kingdom in 297, and perhaps to watch Macedon, where the succession was being contested. Pyrrhus quarrelled with Demetrius, and the death of the latter's wife ended their formal tie. Pyrrhus intervened in the struggle between the sons of Cassander, being summoned by *Alexander V, but Demetrius obtained the throne of Macedon in 292. His estranged wife Lanassa, the daughter of *Agathocles of Syracuse, went over to Demetrius c. 290, whereupon Pyrrhus fought with a Greek anti-Macedonian alliance until 289.

Marble portrait head usually identified as Pyrrhus, king of Epirus. Copenhagen, Ny Carlsberg Glyptotek.

When Demetrius turned to the east, Pyrrhus was persuaded to join the coalition of Ptolemy, *Lysimachus, and *Seleucus I against him in 288. He drove Demetrius out of Macedon, and was proclaimed king by the army in his place in 288. Athens invited him to help their revolt against Demetrius in 287, but he entered the city after the siege had been lifted. The peace-treaty with Demetrius confirmed Pyrrhus as king of Macedon and the partition of the country with Lysimachus. From Macedon he continued to harry Demetrius by attacking Thessaly and his Greek garrisons elsewhere c. 285. Lysimachus, who no longer needed Pyrrhus' help, confronted him in Macedon and Thessaly and drove him back to Epirus in 283.

From 280–275 Pyrrhus fought on behalf of Greeks in Italy and Sicily in a campaign partly financed by some of the Hellenistic kings, who were eager to get him out of the way. A victory over the Romans at Heraclea in 280 was so costly to him that it has passed into tradition as the first proverbial 'pyrrhic victory'.

Returning to Epirus, Pyrrhus opposed Demetrius' son *Antigonus Gonatas, who had established himself on the throne of Macedon and controlled parts of Greece. He drove Antigonus out of Macedonia for a time, and moving south with a large army he invaded the Peloponnese with *Cleonymus of Sparta, and attacked Sparta in 272; they were driven back by Gonatas and *Areus I of Sparta. Continuing the fight against Gonatas at Argos, Pyrrhus was caught in a desperate street battle: struck by a roof-tile, he was killed by a mercenary of Antigonus.

BIBL. G. Nenci, *Pirro* (1953); P. Lévèque, *Pyrrhus* (1957); Hammond, *Epirus*; *Roman World* *Pyrrhus.

Pythagoras Philosopher, late 6th century BC.

Pythagoras (Puthagoras) was born on Samos and went to Croton in southern Italy in about 531 BC, probably to escape *Polycrates' tyranny. There he founded a religious club, which gained political influence, until an uprising by the citizens of Croton forced him to retire to Metapontum, where he died. The club (or clubs) survived, but in the middle of the fifth century further persecution forced the Pythagoreans to disperse to many parts of Greece.

Reverse of a bronze coin of Samos showing Pythagoras holding a sceptre and pointing to a globe mounted on a column.

Even this brief account of his life is uncertain. His beliefs are even more obscure, as he wrote no books, and his followers were noted for secrecy. Legends quickly grew around him, and later Pythagoreans, as well as members of other sects, tended to attribute their own views to him to gain authority. But a few strands of his thought can be disentangled. He had an early reputation as a polymath, according to *Heracl(e)itus. His contemporary *Xenophanes mocked him for believing in the transmigration of souls, and later Pythagorean prohibitions on the eating of meat or beans are probably connected with this (one would not wish to eat old friends). The discovery that concordant musical intervals correspond to simple numerical ratios (octave 2:1; fifth 3:2; fourth 4:3) probably prompted the Pythagoreans to attempt to explain the universe in mathematical terms, and to identify things with numbers (e.g. justice = 4).

These were later developments, but it is possible that Pythagoras made the musical discovery, or knew of it.

'Pythagoras' theorem', in some form, was used long before by the Babylonians. Possibly Pythagoras introduced it to Greece. That he discovered it and celebrated by sacrificing an ox is, sadly, improbable.

BIBL. W. Burkert, *Lore and Science in Ancient Pythagoreanism* (1972).

Pytheas of Massilia Explorer, floruit 325(?)–300 BC.

Pytheas (Putheas) was a mariner from Marseille who made a remarkable voyage beyond the northern parts of his inhabited world. Although not all places mentioned on his route can be certainly located, Pytheas probably went through the Straits of Gibraltar, up the west coast of France, and across to Land's End in Cornwall, from where he began a clockwise circumnavigation of Britain. He visited various groups of northern islands, and an unidentified island 'Thule', which was six days north of Britain and about 65° latitude, judging from the length of its night in midsummer (Norway, Iceland, the Faroe Islands?). The date of this voyage, although uncertain, was probably about the time of *Alexander the Great; the *terminus ante quem* is *Dicaearchus (late fourth century BC), who attacked Pytheas in his writings.

The success of Pytheas' voyage bears witness to his advanced scientific knowledge: he recorded bearings astronomically, and noted the influence of the moon on tides. His findings appeared in a work now lost; he was referred to by several authors (including *Polybius and *Eratosthenes) to whom he was a prime, if not always a credible, source of geographical information. It is now generally accepted that the ancient scepticism over the reality of his journey is unjustified.

BIBL. H. J. Mette, *Pytheas von Massalia* (1954); M. Cary and E. H. Warmington, *The Ancient Explorers* (1929); C. F. C. Hawkes, *Pytheas: Europe and the Greek Explorers* (1977).

Rhianus Scholar and poet, born c. 275 BC?.

Whether he began as a slave in charge of a wrestling-school (*Suda*) or not, Rhianus (Rhianos), a Cretan, was successful as a scholar and poet, presumably at Alexandria. His edition of *Homer, more conservative than *Zenodotus', was rightly respected by later scholiasts. In poetry he apparently sympathized with *Apollonius Rhodius, specializing in ethnographical and historical epics, e.g. *Achaica*, *Thessalica* (tiny fragments remaining). To judge by Pausanias, who used his *Messeniaca* as a source, he 'homerized' history quite effectively. Easy reading for learned poetry, Rhianus was appreciated by the Emperor Tiberius, not least perhaps for his paederastic epigrams.

BIBL. Pausanias iv. 6; *SH* 715–16; Pfeiffer, *Classical Scholarship* i; *Roman World* *Pausanias, *Tiberius.

Roxane Wife of *Alexander the Great, died 311 BC.

Roxane (Rhōxanē) was a Bactrian captive with whom *Alexander fell massively (but, politically speaking, not inconveniently) in love. They were married in an Iranian ceremony in 327 BC, an event depicted in a celebrated painting by Aëtion. Her son *Alexander (IV) became nominal king in 323, and she accompanied him to Macedonia in 320. On *Antipater's death (319) they fled to *Olympias in Epirus, returned with her to Macedonia, and fell into the hands of *Cassander, who executed them seven years later after the Peace of 311. For all the romance of her union with Alexander she was no innocent victim of power politics (note her removal of *Stateira in 323).

BIBL. Berve, *Alexanderreich*, no. 688; Will, *Hist. pol.*

Sacadas Musician and elegiac poet, *c.* 580 BC.

Sacadas (Sakadas) of Argos won the *aulos* competition in the Pythian games of 586, 582, and 578 BC. Pseudo-Plutarch *On Music*, associating him with the Second School of music at Sparta, says he developed the *Three-part* nome (combining Dorian, Phrygian, and Lydian modes) and wrote songs and accompanied elegies (one perhaps a *Sack of Troy*, known to Athenaeus). Nothing survives, but *Strabo and Pollux describe the Pythian nome in which Sacadas apparently depicted in music Apollo's fight with the Delphic snake.

BIBL. Strabo 421C; Pseudo-Plutarch, *On Music* 1134A–B; Pollux iv. 84; West, *IEG*; *Roman World* *Athenaeus.

Sandracottus (Chandragupta) Indian king, *c.* 321–297 BC.

Sandracottus (Sandrakottos, the Indian Chandragupta) was the founder of the Mauryan dynasty in northern India. His capital was at Pataliputra (modern Patna) in Uttar Pradesh, where he received the Seleucid ambassador *Megasthenes. Sandracottus conquered the last ruler of the Nanda dynasty which ruled Maghada (Bihar). He was able to resist an invasion of the Indus basin by *Seleucus I, who ceded the Punjab to him in return for 500 war-elephants in 303 BC. He was the grandfather of *Aśoka (272–231), who united most of north and central India and was instrumental in the spread of Buddhism.

BIBL. R. Thapar, *Aśoka and the Decline of the Mauryas* (1961); R. K. Mookerji, *Chandragupta Maurya and his Times* (4th ed., 1966).

Sappho Lyric poet, *c.* 600 BC.

Perhaps antiquity's greatest love poet, especially admired by a society where women rarely achieved renown as poets or otherwise, Sappho (Phsapphō in the Lesbian dialect of her songs) offered ancient biographers too little information to control speculation. Claimed by both Eresus and Mytilene, she mentioned brothers Charaxus (berated for expenditure on a courtesan in Egypt: frs. 15, 202), Larichus (fr. 203), and probably Erigyius; perhaps her father (Scamandronymus according to *Plato, but other names compete); conceivably her mother Cleis, but that name may be inference from fragment 132, 'I have a beautiful *girl* Cleis', interpreted as 'daughter' but equally probably meaning 'girl-friend'.

It is her girls whom Sappho names most – Anactoria, Atthis, Gongyla – or her rival Andromeda. As men wooed youths in symposia so, in Lesbos at least, women could express and perhaps fulfil homosexual passion in their female counterpart. Sappho naturally lacks *Alcaeus' political preoccupations (albeit mentioning prominent families of Mytilene – and tradition had her exiled to Sicily). Songs sung to her companions focus almost entirely on her love for one of them – whether present, as perhaps in her elaborate but insistent prayer for help to her patron, Aphrodite (fr. 1), or absent, as in a movingly

Sappho and *Alcaeus playing lyres on a vase of *c.* 480–470 BC, by the *Brygus painter. Goluchow.

Inscribed 'portrait' bust of Sappho. Roman period copy of an original of the 4th century BC. Malibu, J. Paul Getty Museum.

simple recollection of parting (fr. 94). Simplicity and intensity culminate in fragment 31, describing her physical responses to a girl's voice and laughter, but are always present, even where she adduces mythology (the beautiful Helen (fr. 16)) to illustrate the overriding compulsion of love, or offers vivid narrative of **Hector and Andromache's wedding (fr. 44). Yet her consummate control of words and themes and tireless variety in approaching the theme of love mark an artist, not an *ingénue*. That she taught her art to débutantes from Lesbos and Ionia (as suggested in antiquity: *Suppl.* 261A) is doubtful – departure of girls to Ionia may have been occasioned otherwise, by exile (which could strike whole households), or marriage, whose intrusion on Sappho's society is clear from her wedding-songs: a book of these (frs. 104–17, compare 103) circulated with or as part of a nine-book edition. Her fame generated stories that she rejected Alcaeus, married one Cercolas of Andros, and committed suicide for love of Phaon.

BIBL. Lobel and Page, *PLF*; Page, *Suppl.*; D. L. Page, *Sappho and Alcaeus* (1955); Campbell, *Lyric Poetry*; Kirkwood, *Greek Monody*.

Satibarzanes Persian satrap, died 330/29 BC.

Although he was one of *Darius III's murderers, Satibarzanes' (Satibarzanēs) prompt surrender to *Alexander the Great secured his life and position as satrap of Areia. He rebelled almost immediately, however, and was killed in single combat by Erigyius.

BIBL. Berve, *Alexanderreich*, no. 697.

Satyrus I and II: see Spartocids

Satyrus Biographer, late 4th or 3rd century BC (?).

The biographer Satyrus (Saturos) was, like his epitomator *Heracleides Lembus, a native of Callatis on the Black Sea. The late third-century date and residence in Egypt traditional in modern scholarship have rested insecurely on identification with the author of an austere work *On the Demes of Alexandria*. If this is challenged, an earlier date and a connection with the Peripatos at Athens can be maintained. A substantial portion of Satyrus' *Life of *Euripides* was found at Oxyrhynchus early this century: elegantly written (in dialogue form), disturbingly anecdotal in flavour, and shameless in extraction of 'facts' from the poet's text, it is probably a representative example of Hellenistic biography (compare *Hermippus of Smyrna).

BIBL. Hunt, *POxy.* (1912) 1176; S. R. West, *GRBS* xv (1974).

Scerdilaidas Illyrian chieftain and king, floruit *c.* 230– before 205 BC.

An Illyrian nobleman who was probably the king's brother, Scerdilaidas (Skerdilaidas) became involved with *Philip V of Macedon, the Aetolians, and Rome. He commanded the Illyrian army when it ravaged Epirus in 230 BC, and, breaking the treaty with Rome of 228 whereby Illyria agreed not to operate south of Lissus, he joined with *Demetrius of Pharos in attacking Pylos in Messenia. Having hired out troops to *Scopas of Aetolia for a foray into Arcadia, Scerdilaidas renounced this agreement in 220–219, when Macedonian money persuaded him to reinforce Philip's fleet. His ships were

used in the attack on Cephallenia, a second infringement of his treaty with Rome. In 217 he broke with Philip over his payment, began piracy against him, and invaded Macedonia, probably with Rome's acquiescence (she gave him ships in 216). Philip drove him back beyond his boundaries by 213/12. Scerdilaidas was a signatory to the Aetolian treaty with Rome in 212/11; he therefore posed a threat to Philip in the First Macedonian War by engaging in border conflicts in 208. He did not sign the Peace of Phoenice, and must therefore have died before 205.

BIBL. *CAH* vii; Walbank, *Philip V*; Hammond, *Epirus*.

Scipio Aemilianus Roman consul, 147 and 134 BC.

An important military and political leader of the second century BC, Publius Cornelius Scipio Aemilianus was born the natural son of L. Aemilius *Paullus (under whom he served in Macedonia in 168), but he was adopted into the Cornelian family by the elder son of *Scipio Africanus. To his admirer and close friend, the historian *Polybius, the young Scipio stood out as a paragon of manly virtues amid a generation corrupted by the influx of luxury and Hellenism, but Scipio coupled a profound regard for traditional Roman austerity with a keen intellectual interest in Greek culture, and was the centre of the 'Scipionic Circle', a group of like-minded friends and protégés which included Greeks such as *Panaetius. In 146 Scipio ended the third war with Carthage by the brutal destruction of the city, and it was probably in 140 that he led an important and wide-ranging embassy to the Greek East, which seems to have involved an investigation into the affairs of many of Rome's client states in the area. After military successes in Spain, he died suddenly in 129, in mysterious circumstances, after his opposition to agrarian legislation had diminished his once considerable popularity.

BIBL. A. E. Astin, *Scipio Aemilianus* (1967); *Roman World*.

Scipio Africanus Roman consul, 205 and 194 BC.

The conqueror of Spain, Africa, and Asia Minor, Publius Cornelius Scipio Africanus stands out more than any other individual as the architect of Rome's world supremacy. By 206 BC he had driven the Carthaginians out of Spain and brought it permanently under Roman control, and he finally defeated the hitherto invincible Hannibal at Zama in 202 BC, for which he took the surname Africanus. Although immensely popular with the people and his soldiers, Scipio had shocked traditional Roman opinion by wearing Greek dress and openly adopting Greek cultural pursuits when he spent a year in Sicily training a new army. In his second consulship (194), with his eye on a possible command against *Antiochus III, Scipio vigorously but unsuccessfully opposed *Flamininus' policy of evacuating Greece. In 190 he led the first Roman army into Asia, nominally as the legate of his brother L. *Scipio Asiagenus. *En route* he established a close friendship with *Philip V (now a vital Roman ally), and scored further diplomatic successes in Asia. He insisted on Antiochus' complete withdrawal from Asia Minor, and granted peace on those terms after the crucial battle of Magnesia. Although Scipio had reached a greatness never previously attained by a Roman, his career revealed several dangerous shifts away from traditional Roman practice towards the cult of personality and Hellenistic kingship. The attacks of his political opponents finally forced his retirement into private life.

BIBL. H. H. Scullard, *Scipio Africanus: Soldier and Politician* (1970); F. W. Walbank, *PCPS* 1967, 54 ff.; A. J. Toynbee, *Hannibal's Legacy* (1965) ii, index; *Roman World*.

Scipio Asiagenus Roman consul, 190 BC.

Of meagre abilities, Lucius Cornelius Scipio Asiagenus owed his advancement to his elder brother *Scipio Africanus, whose fortunes his career followed. He received the consular command against *Antiochus III in 190 BC on the understanding that Africanus would serve as legate and take effective command. He led the first Roman army into Asia, and won a triumph and the surname Asiagenes (-us) for the decisive victory over Antiochus at the battle of Magnesia.

BIBL. H. H. Scullard, *Roman Politics 220–150 BC* (2nd ed., 1973); *Roman World*.

Scopas Sculptor, active 370–330 BC.

Scopas (Skopas) of Paros, a great contemporary of *Praxiteles, was best known as a sculptor of cult-statues,

and seems to have worked mainly in marble. About 30 statues by him are recorded, about 20 of which are cult-statues. He is also recorded as the architect of the temple of Athena Alea at Tegea, begun perhaps in the 360s BC, and, with Bryaxis, Leochares, and *Timotheus (3), as one of the four master-sculptors working on the Mausoleum at Halicarnassus, c. 350 BC (see *Mausolus). He carved one of the 36 relief column-drums of the temple of Artemis at Ephesus, probably in the 340s BC, and was in Thebes sometime before 335 BC (when the town was razed by *Alexander) to make statues of Artemis Eucleia and Athena. Unusually he seems to have made no athletic, genre, or portrait statues.

He is often mentioned in connection with Praxiteles, and later critics seem to have had difficulty telling their styles apart. A nude Aphrodite and statues of Desire ('Pothos') and Yearning ('Himeros') are recorded: they suggest a community of interest with Praxiteles in the feminine and sensual, new to Greek sculpture in the fourth century BC. One of his two statues of Desire, probably that on Samothrace in a group with Aphrodite and perhaps Phaethon, is almost certainly preserved in a figure known in several Roman copies, which is very

Left: Pothos (Desire), by Scopas. Roman period copy, in marble, of a mid-4th-century BC original. Rome, Palazzo dei Conservatori. *Right*: Meleager. Roman period copy, in marble, of a 4th-century BC statue, often attributed to Scopas. Vatican Museum.

similar in conception to the Lizard-slaying Apollo of Praxiteles. There are substantial remains of the sculpture from the Mausoleum and the temple of Artemis at Ephesus, but quite insufficient evidence to recover Scopas' contribution. The remains of the temple at Tegea show it to have been one of the finest of the fourth century BC, and his influence is often detected in the distinctive style of its sculptural decoration; however, he was the architect, and what we know of the roles of architects and sculptors in temple-building (notably at Epidaurus) does not warrant the assumption that he designed or that members of his atelier executed the Tegea sculptures; though it is possible. Other commonly accepted attributions (like the Lansdowne Heracles and the Dresden Maenad) depend either on the Tegea sculptures accurately reflecting his style or on rhetorical and insufficient literary descriptions.

BIBL. Robertson, *History of Greek Art* 452–7; A. F. Stewart, *Skopas of Paros* (1977).

Scopas of Aetolia Aetolian leader and Egyptian mercenary captain, floruit *c.* 221–196 BC.

A prominent member of the war party and frequent *strategus* in Aetolia in the years of the 'Social War' against *Philip V of Macedon (221–217 BC), Scopas (Skopas) led several aggressive raids on the Peloponnese, invaded Macedonia, and wreaked such havoc that cities of the Achaean League hired mercenaries for their own defence. Scopas signed the treaty of 212 which allied Aetolia with Rome against Philip in the First Macedonian War, and led an unsuccessful campaign against Acarnania. From 206 Scopas had imposed strict financial measures throughout Aetolia, and the fear of worse reforms led to his defeat in the election for the *strategia* and his consequent departure for Egypt in 205. After the accession of *Ptolemy V, his minister *Agathocles sent Scopas to Greece to collect mercenaries. In 202 he prepared a counter-offensive against *Antiochus III's invasion of Egypt, and led an abortive revolt against Ptolemy in 196, which caused false reports of the king's death.

BIBL. Walbank, *Philip V*; Will, *Hist. pol.*; *IG* IX. i (2nd ed.) (1), index, s.v. Skopas II.

Scylax Explorer, late 6th century BC.

Between 519 and 512 BC, *Darius (I) asked Scylax (Skulax) of Caryanda in Caria to lead an expedition down the Indus and along the coasts of Persia and Arabia; he reached Suez 30 months later. Scylax wrote an account of his journey which appears to have been used by *Herodotus and *Hecataeus; but the surviving *Periplous* ascribed to him seems to be a fourth-century compilation of earlier reports, including that of *Phileas. He is also said to have written about the exploits of the Carian king Heracleides at the battle of Artemisium in 480 BC.

BIBL. Herodotus iv. 44; *FGrH* iiiC, no. 709. Text of the *Periplous*: Müller, *Geographi Graeci Minores,* i, 15–96. H. Bengston, *Historia* iii (1954).

Seleucus I Nicator (*c.* 358–281 BC) Founder of the Seleucid dynasty.

Seleucus (Seleukos; the later title means 'Conqueror'), son of Antiochus, was one of *Alexander the Great's Macedonian 'Companions', and commanded the Bodyguard during the Indian campaign against King

*Porus. He was made chiliarch by *Perdiccas after Alexander's death, but was one of the officers responsible for Perdiccas' murder in 321/320 BC. At the conference of Triparadeisus he was appointed satrap of Babylonia; the increasing power of *Antigonus forced him to flee to *Ptolemy (I) in Egypt in the spring of 315.

In 312 he defeated an attempt by *Demetrius Poliorcetes to invade Ptolemy's domains at Gaza, and then returned to Babylonia; the date of this return later marked the beginning of the 'Seleucid era' (October 312 by the Macedonian calendar, April 311 by the Babylonian). Confirmed as ruler of the territories east of the Euphrates by the general peace of 311, Seleucus spent the following years fighting to regain the eastern territories of Alexander's empire, including Bactria. In 324 he had married the Persian Apama, daughter of *Spitamenes. In return for ceding the Punjab to the Mauryan king *Sandracottus, Seleucus received 500 war-elephants, providing him with formidable military power. Like the other Macedonian rulers he proclaimed himself king in 305/4.

In 301 Seleucus joined with *Cassander and *Lysimachus to destroy Antigonus at the battle of Ipsus; Syria subsequently became the heartland of the Seleucid state, with a new capital at Antioch. In the following years he campaigned intermittently in Cilicia against

Bronze head from Herculaneum, identified as Seleucus I Nicator because of its similarity to coin-types. Naples, Museo Nazionale.

Demetrius, whose daughter *Stratonice I he married in
299/8 but passed on to his son *Antiochus I in 294/3 (an
incident which provided the basis for a popular theme of
Hellenistic romance). Seleucus captured Demetrius in 286
and held him imprisoned at Apamea; in 281 he conquered
the rest of Asia Minor as a consequence of his victory
over Lysimachus at Corupedium. He followed up this
victory by crossing over to Thrace to annex Lysimachus'
European territories, but was assassinated near Lysimachia
by *Ptolemy Ceraunus.
    BIBL. Bevan, *House of Seleucus*; Will, *Hist. pol.* i.

Seleucus II Callinicus Seleucid king, 246–226 BC.
    The elder son of *Antiochus II and *Laodice (q.v.)
(perhaps re-nominated heir on his father's deathbed),
Seleucus (Seleukos) the 'Triumphant' took the throne in
the face of the claims of the infant son of his step-mother
*Berenice Syra. He thus confronted her brother,
*Ptolemy III, who invaded Syria with a large army to
support her claims. After the murders of Berenice and her
child, Ptolemy is said to have advanced in their names
into the eastern parts of the Seleucid empire as far as
Bactria. When he had to withdraw to Egypt to face
troubles there, Seleucus regained control over the East,
but still faced Ptolemy in Coele-Syria. Seleucus made his
brother *Antiochus Hierax joint ruler c. 242(?) BC, and
their union against Ptolemy forced the conclusion of this
Third Syrian War in 241. Hostilities broke out between
the brothers over the distribution of power, and before
236 they decided to split the empire. Seleucus was freed
of the problem posed by Hierax by the latter's unwise
alliance with the Gauls (Galatians), which led to his defeat
by *Attalus I of Pergamum and death in 226.
    Seleucus regained sole control, but vast areas of
Seleucid Asia Minor now belonged to Pergamum, while in
the East the empire had lost the region north of the Hindu
Kush. It is possible that the king journeyed east and
fought with *Arsaces I of Parthia (c. (?) 230–227). He met
with a fatal accident in 226/5 and was succeeded by his
son, Seleucus III, who ruled from 226–223 BC. This king
set out on an expedition (probably with *Achaeus) against
Attalus to regain former Seleucid territory, but was
murdered *en route*. He was succeeded by his younger
brother, *Antiochus III.
    BIBL. W. Otto, *Bayer. Abh.* xxxiv(1) (1928); M. Cary, *A
History of the Greek World* (1951), App. 8; Will, *Hist. pol.*
i.

The Later Seleucids, after 95 BC.
    Seleucus VI
    Philip I and II
    Demetrius III
    Antiochus X
    Antiochus XI
    Antiochus XII Dionysus
    Antiochus XIII Asiaticus
    The last years of the Seleucid dynasty saw constant
dynastic war among the descendants of *Antiochus
(Antiokhos) VIII and *Antiochus IX. After Seleucus
(Seleukos) VI killed his uncle Antiochus IX in 95 BC, and
was in turn killed by his uncle's son Antiochus X, four
Seleucid kings claimed the throne: three of the four
brothers of Seleucus VI (Philip (Philippos) I and
Antiochus XI in Cilicia, Demetrius (Dēmētrios) III at

Coin portraits of later Seleucid kings (after 95 BC): (*top*) Seleucus
VI and Demetrius III; (*centre*) Antiochus XI; (*bottom*) Antiochus
XII Dionysus, and Antiochus XIII Asiaticus.

Damascus) and their cousin Antiochus X. When
Antiochus X killed Antiochus XI and was subsequently
killed by the Parthians, the conflict narrowed in 88 to the
brothers Philip and Demetrius. The latter had the most
authority, was supported by *Ptolemy IX, and had one
great victory over the Jews (which the fraternal war
prevented him from following up), but he was taken
prisoner by the Parthians. The last brother, Antiochus XII,
tried to replace Demetrius at Damascus in 87, but he was
killed in battle against the Nabataeans. When the
temporary winner, Philip, died in 84/3, his son Philip II
faced Antiochus XIII, the son (probably) of Cleopatra
Selene and Antiochus X.
    The Syrians took matters into their own hands and
offered the throne to *Tigranes I of Armenia in 83.
Antiochus XIII and his brother fled to Rome to defend
their claims, and returned to Antioch in 69, after Tigranes
had lost Syria to Rome. Various struggles with Arab
chieftains and a *coup* by the returning Philip II followed.
In answer to Antiochus' plea to restore him to his throne
in 64, Pompey made Syria a Roman province.
    BIBL. Will, *Hist. pol.* ii; Bellinger, 'The End of the
Seleucids'; *Roman World* *Pompey.

Semonides Iambic poet, c. 630 BC (?).
    Antiquity reckoned Semonides (Sēmōnidēs, according
to the Byzantine scholar Choeroboscus, Simōnidēs in all
quotations) contemporary with *Archilochus, and
disputed which of the two 'invented' iambics. A *Suda*
notice (embedded in that on *Simmias by error of
transmission) says that he led a Samian colony to
Amorgos, and ascribes two elegiac books and one iambic
(though quotation from a second book of iambics (fr. 11)
suggests confusion here too).

Of 42 iambic fragments only two exceed three lines – fragment 1, a pessimistic catalogue of impediments to the fulfilment of man's hopes, and fragment 7, a bitter, male-chauvinistic anatomy of women's characters, compared, over 118 lines, to various animals. Invective against Orodoecides known to Lucian is lost. Elegiacs (fr. 8) quoting *Iliad* vi. 146, scorning youthful optimism and recommending self-indulgence in view of life's brevity, are variously ascribed to Semonides and *Simonides by moderns.

BIBL. West, *IEG*; Campbell, *Lyric Poetry*; H. Lloyd-Jones, *Females of the Species* (1975); *Roman World* *Lucian.

Seuthes Thracian prince, floruit 400–389 BC.

A subordinate ruler under *Amadocus I, Seuthes (Seuthēs) is most extensively known from *Xenophon's *Anabasis* as an ambitious petty ruler in the Thracian Chersonese. He later rebelled against Amadocus, but the two were reconciled by *Thrasybulus and became Athenian allies (390/89 BC).

BIBL. Xenophon, *Anabasis* vii, PW iiA. 2020–1.

Seven Sages

The Seven Sages were the wisest men of ancient Greece, most of them statesmen rather than philosophers. All of them are early sixth-century figures, the original list (traditional as early as *Plato) being apparently *Thales, *Pittacus, *Bias, *Cleobulus, *Solon, *Chilon, and *Periander. The list varied, largely because some authors rejected Periander as being morally and politically unacceptable, and substituted such figures as *Anacharsis. The original story which grouped them together told how a golden tripod was fished up from the sea off Ionia, and an oracle ordered it to be given to 'the wisest'. It was first offered to Thales, but he said that another of the Seven was wiser, and so it went round all of them, until they agreed to dedicate it to Apollo.

BIBL. Plato, *Protagoras* 343A–B; Diogenes Laertius i. 13, 28–33, 40–2; Plutarch, *Banquet of the Seven Sages* (*Moralia* 146B–164D).

Silanion Portrait-sculptor, active *c.* 360–330 BC.

We know of ten works by Silanion (Silaniōn) of Athens: an **Achilles, a **Theseus, a dying Jocasta, and seven portraits – *Sappho, *Corinna, a sculptor Apollodorus, three boxers at Olympia, and a *Plato dedicated in the Academy to the Muses by a Persian. We have copies of portraits of Corinna and Plato which may be his; and there is a fine fourth-century BC bronze portrait-head of a boxer from Olympia which has often been hoped to be his portrait of the boxing champion

Above: Bronze head of a boxer, from Olympia, 4th century BC. Athens, National Museum. (See *Silanion.)

Left: A mosaic from Baalbek showing Calliope surrounded by busts of *Socrates and the Seven Sages – *Solon, *Thales, *Bias, *Cleobulus, *Periander, *Pittacus, and *Chilon – each accompanied by an appropriate maxim. Beirut Museum.

Satyrus. Like other artists, he wrote on 'rules of proportion' (*praecepta symmetriarum*).

BIBL. Moreno, *Enc. Art. Ant.* vii. 288–92; Richter, *Sculpture and Sculptors* 222–3; Robertson, *History of Greek Art* 507–9.

Simias of Rhodes Poet, *c.* 300 BC.

An early Hellenistic scholar-poet on the model of his greater contemporary *Philitas, Simias (sometimes spelled Simmias) produced books both of learned 'glosses' and of miscellaneous short poetry – epigrams, epyllia, and lyric hymns showing serious experimentation with metre (see frs. 9, 13–17). High in curiosity value are three *technopaignia* – bravura poems, imitating on the page the shape of the object described: *Wings*, *Axe*, and *Egg* survive. This whimsical application of learning and technique is characteristically Hellenistic, and engaging or irritating according to taste.

BIBL. Powell, *Coll. Alex.*; Webster, *Hellenistic Poetry*.

Simmias of Thebes Pythagorean philosopher, *c.* 400 BC.

A pupil of *Philolaus, Simmias was one of those who wanted to pay for *Socrates' escape from prison. In *Plato's *Phaedo*, he defends the theory (perhaps of *Philolaus) that the soul is an 'attunement' of the body. Plato evidently thought highly of him as a philosopher.

BIBL. Plato, *Phaedo*.

Simonides (*c.* 557–468/7 BC) Lyric poet and epigrammatist.

Like *Anacreon, Simonides (Simōnidēs) of Ceos travelled widely in the Greek world, settling wherever he could find a market for his poetry. We hear of him at the court of *Hipparchus of Athens, with ruling families in Thessaly, at Athens again at the time of the Persian Wars, and finally at the court of *Hieron I of Syracuse.

In the field of choral lyric he was remembered chiefly for his dirges (his work became proverbial for its pathos) and his victory songs (epinicians, to which he gave the form known to us from *Pindar and *Bacchylides). We also hear of dithyrambs, paeans, and other lyric forms. His style seems to have been simple and elegant. One fragment praises *Leonidas and those who died at Thermopylae; another gives a tender description of Danaë and Perseus adrift on the sea; a poem in which Simonides claims that no man can be truly 'excellent' is discussed in *Plato's *Protagoras*.

Of his epigrams most, if not all, were composed for inscription on tombs or other monuments. A number survive under his name, including several commemorating events in the Persian Wars, but in almost every case the attribution is in some degree doubtful. He may also have written longer elegiac poems.

BIBL. Lesky, *Greek Literature*; *Lyra Graeca* (Loeb) ii; Bowra, *Lyric Poetry*.

Simonides of Amorgos: see **Semonides**

Sitalces King of the Odrysians in Thrace, died 424 BC.

Sitalces (Sitalkēs), son of Teres, established a powerful monarchical state in Thrace, in alliance with Athens. In 429 BC he invaded Chalcidice and Macedonia in support of the pretender Amyntas, but finally concluded a marriage alliance with King *Perdiccas II of Macedon; his nephew and successor Seuthes married Perdiccas' daughter Stratonice. Sitalces died in 424 campaigning against the Triballi.

BIBL. Thucydides ii. 101, iv. 101; Diodorus Siculus xii. 50.

Socrates (*c.* 469–399 BC) Philosopher.

Although one of the most influential Greek philosophers, and the one whose personality and appearance are most familiar of all, Socrates (Sōkratēs) left no written works, except possibly a few poems. He plays a leading part in many of *Plato's philosophical dialogues, but it is disputed whether Plato's portrayal of his character and thought was reliable. Probably the early dialogues are the best evidence we have (though opinions differ). *Xenophon (q.v.) presents him as a much duller character, and the 'Socrates' satirized in *Aristophanes' *Clouds* is a philosophical stereotype.

Socrates did philosophy orally. He would engage in discussions within his circle of friends and admirers, but also with philosophers, politicians, and others who were drawn, sometimes reluctantly, into conversation, and often provoked to anger and abuse. His disciples included not only philosophers, such as Plato, *Eucl(e)ides, *Antisthenes, *Aristippus, and *Phaedo, but also clever young men of politically influential families. Probably his friendship with such unscrupulous politicians as *Alcibiades and *Critias, and his supposed influence on them, was a main cause of his trial and death.

According to *Aristotle, he was only interested in moral questions, and especially in searching for definitions. This fits Plato's picture of him pressing his respondents to define, say, 'courage', 'virtue', or 'justice', and then proving their answers wrong. (Questions like this led Plato to develop his 'Theory of Forms', but it is unlikely that Socrates took that step.) Socrates' method

Part of two epigrams inscribed at Athens in the time of Simonides. The upper one probably commemorates the battle of Salamis, the lower that of Marathon. American School of Classical Studies at Athens.

(called *elenchus*) of making others put forward positive views and then refuting them by a series of questions and answers no doubt earned him a reputation for undermining morals. But he used it not only against dogmatic moral conservatives, but also against more radical sophists who despised moral conventions. Often he appears a defender of traditional values, e.g. in his refusal to escape into exile to avoid the death penalty, on the ground that he owed it to the State to obey its laws. And reports of his courageous behaviour in battle during the Peloponnesian War do not suggest the conduct of a moral nihilist. His well-known mock modesty ('irony'), with which he would plead ignorance of subjects in which others claimed expertise, only to go on to demolish their claims, helps to explain why he enthralled some but enraged others. Some of Plato's earlier positive views on ethics may originate from Socrates. These include the theory that no one ever does wrong voluntarily, but only through ignorance, and indeed that virtue *is* knowledge (or a branch of knowledge).

Few details are known of his life. Born in Athens of a family probably of moderate means, he later grew poor because (so Plato says) he pursued wisdom at the price of neglecting his affairs. His wife *Xanthippe was described as bad-tempered, and later literature made her a notorious shrew. Socrates' frequent expressions of fascination with beautiful young men are jocular. He seems to have advocated sexual self-control and love of others for their minds rather than their bodies. In 399 he was charged with 'not recognizing the gods that the State recognizes and introducing other new divinities' and with 'corrupting the young'. He was convicted and condemned to die by drinking hemlock juice.

BIBL. Plato, *Apology*; W. Jaeger, *Paideia* (1944–5) ii. 2; Guthrie, *Greek Philosophy* iii, part 2.

Solon Athenian lawgiver, 594 BC.

A member of an aristocratic but impoverished family, Solon (Solōn) first became prominent when he persuaded the Athenians to continue a war with Megara for the possession of Salamis, which they were ready to abandon. He did this by means of a poem, and later too he used poetry to express and justify his policies. At this time there was serious discontent in Athens for various reasons. Many poor farmers had become serfs (*hektemoroi*) to their richer neighbours under very oppressive conditions, and the ultimate sanction against these and other debtors, if they defaulted, was that they and their families could be sold into slavery. At the same time, there was a demand for political power from certain people who had hitherto had none. Solon was considered a suitable mediator, and was elected archon (traditionally in 594). He 'shook off the burdens' of the poor ('Seisachtheia') by abolishing hektemorage and debt-slavery and cancelling all debts. Politically his sympathies were with the *demos*, the people who wanted a greater share of power, but he would not grant their more extreme demands. He divided the citizens into four property-classes, each of which was eligible for certain offices. He set up a Council of 400 (100 from each tribe), and increased the powers of the

Relief on the side of a Roman marble sarcophagus showing Socrates conversing with a Muse. Paris, Musée du Louvre.

'Portrait' of Solon, inscribed with his most famous saying,
'Nothing too much'. Panel of a 3rd-century AD mosaic from
Baalbek (see page 189). Beirut Museum.

Assembly. His reforms did not satisfy everybody, and he
found himself bombarded with demands for further
changes, so he decided to leave Athens for ten years,
making the Athenians swear to make no change in his
laws while he was away. During his travels he had his
famous interview with *Croesus. On his return he lived
more or less in retirement, emerging in his old age to
oppose (unsuccessfully) the rise to power of *Peisistratus.

BIBL. Herodotus i. 29–34; Aristotelean *Constitution of
Athens* 5–13; Plutarch, *Life of Solon*; Forrest, *Greek
Democracy*, ch. 6; Andrewes, *Greek Tyrants*, ch. 7.

Sophocles (*c.* 496–406/5 BC) Tragedian.

Sophocles (Sophoklēs) was born at Colonus, near
Athens, into a wealthy family. It is said that as a boy he
led a choir celebrating the victory at Salamis (480 BC), but
that he later had to give up acting in his own plays
because of a weak voice. His first production was in 468,
when he won first prize although competing against
*Aeschylus. He took an active part in public life: the
offices he is known to have held include a generalship in
441/40 as a colleague of *Pericles (it is said that he was
elected to the post on the strength of his *Antigone*, but
that Pericles found him a better poet than general). He
was the priest of a certain hero (Halon?), and, when the
Athenians were establishing a cult of Asclepius, the god
was accommodated in Sophocles' house until a temple
could be built for him. In recognition of this Sophocles
was himself honoured as a hero after his death.

The story that when Sophocles grew old his son Iophon
(also a tragic poet) tried to take over his property is
probably apocryphal. Shortly before his own death
(which had occurred by February 405) he is said to have
dressed a chorus in black in mourning for his dead rival
*Euripides. His career was thus extraordinarily long; he
was still active, and indeed creating such masterpieces as
Philoctetes and *Oedipus at Colonus*, when well into his
eighties. He had the reputation of being amiable and good-
tempered; this is doubtless why the comic poets took little
interest in him.

He is said to have written 123 plays (we know the titles
of over 110) and never to have been placed third in the
competitions (though *Oedipus Tyrannus* belonged to one of
the sets of plays that were placed second). He probably
won 18 victories at the Great Dionysia (making 72
successful plays) and others at the Lenaea. He is said to
have introduced the third actor (but this change is also
attributed to Aeschylus, and evidently occurred in the
period when both poets were competing) and to have
increased the number of the chorus from 12 to 15. If he

ever wrote connected tetralogies, he soon abandoned the
practice.

Non-dramatic works included a paean to Asclepius, a
paean to *Herodotus, an elegiac poem to the philosopher
*Archelaus (of Athens), and (allegedly) a prose treatise on
the chorus.

Seven plays survive: *Ajax*, *Antigone*, *Women of Trachis*
(concerning the death of Heracles), *Oedipus Tyrannus*
(*Oedipus Rex*), *Electra*, *Philoctetes*, and *Oedipus at Colonus*.
That is perhaps the most likely chronological order,
though the only datable plays are *Antigone* (441?),
Philoctetes (409), and *Oedipus at Colonus* (produced
posthumously in 401). Fragments include a large portion
of a satyr play, *Ichneutae* (*Trackers*), concerning the infant
Hermes.

Every Sophoclean play presents a sequence of events
carefully linked together by principles of cause and effect
and of plausible human motivation. At the same time it
always turns out by the end that an oracle or other
prophecy has been fulfilled, in a way that at least some of

Idealized portrait statue of Sophocles. Roman copy (much
restored) of a 4th-century BC Greek original. Vatican Museum.

The theatre at Epidaurus (mid-4th century BC), the best-preserved example of the type of theatre for which Sophocles wrote.

the characters did not expect or intend. This concern with prophecy clearly reflects Sophocles' religious convictions (compare those of Herodotus); it also helps to shape the plays by making the denouement seem inevitable (though prophecy should not be thought to limit human freedom of choice), and to make possible the dramatic irony that pervades Sophocles' work. Certain problems of structure in *Ajax*, *Antigone*, and *Women of Trachis* (arising in each case from the death of a central character well before the end) should not be allowed to obscure Sophocles' concern with giving his plays a satisfying and organic form.

Thus, while each play depicts human suffering (often extreme physical suffering, expressed in harrowing detail) and an abrupt change of fortune (whether for good or ill), such suffering and change can always be seen to form part of a pattern. And this pattern reflects the working of the gods in human affairs. Although those gods do not act justly, in any human sense, they do not act arbitrarily or unintelligibly, and it is this, it seems, that somehow justifies their worship. They have perfect knowledge,

while human beings, however they may strive to act for the best (in *Women of Trachis* and *Oedipus Tyrannus* it is the most well-meaning actions that lead to disaster), constantly find themselves deceived, whether by circumstances or by one another (in *Women of Trachis*, *Electra*, and *Philoctetes* we encounter false messenger-speeches as elaborate and plausible as any real ones).

Schematic attempts to make each play centre on a single 'Sophoclean hero' tend to be unsuccessful (in *Antigone* and *Women of Trachis* they lead to arguments as to who 'the hero' is). Nevertheless each play does contain a character who, while he may be less sympathetic, by normal standards, than those around him, wins our respect by his absolute and uncompromising adherence to some purpose, at whatever cost to himself (and others). Thus **Ajax insists on suicide, Antigone on burying her brother, Heracles (a marginal case) on making extraordinary demands on his son, **Oedipus (*Tyrannus*) on finding out the truth, Electra on opposing her father's murderers, Philoctetes on refusing to come to Troy, Oedipus (*at*

Colonus) on staying at Colonus and on cursing his sons. In the course of the plays each of these characters, while not necessarily rewarded, is in some sense vindicated. There is paradox in the fact that two of them are women (the 'heroism' of Antigone and Electra must have startled the Greek audience), while two others are despised outcasts (Philoctetes and Oedipus (*at Colonus*)), who by the favour of the gods acquire power over other men's lives, and by their own inner strength resist manipulation by those men.

Sophoclean characterization is always fully sufficient to provide a criterion by which actions may be judged plausible, but does not extend beyond this into extraneous detail. The chorus, while less central than in Aeschylus, is resourcefully employed for a variety of purposes.

After his death, though less popular than Euripides, Sophocles was much admired by such critics as *Aristotle (who regarded his *Oedipus Tyrannus* as the ideal tragedy) and Longinus.

BIBL. Lesky, *Greek Literature*; G. H. Gellie, *Sophocles: a Reading* (1972); B. M. W. Knox, *The Heroic Temper* (1964); *Roman World* *Longinus.

Sophron Mimographer, 5th century BC.

The mimes of Sophron (Sōphrōn) of Syracuse were scenes of low life written in a kind of rhythmic prose. It is said that they were admired by *Plato and influenced his use of dialogue form; later they influenced *Theocritus and perhaps *Herodas. We have one fair-sized fragment as well as brief scraps.

BIBL. Lesky, *Greek Literature*; *Literary Papyri* (Loeb).

Sosibius, minister of Ptolemy IV: see **Agathocles**

Sosigenes Astronomer, 1st century BC.

Probably an Alexandrian Greek, Sosigenes (Sōsigenēs) was appointed by Julius Caesar to help reform the Roman calendar. In 46 BC, when the official year had diverged by three months from the solar year, extra days were intercalated to extend the year to 445 days, and the new Julian calendar was introduced, with 365 days and leap years (based on the Egyptian calendar).

BIBL. Pliny, *Natural History* xviii. 25; *Roman World* Gaius Julius *Caesar.

Sositheus: see **The Pleiad**

Sotades Poet, *c.* 280 BC.

A Thracian from Maroneia, Sotades (Sōtadēs) specialized in a brand of scabrous Ionic verse poorly evidenced but clearly close to the abusive tradition of *Hipponax. His notoriously crude attack on *Ptolemy II's incestuous marriage to *Arsinoe II (fr. 1) doubtless reflected widespread Greek revulsion, but allegedly earned Sotades long imprisonment and/or murder by drowning. He showed off his invention of the loose 'Sotadean' metre in several lost works, including a rewritten *Iliad*; what went on under titles like *Adonis* and *Priapus* is mysterious. The educationally moral sotadeans preserved by Stobaeus are not now attributed to our author.

BIBL. Fraser, *Ptolemaic Alexandria*.

Spartocids Bosporan (Crimean) dynasty, 438/7–*c.* 108 BC.

The name Spartocids (Spartokidai) designated the dynasty which ruled in the Milesian colony Panticapaeum (Kertsch) from 438/7 BC (when a Hellenized Thracian Spartocus (Spartokos) I seized power) until the late second century. Spartocus III (304/3–284/3) and his successors called themselves simply kings, but earlier that title was reserved for the dynasts' position *vis-à-vis* non-Greek subjects beyond the Straits of Kertsch, while the term 'archon' was used to describe their standing in 'Bosporus' (i.e. Panticapaeum and other Greek communities either side of the Straits) and Theodosia. Their real position was doubtless justly caught by those who called them tyrants (there is no trace of republican institutions, merely of government by proclamation, with subordinate officials being appointed by the Spartocids), but the dynasty had a generally good reputation, and Stoics instanced Leucon (Leukōn) I (389/8–349/8) when discussing ideal rulers. The creation of 'Bosporus' (see above) may have preceded Spartocid rule, and, apart from the acquisition of nearby Nymphaeum in 405(?), territorial expansion did not come easily. Satyrus (Saturos) I's marriage-alliance with the Sindian king Hecataeus brought no great advantage, and an attack on Theodosia ended in his death (389). Leucon I eventually took Theodosia (despite Heracleote opposition), but then abandoned westward expansion in favour of establishing direct control over the Sindians and other tribes beyond the Straits. With the addition of two more tribes by Paerisades (Pairisadēs) I (sole ruler in 344/3–311/10) the realm reached its widest known extent, for the alleged plans of Eumelus (Eumēlos) (310/309–304/3) to conquer 'all the Pontic nations' were forestalled by his death in a road accident. Eumelus' successors (a very ill-documented lot) weathered the storms caused by Sarmatian migrations, but pressure from Crimean Scythians eventually led Paerisades V to look to *Mithridates VI Eupator of Pontus for help, and when Paerisades succumbed to a revolt by Saumacus, Mithridates took the chance to take direct control.

The Bosporan dynasts generally remained isolated from the political history of Aegean and Mediterranean Greece, but their control of rich sources of (above all) grain gave them considerable economic importance (the golden age being, perhaps, the fourth and early third centuries). Evidence of various dates shows the pursuit of good relations (explicitly or presumably for commercial reasons) with many Greek states, but greatest interest attached to a special relationship with Athens, which can be documented from the 390s until 284 (with a possible break in the period 344–327). Satyrus I (sole ruler in 393/2–389/8) gave occasional advantages to those carrying corn to Athens, and may have started the regular practice (attested for Leucon I, Spartocus II (349/8–344/3), and Paerisades I, and probable for Spartocus III) of allowing them pre-emption and freedom from duty. Additionally, special grants of corn in times of shortage are recorded in the 350s, 320s, and in 286. In return, all the Spartocids just named were given Athenian citizenship, *ateleia* at Athens, and expensive gold crowns; statues of (at least) Paerisades I, Satyrus II (311/10–310/309) and Spartocus III were erected in the city, and (perhaps in 327) Athens undertook to assist in the event of attack on the Spartocid realm.

BIBL. R. Werner, *Historia* iv (1955); S. M. Burstein, *Historia* xxiii (1974), xxvii (1978); *CAH* viii. 561–89; *OCD* (for a list of Spartocid rulers).

Speusippus Philosopher, head of the Academy 347–339 BC.

*Plato chose his nephew Speusippus (Speusippos) to succeed him as head of the Academy on his death. They had previously visited Sicily together, and Speusippus had supported *Dion's (q.v.) attempts to 'liberate' Syracuse from the rule of *Dionysius II. The details are disputed.

His many writings are lost, but some central doctrines from his complicated philosophy can be fairly safely reconstructed. He rejected Plato's Forms, and proposed instead a theory of different levels of reality, which was criticized by *Aristotle as 'disorderly' ('The universe must not be governed badly'). Numbers had a high status in his system (no doubt through *Pythagorean influence), with the One and the Dyad (duality) as first principles. His theory of definitions much influenced Aristotle's biological classifications. In moral philosophy, he argued that pleasure has no moral value, and wrote books criticizing *Aristippus' hedonism.

BIBL. Dillon, *Middle Platonists*; Guthrie, *Greek Philosophy* v.

Sphaerus Stoic philosopher, late 3rd century BC (?).

A pupil of *Cleanthes, Sphaerus (Sphairos) of Borysthenes (or Bosporus) wrote many philosophical works of which none survives. His fellow Stoics thought his definitions particularly good. He visited Sparta, where he helped *Cleomenes III reform the educational system.

BIBL. Diogenes Laertius vii. 177–8.

Sphodrias Spartan general, died 371 BC.

As harmost of Thespiae, Sphodrias undertook (perhaps with *Cleombrotus' approval) an abortive attack on the Piraeus (early 378 BC). His acquittal *in absentia* after *Agesilaus had been persuaded to support him ('the most unjust trial in Spartan history' (*Xenophon)) provoked war with Athens. He died fighting at Leuctra (see *Epaminondas).

BIBL. Poralla, *Prosopographie*, no. 680.

Spitamenes Persian general, died 328 BC.

After betraying the regicide *Bessus to *Alexander the Great, Spitamenes (Spitamenēs) led serious and initially very successful nationalist resistance in the steppe-land of Bactria, Sogdiana, and Scythia (his defeat of a Macedonian force was the starting-point of the discussion which culminated in ('Black') *Cleitus' murder). He was ultimately murdered by some of his Scythian followers.

BIBL. Berve, *Alexanderreich*, no. 717.

Stasinus: see **Cyclic Poets**

Stateira Persian princess, died 323 BC.

A daughter of *Darius III who was captured at Issus (333 BC) by *Alexander the Great, Stateira was offered in marriage to Alexander by her father to seal a proposed division of the Persian empire between them. Alexander refused, but nine years later took her as wife at the mass marriages at Susa. She bore him no children, but *Roxane none the less had her murdered after his death.

BIBL. Berve, *Alexanderreich*, no. 722.

Stesagoras: see **Philaids**

Coin of Thermae Himerenses (2nd century AD) depicting a writer identified as Stesichorus (enlarged).

Stesichorus Lyric poet, *c*. 560 BC.

Linked with south Italian Mataurus or Locri in ancient tradition, but mostly, as by *Plato, with Sicilian Himera (which later commemorated him on coins), Stesichorus (Stēsikhoros) is credited by the *Suda* with inventing choral performances in which singing was accompanied by the lyre: although patently a fabrication based on his name, this does demonstrate that antiquity saw him as a choral poet, a view recently challenged (see West) but supported by the triadic structure of fragments. Closer in scale and treatment to *Homeric epic (with which they were compared) than to other surviving lyric works, his heroic narratives could exceed the length of a papyrus roll (as did his *Oresteia*, see frs. 213–14): new fragments of *Geryoneis* show that it had at least 1,300, probably nearer 2,000 lines and treated Heracles' slaying of Geryon at length (Geryon resists pleas from his mother and Menoetes not to fight (*Suppl*. 9–13)) and with pathos (comparing wilting Geryon to a poppy (*Suppl*. 15)). How closely he could follow *Homer emerges from fr. 209 (perhaps from *Nostoi – Returns of Heroes*); but his most famous poem, *Palinode* (frs. 192–3) ostentatiously challenged Homer's (and *Hesiod's) Trojan story, insisting that Helen went to Egypt and only a phantom to Troy – a *coup de théâtre* which revitalized an old-favourite legend (already treated conventionally by Stesichorus himself (frs. 187–91)) and won him the immortality all poets sought. Musicologists remembered him as adapting the aulodic nome *Harmateios*, perhaps suitable to his dactylic metres, and his tomb was shown at Catana (Sicily).

BIBL. Page, *PMG* and *Suppl*.; M. Davies, *Stesichorus* (forthcoming); Campbell, *Lyric Poetry*; D. L. Page, *JHS* xciii (1973); M. L. West, *CQ* xxi (1971).

Stesimbrotus Sophist, 5th century BC.

Stesimbrotus (Stēsimbrotos) of Thasos taught at Athens, where he wrote lost works about *Homer and the Mysteries of Samothrace, and an anecdotal work entitled *On *Themistocles, *Thucydides [son of Melesias], and *Pericles*; the passages quoted by Plutarch have suggested to some that this was a political pamphlet attacking those leaders of Athenian imperialism who had destroyed the independence of his homeland.

BIBL. *FGrH* iiB, no. 107; *Roman World* *Plutarch.

Stilpon (*c*. 380–300 BC) Philosopher.

The Megarian school of philosophy reached its greatest fame under Stilpon's (Stilpōn) leadership. Philosophers were attracted there from many parts of Greece by his 'inventiveness in argument and his sophistry'. As was usual in the school, his main interest was in logic, but the sparseness of the evidence leaves it unclear how distinguished a logician he was. He denied the existence of universals, arguing that the word 'man' only has meaning if it refers to a particular man. In moral philosophy he was influenced by the Cynic *Crates of Thebes. He attached no value to possessions, and held that wise men should be unaffected by evil. (Thus, when it was suggested to him that his daughter was a disgrace to him, he replied, 'No more than I am an honour to her.')

BIBL. Diogenes Laertius ii. 113–20.

Strabo Geographer, born 64 BC.

A native of Amaseia in Pontus, Strabo (Strabōn) came from a distinguished local family that supported first *Mithridates (VI), then Lucullus. He studied in Rome c. 44–35 BC, and travelled, though selectively, 'from the Euxine [Black Sea] to Ethiopia, from Armenia to Etruria' (II. v. 11); Ethiopia and Arabia he visited with his patron Aelius Gallus, governor of Egypt. He wrote *Historical Memoranda* in 47 books, from the end of *Polybius to (?) the fall of Alexandria to Octavian, and notably 17 books (which survive) of geography – in which he includes much history, legend, antiquities, and ethnography – with explicit awareness of their potential utility to public men. The *Geography* invaluably preserves much information about the work of the earlier Greek geographers, especially the great Alexandrian scholar *Eratosthenes; see also *Agatharchides, *Dicaearchus, *Eudoxus of Cyzicus, *Megasthenes, *Nearchus, and *Pos(e)idonius.

BIBL. *FGrH* 90; Loeb ed. of *Geography* (1917–35); *Roman World* *Lucullus, *Octavian.   N.H.

Stratocles Athenian politician, died after 293/2 BC.

In 324 BC Stratocles (Stratoklēs) attacked *Demosthenes during the *Harpalus investigations, and after the battle of Amorgos (322) he falsely reported an Athenian victory, defending himself, when the truth emerged, by saying 'How have I harmed you, if for two days you have been happy?' But his prominence as democratic leader of Athens belongs later, when he was responsible for the extravagant honours paid to *Antigonus and *Demetrius Poliorcetes in 307 (statues, crowns, divine or quasi-divine honours), for several decrees honouring their adherents and associates, and for a pro-Macedonian policy that lasted, despite opposition (especially when Demetrius interfered to save one Cleomedon from punishment by an Athenian court (303)), until Antigonus' defeat and death at Ipsus (301). A notable example of Stratocles' complaisance to Macedonian whims was his tampering with the calendar which permitted Demetrius to be hastily initiated into the Eleusinian Mysteries at the wrong time of the year (302). After Ipsus political control passed into other hands, but Stratocles survived to see the restoration of Demetrius' influence in 294. His behaviour in 307–301 earned him a bad press (he is described as aping *Cleon, and his association with the prostitute Phylakion was a subject of comment), but it is doubtful whether his political principles were notably worse than those of his contemporaries.

BIBL. Kirchner, *PA*, no. 12938; Davies, *Athenian Families* 494 f.; Ferguson, *Hellenistic Athens.*

Straton of Lampsacus Philosopher, and head of the Peripatetic school c. 287–269 BC.

Straton (Stratōn) succeeded *Theophrastus as head of the Peripatetic school. His main interest was in natural science, although he wrote on many subjects. (Only fragments of his work survive.) He insisted that natural events should be explained by natural causes, and not by appeal to ends or purposes. After his death, little original or interesting work emerged from the school.

BIBL. Wehrli, *Die Schule des Aristoteles* v (1967–9).

Stratonice I Seleucid queen, c. 301–254 BC.

The daughter of *Demetrius Poliorcetes and *Phila I, Stratonice (Stratonikē) was married to *Seleucus I to mark his alliance with her father after *Antigonus and Demetrius were defeated at Ipsus in 301. Ancient sources record a love affair with her stepson *Antiochus I, to whom Seleucus subsequently gave her as wife. Her children were (by Seleucus) Phila the Younger, who married Stratonice's own brother *Antigonus Gonatas, and (by Antiochus) *Antiochus II, a Seleucus, Stratonice II (who married *Demetrius II of Macedon), and Apama (who married *Magas of Cyrene). The range of her descendants makes her comparable with Queen Victoria, and assured the survival of the blood of *Antipater for many generations.

BIBL. Macurdy, *Hellenistic Queens*; Plutarch, *Demetrius* xxxii. 3; xxxiii. 1; Appian, *Syrian Wars* 59–62; Bevan, *House of Seleucus.*

Susarion Iambic poet, 6th–5th century BC (?).

Several ancient writers call Susarion (Sousariōn) the inventor of comedy, and link his name with a tall story about its origin. Some make him a Megarian, others a native of Icaria in Attica. The one fragment attributed to him, however, clearly comes from a non-dramatic poem. Some scholars think him a fictitious character.

BIBL. Pickard-Cambridge, *Dithyramb . . .*; West, *Studies.*

Tachos King of Egypt, c. 362–360 BC.

Succeeding *Nectanebon I in 362 BC after a period of joint rule, Tachos (Takhōs) invaded Palestine in support of (or to exploit) the Satraps' Revolt against Persia. Although he had *Chabrias and *Agesilaus as military advisers, the enterprise failed when a rebellion in Egypt elevated his nephew to the kingship (as *Nectanebon II). Tachos took refuge with the Persians.

BIBL. PW ivA. 1989–95; Kienitz, *Geschichte Ägyptens.*

Taxiles Indian king, floruit 320s BC.

Taxiles (Taxilēs, a 'royal' name: his personal name was Omphis or Mophis) ruled a domain between the Indus and the Hydaspes (Jhelum) with its capital at Taxila. He made friendly overtures to *Alexander the Great before the invasion of India, fought against *Porus (an old enemy) at the Hydaspes (326 BC), and was later co-governor of his erstwhile kingdom with Eudamus.

BIBL. Berve, *Alexanderreich*, no. 739.

T(e)isias Rhetorician, mid-5th century BC.

Together with *Corax, T(e)isias (Teisias) of Syracuse was traditionally held to have been the first professional teacher of public speaking. His pupils are said to have included *Lysias and *Isocrates. The historical context was the replacement of the Syracusan tyranny of the Deinomenids (see *Gelon, *Hieron I) by a democracy; this resulted in substantial changes of land ownership which had to be contested before courts with mass juries, open to rhetorical persuasion.

BIBL. Kennedy, *Art of Persuasion* 58–61.

Telesilla Lyric poetess, 6th–5th centuries BC.

According to legend, Telesilla of Argos saved her city by arming its women after its defeat by *Cleomenes I at Sepeia (c. 494 BC). Her poems seem to have been hymns; hardly anything survives. The metre Telesilleion is called after her.

BIBL. Lesky, *Greek Literature*; *Lyra Graeca* (Loeb) ii; Kirkwood, *Greek Monody*.

Telestes Dithyrambic poet, active c. 400 BC.

A fragment of the dithyramb *Argo* by Telestes (Telestēs) of Selinus defends the *aulos* against *Melanippides' criticisms of it.

BIBL. *Lyra Graeca* (Loeb) iii; Pickard-Cambridge, *Dithyramb . . .*

Teleutias Spartan general, died 381 BC.

Teleutias co-operated with his half-brother King *Agesilaus in operations at Corinth (391 BC), and then served in Rhodes and Aegina (390–388), on one occasion executing a daring raid on the Piraeus. In 382 he led an army against Olynthus, but was killed the following year after starting an engagement in unfavourable circumstances.

BIBL. Poralla, *Prosopographie*, no. 689.

Terpander Musician and poet, c. 670 BC.

From Antissa in Lesbos (as *Timotheus (1) attests)

Terpander (Terpandros) was the first citharode to win at the festival of the Carneia at Sparta, founded 676/3 BC. From Pseudo-Plutarch, *On Music*, we know (on the authority of *Heracleides Ponticus) that he created and named the seven classical citharodic nomes, and to this music set his own or *Homer's words, winning four successive Pythian victories; that Glaucus of Rhegium put him before *Archilochus; that he was responsible for the 'First School' of music at Sparta, where he quelled civil strife; and that he added a seventh string to the lyre, allowing an octave to be played.

His poetry included *prooemia*, comparable to Homeric hymns, and probably dactylic, as are all but one of the (disputed) fragments.

BIBL. Pseudo-Plutarch, *On Music* 1132C–E, 1134B, 1145B–F; Page, *PMG*; W. D. Anderson, *Ethos and Education in Greek Music* (1966); M. L. West, *JHS* ci (1981), 113 ff.

Thales Sage, early 6th century BC.

Thales (Thalēs), a Milesian probably of Phoenician stock, was counted by *Aristotle the first of the natural philosophers, but earlier reports represent him as a man of political and practical ingenuity. He was one of the *Seven Sages (q.v.). *Herodotus credits him with a proposal for a federation of the Ionian states against the threat from Persia, and with a diversion of the river Halys to allow *Croesus' army to pass. He was also said (implausibly) to have predicted an eclipse of the sun, perhaps that of 585 BC. Details of his philosophical or scientific views are scarce. He held that the world rested on and originated from water, and perhaps that it was made from water. But it is unclear whether this amounted to a scientific theory. Other attributed sayings are 'All things are full of gods', and 'The lodestone [or magnet] has

Left: 'portrait', possibly of Thales, from a double herm (the other head represents *Bias). Vatican Museum. *Right*: portrait inscribed 'Thales the Milesian' from the painting of the *Seven Sages in the Palazzo dei Cesari at Ostia.

a soul', attempts, no doubt, to explain how seemingly inanimate things can move. He was said to have introduced geometry to Greece from Egypt, but attribution to him of particular proofs, e.g. on congruent triangles, is unreliable.

BIBL. Guthrie, *Greek Philosophy* i. 45–72.

Thaletas Musician and lyric poet, *c.* 665 BC.

Associated by Pseudo-Plutarch, *On Music*, with the Second School of music at Sparta and the establishment of the Gymnopaedia festival (665 BC), Thaletas (Thalētas) of Gortyn in Crete is credited with paeans (hymns to Apollo), doubtless because he was said to have been summoned by a Delphic oracle and cured Sparta of plague. Attribution of paeans was disputed, and some argued the influence of *Olympus (cretic and paionic rhythms) or *Archilochus.

BIBL. Pseudo-Plutarch, *On Music* 1134B–D, 1145B; PW vA. 1213.

Theaetetus (*c.* 415–369 BC) Mathematician.

Theaetetus (Theaitētos) of Athens was a pupil of *Theodorus of Cyrene, and briefly a friend of *Socrates. He developed a theory of irrationals, and is thought to be largely the source of *Euclid's *Elements*, book x. He was also said to have discovered the regular octahedron and icosahedron. He died, suffering from wounds and dysentery, after fighting courageously in a battle near Corinth.

BIBL. Plato, *Theaetetus*.

Theagenes Tyrant of Megara, *c.* 650 BC.

Theagenes (Theagenēs) became tyrant after slaughtering the cattle of the rich, apparently in the course of a dispute over land. The remains of a fountain-house which he built can still be seen at Megara. He probably supported his son-in-law *Cylon's unsuccessful attempt to make himself tyrant of Athens.

BIBL. Thucydides i. 126; Aristotle, *Politics* 1305a; Andrewes, *Greek Tyrants* 49, 84.

Theagenes of Rhegium Rhapsode and critic, *c.* 525 BC (?).

First to offer allegorical interpretations of *Homer, perhaps reacting against such critics as *Xenophanes, Theagenes (Theagenēs) was also allegedly the first to investigate Homer's biography and Greek usage (*Hellenismos*).

BIBL. Scholiast B on *Iliad* xx. 67; Pfeiffer, *Classical Scholarship* i.

Themistocles Athenian leader, archon 493/2 BC.

The major achievement of Themistocles (Themistoklēs), son of Neocles, was the creation of the fleet which enabled the Greeks to destroy the Persians at Salamis (480 BC), and Athens to control the Aegean through the Delian League. Accordingly, his political career has been interpreted by both ancients and moderns as that of a radical democratic leader who tried systematically to undermine the 'aristocracy'.

Hostile sources claim that Themistocles' background was obscure, and his mother a barbarian; in fact he belonged to a wealthy branch of the Lycomid clan. He was archon, by election, in 493, and a *strategos* at Marathon in 490. The year 487 saw two constitutional

reforms conventionally interpreted as 'democratic' and therefore ascribed to Themistocles: the introduction of ostracism, and the replacement of election by the casting of lots as the method of appointing archons. Neither change need have had anti-aristocratic motives; both would have helped to soothe the bitter feuding between powerful clans like the *Alcmaeonids by removing the archonship from the arena of open competition, and by forcing at least some of the rival leaders into temporary exile. Nor need these reforms be linked to Themistocles in particular. In fact there were concerted attempts to use the ostracism procedure *against* him, since a third of surviving ostraca from the 480s bear his name.

In 483 the discovery of a new vein of silver at the mines of Laureum enabled him to propose the expansion of the navy, ostensibly for war with Aegina. *Xerxes was already preparing his campaign to conquer Greece. In 481 it was Themistocles who proposed the recall of exiles, a Spartan alliance, and other measures to facilitate resistance; an early third-century BC inscription found at Troezen purports to record measures proposed by Themistocles for the evacuation of Attica in the face of the Persian invasion of 480. He himself led Athenian forces in the valley of Tempe in Thessaly and at Artemisium; and it was mainly on his advice that the naval battle at Salamis

Herm bearing the name 'Themistocles', from Ostia. Roman copy of a 5th-century Greek original. Ostia, Museum.

Part of the defensive walls of the Acropolis at Athens, hastily reconstructed (using column drums from destroyed buildings) on the advice of Themistocles, after the Persian retreat in 479 BC.

was fought in a restricted area, thus preventing the Persians from deploying their fleet properly and leading to the decisive Greek victory.

Themistocles' subsequent political role is obscure, and the chronology uncertain. In 479/8 he strongly advocated the reconstruction of the city walls of Athens and the fortification of the Piraeus. In 477/6 he provided the chorus for *Phrynichus' (I) tragedy *The Phoenician Women*. But he was accused of corruption and (at some date) of attempting to negotiate a peace agreement with the Persians; *c*. 471 he was ostracized, probably to resolve the political conflict between himself and the pro-Spartan, anti-Persian *Cimon.

Themistocles went to Argos, where some believe he was involved in attempts to organize an anti-Spartan alliance in the Peloponnese; while he was there, the Spartans accused him of Medizing (in association with *Pausanias (I)), and the Athenians condemned him to death for treason. He fled via Corcyra, Molossia, and Macedonia to Asia Minor; on the way he narrowly avoided capture by the Athenians, probably under Cimon, besieging Naxos (467?). In Asia King *Artaxerxes I (after 465) rewarded him, presumably for trying to arrange peace between Athens and Persia rather than for his trick in warning Xerxes that the Greeks were proposing to cut the bridge across the Hellespont after Salamis: he was granted the three cities of Magnesia, Lampsacus, and Myus. He died soon after (462/59?) at the age of 65, possibly committing suicide.

BIBL. Davies, *Athenian Families*, no. 6669; P. Green, *The Year of Salamis* (1970); A. Podlecki, *The Life of Themistocles* (1975); R. J. Lenardon, *The Saga of Themistocles* (1978).

Theocritus Poet, *c*. 270 BC.

Theocritus (Theokritos), father of pastoral poetry, was a western Greek from Syracuse in Sicily, who apparently moved fairly early to the east, where he knew Cos and Alexandria. The transmitted poems (30 – not all genuine – plus fragments and epigrams, mostly written in literary Doric) give various data without completing the biographical jigsaw puzzle. The flora of the bucolic poems, even those set in southern Italy (*Idylls* iv–v) can tentatively be called characteristic of the eastern Aegean. Theocritus' poetry is remarkable for the number of plants named (twice as many as in *Homer) and for the knowledgeable eye which notes them. This makes attractive the speculation that his evident familiarity with Cos – *Idyll* vii describes a walk which can be taken today – derives from study at the island's famous medical school, where he perhaps met his friend Nicias of Miletus, doctor and litterateur (a scholiast asserts that both were pupils of *Erasistratus). *Idyll* xvi, a fine poem seeking patronage from *Hieron II of Syracuse, datable 275/4 BC, suggests homesickness; but it was apparently from Alexandria that an offer came: *Idyll* xvii is a eulogy of *Ptolemy II datable *c*. 273/2, *Idyll* xv a splendid evocation of bourgeois life in the new city, before 270.

In the mysterious seventh idyll Simichidas (alias Theocritus), recalling an encounter on Cos with one

'Lycidas', reality and fiction tantalizingly mixed, pays tribute to *Asclepiades and *Philitas, and takes a literary stand identical with that of *Callimachus (q.v.). His painstakingly finished pieces are perfect demonstrations of the new poetics (*Idylls* xiii and xxii seem pointedly so, recasting in self-contained form adjacent episodes from *Apollonius Rhodius' *Argonautica*). 'Short poem' is indeed all the later name 'idyll' means. The fame and great influence of Theocritus' few bucolic poems (whence 'idyllic') should not obscure the wide variety of his output, which includes, for example, mythological epyllion (xiii), hymn (xxii), epithalamium (xviii), Aeolic love poems (xxix–xxxi), and epigrams (in mixed metres); nor the experimental freshness of the hexameter bucolic poems themselves. A certain pattern emerges: in a remote landscape evoked by careful detail shepherd meets goatherd, they sit down, they sing, a prize is given. The civilized encounter of *Idyll* i, leading to the set-piece song on the death of the Sicilian bucolic hero Daphnis, inspired the sweet pastoral tradition, in which song and love predominate, of *Moschus, *Bion, Virgil, and Europe in general. But Theocritus could also develop a more spirited realism, e.g. *Idyll* v – an aggressive encounter producing a tit-for-tat capping contest drawing on real-life shepherds' singing-matches. Theocritus brought sub-literary forms, notably the mime, inside his artistically balanced, linguistically and metrically sophisticated new poetry (compare *Herodas). But for all its artifice and concealed learning, his work is sustained by more attractive qualities: a natural dramatic talent (xv, resembling a radio play), a sympathetic insight into people (ii, the revealing monologue of a jilted girl), a gentle humour (xi, recasting Homer's monstrous Cyclops as an overgrown shepherd naïvely in love), and a pervasive melodiousness of language.

BIBL. A. S. F. Gow, ed., *Theocritus* (2nd ed., 1952); K. J. Dover, *Theocritus* (1971); F. T. Griffiths, *Theocritus at Court* (1979); F. Williams, *CQ* xxi (1971); *Roman World* *Virgil.

Theodectes Tragedian and orator, active *c.* 370– *c.* 350 BC (?).

Theodectes (Theodektēs or -tas) of Phaselis in Asia Minor is said to have studied under *Plato, *Isocrates, and (?) *Aristotle, and became known for his tragedies, speeches, works on rhetoric, and verse riddles. Aristotle refers to his work several times, and dedicated a treatise on rhetoric to him.

BIBL. T. B. L. Webster, *Hermes* lxxxii (1954) 302 ff.; Xanthakis-Karamanos, *Fourth-Century Tragedy*.

Theodorus of Cyrene Geometer, 5th century BC.

A pupil of *Protagoras, and probably a *Pythagorean, Theodorus (Theodōros) was distinguished in music and arithmetic, as well as geometry. In *Plato's *Theaetetus*, he is said to have proved that the square root of each non-square number up to 17 was irrational. His pupil *Theaetetus developed a general theory of irrational numbers.

BIBL. Heath, *Greek Mathematics* i. 202–9.

Theognis Elegiac poet, *c.* 540 BC (?).

From mainland Megara (although *Plato says he was Sicilian), Theognis is the only elegist under whose name a corpus has survived in its own manuscript tradition. Unfortunately it cannot all be Theognidean. Rather Book One (1–1220) is a collection of early elegiac poems (assembled by *c.* AD 100) separable into (a) lines 1–18: four hymns; (b) 19–254: an anthology of Theognis' gnomic poems (maxims), probably selected by the fourth century BC, with few intruders (*Solon: 153–4, 227–32), and framed by programmatic and epilogue poems (19 ff., 237 ff.); (c) 255–*c.* 1022: an anthology in which Theognidean poems, convivial and gnomic, are prominent, but quotation elsewhere betrays songs of *Tyrtaeus (1003–6), *Mimnermus (795–6, 1117–22), Solon (315–18, 585–90, 719–28), and Euenus of Paros (467–96, 667–82); others cannot be Theognidean (773–88 by a Megarian in 480 BC, compare 757–64), and doubtless other intruders lurk incognito; (d) *c.* 1023–1220: an anthology which has seven poems also in (b), eleven also in (c), but none demonstrably non-Theognidean. Book Two (only in one manuscript) is a paederastic collection which shares three poems with (d) and one with (c), includes poems of Solon (1253–4), Euenus (1341–50), and Theognis (only 1353–6 demonstrably), and probably circulated independently of Book One in antiquity.

We may rely upon address to Cyrnus to identify Theognis' poems: lines 19–30 show that this is what Theognis intended; rarely – as in 237–54, a brilliant vision of the immortality offered by Theognis' songs and requited by Cyrnus with deceit – is Cyrnus' personality as Theognis' boy-friend discernible. Mostly he is a sounding-board for Theognis' oligarchic preaching: 'Be true to friends', 'Virtue is rare, breeding paramount', 'Beware scoundrels' (viz. men not of Theognis' class).

The unseating of the oligarchy by (in Theognis' terms) worthless *nouveaux riches* probably belongs in the mid-sixth century: since predictions of tyranny (31–52) mention no names, they are unlikely to refer to *Theagenes (*c.* 650 BC (?)) and 1103–4's references to the destruction of Smyrna and Colophon support ancient dating to the 540s BC. Theognis' cantankerous bitching about the *demos* and insistence on clubability secured his poems wide contemporary and posthumous circulation in the symposia of an upper class increasingly under pressure, and we can easily see why they attracted comparable material and became the kernel of an anthology.

BIBL. West, *IEG* and *Studies*; Campbell, *Lyric Poetry*; B. van Groningen, *Théognis: le premier livre* (1966).

Theophrastus (*c.* 370–286 BC) Philosopher.

Born at Eresus in Lesbos, Theophrastus (Theophrastos) became a pupil of *Aristotle, and succeeded him as head of the Peripatetic school. It may have been he who first acquired the Peripatos (a covered area for walking) which gave the school its name, through the influence of his pupil *Demetrius of Phalerum (influence would be needed because neither Aristotle nor Theophrastus was an Athenian citizen).

Not much remains of the 232,808 lines that he was said to have written. Although the subjects of his writings were as varied as those of Aristotle, his main interest was probably in detailed empirical research, notably in botany (two works on plants survive) and political history. His work on metaphysics diverges slightly, but uninterestingly, from that of Aristotle. An important link

Herm bearing the name 'Theophrastus', from a villa near Tivoli. Rome, Villa Albani.

in the tenuous chain of evidence by which we know something of the earliest Greek philosophers was his lost work *Opinions of Natural Philosophers*. The reliability of this work is much disputed. The *Characters*, his most famous work, portrays various ways in which a man's character may diverge from the Aristotelian norm.

BIBL. Diogenes Laertius v. 36–57; E. Zeller, *Die Philosophie der Griechen* (1923) ii. 2. 806.

Theopompus (*c.* 377–320 BC) Historian.

Theopompus (Theopompos) of Chios may have been a pupil of *Isocrates at Athens; at any rate he saw history largely as providing rhetoric with a store of suitable and emotionally coloured subject-matter. In 352 BC he delivered a panegyric at funeral games in honour of King Mausolus. Under *Alexander the Great he was exiled from Chios because of his father Damasistratus' friendship

for Sparta. He lived at the Macedonian court, was restored to Chios in 333/2, but was exiled again after Alexander's death (323), and ended up at *Ptolemy I's court in Egypt.

He wrote 12 books of *Hellenica*, taking *Thucydides' history down to the battle of Cnidos in 394, and 58 books of *Philippica*, dealing with events during the reign of *Philip II of Macedon (359–336), but containing numerous *Herodotean digressions on earlier periods. The pleasure he takes in rhetorical invective leads him to attack the morality both of Athenian statesmen and of Philip and his court. His style is far too rhetorical for him to be identified with the *Oxyrhynchus Historian.

BIBL. *FGrH* iiiB, no. 115; W. R. Connor, *Theopompus and Fifth-century Athens* (1968); A. D. Momigliano, *Terzo Contributo* i (1966), 367 ff.; G. Shrimpton, *Phoenix* xxxi (1977).

Theopompus of Sparta Eurypontid king, *c.* 720–675 BC.

Theopompus (Theopompos) was king during the First Messenian War, and according to *Tyrtaeus it was he and his colleague Polydorus who brought the 'Great Rhetra' (see *Lycurgus of Sparta) from Delphi. It was also supposed to have been during his reign that the ephorate either came into being or acquired more powers than it had had before. It was said that Theopompus' wife reproached him for consenting to this measure, as it would reduce the royal power which their sons would inherit; but Theopompus only replied: 'It'll last all the longer'.

BIBL. Aristotle, *Politics* 1313a; Diodorus VII. xii. 6; Forrest, *History of Sparta* 57–68.

Theramenes Athenian politician, died 404 BC.

The opposition of Theramenes (Thēramenēs) to both radical democracy and extreme oligarchy during the internal strife which marked Athenian public life once control over the empire was shaken by the Sicilian disaster (413 BC) meant that he received a bad press from both sides; the tyrant *Critias called him 'cothurnus', i.e. the stage boot which fits both the right and the left foot. On the other hand he became the favourite of both ancient and modern intellectuals with a belief in rational compromise and moderation, like the author of the Aristotelian *Constitution of Athens*.

As the son of the politician *Hagnon, Theramenes was already well known in 422, when the comic dramatist *Eupolis refers to him. In 411 he was one of the leaders of the oligarchic conspiracy known as the Four Hundred; his father was one of the *probouloi*, the committee of ten wise old men which the conspirators manipulated to get their constitution approved. Theramenes was elected *strategos*, but found himself in opposition to the pro-Spartans among the oligarchs. This group had occupied a fortress at Eëtionea to enable the Spartans to seize the Piraeus. Theramenes destroyed the fortress, and was instrumental in the overthrow of the Four Hundred and the restoration of democracy (September 411). His new constitution, which lasted for only eight months, is described by *Thucydides as the best that Athens ever had: payment for office was abolished, and membership of the Assembly was restricted to the wealthier peasants (those of hoplite census, about 9,000 in number; hence the regime was called (with the number rounded down) 'The Five Thousand').

In the following year (410) Theramenes served the restored radical democracy as *strategos*, operating in the Aegean; he restored a democratic regime at Paros, helped *Alcibiades and *Thrasybulus to defeat the Spartan fleet at Cyzicus, and reimposed Athenian control on the vital cities of Chalcedon and Byzantium.

He served as a trierarch (ship's owner and captain) at the battle of Arginusae in 406. Here he was deputed to save those whose ships had been wrecked in the battle; this proved impossible because of a storm. When the fleet returned to Athens, Theramenes, faced with the anger of the relatives of those who had drowned, lost his nerve and accused the commanding generals of being responsible; six were executed, including *Thrasyllus and a son of *Pericles.

After the destruction of the last Athenian fleet at Aegospotami (405), it was Theramenes who led the peace negotiations with *Lysander. He was said to have refrained from doing anything for three months during the winter so that starvation would encourage the besieged Athenians to accept the humiliation of defeat. He was then sent to Sparta with full powers to make peace. In March 404 Lysander appointed him one of the committee of thirty (the 'Thirty Tyrants') who were to rule Athens on Sparta's behalf; but his opposition to the excesses of his fellow tyrants led to friction, and the oligarchic leader *Critias had him tried and executed. His speech of defence was famous; he was a noted orator who had studied under *Prodicus (hence the fable that he, too, was a Cean, and only adopted by Hagnon), and was himself a teacher of *Isocrates.

BIBL. Davies, *Athenian Families*, no. 7234; P. Harding, *Phoenix* xxviii (1974).

Theron Tyrant of Acragas, 488–472 BC.

A member of the Emmenid family, Theron (Thērōn) became ruler of Acragas in southern Sicily in 488 BC, strengthening his position by marrying his daughter *Demarete to *Gelon of Gela; later he himself married a daughter of Gelon's brother, Polyzalus. In 483 he expelled the tyrant of Himera, Terillus, installing his son Thrasydaeus as ruler; Terillus and his son-in-law *Anaxilas of Rhegium replied by appealing for help to their *xenos* (guest-friend), the Carthaginian *Hamilcar. This resulted in a major Carthaginian invasion, defeated by Gelon and Theron at the battle of Himera (480).

After Gelon's death, Theron was drawn into a conflict between his brothers *Hieron (I) and Polyzalus. Polyzalus fled to Acragas hoping for support from Theron, while the population of Himera expelled Theron's son Thrasydaeus and appealed to Hieron. A compromise is said to have been reached with the help of the poet *Simonides. On his death in 472, Theron was succeeded by Thrasydaeus. The presence of *Pindar at Theron's court is an indication of the wealth and success of the Emmenid tyranny.

BIBL. Herodotus vii. 165–7; Diodorus Siculus xi. 20–6, 48 f., 53; Pindar, *Olympians* ii–iii; Dunbabin, *Western Greeks*, ch. 14.

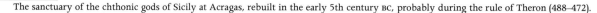

The sanctuary of the chthonic gods of Sicily at Acragas, rebuilt in the early 5th century BC, probably during the rule of Theron (488–472).

Inscribed base of a statue of Thespis (2nd century AD) in the theatre of Dionysus at Athens.

Thespis Poet, *c.* 535 BC.

An Athenian from Icaria, Thespis was famed as the creator of tragedy. *Aristotle and perhaps already *Charon of Lampsacus thought he was the first to introduce an actor who delivered prologues and conversed with the chorus. Later tradition had him meet *Solon, invent the mask, and win the first tragic competition at the Dionysia (535/3 BC). Few accept five attributed fragments (perhaps from tragedies forged in Thespis' name by *Heracleides Ponticus) or the *Suda's* titles (*Pentheus, Phorbas* or *Games for Pelias, Priests*, and *Youths*).

BIBL. Pickard-Cambridge, *Dithyramb . . .*, and *The Dramatic Festivals of Athens* (2nd ed., 1968).

Thestorides: see **Cyclic Poets**

Thibron (1) Spartan general, died 391 BC.

Exiled in 399 BC for his mismanagement of the war with Persia, Thibron (Thibrōn) reappeared in that theatre in 391, but his sloppy generalship (he preferred the company of the *aulos*-player Thersander to military responsibilities) led to defeat and death. *Aristotle mentions a writer on *Lycurgus (of Sparta) named Thibron, who may be the same man.

BIBL. Poralla, *Prosopographie*, no. 375.

Thibron (2) Spartan adventurer, died 322/1 BC.

Using the money and soldiers of his friend *Harpalus, whom he had murdered, Thibron (Thibrōn) attempted to seize Cyrenaica, indirectly causing its annexation to the *Ptolemaic kingdom when *Ophellas was sent to defeat him. Two bronze coins bearing Thibron's name are known.

BIBL. L. Robert, *Hellenica* x (1955), 167–71.

Thorax: see **Aleuadae**

Thrasybulus Athenian democratic leader, died 389 BC.

Nothing certain is known of the family of Thrasybulus (Thrasuboulos), son of Lycus, but he was wealthy enough to be a trierarch. In this capacity he was largely responsible for the oath in favour of the democratic constitution taken by the Athenian navy at Samos when they heard of the oligarchic *coup* of the Four Hundred in 411 BC. The navy chose him as one of its *strategoi*, and he proposed the recall of *Alcibiades. In the same year he won the Athenian victories at Cynossema and Abydos; in the following year he assisted Alcibiades at the victory at Cyzicus.

Thrasybulus was not re-elected after Alcibiades' fall (407); hence he served as trierarch at Arginusae, and survived the victory (see *Theramenes). Under the regime of the Thirty (see *Critias), he retired to Thebes; from here he co-ordinated democratic resistance, occupied Phyle with 70 supporters (winter 404/3), then the Piraeus. Spartan hostility to *Lysander's arrangements led to the fall of the Thirty. Thrasybulus tried, but failed, to have all his supporters (including *Lysias) granted citizenship. He continued to be a prominent leader of the restored democracy, supporting an alliance with Thebes and the Corinthian War against Sparta (395–387). Following *Conon's restoration of Athenian naval hegemony, Thrasybulus led an expedition to recover Thasos, Samothrace, the Chersonese, Chalcedon, and Byzantium (390–389); he was killed near Aspendus on a plundering expedition.

He is to be distinguished from a Thrasybulus son of Thrason who impeached Alcibiades after the battle of Notium (407), was ambassador to Thebes in 377, and was described by *Demosthenes as an excellent and famous public speaker.

BIBL. R. Seager, *JHS* lxxxvii (1967); S. Perlman, *CPhil.* lxiii (1968); G. L. Cawkwell, *CQ* xxvi (1976).

Thrasybulus of Miletus Tyrant, *c.* 625–600 BC.

Thrasybulus (Thrasuboulos) was ruler of Miletus at the time of its successful resistance to *Alyattes. He is best known for his advice to the Corinthian tyrant *Periander. Thrasybulus took Periander's ambassador for a walk through a cornfield, where he knocked the heads off the tallest stalks. Periander rightly interpreted this action as meaning that he should keep his position secure by eliminating prominent men who might become his rivals.

BIBL. Herodotus i. 20–2, v. 92; Andrewes, *Greek Tyrants* 50, 118.

Thrasybulus, son of Thrason: see **Thrasybulus**

Thrasybulus of Syracuse: see **Hieron I**

Thrasyllus Athenian democratic leader, died 406 BC.

In 411 BC Thrasyllus (Thrasullos) was one of those who organized support for the democracy among the fleet at Samos (see *Thrasybulus); elected *strategos*, he helped achieve the naval victories at Cynossema and Abydos. He returned to Athens when the democracy was restored, and repulsed a Spartan attack led by *Agis II. An opponent of *Alcibiades, Thrasyllus was re-elected *strategos* after Alcibiades' disgrace in 407; he was executed as one of the six victorious generals who failed to rescue the Athenians shipwrecked at Arginusae (see *Theramenes).

BIBL. A. Andrewes, *JHS* lxxiii (1953).

Thrasymachus of Chalcedon Sophist, 5th century BC.

Thrasymachus (Thrasumakhos) was primarily interested in rhetorical theory and practice; he produced a handbook (*Megale Techne*, i.e. *The Great Craft*) on how to elicit the required emotional response in an audience, and was the first to analyse *cola* and *perioda*. He published various pamphlets criticizing the decline of political morality, and attacking Macedonian intervention in Thessaly. *Plato depicts him in book i of the *Republic* as advocating the view that 'Justice means the interest of the stronger', but there is no independent evidence of his ethical views.

BIBL. Guthrie, *Greek Philosophy* iii. 294 ff.; Kennedy, *Art of Persuasion* 68 ff.

Thucydides Historian, second half of 5th century BC.

Ancient reconstructions of the life of Thucydides (Thoukudidēs), son of Olorus, are largely speculative. The only reliable evidence other than the text of his *Histories* says that his tomb was to be found among those of *Cimon's family. Cimon's Thracian maternal grandfather was another Olorus, and Thucydides himself says that he had property in Thrace. The Cimonid connection has been adduced to explain Thucydides' supposed 'convert's zeal' for *Pericles. His complicated Greek prose style (especially in the set speeches) has also been implausibly explained as due to his Thracian background; it is rather due to the pleasure he takes in experimenting with the new rhetorical devices analysed by contemporary sophists like *Gorgias. Otherwise we know only that he was 'young' when he began to write his history in 431 BC, was a *strategos* in 424 when he lost Amphipolis to *Brasidas, and was subsequently exiled (probably on a proposal by *Cleon, whom he vilifies); and that he was unaware of *Conon's restoration of Athenian sea-power in 394.

Thucydides considered the *Archidamian War (431–421), the Sicilian Expedition (415–413), and the Decelean and Ionian Wars (413–404) as a single chain of events which rivalled those described by *Homer and *Herodotus – not so much in heroism as in suffering (*pathos*). Like these predecessors he was writing about a war, and chose to narrate only those episodes which were relevant to his subject-matter. He must not, therefore, be blamed for ignoring Athenian or Spartan domestic politics, or the kind of ethnographical material found in Herodotus. F. Cornford's famous thesis (*Thucydides Mythistoricus* (1907)), that Thucydides was unable to appreciate the importance of economic factors, is based on an anachronistic view of the role of the economy in antiquity.

In the Hellenistic period the text was divided into eight books; it breaks off in the winter of 411/10. Book i contains Thucydides' assertion of the importance of his subject-matter (necessitating a comparison with earlier ages, the *Archaeology*: i. 2–19); an account of the Corcyrean and Potidaean affairs, which were the immediate causes of the war; and an analysis of the 'real', underlying cause of the war, Sparta's fear of the continuing growth of Athenian power, requiring a short history of the Athenian empire (the *Pentecontaetia*, i.e. the 'fifty years' between the Persian and Peloponnesian Wars: i. 89–117). Books ii–v. 24 tell the story of the Archidamian War (431–421). The most famous episodes include Pericles' funeral speech (ii. 35–46), the effect of the plague (ii. 47–57), the debates on Mytilene (iii. 35–50; see *Diodotus) and at Plataea (iii. 52–68); the effects of civil war at Corcyra (iii. 82 ff.); the Pylos campaign (iv. 2–41); and Brasidas' campaigns in Thrace (iv. 78 on). Book v. 25–

Bust of Thucydides. Roman copy of an early 4th-century BC original. Holkham Hall, Norfolk.

116, describing the Peace of *Nicias (421–415 BC), includes the Melian Dialogue (85–116). Books vi and vii deal with the Sicilian expedition, and include a digression on the fall of the Peisistratids *Hippias and *Hipparchus (vi. 54–9), and the description of the battle in the Great Harbour at Syracuse, and the destruction of the Athenians (vii. 51–87). Book viii includes the rise (63–72) and fall (89–98) of the regime of the Four Hundred at Athens.

There is a tendency to contrast Herodotus as an oral story-teller who aims to please his audience with Thucydides as the compiler of a factual account of events to be used by future generations (i. 22. 4: *ktema es aei*, 'a possession for all time'). Thus Thucydides was highly regarded in the nineteenth century, when history was thought to be akin to an empirical science. It was noted that he does not introduce the gods to explain human actions, and some of his vocabulary was thought to reflect the influence of *Hippocratic medicine. Scholars today are more interested in Thucydides' skill in selecting material, and in his attitudes to the role of individuals, and to imperialism and the ethics of power-politics.

BIBL. Translations: R. Warner (Penguin Classics, 1954; reprintings after 1972 have an introduction by M. I. Finley); B. Jowett (with introduction by P. A. Brunt (1963)). A. W. Gomme, *A Historical Commentary on Thucydides*, (1945–); J. H. Finley, *Thucydides* (2nd ed., 1947); P. A. Stadter, *The Speeches of Thucydides* (1973); W. R. Connor, *Classical Journal* lxxii (1977).

Thucydides, son of Melesias Athenian political leader, mid-5th century BC.

Thucydides (Thoukudidēs), son of Melesias, was *Cimon's brother-in-law; the standard list which divides Athenian politicians into 'aristocrats' and 'democrats' saw him as the opponent of *Pericles. He was the first to organize his supporters into a 'party' (hetairia); this did not prevent him from being ostracized in 443 BC, for interfering with the foundation of the Panhellenic colony at Thurii. There is no reason to suppose that he had objections in principle to Periclean imperialism (see *Stesimbrotus); nor that his return from exile in 433 led to the prosecution of Periclean figures such as *Anaxagoras, *Pheidias, and *Aspasia, putting pressure on Pericles to begin the Peloponnesian War.

BIBL. Davies, Athenian Families, no. 7268; H. T. Wade-Gery, JHS lii (1932), 205–27 (=Essays (1958), 239–70); N. K. Rutter, Historia xxii (1973).

Tigranes I 'The Great' King of Armenia, 95–56 BC.

A former Parthian hostage, Tigranes (Tigranēs) was placed on the Armenian throne in 95 BC by Mithradates II, after Armenia had become a vassal of Parthia. Parthia's involvement in a long civil war allowed Tigranes to expand his kingdom enormously. He thus appeared as a capable monarch to the inhabitants of Antioch, whose lands had been ravaged by anarchy and the constant fraternal wars of the many Seleucid princes (see Later *Seleucids), and they offered the throne to him as one who could restore order. Syria became an Armenian province, and Tigranes, when he had established control, gave the country peace and prosperity. Fractious Greeks were deported to populate his new capital Tigranocerta. In 69 he captured, exiled, and murdered Cleopatra Selene, the queen mother whose son was claiming the throne at Rome. In the same year, an alliance with *Mithridates VI of Pontus embroiled him in a war with Rome. After his first defeat he was forced to evacuate Syria, Phoenicia, and Cilicia; the last Seleucid, Antiochus XIII (Later *Seleucids), returned to Antioch under Roman protection.

BIBL. PW vi. 970 ff.; R. Grousset, Histoire de l'Arménie des Origines à 1071 (1947); Will, Hist. pol. ii; Roman World.

Timaeus (c. 356–260 BC) Historian.

Timaeus (Timaios), the son of Andromachus the ruler of Tauromenium (Taormina), fled the Sicily of the tyrant *Agathocles of Syracuse (whom he despised) and lived in Athens for 50 years. He studied rhetoric there, and perhaps returned to Sicily during the reign of *Hieron II. He was the author of a history (called the Histories or the Sicelica) which focused on events in the western Mediterranean, despite his long residence in the eastern Greek world and his knowledge of the turbulent affairs there. Timaeus discussed the history, mythology, archaeology, and religious cults of Sicily and Italy, and included Rome and Latium as well as Magna Graecia. He also refers frequently to Carthage. The work apparently began with the earliest period (he knew something of the Trojan foundation legend of Rome) and continued to his own time (certain books deal with Agathocles and *Pyrrhus of Epirus). Originally in 38 books (but now existing in substantial fragments), Timaeus' history was widely known in the third century. *Lycophron, *Callimachus, and *Apollonius Rhodius drew on him for knowledge of the West, and his use by later historians

(*Polybius, *Diodorus Siculus, and many Romans) made him one of the most influential historians well into the Roman period. He presented a fairly impartial view of events (except concerning the hated Agathocles), but was subject to a certain lack of critical judgement, and to the rhetorical tendencies common to many contemporary historians. He was attacked virulently by Polybius on grounds not always comprehensible or justifiable.

BIBL. Roman World; T. S. Brown, Timaeus of Tauromenium (1958); A. Momigliano, Essays in Ancient and Modern Historiography (1977); PW viA. 1076 ff. (Timaios (3)); FGrH 566.

Timocrates (of Athens) Politician, mid-4th century BC.

Timocrates (Timokratēs) was a wealthy Athenian (his two-horse chariot won at Olympia in 352 BC (?)) and associate of *Androtion, in whose interest he proposed a law granting temporary liberty to state-debtors who provided sureties (353). *Demosthenes, Oration xxiv was composed for an ensuing graphe paranomon. Timocrates had earlier supported Demosthenes' guardians, and later was due to speak for *Meidias.

BIBL. Kirchner, PA, no. 13772; Davies, Athenian Families 513 ff.

Timocrates of Rhodes Persian agent, 396/5 BC.

Timocrates (Timokratēs) was sent to Greece in 396/5 BC by *Pharnabazus (or, according to *Xenophon, in 395 by *Tithraustes) to foment anti-Spartan feeling. His payments to leading politicians in Athens, Argos, Corinth, and Thebes were sometimes (simplistically) regarded as the cause of the Corinthian War (395–387/6).

BIBL. Hofstetter, Griechen, no. 326.

Timocreon Lyric poet, after 479 BC.

A native of Ialysos in Rhodes, Timocreon (Timokreōn) was banished from his city, apparently for his Persian sympathies. Then, so he claimed, he bribed *Themistocles to restore him to Ialysos, but was cheated by him. Some fragments survive, probably from drinking-songs, in which he bitterly attacks Themistocles for this and praises *Arist(e)ides. Stories are also told of his rivalry with *Simonides.

BIBL. Lyra Graeca (Loeb) ii; Bowra, Lyric Poetry 349 ff.

Timoleon (died after 338 BC) Liberator of Syracuse.

After helping to thwart the tyrannical ambitions of his brother Timophanes in Corinth (c. 365 BC), Timoleon (Timoleōn) disappears from the record until 345/4, when he was sent from Corinth (the mother-city) to assist Syracuse against *Dionysius II and the Carthaginians. He arrived to find Dionysius trapped in Ortygia by Hicetas of Leontini (who was co-operating with Carthage). By 343/2 he had rescued Syracuse from both Dionysius and Hicetas, but the precise details are reported with irreconcilable differences by the sources. Subsequent years are notable for four themes: (i) the summoning to Sicily of expatriates and new colonists from Greece and Italy, beginning a process of urban renewal strikingly illustrated by archaeology; (ii) oligarchic (?) constitutional reforms in Syracuse; (iii) the defeat of a major Carthaginian attack at the river Crimisus (June 341 (or 339)); and (iv) the overthrow and execution (sometimes public) of the remaining tyrants of eastern Sicily (except Andromachus of Tauromenium), with some of whom Timoleon had earlier co-operated. In *c.* 338 age and blindness forced him to retire from public life, and he ended his days amidst great honour in Syracuse. His career and fate contrast strikingly with those of *Dion.

BIBL. Plutarch, *Timoleon*; R. J. A. Talbert, *Timoleon and the Revival of Greek Sicily* (1974).

Timon of Athens Misanthropist, 5th century BC.

Timon (Timōn), son of Echecratides from the deme Collytus, is first mentioned by *Aristophanes as shunning the world as a result of his evil experiences, and hating all men (but not women). Some of the stories told about Timon appear in a digression in Plutarch's life of Antony; he is referred to by Lucian, Libanius, and Ausonius, and became the subject of Shakespeare's tragedy and of Schiller's 'Der Menschenfeind' (1790).

BIBL. Aristophanes, *Birds* 1549, *Lysistrata* 805 ff.; Plutarch, *Antony* 70; Lucian, *Dialogue* xxv; Libanius, *Declamation* xii; *Roman World* Mark *Antony, *Ausonius, *Libanius, *Lucian, *Plutarch.

Timon of Phlius Philosopher and satirical poet, born *c.* 320 BC.

Chief apostle of the sceptic philosopher *Pyrrhon, Timon (Timōn) led a long and restive life in north and mainland Greece, exercising his fluently contemptuous tongue and pen against all pretensions to knowledge. He wrote prolifically – dramas, elegiacs, and philosophical prose works are attested – but the *mots* preserved come mostly from his influential hexameter *Silloi* (*Lampoons*, in three books), consisting of witty criticism, indebted to *Xenophanes and the Cynic *Crates of Thebes, of rival philosophies. He also attacked the quarrelsome inmates of 'the birdcage of the Muses', Alexandria's Museum, and sardonically commended to *Aratus (it is said) old copies of *Homer, not the newly 'corrected' ones (of *Zenodotus).

BIBL. A. A. Long, *PCPS* xxiv (1978).

Timotheus (1) (*c.* 450–*c.* 360 BC) Lyric poet.

Timotheus (Timotheos) of Miletus and *Philoxenus of Cythera were the leading composers of dithyrambs in the later style – i.e. songs that were wholly or partly astrophic (without overall metrical structure), displayed little or no ritual purpose, and were sung wholly or partly by a soloist to the lyre rather than by a choir to the *aulos*, the music tending to be written in a mixture of different modes and to predominate over the words. The language of such dithyrambs was often criticized as stilted and emptily pretentious. Timotheus also wrote nomes in a similar style, and made innovations in the music of this

A column from the 4th-century BC papyrus of the *Persians* of Timotheus (1). East Berlin, Staatliche Museen.

genre. He is said to have become highly unpopular and to have been comforted for this by *Euripides.

An exceptionally early papyrus (fourth century BC) has given us over 200 lines of his nome *Persians*, in which he describes the battle of Salamis and then defends his own music. The papyrus fully confirms ancient criticisms of his style.

BIBL. Lesky, *Greek Literature*; *Lyra Graeca* (Loeb) iii; Pickard-Cambridge, *Dithyramb*. . . .

Timotheus (2) Athenian general, floruit mid-4th century BC.

Son of the general *Conon, Timotheus (Timotheos) participated in his father's activities in 394–393 BC and was of age in 392, but his recorded military career begins in the 370s. In 375 his acquisition of allies in north-west Greece and victory over Sparta at Alyzeia brought him great honours and encouraged Spartan acceptance of a Common Peace (375/4). In 373 failure to protect Corcyra from the Spartans brought political disgrace (though he was acquitted of treason), and he retired to serve Persia as a mercenary. Between 366 and 362, having returned to favour, he acquired Samos (establishing a cleruchy), Sestos, and Crithote and won allies in Thrace and Macedonia, but failed to regain Amphipolis. His career ended when he failed to engage an enemy fleet at Embata (356), and a 100-talent fine forced his withdrawal to Chalcis, where he died. In his youth he associated with *Plato and with *Isocrates, who praised his generalship in *Oration* xv. (Some comic poets, however, attributed his successes to luck.)

BIBL. Kirchner, *PA*, no. 13700; Davies, *Athenian Families* 509 ff.

Timotheus (3) Sculptor, active *c*. 380–340 BC.

Of unknown origin, Timotheus (Timotheos) worked on the architectural sculpture of the temple of Asclepius at Epidaurus (*c*. 370 BC) and of the Mausoleum (see *Mausolus) at Halicarnassus (*c*. 350). We have substantial remains of both, but on both buildings he was one of four master-sculptors and we cannot identify his work with any confidence. The building accounts at Epidaurus say he made some 'tupoi' (reliefs?) and one of the two sets of acroteria, but whether the east or west set is not clear. Other works connected with him, or rather with the Epidaurus temple sculptures, are an original statue of Hygieia from Epidaurus, and, preserved in Roman copies, a Leda with the Swan and an Athena (the Rospigliosi type); both are interesting and individual works.

BIBL. J. F. Crome, *Die Skulpturen des Asklepiostempels zu Epidauros* (1961); B. Schlörb, *Timotheos* (1965); Robertson, *History of Greek Art* 397–403.

Left: Leda and the Swan, possibly by Timotheus (3). Marble copy of the Roman period. Rome, Capitoline Museum. *Right*: marble acroterion from the temple of Asclepius at Epidaurus, *c*. 370 BC. Athens, National Museum (see Timotheus 3).

Tiribazus Persian satrap, died c. 360 BC.

Tiribazus (Tiribazos) was successively satrap of Armenia and of Sardis, in which latter role he encouraged the Spartan *Antalcidas' negotiations with *Artaxerxes II, unsuccessfully in 393/2 BC and successfully in 388/7. Temporarily disgraced at the end of the war with the Cypriot rebel *Evagoras, he recovered royal favour during the Cadusian war, but later conspired with Artaxerxes' son Darius and was killed when the plot failed.

BIBL. PW viA. 1431–7.

Tisias: see T(e)isias

Tissaphernes Persian commander, died 395 BC.

Tissaphernes (Tissaphernēs) was the grandson of the Hydarnes who led the Persian troops to cut off *Leonidas at Thermopylae (480 BC); he was descended from one of the seven aristocratic conspirators who put *Darius I on the throne in 522. In 413 he replaced the rebel Pissuthnes as satrap of Lydia. He gave Sparta intermittent support in the war against Athens (see *Alcibiades). In 408 he was replaced by *Cyrus the Younger. Cyrus used his conflict with Tissaphernes, who remained satrap of Caria, to move his troops against *Artaxerxes II. Tissaphernes remained loyal to the king, and his cavalry was decisive in defeating Cyrus at Cunaxa (401). He arrested the leaders of Cyrus' Greek mercenaries, and escorted the remainder (the 'Ten Thousand' – see *Xenophon) on their march out of Persian territory. He then returned to Lydia and fought against the Spartans. In 395 *Agesilaus defeated him at the river Pactolus, and Artaxerxes ordered his execution.

BIBL. Olmstead, *Persian Empire*, ch. 27.

Tithraustes Persian vizier, floruit 390s–380s BC.

In 395 BC the chiliarch (vizier) Tithraustes (Tithraustēs) was despatched to Asia Minor to dispose of *Tissaphernes after *Agesilaus' victory at Sardis and, according to *Xenophon, sent *Timocrates of Rhodes to Greece. In the 380s he was involved in an unsuccessful attempt to reconquer Egypt.

BIBL. PW viA. 1522–3. .

Tolmides Athenian general, died 446 BC.

Tolmides (Tolmidēs) commanded a maritime expedition against the Peloponnese in 454 BC, and campaigned in Boeotia in 455/4. In 447 he settled Athenian cleruchs in Euboea and at Naxos. In the following year he commanded the Athenian army which was defeated at Coronea in Boeotia, leading to his own death and the loss of the Athenian land empire in central Greece. There is no need to assume that Tolmides was a 'radical democratic' supporter of *Pericles.

BIBL. Davies, *Athenian Families*, no. 2717.

Tyrannio the Elder Grammarian and metrist, early 1st century BC.

A native of Amisus in Pontus, Tyrannio (Turanniōn: this was a nickname ('imperious') given him by his teacher, his real name being Theophrastus) went to Rome as a prisoner after the Second *Mithridatic War (81 BC). Freed, he was favoured by Pompey and befriended by Cicero, Caesar, and Atticus. A student of both Greek and Latin, he worked also on the library of *Aristotle, which had reached Rome in 86 BC.

BIBL. S. E. Bonner, *Education in Ancient Rome* (1977), 28 ff.; *Roman World* *Atticus, Gaius Julius *Caesar, *Cicero, *Pompey.   N.H.

Tyrtaeus Elegiac poet, c. 640 BC.

Undoubtedly Laconian (although *Plato and *Philochorus already present him as Athenian, and by Pausanias' time he is a lame schoolmaster summoned from Athens to aid Sparta), Tyrtaeus (Turtaios) was remembered for his songs exhorting martial prowess, composed for the crises of the Second Messenian war (hence the *Suda*'s date 640–637 BC) and later sung by Spartans during campaigns. Perhaps there was also an exhortatory element in *Eunomia* ('Good Government'), probably a longer poem, which narrated the **Heracleid Spartans' arrival in Laconia (fr. 2), the conquest of Messenia by King *Theopompus of Sparta two generations before Tyrtaeus (fr. 5), an oracle brought from Delphi by Theopompus and Polydorus (fr. 4), and the contemporary war with Messenia and her allies in which Tyrtaeus claimed a general's part (fr. 8). The exhortatory elegies, like those of *Callinus, exalt the steadfast warrior, contrasting the rewards he gains from his city, dead or alive (fr. 12. 23–42), with the miseries of defeat and dispossession (fr. 10. 1–12). Tyrtaeus' Ionic dialect shows that Ionian elegiacs, and necessarily the symposia where they were performed, had already reached Laconia, as had *Homer, whose influence on Tyrtaeus' language is pervasive.

His five books included 'war-songs' (*Suda*), probably the anapaests mentioned by Pausanias, of which Page, *PMG* fr. 856 may be an example. Presumably these, not elegies, were sung by marching Spartans.

BIBL. West, *IEG*, and *Studies*; Campbell, *Lyric Poetry*; Bowra, *Greek Elegists*; *Roman World* *Pausanias.

Xanthippe Wife of Socrates, later 5th century BC.

Since their three sons Lamprocles, Sophroniscus, and Menexenus were not yet of age when *Socrates was executed at the age of 70, we must assume that Xanthippe (Xanthippē) was considerably younger; an unfounded tradition going back to *Aristotle claims that Socrates had earlier taken another wife, Myrto, the poverty-stricken daughter of *Arist(e)ides. Xanthippe became the exemplar of the nagging wife who tries the philosopher's patience, particularly for Cynic writers; she already appears in this capacity in *Xenophon's *Symposium*.

BIBL. Xenophon, *Symposium* ii. 10.

Xanthippus Athenian leader, early 5th century BC.

Xanthippus (Xanthippos), son of Ariphron, married *Cleisthenes' niece Agariste and was the father of *Pericles; in 489 BC he successfully prosecuted *Miltiades. Like *Megacles, son of Hippocrates, he was one of the politicians ostracized during the 480s on suspicion of supporting the Persians (484/3); he returned to Athens in 480 with the other exiles, was elected one of the *strategoi* for 479, and accompanied *Cimon and *Myronides on the embassy which successfully persuaded the Spartans to participate in the Plataea campaign. He himself served in the fleet which under the command of *Leotychidas destroyed the Persian navy at Mycale. While the Spartans returned home, Xanthippus led the allied fleet to the Chersonese and reconquered Sestos for Athens in the winter of 479/8; control over the route from the Black Sea was vital for Athens' corn imports (see *Spartocids). Subsequently he disappears from the record.

BIBL. Davies, *Athenian Families*, no. 11811; Burn, *Persia and the Greeks*; J. Holladay, *Greece and Rome* xxv (1978).

Xanthus the Lydian Historian, 5th century BC.

Xanthus (Xanthos), son of Candaules from Sardis, wrote a four-volume Greek history of his homeland, probably down to 546 BC. *Ephorus, who quotes from him, claims that he was an older contemporary of *Herodotus and first aroused Herodotus' interest in history.

BIBL. *FGrH* iiiC, no. 765; iiA, no. 90, F 44 ff.; Pearson, *Ionian Historians*, ch. 3.

Xenocrates (*c*. 395–314 BC) Philosopher.

Xenocrates (Xenokratēs) of Chalcedon spent most of his life in Athens studying in *Plato's Academy, and became its third head (after *Speusippus) in 399 BC. Anecdotes suggest that he was slow-witted (which seems unlikely), serious, morally upright, and humane. More than 70 titles were attributed to him, but the works are lost. He divided philosophy into logic, physics, and ethics, but his own contributions in these fields can only be guessed. Probably his work was mainly to organize Platonic philosophy into an orderly and detailed system. This system incorporated much strange theology, with good and bad gods, even a higher and a lower Zeus. His lack of a sense of humour may have led him to take mythical parts of Plato's works more seriously than was intended.

BIBL. Dillon, *Middle Platonists*; Guthrie, *Greek Philosophy* v.

Xenocritus Musician and poet, *c*. 665 BC (?).

Xenocritus (Xenokritos) of Locri in southern Italy, treated by Glaucus of Rhegium as older than *Thaletas, is associated by Pseudo-Plutarch, *On Music*, with Thaletas and others in the establishment of the Gymnopaedia festival (665 BC) and Second School of music at Sparta. His poems involving narration of myth (perhaps like those of *Stesichorus) were variously classed as paeans and dithyrambs. Nothing survives.

BIBL. Pseudo-Plutarch, *On Music* 1134B–E; PW ixA. 1533; M. L. West, *CQ* xxi (1971), 306.

Xenodamus Musician and poet, *c*. 665 BC (?).

Pseudo-Plutarch, *On Music*, associates Xenodamus (Xenodamos) of Cythera with the establishment of the Gymnopaedia festival (665 BC) and the Second School of music at Sparta, classifying his poems as paeans, but admitting that others, including *Pratinas, said they were hyporchemes.

BIBL. Pseudo-Plutarch, *On Music* 1134B–E; PW ixA. 1485.

Xenophanes Poet and philosopher, born *c*. 570 BC.

Born at Colophon in Ionia, Xenophanes (Xenophanēs) left in *c*. 545 BC when it was taken by the Persians, and spent his remaining 67 years travelling around the Greek world, reciting his poems. The surviving fragments of these include theology, philosophy, satirical attacks, and banquet-songs. He attacked traditional accounts of the gods, partly by ridicule, and partly by appealing to what was 'fitting'. He held that God was one, ungenerated, and unmoving, and was particularly contemptuous of anthropomorphism. ('If cattle and horses had hands . . . horses would draw the forms of gods like horses, and cattle like cattle.') He was somewhat sceptical about the scope of human knowledge. His physical and astronomical theories seem to have been less strikingly original than his theology.

BIBL. Kirk and Raven, *Presocratic Philosophers*.

Xenophon Mercenary soldier and writer, died in/after 355/4 BC.

Xenophon (Xenophōn) came from a prosperous Athenian background (sufficiently so to qualify him for cavalry service), and in youth associated with *Socrates. Both circumstances will have encouraged a jaundiced view of radical Athenian democracy, and Xenophon was not one of those who left Athens during the rule of the Thirty Tyrants (404–403 BC: see *Critias) – though (like *Plato) he later expressed strong disapproval of them. In 402/1 he left Athens at the invitation of the Boeotian Proxenus to seek his fortune with *Cyrus the Younger. He thus became involved in the latter's rebellion, and after Cunaxa he took a leading role in the safe return of the

Inscribed herm of the historian and soldier Xenophon, from Cairo. Museum of Alexandria.

army to western Asia Minor. In 399 the 'Cyreans' were incorporated in the army of *Thibron (1), and thereafter Xenophon fought as a mercenary for Sparta, becoming an admirer and friend of *Agesilaus along the way. At the outbreak of the Corinthian War (395) Xenophon elected to remain in Spartan service, and fought at Coronea (394) against his fellow Athenians. This will have caused his exile, if he was not already exiled earlier, as some think, as part of Athenian attempts to win *Artaxerxes II's goodwill. Xenophon never returned permanently to Athens, but the sentence may have been revoked in 370/69 or even earlier; certainly works written in the 360s and 350s display a benevolent interest in Athenian affairs. He settled first at Scillus (on an estate granted by the Spartans), but after the Peloponnesian disturbances following the Spartan defeat at Leuctra (371, see *Cleombrotus, *Epaminondas) he moved to Corinth, where he ended his days.

WRITINGS. (i) The *Hellenica* concerns the history of Greece in 411–362. The bulk (II. iii. 11–end) was written in the 350s, but the rest may date from much earlier. *Hellenica* enjoys no high reputation, and is certainly a work of quirky emphases and omissions; none the less it is an indispensable source. (ii) The *Anabasis* (370s (?)) recounts the adventures of Cyrus' Greek mercenaries from 401 to early 399 with (from book iii onwards) particular emphasis on Xenophon's role in saving the army. Other, and different, accounts existed, to which *Anabasis* may be a self-interested reaction. Some have also seen it as conveying a Panhellenist message. (iii) The *Cyropaedia* (before 362) is an imaginative work about the life of *Cyrus the Great, chiefly concerned with the delineation of techniques of leadership. To most modern tastes it is stunningly dull, but it was popular in certain Roman republican circles. A final chapter excoriates contemporary Persian vices. (iv) The Socratic works are four in number (all of debatable date): *Memorabilia* (a lengthy description of Socrates, largely in the form of reported conversations between him and various interlocutors), *Oeconomicus* (on domestic management), *Symposium* (dinner-table conversation on the theme of the speakers' greatest accomplishments), and *Apology* (a brief defence of Socrates). Xenophontic preoccupations doubtless obtrude, but Xenophon's Socrates, who is more notable for moralizing than philosophizing, might conceivably be truer to life than Plato's (though opinions differ: see *Socrates). (v) Miscellaneous minor works: *Hieron* (after 357 (?): a dialogue between *Hieron I and *Simonides on tyranny), *Agesilaus* (c. 360: a biographical encomium of the dead king), *Respublica Lacedaemoniorum* (date uncertain: an account of the Spartan constitution), *Vectigalia* (355/4: advice to the Athenians about increasing revenue, especially by greater exploitation of Attic silver-mines), *Hipparchicus* (360s: instructions for an Athenian cavalry commander), *De re equestri* (360s: the earliest surviving treatise on general horsemanship). (*Cynegeticus* (on hunting) may well be inauthentic, and *Respublica Atheniensium* certainly is.)

BIBL. J. K. Anderson, *Xenophon* (1974); W. E. Higgins, *Xenophon the Athenian* (1977); introductions by G. Cawkwell in R. Warner (trans.), *The Persian Expedition* and *A History of my Times* (Penguin Classics, 1972, 1979); E. Delebecque, *Essai sur la Vie de Xénophon* (1957); PW ixA. 1569–1982.

Xerxes King of Persia, 486–465 BC.

Xerxes I (Xerxēs; Persian Khshayarsha, 'ruler of men'; Hebrew Ahasuerus) came to the throne on the death of his father *Darius I in 486 BC; an Egyptian revolt was suppressed within a year, and one in Babylon in 482. On the advice of *Mardonius, Xerxes planned to conquer Greece; although he destroyed Athens in revenge for Athenian participation in the Ionian Revolt (see *Aristagoras, *Histiaeus), his navy was decisively defeated at Salamis in 480, and he returned home, leaving Mardonius to be defeated at Plataea in the following year. He was assassinated by the commander of his guard, Artabanus, in 465/4.

BIBL. Burn, *Persia and the Greeks*; Hignett, *Xerxes' Invasion*; Olmstead, *Persian Empire*, chs. 17–19.

Aerial view of Salamis (the top of the picture is about south-east). The Greek allies' defeat of the navy of Xerxes in 480 BC took place in the sound between the island and the mainland (bottom, centre). (See *Themistocles.)

Zaleucus Lawgiver, c. 650 BC (?).

Zaleucus (Zaleukos) is said to have produced for his native city of Locri the first Greek law-code, which was later adopted by other Greek cities in Italy and Sicily. His laws were severe, often prescribing 'an eye for an eye'. He

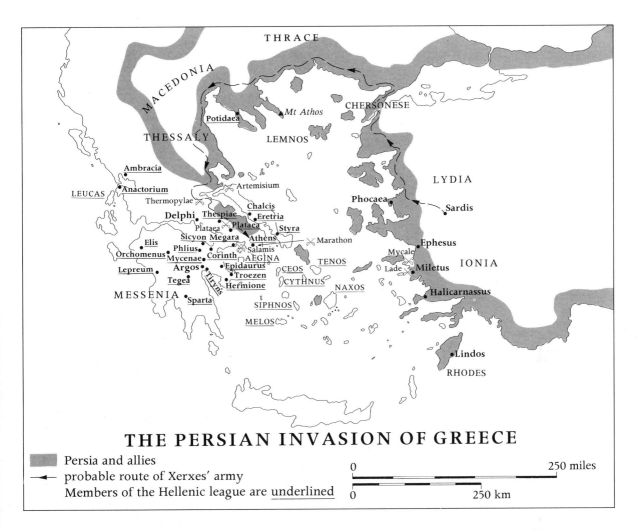

THE PERSIAN INVASION OF GREECE

▨ Persia and allies
← probable route of Xerxes' army
Members of the Hellenic league are <u>underlined</u>

0   250 miles

0   250 km

also made sumptuary laws and settled constitutional disputes.

BIBL. Aristotle, *Politics* 1274a–b; Diodorus Siculus xii. 20–1; Strabo vi. 260.

Zeno of Citium (probably 335–263 BC) Founder of Stoicism.

Probably a Phoenician from Cyprus, Zeno (Zēnōn) arrived in Athens when young, perhaps as a result of a shipwreck. There he eventually taught philosophy in the Stoa Poikile (painted colonnade) which gave his school its name.

His philosophy is hard to disentangle from that of other early Stoics, such as *Cleanthes and *Chrysippus. First attracted to philosophy by *Xenophon's account of *Socrates in his *Memorabilia*, he was later influenced by many other philosophers. From *Heracl(e)itus he borrowed the theory of an eternal fire as the source of things. From *Stilpon the Megarian he learnt logic, and acquired a cautious (though not sceptical) theory of knowledge. His politics owed much to the Cynic *Crates of Thebes. In his *Politeia* (*Republic*), he advocated a world-State in which there would be no money, lawcourts, temples, or gymnasia, and where women would be shared. His main interest was in ethics. He held virtue to be the

Inscribed bust of the philosopher Zeno of Citium. Naples, Museo Nazionale.

end of life: pleasure and pain were of no importance. He ingeniously reconciled moral responsibility with natural necessity. When a slave he was beating complained, 'It was decreed that I should steal', he replied, 'And that you should be whipped too'.

BIBL. Diogenes Laertius vii; Long, *Hellenistic Philosophy*; Rist, *Stoic Philosophy*.

Zeno of Elea Philosopher, born *c.* 490 BC.

According to *Plato, Zeno (Zēnōn) defended the philosophy of his compatriot *Parmenides by the method of *reductio ad absurdum*, i.e. by taking the assertions of Parmenides' opponents and drawing self-contradictory conclusions from them. Thus he argued that what exists is *one*, by showing that if there were many things, they would be both large and small. *Aristotle records four of his arguments against the possibility of motion. The most famous is 'Achilles and the tortoise' (though Aristotle does not mention a tortoise): **Achilles can never overtake the tortoise, because when he reaches the tortoise's starting-point, the tortoise has reached a point ahead of him; when he reaches *that* point, the tortoise is still ahead; and so on *ad infinitum*. Opinions have differed over whether Zeno raised important mathematical questions or produced a collection of sophisms.

BIBL. Aristotle, *Physics* vi. 9; H. D. P. Lee, *Zeno of Elea* (1936).

Zeno: see also **Zenon**

Zenodotus Scholar, born *c.* 325 BC.

As a protégé of *Philitas, Zenodotus (Zēnodotos) was appointed royal tutor and first head of the Library at Alexandria. Here he led *Alexander Aetolus and *Lycophron in the editing of *Ptolemy II's assembled manuscripts, himself tackling the epic and lyric poets. With his fundamental recension of *Homer he pioneered a technique of scientific scholarship based on the comparison of earlier texts. His edition was radical enough to draw the fire of his successors (*Apollonius Rhodius, *Aristophanes of Byzantium, and *Aristarchus of Samothrace), but was probably not as arbitrarily subjective as critics have asserted: he introduced the obelisk to signify suspicion of a line without suppressing it, and the headstrong emendations alleged are poorly evidenced. Critical discussion of the text was apparently confined to Zenodotus' alphabetically arranged *Glosses*, a model for future work. There is evidence for editions of *Hesiod, probably *Anacreon, and *Pindar, where papyrus fragments allow glimpses of Zenodotean variants and the amount of scholarship lost to us.

BIBL. Pfeiffer, *Classical Scholarship* i.

Zenon Secretary of Apollonius, floruit *c.* 262–*c.* 235 BC.

A Greek from Caunus in Caria, Zenon (Zēnōn) was the secretary of Apollonius, the *dioecetes* (finance minister) of *Ptolemies II and III. He has given his name to the Zenon Papyri, a huge archive of documents which preserves his extensive correspondence on the management of Apollonius' estate in Philadelphia in the Fayum, where Zenon settled about 256 BC. Since Apollonius was an absentee landlord, but took a close personal interest in his estate's development, Zenon was responsible for all business: petitions from workers, details of accounts, arrangements for agriculture, livestock, and viticulture, and travel in connection with his work. The letters, both those to and from him, can in many cases be dated precisely, and contain a wealth of information on most aspects of economic life in third-century Egypt.

Apollonius disappeared from public life *c.* 242, and Zenon concentrated on his own business affairs.

BIBL. M. I. Rostovtzeff, *A Large Estate in Egypt in the Third Century B.C.* (1922); C. C. Edgar, *The Zenon Papyri* (1925–40); Cl. Préaux, *Les Grecs en Égypte* (1947).

Zeuxis Painter, active 430–390 BC.

A native of Heraclea in southern Italy, Zeuxis came to Athens as a young man in the 430s or 420s BC, executing an Eros crowned with flowers before 425. Later, like *Euripides, he went to the court of King *Archelaus of Macedon (409–397), where he decorated his palace and gave him a picture of Pan. Continuing the experiments of *Agatharchus, the 'shadow-painter', he was said to have discovered the 'relation of lights and shades' ('luminum umbrarumque ratio'). It is unclear whether his advances in chiaroscuro included highlighting with white; his presumably highly illusionistic painting of some grapes, which he executed in a competition with *Parrhasius and which supposedly fooled some birds, may imply that they did. His most famous pictures were a Helen, apparently nude, and a Centaur family, showing the mother Centaur reclining in the grass suckling her young. He also painted 'monochromes on (or in ?) white' ('monochromata ex albo'). He became wealthy and, like his rival Parrhasius, was ostentatious and extravagantly dressed.

BIBL. Pliny, *Natural History* xxxv. 61 ff.; Robertson, *History of Greek Art* 411 ff.

Zoilus Homeromastix Sophist, died *c.* 330 BC.

Zoilus (Zōïlos) 'Scourge of Homer' was a rhetorician with philosophical interests from Amphipolis. His writings are almost entirely lost; they included a history of Amphipolis as well as a synopsis of world history down to the death of *Philip II of Macedon. There were also rhetorical encomia on paradoxical themes like poverty and exile. His main claims to fame were invectives against *Plato, *Isocrates, and the *Homeric epics; he attacked Homer's style, and pointed out mistakes and inconsistencies in the content. Zoilus' critique of Homer is neither systematic nor serious, but a sophistic exercise, and he should not be seen as a forerunner of the Alexandrian critics (see *Zenodotus).

BIBL. *FGrH* iiA, no. 71; P. M. Fraser, *Eranos* lxviii (1970).

Index of Persons Mentioned but without an Entry

Glossary

Academy: a school founded by *Plato for the training of young men for public life. The Academy still existed in the fifth century AD, when Neoplatonists such as Proclus (see *Roman World*) restored its fame; it was dissolved by Justinian in AD 529. Under its early heads – *Speusippus, *Xenocrates, and *Polemon of Athens – work was apparently concentrated on modifications of Platonic philosophy, with some Pythagorean (q.v.) influence. Under *Arcesilaus of Pitane and, later, *Carneades, it became a centre of scepticism. In the first century BC *Antiochus of Ascalon reintroduced a more dogmatic form of Platonism.

Achaean League: originally a confederacy of the cities of Achaea (founded in 280 BC), which later admitted as members other Peloponnesian cities. Its period of greatest influence was the second half of the third century – see *Aratus of Sicyon.

Acrocorinth: a commanding mountain behind ancient Corinth, used as the city's fortress.

acropolis: the strong point of a Greek city, which could be held against attack even if the rest of the city were lost. It was usually the site of the city's main temples, as at Athens.

acroteria: sculptured elements decorating the apex and corners of temple gables; in the classical period they were often elaborate marble figures or groups.

Aeolic: the dialect (q.v.) of Lesbos and adjacent Asia Minor, used by *Sappho and *Alcaeus as their vernacular and sporadically imitated by later poets.

aetia: stories explaining the origin of a custom, institution, etc., often based on the supposed etymology of its name.

aetiology: explanation of the origin of a custom, ritual, name, etc. (see *aetia*); a special interest of Hellenistic poets, cf. *Callimachus' *Aetia*.

Aetolian League: a close-knit federal State created in the fourth century BC out of the former loose tribal organization of Aetolia (central Greece).

Agoge (Agōgē): the Spartan system of military training and education.

agon: literally 'contest', used to mean a formal contest of words between two or more characters in drama.

agora: the centre of a Greek city, containing important public buildings and temples, as well as shops.

aisymnetes: the title given by *Aristotle to tyrants (q.v.) such as *Pittacus, who were unusual in being elected by their subjects and often in holding power for a limited period only.

Amphictyons, Amphictyonic League: *amphiktuones* means 'dwellers round about', and was applied to states belonging to an organization (Amphictyony) which controlled a major religious centre. The best known is the Amphictyonic League, an association of 12 states responsible for administering the temple of Apollo at Delphi; the League could punish those who had transgressed the Amphictyonic oath, even to the extent of proclaiming a 'Sacred War' (q.v.) against them.

anabasis: a military march from the coast into the interior (literally a 'going up').

Apella: the Spartan popular assembly (q.v.).

archon: literally 'ruler', a title of magistrates in many Greek states. At Athens there were nine: the eponymous (q.v.) archon (the most important), the basileus ('king'), who carried out religious functions once reserved for the monarchy, the polemarch (q.v.), and six thesmothetai ('lawgivers'). The archons were elected (annually in historical times) until about 487 BC, when they began to be chosen by lot; in consequence real power passed to the *strategoi* (q.v.).

Areopagus: the Athenian Council (q.v.) which met on the 'Hill of Ares' near the Acropolis (q.v.). It was originally the only Council of Athens, and was said to have ruled the city in the seventh century, but it lost political power with the creation of the democratic Council by *Solon and *Cleisthenes. From Solon's time onwards it was composed of ex-archons (q.v.), who automatically became members for life. In classical times its chief function was as a lawcourt, trying cases of homicide and religious offences. *Aeschylus in the *Eumenides* described it as having been set up by Athena herself to try Orestes for matricide.

Asclepiadae: famous guild of physicians on Cos, claiming descent from the healing-god Asclepius.

Asianism: term of denigration applied at Rome by adherents of Atticism (q.v.) to an artificial, ornate, and bombastic prose style.

Assembly: a political body which existed in most Greek states, composed of all adult male citizens. The usual name for it was Ecclesia, but some states used different names (see Apella). It was naturally most powerful and important in democratic states; elsewhere it often merely rubber-stamped the decisions of the magistrates (a situation envisaged, for example, in the Spartan

'Great Rhetra' (q.v.)).

astrophic: not consisting of stanzas (strophes) corresponding metrically with one another.

ateleia: immunity from taxation.

atomism: a theory of matter devised by *Leucippus and *Democritus, and adopted with some modifications by the Epicureans (q.v.), according to which the universe consists solely of solid atoms of various shapes and sizes moving around in a vacuum; all the multifarious appearances of things were to be explained by the various conglomerations of atoms, and their effects on sense-organs (themselves, of course, composed of atoms).

Atthis: a work treating the history and institutions of Athens from mythological times onwards. We know of several written c. 350–250 BC, and call their authors 'Atthidographers' (e.g. *Androtion, *Phanodemus, *Philochorus, cf. *Ister).

Attic: dialect of the territory of Athens (Attica), closely related to Ionic (q.v.). Prestigious through Athenian literary achievement (in drama, history, philosophy, oratory), it became the basis of the 'common' Greek (koinē) of the Hellenistic (q.v.) period.

Atticism: a purist movement which sought to imitate the diction and manner of classical Attic prose. See also Asianism.

aulodic: involving a song accompanied by the aulos (q.v.).

aulos: generally translated 'flute', but in fact a reed instrument. It was used to accompany dithyrambs (q.v.), choruses in drama, etc.

black figure: a vase-painting technique invented in Corinth in the seventh century BC, in which the figures and decoration are painted as black silhouettes on to the pale (in Athens, red) body of the vase; internal details are then incised into the black to leave pale lines showing through it.

Boeotarch: title of the chief magistrate of the Boeotian League of cities.

Cadmea: the name of the acropolis (q.v.) at Thebes.

Carneia: a Dorian festival in honour of Karneios, who was assimilated to Apollo; best known in Sparta where in was traditionally founded 676/3 BC. A banquet, musical competitions (see *Terpander), and a ritual pursuit are attested. It was held in July/August.

chiliarch: the Greek equivalent of Old Persian hazarpatish (literally 'leader of a thousand'). The title was particularly associated with a high official of the Achaemenid court (sometimes loosely called a Grand Vizier), who may (originally) have been the commander of the royal infantry bodyguard or of an élite group of 1,000 cavalrymen. The title survived, via its conferment by *Alexander the Great on *Hephaestion and *Perdiccas, into the Hellenistic (q.v.) era.

choliambic: an iambic trimeter (qq. v.) in which the penultimate syllable is not short but long,
i.e. $\bar{u}-\cup-\mid\bar{u}-\cup-\mid\bar{u}---$

choregus: a wealthy citizen who paid most of the expenses of a dramatic production.

chryselephantine: made of gold and ivory, a sumptuous sculpture technique used mainly for cult-statues: gold for the drapery (attached in sheets or hammered on to a cheaper core) and ivory for the face and other visible flesh parts.

citharode: a singer who accompanied himself on the cithara, a form of lyre whose strings were increased in the seventh century from four to seven, traditionally by *Terpander.

citharodic: involving a song accompanied by the cithara (see citharode).

cleruchs: literally 'shareholders' (see kleros); Athenians who were allocated ownership of lands belonging to conquered states (not 'colonists' because they did not necessarily go to live in the territory allotted to them).

cleruchy: a settlement of cleruchs (q.v.).

colon (plural cola): literally 'limb'; small unit within a larger metrical, or syntactical, structure.

comedy: humorous drama of various kinds. Dorian comedy was developed in Sicily c. 500 BC by *Epicharmus and others, and written in Doric (q.v.) Greek. Old Comedy was the earliest Athenian form, produced from c. 490 to c. 390 by *Aristophanes and others, and characterized by fantasy, obscenity, and invective. Middle Comedy was produced from c. 390 to c. 325 by *Antiphanes and others, and combined features of both Old and New. New Comedy was the comparatively restrained and realistic 'comedy of manners' produced after c. 325 by *Menander and others.

Companions (Hetairoi): term designating a body of persons (some 100 in number in the last years of *Alexander the Great's reign) who stood in an especially close personal relationship to a Macedonian king. There is no easy English equivalent, but the Companions, many of whom were military men or technical experts (e.g. doctors or engineers), were in effect the aristocracy of the Macedonian kingdom. The term was also used in connection with the much more numerous 'Companion Cavalry', an élite arm of the Macedonian army.

Council: a political body found in most Greek states, usually called boulē. It was a select body, by contrast with the Assembly (q.v.) of all adult male citizens, but numbers and methods of selection varied widely. The amount of power it held also varied: where the Assembly was subservient, the Council could be the effective ruler of the State.

cretic: the metrical unit $-\cup-$ or (adjectivally) involving that unit.

Cynics: so called (kunikoi, dog-like) after the nickname of *Diogenes of Sinope (kuōn, dog), the Cynics were not an organized 'school' and developed no comprehensive system of philosophy. *Antisthenes was traditionally counted as the first, but Diogenes and *Crates of Thebes are more firmly associated with the Cynics' characteristic attitudes: contempt for convention, outspokenness, and simplicity of life.

Cyrenaic school: a school of philosophy founded by *Socrates' friend *Aristippus at Cyrene in North Africa. Cyrenaics held that immediate pleasures of the body were man's proper goal.

dactylic: involving the metrical unit called a dactyl (from its resemblance to finger (daktulos) joints): $-\cup\cup$ (see hexameter).

Delian League: organization of those Greek states which continued the war against Persia under Athenian leadership when Sparta withdrew in 478 BC; although in theory an alliance, it was effectively the basis of the

Athenian empire.

Delphic oracle: the most famous and influential oracle in Greece, where enquirers consulted a priestess, the Pythia, who went into a trance (possibly drug-induced) and gave answers supposedly inspired by Apollo. Her incoherent utterances were interpreted by temple officials (*prophētai*). Delphi first became prominent when it was consulted by many leaders of colonizing expeditions to Sicily and southern Italy. See also Amphictyons.

deme: the same word as 'demos' (q.v.). Generally, a village or other community; in post-Cleisthenic Athens, the basic unit of administration, membership of which (hereditary from the time of *Cleisthenes) guaranteed citizenship.

democracy: see Outline History, pp. 17–18.

demos: 'the people'. A very tricky word. Exactly who 'the people' were depended on who was using the term and when.

Diadochi: literally 'Successors', a term collectively designating those erstwhile subordinates of *Alexander the Great who partitioned his empire after his death (in most cases adopting the title of King).

dialects: regionally distinct forms of spoken Greek, varying principally in morphology; prominent in literature are Attic, Ionic, Aeolic, and Doric (qq.v.). Particular dialects were conventionally associated with particular literary genres: e.g. epic (q.v.) was written from *Homer on in Ionic fused with elements of Aeolic.

dioecetes: finance minister, or chief financial official, especially in *Ptolemaic Egypt.

dioecism: the destruction of a city-state as a political unit by means of its separation into smaller, distinct communities. See also synoecism.

dithyramb: originally a frenzied choral song in honour of Dionysus, accompanied on the *aulos* (q.v.); radically transformed by *Melanippides and others from the mid-fifth century BC (see *Timotheus (1)); the dithyrambs of *Bacchylides, if rightly so called, represent an intermediate type.

Doric: the dialect (q.v.) spoken in most of the Peloponnese, some islands, and Dorian colonies in Sicily and southern Italy. It was a major contributor to the literary language of choral lyric (e.g. *Stesichorus, *Pindar, and more superficially the Attic tragedians in choral passages), and to that of the idylls of *Theocritus.

eclectic: (a philosopher) selecting elements from the philosophy of several schools (q.v.) or individuals and combining them to form a single system.

Eleatics: a 'school' (q.v.) of philosophy whose best-known members were *Parmenides and *Zeno, both of Elea in southern Italy, and *Melissus of Samos. All of them denied the possibility of change and plurality. The ancient classification of *Xenophanes as Eleatic seems misguided.

elegiac: a metre in which dactylic hexameters (qq.v) alternated with pentameters (q.v.); used chiefly for the poetry of symposia (q.v.) and for epigrams (q.v.).

Eleusinian Mysteries: religious rites celebrated at Eleusis near Athens, which became famous all over the Greek world. The exact nature of the ritual is not known, since it had to be kept secret from the uninitiated (hence the possibility of 'profaning the Mysteries', as *Alcibiades and *Andocides were accused of doing). Its basis seems to have been the myth that it was at Eleusis that the goddess Demeter first taught mankind to grow corn. A Telesterion (Hall of Initiation) was built under *Peisistratus, and a larger and more splendid one under *Pericles.

encaustic: a technique of painting in melted wax.

encomium: a eulogy.; a formal expression of high praise.

ephors: annually-elected magistrates in Doric states, notably Sparta, with executive, judicial, and disciplinary powers. The board of ephors at Sparta (five in classical times) had considerable power even against the kings.

epic: a long narrative poem in dactylic hexameters (qq.v), usually on a heroic theme from mythology (see *Homer), though cosmogony (see *Hesiod) and history also furnished themes (see *Eumelus, *Rhianus).

epicedion (epikēdeion): poem of lament for a dead person.

Epicurean school: a school of philosophy established by *Epicurus at his 'Garden' in Athens, where he and his followers lived a secluded life, pursuing happiness through freedom from trouble (*ataraxia*). The school's ethical doctrines were supposedly derived from a materialistic view of the world, in which men had no grounds for fearing divine intervention in their affairs. Life in the school was apparently quite austere, and later stories of debauchery were no doubt malicious inventions. Other prominent early Epicureans were *Metrodorus, *Colotes, and *Hermarchus.

epinician (epinikion): a choral song celebrating a victory in the Games (q.v.; see *Pindar).

epistoleus: the title of the second-in-command to a Spartan navarch (q.v.).

epode: a poem in which metres of different kinds (e.g. iambic and dactylic, qq.v.) are combined.

eponymous: many Greek communities dated their years by the name of one of the magistrates, who 'gave the year its name'. Thus Sparta had an eponymous ephor (q.v.), Athens an eponymous archon (q.v.).

epyllion: 'little epic' – term applied to a small-scale mythological narrative (about 100–1,000 lines long), often containing another story inset, e.g. *Moschus' *Europa*; developed by Hellenistic (q.v.) poets of *Callimachean persuasion, it reappeared at Rome, e.g. Catullus 64 (see *Roman World*).

fragment: a preserved portion of any literary work that does not survive in its entirety. The two main sources of fragments are quotations by later authors, such as grammarians and anthologists, and portions of ancient rolls of papyrus excavated in Egypt.

Games: athletic (and in some cases musical) competitions held in honour of the gods at various sanctuaries. The most famous took place at Olympia every four years, and others were held at Delphi (Pythian Games), Isthmia, and Nemea. At these four major Games there were no prizes of money or valuables, simply a wreath and glory, which was sufficient to make an Olympic victor a person of some political importance (e.g. *Cylon). Almost but not quite on a level with the major Games were the Panathenaea at Athens, at which prizes were given in the form of olive oil in specially decorated jars.

general: see *strategos*.

genre scenes: representations from everyday life.

Gerousia: the Spartan 'Council [q.v.] of Elders'. It had 30 members including the two kings; the rest were elected from male citizens aged over sixty.

gloss: an obsolete or unusual word, hence an explanation of the meaning of a difficult word.

graphe paranomon: a process in Athenian law for challenging proposed laws or decrees on the grounds of contravention of an existing law.

Great Dionysia (or **City Dionysia**): the main Athenian dramatic festival, held annually in March, at which dithyrambs, tragedies, and comedies (qq.v.) were performed and a prize was awarded to the best poet in each genre. Three tragedians competed with four plays each (normally three tragedies and one satyr play (q.v.)), and five comic poets competed (in wartime perhaps only three) with one play each.

Gymnopaedia: a Spartan festival, traditionally established in 665 BC, involving dances and exercises by naked youths.

gymnosophists: literally 'naked experts', the name given by Greeks to Hindu or Buddhist monks and gurus of India, who prized endurance. They were encountered by *Alexander the Great, and were said (by some rather obscure sources) to have influenced *Pyrrhon in his adoption of a sceptical philosophy.

harmost: Spartan military governor appointed to control an 'allied' city overseas (especially in Asia Minor).

Hektemoroi: literally 'sixth-part men', the serfs at Athens freed by *Solon. The name is derived from the fact that they paid one-sixth of their produce to their master.

Hellenistic: of the period after the death of *Alexander the Great.

helots: the serf population at Sparta, allegedly descended from the pre-Dorian inhabitants of the area, especially the people of Helos, from which the name was derived. After the Spartan conquest of Messenia, the Messenians too were reduced to helot status.

hero: category of being between men and gods. In *Homer the word simply means 'noble'; later it was applied by the Greeks to persons thought to have been of human origin, but who were honoured in ways normally reserved for gods. Men who founded cities or gave them new constitutions were typically honoured as super-human heroes, with a cult paid at their tomb.

hetaira: a euphemistic term for ladies of easy virtue who were protected from being classed as mere prostitutes by their personal accomplishments and/or the social milieu in which they moved.

hexameter: a verse of six metrical units. Its commonest form, the dactylic (q.v.) hexameter

$$- \overline{\upsilon\upsilon} \mid - \overline{\upsilon\upsilon} \mid - \overline{\upsilon\upsilon} \mid - \overline{\upsilon\upsilon} \mid - \overline{\upsilon\upsilon} \mid - -$$

was the regular metre of epic (q.v.) and didactic poetry and is often simply described as 'hexameter'.

hipparch: cavalry commander (an elected civic office).

Hippeis: literally 'horsemen', the second of *Solon's four property-classes, including those who could afford to keep a horse and serve in the cavalry. Often translated 'knights'.

hoplite: the standard classical Greek infantry soldier. Since each man had to provide his own armour, the hoplite had to be of a certain economic standing, and the 'hoplite franchise' was a political system which

extended power to this class.

hymn: a song or poem addressed to a god, generally celebrating his power and achievements and then praying for his help. Developed literary examples in hexameters (q.v.), such as the 'Homeric Hymns' (see *Homer) and those of *Callimachus, consist largely of mythical narrative.

Hyperakrioi: literally 'Men beyond the hills', the party led by *Peisistratus, so called because his geographical base was on the east coast of Attica, separated from Athens by mount Hymettus.

hyporcheme: the word should simply mean a song accompanied by dance, but it is variously and controversially used by ancient writers.

iambic: involving the metrical unit $\overline{\upsilon} - \upsilon -$ (see trimeter).

'Inferiors': the name of a status-group at Sparta ('inferior' with respect to the Spartiates (q.v.)).

Ionic: Greek dialect (q.v.), to which Attic (q.v.) was closely related, widely spoken in the Aegean islands and on the coast of Asia Minor. In literature it was the basis of *Homeric language (with Aeolic (q.v.) admixture), and the dialect of elegiac poetry (*Archilochus, *Tyrtaeus, etc.), of scabrous iambic (q.v.) poetry in the tradition of *Hipponax, and, in prose, of *Herodotus and the *Hippocratic writers of Cos.

kleros: literally 'lot', hence something assigned by lot, especially a portion of land (see cleruchs).

komos: 'revel'; particularly used of the inebriated procession which might leave a symposium (q.v.) to lay siege to the door of the beloved of one of the party.

kore: literally 'girl' or 'maiden', used to refer to a common type of archaic statue of a standing draped girl; they were dedicated as votive offerings in Greek sanctuaries.

League of Corinth: the organization devised by *Philip II after the battle of Chaeronea as a means of controlling the Greek city-states. He himself and his Macedonian successors held the leadership (*hēgemonia*).

Lenaea: an Athenian dramatic festival held about the end of January; less important, especially for tragedy (q.v.), than the Great Dionysia (q.v.).

liturgy: a form of taxation in which a (relatively) rich individual had to finance directly some public activity (e.g. a choral or dramatic performance at a festival or the operation of a warship) or to advance money to the city on behalf of a group of taxpayers.

lyric: for or involving accompaniment by the lyre or related stringed instrument.

Medism: co-operation with the Persian empire; after the Ionian Revolt (499–494 BC) it became a common accusation which might be levelled at any Greek (especially Athenian) statesman by his enemies (see *Alcmaeonids).

Megarian school: a school (q.v.) of philosophy founded by *Eucleides of Megara, mainly known for its work on logic. The Megarians acquired a reputation for sophistry, no doubt helped by their interest in paradoxes such as those of *Eubulides of Miletus. Evidence is scanty, but important developments in logic seem to have been made, notably by *Diodorus Cronus and *Stilpon, and Stoic logic owed much to the school.

metic (metoikos): a resident non-citizen, especially at

Athens, with recognized rights and duties but without full citizen status.

Milesians: traditionally counted the first natural philosophers, *Thales, *Anaximander, and *Anaximenes each developed an explanation of the world as originating from some primary source, or kind of matter. It is not clear in what sense, if any, they constituted a school (q.v.).

mime: a popular theatrical piece, often in 'low' or parodic style, for dramatic performance or semi-dramatic recitation. See *Sophron, *Herodas, *Theocritus.

Museum: *Mouseion*, 'place of the Muses'; most famously the institute of learning supporting scholars and scientists founded and maintained at Alexandria by the *Ptolemies; attached was the great Library. At its zenith in the third to second centuries BC, it was still active under the Roman Empire.

navarch: the title of the Spartan naval commander-in-chief. (The office was held for a period of one year.)

nome: originally (?) a kind of tune, played on the lyre and dedicated to Apollo (see *Terpander); sometimes also the words that were sung to the tune. Some nomes were intended for aulodic, others for citharodic (qq.v.) performance; their development was associated with particular musicians, e.g. *Clonas, *Polymnestus, *Sacadas. See also *Timotheus (1).

Northern League: a confederation of the cities of Heraclea Pontica, Byzantium, and Chalcedon formed in order to preserve each other's independence from further Seleucid rule after the death of *Seleucus I in 281 BC. They were later joined by Pontus, Bithynia, and the Galatians.

ode: song.

oecist (oikistēs): the founder of a new colony or city.

oligarchy: see Outline History, p. 17.

oracle: see Delphic oracle.

Orphic religion: a set of doctrines concerning creation and the after-life, allegedly going back to the Thracian Orpheus.

ostracism: the Athenian device for getting rid of unpopular politicians without bloodshed. Each voter wrote on a potsherd (*ostrakon*) the name of the politician he wanted to remove, and the 'winner' went into exile for ten years, his family and property being left unharmed. Some attributed the practice to *Cleisthenes, but its first certain victims were relatives of the Peisistratids (see *Hippias) and others suspected of Medism (q.v.) in the 480s. Ostracism fell into disuse towards the end of the fifth century BC (see *Hyperbolus).

paean (paian): a song of rejoicing, traditionally addressed to Apollo, but sometimes praising other gods or men.

paeon: a metrical unit with one long and three short syllables ($-\cup\cup\cup$; $\cup-\cup\cup$; $\cup\cup-\cup$; or $\cup\cup\cup-$).

parabasis: the long choral interlude in the middle of an Old Comedy (see comedy), for part of which the chorus steps out of character to become the mouthpiece of the poet.

Paralioi: literally 'Men of the coast', one of the three regionally-based political parties in post-*Solonian Athens. Its natural leaders were the *Alcmaeonids, whose family estates lay in the coastal area between Athens and Cape Sounion.

partheneion: a song for performance by a choir of maidens (*parthenoi*).

Pedieis: literally 'Men of the plain', one of the three political parties in post-*Solonian Athens. The plain in question is that around Athens, where this party had its power-base.

Pentakosiomedimnoi: the highest of the four property-classes introduced by *Solon.

pentameter: a verse of five metrical units. Its commonest form, the dactylic (q.v.) pentameter

$$-\overline{\cup\cup}-\overline{\cup\cup}- \mid -\cup\cup-\cup\cup-$$

alternated with dactylic hexameters (qq.v.) to form the elegiac (q.v.) metre.

periodic style: a major distinction of ancient rhetorical theory was between a 'loose' or 'running' style, in which clauses follow one another with no grammatical connection other than conjunctions, and a 'periodic' style, in which clauses are grouped together within a sentence by means of subsidiary clauses, antitheses, rhythmic clause-endings, etc.

Peripatetic school: a school (q.v.) of philosophy founded by *Aristotle, and named after a covered walking-area (*peripatos*) where he taught. Under Aristotle, *Theophrastus, and *Straton, extensive research was carried out in many fields, but the school declined in the third century under *Lycon's headship. From the first century BC, work in the school seems to have been concentrated on the scholarly study of Aristotle's works, which *Andronicus had acquired and edited.

periplous: a circumnavigation of a body of water, or the title of a written account of such a journey.

polemarch: literally 'ruler in war', an official found in many Greek states, whose primary function was military command. In Athens he also had judicial functions, as president of the court in which cases involving foreigners were tried. From about 487 BC the polemarch was chosen by lot like the other archons (q.v.), and his military duties were taken over by the *strategoi* (q.v.).

Presocratic philosophers: literally those before *Socrates, but often taken to exclude sophists (q.v.) such as *Protagoras who were his elder contemporaries. They include the Milesians, Eleatics, early Pythagoreans, early atomists (qq.v.), and less classifiable individualists such as *Xenophanes, *Empedocles, and *Anaxagoras.

probouloi: the members of committees appointed to draft proposals prior to submission to a plenary Assembly (q.v.).

procurator: a Roman official with fiscal or administrative powers.

proem (prooimion): the introduction to a speech or other work of literature. (See also prooemion.)

prologue: the prologue of a drama is sometimes defined (after *Aristotle) as the part which precedes the first choral song, sometimes as a scene-setting monologue of the kind with which a play of *Euripides or *Menander normally began.

prooemion (prooimion): the introductory section of a literary work, or a song composed specifically to be sung as a prelude to another. (See also proem.)

proskynesis: term used to describe a posture of adoration before a deity, but also applied by Greeks to the gestures of respect from inferior to superior (involving varying degrees of physical abasement) enjoined by Persian social and court custom.

prosodion: a song for singing in procession.

proxenos: the person in each city-state who had an obligation (usually hereditary) to look after all the visitors from some other particular state; the relationship was called *proxenia*. The duties can be compared to those of modern Honorary Consuls.

Pyrrhonism: a sceptical philosophy marked more by a way of life than philosophical doctrines. Avoidance of dogmatism, and suspension of judgement were supposed to result in tranquillity. Apart from *Pyrrhon, the best-known Pyrrhonist was his follower *Timon of Phlius.

Pythagorean school: a society founded in Croton by *Pythagoras, whose aims embraced political influence as well as philosophical enlightenment. In the fifth century BC, persecution led to the dispersal of Pythagoreans from Italy to parts of mainland Greece, where branches of the sect continued to develop 'Pythagorean' doctrines in various directions. These divisions in the school (q.v.), together with its secretiveness, make it hard to reconstruct the school's philosophy and its development. However, central in Pythagorean thought were attempts to explain the universe by numbers, a belief in transmigration of souls, and attempts to achieve purification by ascetic living.

red figure: a vase-painting technique invented as an alternative to black figure in Athens, *c.* 530 BC, in which the figures and decoration are left in the red clay colour of the vase and the background is filled in with black.

rhapsode: a professional reciter of epic (q.v.) poetry, especially that of *Homer, apparently unaccompanied and in a histrionic manner.

rhetra: Spartan term for a law. Great Rhetra: see *Lycurgus of Sparta.

Sacred Wars: wars fought by the states of the Delphic Amphictyony (q.v.) in response to supposed sacrilege against Apollo's shrine and oracle.

Samothracian Mysteries: the cult of the so-called Cabiri (Kabeiroi), Underworld deities (probably of Phrygian origin) who were associated with fertility and the protection of sailors.

satrap (Old Persian *khshatsapavan*): title of Persian provincial governors under the Great King, and preserved as title of similar officials in the East under *Alexander the Great and his Seleucid (see *Seleucus, *Antiochus, etc.) successors.

Satraps' Revolt: a widespread, but ultimately abortive, rebellion against *Artaxerxes II by several western Anatolian satraps (*Ariobarzanes, *Mausolus, *Orontes, Autophradates, and *Datames) in the late 360s BC.

satyr play: a play written by a tragedian on a mythical subject, but treating it in a humorous, burlesque style, and having a chorus of satyrs (wild, lecherous creatures, part man and part animal). See also tetralogy, tragedy.

scepticism: see Pyrrhonism, Academy.

schools of music at Sparta: two stages of musical development; the First School was associated by Pseudo-Plutarch's *On Music* with *Terpander, the Second School with *Polymnestus, *Sacadas, and *Thaletas, *Xenocritus, and *Xenodamus.

school of philosophy: term sometimes applied to groups of very different kinds, e.g. (i) a school in something like the modern sense, where young men received education not only in philosophy, e.g. the Academy (q.v.); (ii) an association for study, with a head, often with its own buildings, and sometimes with communal living, e.g. Peripatetic, Stoic, and Epicurean schools (qq.v.); (iii) (misleadingly) a number of philosophers with similar views and mutual influence, but forming no organized group for teaching or research, e.g. Cynics, and perhaps the Milesians and the Eleatics (qq.v.; though later sources tend to treat them as organized schools).

Second Athenian Confederacy: a modern designation of the alliance system created by Athens in 378 BC. Notable features were Athens' explicit renunciation of the methods of fifth-century imperialism and the establishment of a confederate council which met in Athens but was independent of direct Athenian control.

Seisachtheia: literally 'shaking-off of burdens', the name given to *Solon's measures to relieve the burdens of debt.

skolion: a song for singing at symposia (q.v.) by whichever participant held the myrtle-branch circulating 'crookedly' (*skolion*), i.e. irregularly.

Social War: a war fought between Athens and her allies (*socii* in Latin), viz. certain rebel members of the Second Athenian Confederacy (q.v.), ending in Athens' defeat (357–355 BC). The term is also applied to other wars involving allies, e.g. that fought by *Philip V in 220–217.

sophists: literally 'those who are wise' or 'expert': hence professional teachers, especially of rhetoric.

Spartiates: the ruling population of Sparta, holders of full citizenship, who claimed descent from the Dorian conquerors (see Introduction).

Stoa Poikile: a covered colonnade at Athens, built in the 460s BC; called 'painted' because it was decorated with pictures by *Polygnotus and others.

Stoicism: the Stoic school of philosophy was founded by *Zeno of Citium in the third century BC, and named after the Stoa Poikile (q.v.) where he taught. The doctrines of the school were developed into what became orthodox Stoicism under Zeno's successors *Cleanthes and *Chrysippus (who probably contributed most to the system). Much progress was made in logic, especially propositional logic (which *Aristotle's syllogistic logic did not accommodate), but the Stoics' ethical philosophy, in which virtue based on knowledge was the sole good for man, had the greater influence through its widespread adoption in the Roman world.

strategos: literally 'general'. At Athens, the general elected by each of the ten tribes (q.v.); the ten *strategoi* might command the full army as a committee of equals (as at Marathon in 490 BC), or be allocated independent commands on land or sea. They also had civil powers, and formed the chief executive. See also *strategos autokrator, strategus.*

strategos autokrator: a general with specially enhanced powers of action without reference to other authorities.

strategus (stratēgos): (the Latinized form of the Greek word has been used in this book to distinguish the Macedonian and Hellenistic 'general', very different from the Greek civic office of *strategos* (q.v.).) In the time of *Alexander the Great and his Successors (see Diadochi), the title effectively denoted the viceroy of a specific section of the empire (e.g. *Antipater was *strategus* of Europe, *Antigonus of Asia). It was also applied in Hellenistic times to the elected head of a league of cities such as the Achaean League (e.g. *Aratus of Sicyon).

Successors: see Diadochi.

suffete: the title of the highest magistrate in Punic communities, especially Carthage.

sussitia: the communal messes in which Spartiates (q.v.) ate, also called 'pheiditia'.

symmetria: a technical term of classical art-theory meaning the proportional relation of the various limbs and parts of a statue to each other and to the whole. The complementary term *rhythmos* refers to the design and composition of the figure.

symmories: in fourth-century BC Athens taxpayers were grouped into units called symmories; in 357/6 the system was extended to the upkeep of the navy.

symposium: a drinking-party at which entertainment by conversation, music, and sexual activity were regular (the philosophical discussion of *Plato's *Symposium* was probably exceptional).

synoecism: the creation of a city-state by the political amalgamation of existing smaller communities. See also dioecism.

tagos: Thessalian official title used both of local magistrates and of the elected leader of the Thessalian League.

tetralogy: properly speaking, a set of four plays (normally three tragedies and one satyr play (qq.v.)) written by the same tragedian for performance on the same day at the Great Dionysia (q.v.), *and connected together in subject-matter.* (In this book, however, to avoid confusion, the term 'connected tetralogy' is used in this sense, since 'tetralogy' is ambiguously used by many modern writers.)

tetrameter: a verse of four metrical units, most commonly trochaic (q.v.) with *catalexis* (shortening of the last unit), i.e.

$$-\,\cup\,-\,\bar{\cup}\mid-\,\cup\,-\,\bar{\cup}\mid-\,\cup\,-\,\bar{\cup}\mid-\,\cup\,-$$

tetrarchy: literally 'fourth-rule', originally the title of the four divisions of Thessaly; later used by Hellenistic kings to mean simply a 'principality'.

Theoric Commission: see *theorika*.

theorika: a fund at Athens from which distributions were made to enable poorer citizens to attend the Greater Dionysia (q.v.) and other festivals. As the law stood in the mid-fourth century BC (see *Eubulus) all surpluses of administrative revenue had to be placed in the theoric fund, which was supervised by a Theoric Commission. Money from this accumulated fund could be expended on public works, etc., but its use for military purposes was illegal.

Thetes: the lowest of *Solon's four property-classes. They eventually found their military role as rowers in the fleet.

tragedy: in the fifth century BC this meant the type of drama which had been developed at Athens by *Thespis, *Aeschylus, and others, performed by a small number of actors and a chorus, and treating a theme from myth (or occasionally from history) in a serious and dignified way. In the fourth century the chorus became unimportant, and later tragedy became largely a vehicle for melodramatic displays by actors.

tribes: the citizens of most Greek states were grouped into tribes. The Dorians (see Doric) traditionally had three, and the Ionians (see Ionic) four, but the numbers and usual names were not universally adhered to. *Cleisthenes gave Athens a totally new system of ten tribes.

trierarchs: at Athens, the persons who paid for the provision and upkeep of warships and their crews; thus they were usually the ships' captains.

trilogy: the set of three tragedies from a tetralogy (q.v.).

trimeter: a verse of three metrical units, most commonly iambic (q.v.), i.e.

$$\bar{\cup}\,-\,\cup\,-\mid\bar{\cup}\,-\,\cup\,-\mid\bar{\cup}\,-\,\cup\,-$$

It was the principal metre of Attic tragedy (qq.v.) and (in a looser form) comedy (q.v.).

trochaic: involving the metrical unit $-\,\cup\,-\,\bar{\cup}$ (see tetrameter).

tyrant: not necessarily an oppressive ruler in the modern sense of the word (though some of them were), but one who had come to power by irregular means, or a member of a dynasty which had begun in this way. It may originally have been a Lydian word for 'king'.

xenos: a person from another community ('stranger'), with whom one had reciprocal obligations, usually inherited, to give and receive hospitality and support ('guest-friend').

Zeugitai: the third of *Solon's four property-classes, including those who could afford to equip themselves as hoplites (q.v.).

Bibliography

General Abbreviations

c.   *circa*
cf.   *confer* (compare)
ch(s).   chapter(s)
comm.   commentary (by)
ed.   edited by, edition
f., ff.   following
fr(s).   fragment(s)
n. F.   *neue Folge*
n.s.   new series
Or.   *Oratio*
praef.   *praefatio*
q.v., qq.v.   *quod vide, quae vide*
Suppl.   Supplement
s.v.   *sub voce*
trans.   translated (by)
vol(s).   volume(s)

Abbreviated Titles of Books, Periodicals, etc.

AA   Archäologischer Anzeiger
Accame *Lega Ateniese*   S. Accame, *La Lega Ateniese del IV secolo a.C.* (1940)
AJA   American Journal of Archaeology
AJP   American Journal of Philology
AM   Athenische Mitteilungen
Andrewes, *Greek Tyrants*   A. Andrewes, *The Greek Tyrants* (1956)
Ant. Class.   L'Antiquité Classique
AUMLA   Journal of the Australasian Universities' Modern Language Association
Badian, *Studies*   E. Badian, *Studies in Greek and Roman History* (1964)
Bayer. Abh.   Abhandlungen der Bayerischen Akademie der Wissenschaften (phil.-hist. Klasse)
Beazley, *ABV*   J. D. Beazley, *Attic Black-figure Vasepainters* (1956)
Beazley, *ARV*   J. D. Beazley, *Attic Red-figure Vasepainters* (2nd ed., 1963)
Beazley, *Paralipomena*   J. D. Beazley, *Paralipomena* (1971)
Bellinger, 'The End of the Seleucids'   A. R. Bellinger, 'The End of the Seleucids', *Transactions of the Connecticut Academy of Arts and Sciences* xxxviii (1949)
Berve, *Alexanderreich*   H. Berve, *Das Alexanderreich* ii (1926)

Berve, *Tyrannis*   H. Berve, *Die Tyrannis bei den Griechen* (1967)
Bevan, *House of Seleucus*   E. R. Bevan, *The House of Seleucus* (1902)
BICS   Bulletin of the Institute of Classical Studies
Boardman, *Black Figure*   J. Boardman, *Athenian Black Figure Vases* (1974)
Boardman, *Greeks Overseas*   J. Boardman, *The Greeks Overseas: Their Early Colonies and Trade* (new ed., 1980)
Boardman, *Red Figure*   J. Boardman, *Athenian Red Figure Vases: The Archaic Period* (1975)
Boardman, *Sculpture (Archaic)*   J. Boardman, *Greek Sculpture: The Archaic Period* (1978)
Bosworth, *Arrian*   A. B. Bosworth, *Commentary on Arrian's History of Alexander* (1980)
Bowra, *Greek Elegists*   C. M. Bowra, *Early Greek Elegists* (1938)
Bowra, *Greek Margins*   C. M. Bowra, *On Greek Margins* (1970)
Bowra, *Lyric Poetry*   C. M. Bowra, *Greek Lyric Poetry* (2nd ed., 1961)
Bowra, *Poetry and Life*   C. M. Bowra, in *Greek Poetry and Life* (Festschrift G. Murray, 1936)
Bowra, *Problems*   C. M. Bowra, *Problems in Greek Poetry* (1953)
BSA   Annual of the British School at Athens
Buckler, *Theban Hegemony*   J. Buckler, *The Theban Hegemony, 371–362* (1980)
Burkert, *Pythagoreanism*   W. Burkert, *Lore and Science in Ancient Pythagoreanism* (1972)
Burn, *Persia and the Greeks*   A. R. Burn, *Persia and the Greeks* (1962)
CAH   The Cambridge Ancient History (1923–39; 2nd ed. in progress)
Campbell, *Lyric Poetry*   D. A. Campbell, *Greek Lyric Poetry: A Selection of Early Greek Lyric, Elegiac and Iambic Poetry* (1967)
Campbell: see also *Greek Lyric Poets* (Loeb)
Cawkwell, *Philip* (II)   G. Cawkwell, *Philip of Macedon* (1978)
CPhil.   Classical Philology
CQ   Classical Quarterly
CR   Classical Review
Davies, *Athenian Families*   J. K. Davies, *Athenian Propertied Families 600–300 BC* (1971)
Diels and Kranz, *Vorsokratiker*   H. Diels and W. Kranz, *Die Fragmente der Vorsokratiker* (1956)

Dillon, *Middle Platonists*   J. Dillon, *The Middle Platonists* (1977)

Diogenes Laertius   Diogenes Laertius, *Lives and Opinions of Eminent Philosophers*

Dunbabin, *Western Greeks*   T. J. Dunbabin, *The Western Greeks* (1948)

Edmonds, *Attic Comedy*   J. M. Edmonds, *The Fragments of Attic Comedy* (1957–61)

Edmonds: see also *Greek Elegy and Iambus* (Loeb), *Lyra Graeca* (Loeb)

Enc. Art. Ant.   *Enciclopedia dell' Arte Antica* (1958–66)

Encicl. Ital.   *Enciclopedia Italiana* (1929–)

Ferguson, *Hellenistic Athens*   W. S. Ferguson, *Hellenistic Athens* (1911)

FGrH   F. Jacoby, *Die Fragmente der griechischen Historiker* (1923–)

FHG   C. Müller, *Fragmenta Historicorum Graecorum* (1841–70)

Finley, *Ancient Sicily*   M. I. Finley, *Ancient Sicily* (1968)

Forrest, *Greek Democracy*   W. G. Forrest, *The Emergence of Greek Democracy: The Character of Greek Politics, 800–400 BC* (1968)

Forrest, *History of Sparta*   W. G. Forrest, *A History of Sparta 950–192 BC* (1968)

Fraser, *Ptolemaic Alexandria*   P. M. Fraser, *Ptolemaic Alexandria* (1972)

Gow, *Bucolici Graeci*   *Bucolici Graeci*, ed. A. S. F. Gow (1952)

Gow, *Bucolic Poets*   A. S. F. Gow, *The Greek Bucolic Poets* (1953)

Gow and Page, *Garland of Philip*   A. S. F. Gow and D. L. Page, *The Greek Anthology: The Garland of Philip* (1968)

Gow and Page, *Hellenistic Epigrams*   A. S. F. Gow and D. L. Page, *The Greek Anthology: Hellenistic Epigrams* (1965)

GRBS   *Greek, Roman and Byzantine Studies*

Greek Elegy and Iambus (Loeb)   *Greek Elegy and Iambus*, ed. J. M. Edmonds (Loeb, 1931)

Greek Lyric Poets (Loeb)   *Greek Lyric Poets*, ed. D. A. Campbell (Loeb, 1982– (replacing J. M. Edmonds' unreliable *Lyra Graeca*, 1922–7))

Griffin, *Sikyon*   A. Griffin, *Sikyon* (1981)

GRNSC   Greece and Rome, New Surveys in the Classics (series, Clarendon Press, Oxford)

Guthrie, *Greek Philosophy*   G. K. Guthrie, *A History of Greek Philosophy* (1967–81)

Habicht, *Untersuchungen*   C. Habicht, *Untersuchungen zur politischen Geschichte Athens im 3. Jahrhundert v. Chr.* (1979)

Hamilton, *Sparta's Bitter Victories*   C. D. Hamilton, *Sparta's Bitter Victories: Politics and Diplomacy in the Corinthian War* (1979)

Hammond, *Epirus*   N. G. L. Hammond, *Epirus* (1967)

Hammond, *Studies*   N. G. L. Hammond, *Studies in Greek History* (1973)

Hammond and Griffith, *Macedonia*   N. G. L. Hammond and G. T. Griffith, *A History of Macedonia* (1972–9)

Hansen, *Attalids*   E. V. Hansen, *The Attalids of Pergamum* (2nd ed., 1971)

Heath, *Aristarchus of Samos*   T. L. Heath, *Aristarchus of Samos* (1913)

Heath, *Greek Mathematics*   T. L. Heath, *A History of Greek Mathematics* (1921)

Hignett, *Athenian Constitution*   C. Hignett, *A History of the Athenian Constitution* (1952)

Hignett, *Xerxes' Invasion*   C. Hignett, *Xerxes' Invasion of Greece* (1962)

Hofstetter, *Griechen*   J. Hofstetter, *Die Griechen in Persien* (1978)

HSCP   *Harvard Studies in Classical Philology*

Huxley, *Epic Poetry*   G. L. Huxley, *Greek Epic Poetry from Eumelus to Panyassis* (1969)

IG   *Inscriptiones Graecae* (1873–)

Jacoby, *Atthis*   F. Jacoby, *Atthis* (1949)

JDAI   *Jahrbuch des Deutschen Archäologischen Instituts*

Jebb, *Attic Orators*   R. C. Jebb, *Attic Orators* (1893)

JHS   *Journal of Hellenic Studies*

Jones, *Sparta*   A. H. M. Jones, *Sparta* (1967)

JRS   *Journal of Roman Studies*

Judeich, *Kleinasiatische Studien*   W. Judeich, *Kleinasiatische Studien* (1892)

Kennedy, *Art of Persuasion*   G. Kennedy, *The Art of Persuasion in Greece* (1963)

Kennedy, *Rhetoric*   G. Kennedy, *The Art of Rhetoric in the Roman World* (1972)

Kienitz, *Geschichte Ägyptens*   F. Kienitz, *Die politische Geschichte Ägyptens* (1953)

Kinkel, *EGF*   *Epicorum Graecorum Fragmenta*, ed. G. Kinkel (1877)

Kirchner, *PA*   J. Kirchner, *Prosopographia Attica* (1901–3)

Kirk and Raven, *Presocratic Philosophers*   G. S. Kirk and J. E. Raven, *The Presocratic Philosophers* (1960)

Kirkwood, *Greek Monody*   G. M. Kirkwood, *Early Greek Monody: The History of a Poetic Type* (1974)

Lane Fox, *Alexander*   R. Lane Fox, *Alexander the Great* (1973)

LCM   *Liverpool Classical Monthly*

Lesky, *Greek Literature*   A. Lesky, *A History of Greek Literature*, trans. Willis and de Heer (1966)

Literary Papyri (Loeb)   *Papyri. Literary Selections* (*Poetry*), ed. D. L. Page (Loeb, revised ed., 1950)

Lobel and Page, *PLF*   *Poetarum Lesbiorum Fragmenta*, ed. E. Lobel and D. L. Page (1955); most texts are also printed in *Lyrica Graeca Selecta*, ed. D. L. Page (1968), keeping the same numeration.

Loeb   Loeb Classical Library (texts with English translation)

Long, *Hellenistic Philosophy*   A. A. Long, *Hellenistic Philosophy* (1974)

Lyra Graeca (Loeb)   *Lyra Graeca*, ed. J. M. Edmonds, vols. ii–iii (Loeb, 1924–7) – but see *Greek Lyric Poets* (Loeb)

Macurdy, *Hellenistic Queens*   G. H. Macurdy, *Hellenistic Queens* (1932)

McDonald, *Progress into the Past*   W. A. McDonald, *Progress into the Past* (1967)

Meiggs, *Athenian Empire*   R. Meiggs, *The Athenian Empire* (1972)

Meiggs and Lewis, *Inscriptions*   *A Selection of Greek Historical Inscriptions to the End of the Fifth Century BC*, ed. R. Meiggs and D. Lewis (1969)

Minor Attic Orators (Loeb)   *Minor Attic Orators*, ed. K. J. Maidment and J. O. Burtt (Loeb, 2nd ed., 1953–4)

MusHelv   *Museum Helveticum*

Narain, *Indo-Greeks*   A. K. Narain, *The Indo-Greeks* (1957)

OCD   *The Oxford Classical Dictionary* (2nd ed., 1970)

OGIS   *Orientis Graeci Inscriptiones Selectae*, ed. W.

Dittenberger (1903–5)

Olmstead, *Persian Empire* A. T. Olmstead, *History of the Persian Empire* (1948)

Page, *PMG* *Poetae Melici Graeci*, ed. D. L. Page (1962); most texts are also printed in *Lyrica Graeca Selecta*, ed. D. L. Page (1968), keeping the same numeration.

Page, *Suppl.* *Supplementum Lyricis Graecis*, ed. D. L. Page (1974)

Page: see also *Literary Papyri* (Loeb)

Parke, *Mercenary Soldiers* H. W. Parke, *Greek Mercenary Soldiers* (1933)

PCPS *Proceedings of the Cambridge Philological Society*

Pearson, *Ionian Historians* L. Pearson, *Early Ionian Historians* (1939)

Pearson, *Lost Histories* L. Pearson, *Lost Histories of Alexander the Great* (1960)

Perry, *Ancient Romances* B. E. Perry, *The Ancient Romances* (1967)

Pfeiffer, *Classical Scholarship* i R. Pfeiffer, *History of Classical Scholarship: From the Beginnings to the End of the Hellenistic Age* (1968)

Phillips, *Greek Medicine* E. D. Phillips, *Greek Medicine* (1973)

Pickard-Cambridge, *Dithyramb* . . . A. W. Pickard-Cambridge, *Dithyramb, Tragedy and Comedy*, 2nd ed. revised by Webster (1962)

Poralla, *Prosopographie* P. Poralla, *Prosopographie der Lakedaimonier* (1913)

Powell, *Coll. Alex.* I. U. Powell, *Collectanea Alexandrina* (1925)

POxy. *Oxyrhynchus Papyri*

Proc. Roy. Soc. Med. *Proceedings of the Royal Society of Medicine*

PW A. Pauly, G. Wissowa, and W. Kroll, *Real-Encyclopädie der klassischen Altertumswissenschaft* (1893–)

Rend. Linc. *Rendiconti dell' Accademia Nazionale dei Lincei*

Rend. Pont. Acc. *Rendiconti della Pontificia Accademia Romana di Archeologia*

RFIC *Rivista di Filologia e Istruzione Classica*

RhM *Rheinisches Museum für Philologie*

RIA *Rivista dell' Istituto Nazionale d'Archeologia e Storia dell' Arte*

Richter, *Sculpture and Sculptors* G. M. A. Richter, *The Sculpture and Sculptors of the Greeks* (4th ed., 1970)

Rist, *Stoic Philosophy* J. M. Rist, *Stoic Philosophy* (1969)

Robertson, *History of Greek Art* C. M. Robertson, *A History of Greek Art* (1975)

Rohde, *Der griechische Roman* E. Rohde, *Der griechische Roman und seine Vorläufer* (4th ed., 1961)

Roman World *Who Was Who in the Roman World*, ed. D. Bowder (Phaidon, 1980)

Rostovtzeff, *SEHHW* M. I. Rostovtzeff, *The Social and Economic History of the Hellenistic World* (3rd ed., 1915–24)

Schaefer, *Demosthenes* A. Schaefer, *Demosthenes und seine Zeit* (2nd ed., 1885–7)

Sealey, *Essays* R. Sealey, *Essays in Greek Politics* (1965)

SEG *Supplementum Epigraphicum Graecum* (1923–)

SH H. Lloyd-Jones and P. J. Parsons, *Supplementum Hellenisticum* (1982)

Stewart, *Attika* A. F. Stewart, *Attika: Studies in Athenian Sculpture of the Hellenistic Age* (1975)

Stroheker, *Dionysios I* K. F. Stroheker, *Dionysios I* (1958)

Stuart Jones, *Select Passages* *Select Passages from Ancient Writers Illustrative of the History of Greek Sculpture*, ed. H. Stuart Jones (new ed., revised by A. N. Oikonomides, 1966)

Suda The *Suda* lexicon, an encyclopaedia compiled *c.* AD 980 in Constantinople, chiefly from previous collections and epitomes, the biographical material being drawn from Hesychius of Miletus (sixth century AD). Despite inaccuracy, garbling, and remoteness from its sources it is often the only bearer of valuable information. Edition: A. Adler (1929–38)

Sylloge *Sylloge Inscriptionum Graecarum*, ed. W. Dittenberger (3rd ed., 1915–24)

TAPA *Transactions of the American Philological Association*

Tarn, *Antigonos Gonatas* W. W. Tarn, *Antigonos Gonatas* (1913)

Tarn, *Greeks in Bactria* . . . W. W. Tarn, *The Greeks in Bactria and India* (3rd ed., 1966)

Tod, *Inscriptions* *A Selection of Greek Historical Inscriptions*, ed. M. N. Tod (1946, 1948)

Walbank, *Aratos of Sicyon* F. W. Walbank, *Aratos of Sicyon* (1933)

Walbank, *HCP* F. W. Walbank, *A Historical Commentary on Polybius* (1957–79)

Walbank, *Philip V* F. W. Walbank, *Philip V of Macedon* (1940)

Webster, *Hellenistic Poetry* T. B. L. Webster, *Hellenistic Poetry and Art* (1964)

Webster, *Later Comedy* T. B. L. Webster, *Studies in Later Greek Comedy* (1970)

West, *Delectus* *Delectus ex Iambis et Elegis Graecis*, ed. M. L. West (1980)

West, *IEG* *Iambi et Elegi Graeci*, ed. M. L. West (1971–2); most texts are also printed in West, *Delectus*

West, *Studies* M. L. West, *Studies in Greek Elegy and Iambus* (1974)

Westlake, *Essays* H. D. Westlake, *Essays on the Greek Historians* (1969)

Westlake, *Individuals in Thucydides* H. D. Westlake, *Individuals in Thucydides* (1968)

Will, *Hist. pol.* E. Will, *Histoire politique du Monde hellénistique* (2nd ed., 1979–81)

Woodhead, *Greeks in the West* A. G. Woodhead, *The Greeks in the West* (1962)

Xanthakis-Karamanos, *Fourth-century Tragedy* G. Xanthakis-Karamanos, *Studies in Fourth-century Tragedy* (1980)

YCS *Yale Classical Studies*

ZPE *Zeitschrift für Papyrologie und Epigraphik*

Suggestions for Further Reading

Detailed bibliographical references are to be found at the foot of individual entries consulted; in addition, the above list of abbreviations contains all the works frequently cited. For those in search of general reading matter on various periods and topics of Greek history, the following books (many of them obtainable in paperback editions) are recommended:

A. Cottrell, *The Minoan World* (1979)

J. Chadwick, *The Mycenaean World* (1976)

W. D. Taylour, *The Mycenaeans* (1964)

G. S. Kirk, *The Nature of Greek Myths* (1974)

M. P. Nilsson, *The Mycenaean Origin of Greek Mythology* (1932, re-issued 1972)

O. Murray, *Early Greece* (1980)

L. M. Jeffery, *Archaic Greece* (1976)

A. Andrewes, *The Greek Tyrants* (1956)

W. G. Forrest, *The Emergence of Greek Democracy* (1968)

A. R. Burn, *Persia and the Greeks* (1962)

J. K. Davies, *Democracy and Classical Greece* (1978)

N. G. L. Hammond, *The Classical Age of Greece* (1975)

J. Buckler, *The Theban Hegemony* (1980)

G. T. Griffith, 'The Reign of Philip II', in Hammond and Griffith, *A History of Macedonia* ii, pp. 203–726

R. Lane Fox, *Alexander the Great* (1973)

F. W. Walbank, *The Hellenistic World* (1981)

M. Cary, *A History of the Greek World from 323 to 146 BC* (2nd ed., 1963)

W. W. Tarn and G. T. Griffith, *Hellenistic Civilization* (3rd ed., 1952)

M. I. Rostovtzeff, *Social and Economic History of the Hellenistic World* (2nd ed., 1953)

A. Lesky, *A History of Greek Literature* (English translation, 1966)

Cambridge History of Ancient Literature (forthcoming)

K. J. Dover and others, *Ancient Greek Literature* (1980)

M. R. Lefkowitz, *Lives of the Greek Poets* (1981)

A. A. Long, *Hellenistic Philosophy* (1974)

G. E. R. Lloyd, *Greek Science After Aristotle* (1973)

M. Robertson, *A Short History of Greek Art* (1981)

R. M. Cook, *Greek Art* (1976)

E. R. Dodds, *The Greeks and the Irrational* (1951)

H. Lloyd-Jones, *The Justice of Zeus* (1971)

K. J. Dover, *Greek Popular Morality in the Time of Plato and Aristotle* (1974)

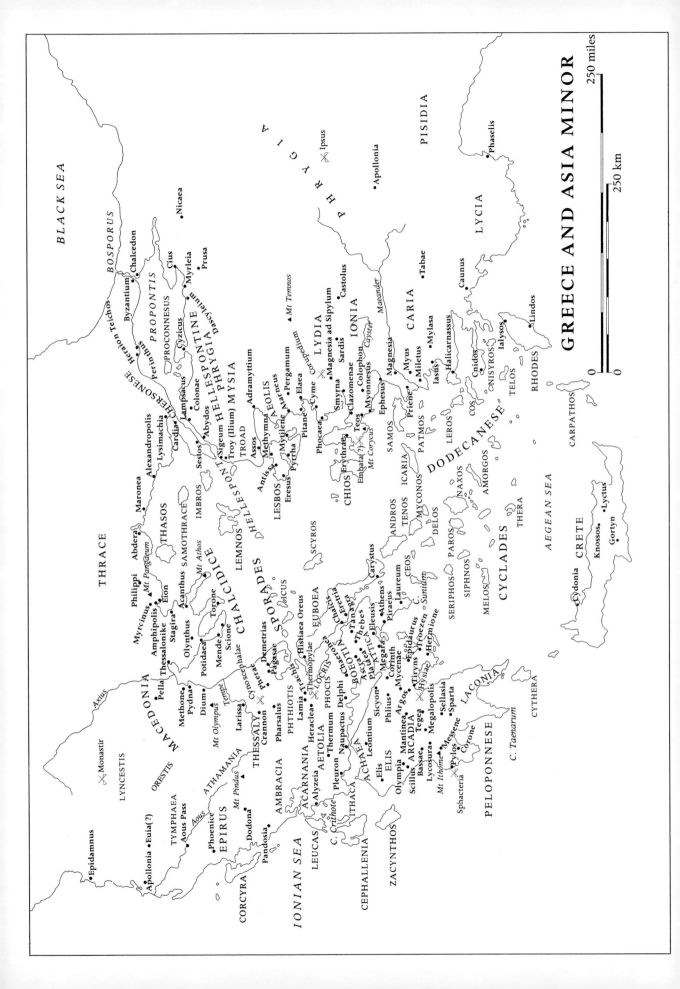

GREECE AND ASIA MINOR

BLACK SEA

BOSPORUS

PROPONTIS

Chalcedon
Byzantium
Nicaea
Cius
Perinthus
Cyzicus
Myrleia
Prusa

CHERSONESE

Heracleum Teichos
Alexandropolis
Lysimachia
Cardia
Lampsacus
Colonae
Abydos
Sestos
Dascylium
Sigeum
Troy (Ilium)
TROAD
Assos
Antissa
Methymna
Mytilene
LESBOS
Eresus
Pyrrha

PHRYGIA

Ipsus
Apollonia
PISIDIA
Phaselis
LYCIA
Caunus
Castolus
Tabae
CARIA
Lindos
RHODES
CARPATHOS
NISYROS
TELOS
COS
Cnidos
Halicarnassus
Mylasa
Iasus
Myus
Miletus
Priene
PATMOS
LEROS
ICARIA
SAMOS
Ephesus
Magnesia
Myonnesus
Colophon
Clazomenae
Teos
Erythrae
Mt Corycus
CHIOS
Phocaea
Cyme
Pitane
Elaea
Pergamum
Atarneus
Mt Temnos
Adramyttium
MYSIA
HELLESPONTINE PHRYGIA
HELLESPONT
LEMNOS
IMBROS
SAMOTHRACE
THASOS
Maronea
Abdera
Mt Pangaeum
Philippi
Myrcinus
Amphipolis
Thessalonike
Pella
Stagira
Acanthus
Mt Athos
Torone
Scione
Mende
Potidaea
Olynthus
CHALCIDICE
SPORADES
ICUS
SCYROS
Demetrias
Pagasae
Pherae
Cynoscephalae
Larissa
Crannon
Pharsalus
PHTHIOTIS
Lamia
Trachis
Heraclea
Thermopylae
Oreus
Histiaea
EUBOEA
Chalcis
Eretria
Carystus
CEOS
Laureum
C. Sunium
ANDROS
TENOS
MYCONOS
DELOS
Andros
PAROS
NAXOS
AMORGOS
THERA
CYCLADES
SERIPHOS
SIPHNOS
MELOS
AEGEAN SEA
CRETE
Cydonia
Knossos
Gortyn
Lyctus

THRACE
MACEDONIA
Monastir
LYNCESTIS
ORESTIS
Mt Olympus
Tempe
THESSALY
Axius
Methone
Pydna
Dium
TYMPHAEA
Aous Pass
ATHAMANIA
Mt Pindus
Phoenice
Dodona
EPIRUS
Pandosia
Apollonia
Euia(?)
Epidamnus
Aous
IONIAN SEA
CORCYRA
LEUCAS
C. Crithote
AMBRACIA
ACARNANIA
Alyzeia
AETOLIA
C. Crithote
Thermum
Pleuron
Naupactus
ITHACA
CEPHALLENIA
ZACYNTHOS
ELIS
Elis
Olympia
Scillus
Lycosura
Bassae
ARCADIA
Mantinea
Tegea
Megalopolis
Mt Ithome
Messene
Pylos
Sphacteria
Corone
Sellasia
Sparta
LACONIA
Hysiae
Tiryns
Argos
Mycenae
Sicyon
Phlius
Corinth
Megara
Eleusis
Athens
Piraeus
ATTICA
Plataea
Thebes
Tanagra
BOEOTIA
Chaeronea
Delphi
PHOCIS
LOCRIS
Leontium
ACHAEA
C. Taenarum
PELOPONNESE
CYTHERA
Troezen
Hermione
Epidaurus

PHRYGIA

Magnesia ad Sipylum
Sardis
Smyrna
LYDIA
Corupedium
IONIA
DODECANESE
Emphata(?)
Maeander
Cayster

0   250 km
0   250 miles

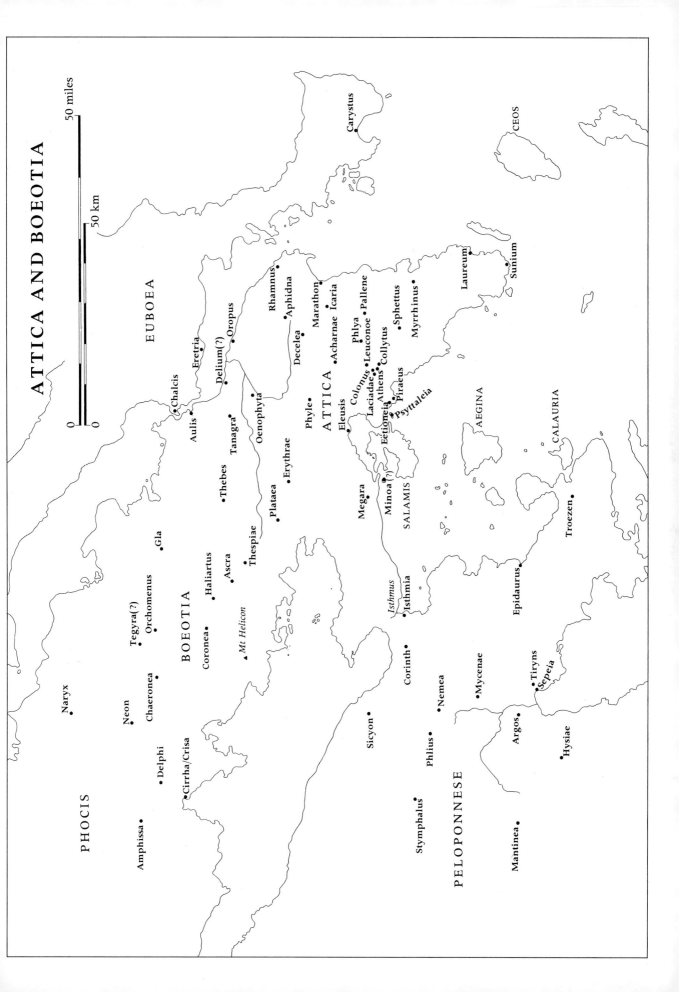

ATTICA AND BOEOTIA

0

50 km

0

50 miles

PHOCIS

Amphissa•

Naryx•

Neon•
•Delphi

Chaeronea•

Cirrha/Crisa•

Tegyra(?)•
Orchomenus•

•Gla

BOEOTIA

Coronea•
Haliartus•

Ascra•
▲ Mt Helicon
•Thespiae

Thebes•

Plataea•

Tanagra•

Oenophyta•

Erythrae•

EUBOEA

Chalcis•

Aulis•

Eretria•

Delium(?)•
Oropus•

Decelea•

Rhamnus•

Aphidna•

Phyle•

Marathon•
Acharnae• Icaria•
Phlya• Pallene•
Colonus• Leuconoe•
Laciadae• Collytus•
Athens• Sphettus•
Piraeus• Myrrhinus•

Laureum•

Sunium•

Carystus•

CEOS

ATTICA

Eleusis•

Eëtioneia
Psyttaleia•

Minoa(?)•

Megara•

SALAMIS

AEGINA

CALAURIA

Troezen•

Sicyon•

Isthmus
Isthmia•

Corinth•

Nemea•

Phlius•

Epidaurus•

Stymphalus•

Mycenae•

Tiryns•
Sepeia•

PELOPONNESE

Mantinea•

Argos•

Hysiae•

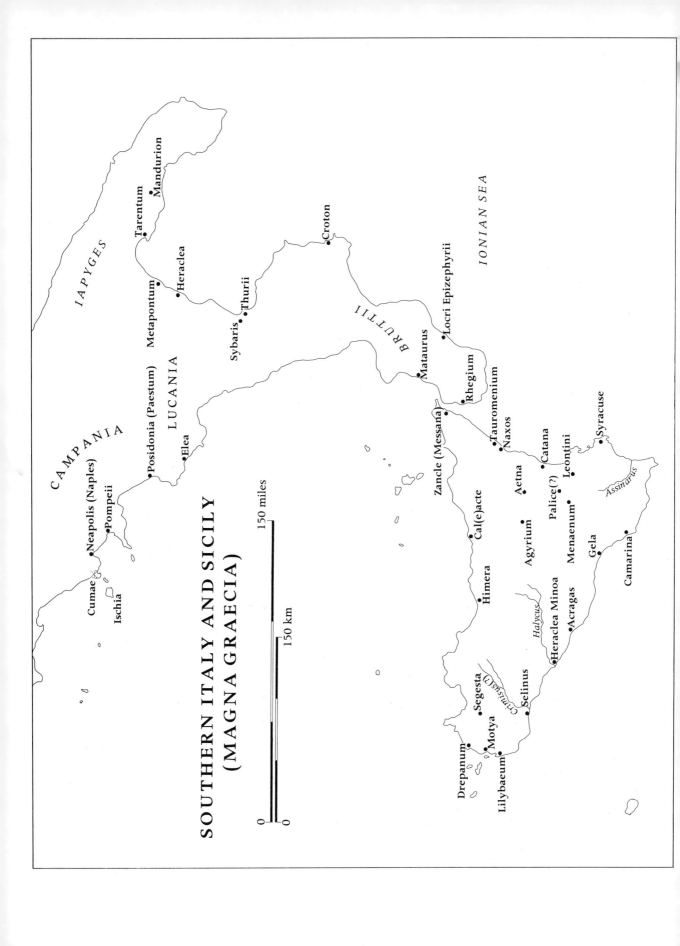

SOUTHERN ITALY AND SICILY (MAGNA GRAECIA)

IAPYGES

CAMPANIA

Cumae
Ischia

Neapolis (Naples)
Pompeii

Posidonia (Paestum)

Elea

LUCANIA

Tarentum
Mandurion

Heraclea

Metapontum

Sybaris
Thurii

Croton

IONIAN SEA

BRUTTII

Locri Epizephyrii

Mataurus

Rhegium

Zancle (Messana)

Tauromenium
Naxos

Catana

Aetna

Palice(?)

Leontini

Syracuse

Assinarus

Cal(e)acte

Agyrium

Menaenum

Gela

Camarina

Himera

Heraclea Minoa

Acragas

Halycus

Segesta

Selinus

Crimissus(?)

Motya

Drepanum

Lilybaeum

150 miles

150 km

0

0

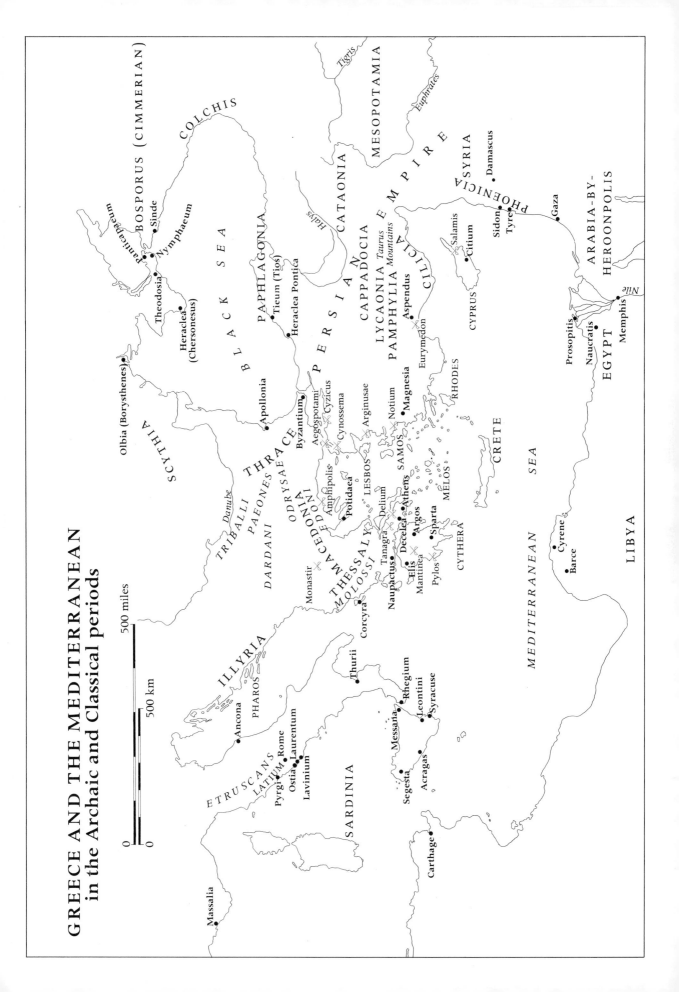

GREECE AND THE MEDITERRANEAN
in the Archaic and Classical periods

500 miles

500 km

Massalia

ILLYRIA

PHAROS

Ancona

ETRUSCANS

LATIUM
Pyrgi Rome
Ostia Laurentum
Lavinium

SARDINIA

Thurii

Rhegium
Messana
Leontini
Segesta
Syracuse
Acragas

Carthage

Monastir

MACEDONIA

THESSALY
MOLOSSI

Corcyra

Naupactus
Tanagra
Elis
Mantinea
Pylos

Decelea
Argos
Sparta

CYTHERA

Athens
Delium

DARDANI

PAEONES

TRIBALLI

Danube

SCYTHIA

Olbia (Borysthenes)

Apollonia

THRACE

ODRYSAE

Amphipolis

Potidaea

Byzantium

LESBOS

SAMOS

MELOS

CRETE

MEDITERRANEAN

SEA

LIBYA

Cyrene

Barce

Panticapaeum
BOSPORUS (CIMMERIAN)
Sinde
Nymphaeum

Theodosia

Heraclea
(Chersonesus)

BLACK SEA

PAPHLAGONIA
Tieum (Tios)
Heraclea Pontica

COLCHIS

Tigris

Halys

CATAONIA

CAPPADOCIA

PERSIA

Aegospotami
Cyzicus
Cynossema
Arginusae
Notium
Magnesia

Eurymedon

RHODES

LYCAONIA Taurus Mountains
PAMPHYLIA
Aspendus

CILICIA

Euphrates

MESOPOTAMIA

ASSYRIA

Damascus

PHOENICIA

Salamis
Citium
CYPRUS

Sidon
Tyre
Gaza

ARABIA-BY-
HEROONPOLIS

Prosopitis
Naucratis
Memphis

EGYPT

Nile

EMPIRE

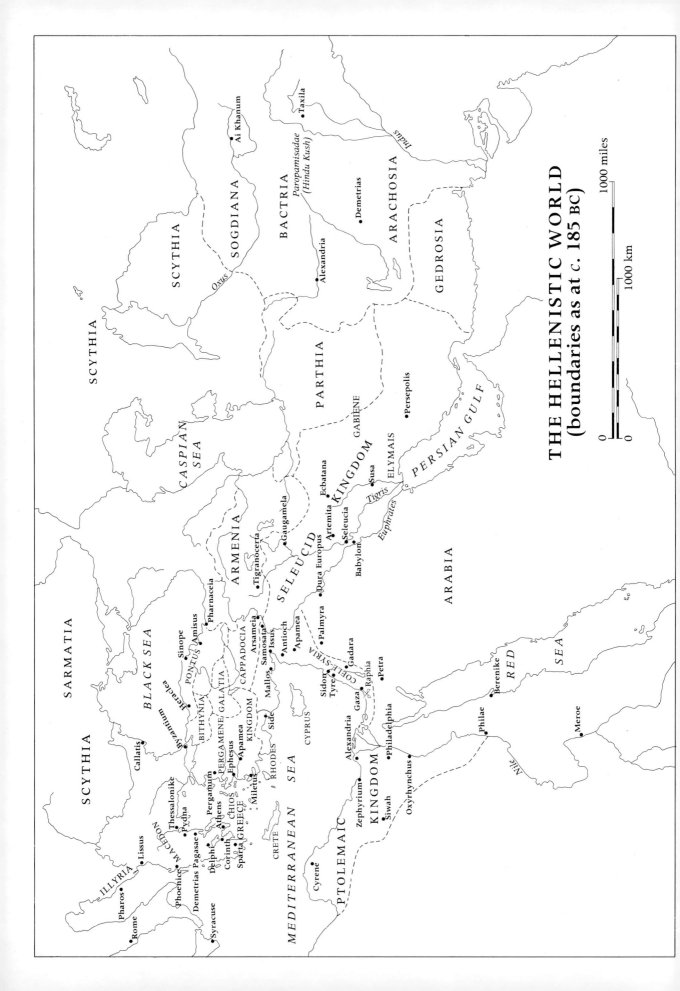

THE HELLENISTIC WORLD
(boundaries as at c. 185 BC)

1000 miles

1000 km

SARMATIA

SCYTHIA

SCYTHIA

SCYTHIA

SCYTHIA

SOGDIANA

•Ai Khanum

•Taxila

BACTRIA

Paropamisadae
(Hindu Kush)

ARACHOSIA

•Demetrias

•Alexandria

GEDROSIA

Indus

Oxus

CASPIAN SEA

PARTHIA

GABIENE

•Persepolis

PERSIAN GULF

ARMENIA

•Gaugamela

•Tigranocerta

SELEUCID

•Dura Europus

•Artemita

•Ecbatana

KINGDOM

•Seleucia

•Susa

ELYMAIS

Tigris

Euphrates

•Babylon

ARABIA

RED SEA

Pharnaceia•

•Amisus

Sinope•

PONTUS

•Arsameia

•Samosata

CAPPADOCIA

•Issus

•Mallos

•Antioch

•Apamea

•Palmyra

COELE-SYRIA

•Gadara

•Sidon

•Tyre

•Raphia

•Petra

•Gaza

•Berenike

•Meroe

•Philae

SCYTHIA

BLACK SEA

Callatis•

Heraclea

Byzantium•

BITHYNIA

PERGAMENE

GALATIA

KINGDOM

•Apamea

Ephesus•

Pergamum•

Thessalonike•

MACEDON

•Pydna

•Athens

Corinth•

Sparta•

GREECE

CHIOS

•Miletus

RHODES

CYPRUS

CRETE

MEDITERRANEAN SEA

ILLYRIA

•Lissus

•Pharos

•Rome

•Syracuse

Phoenice•

•Demetrias

Pagasae•

•Delphi

•Cyrene

•Zephyrium

PTOLEMAIC

KINGDOM

•Alexandria

•Philadelphia

•Siwah

•Oxyrhynchus

Nile

0

0

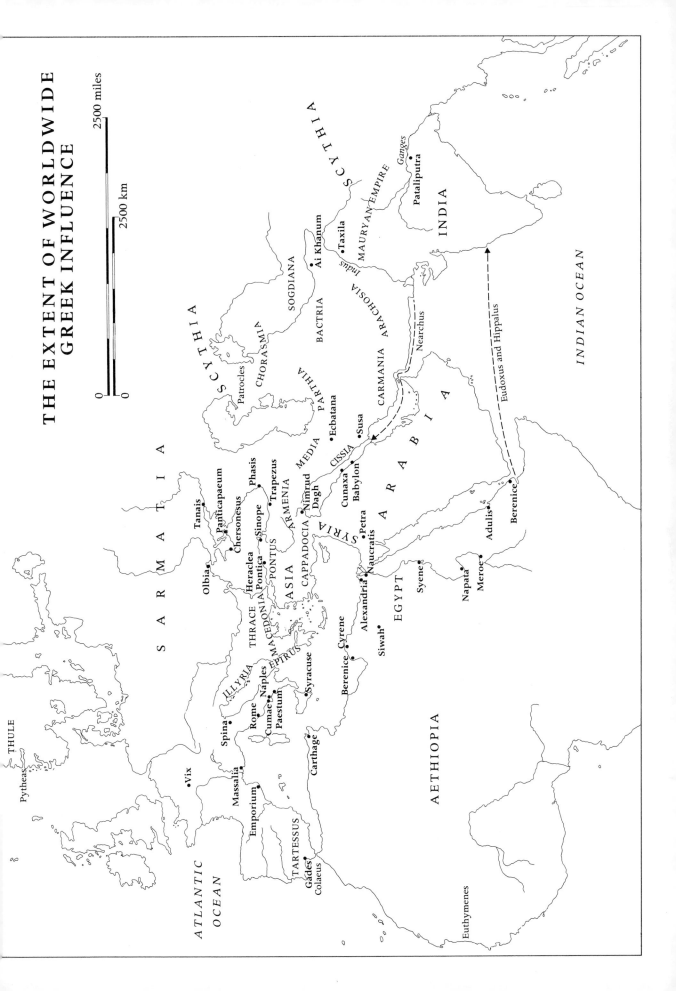

THE EXTENT OF WORLDWIDE GREEK INFLUENCE

2500 miles

2500 km

THULE

Pytheas

ATLANTIC OCEAN

Vix

SARMATIA

SCYTHIA

Olbia

Tanais

Panticapaeum

Chersonesus

Heraclea

Pontica

Sinope

Phasis

Trapezus

THRACE

MACEDONIA

EPIRUS

ILLYRIA

Spina

Rome

Naples

Cumae

Paestum

Emporium

Massalia

TARTESSUS

Gades

Colaeus

Carthage

Syracuse

Berenice

Cyrene

Siwah•

Alexandria

Naucratis

EGYPT

Syene

AETHIOPIA

Euthymenes

Napata

Meroe

Adulis

Berenice

ARABIA

Petra

SYRIA

CAPPADOCIA

ASIA

PONTUS

ARMENIA

MEDIA

CISSIA

Cunaxa

Babylon

Nimrud Dagh

Ecbatana

Susa

PARTHIA

CHORASMIA

Patrocles

SCYTHIA

SOGDIANA

BACTRIA

Ai Khanum

Taxila

ARACHOSIA

CARMANIA

Nearchus

Indus

MAURYAN EMPIRE

Ganges

Pataliputra

INDIA

Eudoxus and Hippalus

INDIAN OCEAN

THE ROYAL FAMILIES OF SPARTA

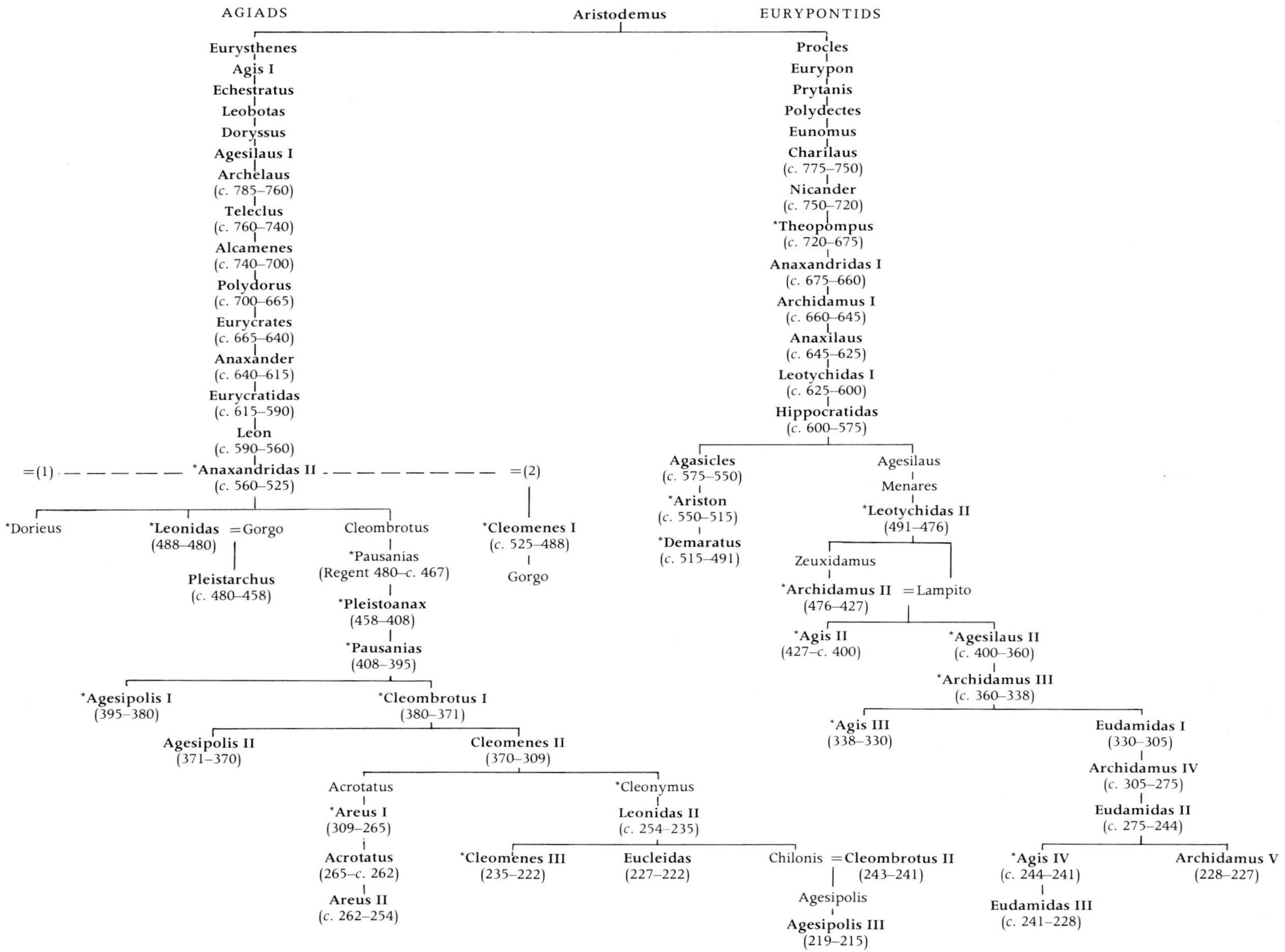

AGIADS   Aristodemus   EURYPONTIDS

AGIADS

Eurysthenes
Agis I
Echestratus
Leobotas
Doryssus
Agesilaus I
Archelaus (c. 785–760)
Teleclus (c. 760–740)
Alcamenes (c. 740–700)
Polydorus (c. 700–665)
Eurycrates (c. 665–640)
Anaxander (c. 640–615)
Eurycratidas (c. 615–590)
Leon (c. 590–560)
*Anaxandridas II (c. 560–525)

=(1) — *Dorieus

=(2)
*Cleomenes I (c. 525–488)
Gorgo

*Leonidas = Gorgo (488–480)
Pleistarchus (c. 480–458)

Cleombrotus
*Pausanias (Regent 480–c. 467)
*Pleistoanax (458–408)
*Pausanias (408–395)

*Agesipolis I (395–380)
Agesipolis II (371–370)
*Cleombrotus I (380–371)
Cleomenes II (370–309)

Acrotatus
*Areus I (309–265)
Acrotatus (265–c. 262)
Areus II (c. 262–254)

*Cleonymus
Leonidas II (254–235)
*Cleomenes III (235–222)
Eucleidas (227–222)

Chilonis = Cleombrotus II (243–241)
Agesipolis
Agesipolis III (219–215)

EURYPONTIDS

Procles
Eurypon
Prytanis
Polydectes
Eunomus
Charilaus (c. 775–750)
Nicander (c. 750–720)
*Theopompus (c. 720–675)
Anaxandridas I (c. 675–660)
Archidamus I (c. 660–645)
Anaxilaus (c. 645–625)
Leotychidas I (c. 625–600)
Hippocratidas (c. 600–575)

Agasilaus
Menares
*Leotychidas II (491–476)

Agasicles (c. 575–550)
*Ariston (c. 550–515)
*Demaratus (c. 515–491)

*Archidamus II = Lampito (476–427)
Zeuxidamus
*Agis II (427–c. 400)
*Agesilaus II (c. 400–360)
*Archidamus III (c. 360–338)
*Agis III (338–330)
Eudamidas I (330–305)
Archidamus IV (c. 305–275)
Eudamidas II (c. 275–244)
*Agis IV (c. 244–241)
Eudamidas III (c. 241–228)
Archidamus V (228–227)

THE PTOLEMIES

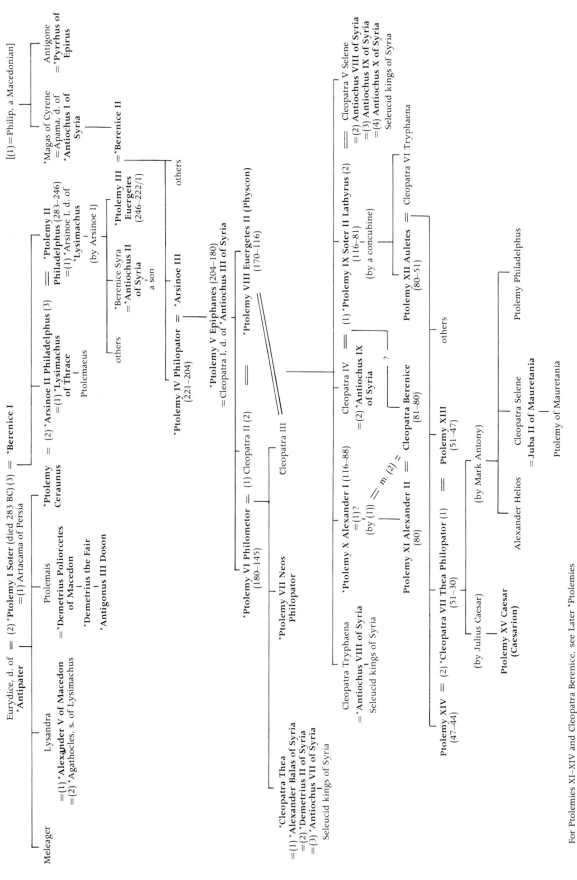

For Ptolemies XI–XIV and Cleopatra Berenice, see Later *Ptolemies

THE SELEUCIDS

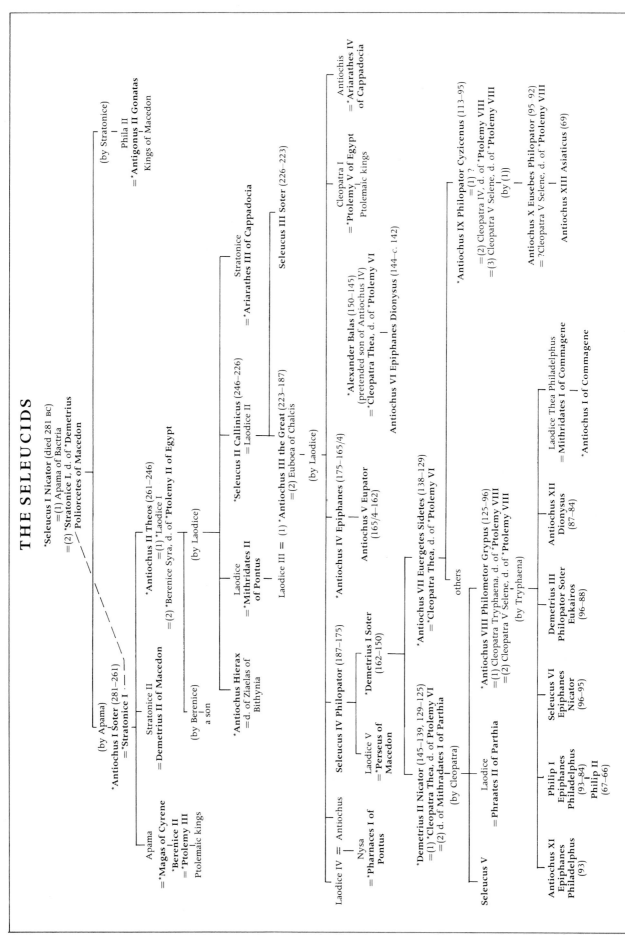

For Antiochus X, XI, XII, and XIII, Demetrius III, Philip I and II, and Seleucus VI, see Later *Seleucids.

THE ANTIGONIDS

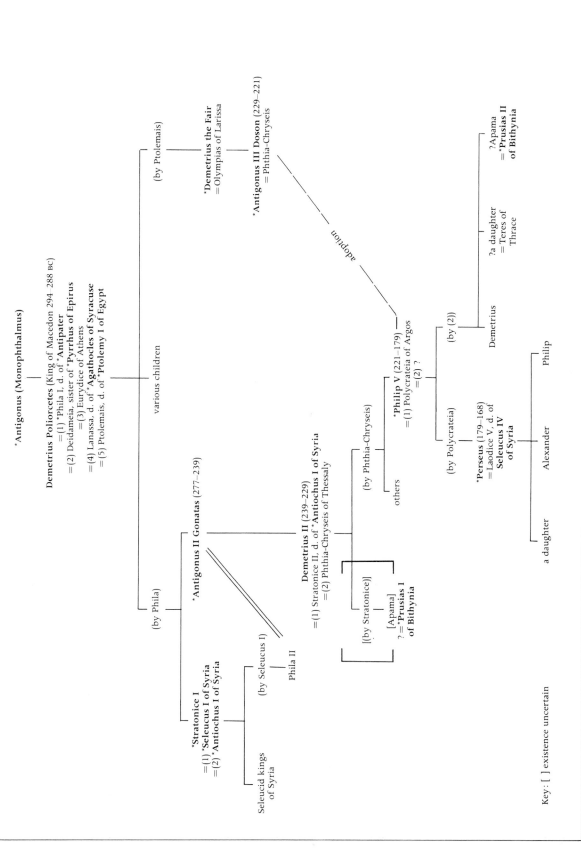

*Antigonus (Monophthalmus)

Demetrius Poliorcetes (King of Macedon 294–288 BC)
=(1) *Phila I, d. of *Antipater
=(2) Deidameia, sister of *Pyrrhus of Epirus
=(3) Eurydice of Athens
=(4) Lanassa, d. of *Agathocles of Syracuse
=(5) Ptolemais, d. of *Ptolemy I of Egypt

(by Phila)

(by Ptolemais)

various children

*Demetrius the Fair
=Olympias of Larissa

*Antigonus III Doson (229–221)
=Phthia-Chryseis

adoption

*Stratonice I
=(1) *Seleucus I of Syria
=(2) *Antiochus I of Syria

(by Seleucus I)

Seleucid kings
of Syria

Phila II

*Antigonus II Gonatas (277–239)

Demetrius II (239–229)
=(1) Stratonice II, d. of *Antiochus I of Syria
=(2) Phthia-Chryseis of Thessaly

[(by Stratonice)]

[Apama]
? = *Prusias I
of Bithynia

(by Phthia-Chryseis)

others

*Philip V (221–179)
=(1) Polycrateia of Argos
=(2) ?

(by Polycrateia)

*Perseus (179–168)
=Laodice V, d. of
Seleucus IV
of Syria

(by (2))

Demetrius

?a daughter
=Teres of
Thrace

?Apama
=*Prusias II
of Bithynia

a daughter   Alexander   Philip

Key: [ ] existence uncertain

THE HOUSE OF ANTIPATER

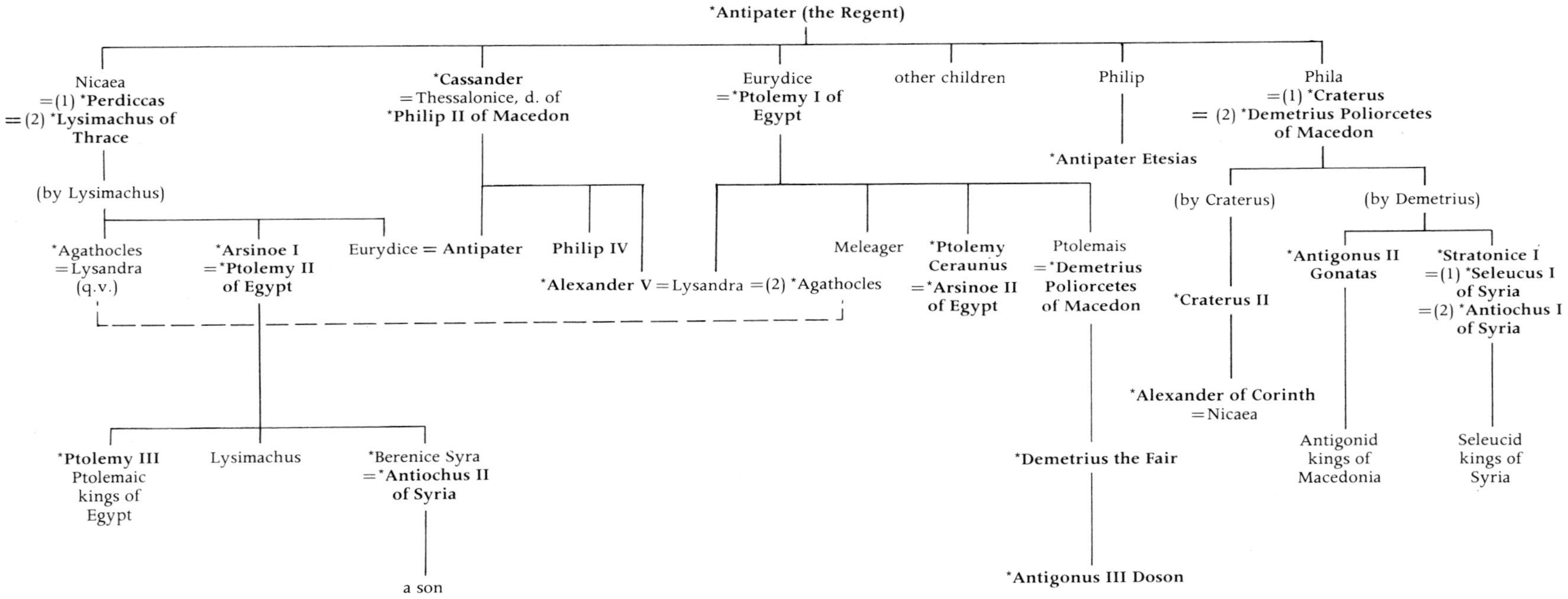

*Antipater (the Regent)

- Nicaea
  = (1) *Perdiccas
  = (2) *Lysimachus of Thrace

- *Cassander
  = Thessalonice, d. of *Philip II of Macedon

- Eurydice
  = *Ptolemy I of Egypt

- other children

- Philip

- *Antipater Etesias

- Phila
  = (1) *Craterus
  = (2) *Demetrius Poliorcetes of Macedon

(by Lysimachus)

*Agathocles = Lysandra (q.v.)

Eurydice = Antipater

Philip IV

*Alexander V = Lysandra = (2) *Agathocles

*Arsinoe I = *Ptolemy II of Egypt

Meleager

*Ptolemy Ceraunus = *Arsinoe II of Egypt

Ptolemais = *Demetrius Poliorcetes of Macedon

(by Craterus)

(by Demetrius)

*Stratonice I
= (1) *Seleucus I of Syria
= (2) *Antiochus I of Syria

*Antigonus II Gonatas

*Craterus II

*Alexander of Corinth = Nicaea

*Demetrius the Fair

Lysimachus

*Berenice Syra = *Antiochus II of Syria

a son

*Ptolemy III
Ptolemaic kings of Egypt

Antigonid kings of Macedonia

Seleucid kings of Syria

*Antigonus III Doson

THE ATTALIDS

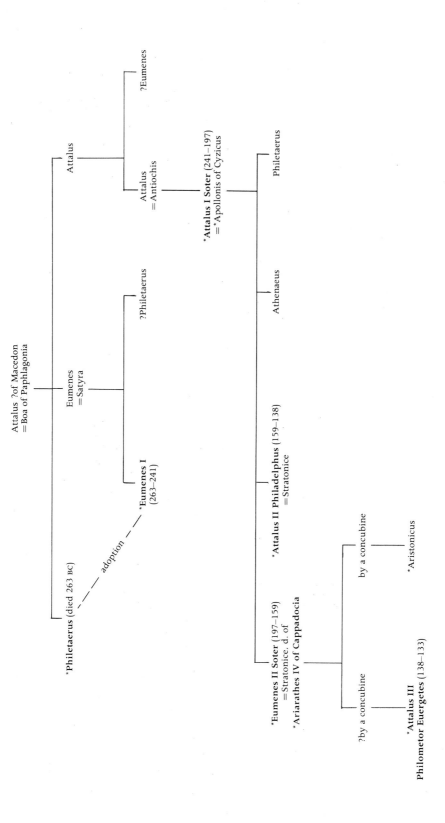

Attalus ?of Macedon
=Boa of Paphlagonia

*Philetaerus (died 263 BC)

--- adoption ---

Eumenes
=Satyra

Attalus

*Eumenes I
(263–241)

?Philetaerus

Attalus
=Antiochis

?Eumenes

*Attalus I Soter (241–197)
=*Apollonis of Cyzicus

Athenaeus

Philetaerus

*Eumenes II Soter (197–159)
=Stratonice. d. of
*Ariarathes IV of Cappadocia

*Attalus II Philadelphus (159–138)
=Stratonice

?by a concubine

by a concubine

*Aristonicus

*Attalus III
Philometor Euergetes (138–133)

Acknowledgements

The publishers wish to thank all the individuals, museums, agencies and other institutions who have supplied photographs and granted permission to use them. Particular thanks are due to the following:

Archivi Alinari, Florence: 27, 49, 51, 80L, 110R, 111R, 113R, 115, 124, 131, 140, 143B, 145R, 147, 159R, 172, 173, 176L,R, 186L, 201.
American School of Classical Studies, Agora Excavations: 56L, 78L, 79, 190L,R.
Ashmolean Library, Oxford: 154L, 206.
Bildarchiv Preussischer Kulturbesitz, Berlin: 47R, 64R.
Bodleian Library, Oxford: 31L.
Boston Museum of Fine Arts: 26R, 62, 180L.
Diana Bowder: 153R.
Viscount Coke: 204.
Délégation Archéologique Française en Afghanistan: 63.
Deutsches Archäologisches Institut, Athens: 53R, 65, 69, 91, 117, 122, 130R, 133, 143T, 150, 153L, 160L, 161, 210.
Egypt Exploration Society, London: 33, 73.
Fitzwilliam Museum, Cambridge: 170.
Giraudon, Paris: 44R, 67T, 88.

Hirmer Fotoarchiv, Munich: 70L, 109R, 113B, 152, 174, 189R, 207L,R.
Metropolitan Borough of Stockport: 58.
Metropolitan Museum, New York: 38, 110L.
Ny Carlsberg Glyptotek, Copenhagen: 30B, 96, 102, 182.
E. E. Rice: 105.
David Robinson, *Excavations at Olynthus*, XII, 1946 (Johns Hopkins University Studies in Archaeology, 36), 125T.
M. Schede, *Die Ruinen von Priene*, 1934, 125B.
Soprintendenza alle Gallerie, Naples: 34, 86, 104, 118R, 187, 211B.
Stockholm, National Museum: 30T.
Christopher Tuplin: 103.
Vatican Museum: 26L, 64L, 68R, 83L, 87, 156L, 166, 186R, 197L.
Wadsworth Athaeneum: 81R.

Illustrations 55, 78R, 120, 139, 156R are reproduced by Courtesy of the Trustees of the British Museum. Many of the photographs in this book are from the Phaidon archive, and include the work of Ilse Schneider-Lengyel.